The Reception of Oscar Wilde in Europe

The Reception of British and Irish Authors in Europe

Series Editor: Elinor Shaffer
School of Advanced Study, University of London

Published Volumes

Volume I: *The Reception of Virginia Woolf in Europe*
Edited by Mary Ann Caws and Nicola Luckhurst

Volume II: *The Reception of Laurence Sterne in Europe*
Edited by Peter de Voogd and John Neubauer

Volume III: *The Reception of James Joyce in Europe*
Edited by Geert Lernout and Wim Van Mierlo

Volume IV: *The Reception of Walter Pater in Europe*
Edited by Stephen Bann

Volume V: *The Reception of Ossian in Europe*
Edited by Howard Gaskill

Volume VI: *The Reception of Byron in Europe*
Edited by Richard Cardwell

Volume VII: *The Reception of H. G. Wells in Europe*
Edited by Patrick Parrinder and John Partington

Volume VIII: *The Reception of Jonathan Swift in Europe*
Edited by Hermann Real

Volume IX: *The Reception of David Hume in Europe*
Edited by Peter Jones

Volume X: *The Reception of W. B. Yeats in Europe*
Edited by Klaus Peter Jochum

Volume XI: *The Reception of Henry James in Europe*
Edited by Annick Duperray

Volume XII: *The Reception of D. H. Lawrence in Europe*
Edited by Dieter Mehl and Christa Jansohn

Volume XIII: *The Reception of Sir Walter Scott in Europe*
Edited by Murray Pittock

Volume XIV: *The Reception of Jane Austen in Europe*
Edited by A. A. Mandal and Brian Southam

Volume XV: *The Reception of S. T. Coleridge in Europe*
Edited by Elinor Shaffer and Edoardo Zuccato

Volume XVI: *The Reception of P. B. Shelley in Europe*
Edited by Susanne Schmid and Michael Rossington

Volume XVII: *The Reception of Charles Darwin in Europe*
Edited by Eve-Marie Engels and Thomas F. Glick

Volume XVIII: *The Reception of Oscar Wilde in Europe*
Edited by Stefano Evangelista

Volume XIX: *The Reception of Charles Dickens in Europe*
Edited by Michael Hollington

Volume XX: *The Literary and Cultural Reception of Charles Darwin in Europe*
Edited by Thomas F. Glick and Elinor Shaffer

Volume XXI: *The Reception of Robert Burns in Europe*
Edited by Murray Pittock

Forthcoming volumes in the series include:

The Reception of Isaac Newton in Europe
Edited by Helmut Pulte and Scott Mandelbrote

The Reception of George Eliot in Europe
Edited by Catherine Brown and Elinor Shaffer

The Reception of William Blake in Europe
Edited by Sibylle Erle and Morton D. Paley

**The Athlone Critical Traditions Series:
The Reception of British and Irish Authors in Europe**

Series Editor: Elinor Shaffer
School of Advanced Study, University of London

The Reception of Oscar Wilde in Europe

Edited by Stefano Evangelista

Bloomsbury Academic
An imprint of Bloomsbury Publishing Plc

B L O O M S B U R Y
LONDON • NEW DELHI • NEW YORK • SYDNEY

Bloomsbury Academic
An imprint of Bloomsbury Publishing Plc

50 Bedford Square   1385 Broadway
London   New York
WC1B 3DP   NY 10018
UK   USA

www.bloomsbury.com

BLOOMSBURY and the Diana logo are trademarks of Bloomsbury Publishing Plc

First published in 2010 by the Continuum International Publishing Group Ltd
Paperback edition first published by Bloomsbury Academic 2015

© Stefano Evangelista and Contributors 2010

Series concept and Series Editor's Preface © Elinor Shaffer

British Library Cataloguing-in-Publication Data
A catalogue record for this book is available from the British Library.

ISBN: HB: 978-1-8470-6005-1
PB: 978-1-4742-4596-8
ePDF: 978-1-4411-7368-3

Library of Congress Cataloging-in-Publication Data
A catalog record for this book is available from the Library of Congress.

Series: The Reception of British and Irish Authors in Europe

Typeset by Fakenham Prepress Solutions, Fakenham, Norfolk NR21 8NN
Printed and bound by CPI Group (UK) Ltd, Croydon, CR0 4YY

FSC
www.fsc.org
MIX
Paper from
responsible sources
FSC® C013604

Contents

Series Editor's Preface:
The Reception of Oscar Wilde in Europe

The reception of British authors in Britain has in good part been studied; indeed, it forms our literary history. By contrast, the reception of British authors in Europe has not been examined in any systematic, long-term or large-scale way. With our volume on Jonathan Swift (2005), we altered our Series title to 'The Reception of British and Irish Authors in Europe', as a reminder that many writers previously travelling under the British flag may now be considered or claimed as belonging to the Republic of Ireland (1948), or Eire. With Swift, Joyce, Yeats, and Wilde, our 'Irish shelf' is now substantial.

All these authors had complex relations with 'the language of Shakespeare' they were, as Wilde put it, 'condemned' to write. That phrase speaks of a high ambition as well as of resentment. If Swift's career in England was as prominent and embattled as his career in Ireland, while Joyce in 'silence, exile and cunning' recreated himself as a European, it is the name of William Butler Yeats that has come by his own fierce choice to stand for 'his country's biography', the life history of Ireland, as his most recent biographer has put it (R. F. Foster, 1: xviii). In his lifetime the crucial moment was the founding of the Irish Free State in 1922. When the Commonwealth was founded a decade later, Ireland became a full member of it, though the Republic of Ireland did not come into being until 1948. Not only did Yeats's poetry and drama help forge a nation and a national identity, but it did so although he wrote in English and came to rank as a major English poet, even while his status as an 'Irish poet' was marked out in the award citation of the Nobel Prize in 1923.

Wilde's case is a powerful variant on these; born in Ireland, of notable Irish parents, it was nevertheless in England that he made his name, for both good and ill; and as this volume demonstrates, it was on the continent of Europe, in France, Germany, and the Austro-Hungarian Empire, that he was overwhelmingly received, welcomed, performed, and greeted with much sympathy, as a man and as a writer. He had wished to be a French writer, and his *Salomé*, his most widely received play on the continent, was written in French; and he died and was buried in France. Yet today he is also claimed back by England and above all by Ireland.

It is the aim of this Series to initiate and forward the study of the reception of British and Irish authors in continental Europe, or, as we would now say, the rest of Europe as a whole, rather than as isolated national histories with a narrow national perspective. The perspectives of other nations greatly add to our understanding of individual contributors to that history. The history of the reception of British authors extends our knowledge of their capacity to stimulate and to call forth new responses, not only in their own disciplines but in wider fields and to diverse publics in a variety of historical circumstances. Often these responses provide quite unexpected and enriching insights into our own histories, politics and culture. Individual works and personalities take on new dimensions and facets. They may also be subject to enlightening critiques. Our knowledge of the writers of the British Isles is simply incomplete and inadequate without these reception studies.

By 'authors' we intend writers in any field whose works have been recognized as making a contribution to the intellectual and cultural history of our societies. Thus the Series includes literary figures, such as Laurence Sterne, Virginia Woolf and James Joyce, philosophers such as Francis Bacon and David Hume, historians and political figures such as Edmund Burke, and natural scientists such as Charles Darwin and Isaac Newton, whose works have had a broad impact on thinking in every field. In some cases individual works of the same author have dealt with different subjects, each with virtually its own reception history; so Burke's *Reflections on the French Revolution* (1790) was instantaneously translated and moulded thinking on the power struggles in the Europe of his own day; his youthful *A Philosophical Enquiry into the Origin of our Ideas of the Sublime and Beautiful* (1757) exerted a powerful influence on aesthetic thought and the practice of writing and remains a seminal work for certain genres of fiction and of art. Similarly, each of Laurence Sterne's two major works of fiction, *Tristram Shandy* and *A Sentimental Journey*, has its own history of reception, giving rise to a whole line of literary movements, innovative progeny and concomitant critical theory in most European countries. Note that both Burke and Sterne may be accounted Irish.

The research project examines the ways in which selected authors have been translated, published, distributed, read, reviewed and discussed on the continent of Europe. In doing so, it throws light not only on specific strands of intellectual and cultural history but also on the processes involved in the dissemination of ideas and texts. The project brings to bear the theoretical and critical approaches that have characterized the growing fields of reader response theory and reception studies in the last quarter of the twentieth century and into the twenty-first century. These critical approaches have illuminated the activity of the reader in bringing the text to life and stressed the changing horizons of the reading public or community of which the reader is a part. The project also takes cognizance of the studies of the material history of the book that have begun to explore the production, publication and distribution of manuscripts and books. Increasingly, other media too are playing a role in these processes, and to the history of book illustration must be added lantern slides (as in the popular versions of both Scott's and Dickens's works), cinema (whose early impact forms an important part of our H. G. Wells volume), and more recently television (as recounted in the Jane Austen volume). Byron's writings, like Ossian's and Scott's, have almost as extensive a history in images and in sound as in prose and poetry. Performance history requires strenuous tracing, beyond the texts, whether for works written for the stage or for adaptations, and for the first time, in this volume we present a separate Performance Timeline in conjunction with the general Timeline (which contains the first English productions). If Yeats's poetic drama had remarkable resonances across Europe, extending to Catalan nationalism and Basque revolution, Wilde's dramatic productions have had an extraordinary career across the theatres of Europe, first with *Salomé* (banned in England), then with the society dramas, especially (but by no means only) *The Importance of Being Earnest*, as well as stage versions of his novel *The Portrait of Dorian Gray* and his popular fairy tales. The avant-garde in Paris and Berlin took up *Salomé*, leading to Richard Strauss's dazzling operatic version; and actresses made theatre history with their brilliant interpretations of the role. We have only begun the work of collecting the full evidence of the performance history; for it is also present in ballet and many kinds of musical form, as well as in literary and political cabaret, and private performances of many kinds difficult to trace. As with Shelley's banned play *I Cenci*, underground productions flourished.

The study of material history forms a curious annexe, that is of the objects that form durable traces of the vogue for a particular author, which may be parts of himself (as with the macabre story told in our Shelley volume of the wish to possess the poet's heart), or items of his wardrobe (as with Byronic shirtsleeves), or souvenir objects associated with his characters, or the more elaborate memorial gardens and graveyards such as linked Rousseau and Sterne in France. The moving of Yeats's grave in Roquebrune to his birth-place in Ireland is an aspect of such history; Wilde's grave in the celebrated Paris cemetery of Père Lachaise is one of the most visited, and sometimes desecrated. The author's own image may achieve iconic status, as with Byron 'in Albanian dress', or Wilde, the quintessential dandy and aesthete, with a green carnation in his buttonhole. The significance of such cults and cult objects requires further analysis as the examples multiply and diversify.

The Series as published by Continuum, now Bloomsbury, is open-ended and multi-volumed, each volume based on a particular author. The authors may be regarded according to their discipline, or looked at across disciplines within their period. Thus the reception of philosophers Bacon and Hume may be compared; or Hume may be considered as belonging to an eighteenth-century group that includes writers like Swift and Sterne, historians and political figures such as Gibbon and Burke. As the volumes accumulate they enrich each other and our awareness of the full context in which an individual author is received. The Swift volume shows that in many places Swift and Sterne were received at the same time, and viewed sometimes as a pair of witty ironists, and sometimes as opposites representing traditional satire on the one hand (Swift) and modern sentimentalism on the other (Sterne), and equally or diversely valued as a result. The Romantic poets were carried forward into mid-century nationalist movements and late nineteenth-century symbolist movements; Yeats often appeared to be their coeval. The *fin-de-siècle* aspects of Pater, Wilde, early Yeats, James, Woolf and Joyce are interwoven in a wider European experience. In the twentieth century, Sterne was paired with Joyce as subversive of the novel form; and Joyce and Woolf became Modernists.

These chronological shifts, bringing different authors and different works into view together, are common to the reception process, so often displacing or delaying them into an entirely new historical scene or set of circumstances. Thus Byron's two major works, *Childe Harold* and *Don Juan*, came to stand, after his death, for whole epochs of feeling in Europe, first the melancholic, inward post-Napoleonic *Weltschmerz*, then the bitter and disillusioned mocking tones of the failed Revolution of 1848. Yeats's own distinct creative phases, brought into conjunction with those of his period, make him an epitome of the process: his early mythological poetry culminated in the founding of the

Abbey Theatre Dublin and a national drama; his later poetry stood more aloof. His identification with Ireland both forwarded and impeded his reception abroad. In some countries, a fight for liberty and national identity associated with folk tradition raised immediate sympathies well established from the mid-nineteenth century. In Poland, Yeats's drama coincided with the first, much delayed performances of the exiled Romantic Mickiewicz's national drama; in Hungary and Croatia the ossianic laments for a lost society and the byronic summons to liberty seemed come again. By contrast, the early poetry might be regarded favourably as quite the reverse of animating a local 'folk' spirit but rather as part of a European movement of Symbolism and aestheticism, as in France (where he was associated with Mallarmé) and in Russia. In either case, the later 'mature' poetry might be ignored or deprecated. Yet a succession of first-rate poet-translators recognized the 'mature' poetry; and in the many fine translations Yeats sometimes seems to move body and soul into another age. The kaleidoscope of reception displays and discovers new pairings and couplings, new milieux, new matches and mismatches, and, of course, new valuations.

In the case of Wilde, the differing legal status of the offences that led to his conviction and imprisonment is a significant historical factor that played a role in every country. His conviction under English law led not only to libertarian and avant-garde championship of his work abroad, but to religious and philosophical support for his own cry from the depths, *De profundis*; he presents an altogether deeper, tormented consciousness, and comparisons to Tolstoy and Nietzsche are made. With the change in the English laws in 1959, after the Wolfenden Report, decriminalizing homosexual activity between consenting adults, open adoption of him as a hero and martyr of the cause became possible. But in other countries he had long since been so, a new instance of a Chatterton, or the Romantic *poète maudit*. A legal turning-point is a special and especially well-marked case of historical shifts of perspective. For Wilde, it also meant that his stature and wide and diverse reception as a writer could at last come into full and unobscured view.

In period terms one may discern within the Series a Romantic group; a Victorian group; a *fin-de-siècle* and an early Modernist group. Period designations differ from discipline to discipline, and are shifting even within a discipline: Blake, who was a 'Pre-Romantic' poet a generation ago, is now considered a fully fledged Romantic. Virginia Woolf may be regarded as a *fin-de-siècle* aesthete and stylist whose affinities are with Pater or as an epoch-making Modernist like Joyce. Terms referring to period and style often vary from country to country. What happens to a 'Victorian' author transplanted to 'Wilhelmine' Germany? Are the English Metaphysical poets to be regarded as 'baroque' in continental terms, or will that term continue to be borrowed in English only for music, art and to an extent architecture? Is the 'Augustan' Swift a classicist in Italian terms, or an Enlightenment thinker in French terms? What does it mean that Wilde is embraced in the Austro-Hungarian Empire, a political entity that no longer exists? It is most straightforward to classify them simply according to century, for the calendar is for the most part shared. But the various possible groupings will provide a context for reception and enrich our knowledge of each author.

Division of each volume by country or by linguistic region is dictated by the historical development of Europe; each volume necessarily adopts a different selection of countries and regions, depending on period and on the specific reception of any given author. Countries or regions are treated either substantially, in several chapters or sections where this is warranted, for example, the French reception of Yeats, Woolf, Joyce and Wilde (and nearly all English-language works until after World War II pass first through the medium of French language and the prism of French thought), or on a moderate scale, or simply as a brief section. In some cases, where a rich reception is located that has not been reported or of which the critical community is not aware, more detailed coverage may be justified. In general, comparative studies have neglected Spain in favour of France, Germany and Italy, and this imbalance needs to be righted. For example, we have shown the reception of Woolf in the different linguistic communities of the Iberian peninsula, and given a detailed treatment of a play of Yeats in Catalan, Galician and Basque. Wilde's reception calls attention to theatrical performances not only in Berlin or Vienna, but also in Breslau, Cracow, Budapest and Zagreb – and in Spain and Catalonia. Brevity does not indicate lack of interest. Where separate coverage of any particular country or region is not justified by the extent of the reception, relevant material is incorporated into the bibliography and the Timeline. Thus an early translation may be noted, although there was subsequently a minimal response to the author or work, or a very long gap in the reception in that region.

This kind of material will be fully described in the database (see below). It is, of course, always possible, and indeed to be hoped and expected that further aspects of reception will later be uncovered, and the long-term research project forwarded, through this initial information. Reception studies often display an author's intellectual and political impact and reveal effects abroad that are unfamiliar to the author's compatriots. Thus, Byron, for example, had the power of carrying and incarnating liberal political thought to regimes and institutions to whom it was anathema; it is less well known that Sterne had the same effect, and that both were charged with erotically tinged subversion; and that Pater suggested a style of aesthetic sensibility in which sensation took precedence over moral values. Woolf came to be an icon for women writers in countries where there was little tradition of women's writing. Pater's pupil, Wilde in his imprisonment became a hope for personal liberty. By the same token, the study of censorship, or more broadly impediments to dissemination, and of modes of circumventing control, becomes an important aspect of reception studies. In Bacon studies, the process of dissemination of his ideas through the private correspondence of organized circles was vital. Certain presses and publishers also play a role, and the study of modes of secret distribution under severe penalty is a particularly fascinating subject, whether in Catholic Europe or Soviet Russia. Much translation was carried out in prisons. Irony and aesopian devices, and audience alertness to them, are highly developed under controlling regimes. A surprising number of authors live more dangerously abroad than at home. Where Yeats or Joyce was at home was moot point; Wilde, unusually, lived more dangerously at home, in England and Ireland, than abroad; but then he too might suggest that France had always been his home.

Translation itself may provide a mode of evading censure. There is probably no more complex and elaborated example in the annals of Europe of the use of translation to invent new movements, styles, and political departures than that of Ossian, the fabled early Scottish oral poet, which became itself a form of 'pseudo-translation', that is works by writers masquerading under pseudonyms suggestive of 'dangerous' foreigners but providing safety for mere 'translators'. 'Ossian' became the cover name for new initiatives, as 'Byron' flew the flag of liberation. 'Wilde' the dandy who would speak French but perforce spoke Shakespeare's language became an explorer of the divided modern psycho-social self.

New electronic technology makes it possible to undertake reception studies on this scale. An extensive database stores information about editions, translations, accompanying critical prefaces or afterwords, illustrations, biographies and correspondence, early reviews, important essays and book-length studies of the authors, and comments, citations and imitations or reworkings, including satire and pastiche by other writers. Some, as often Pater, live in the echoes of their style as understood in another language.

The recording of full details of translations and translators is a particular concern, since often the names of translators are not supplied, or their identity is concealed behind pseudonyms or false attributions. The nature of the translation is often a determining factor in the reception of a work or an author; yet often the work was translated from a language other than English. The database also records the character and location of rare works. Selected texts and passages are included, together with English translations. The Project website www.clarehall.cam.ac.uk/rbae provides further information about the Project's history, advisory board, conferences, colloquia and seminars, as well as reviews of its volumes. The database is currently an open-access bibliographical resource, available online via the Project website and containing all the bibliographies published so far in the Series as well as supplementary information and bibliography relating to the authors.

Professor Elinor Shaffer, FBA
Director, Research Project
Reception of British and Irish Authors in Europe

Acknowledgements

The Research Project on the Reception of British and Irish Authors in Europe is happy to acknowledge the support of the British Academy, the Leverhulme Trust, the Arts and Humanities Research Board, the Modern Humanities Research Association, the European Science Foundation, and other funding bodies.

We are also greatly indebted to the School of Advanced Study, University of London, to the Institute of Germanic Studies, and the Institute of Romance Studies (merged as the Institute of Germanic & Romance Studies, and now the Institute of Modern Languages Research), the Institute of English Studies, and the Institute of Historical Research, with whom we have held a series of seminars, colloquia and conferences on Reception Studies since 1998, when the Project was launched in the British Academy. We are grateful to Clare Hall College, Cambridge, which has provided the Project with a second institutional home from 2003.

We also gratefully acknowledge the advice and guidance of the Advisory Board of the Project, which has met regularly since the launch of the Project. The Research Director, Elinor Shaffer, is also pleased to acknowledge the indispensable services of the staff of the Research Project during the preparation of this volume: the MHRA Research Associate, Alessandra Tosi; and the Project Officer, Lachlan Moyle. We are grateful in particular to Paul Barnaby, the first Research Fellow of the Project, who has worked with us throughout the Series on assembling the Timelines, and in this case has pioneered the orchestration of the Timeline with the first separate Performance Timeline, which embodies major research findings of this volume

The Volume editor would like to thank Joseph Bristow, Philip Ross Bullock, Raquel Merino Álvarez, Jacqueline Hurtley, Mária Kurdi, Bernard O'Donoghue, Giuliana Pieri and Florina Tufescu for their expert advice, and Kristin Ewins for her assistance. The Volume editor would also like to express his gratitude to the English Faculty of the University of Oxford for providing generous funding towards the Colloquium held in Trinity College in March 2007 and to Professor Gesa Stedman and the Centre for British Studies of the Humboldt University, Berlin, for kindly hosting him in early 2009. Research on the volume was made possible thanks to a fellowship awarded by the William Andrews Clark Memorial Library, University of California, Los Angeles; Scott Jacobs from the Clark Library deserves special thanks for his help and kindness. The final stages of the editing process took place during a term of leave funded by the John Fell OUP Research Fund. Trinity College, Oxford, provided support throughout the project. The Volume editor would also like to thank the William Andrews Clark Memorial Library for permission to quote from Robert Ross's manuscript.

Ton van Kalmthout provided the Dutch-language material from which the data for the timeline has been drawn. David Rose provided invaluable help both at the time of the Oxford colloquium and in establishing contact with other European Wildeans through the extensive network of *The Oscholars*.

The contributors to the volume would also like to acknowledge support in the preparation of their chapters. Joseph Bristow would like to thank Lucy

Baines, archivist at Queen's College, London, for information about Walter Rippmann. Richard Hibbitt would like to thank the British Academy for awarding him a Small Research Grant to fund archival research. Marta Mateo records her gratitude to Raquel Merino and the TRACE research group on censorship – a joint project between the Universidad de León and the Universidad del País Vasco – for making available the data they have collected on Wilde and sharing their ideas on the situation of Wilde's works under the censorship in Franco's regime and the issue of homosexuality. She would also like to thank the Biblioteca Española de Música y Teatro Contemporáneos of the Fundación Juan March in Madrid. Lene Østermark-Johansen would like to thank Dag Heede, Knud Arne Jürgensen, Wilhelm von Rosen and the librarians in the Royal Library in Copenhagen, the Danish Theatre Museum, the Royal Theatre Archives and in the Danish Film Museum. Material cited from Evgenii Bershtein, 'The Russian Myth of Oscar Wilde', in *Self and Story in Russian History*, edited by Laura Engelstein and Stephanie Sandler, is used by permission of Cornell University Press (© 2000 Cornell University).

The Editors are grateful to the William Andrews Clark Memorial Library, University of California, Los Angeles, for the cover portrait of Oscar Wilde.

List of Contributors

Paul Barnaby gained his Ph.D. (Edinburgh) on the reception of French Naturalism in Italy. He was Bibliographer/Researcher for BOSLIT (Bibliography of Scottish Literature in Translation), a joint project of the University of Edinburgh and the National Library of Scotland, and AHRB Research Fellow to the Research Project on the Reception of British Authors in Europe, 1999–2000. He is currently Editor of the Walter Scott Digital Archive, an online resource based around the Corson Collection of Walter Scott materials at Edinburgh University Library. He has published on the Italian reception of French Naturalism, on the reception and translation of twentieth-century Scottish literature and on French translations of Walter Scott (in the volume on Walter Scott in the present Series). He co-authored (with Tom Hubbard) four chapters on the international reception of Scottish literature for *The Edinburgh History of Scottish Literature* (2007). He has contributed the Timeline to most of the volumes in the present Series.

Zdeněk Beran is a lecturer in English Literature and Literary Translation at the Department of Anglophone Literatures and Cultures, Charles University, Prague. He has published articles (including '*Teleny* and the question of *Fin-de-Siècle* Sexuality') in *Prague Studies in English* and other academic journals. His recent research includes the Czech reception of major English writers, such as Conrad, Wilde and Dickens. He translates fiction and non-fiction, is a member of *Obec překladatelů* (Translators' association) and presides over the prestigious Cena Josefa Jungmanna (Josef Jungmann Award) for the best Czech translation of the year.

Evgenii Bershtein is Associate Professor and Chair of the Russian Department at Reed College in Portland, Oregon, where he teaches twentieth-century Russian literature and culture. He has published on Western sexual ideologies in Russian Symbolism (the topic of his forthcoming book) as well as eighteenth-century Russian poetry and contemporary Russian literature and film.

Elisa Bizzotto is a lecturer at IUAV University in Venice. She has worked on Walter Pater, Oscar Wilde, Vernon Lee and other *fin-de-siècle* authors and is especially interested in genre, gender, myth and inter-art and comparative approaches. She is the author of *La mano e l'anima* (Hand and soul) (2001) and has co-edited with Paola Spinozzi the Pre-Raphaelite magazine *The Germ: Thoughts towards nature in Poetry, Literature and Art* (2008).

Joseph Bristow is Professor of English at the University of California, Los Angeles. His most recent books include *Oscar Wilde and Modern Culture: The Making of a Legend* (Ohio University Press, 2008). During 2010–11 he is directing a year-long programme, 'Cultures of Aestheticism', at the William Andrews Clark Memorial Library, Los Angeles. He is International Editor of the *Journal of Victorian Culture* (Routledge) and series editor of Palgrave Studies in Nineteenth-Century Writing and Culture.

Richard A. Cardwell is Emeritus Professor of Modern Spanish Literatures at the University of Nottingham, United Kingdom. He is the author of over one hundred and twenty articles and over twenty books and editions on Castilian, Catalan and Galician writers in the modern period. He has also published comparative essays on European Romanticism, including Keats and Byron. He edited the special bi-centennial issue of *Renaissance and Modern Studies* (1988) on 'Byron and Europe' and *Lord Byron the European, Essays from the International Byron Society, July 1994* (1997). More recently he was the volume editor of *The Reception of Lord Byron in Europe*, in two volumes (2005), in the present Series. In 2007 this book was awarded the prestigious literary prize, the Emma Dangerfield Award for Scholarship on Lord Byron. His comparative essays include, among other authors, Musset, Coppée, Baudelaire, Verlaine, Mendès, Régnier, Mallarmé and Oscar Wilde. He is a Corresponding Member of the Academia de Buenas Letras de Sevilla, Spain.

Noreen Doody lectures in English Literature at St Patrick's College, Drumcondra, a college of Dublin City University, where she is Director of the MA in Theatre Studies. Her research interests are in Irish Studies and nineteenth-century literature, especially the work of Oscar Wilde and W. B. Yeats. She has published widely in this area and is currently working on a book on the influence of Wilde on Yeats.

Emily Eells is Professor of English at the University of Paris Ouest at Nanterre and head of the department's research centre. She teaches translation and nineteenth-century British literature, art and aesthetic theory, and focuses her research on the cultural exchange between Britain and France at the end of the nineteenth century. Her monograph, *Proust's Cup of Tea: Homoeroticism and Victorian Culture* was published by Ashgate in 2002. She contributed to *The Reception of Walter Pater in Europe* in this series, edited by Stephen Bann. The working title for her next book is *The French Oscar Wilde*.

Stefano Evangelista is Fellow and Tutor in English at Trinity College and Associate Professor in English at the University of Oxford. His research interests are in nineteenth-century English literature (especially aestheticism and Decadence), comparative literature, the reception of the classics and the relationship between literary and visual cultures. His monograph, *British Aestheticism and Ancient Greece: Hellenism, Reception, Gods in Exile*, was published by Palgrave Macmillan in 2009. He is currently working on a book on cosmopolitanism in English nineteenth-century literature.

Irena Grubica is a Lecturer in the English Department at the University of Rijeka, Croatia, where she teaches English Neo-Classicism and Romanticism and modern Irish literature. She graduated in English and comparative literature from the University of Zagreb and defended her Master's thesis on the two Croatian translations of *Ulysses*. She is currently working on a doctoral thesis on cultural memory in Joyce's novels. Her interests also include twentieth-century English and Irish literature, translation studies and cultural criticism. She has published several articles on English authors in various periodicals and a foreword to the first Croatian translation of Beckett's *Molloy*.

Richard Hibbitt is Lecturer in French at the University of Leeds. His research interests are in comparative literature and, in particular, in cultural exchange in the late nineteenth century. He is the author of *Dilettantism and its Values: From Weimar Classicism to the Fin de Siècle* (Legenda, 2006) and Assistant Editor of *Comparative Critical Studies*, the house journal of the British Comparative Literature Association. His publications include a further piece on Wilde entitled 'Oscar Wilde et Paul Bourget', in the online Wilde journal *Rue des beaux-arts* (November 2008). <http://www.oscholars.com/RBA/Rue_des_beaux_arts.htm>.

Rainer Kohlmayer is a Senior Lecturer in translation studies and linguistics at Mainz University at Germersheim. In 1980 he founded the Germersheim University Theatre (Uni-Bühne Germersheim) with which he produced almost thirty plays, often in new translations (Wilde, Maugham, Dumas, Molière, Corneille etc.). His translations have been staged all over Germany. He is the author of several plays, numerous cabaret sketches, aphorisms and poems. He has written a book and a number of essays on the reception of Oscar Wilde's plays in German-speaking theatres. His current research is concerned with literary translation in general. He is the editor and main contributor of *Die Schnake*, a literary and satirical fringe journal, founded in 1981, and still going. For more information see <www.rainer-kohlmayer.de>.

Lucia Krämer is a Lecturer in British literature and culture at Leibniz Universität, Hannover. She obtained her Ph.D. in 2002 at the University of Regensburg with a study on the biofictional representation of Oscar Wilde: *Oscar Wilde in Roman, Drama und Film* (Oscar Wilde in novels, drama and films, 2003). She continues to work on Wilde as an associate editor of the electronic journal *The Oscholars*. Other research areas, on which she has published various articles, include the British heritage culture and the theory and practice of adaptation. Her current main research project concerns the reception of popular Indian cinema in Britain.

Mária Kurdi is professor in the Institute of English Studies at the University of Pécs, Hungary. Her books include a volume of essays entitled *Codes and Masks: Aspects of Identity in Contemporary Irish Plays in an Intercultural Context* (Peter Lang 2000), and a collection of interviews with Irish playwrights, published in 2004. She is editor-in-chief of the journal *Focus: Papers in English Literary and Cultural Studies*, and has guest-edited special issues on Brian Friel and Arthur Miller for the *Hungarian Journal of English and American Studies*. With Donald E. Morse and Csilla Bertha she co-edited the book *Brian Friel's Dramatic Artistry: "The Work Has Value"* (Carysfort 2006). In 2009 Carysfort published her edited volume entitled *Literary and Cultural Relations: Ireland, Hungary, and Central and Eastern Europe*.

Marta Mateo is a Lecturer in English at the University of Oviedo, Spain, where she teaches English and literary translation. She completed her Ph.D. on the translation of English comedies into Spanish in 1992, and has since published articles and presented conference papers on the translation of humour, drama and opera. Her research interests also include translation theory, audiovisual translation and the teaching of English phonetics. She is the Spanish translator of Egil Törnqvist's *Transposing Drama* and Chester Himes's novel *If He Hollers, Let Him Go*. She has recently embarked on the translation of Tobias Smollet's *Humphrey Clinker*.

Sandra Mayer completed her PhD thesis at the University of Vienna on the reception of Wilde's plays on the Viennese stages in the twentieth century as part of the Austrian Science Fund project *Weltbühne Wien* (World Stage Vienna) on the reception of Anglophone plays in Vienna. She is now working on a post-doc project that explores the intersections of authorship, literary celebrity and politics in Victorian Britain.

Lene Østermark-Johansen is Associate Professor of English at the University of Copenhagen. She is the author of *Sweetness and Strength: The Reception of Michelangelo in Late Victorian England* (1998), and is the editor of a volume of essays on British Romanticism (2003) and of *Victorian and Edwardian Responses to the Italian Renaissance* (2005). She has published several articles on Pater, Swinburne and Wilde. Her monograph *Walter Pater and the Language of Sculpture* will be published by Ashgate in 2010.

Michelle Paull has worked as the Curator of Modern Literary Manuscripts at the British Library, as a researcher for the PeoplePlay project at the Theatre Museum in London and as an archivist on the Leyhausen-Spiess Collection at the Archive of Performances of Greek and Roman Drama in Oxford. She now lectures in Drama at St Mary's University College, Strawberry Hill, Twickenham, where her special interests include Irish drama – particularly Sean O'Casey and Oscar Wilde – Daphne du Maurier and adaptation studies. She is currently working on her book, *Sean O'Casey: The Critic and the Canon*, is the editor of the online Sean O'Casey journal, *Drummings,* and theatre-reviews editor for the online journal *The Oscholars*.

Victoria Reid is Lecturer in French at the University of Glasgow. She is the author of *André Gide and Curiosity* (Rodopi, 2009) and of the comparative articles 'André Gide and James Hogg: Elective Affinities' (*Studies in Hogg and His World*, 2007) and 'Gide et Rembrandt: la leçon d'anatomie' ('Gide and Rembrandt: The Anatomy Lesson', *Bulletin des amis d'André Gide*, 2007). Her area of research is French literature and culture from the late nineteenth century to the present, and her current focus is the representation of ageing in contemporary fiction and cinema.

Rita Severi teaches English Literature and Theatre Studies at the University of Verona (Italy). Her books, editions and essays on Oscar Wilde include: *Il Quinto Vangelo* (The fifth gospel) (1997), *La ballata del carcere di Reading* (BRG)

(1998), the exhibition catalogue 'Oscar Wilde: L'anima dell'uomo; Oscar Wilde in Italia' (Oscar Wilde: The soul of man; Oscar Wilde in Italy) (1998), *Wilde and Company: Sinestesie Fin de Siècle* (Wilde and Co: *fin-de-siècle* synaesthesias) (2001), *La Vita come Arte: Oscar Wilde, le Arti e l'Italia* (Life as art: Oscar Wilde, the arts and Italy) (with Masolino D'Amico, 2001) and *La Biblioteca di Oscar Wilde* (The library of Oscar Wilde) (2004). She has just published a book entitled *Rinascimenti: Shakespeare and Anglo/Italian Relations*.

Robert Vilain is Professor of German and Comparative Literature at Royal Holloway, University of London. He has published widely on German and French literature in the late nineteenth and early twentieth centuries, including monographs on Hugo von Hofmannsthal (OUP 2000) and Yvan Goll (forthcoming). He is co-editor of *Austrian Studies* and of a number of books including two volumes of essays on Rilke (CUP and Wallstein, 2009) and essays on detective fiction (Macmillan 2000).

Chris Walton was born in northern England and studied at the universities of Cambridge, Oxford, Zurich and Munich. From 1990 to 2001 he was head of the Music Division at the *Zentralbibliothek Zürich* (Zurich Central Library) and from 2001 to 2008 he was a professor in musicology at the music department at the University of Pretoria, which he also headed from 2001 to 2005. He is now an extraordinary professor at the University of Stellenbosch and managing director of the Orchestre Symphonique Bienne in Switzerland. He has published widely in English and German on topics ranging from the Swiss Renaissance to contemporary South African composers, but his main field of research is Romanticism in the German-speaking world, specifically Richard Wagner, Richard Strauss and Othmar Schoeck.

Abbreviations

The following abbreviations of titles of works by Oscar Wilde are used throughout the book.

BI	'The Birthday of the Infanta'
BRG	*The Ballad of Reading Gaol*
CA	'The Critic as Artist'
CG	'The Canterville Ghost'
DF	'The Devoted Friend'
DG	'The Doer of Good'
DL	'The Decay of Lying'
DP	*De Profundis*
DOP	*The Duchess of Padua*
ERA	'The English Renaissance of Art'
FHS	'The Fisherman and his Soul'
FT	'A Florentine Tragedy'
HJ	'The House of Judgement'
HOP	*A House of Pomegranates*
HP	'The Happy Prince'
HPOT	*The Happy Prince, and Other Tales*
IBE	*The Importance of Being Earnest*
IH	*An Ideal Husband*
LASC	'Lord Arthur Savile's Crime'
LASCOS	*Lord Arthur Savile's Crime and Other Stories*
LWF	*Lady Windermere's Fan*
MM	'The Model Millionaire'
NR	'The Nightingale and The Rose'
PA	'The Priest and the Acolyte'
PDG	*The Picture of Dorian Gray*
PMWH	'The Portrait of Mr. W. H.'
PP	'Poems in Prose'
PPP	'Pen, Pencil and Poison' (1889)
PPUY	'Phrases and Philosophies for the Use of the Young'
RR	'The Remarkable Rocket'
SC	'The Star-Child'
SCo	'La Sainte Courtisane'
SG	'The Selfish Giant'
SMUS	'The Soul of Man under Socialism'
SWS	'The Sphinx without a Secret'
TM	'The Truth of Masks'
VN	*Vera: or the Nihilist*
WNI	*A Woman of No Importance*
YK	'The Young King'

Timeline of the European Reception of Oscar Wilde

Compiled by Paul Barnaby

Under 'Translations', the Timeline records the first translations of individual works by Wilde for each European country, and in addition a number of significant retranslations. Under 'Criticism', it lists all European book-length monographs on Wilde, together with a number of significant reviews, articles, chapters and theses. 'Other' covers literary, artistic, and musical works inspired by Wilde, adaptations into other media, and significant events connected to Wilde's life and works.

In addition to bibliographical data supplied by the contributors to this volume, the Timeline draws on the national bibliographies, national library catalogues, or union catalogues of the following countries: Austria, Belgium, Bosnia-Herzegovina, Bulgaria, Croatia, Czech Republic, Denmark, Estonia, Finland, France, Germany, Greece, Hungary, Iceland, Ireland, Italy, Latvia, Lithuania, Macedonia, Moldova, Netherlands, Norway, Poland, Portugal, Romania, Serbia, Slovakia, Slovenia, Spain, Sweden, and Switzerland. Further data was extracted from UNESCO's *Index Translationum* database and the *WorldCat* global catalogue of library collections. For musical adaptations of Wilde, the principal sources were *Die Musik in Geschichte und Gegenwart: allgemeine Enzyklopädie der Musik, Personenteil*, 2nd rev. edn, ed. Ludwig Finscher (Kassel: Bärenreiter, c1994–2007), XVII (2007): 918–22, and Kurt Gänzl's *The Encyclopedia of the Musical Theatre*, 2nd edn (New York: Schirmer Books, 2001), III, 2193–95. The Timeline also draws on the following online bibliographies and scenographies:

Stumbea, Camelia, Chris Tanasescu, and Florina Tufescu, 'Oscar Wilde: A Romanian Bibliography of Secondary Sources' <http://www.oscholars.com/TO/Appendix/Bibliographies/romanian1.htm>

Stumbea, Camelia, Chris Tanasescu, and Florina Tufescu, 'Oscar Wilde: A Romanian Scenography' <http://www.oscholars.com/TO/Appendix/Scenographies/Romania/romania.htm>

Vernadakis, Emmanuel, 'Inventory of Plays and Dramatic Adaptations by Oscar Wilde Produced in Greece, 1900–1992' <http://www.oscholars.com/TO/Appendix/Scenographies/Greece/greece.htm>

Oscar Wilde is one of the world's most widely translated and discussed authors. According to UNESCO's *Index Translationum*, only Shakespeare, Conan Doyle, Stevenson and Dickens, among British or Irish literary figures, have appeared more widely in translations over the past thirty years. The Timeline records translations into forty-seven European tongues, including regional or minority languages such as Basque, Breton, Chuvash, Scottish Gaelic, and West Frisian, and into transnational languages such as Yiddish and Hebrew. In German alone, over seventy critical or biographical monographs have been published. Particularly in recent decades, the extent of Wilde's critical and popular reception far exceeds that of any previous writer treated in this series. The Timeline is thus by necessity longer than in previous volumes but also more selective. While it aims to record all first translations, subsequent significant translations and all critical monographs, space constraints have limited its coverage of articles, chapters and theses. While not exhaustive, then, it nonetheless offers an extensive and detailed overview of Wilde's European reception.

Date	Translations	Criticism	Other
1877		**Ireland:** *Freeman's Journal* commends Wilde's poetic contributions to *The Illustrated Monitor* and his article on the Grosvenor Gallery in the *Dublin University Magazine*	
1878		**Ireland:** *Irish Times* celebrates award of Newdigate Prize to Wilde	**Publication of 'Ravenna'**
1880			**Premiere of *VN***
1881			**Publication of *Poems***
1883		**France:** Wilde's comments on Swinburne noted in E. de Goncourt's diary (pub. during Wilde's 1891 visit to Paris)	**Composition of *DOP* (premiered 1891)**
			France: Wilde visits Paris
			Ireland: Wilde gives lectures 'The House Beautiful' and 'Personal Impressions of America' at the Gaiety Theatre, Dublin
1885			**Ireland:** Wilde gives lectures 'Dress' and 'The Value of Art in Modern Life' at the Gaiety Theatre
1887			**Publication of CG**

Date	Translations	Criticism	Other
1888			**Publication of** *HPOT*
			Ireland: Yeats meets Wilde in London
1889	**France:** BI (Merrill)		**Publication of** *DL*
	Netherlands: BI, HP, NR, SG (Ritter)		
1890	**Italy:** *VN*	**Bohemia (Czech):** H. G. Schauer, 'O úkolech naší kritiky'	**Publication of** *PDG*
1891	**France:** SG (Schwob)	**France:** 1) J. Daurelle interviews Wilde for *L'Echo de Paris* 2) E. de Goncourt's 1883 *Journal* entry published, provoking open letter from Wilde 3) H. Le Roux, 'OW' 4) Mallarmé praises *PDG* in letter to Wilde	**Publication of** *HOP,* *Intentions, LASCOS,* *SMUS;* **premiere of** *DOP*
			Austria: Hofmannsthal's verse drama *Gestern*
		Ireland: 1) Yeats, 'OW's Last Book' 2) *Irish Times* reviews *HOP, Intentions, LWF,* and *WNI*	**France:** 1) Wilde returns to Paris, meets Gide, Loüys, Mallarmé, Proust; Barrès gives dinner in his honour 2) Gide's essay *Le Traité du Narcisse* 3) J. Lorrain and M. Schwob dedicate tales to Wilde
		Spain: Nicaraguan essayist E. Gómez Carrillo discusses *Intentions* in *Sensaciones de arte*	
			Spain: Gómez Carrillo meets Wilde in Paris
1892	**France:** *LWF* (Bonnefont)	**France:** 1) H. Bauër discusses London banning of *Salomé* in *L'Echo de Paris* 2) Gide records fear of Wilde's influence in *Journal* 3) T. de Wyzewa, 'M. OW et les jeunes littérateurs anglais'	**Premiere of** *LWF*
	Italy: Extracts from SMUS in Sicilian journal *L'uguaglianza sociale*		**Austria:** Hofmannsthal announces intention to write essay on Wilde
	Netherlands: *LWF* (Ising)		**Germany/Hungary:** M. Nordau, *Entartung*
		Spain: Gómez Carrillo, *Esquisses*	
1893	**Netherlands:** *PDG* (Baud)	**France:** 1) A. France praises Wilde in *L'Univers illustré* (incl. translated extract from CA) 2) S. Merrill, 'OW'	**Publication of** *Salomé* **in Paris; premiere of** *WNI*
	Sweden: *Intentions* (Alkman)		**Austria:** Hofmannsthal's verse drama *Der Tor und der Tod* and essay 'Algernon Charles Swinburne'

Date	Translations	Criticism	Other
1894	**Austria:** DL	**Austria:** 1) H. Bahr, 'Décadence' 2) Hofmannsthal's notebook compares Wilde unfavourably with Ruskin, Pater, Madox Brown, Rossetti and Burne-Jones	**Publication of PP, PPUY, 'The Sphinx'** **France:** Gide encounters Wilde and Douglas in Florence **Italy:** 1) A. Conti, *Giorgione* 2) D'Annunzio's novel *Trionfo della morte*
1895	**Bohemia (Czech):** DL (Kosterka) in *Moderní revue* **France:** *PDG* (Tardieu/Maurevert) **Sweden:** *Salomé* (Alkman)	**Bohemia:** J. Karásek and A. Procházka defend Wilde in *Moderní revue* against attacks in the Czech press sparked by his trial and conviction **France:** 1) Following arrest, Wilde defended by P. Adam, Bauër, L. Lormel, H. Rebell, H. de Régnier, and L. Tailhade 2) Merrill and L. Deschamps launch petition demanding Wilde's release 3) A. Goldemar (*Le Gaulois*) and O. Mirbeau (*Le Journal*) report on conditions of hard labour 4) M. A. Raffalovich, 'L'Affaire OW' 5) *PDG* reviewed by C. Mauclair (*Le Mercure de France*), Mirbeau (*Le Journal*), A. Retté (*La Plume*), Tailhade, and Willy (both *L'Echo de Paris*) **Italy:** 1) B. Alimena, 'I reati contro il pudore e i reati contro la natura nel diritto inglese: a proposito del processo a carico di OW' 2) G. A. Sartorio, 'Esposizione di Venezia: nota sulla pittura in Inghilterra' **Russia:** 1) Wilde's trials extensively covered in popular daily *Novoe Vremya* 2) Argus, 'Oskar Uail'd i oskar uail'dizm' 3) A. Volynskii reviews *Intentions* for *Severnyi vestnik*	**Premieres of *IBE*, *IH*; Wilde's trials and imprisonment** **Austria:** Hofmannsthal's tale 'Das Märchen der 672. Nacht' **France:** 1) Gide meets Wilde and Douglas in Algeria 2) Gide corresponds with Douglas during Wilde's trials 3) 'Métamorphoses d'OW', parody of *PDG* published in *La Lanterne* **Italy:** D'Annunzio's 'Proemio' to first issue of *Convito*

Date	Translations	Criticism	Other
1896	**Bohemia (Czech):** Preface to *PDG* (Procházka) in *Moderní revue*	**France:** 1) Gide in his *Journal* considers Wilde's life more important than his works 2) Lorrain, 'Salomé et ses poètes' 3) Rachilde, 'Questions brûlantes' 4) Raffalovich, *Uranisme et unisexualité* 5) G. Saint-Paul, *Perversion et perversité sexuelle* 6) *Salomé* extensively reviewed, incl. by Bauër, L. Bernard-Derosne, G. Boyer, H. Céard, J. Du Tillet, J. Des Gachons, G. Geffroy, C. Le Senne, P. Marrot, C. Mendès, F. Sarcey, A. Segard, J. de Tinan, G. Vanor, and 'Les Treize' 7) *LWF* negatively reviewed by Lorrain **Austria:** Hofmannsthal rejects Wilde's aestheticism in letter to Bahr **Germany:** 1) J. Gaulke, 'OW' 2) O. Sero, *Der Fall Wilde und das Problem der Homosexualität* **Russia:** Volynskii, 'Oskar Uail'd' **Spain:** Nicaraguan poet Rubén Darío's essays *Los raros*	**Premiere of *Salomé* in Paris** **Italy:** 1) D'Annunzio/Gargano, 'Prologo' to first issue of *Il Marzocco* 2) Italian trans. of Raffalovich's 'L'Affaire OW' **Russia:** Gippius's short story 'Zlatotsvet'
1897	**Germany:** CG (Boehn) **Italy:** Private reading in Naples of trans. of *Salomé* (Rocco), pub. 1901 **Russia:** *LWF* (Vasil'ev) **Sweden:** *LWF* (Alkman)	**Italy:** M. Serao announces Wilde's presence in Naples in *Il Mattino* **Russia:** N.V., 'Oskar Uail'd i angliiskie estety'	**Austria:** Hofmannsthal's verse play *Der Kaiser und die Hexe* **France:** 1) Gide visits freed Wilde in Berneval-sur-Mer 2) Gide's novel *Les Nourritures terrestres* **Italy:** 1) Wilde in Naples 2) U. Ojetti's 'Dialoghi dei vivi' **Russia:** Tolstoy's treatise 'Chto takoe iskusstvo' (through 1898)

Date	Translations	Criticism	Other
1898	**France:** *BRG* (Davray) **Russia:** DF, HP ('M.')	**Italy:** Ojetti reviews French trans. of *BRG* in *Il Marzocco* (with trans. of extracts) **Russia:** L. Shestov, *Dobro i zlo v uchenii Grafa Tolstogo i F. Nitsshe* **Spain:** Anon., 'Los estetas' in *Vida nueva*	**Publication of *BRG***
1899	**Bohemia (Czech):** 'The Artist', 'The Disciple' (Procházka) **France:** PP (Davray) **Russia:** DL (Solov'eva)	**France:** L. Sougenet praises *BRG* in *La Plume* **Germany:** Wilde trials discussed in *Jahrbuch für sexuelle Zwischenstufen* **Italy:** A. Conti, 'Il poeta', 'Le vicende dell'arte'	**France:** Gide's play *El Hadj* **Germany:** T. Mann's short story 'Gerächt'
1900	**Austria:** First German trans. of *Salomé* (Lachmann); 'The Disciple', 'The Master' (Kassner) **Bohemia (Czech):** 'The Master' (Procházka) **Croatia:** 'The Artist' (Jelovšek) **France:** NR (Merrill) **Germany:** LASC, PMWH (Greve) **Sweden:** 59 stanzas of *BRG*	**Austria:** R. Kassner, 'Zum Tode Oskar Wildes' **France:** Obituaries by E. La Jeunesse, Lorrain, Merrill, and L. Muhlfeld **Italy:** The *Giornale di Sicilia* notes Wilde's presence in Palermo, translating aphorisms and extracts from *BRG* **Spain:** Rubén Darío, 'Purificaciones de la piedad'	**Death of Wilde in Paris, burial in Bagneux cemetery** **Bohemia (Czech):** 1) H. Boettinger's painting *Salome* (approx. date) 2) J. Jakší's painting *The Beheading of St John the Baptist* 3) S. K. Neumann's poem 'Salome' **France:** Mirbeau portrays Wilde as Sir Harry Kimberly in *Le Journal d'une femme de chambre* **Italy:** Conti's treatise *Beata riva*
1901	**Bohemia (Czech):** *BRG* (Živný) **Germany:** *PDG* (Gaulke) **Italy:** Publication of *Salomé* (Rocco) **Latvia:** DG (Lejas-Krūmiņš) **Russia:** CA (Solov'eva)	**Bohemia:** Karásek, 'OW' **Croatia:** A. G. Matoš, 'Pismo iz Pariza' **Germany:** 1) Gaulke, 'Oskar Wildes Dorian Gray' 2) E. Mayer, 'Von den Londoner Theatern' (through 1902) 3) N. Prätorius, 'Oskar Wilde: ein Bericht'	**Bohemia:** *Moderní revue* prints A. C. Sterner's portrait of Wilde in pen and ink and a trans. of Merrill's obituary (Procházka) **France:** Wilde is model for Lord Ethal in Lorrain's novel *Monsieur de Phocas*

Date	Translations	Criticism	Other
1902	**Bohemia (Czech):** *Salomé* (Anon.)	**Croatia:** Matoš, 'Oskar Wilde'	**Croatia:** Matoš's short story 'Ugasnulo svjetlo'
	France: *HOP* (Khnopff)	**France:** Gide, 'Hommage à OW'	**France:** 1) Gide's novel *L'Immoraliste*
	Germany: *IBE, Intentions, PPUY,* new *PDG* (Greve); *LWF, WNI* (Pavia/Teschenberg)	**Germany:** *Salomé* and *IBE* reviewed by A. Eloesser, S. Jacobsohn, and I. Landau	2) Wilde is model for Filde in Lorrain's *Le Vice errant*
		Hungary: 1) G. Szilágyi, 'Wilde Oszkár' 2) G. Szini, 'Wilde Oszkár'	**Germany:** Trans. of Sherard's *OW*
	Spain: *Salomé* (Pérez Jorba/Rodríguez)		
1903	**Bohemia (Czech):** *CA* (Šalda; through 1904)	**Austria:** 1) K. Kraus refutes F. Schütz's charge that *Salomé* is anti-semitic 2) F. Salten, 'Von OW'	**France:** Gide's drama *Saül*
	Denmark: *Salomé* (Sarauw)		**Germany:** Trans. of Gide's 'Hommage à OW'
	Germany: *HPOT* (Gaulke), *IH*, new *Salomé* (Pavia/Teschenberg), new *IBE* (Teschenberg)	**Denmark:** Dagmar Theatre production of *Salomé* reviewed in *Politiken* and *Teateret*	**Italy:** B. Chiara's collection of tales *L'umano convito*
		Germany: 1) F. C. Gerden, *OW* 2) F. P. Greve, *Randarabesken zu OW* 3) M. Meyerfeld, 'OW in Deutschland'	
	Hungary: *LWF* (Moly)		
	Italy: LASC (Corsi)		
	Poland: *Salomé* (Fromowicz)	**Hungary:** 1) *LWF* reviewed by Lukács and E. Osvát 2) *Salomé* praised by Lukács	
	Russia: *BRG* (Norm), BI (Sherstobitova), NR ('Z.T.')	**Italy:** Alastor, 'Arte e democrazia'	
1904	**Bohemia (Czech):** *HOP, HPOT* (Jesenská, introd. Bartoš)	**Austria:** 1) F. Blei (ed.), *In Memoriam OW* 2) Kraus praises *BRG, PDG,* and SMUS in *Die Fackel*	**Denmark:** Bang's novel *Mikaël*
	Germany: *DOP* (Meyerfeld), *HOP* (Greve), SMUS (Lachmann/Landauer)	**Bohemia:** V. Tille, 'Oskar Wilde'	**Germany:** Trans. of D. Young's *Apologia pro OW* (Greve)
	Hungary: *HPOT* (Iván), *PDG* (Konkoly)	**Germany:** C. Hagemann, *OW*	
	Italy: HP (Bianco)	**Italy:** L. Gamberale, 'Il processo e l'estetica di OW'	

Date	Translations	Criticism	Other
	Netherlands: *Salomé*	**Russia:**	
		1) V. Artaban, 'Gnilaia dusha'	
	Russia: *Salomé* (V. &	2) K. Bal'mont, 'Poeziia	
	L. Andruson), new	Oskara Uail'da'	
	BRG (Bal'mont)		
1905	**Bohemia (Czech):**	**Austria:**	**Posthumous**
	IBE (Lorenc), *IH*	1) P. Altenberg, '*Der*	**publication of *DP***
	(Linková), *PDG*	*Sozialismus und die Seele*	**(preceded by German**
	(A. Tille/Borecký),	*des Menschen*, von OW'	**trans. of *MS*) and**
	2 x new *Salomé*	2) Hofmannsthal, 'Sebastian	***The Rise of Historical***
	(Adi-Hidári-Ho;	Melmoth'	***Criticism***
	Theer, introd. V. Tille)	3) A. Polgar, 'OWs Lustspiele'	
			Bohemia (Czech):
	Croatia: *Salomé*	**Austria/Ireland:** Shaw,	1) O. Schneiderová's
	(Benešić /N. Andrić)	'Oskar Wilde' in *Neue Freie*	painting *Pride*
		Presse	*(Salome)* (approx.
	Denmark: *PDG*		date)
	(Drewsen)	**Denmark:** P. Levin reviews	2) J. Wenig's painting
		PDG in *Politiken*	*Salome*
	England (Yiddish):		
	SMUS	**Finland (Swedish):** English	**Croatia:** F. Galović's
		DP reviewed in *Euterpe*	poem 'Saloma' (revised
	Finland: *IH*, *Salomé*		1911)
		France: Gide, 'Le *De*	
	Finland (Swedish):	*Profundis* d'OW'	**Germany:**
	CG, LASC		1) Premiere of Strauss's
	(Gripenberg/Wendt)	**Germany:** Meyerfeld,	*Salome* (with libretto
		'Wilde, Wilde, Wilde...'	based on Lachmann's
	France: *Intentions*		trans.)
	(Renaud); *HPOT*,	**Ireland:** G. Moore compares	2) Premiere of
	LASC (Savine); *DP*	Synge and Wilde in letter to	Simplizissimus's
	(Davray)	*Irish Times*	burlesque opera
			Das Gespenst von
	Germany: *DP*	**Italy:**	*Matschatsch* (after
	(Meyerfeld); The	1) Anon., 'La psicologia di	CG)
	Sphinx' (Dörmann),	Cristo'	
	new *Intentions*	2) Gamberale, 'Un più reale	**Russia:** Trans. of Gide's
	(Roessler), new CG	OW'	'Le *De Profundis* d'OW'
	and other stories	3) G. Lipparini, '*De Profundis*	
	(Blei)	di O. Wilde'	
	Hungary: *DOP*	**Sweden:** English *DP*	
	(Kosztolányi), *DP*	reviewed in *Svenska Dagbladet*	
	(Sztankay)		
	Italy: *LWF*; *PDG*		
	(Chiara), *DP*		
	(Bicchierai)		
	Netherlands: 2 x		
	DP (Boutens, van der		
	Borch)		
	Poland: Selected tales		
	(Feldmanowa)		

Date	Translations	Criticism	Other
	Russia: *PDG* ('A.T.'); *DP*, with selected poems, prose, letters, and aphorisms (Andreeva); Collected Works (Sablin edition; through 1909)		
	Sweden: *PDG* (Selander), *DP* (Lamberg)		
1906	**Austria/Germany:** Vols I–VI of Wiener edition of Collected Works, comprising first German trans. of *Poems* (Hauser) and *Essays* (Löwenkreuz) plus new *PDG* (Fred) and *Intentions* (Wertheimer)	**Austria:** 1) R. Auernheimer, 'Paradoxe Aesthetik' 2) Blei, 'Das ästhetische Leben' 3) G. Landauer, 'Drei Dramen und ihre Richter'	**Austria/Belgium:** Premiere in Vienna of dancer Maud Allan's *The Vision of Salome* (with music by Belgian composer M. Rémy)
	Belgium: First French trans. of SMUS (Grosfils)	**Denmark/Germany:** H. Langgaard, *Oskar Wilde: die Saga eines Dichters*	**Croatia:** Galović's one-act play *Tamara* (rewritten in verse, 1907)
	Bohemia (Czech): *DP* (Starý, introd. Marten)	**Germany:** H. Ernstmann, *Salome an den deutschen Hofbühnen: ein Kulturbild*	**Germany:** PA translated and attributed to Wilde
	Croatia: DG, HJ, 'The Master', 'The Teacher of Wisdom', new 'The Artist' (Mel); 'The Disciple' (Laetus; through 1907)	**Hungary:** *WNI* reviewed in *Budapest Hírlap*	**Russia:** Kuzmin's novel *Kryl'ya*
		Ireland: Wilde's trans. from Aeschylus and Euripides praised in *Irish Times*	**Sweden:** Trans. of Sherard's *OW*
	Finland: *PDG* (Setälä)	**Italy:** 1) P. Borrelli, 'OW' 2) G. S. Gargano, 'Precetti di estetica wildiana'	
	Finland (Swedish): *IBE*	**Poland:** A. Nowaczyński, *Oskar Wilde*	
	France: CG, MM, PMWH, SMUS, SWS (Savine); *IH*, *WNI* (Arnelle); new *Intentions* (Rebell)	**Russia:** 1) M. Kuzmin and V. Ivanov debate Wilde 2) V. Uspenskii, 'Religiia Oskara Uail'da i sovremennyi asketizm'	
	Germany: FT (Meyerfeld); *Poems*; ERA (Blei)		
	Hungary: *WNI*		

Date	Translations	Criticism	Other
	Italy: *BRG* (Vannicola; through 1907); *Intentions* (Piccoli), with introduction incl. translated extracts from *DP*, PP, and selected poems; *WNI*		
	Latvia: *HOP* (Upīts)		
	Netherlands: *HPOT* (Oosterzee)		
	Poland: *Intentions* (Feldmanowa)		
	Russia: *Intentions* (Mintslova)		
	Spain (Catalan): CG, DF, HP, LASC, MM, NR, SG (Montoliu)		
	Sweden: CG, *HOP*, *HPOT*, LASC, PMWH (Lundquist); *IH*		
1907	**Bohemia (Czech):** *LWF* (Havlasa)

Croatia: *PDG* (Schneider) serialized in *Hrvatska smotra*; *LWF* (Bogdanović); 'Sonnet on Hearing the Dies Irae Sung in the Sistine Chapel' (B.D.)

England (Yiddish): *Salomé*; HP, NR, SG (Frumkin)

Finland: *HPOT*, *DP* (Setälä)

Finland (Swedish): *BRG* (Gripenberg)

France: *Poems* (Savine) | **Austria:**
1) T. Antropp reviews *WNI* in *Österreichische Rundschau*
2) R. Lothar comments on Viennese vogue for Wilde in *Bühne und Welt*
3) *LWF* reviewed in *Illustrirtes Wiener Extrablatt*

Croatia: V. Lunaček reviews *LWF* in *Obzor*

Hungary:
1) D. Kosztolányi reviews *IBE*, *IH*, *Salomé*, and dramatization of *PDG* in *Budapesti Napló*
2) *Salomé* attacked by B. Tóth and defended by Endre Ady

Ireland: *LWF* praised in *Irish Times* | **Bohemia (Czech):**
1) Karásek's novel *Román Manfreda Macmillena* and play *Sen o říši krásy*
2) J. Konůpek's portrait of Wilde (oil)

Denmark: Bang's short story 'Stærkest'

France:
1) Premiere of F. Schmitt's ballet *La Tragédie de Salomé*, interpreted by L. Fuller, in a costume of 4,500 peacock feathers based on Beardsley's drawing
2) Cinematic *Salomé* produced by Gaumont studio
3) PA translated and attributed to Wilde |

Date	Translations	Criticism	Other
	Germany: *BRG* (Unus), new *HOP* (Greve), 3 x new *PDG* (Lachmann/ Preiß/Oehlschlägel/ Landauer), new CA, DL (Lachmann/ Landauer)	**Russia:** Anon., *Literaturnye siluety*	**Hungary:** Trans. of Langgaard's *Oskar Wilde*
	Hungary: Aphorisms (Radó), FT (Benedek), *IBE* (Mikes), *IH* (Mihály), *Salomé* (Battlay)		
	Italy: *HOP*, NR, 'The Master of Wisdom' (Chiara); *IH* (Palmieri)		
	Latvia: *Salomé*		
	Russia: FT (Likiardopulo/ Kursinkski), *IH* (Popova), SMUS (Golovkina)		
	Spain: New *Salomé* serialized in *El nuevo mercurio*		
	Sweden: *IBE*		
1908	**Austria/Germany:** Vols VII–X of Wiener edition of Collected Works, comprising first German trans. of *VN* (Neumann), new trans. of *IBE* (Greve), *IH* (Neumann), *LWF* (Brieger), *Salomé* (Uhl), and *WNI* (Greve)	**Germany:** 1) L. Feuchtwanger, *Heinrich Heine und OW* 2) E. Weisz, *Psychologische Streifzüge über OW*	**Posthumous publication of FT, SCo**
		Hungary: Z. Szász, 'Wilde Oszkár'	**Austria:** Premiere of F. Schreker's ballet-pantomime *Der Geburtstag der Infantin* (after BI)
	Belgium (Dutch): *IBE*	**Italy:** 1) G. Barini, 'La morale nelle opere di OW' 2) G. Vitaletti, *Salome nella leggenda e nell'arte*	**France:** 1) Theatrical adaption of *PDG* by Cocteau and Renaud (posthumously pub. in 1978) 2) Premiere of A. Mariotte's opera *Salomé*
	Bohemia (Czech): CG, LASC, MM, PP, SWS (Procházka); FT (Krecar)	**Russia:** N. Minskii, 'Smysl Salomei'	
		Spain: Review of Methuen edition of Wilde in *Prometeo*	
	Croatia: FT (Vojnović); *PDG* (Schneider) in book form; NR	**Sweden:** N. Söderblom, 'Kristusbilden i OWs *De profundis*'	**Hungary:** Szini's essay 'A mese alkonya'

Date	Translations	Criticism	Other
	England (Yiddish): *BRG* (Rosenblatt) **Estonia:** SG **Germany:** New *Salomé* (Meyerfeld) **Greece:** FT, *Salomé* (Poriotis)*; IBE* **Hungary:** *BRG* (Radó), *HOP* (Mikes), SMUS (Kelen), selected fiction and prose, selected essays **Italy:** New *Salomé* (Vannicola); new LASC (Verdinois, introd. Rocco) **Netherlands:** FT (Raaf), *IH* **Poland:** *IH* (Rakowski), *WNI* (Beaupré), SMUS (Belmont) **Portugal:** First Portuguese-language trans. of *Salomé* (Rio) pub. simultaneously in Paris and Rio de Janeiro **Russia:** *IBE* (Popilov/von Minkvits), SCo (Likiardopulo), PMWH (Berdyaev) **Spain (Catalan):** *Salomé* (Pena) **Ukraine:** Selected tales		**Russia:** 1) Premiere of A. Glazunov's ballet *Salomé* (choreography by M. Fokine, interpreted by I. Rubinstein) 2) S. Vasilenko's symphonic poem *The Garden of Death* (inspired by CG) 3) Trans. of Langgaard's *Oskar Wilde*

Date	Translations	Criticism	Other
1909	**Bohemia (Czech):** ERA, PMWH, SMUS, 'L'Envoi', 'Personal Impressions of America' (Procházka); new CA (Novák); selected poems (Klášterský) **Croatia:** *IH* (Šenoa), *FT* (Vojnović) **England (Yiddish):** *DP* (Marmor) **France:** Vol. I of Collected Theatre (Savine), incl. first trans. of *DOP*, *VN* **Netherlands:** *HOP* (Oosterzee), *IBE* **Russia:** *VN* (Solov'ev) **Spain:** *BRG* (Baeza), *HOP* (Emeterio Mazorriaga)	**Croatia:** National Theatre production of *IH* reviewed by J. Benešić and 'Ld.' **France:** J. Adelswärd-Fersen, 'Sur la glorification du vierge dans la religion d'OW' **Germany:** Reimarus Secundus, *Geschichte der Salome: von Cato bis OW* **Hungary:** 1) C. V. H. de Rozsnyay, *Emlékek* 2) M. Lengyel praises *DOP* in *Nyugat* **Italy:** 1) E. Pappacena, 'Nei pomeriggi d'estate' 2) P. Valera, *I gentiluomini invertiti* **Italy/Ireland:** Joyce, 'OW: il poeta di *Salomè*' in Triestine daily *Il Piccolo della Sera* **Russia:** H. Y. Abramovich, *Religiia krasoty i stradaniia: O. Uail'd i Dostoevsskii*	**Wilde's remains moved from Bagneux to Père Lachaise cemetery, Paris** **Austria:** Schoenberg's monodrama *Erwartung* (premiered in Prague, 1924) **Bohemia (Czech):** 1) A. Breisky's 'Kvintesence dandysmu' and 'Harlekýn – kosmický klaun' (essays) and 'Báseň v próze' and 'Zpověď grafomanova' (tales purportedly translated from Stevenson) 2) J. Váchal's first woodcut *Salome* **France:** Cocteau's *La Lampe d'Aladin* includes 4 poems based on *Salomé*
1910	**Armenia:** LASC and other tales (Khashmanean) **Croatia:** *IBE* (Begović) **Denmark:** *BRG* (O. V. Andersen); *IBE*; *IH* (Høyer) **France:** Vol. II of Collected Theatre (new trans. of *LWF*, *WNI*) **Germany:** Collected tales (Blei) and fairy tales (Greve)	**Denmark:** Trans. of *BRG*, Ny Teater production of *IH*, and Frederiksberg Teater production of *IBE* all reviewed in *Politiken* **France:** 1) Gide, *OW* (incl. revised versions of 'Hommage à OW' and 'Le *De Profundis* d'OW') 2) R. Laurent, *Etudes anglaises* **Italy:** Marinetti, *Futurist Speech to the English* **Netherlands:** C. Van Balen, *OW*	**Bohemia (Czech):** 1) Breisky's short stories *Triumf zla* 2) Konůpek's drawings *Ecstasy (Salome)* and *Black Flame (Salome)*, etching *Salome*, and print *Salome* (drypoint) 3) J. Zrzavý's drawings *The Head of St John the Baptist* and *Garlanded Nude Woman (Salome)* **Denmark:** A. Strøm's film *Dorian Grays Portræt* (after *PDG*)

Date	Translations	Criticism	Other
	Greece: *DP*	**Spain (Catalan):** R. Portusach reviews Teatro principal de Barcelona production of *Salomé*	**France:** 1) First illustrated ed. of *PDG* (ill. Thiriat and Dété) issued by Carrington 2) Cocteau's poems 'Mr W. H.' and 'Le Dieu nu'
	Netherlands: *BRG* (Nijhoff)		
	Portugal: *Salomé* (Souto)	**Sweden:** E. P. Bendz, 'Some Stray Notes on the Personality and Writings of OW'	
	Serbia: *LWF* (Grčić)		
	Spain: New *Salomé* (Pérez Jorba)	**Ukraine (Hebrew):** S. Gorelik, *Partsufim sifrutiyim kovets maamre bikoret*	**Spain:** PA translated and attributed to Wilde
1911	**Armenia:** SG (Mirianian)	**Croatia:** 1) Matoš, 'Wilde i Mac Neill Whistler' 2) A. Wenzelides, 'O Oskaru Wildeu'	**Bohemia (Czech):** 1) E. Filla's painting *Salome* 2) J. Hořejší's sonnet 'U hrobu Oscara Wilda'
	Bohemia (Czech): *DOP* (Procházka), TM (Novák)		
	Croatia: *HPOT*	**Hungary:** 1) Lukács, *A modern dráma fejlődésének története* 2) Rozsnyay, *Jegyzetek Oscar Wilderól*	**Germany:** Trans. of Gide's *OW*
	Denmark: DF, HP, NR, SG (O. V. Andersen)		**Hungary:** Trans. of S. Mason's *OW: Art and Morality*
		Italy: 1) D. Oliva, *Note di uno spettatore* 2) G. Rosadi, 'OW in carcere' 3) A. Sorani, 'OW e sua madre'	
	England (Yiddish): *PDG* (Meyer)		**Italy/France:** D'Annunzio's mystery play *Le Martyre de Saint Sébastien*
	France: Vol. III of Collected Theatre (first trans. of *IBE* and new *IH*)		
			Russia: Prokofiev's *Maddalena* (through 1913), an operatic version of *FT* (premiered in Austria, 1981)
	Germany: PP (in trans. of Gide's *OW*)		
	Greece: Chapter 1 of *PDG* (Raissi) in *Nea hestia*		
	Hungary: *VN* (Rozsnyay)		

Date	Translations	Criticism	Other
1911 (*cont*)	**Netherlands:** *WNI* **Poland (Yiddish):** HP, SC, YK (Vaynberg) **Romania:** FHS (Anghel) **Spain:** *WNI*, PP (Baeza)		
1912	**France:** Collected essays, criticism, and letters, 1877–85 (Savine) **Hungary:** SMUS (Winkler) **Italy:** *HPOT* (Misa), first complete SMUS (Agresti), SWS (Vannicola) **Latvia:** *HPOT* (Skalbe; pub. Russia) **Portugal:** First Portuguese-language trans. of *Intentions* (Rio) pub. simultaneously in Paris and Rio de Janeiro **Russia:** Collected Works (ed. Chukovskii) **Spain:** DL **Sweden:** *WNI*	**Austria:** Blei, *Der Dichter und das Leben* **Russia:** Z. Vengerova, 'Sud nad Oskarom Uail'dom' **Spain:** Rubén Darío, *Autobiografía*	**Germany:** T. Mann's novella *Der Tod in Venedig*

Date	Translations	Criticism	Other
1913	**Croatia:** 210 lines of *BRG* (K. Kovačić); YK (Galović); CG, HP, MM, SG **Estonia:** HP (Kurs-Olesk) **France:** Collected essays, criticism, and letters, 1887–90 (Savine) **Italy:** New SMUS (Fabbri) **Netherlands:** SMUS (Boutens) **Poland:** *PDG* (Jaroszyński) **Spain:** *Intentions* (Gómez de la Serna) **Sweden:** SMUS (Höglund)	**Germany:** 1) E. J. Bock, *Walter Pater's Einfluss auf OW* 2) F. K. Brass, *OWs 'Salome': eine kritische Quellenstudie* **Italy:** 1) A. Soffici comments on Wilde's trials in his diary 2) G. Vannicola, 'OW e l'edonismo'	**Bohemia (Czech):** 1) Photograph and two oleo prints by F. Drtikol all entitled *Salome* 2) Kobliha's woodcut *Salome* (approx. date) 3) Váchal's second woodcut *Salome* **Croatia:** Galović's short story 'Začarano ogledalo' **France:** Gide's *Journal* records ambition to be an explicator of Wilde **Germany:** B. Sekles's ballet *Der Zwerg und die Infantin* (after BI) **Italy:** 1) PA (Chiara) translated and attributed to Wilde 2) G. Papini, et al., 'Introibo' to *Lacerba* **Russia:** Ballets Russes present Schmitt's *La Tragédie de Salomé* (choreography: B. Ramonov)
1914	**Bohemia (Czech):** *WNI* (Hanušová/ Linhart) **France:** Selected essays and aphorisms (Cantel) **Italy:** CG, new LASC (Vannicola), FT (Moschino), PP (von Tigerström), *BRG,* new *DP* (De Naro) **Lithuania:** *HOP* (Puida; pub. USA, first Lithuanian edition: 1923) **Romania:** *IH* **Spain:** *IH* (Jori)	**Italy:** Anon., 'OW e il pubblico' **Poland:** K. Bukowski, *Sylwetki: studya z literatury i sztuki* **Sweden:** Bendz, *The Influence of Pater and Matthew Arnold in the Prose-Writings of OW*	**Bohemia (Czech/ German):** E. Schulhoff's *Rosa Mystica*, song settings of 'E tenebris', 'Madonna mia', and 'Requiescat' **France:** 1) Gide's novel *Les Caves du Vatican* 2) Trans. of Douglas's *OW and Myself* 3) Trans. of Ransome's *OW* **Italy:** D. Campana's poem 'OW a San Miniato' (approx. date)

Date	Translations	Criticism	Other
1915	**Croatia:** New *Salomé* (Mitrović; trans. from Lachmann's libretto to Strauss's *Salome*) **Lithuania:** *Salomé* (Michelsonas; pub. USA) **Greece:** Aphorisms, etc. **Norway:** 2 x *BRG* (Lippe Konow, Twedt), *LASCOS* (Fermann), *DP* (Lippe Konow) **Serbia:** *DP* (Sekulić) **Ukraine:** SWS and other tales (Makovska)	**Italy:** 1) G. A. Borgese, *Studi di letteratura moderna* 2) Vannicola, 'Il segreto di OW' **Norway:** J. O. Dedekam, *Bemerkninger om OW og hans 'Society plays'*	**Russia:** *Portret Doriana Greya*, film directed by V. Meyerhold and M. Doronin
1916	**Greece:** *BRG* (Marpoutzoglou), PP **Hungary:** Selected poems (Babits) **Italy:** Selections from *Oscariana* (Stocchetti) **Romania:** Selected tales (Davidescu), LASC (Ardeleanu)		**Hungary:** M. Babits's novel *A gólyakalifa*
1917	**Bohemia (Czech):** SCo (Reichmann) **Bosnia-Herzegovina:** *DP* **Greece:** *IH*, SCo, selected tales **Spain:** *HPOT* (Baeza); new *WNI* (Plañiol)	**Austria/Germany:** E. Friedell, 'Das Bild des Dorian Gray' **France:** Lady Gargiles, *Petit essay sur le 'Portrait de Dorian Gray' d'OW* **Norway:** T. L. Findahl, *OW og den engelske societet* **Spain:** 1) R. Pérez de Ayala, 'Las comedias modernas de OW' and 'OW o el espíritu de la contradicción' 2) Adamuz and García Ortega company productions of *IH* and *WNI* reviewed in *ABC*	**Bohemia (Czech):** M. Marten's 'testament' *Nad městem* **Germany:** 1) Premiere of Zemlinsky's opera *Eine florentinische Tragödie* (after FT) 2) R. Oswald's film *Das Bildnis des Dorian Gray*

Date	Translations	Criticism	Other
1918	**Belgium (Dutch):** *BRG* (van Akkergem/ van Beugem Verdoodt) **Croatia:** *HOP* (Velikanović) **Estonia:** CG (Johannson) **France:** FT, SCo, *The Cardinal of Avignon* (Georges–Bazile) **Hungary:** *Intentions* (Halasi) **Iceland:** YK (Jónsson) **Poland:** SG (Langerowa) **Spain:** *PDG* (Gómez de la Serna), PPUY (Baeza)	**Germany:** 1) B. Fehr, *Studien zu OW's Gedichten* 2) T. Mann, *Betrachtungen eines Unpolitischen* **Spain:** R. Baeza refutes Pérez de Ayala's critique of Wilde in *La correspondencia de España*	**Bohemia (Czech):** Trans. of Gide's *OW* **Croatia:** M. Krleža's poem 'Saloma' **Hungary:** Premiere of M. Radnai's ballet *Az infánsznö születésnapja* (after BI)
1919	**Czechoslovakia (Czech):** *Intentions* **Estonia:** *Salomé* (Visnapuu); 'The Artist', 'The Master' **Finland:** SMUS (Vehkamäki) **France:** 'The Harlot's House', letters to the *Daily Chronicle* on living conditions in prison (Savine) **Germany:** New *Salomé* (Moreck) **Hungary:** Selected essays (Hevesi) **Italy:** SCo (Moschino), new *BRG*, *DP* (Manzotti Bignone)	**Czechoslovakia (Czech):** J. Reichmann, 'OW a české písemnictví' **Hungary:** Kosztolányi comments ironically on cult of Wilde **Italy:** G. Sgroi, 'Il *De Profundis* di OW' and 'Le idee estetiche e la critica letteraria di OW' **Spain:** 1) A. Alcalá Galiano, 'OW: una semblanza' (compiled from articles originally pub. 1918) 2) R. Cansinos-Assens, *Salomé en la literatura: Flaubert, Wilde, Mallarmé, Eugenio de Castro, Apollinaire*	**Czechoslovakia (Czech):** PA translated and attributed to Wilde **Hungary:** Trans. of Douglas's *OW and Myself*

Date	Translations	Criticism	Other
	Norway: SMUS (Mikkelsen)		
	Poland (Hebrew): *IBE* (Tawiow), *DP* (Frischmann)		
	Romania: PP (Stamatiad)		
	Slovenia: Selected fairy tales (Gradnik)		
	Spain: *IBE* (Baeza); *DP*, SMUS (Vasseur); LASC (Gómez de la Serna)		
	Ukraine: *Salomé*		
1920	**Armenia:** RR (Mikayelian; pub. Russia)	**Croatia:** M. Begović reviews *Salomé* in *Novosti*	**Bohemia (Czech):** F. T. Šimon's wood engraving *Salome* (approx. date)
	Croatia: *LASCOS* (Drvodelić), *PDG* (Schneider)	**Denmark:** N. T. Thomsen, *OW: literaturbilleder fra det moderne England.*	**France:** 1) J. Ibert's symphonic poem *La Ballade de la geôle de Reading*
	Germany (Hebrew): Fairy tales (Ben Eliezer)	**France:** L. Thomas, *L'Esprit d'OW*	2) Edition of *PDG* with woodcuts by F. Siméon issued by Mornay
	Hungary: CG (Tímár)	**Italy:** Sorani, 'Le recensioni di OW'.	
	Italy: ERA, 'Art and the Handicraftsman', 'House Decoration', 'Lecture to Art Students', 'London Models', 'The Rise of Historical Criticism' (Bondois); The Harlot's House' (Chiavolini)	**Spain:** Gómez Carrillo, *En plena bohemia* (approx. date)	**Netherlands:** H. Zagwijn's *Kerker-Ballade* (setting of *BRG*)
	Latvia: *IBE*		
	Poland (Hebrew): *LWF, PDG* (Tawiow)		
	Romania: BI, SC (Ghetu)		

Date	Translations	Criticism	Other
	Serbia: *PDG* (Pijade)		
	Slovakia: NR ('J.A.M')		
	Spain: *LWF* (Baeza); ERA and other essays (Felipe)		
	Ukraine: SC		
1921	**Bosnia-Herzegovina:** CG and other tales (Slijepčević)	**Croatia:** Begović reviews *LWF* in *Novosti*	**Czechoslovakia (Czech):** Trans. of transcripts of Wilde's trials (Krecar)
	Germany: SCo (Behmer)	**Germany:** 1) E. Ebertin, *Historische und zeitgenössische Charakterbilder* 2) F. Engel, *OW und seine besten Bühnenwerke*	**France:** Proust, *Le Côté de Guermantes II, Sodome et Gomorrhe I*
	Greece: CG		
	Lithuania (Yiddish): *Salomé* (Steiman)	**Hungary:** L. Szabó, 'Tóth Árpád Wilde-fordítása'	
	Portugal: NR and other fairy tales (Paiva)	**Italy:** E. Cecchi refers to Wilde's homosexuality in letter to Praz	
	Russia (Yiddish): HP (Wendroff)	**Netherlands:** 1) L. Couperus, 'Erkenning van officieele zijde: de Oscar-Wilde-vrouw' 2) J. Greshoff, 'Alfred Douglas en OW'	
	Serbia: CG and other tales (Petrović)		
	Slovenia: *LWF* (Rehar), selected fairy tales ('M.J.')	**Norway:** T. Lunden, *OW: en studie*	
		Poland: J. Parandowski, *Antinous w aksamitnym berecie*	
		Sweden: Bendz, *OW: A Retrospect*	

Date	Translations	Criticism	Other
1922	**Bosnia-Herzegovina:** CA (Ilić) **Denmark:** New *IBE* (Thomsen) **Hungary:** LASC (Tímár), selected essays (Supka) **Hungary (Romanian):** *Salomé* **Iceland:** 'The Teacher of Wisdom' (Jónsson) **Italy:** *IBE* (Nori Giambastiani) **Poland:** FT (Rogowicz), *LASCOS* (Centnerszwerowa), 2 x *DP* (Centnerszwerowa, Markowski), HP (Storożyński/ Szygowski), aphorisms (Wierzbiński)	**Austria:** Blei, *Das große Bestiarium der Literatur* **Denmark:** S. Placzek compares Wilde and Bang in his introduction to Bang's posthumous *Gedanken zum Sexualitätsproblem* **Germany:** P. Aronstein, *OW: sein Leben und Lebenswerk* **Poland:** W. Rogowicz, *Miłość w dramatach Oskara Wilde'a* **Russia:** N. V. Korneichuk, *Oskar Uail'd*	**France:** 1) Theatrical adaptations of *PDG* by S. Mercey and G. C. Lounsbery/F. Nozière 2) Proust, *Sodome et Gomorrhe II* **Germany:** Premiere of Zemlinsky's opera *Der Zwerg* (after BI; libretto: G. Klaren) **Ireland:** Joyce, *Ulysses* **Poland:** PA translated and attributed to Wilde
1923	**Estonia:** NR **Greece:** *PDG* **Hungary:** SCo, new FT, *PDG*, *Salomé* (Kosztolányi); *For Love of the King* (Bálint); selected essays (Hevesi) **Lithuania:** *HOP* (Puida; originally pub. USA, 1914) **Norway:** 2 x *PDG* (Kvam, Dale) **Poland:** *BRG* (Kasprowicz)	**France:** G. Duthuit, *Le Rose et le Noir: de Walter Pater à OW* **Hungary:** A. Cserna, *Wilde-breviárium* **Poland (Yiddish):** Y. Y. Trunk, *'Doryan Grey': ophandlung vegen kunst un virklikhkayt* **Russia:** L. I. Aksel'rod, *Moral' i krasota v proizvedeniiakh Oskara Uail'da*	**Czechoslovakia (Czech):** Karásek's novel *Zastřený obraz* **Germany:** Trans. of Harris's *OW*

Date	Translations	Criticism	Other
	Portugal: *HOP* (Paiva); first Portuguese-language trans. of *PDG* (Rio) pub. simultaneously in Paris and Rio de Janeiro		
	Romania: HP (Floru)		
	Spain (Catalan): *LWF* (Jordá/ Pujols)		
1924	**Denmark:** *WNI* (Thomsen)		**France:** 1) J.-E. Blanche's portrait of Sir Coleridge Kennard exhibited as *Le Portrait de Dorian Gray* 2) Gide's Socratic dialogues *Corydon* (previously pub. privately in 1911 and 1920)
	France: New *PDG* (Jaloux/Frapereau)		
	Germany: New *PDG* (Sander)		
	Hungary: Selected poems (Radó)		
	Lithuania: Fairy tales (Jablonskis)		**Spain:** Valle-Inclán's *esperpento* play, *La cabeza del Bautista*
	Poland: Selected poems (Kasprowicz), aphorisms (Ostrowski-Naumoff)		
	Slovenia: CG; *PDG* (Vurnik)		
1925	**Germany:** Last letters (Meyerfeld)	**Austria:** Polgar, 'Die Frau ohne Bedeutung'	**Czechoslovakia (Czech):** Karásek's novel *Ganymedes*
	Italy: *LASCOS*	**Czechoslovakia (Czech):** F. X. Šalda, 'Orientace staré a nové'	**Germany:** 1) C. Sternheim's biographical drama *Oskar Wilde* 2) Trans. of L. Houseman's *Echo de Paris*
	Slovakia: *Salomé*	**Spain:** C. González Ruano, *Notas sobre OW*	**Hungary:** Trans. of Gide's *OW*
			Spain: Trans. of Douglas's *OW and Myself*

Date	Translations	Criticism	Other
1926	**Belarus:** *BRG* (Dubrouski) **Hungary:** Selected poems (Kosztolányi) **Iceland:** *DP* (Jóhannesson) **Portugal:** Aphorisms, etc. (Paiva) **Romania:** CG (Budaru) **Spain:** CG (Donday)	**Austria/Germany:** K. Mann, 'Wildes letzte Briefe' **Hungary:** 1) I. Boross, *Balzac Wilde és Babits* 2) A. Schöpflin reviews Nemzeti Színház production of *IH* **Italy:** Anon., 'Perversioni' in *Il popolo d'Italia*, official organ of the Fascist Party	**France:** Gide's autobiography *Si le grain ne meurt* (previously pub. privately in 1920 and 1921)
1927	**Spain (Basque):** Selected fairy tales (Altuna) **Czechoslovakia (Czech):** *The Cardinal of Avignon* (Hruška) **Denmark:** *DP* (Gamél) **Iceland:** HP (Gunnarsson) **Spain:** FT, *DOP* (Baeza); *LASCOS* (Humanes/Baeza)	**France:** 1) L. F. Choisy, *OW* 2) Gide's *Journal* discusses Wilde's Aestheticism 3) Maurois, *Etudes anglaises* 4) F. Porché, *L'Amour qui n'ose pas dire son nom* **Germany:** K. Lück, *Das französische Fremdwort bei OW als stilistisches Kunstmittel*	**Croatia:** Stage adaptation of SC (Širola) **Spain:** Wilde ranked fourth favourite author in survey of female readers carried out by *El Sol* **Switzerland/ Germany:** Premiere of O. Schoeck's opera *Penthesilea* in Dresden
1928	**Germany:** *HPOT* (Sander) **Greece:** BI and other tales **Italy:** *DOP* (Motta) **Lithuania:** CG, SMUS **Sweden:** FT, SCo (Olsson); PPP (Neymark)	**Denmark:** Thomsen's entry on Wilde in *Salmonsens Konversationsleksikon* **France:** H.-D. Davray, *OW, la tragédie finale* **Hungary:** Schöpflin reviews Kamaraszínház production of *IBE* **Italy:** Cecchi, 'Il mito di O. Wilde'	**France:** Trans. of Harris's *OW* **Spain:** Trans. of Harris's *OW*

Date	Translations	Criticism	Other
1929	**Estonia:** *PDG* (Tammsaare), YK **Finland:** *BRG* (Jylhä) **Romania:** *HPOT* (Boureanu), *WNI* **Spain:** Last letters (Baeza/Mesa); aphorisms, etc., selected essays (Baeza)	**France:** 1) L. Delarue-Mardrus, *Les Amours d'OW* 2) Yourcenar, 'Abraham France traducteur de Virgile: OW' **Hungary:** Ignotus, 'Faj és művészet' in *Nyugat* **Norway:** S. Bryn, *Omkring OW*	**Czechoslovakia (Czech):** Premiere of J. Křička's opera *Bílý pán* (after CG) **Germany:** Trans. of *The Autobiography of Lord Alfred Douglas* **Russia:** A. Krein's symphonic poem *Salome* **Switzerland:** Premiere of R. Flury's opera *Eine florentinische Tragödie* (after FT)
1930	**Czechoslovakia (Czech):** Three letters (Smetánka/ Svoboda) **Germany:** New ed. of Wiener Collected Works, introd. A. Zweig **Romania:** *LWF* **Spain (Catalan):** *PDG* (Tasis)	**Austria:** Blei, 'OW' **Croatia:** Begović reviews Eugen Robert's production of *IH* in *Novosti* **Italy:** M. Praz, *La carne, la morte, e il diavolo nella letteratura romantica* **Norway:** Ø. F. Helseth, *OW og England*	**France:** 1) P. Capdevielle's *Deux Apologues d'OW*, recitation for voice and orchestra 2) Trans. of *The Autobiography of Lord Alfred Douglas* **Germany:** Premiere of R. Wagner-Régeny's musical drama *La Sainte Courtisane* **Poland:** Parandowski's fictionalized biography of Wilde *Król życia*
1931	**Serbia:** LASC	**France:** 1) L. Lemonnier, *Vie d'OW* 2) L. M. Rosenblatt, *L'Idée de l'art pour l'art dans la littérature anglaise pendant la période victorienne*	**Italy:** *HPOT* introduced as English primer in Italian schools
1932	**Lithuania:** *PDG* (Češūnas) **Serbia:** *Salomé* **Slovakia:** FT (Roy)	**Denmark:** Thomsen, *OW (1856–1900): An Introduction to the Performance of 'The Importance of Being Earnest'* **Germany:** L. M. Price, *The Reception of English Literature in Germany*	

Date	Translations	Criticism	Other
1933	**Croatia:** *DP* (V. M.) **Czechoslovakia (Czech):** First complete *DP* (Vendyš) **Latvia:** *PDG* (Kroders) **Lithuania (Yiddish):** HP (Bastomski)	**France:** 1) H. Pacq, *Le Procès d'OW* 2) Sherard/Renier, *André Gide's Wicked Lies about the Late Mr. OW in Algiers in January, 1895* **Germany:** E. Schirmann, *Die literarischen Strömungen im Werke OWs* **Netherlands:** G. J. Renier, *OW* **Switzerland:** F. K. Baumann, *OW als Kritiker der Literatur*	**Italy:** N. De' Colli's play *OW*
1934	**Germany:** New *LWF*, *WNI* (Lerbs)	**Germany:** 1) R. Defieber, *OW: der Mann und sein Werk im Spiegel der deutschen Kritik und sein Einfluß auf die deutsche Literatur* 2) E. Ihrig, *Das Paradoxon bei OW* **Italy:** A. Zanco, *OW* **Poland:** 1) S. J. Imber, *Pieśń i dusza Oskara Wilde'a* 2) M. Siwy, *Oskar Wilde: tragedja poety — homoseksualisty* **Switzerland:** E. Müller, *OW: Wesen und Stil*	**France:** Trans. of *Teleny*, sometimes attributed to Wilde **Spain:** Trans. of Cooper-Prichard's *Conversations with OW*
1935	**Estonia:** *HOP*, *HPOT* (Truu) **Germany:** New *IH* (Lerbs)	**Czechoslovakia (Czech):** R. Wellek, *D'lo Oscara Wildea* **France:** K. Hartley, *OW: l'influence française dans son œuvre* **Germany:** K. Lerbs, 'Warum spielen wir heute Wilde?' and 'Der zeitnahe Wilde'	**France:** M. Rostand's drama *Le Procès d'OW* **Germany:** H. Selpin's film *Ein idealer Gatte* (after *IH*)

Date	Translations	Criticism	Other
1936	**Denmark:** New *IBE* (Lindemann/K. N. Andersen) **Iceland:** NR (Guðmundsson) **Latvia:** BI (Adamsons) **Netherlands:** 'Ravenna' (Koppeschaar) **Serbia:** Fairy tales	**Denmark:** Lindemann/ Andersen *IBE* reviewed by *Berlingske Tidende*	**Germany:** H. Steinhoff's film *Eine Frau ohne Bedeutung* (after *WNI*) **Hungary:** Premiere of J. Hubay's opera *Az Önző óriás* (after SG)
1937	**Croatia:** 'Requiescat' (Smerdel) **Germany:** Complete Works reprinted with new introd. by Goetz **Greece:** *LWF* (Heliopoulos) **Romania:** *BRG*, selected tales and fairy tales (Stamatiad) **Spain (Catalan):** *BRG*, PP (Janés)	**Denmark:** A. Schmidt, *I Liv og Kunst* (incl. account of confronting Bang in 1904 over similarities between *PDG* and *Mikaël*) **France:** L. Guillot de Saix, '*Jézabel*', *essai de reconstitution* **Germany:** 1) K. Mann, 'OW entdeckt Amerika' 2) A. Schlösser, *Die englische Literatur in Deutschland von 1895 bis 1934* **Italy:** C. M. Franzero, *Vita di OW*	**France:** J. Choux's film *Une femme sans importance* (after *WNI*)
1938	**Iceland:** *BRG* (Ásgeirsson) **Romania:** *IBE* **Serbia:** HP (Milosavljević) **Spain (Catalan):** *IBE* (Artells)		**Italy:** Premiere of R. Bossi's opera *Rosa rossa* (after NR) **Latvia:** Premiere of J. Kalnins's ballet *Lakstigala un roze* (after NR)
1939	**Lithuania:** *IBE* **Portugal:** HP (Vilela)		**France:** Trans. of M. Birnbaum's *OW* **Germany:** Premiere of H. Leger's opera *Das Bildnis des Dorian Gray* (libretto: C. Creutzer)

Date	Translations	Criticism	Other
1940	**Greece:** *WNI* (Speliotopoulos)		
1941		**Czechoslovakia (Czech):** F. Soldan, *Jiří Karásek ze Lvovic* **Norway:** M. Berge, *OW: en utviklingsstudie*	**Switzerland:** Premiere of F. Tischhauser's ballet *Der Geburtstag der Infantin* (after BI)
1942	**France:** Collection of Wilde's spoken tales and aphorisms, largely drawn from Gide (ed. Guillot de Saix)		**Czechoslovakia (Czech):** O. Zítek's ballet *O růži* (after BI)
1943	**Portugal:** CG (Frias), *PDG* (Leite), LASC (Fernandes), selected tales (Cardoso) **Spain:** Collected Works (trans. and introd. Gómez de la Serna)	**Switzerland:** A. Stocker, *L'Amour interdit*	
1944	**Albania:** *HPOT* **Denmark:** *CG*, LASC (Adamsen) **Greece:** CA **Portugal:** *BRG, DP* (Leite)	**Denmark:** Royal Theatre production of *IBE* reviewed by *Berlingske Aftenavis* (Lindeballe), *Børsen* (Hauch), *Ekstra Bladet* (Soya), *Fædrelande* (Barfod), and *Kristeligt Dagblad* (Geismar) **Netherlands:** J. C. Ten Horst, *OW: 1854 – 16 October, 1944*	**Greece:** Trans. of Gide's *OW*
1945	**Belgium (Dutch):** *HPOT* (van Tichelen) **Greece:** SWS **Portugal:** *IBE, IH, LWF, WNI* (Cardoso) **Slovakia:** *HPOT* (Procházka) **Ukraine:** DF, NR, SG (Vasyl'; pub. Munich)	**Austria:** Volkstheater production of *LWF* reviewed in *Kleines Volksblatt*	**Italy:** Trans. of Gide's *OW* **Spain:** Trans. of Gide's *OW*

Date	Translations	Criticism	Other
1946	**Denmark:** First published trans. of *IBE* (Lind) **Greece:** LASC **Iceland:** *PDG* (Einarsson) **Romania:** *PDG* (Holda/Luca); trans. of Guillot de Saix's 1942 French selection of Wilde's spoken tales and anecdotes (Stamatiad) **Slovakia:** *BRG* (Beniak), *HOP* (Procházka)	**Czechoslovakia (Czech):** A. Novák, R. Havel, and A. Grund, *Stručné dějiny literatury české* **Germany:** O. Flake, *Versuch über OW*	**Portugal:** Trans. of Stocker's *L'Amour interdit*
1947	**Belarus:** HP (Khval'ko) **Croatia:** 'Easter Day', 'The Harlot's House', 'Impression du matin' (I. G. Kovačić) **Estonia:** LASC (Oinas; pub. Germany) **Germany:** New *IBE, IH, LWF, WNI* (Hagemann) **Poland:** DF, NR (Feldmanowa/ Federowic; pub. Scotland) **Portugal:** FT (Machado) **Slovakia:** *PDG* (Mihál)	**France:** R. Merle, *OW* **Norway:** A. E. Haug, *OW: The Influence of Contemporary and Previous Writers in his Work*	**Germany:** 1) T. Mann's novel *Doktor Faustus* 2) Trans. of E. Roditi's *OW* **Italy:** Premiere (in USA) of M. Castelnuovo-Tedesco's ballet *The Birthday of the Infanta* **Sweden:** Trans. of Pearson's *OW* **Switzerland (German):** Trans. of Pearson's *OW*
1948	**Belarus:** NR (pub. USA) **Estonia:** SWS (Oinas; pub. Germany) **Italy:** Collected Theatre (ed. Franzero/ Gigli) **Slovakia:** SWS (E. & K. Terebessy)		**Spain:** Trans. of Pearson's *OW* **Switzerland:** H. Schaeuble's opera *Dorian Gray* (premiered in USA, 2004)

Date	Translations	Criticism	Other
1949	**Italy:** MM, PMWH, new SWS (Valbia)	**Austria:** R. Alewyn, 'Hofmannsthals Wandlung'	**Germany:** T. Mann's essay 'Nietzsches Philosophie im Lichte unserer Erfahrung'
		Hungary: Művész Színház production of *IH* reviewed by S. Darvas, G. Faludy, and L. Vass	
		Netherlands: H. Kapteijns, *Autonome dichters: typen van 'poètes maudits'*	
1950	**Estonia:** *IH*	**Denmark:** C. Houmark, *Timer der blev til Dage* (incl. anecdote in which Bang expresses his opinion of Wilde)	**France:** Trans. of Queensberry/Colson, *OW and the Black Douglas*
	Greece: Fairy tales		
	Norway: CG (Magnus), *IH* (Heiberg)		**Germany (West):** Premiere of W. Fortner's ballet *Die weisse Rose* (after BI)
			Italy: Broadcast of R. Bossi's radio opera *Il principe felice* (after HP)
1951	**Greece:** 'Charmides' and other poems (Psara)		**France:** Trans. of Hyde's *The Trials of OW*
	Italy: Collected Works (ed. Camerino; through 1952)		**Germany (West):** Trans. of Rostand's *Le Procès d'OW*
1952	**Denmark:** SMUS (Kehler)		
1953	**Croatia:** New *PDG* (Gorjan)	**Croatia:** I. Hergešić, 'OW ili tisuću i jedan paradoks'	**Italy:** Trans. of Pearson's *OW*
	Denmark: *Intentions* (Kehler); new *PDG* (Jørgensen)	**Spain:** A. C. Atienza y Bermejo, *OW, se llamaba 'El hijo pródigo'*	
	Netherlands (West Frisian): *BRG* (Sikkema)		
1954	**France:** *Love is Law* (Guillot de Saix); new *IBE* (Anouilh/ Vincent)	**Germany (West):** E. Eberymayer, *Das ungewöhnliche Leben des OW*	**Centenary of Wilde's birth**
			Germany: T. Mann's novel *Die Bekenntnisse des Hochstaplers Felix Krull*
	Serbia: MM, SWS	**Finland:** A. Ojala, *Aestheticism and OW* (through 1955)	
		Ireland: Flann O'Brien sparks debate on Wilde's Irishness in *Irish Times*	**Greece:** Trans. of Franzero's *Vita di OW*
			Ireland: Plaque erected at Wilde's Dublin birthplace

Date	Translations	Criticism	Other
1955	**Denmark:** New *BRG* (Geddebro)	**Austria:** E. Lothar's production of *IBE* reviewed by *Der Abend* (Singer), *Neues Österreich* (Basil), *Die Presse* (Fontana), *Volksstimme* (Kauer), *Wiener Zeitung* (Rollett)	**France:** Trans. of V. Holland's *Son of OW*
	Germany (West): Trans. of Guillot de Saix's 1942 French selection of Wilde's spoken tales and anecdotes		**Germany (West):** Trans. of V. Holland's *Son of OW*
1956	**Bosnia-Herzegovina:** Fairy tales (Kršić)	**Czechoslovakia (Czech):** A. Skoumal, *OW, 1854–1900*	**Iceland:** Trans. of Pearson's *OW*
	Croatia: SMUS (Kostić) 'The Harlot's House' (Slamnig/Šoljan)	**France:** Guillot de Saix, 'OW disait "moi je pense en contes"'	**Spain:** Trans. of Merle's *OW*
	Serbia: *HOP, HPOT* (Grujić)	**Norway:** A. K. Lund, *The Moral Attitude of OW*	
	Slovakia: *IH* (Dlouhý)		
1957	**Greece:** *DOP*	**Croatia:** T. Blažeković, 'Engleska književnost i njene veze s Hrvatskom Modernom (1900–1914)' (doctoral thesis, Zagreb)	**Italy:** L. Dallapiccola's choral setting of 'Requeiscat' (through 1958)
	Hungary: MM, SWS (Honti)		
	Poland: Selected essays, tales, fairy tales, and prose poems (ed. Żuławski)	**France:** J. Delay, *La Jeunesse d'André Gide*	
	Sweden: Aphorisms (Berndal)	**Germany:** G. Glur, *Kunstlehre und Kunstanschauung des Georgekreises und die Aesthetik Oscar Wildes* (pub. Switzerland)	
		Italy: G. Pellegrini, *Appunti di letteratura inglese*	
1958	**Lithuania:** *HPOT*	**Austria:** E. Lothar's production of *WNI* reviewed by O. Basil in *Neues Österreich*	
	Netherlands: Aphorisms, etc.		
	Norway: SG (Stixrud)	**Italy:** M. T. Dainotti Cerutti, *OW e il suo problema religioso*	
	Ukraine: *BRG* (Osmack; pub. Neu-Ulm, West Germany)		

Date	Translations	Criticism	Other
1959	**Bulgaria:** *IH* **Germany (East):** New collected tales and fairy tales (Seiffert) **Slovenia:** *HOP*, *HPOT* (Kosmač)	**Estonia/Finland:** H. Salu, 'A. H. Tammsaare, OW und Eino Leino' **Hungary:** 1) Nemzeti Színház Pécs production of *IBE* reviewed by G. Lemle 2) Madách Kamara Színház production of *LWF* reviewed by I. Hermann	
1960	**Georgia:** *HOP*, selected fairy tales, incl. HP & NR (Gamsakhurdia) **Iceland:** SC (Níelsson) **Romania:** *HPOT* (Archip) **Slovakia:** *IBE* **Slovenia:** *BRG* (Vidmar)	**Hungary:** Szeged production of *IBE* reviewed by I. Simon **Russia:** K. Chukovskii, *Liudi i knigi* **Spain:** S. Juan Arbó, *OW*	**Publication of *The Letters of OW*** **Hungary:** Premiere (in E. Germany) of E. Szönyi's opera *Firenzei tragédia* (after FT) **Ireland:** First performance of M. MacLiammóir's one-man show, *The Importance of Being Oscar*
1961	**Croatia:** First complete *BRG* (Gorjan) **Poland:** *IBE*, *LWF* (Lewik/Pudełek/ Wojewoda) **Serbia:** *IH*	**Croatia:** Hergešić, 'OW ili život kao umjetnina' **Netherlands/Belgium:** R. Breugelmans, 'De weerklank van OW in Nederland en Vlaanderen, 1880–1960'	**Germany (West):** Premiere of F. Voss's ballet *Die Nachtigall und die Rose* (after NR) **Sweden:** Trans. of V. Holland's *OW: A Pictorial Biography*
1962	**Denmark:** New *DP* (Buhl) **Norway:** *Poems* (Bjerke)	**Italy:** P. Scarfo, *OW: profilo letterario* **Portugal:** A. C. da Silva, *Eça e Wilde*	**France:** Trans. of V. Holland's *OW: A Pictorial Biography* **Germany (East):** Premiere of R. Hansell's opera *Dorian Gray*
1963	**Bosnia-Herzegovina:** *HPOT* (Kršić) **Germany (West):** Plattdeutsch trans. of DF (Petersen)	**Greece:** G. Syriotis, *E tragodia tou Oskar Uaild*	**Austria:** P. W. Fürst's unperformed ballet *Dorian Gray* (libretto: E. Jandl) **Croatia:** Krleža's one-act play *Saloma*

Date	Translations	Criticism	Other
			Germany (West): Premiere of F. Grothe's opera *Der Ideale Gatte* (after *IH*; libretto: H. Mostar)
			Poland: Trans. of Pearson's *OW*
1964	**Kosovo (Albanian):** *HPOT* (Dino)	**Spain:** F. Agustinoy, *OW*	**Germany (East):** Premiere of G. Natschinski's musical comedy *Mein Freund Bunbury* (after *IBE*; libretto: J. Degenhardt/H. Bez)
			Germany (West): Trans. of Hyde's *OW: The Aftermath*
			Slovenia: Trans. of Pearson's *OW*
			Switzerland/ West Germany: H. Sutermeister's opera *Das Gespenst von Canterville* (after *CG*) broadcast on West German television
1965	**Germany (East):** New *HOP* (Hoeppener)	**Estonia/Finland:** Salu, *Tuul üle mere ja muid lühiuurimusi Eesti kirjandusest*	**Denmark:** Trans. of Hyde's *The Trials of OW*
	Slovakia: *LWF* (Blaho)	**Germany (West):** R. Schaffner, *Die Salome-Dichtungen von Flaubert, Laforgue, Wilde und Mallarmé*	**Germany (West):** Trans. of V. Holland's *OW: A Pictorial Biography*
		Portugal: C. Malpique, *Óscar Wilde: esteta paradoxal*	**Switzerland:** Premiere of P. Burkhard's musical comedy *Bunbury* (after *IBE*; libretto: H. Weigel)
1966	**France:** *The Letters of OW* (Boissard)	**Sweden:** W. Nelson, *OW in Sweden*	**Italy:** Trans. of Hyde's *The Trials of OW*
	Germany (West): *The Letters of OW* (Soellner)		**Switzerland:** Premiere of M. Lang's ballet *Dorian Gray* (choreography: V. Orlikowsky)
	Portugal: *DF* (Vilela)		

Date	Translations	Criticism	Other
1967	**Romania:** Selected plays (A. & A. Bantas) **Slovenia:** *IBE* (Mihelič)	**France:** P. Jullian, *OW* **Italy:** D. Spano, *Psicologismo estetico nella filosofia wildiana*	**Czechoslovakia:** Dramatic adaptation of *CG* by J. Skopeček.
1968	**Germany (East):** New CG, LASC, MM, PMWH, PP, SWS (Hoeppener) **Norway:** HP (Huse) **Slovakia:** CG **Ukraine:** *PDG* (Dotsenko)	**Hungary:** Ódry Színpad production of *IBE* reviewed by A. Rajk **Italy:** R. Weiss, 'D'Annunzio e l'Inghilterra' **Sweden:** B. Borelius, *OW, Whistler and Colours*	**France:** Trans. of Hyde's *OW: The Aftermath*
1969	**Slovakia:** Selected tales and fairy tales (Marušiaková/ Peková-Kresáková/ Vanovičová)	**France:** H. P. Clive, 'Pierre Louÿs and OW: A Chronicle of their Friendship' **Germany (West):** P. Funke, *OW: in Selbstzeugnissen und Bilddokumenten* **Spain:** J. A. García Blázquez, *OW*	
1970	**Armenia:** *PDG* (Morchikean; pub. Lebanon) **Croatia:** 'E tenebris' (Mlač) **Germany (East):** New *BRG* (Mund) **Greece:** Selected tales; aphorisms, etc.	**France:** Clive, 'OW's First Meeting with Mallarmé' **Slovenia:** M. Stanovnik, '*OW* v slovenskem tisku do leta 1914'	
1971	**Germany (West):** New Collected Theatre (Schmitz) **Macedonia:** DF (Siljanovski)	**Austria:** E. Weber, 'Hofmannsthal und OW' **France:** A. Caillas, *OW tel que je l'ai connu* **Hungary:** Szigligeti Színház, Szolnok production of *IBE* reviewed by I. Csík **Switzerland:** F. Massara, *I processi dell'eccentricità: OW*	**Russia:** B. Arapov's ballet *Portret Doriana Greia* **Spain:** 1) L. A. de Villena's poetry collection *Sublime solarium* 2) Trans. of Rostand's *Le Procès d'OW*

Date	Translations	Criticism	Other
1972	**Norway:** *IBE* (Pierstorff)	**Russia:** S. A. Kolesnik, *Proza Oskara Uail'da*	**Finland:** Trans. of *Teleny*
	Romania: *Intentions* (Radulescu)		**Germany (West):** Trans. of Jullian's *OW*
	Slovenia: *Salomé* (Flerè)		**Italy:** Trans. of Jullian's *OW*
			Spain: Trans. of Funke's *OW*
			Switzerland (German): Trans. of Whistler's *The Gentle Art of Making Enemies*
1973	**Germany (East):** New *IH* (Jung-Alsen)	**Italy:** M. D'Amico, *OW: il critico e le sue maschere*	
	Iceland: 'The House of Judgement' (Þórðarson)	**Norway:** A. Kleppe, *The Theatre of OW*	
	Portugal: *LASCOS* (Romão)	**Spain:** L. E. Davis, 'OW in Spain'	
1974	**Poland:** Aphorisms (Dobrosielski)		**Netherlands:** Premiere of H. Kox's opera *Dorian Gray*
			Russia: Premiere of A. Knayfel's opera *Kentervil'skoe prividenie* (after *CG*; libretto: T. Kramarova)
1975	**France:** First Collected Works (ed. Langlade; through 1977)	**France:** 1) J. de Langlade, *OW, écrivain français* 2) F. J.-L. Mouret, 'Quatorze lettres et billets inédits de Lord Alfred Douglas à André Gide, 1895–1929'	**Germany (West):** 1) Premiere of B. Wefelmeyer's musical comedy *Lord Arthurs pflichtbewusstes Verbrechen* (after *LASC*; libretto: G. Hornawsky)
	Germany (East): New Collected Theatre (Hoeppener)	**Russia:** Y. Y. Kissel, *Okkazional'noe ispol'zovanie frazeologicheskikh edinits v proizvedeniiakh B. Shou i O. Uail'da*	2) Premiere of musical comedy *Piccadilly Circus* (after *IH*; music: H. Osterwald/ C. Prina; libretto: H. Schachner/D. Price)
	Macedonia: *PDG* (Jovanovski)		
	Norway: *Salomé* (Bjerke)		
	Portugal: *SMUS* (Sarmento)		3) Trans. of Osborne's stage adaptation of *PDG*

Date	Translations	Criticism	Other
1976	**Germany (East):** Collected Fiction (incl. new *PDG* by Hoeppener)	**Croatia:** V. Sepčić, 'Matoš između Wildea i Poea' **Germany (West):** N. Kohl (ed.), *OW: Leben und Werk in Daten und Bildern*	
1977	**Bulgaria:** *HPOT* **Faeroe Islands:** HP (Ódn)	**Austria:** L. Muerdel–Dormer, 'Die Truggestalt der Kaiserin und OW: zur Metaphorik in Hofmannsthals Drama *Der Kaiser und die Hexe*' **Italy:** 1) D'Amico, *Vita di OW attraverso le lettere* 2) G. Franci, *Il sistema del dandy: Wilde-Beardsley-Beerbohm*	
1978	**Croatia:** New *BRG* (I. Andrić)	**Germany (West):** R. Omasreiter, *OW: Epigone, Ästhet und "wit"* **Hungary:** T. Mészáros reviews Summer Theatre of Pécs production of *Salomé* **Spain:** Villena, *Conocer OW y su obra*	**Hungary:** E. Petrovics's ballet *Salome*
1979	**Belarus:** NR **Belgium (Dutch):** LASC (van Malderen) **Italy:** Selected works (ed. D'Amico)	**Italy:** E. De Michelis, 'Giuseppe Vannicola fra D'Annunzio e Wilde'	**Croatia:** Premiere of B. Papandopulo's opera *Kentervilski duh* (after CG; libretto: N. Turkalj) **Spain:** Villena's poetry collection *Hymnica*
1980	**Armenia:** Selected fairy tales and plays (Hakhverdiane) **Bulgaria:** *BRG, PDG*, selected fairy tales and plays (Todorova) **Scotland (Gaelic):** SG (Macleòid)	**Austria:** A. Roitinger, *OW's Life as Reflected in his Correspondence and his Autobiography* **Croatia:** L. Paljetak, 'OW gospodin sa suncokretom' **Germany (West):** Kohl, *OW: Das literarische Werk zwischen Provokation und Anpassung* **Italy:** G. Falzone, 'OW a Palermo'	**Croatia:** Trans. of Gide's OW **Spain:** Trans. of *Teleny*

Date	Translations	Criticism	Other
1981	**Germany (West):** New *IBE* (Kohlmayer) **Greece:** *HPOT*; SMUS (Pesketze)	**Austria:** A. Stillmark, 'Hofmannsthal and OW' **Hungary:** E. Ézsaiás reviews Veszprém theatre production of *IH* **Italy:** 1) P. F. Gasparetto, *OW: l'importanza di essere diverso* 2) R. Severi, 'OW e il mito di Salomé'	**Russia:** V. Georgiyev's film *Idealny Muzh* (after *IH*)
1982	**Bulgaria:** CA and other essays **Finland:** CG (Starck) **Georgia:** *PDG* **Greece:** PMWH with selected poems **Portugal:** SG **Spain (Catalan):** *HPOT* (Vallverdú)	**France:** Yourcenar, 'Wilde rue des Beaux-Arts' (revised version of 1929 article) **Germany (West):** R. Italiaander, *Der Fall OW* **Italy:** P. Bà, *Dorian Gray: un mito vittoriano*	**Italy:** 1) Trans. of Douglas's *OW and Myself* 2) Premiere of F. Mannino's opera *Il ritratto di Dorian Gray* (libretto: P. Masino/B. De Tomasi)
1983	**Spain (Galician):** CG, HP, LASC, NR, SG, YK (Luca de Tena) **Greece:** *HOP*	**Germany (West):** G. Müller, *Philosophische Ästhetik versus ästhetisches Manifest: Rekonstruktion und systematischer Vergleich der ästhetischen Theorien Kants und OWs* **Hungary:** P. Egri, *Törésvonalak: Drámai irányok az európai századfordulón* **Ireland:** R. Pine, *OW* **Spain:** Villena, *Corsarios de guante amarillo: sobre el dandysmo*	**Germany (West):** E. Schneider's opera *Das Salome-Prinzip* (premiered in 2002) **Italy:** Trans. of *Teleny*

Date	Translations	Criticism	Other
1984	**Armenia:** *VN*, *DP* (Papazian; pub. Cyprus)	**Denmark:** B. Green Jensen, *'De profundis' og lidelsens mening*	**France:** Trans. of P. Ackroyd's novel *The Last Testament of OW* and Amor's *Mrs. OW*
	Bulgaria: *DOP*, selected fiction, fairy tales, and poems	**Germany (West):** 1) Kleine Komödie Munich production of *IBE* reviewed by J. Kaiser	**Germany (West):** Trans. of *Teleny* and of Whistler's *The Gentle Art of Making Enemies* (also pub. East Germany)
	Netherlands: PP (Lemmens)	2) W. Maier, *OW, 'The Picture of Dorian Gray': eine kritische Analyse der anglistischen Forschung von 1962 bis 1982*	
	Slovakia: *WNI* (Ruppeldtová)	3) H. Schroeder, *OW, 'The Portrait of Mr W.H.': Its Composition, Publication, and Reception*	**Netherlands:** Trans. of *Teleny*
	Spain (Catalan): *LASCOS* (Sorribas)		**Portugal:** Trans. of *Teleny*
		Italy: G. Micks La Regina, *Le verità di una maschera: il pensiero estetico di OW*	
		Netherlands: J. Brockway, *De bittere laurier*	
1985	**Belgium (Dutch):** CG, MM, PMWH, SWS	**France:** P. Delaveau, 'André Gide et OW'	**Italy:** Trans. of Ackroyd's *The Last Testament of OW*
	Georgia: SC (Maharadze)	**Italy:** 1) G. D'Elia, *Il quadro in movimento di OW*	
	Latvia: PP (Sērmūkša)	2) Severi, 'OW, la femme fatale and the Salomé Myth'	
	Spain: New *Salomé* (Moix)	**Spain:** A. Coletes, 'OW en España, 1902–1928'	
1986	**Azerbaijan:** HP and other fairy tales	**Germany (West):** 1) A. Barth, *Moderne englische Gesellschaftskomödie*	**Germany/Sweden:** E. Eyser's unperformed opera *Dorian Gray*
	Ireland: HP (Ní Ghallchóir), SG (Ó Dúgáin)	2) A. Höfele, *Parodie und literarischer Wandel* 3) M. Pfister, *OW: 'The Picture of Dorian Gray'*	**Greece:** Trans. of Pearson's *OW*
	Latvia: *LASCOS* (Sērmūkša)	4) E. Schönfeld, *Der deformierte Dandy: OW im Zerrspiegel der Parodie*	**Spain:** Trans. of Ackroyd's *The Last Testament of OW*
	Netherlands: Selected tales (Schuchart)	5) Schroeder, *Annotations to OW, 'The Portrait of Mr. W. H.'*	**Sweden:** Trans. of Ackroyd's *The Last Testament of OW*

Date	Translations	Criticism	Other
	Russia (Chuvash): Fairy tales	**Switzerland (German):** G. Debon, *OW und der Taoismus*	
	Spain (Basque): *PDG* (Hidalgo)		
	Spain (Catalan): *DP* (Ayala)		
	Sweden: Selected writings (Hallén/ Sundborg/ Olausson)		
1987	**Croatia:** *BRG* and other poems (L. Paljetak)	**France:** 1) M. de Belleroche, *OW, ou, L'Amour qui n'ose dire son nom* 2) Langlade, *OW, ou, La Vérité des masques*	**Italy:** Premiere of Mannino's opera *Il principe felice* (after HP; libretto: M. S. Sernas)
	Norway: *HOP, HPOT* (Lange)		**Netherlands:** Trans. of Ackroyd's *The Last Testament of OW*
	Spain: Letters to Lord Alfred Douglas (Villena)	**Italy:** 1) F. Ceragioli, '"OW a S. Miniato" di Dino Campana' 2) F. Mei, *OW*	
	Spain (Basque): *HPOT* (Mendiguren); *Salomé* (Mujika)	**Netherlands:** N. Maas, *Nederlandse reacties op Oscar Wilde*	
		Serbia: S. Kusturin, *Oskar Vajld*	
1988	**Greece:** *DL; MM* (Andreou)	**France:** P. Masson, 'Pour une relecture de l'*OW* d'André Gide'	
	Kosovo (Albanian): Selected tales (Hoxha)	**Germany:** S. L. Gilman, 'Strauss, the Pervert, and Avant Garde Opera of the Fin de Siècle'	
	Netherlands: *CG* (Leistra)		
	Norway: *DL* (Claussen)	**Italy:** R. De Cadaval, *La vita 'recitata' di OW*	
	Poland: Fairy tales (Ewa Berberyusz/ Feldmanowa/Lewik)	**Netherlands:** J. Polak, *OW in Nederland*	
	Sweden: Selected aphorisms, essays, and tales (Olausson)		

Date	Translations	Criticism	Other
1989	**Macedonia:** *HPOT* (Stanoeska)	**Croatia:** D. Gašparović, 'O Wildeovu apokrifu'	**Italy:** Trans. of Ellmann's *Four Dubliners*
	Spain (Galician): *Salomé* (adapt. Vidal/ Eastham)	**Germany (West):** 1) T. Klugsberger, *Verfahren im Text: Meerjungfrauen in literarischen Versionen und mythischen Konstruktionen von H. C. Andersen, H. C. Artmann, K. Bayer, C. M. Wieland, O. Wilde* 2) Schroeder, *Additions and Corrections to Richard Ellmann's 'OW'*	
		Hungary: A. Török, *OW világa*	
		Spain: Villena, *OW*	
1990	**Spain (Bable):** CG, LASC (Rodríguez Cueto) **Poland:** *HPOT* (Tuziak)	**Austria/Germany:** M. Hänsel-Hohenhausen, *Die frühe deutschsprachige Oscar-Wilde-Rezeption (1893–1906): Bibliographie* **Croatia/Serbia/Bosnia-Herzegovina:** Z. Petković, 'Recepcija dela Oskara Vajlda na srpskohrvatskom jezičkom području: (1901–1970)' **Germany:** R. Kohlmayer, 'Ein Dandy "bester Zucht": OWs Gesellschaftskomödie *An Ideal Husband* in Karl Lerbs' Bühnenbearbeitung aus dem Jahre 1935' **Italy:** M. Slawinski, 'La metamorfosi di Ariele: D'Annunzio, il romanzo inglese e la voce del vate' **Poland:** A. Bojarska, *Pięć śmierci* **Russia:** B. F. Moeller-Sally, 'OW and the Culture of Russian Modernism' **Spain:** D. Dougherty/M. F. Vilches, *La escena madrileña entre 1918 y 1926* **Ukraine (Russian):** M. G. Sokolianskii, *Oskar Uail'd*	**Germany:** Trans. of Ellmann's *Four Dubliners* **Hungary:** Premiere of M. Várkonyi's musical *Dorian Gray* (libretto: G. Braunke, et al.) **Spain:** 1) Trans. of Ellmann's *OW* and *Four Dubliners* 2) A. Sastre's libretto *Bunbury* (from *IBE*) **Slovenia:** Trans. of K. Brandys's 'Hôtel d'Alsace' **Sweden:** Trans. of Ellmann's *OW*

Date	Translations	Criticism	Other
1991	**Denmark:** Fairy tales (Holst/Grønborg) **Germany:** New *IH* (Kohlmayer) **Portugal:** DL (Sampaio) **Spain (Basque):** CG (Mendiguren)	**Germany:** Kohlmayer, 'Ambiguität und Ideologie als Probleme deutscher Wilde-Übersetzungen' **Greece:** M. K. Makrakis, *Techne kai ethike sto 'portraito' tou OW* **Poland:** Brandys, *Charaktery i pisma* (incl. 'Hôtel d'Alsace'; pub. London) **Russia:** T. Pavlova, 'Oskar Uail'd v russkoi literature (konets XIX–nachalo XX vv.)'	**Belgium:** P. Jacobs's short stories *De kus van OW* **Germany:** 1) Premiere (in Austria) of C. R. Hirschfeld's opera *Bianca* (after FT) 2) Trans. of Ellmann's *OW* **Italy:** Trans. of Ellmann's *OW* and Brandys's *Charaktery i pisma* **Spain:** Trans. of R. Brown's *Sherlock Holmes and the Mysterious Friend of OW*
1992	**Estonia:** *DP* (Kaer) **France:** New Collected Works (ed. Delahaye) **Portugal:** *Intentions* (Feijó) **Serbia:** *BRG* (Andrić) **Spain:** *The Letters of OW* (Balseiro); new *LWF* (Diosdado) **Spain (Basque):** LASC (Juaristi) **Spain (Catalan):** SC	**Germany/Ireland:** J. W. Pesch, *Wilde about Joyce* **Serbia:** S. M. Ignjačević, 'Andrićev prevod Vajldove balade' **Spain:** 1) Teatro Alcázar production of *LWF* reviewed by E. Centeno, E. Haro Tecglen, and F. Umbral 2) J. Marías, *Vidas escritas*	**Estonia:** Trans. of Ackroyd's *The Last Testament of OW* **France:** Trans. of Brandys's *Charaktery i pisma* **Poland:** 1) Trans. of *Teleny* 2) A. Bojarska's biographical fiction *Biedny Oskar* **Spain:** J. A. Vitoria's play *OW no tiene nombre* (inspired by *DP*) and A. Diosdado's drama *La importancia de llamarse Wilde*
1993	**Bulgaria:** Aphorisms, etc. **Netherlands:** MM (Leistra) **Poland:** BI (Łoza-Lipszyc) **Slovenia:** *DP*, SMUS (Gabrijelčič)	**Bulgaria:** L. Grigorova, *Drama na paradoksa: Oskar Uajld v bălgarski kulturen kontekst* **Germany:** 1) Kohlmayer, 'Sprachkomik bei Wilde und seinen deutschen Übersetzern' 2) J. Rattner (ed.), *Kunst und Krankheit in der Psychoanalyse*	**Russia:** Trans. of Ackroyd's *The Last Testament of OW* **Spain:** Premiere of M. Balboa's opera *El secreto enamorado* (libretto: A. Rossetti)

Date	Translations	Criticism	Other
	Spain (Galician): *HPOT* (Fernández Salgado)	**Italy:** 1) P. Bertelli, *Elogio della diversità e sabotaggio della civiltà dello spettacolo* 2) C. Samson Ciacca, *OW: il teatro del paradosso*	
		Spain: A. N. Delmar, *Vida de OW*	
		Sweden: F. Skjoldbjærg, *Tekstens nytelser: en lesning i og omkring OWs roman 'The Picture of Dorian Gray'*	
1994	**France (Breton):** Selected tales (Miossec)	**Austria/France:** C. Satzinger, *The French Influences on OW's 'The Picture of Dorian Gray' and 'Salome'*	**France:** Trans. of Ellmann's *OW*
	Italy: New Complete Works (ed. D'Amico)	**Croatia:** L. Paljetak, 'OW i njegove bajke'	**Russia:** Premiere (in London) of E. Firsova's opera *The Nightingale and the Rose*
	Netherlands: *Intentions* (Kuil)	**France:** 1) E. Brunet (ed.), *Pour OW: des écrivains français au secours du condamné*	**Spain:** J. Duggan's performance piece *OW* produced in Madrid
	Netherlands (West Frisian): *HPOT*	2) Langlade, *La Mésentente cordiale: Wilde-Dreyfus*	
	Portugal: *HPOT* (Marcela C.)	3) P. Pollard, 'OW et le paradoxe gidien'	
	Spain (Galician): *DP* (Seco Vilariño/ Cao Losada)	**Germany:** 1) Kohlmayer, 'OW's Society Comedies and the National Socialist Message' 2) Schroeder, *Alice in Wildeland* 3) J. Zelter, *Sinnhafte Fiktion und Wahrheit*	
		Italy: 1) M. Amendolara, *Indagine su OW* 2) D'Amico, 'OW in Naples'	
		Romania: M. Irimia, 'OW: A Case Study of a "Personality Cult" in Romanian Criticism (1900–1918)'	

Date	Translations	Criticism	Other
		Spain: 1) M. Dalmau, *Yo, Wilde* 2) R. Merino, *Traducción, tradición y manipulación: teatro inglés en España 1950–1990*	
1995	**Bulgaria:** *HOP* **Spain:** New *IBE* (Villena; from four-act version)	**Austria/Germany:** R. Blackburn, '"The Unutterable and the Dream": Aspects of Wilde's Reception in Central Europe 1900–1922' **Croatia:** I. Vidan, *Engleski intertekst hrvatske književnosti* **France:** 1) S. Gendre-Dusuzeau, *OW: 'père, j'ai mal à l'oreille'* 2) J.-M. Varaut, *Les Procès d'OW* 3) O. Vallet, *L'Affaire OW* **Germany:** 1) R. Gentz, *Das erzählerische Werk OWs* 2) M. Schramm, *Der soziale Auftrag der absoluten Kunst: Gesellschaftskritik in OWs 'An Ideal Husband'* **Ireland:** 1) D. Coakley, *OW: The Importance of Being Irish* 2) D. Kiberd, *Inventing Ireland* 3) Pine, *The Thief of Reason: OW and Modern Ireland* **Netherland:** C. Wintermans, *Lord Alfred Douglas* **Norway:** M. Claussen, *Finn en mening den som kan: essays om humaniora, Sterne, Wilde, Kafka og Beckett* **Slovenia:** D. Čater, *OW*	**France:** Trans. of W. Satterthwait's novel *Wilde West* and Whistler's *The Gentle Art of Making Enemies* **Hungary:** Trans. of Brandys's *Charaktery i pisma* **Ireland:** Dublin's Oscar Wilde Society commissions P. Lamb to design a stained glass window of the Happy Prince for Wilde's Merrion Square home **Italy:** Trans. of J. L. Borges's 1946 essay on Wilde

Date	Translations	Criticism	Other
		Spain: 1) M. Mateo, *La traducción del humor: las comedias inglesas en español* 2) Teatro Reina Victoria production of *IBE* reviewed by Centeno, Haro Tecglen, L. López Sancho, E. Pérez-Rasilla, and J. Villán	
1996	**Albania:** Aphorisms, etc. (Myftiu) **France:** Pléiade edition of Wilde's works (ed. Gattégno) **Italy:** *The Uncollected OW* (Zazo) **Latvia:** Aphorisms, etc. **Lithuania:** *DP* (Česonienė) **Norway:** Aphorisms (Fosli) **Romania:** *DP* (Izverna) **Spain:** New *IH* (Arteche) **Spain (Bable):** FHS (Trapiella)	**Austria:** H. R. Brittnacher, "'Der Geck war tragisch'': Hofmannsthals Nachruf auf OW' **Austria/Germany:** Kohlmayer, *OW in Deutschland und Österreich* **Finland:** P. Suhonen, *Rooli ja kohtalo* **France:** 1) H. Catsiapis (ed.), *L'Actualité d'OW* 2) N. Erber, 'The French Trials of OW' **Germany:** B.-S. Ahn, *Dekadenz in der Dichtung des Fin de siècle* **Hungary:** Kaposvár Theatre production of *Salomé* reviewed by P. Müller **Italy:** 1) M. L. Lolli Pozzi, *Guide alla lettura* (Reading Guides) to *PDG* and *CG* 2) M. Quadri, *L'arte della menzogna: i racconti di OW* 3) G. Zappu, *Guida alla lettura* to *IBE* **Spain:** 1) O. González de Cardedal, *Cuatro poetas desde la otra ladera: Unamuno, Jean-Paul, Machado, OW* 2) M. C. Sanza Casares, *El universo de los cuentos de OW* 3) Teatro Alcázar production of *IH* reviewed by Haro Tecglen in *El País*	**France:** Trans. of M. Holland's *The Wilde Album* and Gardiner's *OW: A Life in Letters, Writings and Wit* **Germany:** J. Müller-Wieland's chamber opera *Die Nachtigall und die Rose* (after *NR*; libretto: H. Neves) **Serbia:** Trans. of Ackroyd's *The Last Testament of OW* **Spain:** Trans. of Gardiner's *OW* **Switzerland (German):** Trans. of Satterthwait's *Wilde West* (pub. in Germany, 1998)

Date	Translations	Criticism	Other
1997	**Albania:** *Salomé* (Mita), SC (Papleka) **Croatia:** *VN* (Varga) **Italy:** Trans. of Guillot de Saix's 1942 French selection of Wilde's spoken tales and anecdotes (Severi) **Netherlands:** Selected letters (Janzen)	**France:** J. Fryer, *André and Oscar: Gide, Wilde and the Gay Art of Living* **Germany:** 1) B. Hermes, *Félix Paul Greve als Übersetzer von Gide und Wilde* 2) Kohlmayer, 'Wildes *Bunbury* auf braunen Bühnen' 3) U. Kunz, 'Der Zeit ihre Kunst, der Kunst ihre Freiheit': ästhetizistischer Realismus in der europäischen Décadenceliteratur um 1900 4) K. Sauerland, 'Das Spiel mit dem abgeschlagenen Haupt, oder, Der Salome-Stoff bei Heine, Flaubert, OW und Jan Kasprowicz' **Italy:** 1) O. Bonamici, *Impossible but Inevitable: (Oscar F. Wilde and Jack London, Illusionists Thirsting for Illusions)* 2) A. Iannucci, 'Giornalista a tempo pieno: la difesa di O. Wilde e la *Rivista d'Italia*' **Spain:** D. Rodríguez Fonseca, *Salomé: la influencia de OW en las literaturas hispánicas*	**Germany:** Premiere of *Der glückliche Prinz*, S. Heucke's musical setting of HP **Ireland:** Sculptor D. Osborne's Wilde Monument unveiled in Merrion Square **Spain:** Villena's novel *El charlatán crepuscular: Óscar y Bosie*
1998	**Finland:** DL (Anhava) **Spain (Catalan):** FHS, YK (Ribera)	**Germany:** T. Bruncken's production of *IBE* reviewed by U. Deuter **Ireland:** 1) J. H. MacCormack (ed.), *Wilde the Irishman* 2) V. Mahaffey, *Wilde, Yeats, Joyce, and the Irish Experiment* **Italy:** 1) S. Arcara, *OW e la Sicilia* 2) R. Miracco (ed.), *OW, verso il sole: cronaca del soggiorno napoletano* 3) Severi, *L'anima dell'uomo: OW in Italia* 4) G. Silvani, *Il cerchio di Narciso: figure e simboli dell'immaginario wildiano*	**Germany:** Trans. of M. Holland's *The Wilde Album* **Ireland:** Oscar Wilde Centre for Irish Writing opened in Wilde's birthplace, Westland Row, Dublin **Italy:** 'Wilde Days' festival in Palermo to mark centenary of *BRG*, including conference 'La vita come arte: OW, le arti e l'Italia' and exhibition of first Italian editions of Wilde

Date	Translations	Criticism	Other
		Russia: 1) E. Bershtein, 'Western Models of Sexuality in Russian Modernism' (Ph.D. thesis, California, Berkeley) 2) R. Polonsky, *English Literature and the Russian Aesthetic Renaissance*	**Norway:** Trans. of M. Holland's *The Wilde Album* **Sweden:** Trans. of M. Holland's *The Wilde Album* and M. Kaufman's play *Gross Indecency*
		Serbia: B. Živojinović, 'O Andrićevom prevodu Vajldove Redinške tamnice'	
1999	**Croatia:** Aphorisms **Bulgaria:** Poems (Todorov) **Finland:** CA **Macedonia:** *IBE* (Mihajlovski) **Serbia:** Aphorisms, etc. (Bogdanović) **Spain:** Collected Poems **Spain (Galician):** *IBE* (Pérez Romero) **Spain (Catalan):** *IH* (Sala)	**General:** R. Tanitch, *OW on Stage and Screen* **Austria:** R. Weiss, 'Terra Incognita, Populärkultur, intellektuelle Akrobatik: das englische Drama im Wiener Theater der Jahrhundertwende' **Czech Republic:** L. Zadrazil, *Východoevropská moderna a její evropský kontext* **Denmark:** E. Bredsdorff, *Syndebukken: en bog om OW* **Finland:** 1) A. Halmesvirta/R. Valta (eds), *Aatteiden kamppailu elintilasta* 2) H. Welling, *Turhamainen mies: narri vai sankari?* **France:** 1) D. Eribon, *Réflexions sur la question gay* 2) D. Sweetman, *Explosive Acts: Toulouse-Lautrec, OW, Félix Fénéon and the Art & Anarchy of the Fin de Siècle* **Germany:** 1) P. Bridgwater, 'OW and Germany, Germany and OW' and 'Masked Men: Nietzsche, Pater and Wilde' 2) Höfele, 'OW, or, The Prehistory of Postmodern Parody'	**France:** Trans. of Kaufman's *Gross Indecency* **Germany:** Trans. of Ackroyd's *The Last Testament of OW* and Kaufman's *Gross Indecency* **Italy:** A. V. U. Zioni's biography of Lord Alfred Douglas *Il garofano blu* **Russia:** Trans. of Langlade's *OW, ou, La Vérité des masques* **Switzerland (German):** Trans. of S. Fry's 'Playing Oscar'

Date	Translations	Criticism	Other
		3) G. Krämer, 'Der Mord als eine schöne Kunst betrachtet': zur ästhetischen Valenz eines Motivs bei Thomas de Quincey, OW und Marcel Schwob 4) L. Krämer, Das Bildnis des OW **Netherlands:** Wintermans, Alfred Douglas: de boezemvriend van OW **Norway:** C. Krohg, Fire portretter **Poland:** D. Pestka, OW: Between Aestheticism and Anticipation of Modernism **Slovenia:** M. Grosman, Solska ura s Salomo Oscarja Wilda **Spain:** L. Alonso Gómez, La magia celta según Gustavo Adolfo Bécquer, OW y la literatura artúrica actual	
2000	**Albania:** DL, SMUS, TM (Gjana) **Czech Republic:** Aphorisms, etc. (Samek) **Denmark:** HOP, HPOT (Have) **France:** New Collected Works (ed. Aquien) **Hungary:** Collected Works (ed. Szántai) **Portugal:** Aphorisms (Condinho), selected prose (Gorman)	**Austria:** S. Arlaud, Les Références anglaises de la modernité viennoise **Bulgaria:** E. Lazarova, Eticheskite urotsi na prints paradoks, ili, Nepoznatiiat Uaild **Croatia:** N. Batušić, 'Galovićeva Tamara i Wildeova Saloma' **France:** 1) D. Durosay, 'Gide et Wilde, paradoxe de l'In memoriam' 2) L. Louvel, 'The Picture of Dorian Gray', OW: le double miroir de l'art 3) M. N. Zeender, Le Triptyque de Dorian Gray: essai sur l'art dans le récit d'OW	Centenary of Wilde's death **Revised and expanded edition of The Letters of OW** **Greece:** Trans. of M. Holland's The Wilde Album **Russia:** Trans. of Ellmann's OW **Spain (Basque):** Trans. of Teleny **Switzerland (German):** Trans. of Belford's OW

Date	Translations	Criticism	Other
	Serbia: *Intentions* (Ćirjanić)	**France/Germany:** J. Rosteck, *Die Sphinx verstummt: OW in Paris*	
	Spain: New *Salomé* (González Carreño)	**Germany:**	
	Spain (Basque): *IBE* (Olano Irurtia)	1) C. Juranek (ed.), *Die Erfindung des Schönen: OW und das England des 19. Jahrhunderts* (exhibition catalogue: Schloß Wernigerode Verwaltungs- und Betriebsgesellschaft)	
	Spain (Catalan): 'The Sphinx' (Cabré)		
	Switzerland (German): *Oscariana* (Mohr)	2) Kohl (ed.), *OW im Spiegel des Jahrhunderts* 3) J. W. Rademacher, *OW* 4) K. Tebben (ed.), *Frauen – Körper – Kunst: literarische Inszenierungen weiblicher Sexualität*	
		Greece: Makrakis, *O amartolos 'Agios'*	
		Italy: 1) M. Veronesi, 'Da Poe a Wilde: intorno ad alcune fonti del concetto di critica tra il *Convito* e il primo *Marzocco*' 2) Zioni, *OW: aneddoti romanzati*	
		Norway: B. Angvik, *OW*	
		Russia: 1) Bershtein, 'The Russian Myth of OW' 2) Y. A. Roznatovskaya, *Oskar Uail'd v Rossii: bibliograficheskii ukazatel', 1892–2000*	
		Spain: González Carreño production of *Salomé* favourably reviewed by P. M. Víllora in *ABC*	
		Sweden: Nelson, *OW and Sweden: A Summing-Up*	

Date	Translations	Criticism	Other
2001	**Albania:** *BRG, DP* (Toto/Shopllo); *HPOT, LASCOS* (Briçi)	**Austria/Germany:** B. Barboni, 'OW nella letteratura tedesca di fine Ottocento' (through 2002)	**Germany:** Trans. of MacGinn's *Ethics, Evil, and Fiction* and Wintermans's *Alfred Douglas*
	Finland: Selected essays (Rissanen)	**Belgium:** J. Franck, *OW, ou, Le Festin avec les panthères*	**Hungary:** Trans. of Rademacher's *OW*
	Iceland: *SG* (Óskarsson)	**Croatia:** 1) A. Paljetak, 'Tragovi Oscara Wildea u djelu Srećka Kosovela'	**Spain:** J.-M. Quirós Lobo's novel *Serenata para dos amores*
	Romania: *DL* and other essays (Teodorescu)	2) L. Paljetak, 'Fi(jo)rentinska tragedija, dodirna točka Wildea i Vojnovića'	
	Serbia: Selected plays (Petrović/ Erdeljanović/Nikolić)	**France:** 1) C. Beausoleil, *OW: pour l'amour du beau*	
	Slovenia: *LASCOS* (Zabel)	2) E. Asselot, *OW, lecteur de l'antiquité gréco-latine*	
	Spain (Bable): *IBE* (Iglesias Fernández)	**Germany:** 1) U. Böker/J. Hibbard (eds.), *Processes of Institutionalisation*	
	Spain (Catalan): SMUS (Solé)	2) W. E. Davis, 'OW, *Salome,* and the German Press 1902–1905'	
		3) W. G. Klee, *Leibhaftige Dekadenz: Studien zur Körperlichkeit in ausgewählten Werken von Joris-Karl Huysmans und OW*	
		4) I. Krauss, *Dichtung und Psychologie*	
		Germany (East): A.-C. Giovanopoulos, 'Censorship and the Institutionalisation of Meaning: OW in East Germany'	
		Italy: 1) D'Amico/Severi (eds), *La vita come arte: OW, le Arti e l'Italia* (proceedings of Palermo 1999 conference)	
		2) Severi, *OW & company*	

Date	Translations	Criticism	Other
		Russia: A. G. Obraztsova, *Volshebnik ili shut?: teatr Oskara Uail'da*	
		Spain: 1) M. Armiño/A. Peláez, Ciclo de conferencias en torno a OW 2) Villena, *Wilde total, Los andróginos del lenguaje,* and *Diccionario esencial del fin de siglo*	
		Switzerland: Special issue of journal *Boèce* devoted to Wilde	
2002	**Bulgaria:** *IBE* (Ignatovski)	**General:** Böker/Corballis/ Hibbard (eds), *The Importance of Reinventing Oscar: Versions of Wilde during the Last 100 Years*	**Germany:** Premiere of *Der selbstsüchtige Riese,* Heucke's musical setting of SG
	Croatia: New PP (Paljetak)		
	Estonia: *Table Talk* (Suursalu), aphorisms, etc. (Seinberg/Rajand)	**France:** 1) F. Guého, *Berneval: terre d'exil d'OW* 2) Masson, 'Wilde dans *Les Caves*'	**Italy:** Trans. of M. Holland's *The Wilde Album*
	Germany: *Table Talk* (Mill)		**Spain:** 1) C. Saura's film *Salomé*
	Greece: Selected essays	**Germany:** 1) Bridgwater, 'Some German OWs' (in Böker, Corballis, and Hibbard) 2) W. Schwandt, *Bekenntnis, Pose, Parodie: OW und das Ästheten-Stereotyp*	2) Series of Wilde-themed lectures delivered in Madrid
	Latvia: *DP* (Sērmūkša)		3) Trans. of Gaunt's *The Aesthetic Adventure* and Schenkar's *Truly Wilde: The Unsettling Story of Dolly Wilde*
	Portugal: PP (Cachapa), *Table Talk* (Ferrari)	**Germany (East):** Giovanopoulos 'Wilde in the East: Processes of Mediation' (in Böker/Corballis/ Hibbard)	
	Romania: PMWH (Bantas)		
	Spain (Galician): *IH*	**Germany/Italy:** S. Kleine-Roßbach, 'Todes-Lieben bei Gabriele D'Annunzio, OW und Thomas Mann'	
		Greece: E. Kakuris, *Tò 'chimoniatiko rodo' tou OW*	

Date	Translations	Criticism	Other
		Italy: 1) Franci/R. Mangaroni, *Le mille e una maschera di OW* 2) L. Re, 'D'Annunzio, Duse, Wilde, Bernhardt: il rapporto autore/attrice fra decadentismo e modernità' **Russia:** O. V. Kovaleva, *O. Uail'd i stil' modern* **Spain:** 1) J. Herrero Senés, *La inocencia del devenir: la vida como obra de arte según Friedrich Nietzsche y OW* 2) J. Navarro de Zuvillaga (ed), *Homenaje a Calderón, Wilde y Saint-Exupéry* 3) D. Puente, *De profundis: literatura y perdón (Tennyson, Baudelaire, Wilde)* 4) Villena, *Máscaras y formas del fin de siglo*	
2003	**Albania:** *IBE, PDG* (Kalldrëmxhi) **Bulgaria:** *LASCOS* **Estonia:** LASC, MM, SWS (Peetersoo/Luts) **Hungary:** New *IBE* (Nádasdy) **Italy:** Letters to Douglas (Carantini) **Lithuania:** Aphorisms, etc. (Vanagienė) **Moldova:** *PDG* (Mazilu) **Romania:** 'Impression de voyage' (Tartler) **Serbia:** 'Athanasia' (Kostić)	**Finland:** S. Anhava, *Minä kirjoitan sinulle kaukaisesta maasta* **France:** S. Heurtel, *OW, ermite mondain* **Germany:** 1) S. Bach, *Theatralität und Authentizität zwischen Viktorianismus und Moderne* 2) L. Krämer, *OW in Roman, Drama und Film* 3) S. Lange, *Ästhetische Lebensalternativen im Werk OWs* **Hungary:** Győr production of *IBE* reviewed by V. L. in *Kisalföld* **Italy:** 1) Franci/Silvani (eds), *The Importance of Being Misunderstood: Homage to OW* 2) M. Tomatis, *OW: l'insostenibile leggerezza del piacere*	**Estonia:** Trans. of Belford's *OW* **Germany:** Trans. of M. Holland's *Irish Peacock and Scarlet Marquess* **Hungary:** Trans. of *Teleny* **Lithuania:** Trans. of Ackroyd's *The Last Testament of OW* **Portugal:** Trans. of Funke's *OW* **Spain (Galician):** X. Agrafoxo's short story collection *O triángulo de Óscar Wilde*

Date	Translations	Criticism	Other
	Slovakia: Aphorisms, etc. **Spain (Galician):** *BRG* (Salvado/Lopo)	**Netherlands:** Wintermans (ed.), *Dear sir: brieven van het echtpaar Couperus aan Oscar Wilde* **Russia:** A. Kurpatov, *Salomeia i Oskar Uail'd Romana Viktiuka* **Spain:** 1) R. Cardwell, 'Madman, Martyr and *Maudit*: OW and Spain' 2) A. Mira, 'La importancia de no ser fiel: a propósito de una nueva traducción de OW'	
2004	**Austria:** *IBE* (adapt. E. Jelinek/K. Rausch) **Estonia:** *BRG* (Ilmet) with selected essays (Kaer); selected verse and prose (J. Linnart/M. Linnart) **Finland:** New *PDG* (Kaila) **Germany:** 'Neue Zürcher' edition of Collected Works **Macedonia:** *Salomé* (Papazovska-Levkova) **Romania:** Selected prose, poetry, and essays (Ripeanu); MM (Poantă)	**Austria:** 'Die Übersetzung schmiegt sich an das Original wie das Lamm an den Wolf': Jelinek's interview with C. Augustin **France:** 1) P. Aquien, *'The Picture of Dorian Gray'*, *OW: pour une poétique du roman* 2) K. Brown Downey, *Perverse Midrash: OW, André Gide, and Censorship of Biblical Drama* 3) D. Morris, *L'Ami de Bunbury, ou, Si OW m'était conté* **Germany:** 1) K. Decker, *OW für Eilige* 2) H. Haase, *Oscar für alle: die Darstellung OWs in biofiktionaler Literatur* 3) C. Holzschuh *Gesellschaftskritik in viktorianischen Kunstmärchen* 4) M. Middeke, *Die Kunst der gelebten Zeit* 5) H.-C. Oeser, *Oscar-Wilde-ABC* **Hungary:** 1) A. Vámos interviews P. Valló, director of the Radnóti Színház production of *IH* 2) *IH* production reviewed by J. Szántó	**Croatia:** B. Senker's play *Dandy ili san glavosječke noći* **Ireland/Estonia:** City of Tartu presents Galway city with statue of imagined meeting between Wilde and Estonian writer E. Vilde **Poland:** Trans. of Fisher's *Oscar and Bosie* **Spain:** 1) Premiere of F. Savater's dramatic adaptation of *PDG* 2) Villena's novel *El bello tenebroso*

Date	Translations	Criticism	Other
		Italy: 1) A. Sacco, *I tre processi di OW* 2) Severi, *La biblioteca di OW* 3) Veronesi, 'D'Annunzio e Wilde' **Russia:** M. A. Cebrakova, *Issledovanie obscich charakteristik, struktur i zagadok tekstov skazok Oskara Uajl'da* **Spain:** Savater's theatrical adaptation of *PDG* reviewed by Centeno	
2005	**Croatia:** SWS (Demirović) **Germany:** *A Life in Letters* **Greece:** *A Life in Letters* **Malta:** *PDG* (Palma) **Poland:** Selected letters (Piestrzyńska) **Portugal:** *Poems* (Gato) **Serbia:** Aphorisms, etc. (Krznarić) **Spain:** *A Life in Letters*; new *Salomé* (Armiño)	**Austria:** 1) Jelinek, 'OW' and F. Richter, 'Pointenporno: Notizen zu Bunbury' in theatre programme for *Ernst ist das Leben*, the Jelinek/Rausch adaptation of *IBE* 2) Jelinek interviewed by E. Hirschmann-Altzinger for *Die Bühne* 3) Jelinek/Rausch *IBE* reviewed by *Die Presse* (Petsch), *Profil* (Schneeberger), *Salzburger Nachrichten* (Thuswaldner), and *Der Standard* (Pohl) 4) F. Richter, producer of Jelinek/Rausch *IBE* interviewed in *Der Standard* 5) Actors R. Koch and M. Maertens interviewed in *Die Bühne* on role in Jelinek/Rausch *IBE* **Austria/Germany:** Jelinek/Rausch *IBE* reviewed in *Frankfurter Allgemeine Zeitung* (Stadelmaier), *Frankfurter Rundschau* (Michalzik), *Süddeutsche Zeitung* (Dössel), and *Der Tagesspiegel* (Krug) **Austria/Switzerland:** Jelinek/Rausch *IBE* reviewed by V. Heilig in *Neue Zürcher Zeitung*	**France:** Trans. of M. Holland's *Irish Peacock and Scarlet Marquess* **Germany:** Trans. of Pearce's *The Unmasking of OW* **Ireland:** C. Ó Searcaigh's *Oíche dhrochghealaí*, an Irish-language adaptation of *Salomé* **Latvia:** Trans. of Ackroyd's *The Last Testament of OW* **Russia:** Trans. of *Teleny* **Spain (Galician):** Theatrical adaptation of Schenkar's *Truly Wilde* **Sweden:** Karl Lagerfeld's photographic album *A Portrait of Dorian Gray*

Date	Translations	Criticism	Other
		Finland: I. Reiners, *Kaipausta ja kannibalismia*	
		France: I. de Saint-Pierre, *Bosie and Wilde: la vie après la mort d'OW*	
		Ireland: J. Killeen, *The Faiths of OW*	
		Italy: B. Siviglia, *'Il piacere' e 'The Picture of Dorian Gray': estetica decadente a confronto*	
		Russia: V. A. Lukov & N. V. Solomatina, *Fenomen Uajl'da*	
		Spain: 1) Savater's theatrical adaptation of *PDG* reviewed by Haro Tecglen 2) Mateo, 'La traducción de *Salomé* para distintos públicos y escenarios'	
		Sweden: 1) I. Holm, *De olydigas litteraturhistoria och andra essäer* 2) C.-J. Malmberg, *Sår: i myt, kult, bild och dikt*	
2006	**Denmark:** New *PDG* (Dinesen) **Finland:** Selected essays (Hännikäinen) **Latvia:** Aphorisms, etc. **Macedonia:** *DP* (Kalpakovski) **Norway:** PMWH (Lausund) **Serbia:** Four prison letters (Bulatović) **Spain (Galician):** *HOP* (Cuba; with new *HPOT*)	**Austria:** 1) C. H. Hammond, 'Blind Alleys: Hugo von Hofmannsthal, OW and the Problem of Aestheticism' (doctoral thesis, California, Irvine) 2) Hollmann's production of *IBE* reviewed by *Kurier* (Tartarotti) and *Die Presse* (Petsch) **Croatia:** A. Primorac, 'Dvije Salome: *Saloma* Oscara Wildea i *Saloma* Miroslava Krleže' **France:** 1) Acquien, *OW: les mots et les songes* 2) E. Egnell, *Quatuor irlandais* 3) T. Todorov, *Les Aventuriers de l'absolu*	**Czech Republic:** 1) Premiere of *Obraz Doriana Graye*, M. Pavlíček's musical adaptation of *PDG* (libretto: J. S. Hedl) 2) Trans. of Ackroyd's *The Last Testament of OW* **Germany:** Premiere of H. Albrecht's 'orchestral radio play' *Das Gespenst von Canterville* **Russia:** Trans. of M. Holland's *Irish Peacock and Scarlet Marquess* and V. Holland's *Son of OW* **Spain:** Trans. of Pearce's *The Unmasking of OW*

Date	Translations	Criticism	Other
		Germany: Bruinier's production of *IBE* reviewed by C. Wahl in *Tagesspiegel*	
		Italy 1) F. Marucci, 'Wilde' in *Storia della letteratura inglese* 2) Veronesi, *Il critico come artista dall'estetismo agli ermetici*	
		Latvia: I. Kačāne. *O. Vailds-K. Skalbe: dubultportrets*	
		Romania: C. Cheveresan, *Wounds and Deceptions: Decadent and Modernist Sensitivities on the Edge*	
		Spain: 1) N. González de la Llana, *Adán y Eva, Fausto y Dorian Gray: tres mitos de transgression* (pub. Germany) 2) N. Rivas Bravo (ed.), *OW* (anthology of early Spanish criticism)	
2007	**Germany:** New *PDG* (Breitkeutz) **Lithuania:** LASC, MM, SWS (Traškevičiūtė) **Macedonia:** LASC (Tudžarovska) **Malta:** *DP* (Palma) **Spain:** New *IBE* (Pérez/Galán) **Spain (Basque):** *DP*, PMWH (Arana) **Spain (Catalan):** *LWF* (Sellent)	**Austria:** S. Mayer/B. Pfeifer, 'The Reception of OW and Bernard Shaw in the Light of Early Twentieth-Century Austrian Censorship' **France:** 1) Ferney, *OW, ou, Les Cendres de la gloire* 2) B. De Saint-Mont, *OW: et si mon coeur doit se briser* **France/Spain:** I. Ramos Gay, *Óscar Wilde y el teatro de boulevard francés* **Germany:** F. Apel, *Konservative Anarchie: Individualismus als Politik bei OW, Karl Kraus, Peter Altenberg und Hugo von Hofmannsthal* **Italy:** 1) A. R. Falzon, *Le nozze alchemiche di Salomè: OW e la tradizione ermetica*	**France:** Trans. of Lottman's *OW in Paris* **Ireland:** 1) Taoiseach B. Ahern underlines Wilde's 'uniquely Irish' perspective in speech to two Houses of British Parliament 2) Irish Ferries name cruise ship *Oscar Wilde* **Spain:** 1) *Wild Oscar: Prisionero del pasado* staged by secondary-school students at Teatro López de Ayala, Badajoz 2) Spanish and Catalan productions of M. Ravenhill's *Handbag*

Date	Translations	Criticism	Other
		2) L. Giovannelli, *Il principe e il satiro: (ri)leggere 'Il ritratto di Dorian Gray'* 3) F. Paglieri, *La donna nei society dramas di OW* 4) M. Vignolo Gargini, *OW: il critico artista* **Russia:** V. Kharchenko/E. Koreneva, *Iazyk frustratsii: M. Lermontov, M. Gor'kii, O. Uail'd, S. Esin* **Spain:** M. N. Pastor Caparrós (ed.), *Remembering Wilde: Parallel Translations and Activities* **Spain (Basque):** A. Arana (ed.), *OW euskaraz: 1927–2007*	
2008	**Czech Republic:** First complete PMWH (Josek), Aphorisms, etc. (Tomský) **Estonia:** Aphorisms, etc. (Talivee) **Finland:** TM and other essays (Hännikäinen) **Hungary:** Aphorisms, etc. (Molnár) **Slovenia:** Collected Theatre, incl. first pub. trans. of *DOP*, *FT*, *IH*, SCo *VN*, and *WNI* **Spain (Basque):** *IBE* **Spain (Galician):** *LWF*	**Austria/Germany:** K. Kuschel, 'Der Künstler zwischen Christusrolle und Judasrolle: OW, Rainer Maria Rilke, Gottfried Benn' **Croatia:** J. Novaković, 'Rasprava za svakoga i ni za koga: OW – i Friedrich Nietzsche – fin de siecle potpaljivači' **France:** 1) C. Queffélec, *L'Esthétique de Gustave Flaubert et d'OW* 2) D. S. Schiffer, *Philosophie du dandysme: une esthétique de l'âme et du corps: Kierkegaard, Wilde, Nietzsche, Baudelaire* **Germany:** 1) A. Eilers, *Im Auftrag der Schönheit: OWs Amerika-Tournee* 2) S. Neuhaus, 'The Politics of Fairytales: OW and the German Tradition'	**France:** Trans. of Brandreth's novel *OW and the Candlelight Murders* **Italy:** Trans. of Brandreth's *OW and the Candlelight Murders* and *OW and the Ring of Death* **Portugal:** Trans. of Brandreth's *OW and the Candlelight Murders* and *OW and the Ring of Death* **Romania:** Trans. of Brandreth's *OW and the Candlelight Murders* and *OW and the Ring of Death* **Russia:** Trans. of Brandreth's *OW and the Candlelight Murders* **Spain:** Trans. of M. Holland's *Irish Peacock and Scarlet Marquess* and *Coffee with OW* and of D. Hare's *The Judas Kiss*

Date	Translations	Criticism	Other
		Italy: 1) S. Mondardini, *L'infame Sant'Oscar di Oxford, poeta e martire* 2) M. Pelliccioli, *Un dandy a teatro: OW e Woody Allen* 3) Transcript of first Wilde trial, ed. P. Orlandelli/ P. Iorio	**Spain (Basque):** Trans. of Douglas's *OW and Myself*
		Poland: K. Krasuska, 'Undoing Gender Masquerade: Maria Komornicka's Oscar Wilde, An Ideal Apocryphon'	
		Russia: O. V. Akimova, *Etika i estetika Oskara Uail'da*	
		Spain: Olivares's production of *IBE* reviewed by A. Cortina, M. S. Moreno	
2009	**Bulgaria:** *DP*, SMUS (Minchev) **Croatia:** *Intentions* (Lalović); new *HPOT* (Paljetak) **Denmark:** New SMUS (Schmidt-Madsen) **Finland:** New *PDG* and *HPOT* (Kapari-Jatta) **Portugal:** New *DP* (Coutinho) **Serbia:** SMUS (Maljković), selected poems (Jagličić) **Slovenia:** Selected works (Groselj) **Spain (Catalan):** PPUY, 'Art and the Handicraftsman', 'Lecture to Art Students' (Subirats)	**Austria:** C. Bianchi, *Karl Kraus als Leser von Charles Baudelaire und OW* **France:** 1) F. Pierobon, *Salomé, ou, La tragédie du regard: OW, l'auteur, le personnage* 2) V. Reid, *André Gide and Curiosity* 3) Schiffer, *OW and Le dandysme, dernier éclat d'héroïsme* **Germany:** M. R. Müller, *Stil und Individualität: die Ästhetik gesellschaftlicher Selbstbehauptung* **Hungary:** 1) S. Tóth, *Lázadásból hagyomány: tanulmányok a modernizmusról és az avantgárdról* 2) G. Vöő, 'A Congenial Race: Reflections on Irish Literature and National Character in the Hungarian Literary Journal *Nyugat*'	**France:** Trans. of Brandreth's *OW and the Ring of Death* **Greece:** Trans. of A. Cravan's hoax article 'OW est vivant!' **Lithuania:** Trans. of Brandreth's *OW and the Candlelight Murders* **Portugal:** Trans. of Brandreth's *OW and the Dead Man's Smile* **Slovenia:** Premiere of I. Petrić's symphonic poem *Slika Dorian Gray* **Spain:** Trans. of Brandreth's *OW and the Ring of Death* and Lottman's *OW in Paris* **Spain (Basque):** Arana's novelized biography *Oscar eta Sebastian edo Oscar Wilderen bizitza*

Date	Translations	Criticism	Other
		Italy: P. Gulisano, *Il ritratto di OW*	
		Russia: A. S. Ivanova, *K.D. Bal'mont, perevodchik angliiskoi literatury*	
		Spain: S. Constán, *Wilde en España: la presencia de OW en la literatura española, 1882-1936*	
		Spain/Germany: N. González de la Llana, *Adán y Eva, Fausto y Dorian Gray: tres mitos de transgresión* (pub. Germany)	
2010	**Albania:** New DL (Marku)	**General:**	**Bulgaria:** Trans. of Todorov's *Les Aventuriers de l'absolu*
	Bulgaria: *LWF, La Sainte Courtisane, Salomé, VN* (Minchev)	1) A. M. Fischer, *Dédoublement: Wahrnehmungsstruktur und ironisches Erzählverfahren der Décadence (Huysmans, Wilde, Hofmannsthal, H. Mann)*	**France:**
			1) C. Merlhiot's film *Le Procès d'OW*
	Croatia: Selections (Bartolec); new CG (Posarić), *IH* (Roić), *Salomé* (adapt. Udovičić/Zlatar Frey)	2) J. Streicher, 'Per la fortuna musicale di OW: da Richard Strauss a Lino Bianchi e oltre'	2) Publication of L. Ferreira's play *L'Ombre d'OW*
			3) M. Bulteau's novella *OW à Hollywood*
	Czech Republic: New *IH* (Strnad)	**France:**	4) Trans. of Brandreth's *OW and the Dead Man's Smile*
		1) M. Drugeon (ed.), *Studies in the Theatre of OW*	
	France: 'Hellenism', 'The Women of Homer' (Aquien), selected journalism (Dantzig); new SMUS (Shelledy)	2) Eells, *Two 'Tombeaux'* to OW: Jean Cocteau's 'Le Portrait surnaturel de Dorian Gray' and Raymond Laurent's Essay on Wildean Aesthetics	**Italy:**
			1) Trans. of Todorov's *Les Aventuriers de l'absolu* and Brandreth's *OW and the Dead Man's Smile*
	Italy: New selection of spoken tales (Di Noto Ascenzo)	3) P. Poivre d'Arvor, *Faut-il brûler ce livre?:* écrivains en procès	2) New ed. of *Divagazioni sulla felicità* pub. by 'Oscar Fingal', in Italy, 1919, proposes that it is by OW
	Lithuania: New *PDG* (Vanagienė)	4) J. Vebret (ed.), *Le procès d'Oscar Wilde: l'homosexualité condamnée*	
			Poland: M. Lechowski's novel *Oscar i ja*
	Portugal: New *WNI* (Pires)		

Date	Translations	Criticism	Other
		Germany: 1) J. Kurz, *Der schöne Mann: Playboys, Dandys, Lebenskünstler* 2) S. Stauss, *Zwischen Narzissmus und Selbsthass: das Bild des ästhetizistischen Künstlers im Theater der Jahrhundertwende und der Zwischenkriegszeit* **Italy:** 1) W. Badford, *Dossier OW* 2) P. Zichella, *OW: vita, personalità, opere* **Poland:** J. Pol, *OW o sztuce i zyciu* **Serbia:** B. Jevtović, 'Recepcija bajke "Srećni princ" Oskara Vajlda u mlađim razredima osnovne škole' **Slovakia (Hungarian):** K. Galgóczi, *A századvég titokzatos tárgya: démonikus nok a modern drámában* **Slovenia:** M. Blazic, 'Primerjalna analiza mladinskih besedil Oscarja Wilda na Cirila Kosmaca'	**Spain:** 1) Trans. of Brandreth's *OW and the Candlelight Murders* 2) Arana's *Oscar eta Sebastian edo Oscar Wilderen bizitza* trans. into Castilian **Switzerland:** Publication of J. Marschall's Swiss-German play of CG
2011	**Albania:** Selected poems (Balli) **Austria:** *IH* (adapt. Jelinek/Rausch) **Bulgaria:** CG (Damyanov) **Czech Republic:** New *PDG* (Hilská) **Germany:** Uncensored *PDG* (Rademacher)	**Austria:** Jelinek/Rausch *IH* reviewed in *TLS* (Evangelista) **Germany:** 1) Eilers, 'Englische Aphorismen in deutscher Übersetzung am Beispiel von OW' 2) K. Tausche, 'Salome bei OW und Richard Strauss'	**Czech Republic:** 1) Trans. of Brandreth's *OW and the Candlelight Murders* 2) Trans. of *Lady Pokingham*, with OW given as author **France:** 1) Exhibition 'Beauté, morale et volupté dans l'Angleterre d'OW', Musée d'Orsay, Paris 2) Trans. of Brandreth's *OW and the Nest of Vipers*

Date	Translations	Criticism	Other
	Italy: *Selected Prose of OW* (Chondrogiannis), selected poems (Russo)	**Italy:** 1) V. Iannella, *Gli spazi oscuri della metropoli: un viaggio misterioso nell'immaginario di OW* 2) Transcript of both Wilde trials, ed. Orlandelli/Iorio 3) L. Terzo (ed.), *Assurdo, paradosso, follia: Samuel Beckett, OW, William Shakespeare*	**France/Spain:** E. Jiménez Corominas's graphic novel *Dorian Gray* (pub. in French; Spanish version pub. 2012)
	Lithuania: *Intentions* (Neverauskytė-Brundzienė)		
	Macedonia: CG (Dimkova)		**Latvia:** Trans. of Brandreth's *OW and the Candlelight Murders* and *OW and the Ring of Death*
	Netherlands: Selected poems (Wiebes, Berg)	**Poland:** A. Mitek-Dziemba, *Literatura i filozofia w poszukiwaniu sztuki zycia: Nietzsche, Wilde, Shusterman*	**Spain:** 1) A. Percy's self-help manual *El coaching de OW*
	Portugal: New *DP* (Correia)	**Slovenia:** Stanovnik, 'Wildovi aforizmi v slovenskih prevodih'	2) Trans. of Brandreth's *OW and the Dead Man's Smile* and M. Holland's *The Real Trial of OW*
	Spain: New *DP* (Briggent), SMUS (Palmer)	**Spain:** 1) A. Lázaro, 'Reading OW in Post-War Spain: *The Picture of Dorian Gray* under the Microscope'	**Spain (Catalan):** Trans. of Culbard/ Edginton's graphic novel of *PDG*
	Spain (Basque): New *PDG* (Arana)	2) M. Morales Ibáñez, *Doce juicios que cambiaron la historia*	
	Spain (Galician): Selected stories (Luca de Tena)		
	Spain (Romani): *PDG* (Arana)	**Ukraine:** O. I. Onishchenko, *Pys'mennyky iak doslidnyky*	
2012	**Albania:** New *Salomé* (Qazimi)	**Austria:** C. Badiou, '"It was the portrait that had done everything": zur OW-Rezeption von Franz Schreker'	**Czech Republic:** Trans. of Brandreth's *OW and the Ring of Death*
	Bulgaria: *HPOT*		
	Czech Republic: New *IBE* (Dominik)	**Bulgaria:** M. Anastasova, 'Translation of Catholic Lexis from English into Bulgarian in the Context of a Novel by OW'	**France:** Trans. of Brandreth's *OW and the Vatican Murders*
	France: New *LWF* (Aquien)		**Greece:** Trans. of Percy's *El coaching de OW*
	Italy: New *Salomé* (Ciambella)		

Date	Translations	Criticism	Other
	Spain: Selected essays (Temprano García), 'Personal Impressions of America', PPP (both Carral); new *Intentions* (Hernández Arias)	**France:** 1) P. Honoré, *L'Importance d'être Wilde* 2) A. Mouy, *Oscar Fingal O'Flahertie Wills Wilde* 3) F. Tamagne, 'Dialogues franco-anglais sur l'homosexualité, de OW à Édith Cresson' **Germany:** 1) H. U. Seeber, *Literarische Faszination in England um 1900* 2) B. Seemann, '*Mit den Besiegten': Hedwig Lachmann (1865-1918), deutsch-jüdische Schriftstellerin und Antimilitaristin* **Hungary:** Vöő, 'The Rise of the Hungarian Dandy: OW's Contribution to the Experience of Modernity in Early-Twentieth-Century Hungary' **Italy:** 1) D. Chiapello, *Il fantasma bulimico: OW e la constitutio vittoriana* 2) G. Galigani, *Salomè, mostruosa fanciulla* **Russia:** M. Bessarab, *Prints Paradoks: Oskar Uail'd* **Spain:** J. Esteban, *Los amigos españoles de OW*	**Italy:** D. Capelli's book of aphorisms *Jim Morrison è morto, OW è morto e anch'io non mi sento molto bene* **Spain:** Trans. of S. Sebag Montefiore's *Titans of History* **Sweden:** Å. Axelsson's novel *OW på Öland*
2013	**Belarus:** *Salomé* (Matsieuskaia) **Czech Republic:** New *PDG* (Suvová) **France:** 2 x new *IBE* (Besset, Dantzig)	**General:** 1) A. M. Magid, *Wilde's Wiles: Studies of the Influences on OW and his Enduring Influences in the Twenty-First Century* 2) K. Powell/P. Raby (eds), *OW in Context*	**Croatia:** Trans. of G. Hanberry's *More Lives than One* **France:** Trans. of Brandreth's *OW and the Murders at Reading Gaol*

Date	Translations	Criticism	Other
	Germany: New *PDG* (Wolff) **Italy:** New *BRG* (Davico Bonino) **Latvia:** Selected poems (Dreika) **Macedonia:** CA (Dimkova) **Netherlands:** 2 x selected poems (Schoneveld) **Spain:** Letters to Whistler (Martínez Muñoz); new *DP* and prison writings	**Croatia:** 1) R. Bartolec, *England made me: libertinska misao o engleskoj književnosti via Pater, Brummell, Disraeli, Swinburne, Wilde, Larkin* 2) G. Schmidt, 'Foreignization and Domestication in the Croatian Translations of OW's *The Picture of Dorian Gray*' **France:** 1) O. Darcos, *Oscar a toujours raison* 2) Ferreira, *OW* 3) V. Tolmatchoff, 'OW as a Reader of French Naturalism' **Germany:** 1) A.-C. Esseln, *Evil Women and Helpless Men: The Femme Fatale in English Literature and European Arts, 1796-1927* 2) W. G. Müller, *Detektiv, Flaneur, Dandy: drei mythische Figuren der Stadtkultur des 19. Jahrhunderts und ihre Aktualität* **Italy:** 1) F. Ciambella, *Testo, danza e corpo nell'Ottocento inglese* 2) R. Genovese, *Il destino dell'intellettuale* **Russia:** S. Lukanitschewa, *Das Theatralitätskonzept von Nikolai Evreinov*	**Italy:** B. Arixi's autobiography *Sono figlio di OW* **Spain:** Trans. of F. Moyle's *Constance*
2014	**Germany:** New *PDG* (Schönfeld) **Italy:** Uncensored *PDG* (Piumini)	**France:** 1) Aquien/X. Giudicelli (eds), 'The Importance of Being Earnest' d'OW	**France:** Publication of Ferreira's play *Pour l'éternité*

Date	Translations	Criticism	Other
	Macedonia: DL (Dimkova) **Spain:** 'Art and the Handicraftsman' (García Simón) **Spain (Catalan):** DL (Cañigueral)	2) E. Degroisse, *The Paradox of Identity: OW's 'The Importance of Being Earnest'* 3) Drugeon/E. Vernadakis, *OW: 'The Importance of Being Earnest'* 4) Eells (ed.), *Wilde in Earnest* 5) D. Guérin-Rose, *OW* 6) Institut catholique d'études supérieures (La Roche-sur-Yon), *Wilde, Waugh, Chesterton: trois humeurs britanniques; actes des journées d'études, le 23 et 24 avril 2012* 7) Schiffer, *OW: splendeur et misère d'un dandy* **Germany:** 1) Rademacher, *Oscar Wilde Kalender* and *The Picture of Dorian Gray: A Reconstruction of the Uncensored Wording of the Lippincott's Text* 2) R. T. Schröder, *Künstlerische Freiheit!?: OWs Autonomie des Schönen in Anlehnung an Immanuel Kant* 3) D. Tappen-Scheuermann, *Literarischer Narzissmus: Spiegelverhältnisse zwischen Autor, Text und Leser* 4) L. Yotov, *The Uses of the Late Victorian and Neo-Victorian Gothic* **Italy:** G. Gozzelino, *OW's Wit: The Question of Translation* **Russia:** A. Livergant, *Oskar Uail'd*	**Germany:** Trans. of J. Kemp's novel *London Triptych* **Lithuania:** Trans. of N. McKenna's *The Secret Life of OW* **Poland:** English/Polish parallel text of *PDG* pub. for English learners **Slovenia:** Trans. of *Teleny* **Sweden:** Trans. of *Teleny* and of T. Eagleton's play *Saint Oscar*

Performance Timeline of the European Reception of Oscar Wilde

Compiled by Michelle Paull

Gathered here are details of the first and other significant stage performances of Wilde's plays in Europe. Richard Strauss's operatic adaptation of *Salomé* was increasingly influential in the proliferation of Wilde's work across Europe, sometimes reaching public performance before Wilde's own play. Thus I have included details of this opera but excluded other adaptations of Wilde's work, including films and dramatizations of his tales, which are listed in Paul Barnaby's Timeline in this volume, as a form of creative reception.

The Timeline brings together the data supplied by the contributors to this volume, to which I have added information drawn from Robert Tannitch's *Oscar Wilde on Stage and Screen* (London: Methuen, 1999), the increasing number of performance timelines compiled by *The Oscholars* <www.oscholars. com>, several individual theatre websites and personal communication with a number of scholars, including Koenraad Claes, Kate Dorney, Tine Englebert, Valerie Fehlbaum, Danielle Guérin, Irena Grubica, Eleftheria Ioannidou, Ilze Kacane, Nevin Koyuncu, Krisztina Lajosi, David Rose, Michael Seeney, Laurence Senelick, Tijana Stajic, Chris Tanesescu, Florina Tufescu and Caspar Wintermans. The Swedish data comes from Walter W. Nelson, *Oscar Wilde in Sweden and Other Essays* (Dublin: Dublin University Press, 1965); the Dutch-language data is drawn from R. Breugelmans, 'De weerklank van Oscar Wilde in Nederland en Vlaanderen (1880–1960)', *Studia Germanica Gandensia*, 3 (1961): 53–144; the Polish data comes from <www.e-teatr.pl> [accessed 28 July 2009]. Steven Halliwell provided invaluable assistance in the construction and organization of the timeline.

The Timeline aims to be as comprehensive as possible, but some details of the exact venues, as well as information regarding directors and actors, are inevitably missing. Where it has been impossible to trace the translated title of a play, this has been listed under its original title in English. The list is not exhaustive but represents the beginning of an attempt to provide a comprehensive account of the rich European stage history of Wilde's dramas. Performance research is a growing area of interest in Wilde scholarship, and I hope that this Timeline will encourage further investigations into the European productions of Wilde.

Date	Venue	Play	Additional Information
1890	**Italy:** Teatro Diana, Milan	*VN*	Company of Andrea Maggi and Clara Della Guardia.
1892	**England:** St James's Theatre, London	*LWF*	**World Premiere**.
	Netherlands: 1) Amsterdam	*De Waaier* (*LWF*)	Produced by De Koninklijke Vereeniging het Nederlandsch Tooneel; trans. A. Ising
	2) Koninklijke Schouwburg, The Hague	*De Waaier* (*LWF*)	Produced by De Koninklijke Vereeniging het Nederlandsch Tooneel; trans. A. Ising
1893	**England:** Theatre Royal, London	*WNI*	**World Premiere**.
1895	**England:** 1) Theatre Royal, London	*IH*	**World Premiere**. Transferred to Criterion Theatre on 13 April.
	2) St James's Theatre, London	*IBE*	**World Premiere**.
1896	**France:** 1) Nouveau Théâtre, Paris	*La Passante* (*LWF*)	Adaptation by G. Bertal. Double bill with *Salomé*.
	2) Nouveau Théâtre, Paris	*Salomé*	Lina Munte in the title role. Double bill with *LWF*.
	3) Théâtre de L'Oeuvre, Paris	*Salomé*	**World Premiere.** Directed by Aurélien Lugné-Poë; with Aurélien Lugné Poë (Hérode), Lina Munte (Salomé) Gina Barbieri (Hérodiade). Programme designed by Toulouse-Lautrec. Single performance.
1897	**Sweden:** Vasa Theatre, Stockholm	*LWF*	Tans. Edvard Alkman.
1901	**Ireland:** 1) Grand Opera House, Belfast	*IBE*	Performance by the George Alexander Company.

Date	Venue	Play	Additional Information
	2) Theatre Royal, Dublin	*LWF*	Performance by the George Alexander Company.
	Poland (German): Breslau	*Salomé*	German language premiere. Trans. Dr Kisper.
	Sweden	*LWF*	Revival of 1897 production.
1902	**Germany:** 1) Kleines Theater, Berlin	*Bunbury (IBE)*	Double bill with *Salomé*. Produced by Max Reinhardt. Private performance. Trans. Felix Paul Greve.
	2) Kleines Theater, Berlin	*Salomé*	Directed by Max Reinhardt. Private performance. Gertrud Eysoldt in the title role. Specially invited audience including Richard Strauss. Trans. Hedwig Lachmann.
	Poland (German): Lobe Theatre, Breslau	*LWF*	German premiere.
1903	**Austria:** Deutsches Volkstheater, Vienna	*Salomé*	Premiere, revived in 1906. Directed by Richard Fellner.
	Denmark: Dagmar Theatre, Copenhagen	*Salomé*	Possibly the only early production in Denmark, translated into Danish.
	Germany: 1) Neues Theater, Berlin	*Salomé*	First public performance of Max Reinhardt's production.
	2) Stuttgart	*Salomé*	Directed by Alfred von Berger.
	3) Munich	*Salomé*	Lily Marburg in the title role.
	4) Neues Theater, Berlin	*Eine Frau ohne Bedeutung (WNI)*	German premiere. Directed by Richard Vallentin.
	Hungary: 1) Budapest	*Salomé*	Performed by the Kleines and Neues Theater from Berlin, directed by Max Reinhardt.
	2) Nemzeti Színház, Budapest	*Lady Windermere legyezője (LWF)*	Mari Jászai as Mrs Erlynne.
1904	**Germany:** 1) Hamburg	*DOP*	German premiere, from text by Max Meyerfeld.

Date	Venue	Play	Additional Information
	2) Stadttheater Altona, Hamburg	*Bunbury (IBE)*	First major German production. Directed by Siegfried Jelenko.
	Italy: Teatro dei Filodrammatici, Milan	*Salomé*	Mario Fumagalli as Herod and Edvige Reinach in the title role. Trans. G. Bonaspetti and S. Benelli.
	Netherlands: Tivoli Theatre, Rotterdam	*Salomé*	Directed by Brondgeest. Dutch translation. Also staged in The Hague and Delft in the same year.
1905	**Austria:** Deutsches Volkstheater Vienna	*Eine triviale Komödie für seriöse Leute (IBE)*	Directed by Richard Vallentin.
	Bohemia (Czech): National Theatre, Prague	*Salomé*	Directed by Jaroslav Kvapil. Trans. Otakar Theer.
	Croatia: Croatian National Theatre, Zagreb	*Salomé*	Directed by Josip Bach. Hermina Šumovska in the title role. Trans. Nikola Andrić and Julije Benešić.
	England: Bijou Theatre, London	*Salomé*	Two private performances by the New Stage Club.
	Finland: 1) Finnish Theatre, Helsinki	*IH*	Performed in Finnish.
	2) Finnish Theatre, Helsinki	*Salomé*	Performed in Finnish.
	Germany: 1) Royal Opera House, Dresden	*Salome* (Strauss)	**World premiere.**
	2) Residenz Theater, Munich	*IH*	Premiere. Trans. Pavia and Teschenberg.
	Italy	*LWF*	Actresses Teresa Franchini, Evelina Poli, Elisa Berti Masi, with scenes by Rovescalli and costumes by Caramba.
	Poland: Teatr Miejski, Lwów	*Birbant (IBE)*	
	Slovenia: Slovenian National Theatre, Ljubljana	*Salomé*	Premiere. Directed by the Czech Adolf Dobrovolny. Czech actress Josipina Kreisova in the title role.

Date	Venue	Play	Additional Information
1906	**Austria:** 1) Theater in der Josefstadt, Vienna	*Ein idealer Gatte* (*IH*)	
	2) Grazer Oper, Graz	*Salome* (Strauss)	Austrian premiere, conducted by Strauss.
	Bohemia (Czech): 1) National Theatre in the Na Veveří Theatre building, Brno	*Ideální manžel* (*IH*)	Directed by Adolf Dobrovolný. Trans. Adrienna Linková.
	2) National Theatre in the Na Veveří Theatre building, Brno	*Salomé*	Directed by Jaroslav Pulda. Trans. Otakar Theer.
	England: 1) King's Hall, London	FT	Performed by the Literary Theatre Club. Directed by C. S. Ricketts. Double bill with *Salomé*.
	2) King's Hall, London	*Salomé*	Performed by the Literary Theatre Club. Directed and costume designs by C. S. Ricketts. Double bill with FT.
	Finland: Swedish Theatre, Helsinki	IBE	This production goes to Stockholm in 1907.
	Germany: 1) Berlin	DOP	
	2) Deutsches Theater, Berlin	FT	Trans. Max Meyerfeld.
	3) Königliches Schauspielhaus, Dresden	*Bunbury* (*IBE*)	In three acts; directed by Carl Zeiß; trans. Franz Blei.
	4) Thalia Theater, Hamburg	IH	Trans. Pavia and Teschenberg.
	5) Kölner Festspiele, Cologne	*Salome* (Strauss)	Directed by Strauss.
	6) Bayerische Staatsoper, Munich	*Salome* (Strauss)	
	7) Staatsoper unter den Linden, Berlin	*Salome* (Strauss)	Conducted by Strauss.
	Hungary: Nemzeti Színház, Budapest	*A jelentéktelen asszony* (*WNI*)	

Date	Venue	Play	Additional Information
	Italy: 1) Turin	*Salome* (Strauss)	Italian premiere, conducted by Strauss. Gemma Bellincioni in the title role.
	2) La Scala, Milan	*Salome* (Strauss)	Conducted by Arturo Toscanini. Scala debut of Salomea Krusceniski (Solomiia Krushelnytska) in the title role.
	3) Teatro Argentina, Rome	*Una Donna di Nessun Conto* (*WNI*)	
	Poland: 1) Teatr Miejski, Kraków	*Wachlarz Lady Windermere* (*LWF*)	
	2) Oper Breslau, Breslau	*Salome* (Strauss)	Conducted by Julius Prüwer, Fanchette Verhunk in the title role.
	Sweden: Stockholm	*IH*	In Swedish.
1907	**Austria:** 1) Bürgertheater, Vienna	*Lady Windermeres Fächer* (*LWF*)	
	2) Deutsches Volkstheater, Vienna	*Eine Frau ohne Bedeutung* (*WNI*)	Directed by Richard Vallentin.
	3) Kleines Schauspielhaus, Vienna	*Dorian Grays Bildnis* (*PDG*)	Directed by Ferdinand Skuhra. German stage version of *PDG*.
	4) Theater in der Josefstadt, Vienna	*Dorian Gray* (*PDG*)	Directed by Josef Jarno. German stage version of *PDG*.
	Belgium: Théâtre royal de la Monnaie, Brussels	*Salome* (Strauss)	French Production.
	Bohemia (Czech): 1) National Theatre, Prague	*Ideální manžel* (*IH*)	Directed by Karel Mušek. Trans. V.A. Jung.
	2) Vinohrady Theatre, Prague	*Vějíř lady Windermerové* (*LWF*)	Directed by Jaroslav Kamper. Trans. Jan Havlasa.
	Croatia: Croatian National Theatre, Zagreb	*Lepeza Lady Windermerove* (*LWF*)	Directed by Andrija Fijan who also played Lord Windermere. Trans. Milan Šrabec (Bogdanović).
	England: St. James's Theatre, London	*DOP*	One performance for copyright purposes.

Date	Venue	Play	Additional Information
	France: 1) Le Petit Théâtre, Paris	*Salome* (Strauss)	Private performance. Conducted by Walther Straram.
	2) Théâtre du Châtelet, Paris	*Salome* (Strauss)	German production by Hans Loewenfeld. Conducted by Strauss.
	Hungary: 1) Vígszínház (Comedy Theatre), Budapest	*Bunbury* (*IBE*)	English version. The main roles were given to German actors.
	2) Nemzeti Színház, Budapest	*Az eszményi férj* (*IH*)	
	3) Vígszínház (Comedy Theatre), Budapest	*Salomé*	Trans. Gyula Színi.
	4) Magyar Színház, Budapest	*PDG*	dramatized version
	Netherlands: 1) Stadsschouwburg, Amsterdam	*Salome* (Strauss)	Opera-Vereeniging. German singer Leonore Sengern in the title role.
	2) Gebouw voor Kunsten en Wetenschappen, The Hague	*Salome* (Strauss)	Opera Italiana, conducted by Strauss.
	Poland: Teatr Miejski, Kraków	*Mąż idealny* (*IH*)	
	Russia: Korsh's, Moscow	*LWF*	Premiere.
	Sweden: 1) Vasa Theatre, Stockholm	*IBE*	
	2) Hippodrom Theatre, Malmö	*Salomé*	Knut Lindroth's Company.
1908	**Belgium:** Ghent	*Het belang van Ernst* (*IBE*)	Performed by the company Fronttoneel, a Flemish offshoot of the 'Theater van de Koningin'.
	Bohemia (Czech): 1) Vinohrady Theatre, Prague	*Na čem záleží* (*IBE*)	Directed by Jaroslav Kamper. Trans. Jan Lorenz.

Date	Venue	Play	Additional Information
	2) National Theatre in the Na Veveří Theatre building, Brno	*Salomé*	Directed by Antoš J. Frýda. Trans. Otakar Theer.
	Croatia: Croatian National Theatre, Zagreb	*Fiorentinska tragedija* (FT)	Premiere. Directed by Andrija Fijan. Trans. Ivo Vojnović.
	Greece: 1) Demotiko Theatro Athinon, Athens	*Florentiní tragodía* (FT)	Directed by Thomas Economou. Company of Thanasis Megoulas. Trans. Nicolaos Poriotis.
	2)	*Bunbury* (IBE)	Thomas Economou Company.
	3) Syntagma Theatre, Athens	*Salómi*	Directed by Thomas Economou. Company of Rozalia Nicas. Trans. Nicolaos Poriotis.
	Netherlands	*IH*	
	Sweden: Stockholm	*Salome* (Strauss)	Swedish premiere.
1909	**Austria:** Johann Strauss Theater, Vienna	*Eine florentinische Tragödie* (FT)	Austrian premiere.
	Belgium: Antwerp	*Een ideale echtgenoot* (IH)	Performed by de Koninklijke Nederlandse Schouwburg (Royal Dutch Theatre). Belgian premiere.
	Bohemia (Czech): National Theatre, Prague	*Florentská tragedie* (FT)	Directed by Jaroslav Kvapil. Trans. Jarmila Dušková (Jaroslav Kvapil).
	Croatia: Croatian National Theatre, Zagreb	*Idealni muž* (IH)	Directed by Josip Bach. Trans. Milan Šenoa.
	France: Théâtre des Arts, Paris	*L'Éventail de Lady Windermere* (LWF)	Trans. Maurice Rémond and J. Chalençon.
	Hungary: Magyar Színház, Budapest	*Pádua hercegnője* (DOP)	
	Netherlands	*De belangrijkheid van Ernst* (IBE)	Performed by the Haghespelers. Directed by Eduard Verkade.
	Russia: 1) Maly Theatre, Moscow	*IH*	Premiere.

Date	Venue	Play	Additional Information
	2) Vera Komissarzhevkaya's Theatre, St Petersburg	*Salomé*	Directed by Nikolai Evreinov. Banned by the Holy Synod before it opened.
1910	**Austria:** Volksoper, Vienna	*Salome* (Strauss)	Conducted by Alexander Zemlinsky.
	Croatia: Croatian National Theatre, Zagreb	*Važno je da se zove Ernest* (*IBE*)	Directed by Ivo Raić. Trans. Milan Begović.
	Denmark: 1) Det Ny Teater	*IH*	Danish fringe theatre. Trans. Edgard Høyer.
	2) Frederiksberg Teater, Copenhagen	*Hvad hedder han?* (*IBE*)	Danish fringe theatre.
	England: Royal Opera House, London	*Salome* (Strauss)	Premiere.
	France: Opéra Garnier, Paris	*Salome* (Strauss)	Directed by André Messager. Produced by Paul Stuart.
	Netherlands	FT	
	Romania: Davila Theatre, Pitesti	*Salomé*	Marioara Voiculescu in the title role.
	Spain (Catalan): Teatro Principal, Barcelona	*Salomé*	Catalan version by Joaquim Pena. Margarita Xirgu in the title role.
1911	**Bohemia (Czech):** National Theatre in the Na Veveří Theatre building, Brno	*Florentská tragedie* (FT)	Directed by Josef Fišer.
	France: Paris	*De l'Importance du Sérieux* (*IBE*)	
	Italy: Teatro Apollo, Rome	*Salomé*	Compagnia Drammatica Italiana Ruggieri.
	Netherlands	*WNI*	
	Russia: Suvorin's Maly, St Petersburg	*IH*	

Date	Venue	Play	Additional Information
1912	**Belgium:** Antwerp	*Salomé*	Performed by de Koninklijke Nederlandse Schouwburg (Royal Dutch Theatre).
	Bohemia: National Theatre, Prague	*Salome* (Strauss)	Olga Grovskaya as Salome.
	France: Théâtre du Chatelet, Paris	*Salomé*	Ida Rubinstein in her first public performance as Salomé. Sets designed by Léon Baskst.
	Hungary: Opera House, Budapest	*Salome* (Strauss)	
	Italy: Venice	*Salomé*	Compagnia Drammatica Italiana Ruggieri.
	Russia: 1) Maly Theatre, Moscow	*DOP*	Premiere.
	2) Terijoki Summer Theatre, St. Petersburg	*IBE*	Directed by Vsevolod Meyerhold.
	Sweden: Intimate Theatre, Stockholm	*WNI*	
1913	**Austria:** Neue Wiener Bühne, Vienna	*Salomé*	Guest performance by Gertrud Eysoldt.
	Spain: Teatro de la Princesa, Madrid	*Salomé*	Margarita Xirgu in the title role. Spanish version, possibly from Catalan, by Joaquim Pena.
1914	**Bohemia (Czech):** Vinohrady Theatre, Prague	*Bezvýznamná žena* (*WNI*)	Directed by Karel Hugo Hilar. Trans. A. Hanušová and František Linhart.
	Greece: Royal Theatre, Athens	FT	Part of a concert of the 'Music Academy'.
	Romania: Teatrul Modern, Bucharest	*Soţul ideal* (*IH*)	Voiculescu-Bulandra Company. Lucia Bulandra as Lady Chiltern, Marioara Voiculescu as Mrs Cheveley.
1915	**Bohemia (Czech):** Vinohrady Theatre, Prague	*Vějíř lady Windermerové* (*LWF*)	Directed by František Hlavatý.

Date	Venue	Play	Additional Information
	Croatia: Croatian National Theatre, Zagreb	*Salome* (Strauss)	Directed by Ivo Raić-Lonjski. Trans. Andro Mitrović.
	Netherlands	*Een Ideaal Echtgenoot* (*IH*)	Performed by the Haghespelers.
	Sweden: Swedish Theatre, Stockholm	*Salomé*	
1917	**Greece:** Theatre Cybele	*Enas idanikós ouzygos* (*IH*)	Greek Company of Dramas and Comedies.
	Netherlands: Stadion, Amsterdam	*Salomé*	
	Russia: Kamerny Theatre, Moscow	*Salomé*	Premiere. Directed by Aleksandr Tairov. Cubist-inspired sets and costumes. Trans. Konstantin Balmont.
	Spain: 1) Príncipe Alfonso, Madrid	*Un marido ideal* (*IH*)	Performed by Ana Adamuz and García Ortega's company (Ana Adamuz as Lady Chiltern). Trans. Ricardo Baeza.
	2) Teatro de la Princesa, Madrid	*Una mujer sin importancia* (*WNI*)	Francisco García Ortega's company, with García Ortega as Lord Illingworth and Ana Adamuz as Mrs Arbuthnot. Trans. Antonio Plañiol.
1918	**Latvia:** Riga Latvian Theatre, Riga	*Salomé*	
	Netherlands 1)	*De ernst van Ernst* (*IBE*)	Produced by Nederlandsch Tooneel.
	2) Amsterdam	*Salomé* and *Florentijns Treurspel* (FT)	Produced by Het Groot Tooneel.
	Spain: Teatro Goya, Madrid	*Una mujer sin importancia* (*WNI*)	Performed by García Ortega's company. Trans. Ricardo Baeza.
	Switzerland: Theater zu Kaufleuten, Zurich	*IBE*	English Players' first production. James Joyce as business manager.

Date	Venue	Play	Additional Information
1919	**Czechoslovakia (Czech):** Moravian–Silesian National Theatre, Ostrava	*Vějíř lady Windermerové* (*LWF*)	Trans. Jan Havlasa.
	Poland: Teatr Mały, Warszawa	*Brat marnotrawny* (*IBE*)	Directed by Julius Osterwa.
	Spain: Teatro de la Princesa, Madrid	*La importancia de llamarse Ernesto* (*IBE*)	Trans. Ricardo Baeza and performed by his theatre company, Atenea.
1920	**Estonia:** Theatre Ugala, Viljandi	*Salomé*	First professional open-air play in Estonia.
	Spain: Teatro de la Princesa, Madrid	*El abanico de Lady Windermere* (*LWF*)	Performed by the Guerrero-Díaz de Mendoza company. Trans. Ricardo Baeza.
1921	**Netherlands**	*De ernst van Ernst* (*IBE*)	Performed by the Haghespelers.
	Poland: 1) Teatr Miejski im. Juliusza Słowackiego, Kraków	*Tragedia florencka* (*FT*)	Directed by Józef Sosnowski.
	2) Teatr Miejski im. Juliusza Słowackiego, Kraków	*Salomé*	Directed by Teofil Trzciński.
1922	**Croatia:** Croatian National Theatre, Zagreb	*Salome* (Strauss)	Directed by Branko Gavella. Conducted by Milan Sachs.
	Denmark: Dagmar Theatre, Copenhagen	*IBE*	Trans. Niels Th. Thomsen.
	France: Comédie des Champs-Elysées, Paris	*Salomé*	Adaptation by Maurice Bourgeois.
	Ireland: Abbey Theatre, Dublin	*IBE*	A production by the repertory company of Madam Kirkwood Hackett.

Date	Venue	Play	Additional Information
	Romania: Sidoli Circus Arena	*Salomé*	Opening night for 'Marioara Voiculescu' Theatre. Reinhardt-inspired scenography. Marioara Voiculescu in the title role.
1923	**Czechoslovakia (Czech):** National Theatre in the Nobility Theatre building, Prague	*Bezvýznamná žena* (*WNI*)	Directed by Miloš Nový. Trans. A. Hanušová and František Linhart.
	Netherlands: Amsterdam	*Lady Windermere's Waaier* (*LWF*)	Produced by Het Hollandsch Tooneel.
1924	**Czechoslovakia (Czech):** 1) City Theatre, Brno	*Vějíř lady Windermerové* (*LWF*)	Directed by Rudolf Walter. Trans. Bořivoj Prusík.
	2) **(Czech):** City Theatre, Brno	*Salomé*	Directed by Vilém Skoch. Trans. Otakar Theer.
	Denmark: Dagmar Theatre, Copenhagen	*WNI*	Trans. Niels Th. Thomsen.
	Hungary: Vígszínház (Comedy Theatre), Budapest	*Bunbury* (*IBE*)	
	Spain: 1) Teatro Centro, Madrid	*La importancia de llamarse Ernesto* (*IBE*)	Performed by López Alarcón's company.
	2) Teatro Reina Victoria, Madrid	*Una mujer sin importancia* (*WNI*)	Performed by Ana Adámuz and Manuel González's company. Trans. Ricardo Baeza.
1925	**Austria:** Raimundtheater, Vienna	*Salomé*	Guest performance by Alexander Tairov's Moscow Chamber Theatre.
	Czechoslovakia (Czech): 1) National Theatre in the Na Veveří Theatre building, Brno	*Ideální manžel* (*IH*)	Directed by Vladimír Šimáček. Trans. Adrienna Linková.

Date	Venue	Play	Additional Information
	2) Moravian-Silesian National Theatre, Ostrava	*Na čem záleží* (*IBE*)	Directed by Karel Prox. Trans. Jan Lorenc.
	Spain: 1) Teatro Infanta Beatriz, Madrid	*Un marido ideal* (*IH*)	Performed by Ernesto Vilches's company. Trans. Ricardo Baeza.
	2) Teatro Infanta Beatriz, Madrid	*Una mujer sin importancia* (*WNI*)	Performed by Ana Adámuz and Manuel González's company. Trans. Ricardo Baeza.
1926	**Croatia:** National Theatre for Dalmatia, Split	*Idealan muž* (*IH*)	Directed by Rade Pregarc. Trans. Milan Šenoa.
	Hungary: Nemzeti Színház, Budapest	*IH*	
	Ireland: Abbey Theatre, Dublin	*IBE*	Directed by Lennox Robinson.
1928	**Czechoslovakia (Czech):** Moravian-Silesian National Theatre, Ostrava	*Florentská tragedie* (*FT*)	Directed by Miloš Nový. Trans. Jarmila Dušková (Jaroslav Kvapil).
	Hungary: Kamaraszínház (Chamber Theatre), Budapest	*Bunbury* (*IBE*)	
	Ireland: Gate Theatre, Dublin	*Salomé*	Directed by Hilton Edwards, Micheál Mac Liammóir as Jokanaan.
	Romania: Regina Maria Theatre, Bucharest	*Soţul ideal* (*IH*)	
	Spain: 1) Teatro Infanta Beatriz, Madrid	*Un marido ideal* (*IH*)	Performed by Irene López Heredia's company. Trans. Ricardo Baeza.
	2) Teatro Reina Victoria, Madrid	*Una mujer sin importancia* (*WNI*)	Performed by Ana Adámuz and Manuel González's company. Trans. Ricardo Baeza.

Date	Venue	Play	Additional Information
1929	**Czechoslovakia (Czech):** National Theatre in the Nobility Theatre building, Prague	*Na čem záleží* (*IBE*)	Directed by Vojta Novák. Trans. Josef Hrůša.
	Netherlands	*Een Ideaal Echtgenoot* (*IH*)	Produced by Vereenigt Tooneel.
	Romania: Teatrul National, Bucharest	*O femeie fara importanta* (*WNI*)	
	Spain: Teatro Centro, Madrid	*El abanico de Lady Windermere* (*LWF*)	Performed by Lola Membrives's company (an Argentine company).
1930	**Greece:** Laiko Theatro, Athens	FT	
	Romania: Regina Maria Theatre, Bucharest	*Evantaiul dnei Windermere* (*LWF*)	
1931	**Austria:** Deutsches Volkstheater, Vienna	*Bunbury* (*IBE*)	Directed by Herbert Furreg, starring Adele Sandrock as Lady Brancaster.
	Romania: Bucharest National Theatre, Bucharest	*Evantaiul dnei Windermere* (*LWF*)	
	Spain: Teatro Español, Madrid	*El abanico de Lady Windermere* (*LWF*)	Performed by the Guerrero-Díaz de Mendoza.
1933	**Ireland:** Gate Theatre, Dublin	*IBE*	Directed by Hilton Edwards.
	Netherlands: Openluchttheater, Zandvoort	*Salomé*	Directed by Anton Verhagen
1934	**Croatia:** Croatian National Theatre, Zagreb	*Salome* (Strauss)	Directed by Petar Raičev, conducted by Lovro Matačić, scenography by Ljubo Babić.

Date	Venue	Play	Additional Information
	Switzerland: Schauspielhaus, Zurich	*Bunbury (IBE)*	
1935	**France:** La Petite Scène, Paris	*WNI*	Directed by Marie-Ange Rivain. Adapted by L. Guillot.de Saix and M.Saint-Marc.
	Germany: 1) Hamburg	*IH*	Trans. Karl Lerbs.
	2) Neues Theater, Hamburg	*Vor allem Ernst! (Bunbury) (IBE)*	Text by Ernst Sander, contemporary setting and ironic references to Nazi ideology.
	Switzerland: Schauspielhaus, Zurich	*LWF*	
1936	**Germany:** Mannheim	*WNI*	Trans. Karl Lerbs.
	Serbia: Serbian National Theatre, Belgrade	*LWF*	Produced by Dragutinovic (also playing Lord Windermere) and starring Mrs Riznic.
1937	**Czechoslovakia (Czech):** National Theatre in the Na Veveří Theatre building, Brno	*Na čem záleží (IBE)*	Directed by Jan Škoda. Trans. Jan Lorenc.
	Germany: Staatstheater, Berlin	*Bunbury (IBE)*	Directed by Paul Bildt. Trans. Franz Blei and Carl Zeiß.
	Greece: Royal Theatre, Athens	*I Ventália tīs Laídis Ouídermier (LWF)*	Directed by Dimitri Rontires. Company of the Theatre Royal. Trans. Vassili Heliopoulos.
1938	**Austria:** Burgtheater, Vienna	*Bunbury, oder die Bedeutung, Ernst zu sein (IBE)*	Based on the German adaptation by Ernst Sander.
	Greece: National Theatre of Greece, Athens	*Enas idanikós ouzygoz (IH)*	Directed by Dimitri Ronteres. Trans. D. S. Devaris.

Date	Venue	Play	Additional Information
	Romania: Bucharest National Theatre, Bucharest	*Bunbury* (*IBE*)	
1939	**Croatia:** Little Theatre, Zagreb	*IBE*	Directed by Hilton Edwards. Dublin Gate Theatre touring performance, in English.
	Czechoslovakia (Czech): National Theatre in the Na Veveří Theatre building, Brno	*Ideální manžel* (*IH*)	Directed by Jan Škoda. Trans. Adrienna Linková.
	Hungary: National Theatre, Budapest	*Bunbury* (*IBE*)	Performed by students of acting
	Romania: Bucharest	*Bunbury* (*IBE*)	Directed by Hilton Edwards. Dublin Gate Theatre touring performance, in English.
1940	**Greece:** Theatre d'Art	*Mía gynaíka chōrís sīmasía* (*WNI*)	Company of Carolos Koun. Trans. Stamatis Speliotopoulos.
1941	**Spain:** Teatro Bretón, Madrid	*Una mujer sin importancia* (*WNI*)	Irene López Heredia and Mariano Asquerino as main actors.
	Switzerland: Schauspielhaus, Zurich	*Bunbury* (*IBE*)	
1942	**Italy:** Teatro Manzoni, Milan	*La Duchessa di Padova* (*DOP*)	Directed by Alessandro Brissoni, with scenes and costumes by Titina Rota and musical accompaniment by Guido Soresina.
	Romania: Theatre Municipal, Bucharest	*Soţul ideal* (*IH*)	Directed by Soare Z. Soare. With Tony Bulandra, Pop Marţian, Marieta Anca, Maria Mohor.
	Spain: Teatro Beatriz, Madrid	*Una mujer sin importancia* (*WNI*)	Irene López Heredia and Mariano Asquerino as main actors.

Date	Venue	Play	Additional Information
1944	**Denmark:** Royal Theatre, Copenhagen	*IBE*	During the German occupation. Directed by Holger Gabrielsen, with Ebbe Rohde, Mogens Wieth, Karin Nellemose, Bodil Kjer and the legendary Clara Pontoppidan.
1945	**Austria:** Deutsches Volkstheater, Vienna	*Lady Windermeres Fächer* (*LWF*)	Directed by the Viennese actor Hans Thimig.
	Greece: National Theatre of Greece, Athens	FT	
	Romania: Marin Sorescu Theatre, Craiova	*Evantaiul Doamnei Windermere* (*LWF*)	Directed by Ion Olteanu. Trans. Petru Comarnescu.
1946	**Czechoslovakia (Czech):** 1) City Theatre, Most	*Na čem záleží* (*IBE*)	Directed by Josef Schettina. Trans. Jan Lorenc.
	2) National Theatre in the Na Veveří Theatre building, Brno	*Bezvýznamná žena* (*WNI*)	Directed by Vladimír Vozák. Trans. Josef Kaňka.
1947	**Czechoslovakia (Czech):** 1) Realistic Theatre, Prague	*Jak je důležité míti Filipa* (*IBE*)	Directed by Ota Ornest. Trans. J.Z.Novák.
	2) Vinohrady City Theatre, Prague	*Vějíř lady Windermerové* (*LWF*)	Directed by Bedřich Vrbský. Trans. Zdeněk Vančura.
1948	**Austria:** Theater an der Wien, Vienna	*Salome* (Strauss)	Ljuba Welitsch in the title role. Trans. Hedwig Lachmann.
1949	**Czechoslovakia (Czech):** Zdeněk Nejedlý City Theatre, Opava	*Jak je důležité míti Filipa* (*IBE*)	Directed by Vladislav Hamšík.

Date	Venue	Play	Additional Information
	Hungary: Művész Színház (Arts Theatre), Budapest	*IH*	Performed only three times before the theatre is closed down.
1950	**Netherlands:** 1) Stadsschouwburg, Amsterdam	*IBE*	Produced by Birmingham Repertory Company under Sir Barry Jackson.
	2)	*De ernst van Ernst (IBE)*	Performed by the Haagse Comedie and directed by Paul Steenberger.
1951	**Czechoslovakia (Czech):** State Theatre, Brno	*Jak je důležité míti Filipa (IBE)*	Directed by Miroslav Kratochvíl.
1953	**Serbia:** Serbian National Theatre, Belgrade	*LWF*	
1954	**Croatia:** Croatian National Theatre, Zagreb	*Lepeza Lady Windermere (LWF)*	Directed by Vlado Habunek. Trans. Vlado Habunek.
	Czechoslovakia (Czech): 1) National Theatre in the Josef Kajetán Tyl Theatre building, Prague	*Ideální manžel (IH)*	Directed by Otmar Krejča. Trans. Frank Tetauer.
	2) East Bohemia Theatre, Pradubice	*Vějíř lady Windermerové (LWF)*	Directed by Zdeněk Bittl. Trans. Zdeněk Vančura.
	France: Théâtre Comédie des Champs-Élysées, Paris	*Il est important d'être aimé (IBE)*	Directed by Claude Sainval. Adaptation by Nicole and Jean Anouilh.

Date	Venue	Play	Additional Information
1955	**Austria:** Burgtheater in the Ronacher Theatre, Vienna	*Bunbury, oder die Komödie des Ernst-Seins (Bunbury, or the Comedy of Being Earnest) (IBE)*	Directed and newly adapted for the stage by Ernst Lothar.
	Czechoslovakia (Czech): Zdeněk Nejedlý Theatre, Opava	*Bezvýznamná žena (WNI)*	Directed by Tomáš Bek.
	France: Théâtre Hébertot, Paris	*L'Éventail de Lady Windermere (LWF)*	Directed by Marcelle Tassencourt. Adapted by Michelle Lahaye.
1956	**Hungary:** Déryné Színház, Miskolc	*Firenzei tragédia (FT)*	
	Romania: 1) Arad Theatre, Arad	*Soţul ideal (IH)*	Directed by Savel Grunea.
	2) Marin Sorescu Theatre, Craiova	*Bunbury/Ce inseamna sa fii onest (IBE)*	Directed by Val Mugur. Trans. Alexandru Alcalay and Sima Zamfir.
1957	**Ireland:** International Theatre Festival, Dublin	*IBE*	Margaret Rutherford as Lady Bracknell.
1958	**Czechoslovakia (Czech):** Petr Bezruč Theatre, Ostrava	*Jak je důležité míti Filipa (IBE)*	Directed by Václav Kyzlink.
1959	**Bulgaria:** Bulgarian National Theatre, Sofia	*IH*	
	Hungary: 1) Madách Kamara Theatre, Budapest	*LWF*	
	2) National Theatre, Pécs	*Bunbury (IBE)*	

Date	Venue	Play	Additional Information
1960	**Czechoslovakia (Czech):** Theatre of the Beskydy Mountains, Nový Jičín	*Ideální manžel* (*IH*)	Directed by R. Chmelík.
	Hungary: National Theatre, Szeged	*Hazudj igazat* (*IBE*)	
1961	**Serbia:** Yugoslav Drama Theatre, Belgrade	*IH*	Staring Branko Plesa and Marija Crnobori.
1965	**Czechoslovakia (Czech):** 1) Janáček Academy of Performing Arts, Brno	*Jak je důležité míti Filipa* (*IBE*)	Directed by Libor Pleva.
	2) State Theatre, Ostrava	*Jak je důležité míti Filipa* (*IBE*)	Directed by Alois Hajda.
	3) City Theatre, Kolin	*Bezvýznamná žena* (*WNI*)	Directed by Karel Lhota.
1967	**Czechoslovakia (Czech):** 1) Theatre of South Bohemia, České Budějovice	*Jak je důležité míti Filipa* (*IBE*)	Directed by Zdeněk Míka.
	2) Regional Theatre, Kolin	*Vějíř lady Windermerové* (*LWF*)	Directed by Karel Lhota.
	Romania: Victor Ion Popa Theatre, Barlad	*Evantaiul Doamnei Windermere* (*LWF*)	Directed by Moruzan Constantin. Trans. Andrei Bantas.
1968	**Czechoslovakia (Czech):** Workers Theatre, Gottwaldov	*Ideální manžel* (*IH*)	Directed by K. Pokorný.
	Hungary: Ódry Színpad, Budapest	*Bunbury* (*IBE*)	

Date	Venue	Play	Additional Information
	Romania: German Theatre, Timisoara	*Bunbury (IBE)*	Directed by Hans Schuschnig. Trans. Kurt Jung Alsen.
1969	**Croatia:** Diocletian's Palace, Split	*Salome* (Strauss)	Directed by Danijel Marušić, conducted by Mladen Bašić. Produced in cooperation with Croatian Radio and Television (Zagreb).
1970	**Romania:** 1) **(Hungarian):** Hungarian Theatre, Cluj	*Hazudj Igazat (IBE)*	Directed by Bela Horvath. Trans. Ferenc Karinthy.
	2) Lucian Blaga Theatre, Cluj	*O femeie fara importanta (WNI)*	Directed by Taub Ianos. Trans. Andrei Bantas and Crisan Toescu.
1971	**Hungary:** Szigligeti Theatre, Szolnok	*Hazudj igazat (IBE)*	
	Romania: 1) **(German):** Radu Stanca Theatre, Sibiu	*Bunbury Oder Keine Hochzeit ohne Ernst (IBE)*	Directed by Hans Schuschnig. Trans. Paul Felix Greve.
	2) **(Hungarian):** Tompa Miklos Theatre Company, Targu Mures	*Lady Windermere Legyezoje (LWF)*	Directed by Constantin Anatol. Trans. Tamás Moly.
1972	**France:** Théâtre Marigny, Paris	*Un Mari Idéal (IH)*	Directed by Raymond Rouleau.
1973	**France:** Théâtre du Globe, Paris	*Salomé*	Produced by Francis Sourbié. All male cast.
	Ireland: Abbey Theatre, Dublin	*IBE*	Directed by Alan Barlow.
1975	**Czechoslovakia (Czech):** East Bohemia Theatre, Pradubice	*Vějíř lady Windermerové (LWF)*	Directed by Oto Ševčík.

Date	Venue	Play	Additional Information
	Romania: Mihai Eminescu Theatre, Timisoara	*Evantaiul unei lady* (*LWF*)	Directed and Trans. Constantin Anatol.
1976	**Czechoslovakia (Czech):** Vítězslav Nezval Theatre, Karlovy Vary	*Bezvýznamná žena* (*WNI*)	Directed by Svatoslav Papež.
1978	**Czechoslovakia (Czech):** Regional Theatre, Příbram	*Ideální manžel* (*IH*)	Directed by Emil Kadeřávek. Trans. J. Z. Novák.
	Hungary: Nyári Theatre, Pécs	*Salomé*	Directed by Imre Eck
1979	**Czechoslovakia (Czech):** Vítězslav Nezval Theatre, Karlovy Vary	*Jak je důležité míti Filipa* (*IBE*)	Directed by Jiří Dalík. Trans. J. Z. Novák.
1980	**Croatia:** Croatian National Theatre, Rijeka	*Idealan muž* (*IH*)	Directed by Radoslav Zlatan Dorić. Trans. Nada Čurčija-Prodanović. Also performed at the Croatian professional theatres meeting in Slavonski Brod, Croatia, on 26 September 1981.
	Germany: Freie Volksbühne, Berlin	*Bunbury* (*IBE*)	Directed by Peter Zadek.
1981	**Hungary:** 1) Veszprém	*IH*	
	2) Ódry Színpad, Budapest	*Salomé*	
1983	**Czechoslovakia (Czech):** E. F. Burian Theatre, Prague	*Vějíř lady Windermerové* (*LWF*)	Directed by Josef Palla. Trans. Milan Lukeš.

Date	Venue	Play	Additional Information
1984	**Czechoslovakia (Czech):** Oldřich Stibor State Theatre, Olomouc	*Vějíř lady Windermerové* (*LWF*)	Directed by Jiří Vrba. Trans. Milan Lukeš
	Ireland: Gate Theatre, Dublin	*WNI*	Directed by Patrick Mason.
1985	**Czechoslovakia (Czech):** Theatre of the Horácko Region, Jihlava	*Bezvýznamná žena* (*WNI*)	Directed by Michael Junášek Trans. J.Z.Novák
	Romania (Hungarian): Oradea Theatre, Oradea	*Hazudj Igazat* (*IBE*)	Directed by Katy Gabor. Trans. into Hungarian by Sandor Hevesi.
	Spain: Festival de Teatro Clásico, Mérida	*Salomé*	Directed by Mario Gas and performed by Nuria Espert; adaptation by Terenci Moix. Dance choreography by contemporary ballet dancer Cesc Gelabert.
1986	**Czechoslovakia (Czech):** Theatre of the Slovácko Region, Uherské Hradiště	*Jak je důležité míti Filipa* (*IBE*)	Directed by Hugo Domes. Trans. J. Z. Novák.
1987	**Ireland:** Gate Theatre, Dublin	*IBE*	Directed by Patrick Mason.
1988	**Croatia:** Croatian National Theatre, Zagreb	*Salome* (Strauss)	Directed by Tobias Richter, conducted by Miro Belamarić.
	Czechoslovakia (Czech): F.X.Šalda State Theatre, Liberec	*Salomé*	Directed by Václav Martinec. Trans. Drahoslava Janderová.
	Ireland: Gate Theatre, Dublin	*Salomé*	Directed by Steven Berkoff.

Date	Venue	Play	Additional Information
1989	**Ireland:** Gate Theatre, Dublin	*IH*	Directed by Ben Barnes.
	Spain (Galician): Centro Dramático Galego, Santiago de Compostela	*Salomé*	Adapted by Roberto Vidal and John Eastham.
1990	**Hungary:** Móricz Zsigmond Theatre, Nyíregyháza	*Bunbury (IBE)*	Directed by László Salamon Suba
1991	**Romania:** Fani Tardini, Galati	*Salomé*	Directed by Gheorge Jora. Trans. Adriana and Andrei Bantas.
1993	**Ireland:** Rough Magic, Dublin	*LWF*	Directed by Lynne Parker. All male cast.
1994	**Germany:** Bayerisches Staatsschauspiel, Munich	*IBE*	Directed by Leander Haußmann.
	Spain	*La importancia de llamarse Ernesto (IBE)*	Theatre group La Ruina, directed by Francisco José Redondo Navalón.
1995	**France:** Théâtre Antoine, Paris	*Un Mari Idéal (IH)*	Directed by Adrian Brine. Adapted by Pierre Laville.
	Hungary: 1) Nemzeti Theatre, Miskolc	*Salomé*	Interpretation by Zoltán Kamondi.
	2) Józsefvárosi Theatre, Budapest.	*Bunbury (IBE)*	Directed by Miklós Gábor
1996	**France:** Théâtre National de Chaillot, Paris	*L'Importance d'Etre Constant (IBE)*	Directed by Jérôme Savary. Trans. Jean-Michel Départs.
	Greece: Theatre Lampeti, Athens	*IBE*	Directed by Marios Plorites.

Date	Venue	Play	Additional Information
	Ireland: Abbey Theatre, Dublin	*WNI*	Directed by Ben Barnes.
	Hungary: Csiky Gergely Theatre, Kaposvár	*Salomé*	
	Spain: 1) Teatro Alcázar, Madrid	*Un marido ideal* (*IH*)	Directed by Alfonso Zurro. Produced by Juanjo Seoane. Actors: Ana Marzoa, José Goyanes, Víctor Valverde, Jaime Blach. Trans. Juan José de Arteche from a French version by Pierre Laville.
	2) Escuela Superior de Arte Dramático, Murcia	*Salomé*	Directed by Antonio Saura. Trans. Antonio Saura.
1997	**Czech Republic:** 1) Prague City Theatres – ABC, Prague	*Ideální manžel* (*IH*)	Directed by Radovan Lipus. Trans. Jiří Strnad.
	2) City Theatre, Mladá Boleslav	*Jak je důležité míti Filipa* (*IBE*)	Directed by Ladislav Vymětal.
	Ireland: Gate Theatre, Dublin	*LWF*	Directed by Alan Stanford.
1998	**Czech Republic:** Academy of Performing Arts, Prague	*Salomé*	Directed by Eva Leinveberová.
	Germany: Renaissance Theatre, Berlin	*IBE*	All male production. Directed by Hans Hollmann.
1999	**Croatia:** Lisinski Concert Hall, Zagreb	*Salome* (Strauss)	Directed by Christian Romanowski, conducted by Kazushi Ōno. Dunja Vejzović in the title role.
	Spain: Teatro Juan Bravo, Segovia	*Una mujer sin importancia* (*WNI*)	Directed by Tomás Gayo and Julio Escalada. Produced by Escalada Teatral. Performed by Silvia Tortosa, Claudio Sierra, Enriqueta Carvalleira and Mara Goyanes.

Date	Venue	Play	Additional Information
2000	**Spain:** Teatro Galileo, Madrid	*Salomé. La Hija de Herodías (Salomé. Herodias' Daughter)*	Directed by Luis González Carreño. Costumes and set also by Carreño.
2001	**Austria:** Theater in der Josefstadt, Vienna	*Ein Idealer Gatte (IH)*	Directed by Michael Gampe. Trans. Rainer Kohlmayer.
2002	**Spain (Galician)**	*Un marido ideal (IH)*	Theatre group from the Universidade de Vigo, directed by Iago Vázquez Brea. Trans. Xerigonza.
2003	**Czech Republic:** City Theatre, Brno	*Jak je důležité míti Filipa (IBE)*	Directed by Jana Kališová.
	France: Théâtre du Palais Royal, Paris	*L'Éventail de Lady Windermere (LWF)*	New version by Pierre Laville.
	Hungary: 1) Radnóti Theatre, Budapest	*IH*	Directed by Péter Valló.
	2) József Attila Theatre, Budapest	*Bunbury, avagy Szilárdnak kell lenni (IBE)*	Incorporating a musical accompaniment. New translation by Ádám Nádasdy.
	3) National Theatre, Győr	*Bunbury, avagy a határozott lét fontossága (IBE)*	
	Romania (German): German Theatre, Timisoara	*Bunbury (IBE)*	Directed by Marina Tiron Emandi. Trans. Rainer Kohlmayer.
2004	**Austria:** Akademietheater, Vienna	*Salomé*	Directed by Dimiter Gotscheff, German adaptation by the Austrian poet Gerhard Rühm.
	Romania: Vasile Alecsandri Theatre, Iasi	*Salomé*	Directed by Alexandru Hausvater.
2005	**Austria:** Akademietheater, Vienna	*Ernst ist das Leben (IBE)*	Produced by Falk Richter. German stage adaptation by Elfriede Jelinek on the basis of a translation by Karin Rausch.

Date	Venue	Play	Additional Information
	Spain: Teatro Álbeniz, Madrid	*Salomé*	Directed by Miguel Narros, included a dance choreographed by Víctor Ullate. Trans. Mauro Armiño.
2006	**Austria:** Theater in der Josefstadt, Vienna	*Bunbury (IBE)*	Produced by Hans Hollmann. All male cast.
	France: 1) Théâtre Antoine, Paris	*L'Importance d'être Constant (IBE)*	
	2) Théâtre 14 Jean-Marie Serreau, Paris	*L'Éventail de Lady Windermere (LWF)*	Produced by Sébastien Azzopardi. New version by Pierre Laville.
	3) Théâtre de Nesle, Paris	*Salomé*	Kelly Rivière as Salomé.
	Germany: 1) Schauspielhaus Bochum, Bochum	*Ein idealer Gatte (IH)*	Directed by Armin Holz.
	2) Deutsches Theater, Berlin	*Bunbury – Ernst ist das Leben (IBE)*	Directed by Bettina Bruinier. Trans. Rausch/Jelinek.
	Switzerland: Pfauen, Zurich	*Bunbury (IBE)*	Directed by Werner Düggelin. Trans. Rainer Kohlmayer.
2007	**Croatia:** Croatian National Theatre, Zagreb	*Važno je zvati se Ernest (IBE)*	Directed by Tomislav Pavković. Trans. Martina Aničić.
	Czech Republic: Vinohrady Theatre, Prague	*Ideální manžel (IH)*	Directed by Jana Kališová.
	Denmark: Royal Theatre, Copenhagen	*IBE*	
	France: 1) **(English):** Théâtre Sylvia Montfort, Paris	*IBE*	Directed by Lucile O'Flanagan. Adaptation by Andrew Loudon and Emma Reeves.
	2) Théâtre des Bouffes Parisiens, Paris	*L'Éventail de Lady Windermere (LWF)*	Produced by Sébastien Azzopardi. New version by Pierre Laville.

Date	Venue	Play	Additional Information
	Spain: 1) Colegio Mayor Universitario Isabel de España, Madrid	*Un marido ideal* *(IH)*	Amateur production by Grupo Tilmun Teatro, a university theatre group, directed by Jose Antonio Díaz and Sara Sánchez.
	2) Teatro Cervantes, Valladolid	*La importancia de llamarse Ernesto* *(IBE)*	Directed by Gabriel Olivares. Performed by actors Patxi Freytex, Fran Nortes, Yolanda Ulloa, and Carmen Morales. Toured around Spain in 2008. Trans. Daniel Pérez and Eduardo Galán.
	3) (Catalan): Teatre Nacional de Catalunya, Barcelona	*El ventall de Lady Windermere* *(LWF)*	Directed by Josep Maria Mestres Quadrany. Teresa Lozana as Lady Windermere. Trans. Joan Sellent.
2008	**Austria:** 3raum-Anatomietheater, Vienna	*LWF*	Directed by Hubsi Kramar, with drag artist Lucy McEvil as Mrs Erlynne.
	Hungary: Radnóti Miklós Theatre, Budapest	*Bunbury (IBE)*	Directed by Péter Valló New translation by Ádám Nádasdy.
	Spain (Galician): Mostra de Teatro Universitario de Galicia, Santiago de Compostela	*O abanico de lady Windermere* *(LWF)*	Performed in Galician by Tangatutanga Teatro, from the Universidade de Santiago de Compostela.
2009	**Austria:** 3raum-Anatomietheater, Vienna	*IH*	Directed by Hubsi Kramar, with drag artist Lucy McEvil as Mrs Cheveley.
2010	**Austria:** 1) Burgtheater – Vestibül, Vienna	*Dorian Gray (PDG)*	Stage version of *PDG*, directed by Bastian Kraft.
	2) 3raum-Anatomietheater, Vienna	*IBE*	Directed by Hubsi Kramar, with drag artist Lucy McEvil as Lady Bracknell.
	Croatia: Istarsko narodno kazalište, Pula	*Salome*	Directed by Damir Zlatar Frey.
2011	**Austria:** Akademietheater, Vienna	*Der ideale Mann* *(IH)*	Directed by Barbara Frey. German stage adaptation by Elfriede Jelinek on the basis of a translation by Karin Rausch.

Date	Venue	Play	Additional Information
	Spain: Teatro de la Abadía, Madrid	*Wild, Wild, Wilde*	Stage version of *DP*, text by José Ramón Fernández, directed by Fefa Noia.
2013	**Spain:** Teatro Fernán Gómez, Madrid	*La importancia de llamarse Ernesto* (*IBE*)	Directed by Alfredo Sanzol. Adaptation by Sanzol and José Padilla.

Introduction: Oscar Wilde: European by Sympathy

Stefano Evangelista

'Français de sympathie, je suis Irlandais de race, et les Anglais m'ont condamné à parler le langage de Shakespeare.' (Wilde 2000, 505)[1]

This epigrammatic autobiographical statement, addressed to the French writer Edmond de Goncourt in 1891, alerts us to the complexities of Oscar Wilde's identity and intellectual allegiances. Wilde juxtaposes the variables of desire, heredity and language with a characteristic mixture of immodesty and extreme graciousness. If the language of Shakespeare is a burden to which the English colonizers have condemned Wilde (the knowing reader must feel an eerie premonition of a much harsher sentence that, at this point, was less than four years in the future), then the language of Baudelaire – and, of course, Goncourt – is the author's chosen intellectual homeland. This view was borne out by many of Wilde's early English critics, for whom Wilde's works possessed a certain foreign or, more precisely, French quality which derived no doubt from his following of French writers such as Théophile Gautier and Joris-Karl Huysmans and from his role as an important intermediary in the diffusion of French Symbolism into England. A sharp observer of the literary culture of his time, Wilde understood the cultural dynamics of nineteenth-century cosmopolitanism and exploited this knowledge to forge an incredibly successful public image as iconoclastic critic of middle-class culture and society. The mixture of French-inflected cosmopolitanism, Englishness and Irishness expressed to Goncourt made him then and still makes him now difficult to assimilate into a single national tradition.

Wilde's fame was built across national borders: his notoriety in Britain was cemented by his American lecture tour of 1882, years before he wrote any of his major works. On his return from America, Wilde started making regular trips to France, where he was always eager to make contact with the most prominent authors and artists of the day. He loved the French language (as much as he disliked German) and spoke excellent French – even Gide had to admit as much. This facilitated his introduction into the local artistic

---

[1] 'French by sympathy, I am Irish by birth, and the English have condemned me to speak the language of Shakespeare.'

circles, where he met, among others, Sarah Bernhardt, Debussy, Degas, Hugo, Mallarmé, Proust, Toulouse-Lautrec (who painted a portrait of him), Verlaine and Zola. Wilde's ambition to *belong* to French culture culminated in the composition of *Salomé* in 1891, around the time of his letter to Goncourt. The choice to write one of his major literary works in French makes Wilde unique among nineteenth-century Anglophone authors. This Francophilia – intensified by his wide-ranging knowledge of French literature and his spectacular clashes with English law – has shaped Wilde's reputation both during and after his life-time.[2] It seems symbolically fitting that he should be buried in Paris, where he died a voluntary exile in November 1900, and where his funeral monument sculpted by Jacob Epstein has alternately been the object of desecration and veneration, and is today among Europe's best-known sites of literary pilgrimage.

Wilde was often impatient with the provincialism and narrow moral values of English literary culture. The following attack on the editor of the *St James's Gazette* is characteristic. It was part of a public diatribe that followed the publication of *PDG*:

> Such an article as you have published really makes one despair of the possibility of any general culture in England. Were I a French author, and my book brought out in Paris, there is not a single literary critic in France, on any paper of high standing, who would think for a moment of criticising it from an ethical standpoint. If he did so, he would stultify himself, not merely in the eyes of all men of letters, but in the eyes of the majority of the public. (Wilde 2000, 432)

Wilde's authority as writer and public intellectual and his own self-myth were rooted in this sense of alienation from the English public – a feeling of being misunderstood or only half understood together with a conviction of being fully appreciated only abroad, whether in Continental Europe or the United States.

As an Irish writer, Wilde had a much more pronounced European outlook than his contemporary W. B. Yeats who, as Klaus Peter Jochum explains in the Yeats volume in this series, had a poor command of foreign languages, established few contacts with European intellectuals and was comparatively less interested in the European reception of his work (2006). It is tempting to think of Wilde as anticipating a tradition of cosmopolitan Irish writers of the twentieth century best represented by Joyce, whose writings emerge from a European (rather than national) literature while maintaining a distinctively Irish interest and character (see Lernout 2004). The works of Beckett could be seen to represent a similar case. In his life and work Wilde was, however, much more deeply invested in England and Englishness than Joyce. As a journalist and then as a playwright, he worked, most of his life, for the English culture industry. Ireland does not play a conspicuous role in any of his writings. Yet Wilde also saw that his Irish identity put him in a position of

---

2   In 1975, the critic Jacques de Langlade paid tribute to Wilde's Frenchness in his monograph *Oscar Wilde: Ecrivain français* (Oscar Wilde: French writer).

marginality that he could turn into cultural authority. As he wrote in a letter to George Bernard Shaw in 1893, 'England is the land of intellectual fogs but you have done much to clear the air: we are both Celtic, and I like to think that we are friends' (1962, 332). By implication, the Celtic bond that unites the two writers is what equips them to criticize modern England with a clarity that is unavailable to natives. As in the letter to Goncourt, graciousness and immodesty blend into one another.

The history of Wilde's reception in Europe must start from a reflection on this tripartite dialogue between Irishness, Englishness and a heavily French-accented cosmopolitanism. As the essays in this volume make clear, this is a rich and complex history, marked by an abundance of translations, perform-ances, adaptations and critical and creative responses. The circulation of Wilde's work in Europe started when the author was still alive, in the 1890s, and continues today with a flourishing of new translations and theatrical produc-tions. The popular interest in Wilde is matched by renewed attention in the academy, stimulated by neo-historicist and post-colonial approaches, identity politics and queer studies. For the editor of a volume such as the present one, the richness of the material in hand poses difficult choices. As the timeline reveals, Wilde is one of the most widely translated Anglophone authors of all times, his works appearing at one point or another in all European languages, including Basque, Yiddish and Faroese. A further layer of richness is added by the circumstance that, aside from the textual history, Wilde's reception also takes place through the performance of his dramas. Given Wilde's enduring presence in the press, on the stage and in popular culture, all European countries could have been represented here, each of them offering a unique and no doubt engaging tessera to help us reconstruct the large mosaic of Wilde's presence on the map of Europe, from the end of the nineteenth century to the present. But the wealth of material rules this out, and indeed has induced several of the authors to privilege the crucial period that runs, roughly, from the 1890s to the 1920s (the decades of the Symbolist legacy and early modernism), exploring the conditions of Wilde's early impact and dissemination. The contributions in this volume focus on individual countries and at the same time identify important connections, trends and patterns in the history of Wilde's European reception more generally. They have been selected to convey geographical breadth – stretching from Spain to Russia, from Denmark to Italy – as well as to maintain a balance between textual reception and performance history.

Wilde's public disgrace following his trials and imprisonment has given rise to a unique history in which the early Anglophone reception, marked by silence, is a striking anomaly within the larger context of Europe. The volume therefore opens with chapters devoted to Britain and Ireland, which chart parallel narratives of rejection, followed by rehabilitation and then enthusi-astic acceptance. The European reception, properly understood, started from France, Wilde's self-proclaimed intellectual homeland and his main home in the voluntary exile that followed his release from prison. France was both the first European country to show widespread awareness of Wilde and, given the dominance of Francophone culture on much of the Continent, it was also the centre from which his work reached countries such as Italy and

Spain, which are the subjects of the next set of essays. But already from the early twentieth century, the German-language reception had begun to rival the French one in extent and influence. The German and Austrian chapters document Wilde's strong presence in the literary culture and in the theatre of these countries, which were also home to an influential tradition of musical settings of Wilde's works, the most famous of which is undoubtedly Richard Strauss's opera, *Salome*. The last set of essays examines examples from Scandinavia, Central Europe – where, given the dominance of the Austro-Hungarian Empire until World War I, the reception was initially intimately connected with the German-language model – and Russia.

The trials and early reception

One of the circumstances that make Wilde's career exceptional is that he had already become famous before he published any of the writings for which he is remembered today. When he brought out his coldly-received *Poems* in 1881, he was already a familiar presence in the British press, where he had often featured as a striking society figure, the author of quotable *bons mots* and the much caricatured public face of aestheticism. By the early 1890s his fame had extended to France, where, as Richard Hibbitt shows, he 'became a newsworthy figure for the vast number of daily newspapers and literary period-icals'. Translations were still relatively scarce at this point, being largely limited to poems or extracts published in magazines. The first important breakthrough in Wilde's European reputation came with the publication of Max Nordau's *Entartung* (*Degeneration*) in 1892. Nordau, a Hungarian-born social critic, built on the theories of the Italian criminologist Cesare Lombroso in order to launch an influential attack on Decadence, Symbolism and the notion of art for art's sake, providing an infamous reading of these literary movements in terms of pathology. Drawing both on Wilde's writings (which he saw as an imitation of French models, especially Baudelaire and Huysmans) and on his public image, Nordau criticized Wilde for his 'ego-mania' and antisocial tendencies. Nordau's intent was of course to warn readers against Wilde. But, as *Degeneration* sent ripples across Europe, Wilde gained a reputation as one of the main exponents of the international artistic currents that Nordau was trying to repress. It is, in other words, in the unlikely context of this pseudo-scientific treatise that we find the first important canonization of Wilde who, in *Degeneration*, rubbed shoulders with such great figures of European culture as Baudelaire, Wagner and Nietzsche. Therefore, as Richard Cardwell argues here, progressive readers like the Nicaraguan poet Rubén Darío could reverse the negative argument advanced by Nordau and use it instead as a platform to promote the rising internationalist movements of aestheticism and Decadence identified with Wilde's influence.

Degeneration* was only a premonition of the type of negative exposure that was to come. For the most significant episodes in Wilde's early reception are certainly his trials and imprisonment. As is well known, in 1895 Wilde was found guilty of 'gross indecency' and sentenced to two years of hard labour. Wilde's trials were not, strictly speaking, literary trials. But even though the accusations of criminal behaviour concerned Wilde's private life rather than any of his works, the prosecution used passages from Wilde's writings (especially *PDG*) as evidence against him: it successfully argued that Wilde's novel and theories of art showed the outward signs of the moral corruption evidenced by his private sexual practices. The trials have been described as a 'ritual of purification' of late-Victorian society (see Dowling 1996, 99). Their outcome unleashed a sensational onslaught against the alleged degeneracy of aestheticism and Decadence. The British press was almost unanimous in wishing for a return to moral health and stricter self-censorship on the part of writers and artists. In the eyes of the public Wilde became a criminal and the object of scorn and ridicule. His cosmopolitanism was declared 'unsuited to British soil'. Commentators directly or indirectly invoked nationalism, philistinism and homophobia as cures for the 'aesthetic craze' and sometimes openly relied on Nordau's pseudo-science to substantiate their views.[3]

The news of the trials was reported extensively in the European press. In some countries, such as Russia, this preceded Wilde's literary fame, leaving a profound mark on the modes of his subsequent reception. Evgenii Bershtein shows how closely the Russian papers followed the court proceedings in London, linking the Wilde case to issues of public morality and political debates at home. The same was true of France, where, as Richard Hibbitt argues, the 'court cases and sentence generated an enormous amount of press coverage [...], polarizing opinion and eliciting comments on British morality and parallels with the ongoing Dreyfus case.' There were of course enormous differences in the ways in which European countries dealt with homosexuality from the point of view of the law. In France, homosexual acts had been decriminalized since the time of the Revolution and, in general terms, the European countries that followed the *Code Napoléon* adopted this progressive practice. But in other countries such as Britain and the newly unified Germany (which had extended Prussian law to its entire territory) homosexuality was punished by imprisonment.

Whatever the local legislation, male homosexuality was a taboo topic everywhere in nineteenth-century Europe. For instance in Italy, where same-sex relations were not technically outlawed, Catholicism imposed silence on such topics and therefore the precise nature of Wilde's crime was never explicitly mentioned in the press reports. Noreen Doody shows that the Irish press reports followed a similar practice, leaving unsuspecting readers at a loss about the 'unspeakable' events. In fact, as Doody demonstrates, most Irish newspapers were remarkably reticent in their coverage of Wilde's trials and charge, perhaps out of nationalist feeling. In general, cries against Wilde and the immorality of the age seem to have outnumbered defences in the European press. I will come back to the specific significance of the public knowledge of Wilde's homosexuality for his European reception. For the moment it suffices

---

[3] Respectively from Stutfield 1895, 834 and Quilter 1895, 763. Both are quoted in Evangelista 2009, which contains a fuller discussion of xenophobia and chauvinism in British reactions to the Wilde trials.

to add that the Wilde trials functioned as a symbolic event in the twin histories of anti-homosexual legislation and homosexual liberation in Europe: they were probably the most spectacular and certainly the most literary in a series of homosexual scandals large and small, hushed-up and full-blown, that came to the attention of the European media around the turn of the twentieth century. In Germany, for instance, the Wilde trials had a determining influence in the formulation and growth of an organized political movement for the emancipation of homosexuals, which challenged the legal and medical cultures of the times (Keilson-Lauritz 1997).

The prison sentence caused a bifurcation in early responses to Wilde that is a fundamental factor in the later history of reception. In Britain and Ireland Wilde was engulfed in silence: his plays were taken off the London stage, his name soon disappeared from the newspapers and his printed works became harder to find; while all over Europe the trials generated an extreme interest in both the author and the man: the prison sentence made Wilde into a literary celebrity and promoted the activities of translation and critical dissemination. As in the case of Byron – to whom, as Irena Grubica shows in the Croatian context, Wilde was sometimes openly compared – this interest, fuelled by the media, laid the foundations for a veritable mythology around the figure of Wilde. The Wilde myth, which seems to have been strongest in Central and Eastern Europe, including Russia, reached its peak just after the author's death, in the early twentieth century. Mária Kurdi records that, during these years of 'Wilde fever', Hungarian 'fashion-crazy youngsters' were in the habit of imitating Wilde's dress. Wilde's reputation as a transgressive figure made him the ideal object of such forms of cultish devotion, which were not confined to the literary milieus. This type of visibility, borne out by a remarkably successful history of early translations and by the appearance of the first critical portraits in foreign languages, generated great curiosity about Wilde's life among European readers. As Rita Severi shows here, journalists even circulated apocryphal stories according to which Wilde was still alive and hiding in a Spanish convent. Wilde embodied the type of the tortured romantic artist who had been misunderstood, marginalized and eventually quashed by the narrow morality of bourgeois society – a reputation that was consolidated by his autobiographical portrayal in *DP*.

It is largely due to the appetite for biographical detail that Wilde's prison writings, especially *BRG*, immediately proved immensely popular. The autobiographical prison writings simultaneously hark back to a Romantic tradition of confessional writing, best typified by Rousseau, and feed into a modern taste for sensationalist accounts of the literary author as celebrity, fuelled by the increasing power of the mass media, which played a key role in the creation of Wilde's European reputation. Unexpectedly perhaps, in some countries the early reception of the prison writings tapped into local religious sensibilities. Elisa Bizzotto suggests that Italian readers, steeped in Catholic culture, appreciated the 'redemptive quality' of *BRG*; and Evgenii Bershtein shows that a similar preoccupation informed the Russian reception of this work, which focused on issues of guilt, suffering and redemption.

The European success of *Salomé*

Wilde's early European reception is dominated by the work that has traditionally enjoyed the least success in Anglophone countries: *Salomé*. Written by Wilde in French and translated into English (badly, according to Wilde) by his lover Alfred Douglas, *Salomé* was banned in Britain by the Lord Chamberlain in 1892, as rehearsals were under way with the French diva Sarah Bernhardt in the title role. The first performance of *Salomé* took place while Wilde was in prison, in 1896. It was staged in the experimental *Théâtre de l'Oeuvre* in Paris to mixed critical reviews (Eells). Wilde set great store by this work and, as Rita Severi shows here, he personally oversaw its translation into Italian during his stay in Naples in 1897, when he vainly tried to persuade the celebrated Italian actress Eleonora Duse to perform in the title role. In the British context, critics have often branded *Salomé* as derivative, following the dominant strand of negative criticism against Wilde that had regularly appeared in the press since the time of *Poems*. This has determined its conspicuous absence from the British stage, even in the recent renascence of interest in Wilde. But this most neglected amongst Wilde's works has been crucial in consolidating and broadcasting Wilde's reputation in Europe. In the speech given at a dinner held to mark the launch of the first complete edition of Wilde's works in 1908, on the eighth anniversary of his death, Wilde's literary executor Robbie Ross revealed that it was largely thanks to the profits of the German performances of *Salomé* that he had been able to pay off all Wilde's creditors in full. Ross added that it may be said 'with truth that Oscar Wilde's regenerated reputation was made in Germany' – a statement for which he felt he must publicly excuse himself at a time of growing Anglo-German tensions (Ross 1908, 4).

The European success of this experimental play, inspired by the paintings of Gustave Moreau and the dramatic techniques of the Belgian Symbolist Maurice Maeterlinck, was largely due to the work of the Austrian director Max Reinhardt. In 1902, Reinhardt staged a private performance of *Salomé* in the *Kleines Theater* (Small Theatre) in Berlin in front of a select audience of three hundred artists and critics. This production, in which Reinhardt laid the foundations for his experiments in post-naturalistic theatre, was of enormous 'significance for the reception of Wilde as a modernist classic as well as for the development of German theatre' (Rainer Kohlmayer and Lucia Krämer). *Salomé* was transferred to Berlin's *Neues Theater* (New Theatre) the following year and, from there, it toured the major cities of Germany and the Austro-Hungarian Empire. In the wake of the German success, the early twentieth century witnessed a spate of experimental productions of *Salomé* in major European playhouses. Wilde's play became a vehicle for experimental theatre and for the modernization of directing and acting styles, especially, but not only, in the countries where the influence of German culture was most strongly felt. Zdeněk Beran shows that *Salomé* was 'the nexus of Oscar Wilde's presence in Czech Decadence', providing shared thematic material for literature, theatre and the visual arts. The Czech example is representative of Central Europe, where its fame soon outstripped that of Wilde's other works. The European success of Wilde's Symbolist tragedy was also linked to the memorable performances of internationally-renowned actresses – from the

German Gertrud Eysoldt to the Croatian Hermina Šumovska – for whom
the role of the blood-thirsty Princess became a prestigious part to add to
their repertoire. As several of the essays in this volume show, the play did
experience difficulties with the local authorities of some of the countries
(notably Germany) that would seal its fame. Nevertheless, audiences in Berlin,
Vienna, Budapest and Copenhagen enjoyed it as an experimental classic of
modern drama before its London debut as a private performance in 1905. In
Wilde's native Ireland, *Salomé* had its first public staging in the Gate Theatre
in Dublin in 1928 (Doody); while in Britain the Lord Chamberlain's ban on
the play was finally lifted only in 1931.

The German composer Richard Strauss was among those select three
hundred who attended the first private performance of *Salomé* in Berlin.
Strauss was clearly struck by the ambiguous and protean nature of this work,
which makes it highly suited for dramatic experimentation. Three years
afterwards his own opera, *Salome*, was premiered in Dresden to great critical
acclaim. As Chris Walton shows here, 'the phenomenal success of *Salome* made
it arguably the real progenitor of the widespread twentieth-century vogue
for *Literaturoper*, the genre to which some of the finest operas of the century
belong'. The operatic version soon took over the play as a medium for the
dissemination of Wilde's avant-garde work. This move from the French of
Wilde's original text to the German of Strauss's libretto (based on Hedwig
Lachmann's translation) is symbolic of a general shift that took place at this
point: Germany and the Austro-Hungarian Empire took over from France as
the main focus of the European reception. Strauss's opera was instrumental in
guaranteeing Wilde's survival within progressive literary and artistic circles in
Europe well into the early decades of the twentieth century, at a time when his
writings started to seem less interesting to exponents of literary modernism.
In other words, as Wilde's works risked appearing dated precisely because
they were so representative of a now superseded Decadent aesthetics, Strauss's
opera, with its enormous critical success and its experimental music, kept alive
audiences' interest in Wilde as a modern and daring author. Strauss's *Salome*, a
work that still features regularly in the main European opera houses, has now
for several decades been the main medium for the survival of Wilde's tragedy,
which declined in popularity after its heyday in the early twentieth century,
though, like several of Wilde's works, it has also enjoyed a life in ballet.

The society plays

The reception history of Wilde's society plays highlights another divergence
between the Anglophone and Continental receptions. The comedies, written
in the short period between 1892 and 1895, marked the apogee of Wilde's
popular success in Britain. Joseph Bristow shows that revivals of Wilde's
comedies 'resumed as early as 1901 with performances of *LWF* and *IBE* at
the Coronet Theatre, London', starting the slow process of rehabilitation of
Wilde's works after the trials. As Noreen Doody relates, these productions
were immediately transferred to Ireland. In Europe, though, the comedies
arrived comparatively late: *IBE*, for instance, received its premiere in Italy and

Denmark only in 1922. This delay meant that Wilde's reputation as the author of comic dramas in most cases followed his reputation as critic, novelist and as the tragic poet of *Salomé*. With the notable exception of France, the society comedies proved popular abroad, replicating to some extent Wilde's success on the English stage. Despite the obvious difficulties of adapting Wilde's language-driven, punning style to foreign languages (the title of *IBE* tested the resourcefulness of many translators), European reviewers and, one must suspect, theatre goers enjoyed the comedies as witty portrayals of the English bourgeoisie. In some cases, such as with *LWF*, critics noted the socially progressive message of Wilde's work, aligning him to his contemporaries Shaw and Ibsen.

The performance timeline at the beginning of this volume charts the impact and early presence of Wilde on the European stages. His popularity is attested, for instance, by the fact that just in the year 1907, as Mária Kurdi shows, there were Hungarian productions of *IH*, *IBE*, *Salomé* and a dramatized version of *PDG*. Wilde's success as a dramatist is undoubtedly at its greatest in the German-language reception. Rainer Kohlmayer and Lucia Krämer record that, from the beginning of Wilde's reception to today, the comedies 'have been performed thousands of times in Germany's bigger cities and provincial theatres', undergoing 'remarkable ideological trans-formations' as the country's volatile twentieth-century history unfolded. In the beginning, German and Austrian audiences – as, no doubt, their counterparts in other European countries – came to enjoy the comedies as expressing a quintessentially English preoccupation with form and social conventions. This was especially the case in Vienna, where, as Sandra Mayer argues, 'the society plays also appeared to evoke a sense of nostalgia for a lost world of elegance and splendour, promoted by the specific local colouring of period productions'. The emphasis on elegance and, as time passed, on the period portrayal of an ever more distant and faded Victorian England, risks diluting the satirical content, robbing Wilde's humour of its subversive quality. Many European productions, from the early twentieth century to this day, have chosen to run this risk, opting for decidedly mannered inter-pretations – with directors in some cases even asking actors to recite their lines in fake English accents.

In the years leading up to World War I, the vogue for expressionism that had sealed the success of *Salomé* made the society plays less suitable for innovative productions. But precisely because they could be read as anodyne and de-politicized comedies of manners, Wilde's society dramas achieved tolerance and popular success in otherwise inauspicious times and places. Elisa Bizzotto notes that in Italy the plays continued to be performed and enjoyed under Fascism, because they were 'considered less threatening to hegemonic culture than the rest of his output'. The same was true of the Third Reich, where the society plays became 'perfectly integrated into the theatre world', surprisingly 'transforming Wilde into a champion of collectivism and moral conformism' (Rainer Kohlmayer and Lucia Krämer). Nevertheless, some directors realized that the superficial conformity to social conventions of these works could also be exploited, just as Wilde himself had done, to convey social satire and progressive criticism. Lene Østermark-Johansen shows that, in 1936, Danish theatre goers experienced an unexpectedly political Wilde in a vaudeville version of *IBE* in Copenhagen, which deliberately exaggerated Wilde's playful jibes at the German language, turning them into thinly-veiled satire. And when the same play was produced at the Royal Theatre in Copenhagen in 1944, during the German occupation of the country, Wilde's humour, and of course his association with England, were used to disseminate a message of political dissent that only managed to escape censorship thanks to the frivolous surface behind which it was effectively hidden. As Marta Mateo argues in the Spanish context, the comedies also dodged censorship during Franco's post-war regime, this time because of Wilde's status as a classic.

After World War II, directors faced the challenge of how to bring up to date works that had originally appealed to the popular audience of half a century earlier. A renewed appetite for experimental and political theatre made the comedies seem outdated and determined the fact that they survived largely as period pieces or light entertainment. But in more recent years European audiences have experienced a revival of the subversive Wilde. The emblem of this new trend is the 2005 adaptation of *IBE* by Austrian feminist novelist and playwright Elfriede Jelinek, analyzed by Sandra Mayer in this volume. This production rereads Wilde's portrayal of genteel society through a fascination with the low, trashy and vulgar, turning Wilde's poise into brash and openly gay, post-modern excess. Jelinek's *IBE* attracted the attention of critics well beyond the German-speaking world. It is the most evident manifestation of a rediscovery of a playful and 'queer' Wilde that is emerging in theatrical productions from Copenhagen to Madrid. As the interest in Wilde's personality gains new momentum, directors strive to produce biographically-inflected renderings of the comedies, which are sometimes interpreted as the projection of Wilde's own homosexual desire. This new trend has produced some recent experiments with all-male casts, as in Conall Morrison's 2005 rendition of *IBE* in Dublin's Abbey Theatre, discussed here by Noreen Doody, and a 2006 production of *Bunbury* (*IBE*) in the *Theater in der Josefstadt* (Theatre in the Josefstadt) in Vienna.

These transgressive productions that have been housed by prominent venues in recent years have brought into the open a tradition of counter-cultural appropriations and performances of Wilde which are marginal to mainstream culture and therefore more difficult to reconstruct from our perspective in the twenty-first century. There is undoubtedly a large underground reception of private and cabaret performances of various kinds that can be only partially recovered. The contents of much of the well-known Munich *Elf Scharfrichter* (Eleven Sharpshooters) cabaret, for example, were reconstructed only in the 1990s through the survival of the Bavarian secret service reports on the cabaret before it was closed in 1903. Here, Zdeněk Beran mentions a successful 1910 parody of *Salomé* by one of the most famous Prague cabarets, Červená sedma (The red seven), in which 'Salomé is finally presented with a pig's head on a plate and marries Narraboth'. As we will see with the issue of homosexuality, much of Wilde's reception takes place in this shifting cultural space that lies between the high and low, the spectacular and the hidden.

Quintessentially 'English'

The early European reception was crucial for the survival of Wilde's reputation into the twentieth century: it is the link between his early silencing in Britain and Ireland and his recent rehabilitation and apotheosis. Wilde's son, Vyvyan Holland, remembered that around 1905, during his time as a Cambridge student, Wilde's name was 'frequently mentioned' (although mainly in 'unflattering' terms) but his works were very difficult to get hold of before the first complete edition of 1907: 'no authorized edition of any of his works had been published for years. Even the copies sometimes to be found in secondhand bookshops were usually badly printed and were often inaccurate piracies' (Holland 1954, 202 and 179). Joseph Bristow argues here that Wilde's 'presence in [British] literary culture was hardly eclipsed' even in the decades that immediately followed his public disgrace; but that his name remained, for a long time, taboo in polite society because of its embarrassing associations with homosexuality. This British embarrassment about Wilde was seriously challenged for the first time with the publication of Vyvyan Holland's *Son of Oscar Wilde* (1954) – a brave autobiographical account of the Wilde family's life after the trials, which laid the foundations for an open discourse that overcame secrecy and shame.

1905, the year of Strauss's *Salome* and of the first English edition of *DP*, was an important turning point in the history of Wilde's reception. *DP* was immediately translated into German, Hungarian, Italian, Dutch, Russian and Swedish. Robert Vilain dates to 1905 the beginning of a 'Wilde-mania' in the German-speaking world, and the statistics of Wilde's German translations are indeed staggering: there were no fewer than 250 of them between 1900 and 1934 (quoted in Vilain). *PDG*, which has enjoyed a particularly strong reputation in Germany, went through 13 editions and reprints between 1901 and 1927 (Grubica). This is remarkable even when compared to France, where the novel was also very successful and its 1895 translation was reprinted five times between its first publication and 1911 (Eells). The timeline in this volume reveals the extent and breadth of the dissemination of Wilde's works in the period of the early peak of his popularity, which roughly spans from 1905 until the end of the 1920s. In those years Wilde was a notorious figure and a popular author throughout Europe. These were the years of the Wilde myth described above. A recurrent view in European critical and popular appraisals was that Wilde had been a symbolic victim to a specifically English brand of middle-class hypocrisy.

Yet it was only very rarely that early European commentators noted Wilde's Irish identity as a possible reason for his critique of English institutions. There were of course exceptions to this pattern, notably in Wilde's native Ireland, as Noreen Doody shows here. In an early review of *LASCOS* for the Irish press, W. B. Yeats remarked on England's inability to understand Wilde: '*We* should not find him so unintelligible – for much about him is Irish for the Irish. I see in his life and works an extravagant Celtic crusade against Anglo-Saxon stupidity' (Yeats 1891). We have had to wait until the late twentieth century and the advent of post-colonial criticism for this image of a frankly Irish Wilde to reach the wider European public. The parallel with Yeats is telling. In the comparatively more patchy history of Yeats's European reception, Irishness immediately played a crucial role, no doubt because of Yeats's open interest in Irish nationalism, making his work attractive to readers from small, marginal or developing nationalities (see the Yeats volume in this series and especially Jacqueline A. Hurtley's essay on the Catalan, Galician and Basque receptions). Similar nationalist readings of a strongly Irish Wilde occur for instance in early twentieth-century Italy, thanks to Joyce's contributions to the local press of the Austrian-occupied Trieste, and in the depleted Hungary of the 1920s, which had lost a large portion of its former territory (analyzed respectively by Elisa Bizzotto and Mária Kurdi). As we will see, homosexuality rather than nationality provided the more common catalyst for such 'minority' appropriations of Wilde.

Aside from these comparatively rare instances, though, the early reception tends to privilege a quintessentially 'English' Wilde, who writes about England and Englishness and who is a problematic product of certain strands of Victorian liberalism: individualism, provocative iconoclasm, neurosis. The paradox here is that the modes of Wilde's cultural resistance – his aestheticism, dandyism and even his homosexuality – were seen to be at once fundamentally English and fundamentally opposed to mainstream English values, as his satirical writings and his public disgrace proved in different ways. This ambiguity, which was carefully engineered by Wilde himself through his use of parody and paradox in his writings, is at the heart of the reception of Wilde's 'English' identity. For Lucia Krämer and Rainer Kohlmayer, Wilde's critical stance towards England and his victimization by it, determined that 'his case could be used in the service of anti-British propaganda in the context of the mounting tensions between Germany and Britain in the years leading up to World War I'. The same was true, to a certain extent, of Nazi Germany and Fascist Italy, which therefore tolerated Wilde in spite of his Englishness and his well-known sexual perversion. But the relative tolerance practised by right-wing dictatorships also gave attentive readers the freedom to rediscover the subversive and dangerous Wilde who believed in political resistance, individualism and sexual freedom. This is the Wilde that audiences enjoyed so much in German-occupied Denmark: here his defence of individualism was read, perhaps in a simplified version, as a fundamental critique of right-wing totalitarianism and was identified with the English tradition of political liberalism – the same tradition by which he had, paradoxically, been sent to hard labour.

There is another, curious, way in which Wilde has been received as representative of Englishness by non-Anglophone readers: his works, mainly the comedies and children's tales, have been extensively used as language primers for learners of the English language. Vyvyan Holland claims that Wilde's works were already being used as 'textbooks of English' in Germany when he was sent to school there as a boy in the end of the nineteenth century (Holland 1954, 87). And in an essay on Wilde written in 1946, the Argentine author Jorge Luis Borges, who translated HP at the precocious age of nine years, writes on the simplicity of Wilde's syntax, arguing that of all 'British' writers, none is so accessible to foreigners (Borges 1999). This stylistic clarity identified by Borges has guaranteed Wilde's circulation in schools and universities even in such different contexts as Fascist Italy and the Soviet Union, where this pedagogic use of Wilde's writings was also a way of circumventing communist censorship.

The modernist reception

In the early twentieth century Wilde became the iconic representative of English aestheticism in Europe. His reception can therefore be seen to mask or contain within it the legacies of Pater, Swinburne and the Pre-Raphaelites, all of whom had had a strong influence on the development of Wilde's own work, and whose presence in Europe was played out, as Stephen Bann has argued in his introduction to the Pater volume in this series, in the shadow of the more visible Wilde (Bann 2004). It is largely through Wilde that English aestheticism – a movement that argued for the modernization of the nineteenth-century culture of art – exercised its influence on the many local Decadent and proto-modernist movements that blossomed around Europe at the turn of the twentieth century. At this time Wilde's work did not circulate only in the form of book-length translations: his provocative and highly memorable statements on literature and aesthetics were anthologized or simply imitated in Symbolist and avant-garde magazines such as the Czech *Moderní revue* (Modern review) or the Italian *Marzocco*. Wilde's early European reception lights up a constellation of more or less prominent figures of European Decadence such as the French Jean Cocteau, the Czech Jiří Karásek and Arthur Breisky and the Russian Konstantin Bal'mont. Some of them were early critics, and perhaps even translators, of Wilde as well as authors in their own right (Karásek brought out a trilogy of Decadent novels of clear Wildean derivation, analysed here by Zdeněk Beran). Reading through the essays in this volume, Wilde emerges as an enduring presence in the networks of influence and cultural contamination that criss-cross the cosmopolitan circles of European Decadence. Elisa Bizzotto unveils how the iconic Italian Decadent poet Gabriele D'Annunzio, who gathered around him an influential clique of critics and authors, made 'frequent, yet often oblique and unacknowledged reference to Wilde' in his works. Wilde's impact reached the D'Annunzio circle via Paris and the Francophile networks of late nineteenth-century Italian culture, proving that Wilde's determination to participate in the French literary scene shaped the patterns of the later dissemination of his work. The French connection was also important in the case of the Danish writer and dandy Herman Bang, examined by Lene Østermark-Johansen. Bang's 'ongoing dialogue with Wilde was one of plagiarism, denial, subtle allusion and appropriation, on both a personal and a professional level'; his Decadent novel, *Mikaël* (1904), for instance, borrows from Wilde the theme of an obsessive relationship between an artist and his male model. The examples of D'Annunzio and Bang are very important, as they show Wilde's influence directly at work on canonical authors whose legacies extend well into the twentieth century, both on a national and international level.

The most influential figure in this first generation of mediators, though, is undoubtedly the French author André Gide. Gide met Wilde for the first time in 1891 and, as Victoria Reid demonstrates here, developed a conflicting relationship of discipleship and hostility towards him. Gide's 'Hommage à Oscar Wilde' (Homage to Oscar Wilde), was first published in *L'Ermitage* in 1902. It was translated into German the following year, it appeared in English in 1905 and has been widely disseminated well beyond Francophone countries. Gide's essay has often been reprinted in translations of Wilde's works, providing an authoritative (given Gide's rising European fame) but highly personal lens through which Wilde's writings were presented to readers across Europe. Gide, at first entranced by Wilde the man, is frank about his low opinion of the quality of Wilde's writings. His assessment of Wilde revolves around the assumption that the personality and the man, and not the written word and text, represent the 'truth' about Wilde. Wilde's works are for Gide only an imperfect reflection of Wilde's genius, which found its best expression in conversation and improvisation, and are therefore ultimately deceptive. Gide's views contributed to the growth of Wilde's fame as legendary poet-artist, but they also detracted from the value of his work, which was presented as imperfect, second-best and, paradoxically, somewhat marginal to a full understanding of the author. In the eyes of the influential school of inter-pretation initiated by Gide, Wilde's works should be seen as masks or cryptic inscriptions of the personality: they should be valued inasmuch as they reveal the secret – especially the sexual secret – behind them. For Gide, as for many later critics, the knowledge of Wilde's 'secret' homosexuality provides the ultimate key to his literary works. Gide's ambiguous response to Wilde was undoubtedly rooted in the story of his personal development as an author and as a practising homosexual man; but his feeling of ambivalence was shared by several writers of the early twentieth century: as modernism advanced, authors started to question the real value of Wilde's aestheticism.

In 'Nietzsches Philosophie im Lichte unserer Erfahrung' ('Nietzsche's Philosophy in the light of Contemporary Events'), an essay discussed by Robert Vilain in this volume, Thomas Mann paired Wilde and Nietzsche as the exponents of a modern European crisis of values (Mann 1947, 18). Writing in the aftermath of World War II, Mann tries to recuperate Nietzsche, distancing him from the wrongful appropriation of his thought by the defeated forces of right-wing totalitarianism. He wants to show that Nietzsche's belief in counter-cultural critique is fundamentally hostile to the ethos of conformity that is the principle of Nazism. Arguably, Mann's parallel invests Wilde with a cultural influence that may seem exaggerated. Yet the association with Nietzsche is a recurrent element of Wilde's European reception, as several of the essays in this volume attest. Wilde and Nietzsche were paired as rebel thinkers who defended the anti-rational forces of passion and desire as weapons against the pressure to conformity enforced on the individual by modern European civilization. They were seen to have spoken out in similar ways against the integrity of bourgeois subjectivity, calling both artists and ordinary men and women to withdraw from social norms and widely accepted notions of morality. In this reading, their writings are harbingers of the forces threatening the disintegration of bourgeois art and culture that would erupt in the early twentieth century in the form of modernism and avant-garde movements such as Czech synthetic art and Italian Futurism. As Evgenii

Bershtein argues here, the parallel between Wilde and Nietzsche flourished in Russia, where the concept of life as art promoted by both thinkers deeply engaged the modernist innovators of Russian Silver-Age literature, notably the Symbolist poet and philosopher Vyacheslav Ivanov. In Russia the association of Wilde with Nietzsche acquired a peculiar Christological dimension: their ideas were perceived to have been validated by extreme personal suffering – the struggle with mental illness in Nietzsche's case and the prison sentence in Wilde's.

In 1949, Mann's revaluation of Wilde was atypical of its times and should probably be read as a rare public record of a private history of largely submerged influence. By this point the general trend of Wilde's reception by European authors followed Gide's model: Wilde's aestheticism and his paradoxical, epigrammatic style were seen as a dead end: they had been momentarily liberating but were deemed to be unsustainable in the longer term (as Robert Vilain shows, Hugo von Hofmannsthal is another case in point). Richard Cardwell observes this disenchantment at work already in early-twentieth-century Spain, where Wilde and aestheticism more broadly 'seemed to have no positive role to play in the process of national regeneration', as writers such as Juan Ramón Jiménez and Antonio Machado turned away from Decadence and began 'to create a poetry which sought to "redeem" and "regenerate" the national spirit.' There is no doubt that Wilde's sense of belatedness and over-refinement attracted opposition from several similar quarters. The early twentieth century brought a return to active political engagement and the revaluation of an ideal of primitivism, sometimes identified with conservative notions of masculinity, that were in explicit reaction to the sophisticated individualism of the *fin de siècle*. While the ongoing production of new editions of his works and performances of his dramas indicate that Wilde's popular appeal survived the critical turn that was brought about by the consolidation of modernism, his strong intellectual impact was consigned to the past. Emblematic of this change in fortune are the judgements of Theodor Adorno, for whom all the mysteries of Wilde's paradoxes had been solved. According to Adorno, the motto 'art for art's sake' was a cover for its opposite ('die Parole l'art pour l'art [war] das Deckbild ihres Gegenteils'): Wilde's aestheticism was actually in alliance with the commercial culture it purported to despise (Adorno 2003, 355). For Adorno, Wilde's theories and works expanded the domain of aesthetic allure, making it available to a larger middle-class readership and possible to produce by the modern culture industry. Wilde was therefore not a rebel but rather an ally of the bourgeoisie whose values he ridiculed. To modernist critics like Adorno, Wilde's writings appeared kitsch, sentimental, decorative and, above all, politically suspect. It is worth noting, though, that while Adorno dismissed Wilde, he still took his failure as emblematic of the doctrines of aestheticism and art for art's sake – that is, he indirectly confirmed his position of prominence.

The ideological critique advanced by Adorno was of course exacerbated in the contexts of the East European countries under communist rule. As the translation timeline shows, Wilde's fairy tales enjoyed undiminished popularity in Central and Eastern Europe all through the second half of the twentieth century. But *PDG*, the critical essays and the dramas posed deeper ideological problems. Reflecting on the paucity of performances of Wilde's plays during the Stalinist period in Hungary, Mária Kurdi argues that a 'playwright such as Wilde was considered too "bourgeois" to serve the goals of the new cultural politics, and was deemed to have no place in the theatre programmes.' After Stalin's death in 1953, state-enforced censorship relaxed all across the former Eastern Bloc. Even so, Wilde could hardly be seen to fit within the principles of socialist realism, the aesthetic doctrine which governed the cultural politics of the former communist regimes. Wilde's homosexuality and his dandyism were likewise not tolerated by the dominant socialist ideology. Yet editors, translators and critics in Eastern Europe managed to circumvent censorship by emphasizing the satirical aspect of his works, interpreting them as critiques of the aristocracy and of the hypocritical trappings of the bourgeois mentality. In other words, the ideological problems posed by Wilde's individualism and his espousal of decadence and artifice could be bypassed by reading him as a critic of capitalism – the author of SMUS above all else. If, as Irena Grubica points out with reference to 1950s Croatia, 'the views expressed in that essay were easily absorbed into the political discourse of the time', then SMUS could be used as a tool to lend political respectability to the entirety of Wilde's oeuvre. The long history of reception of SMUS makes Wilde the perhaps surprising ally of international socialism, anarchism and revolutionary ideology. Rita Severi shows that, following a practice already established by French, Spanish and German-language periodicals, extracts from SMUS were published in an Italian anarchist paper as early as 1892. She also records that the immediate aftermath of World War II saw at least five new Italian editions of the essay, in which Italian readers found a popular intellectual antidote to the doctrines of Fascism.

Homosexuality

The issue of Wilde's homosexuality deserves special attention in an overview of his European reception. Gide was by no means unique in thinking that the sexual issue – homosexual desire and its modes of revelation and concealment – lay at the heart of Wilde's work. The spectacular events of the trials, with the publicity they received in various European countries, made Wilde a rare public person in the otherwise secret history of male homosexuality in the nineteenth century. Wilde's very name entered into the international vocabulary of sexual perversion: E. M. Forster's use of it as a euphemism for the otherwise 'unspeakable' homoerotic desire (Bristow) has an Italian equivalent in the clumsy 'oscarwildismo' (Bizzotto), while in France '"Dorian Gray" circulated in initiated circles as a code-name for homosexuality' (Eells). The reception of Wilde's homosexuality brings to light different sociological and creative responses, which are coloured by the different local histories of the legal, medical and artistic cultures in which the discourse of homosexuality developed around Europe.

Wilde's homosexuality provoked debates in prominent journals such as the Czech *Moderní revue* and the Russian *Vesy* (Libra), which combined polemics against sexual intolerance with reflections on aesthetic questions. But side by side with these public treatments, Wilde was undoubtedly also the object of an underground reception, more ephemeral and therefore more difficult to piece together, which took place in venues like cafés, clubs or private homes (such as Vyacheslav Ivanov's St Petersburg apartment, as Evgenii Bershtein uncovers) around which European homosexual subcultures gathered in the years that preceded homosexual emancipation. In these milieus, as in the Wilde trials, 'high' culture brushed shoulders with danger and the low life. All in all, progressive discussions of the Wilde case seem to have been far more widespread in Continental Europe – with the exception of the Catholic Southern nations – than in Britain or Ireland. The conditions for this open discourse were created by the sense of geographical and cultural distance: paradoxically, the Wilde case became so important precisely because it was far from home and could therefore be talked about more freely by commentators outside of Britain, who did not have to fear accusations of having a personal interest in the issue.

Sexology provided a culturally acceptable forum in which Wilde's homosexuality could be discussed as a case study, with what appeared to be a purely scientific interest. One of the most influential sexological responses to the Wilde case came from his one-time friend Marc André Raffalovich, a Decadent author and Catholic convert whose *Uranisme et Unisexualité* (Uranism and unisexuality) appeared in French in 1896. Like other progressive sexologists, Raffalovich was haunted by the spectre of Nordau, who had drawn attention to Wilde's psychological aberrations before his 'perversion' had become common knowledge. As noted above, the Wilde case attracted the interest of commentators and campaigners for the legal and medical emancipation of homosexuality especially in Germany, where sexological science was particularly advanced. Wilde's name was often to be found in the pages of the pioneering German homophile journals *Jahrbuch für sexuelle Zwischenstufen* (Journal of sexual abnormalities), active from 1899 to 1923 and explicitly addressed to the medical and legal professions, and the more literary *Der Eigene*, which ran from 1896 to 1932. The precocious development of a local movement for homosexual emancipation made Germany the first country in which Wilde could be received among organized networks of readers interested in homosexuality. The Leipzig publishing house Max Spohr (the publisher of the *Jahrbuch für sexuelle Zwischenstufen*) brought out some of the first German translations of Wilde's works in the context of a highly specialized list that comprised sexological studies, treatises on the sociological and cultural history of homosexuality, fiction and poetry on homosexual and masochistic themes and books on hygiene, ecological topics and macrobiotics. This eclectic grouping shows that, already at the very beginning of the century (the Spohr *PDG* dates from 1901), Wilde was being marketed to cater for the specific tastes of a homosexual readership. More than that, Wilde's works were influencing the formation of a nascent twentieth-century homosexual taste.

The scientific and sociological interpretation of Wilde promoted by sexologists and psychologists tended to sideline discussions of Wilde's literary merit. An exception to this trend is Raffalovich, who used sexology as a springboard for an analysis of the persistent connection between sexual 'inversion' and

artistic genius. But Wilde's influence assumed a particularly strong significance for male homosexual authors, who felt forced to write in the shadow
of this most visible among gay writers. Several essays in this volume therefore
explicitly address the question of how Wilde was received by homosexual
authors such as Bang, Mikhail Kuzmin, Gide and Proust. The case of Gide is
once again emblematic. As Victoria Reid shows, Gide's influential assessments
of Wilde took place within a tortuous process of private and public recognition of his own homosexuality. On the one hand, Wilde helped writers such
as Gide to find a language to write about the difficult topic of homoeroticism
but, on the other, his personal story of ostracism and punishment became a
taboo for homosexual authors who feared exposure and marginalization. It is
for these reasons that Wilde's influence is often found buried and sometimes
concealed within their texts. Wilde was an enabling precedent but he was also
a figure to exorcize, especially for those writers who strove to depart from a
nineteenth-century tradition of bourgeois literature with which they rightly
or wrongly associated Wilde's work. At the heart of this tension is the ramified
problem of the self-representation of the homosexual author in the face of a
largely hostile public. To use Emily Eells's evocative expression, Wilde's name
is 'invisibly inscribed' in the writings of such giants of twentieth-century
European literature as Proust and Mann, who are fascinated by the emotional
possibilities of homoerotic desire.

As we have seen, Wilde's fall from artistic glory to public disgrace has
sparked a Romantic mythology that has seen in him the ultimate type of
the tortured Romantic artist who sacrifices his life for art and a higher
ideal. Within homophile literary circles, this mythology has given rise to a
tradition of interpreting Wilde's downfall in terms of martyrdom. According
to this view, Wilde's suffering in prison and eventual death are explained as
a necessary sacrifice in the progress towards homosexual emancipation and
sexual freedom. Some critics have rejected the pejorative connotations of
this mythology, which locks the representation of homosexual desire into
a narrative of suffering and redemption. An early model for resistance can
be found in Kuzmin's novel, *Wings* (1906), in which homosexual desire is
openly and sympathetically portrayed in terms of happy fruition. As Evgenii
Bershtein argues here, although Kuzmin is often referred to as the 'Russian
Wilde', *Wings* draws on and yet rejects the powerful legacy of the homosexual
Wilde by freeing love between men from patterns of 'tragic rebellion and
voluntary suffering'. The different and sometimes conflicting receptions of
Wilde's homosexuality analyzed in this volume all point to his central role
in the formation of a twentieth-century canon of openly gay writing. This
homosexual Wilde gained special prominence in the last two decades of the
twentieth century, as the growing fields of gender and 'queer' studies provided
a dynamic and innovative forum for Wilde scholarship, contributing to the rise
of his reputation in the academy. In the wake of the homosexual emancipation
of recent years, Wilde has gained further visibility even as homosexuality has
become increasingly acceptable within mainstream culture: contemporary gay
writing recognizes Wilde as an important precursor, while the Wilde myth
continues to play into popular culture and art within gay cultures and subcultures around Europe.

Conclusion

In the wake of the controversy that followed the publication of *PDG*, Wilde wrote to the editor of the *Scots Observer* that it was a pity 'that Goethe never had an opportunity of reading *Dorian Gray*. I feel quite certain that he would have been delighted by it, and I only hope that some ghostly publisher is even now distributing shadowy copies in the Elysian fields, and that the cover of Gautier's copy is powdered with gilt asphodels' (Wilde 2000, 446). This good-humoured fantasy of canonization, in which Wilde imagined himself in the Olympus of European letters, seems to have, at least partially, come true. The reception of Oscar Wilde in Europe is by and large a tale of popularity and success. Several of the contributors to this volume employ the word 'classic' to define Wilde's reputation in their country, and the quantity of translations, adaptations and critical studies of Wilde's works in all European languages certainly seems to bear out this assessment. The trajectory of Wilde's reputation seems therefore to have gone from *succès de scandale* to best-selling author to classic.

The end of the twentieth century and the beginning of the twenty-first have inaugurated a new phase in Wilde's international success, of which this volume is both product and testimony. The collapse of modernist ideology, which had always viewed Wilde's aestheticism with suspicion, has brought Wilde closer to the sensibilities of contemporary readers, who can find in his writings the foreshadowings of post-modern irony, moral relativism, late-capitalist materialism, postcolonial rewriting and, of course, 'queer' identity politics and sexual liberation. Readers trained in deconstruction feel they understand the ambiguity and contradictory intellectual allegiances of works such as PMWH and *PDG*, which stubbornly resist fixed or univocal interpretations. Wilde holds a particular appeal to sophisticated readers interested in the duplicitous nature of language: as his well-known aphorisms demonstrate, Wilde shows that words are always unsettlingly close in meaning to their semantic opposites; his texts contain their own negations in the form of irony, self-parody and the continuous rejection of the obvious and the dominant. But Wilde is also, importantly, a popular author. His transgressions have always managed to seduce bourgeois readers. Above all, Wilde is a brilliant popularizer who translated complex and radical ideas into pleasurable works that, as these essays make clear, have had an immediate impact and a lasting legacy on the heterogeneous community of European readers, authors, artists, directors, composers and actors.

1 Picturing His Exact Decadence: The British Reception of Oscar Wilde

Joseph Bristow

'Our English Nietzsche': re-evaluating Wilde, from the turn of the century to World War I

In a letter dating from the spring of 1909, the twenty-year-old New Zealand writer Katherine Mansfield puts the following question to Ida Constance Baker, the lifelong friend with whom she enjoyed an intimate affair during their schooldays at Queen's College, London: 'Did you ever read the life of Oscar Wilde – not only read it but think of Wilde – picture his exact decadence?' (Mansfield 1984–2008, I: 89).[1] Written eight and a half years after Wilde died from meningitis in a shabby Parisian hotel room, Mansfield's correspondence provides a helpful starting-point to comprehend the Irish writer's critical reception in Britain. As I show in this chapter, the complex ways in which Wilde's writings had taken hold of Mansfield's powerful teenage imagination point to the divided response that most commentators expressed toward his legacy in the earliest years of the twentieth century. On the one hand, there were aspects of Wilde's decadent style that she could never shake off from her increasingly experimental writing. On the other hand, Mansfield was agonized by the thought that such a brilliant author could have led a sexually perilous life, one that resulted in his brutal two-year jail sentence. Even though she was captivated by Wilde's works, Mansfield's early struggles with his posthumous reputation accentuate some of the broader difficulties that succeeding generations would experience when trying to assess both the extent of his literary influence and the precise nature of his homosexuality.

More than anyone else, Baker understood why Mansfield became entranced by Wilde. In the memoir she published under the initials 'LM' (as Mansfield affectionately called her), Baker reminds us that once the young author had completed her education in 1906 she was filling her notebooks with Wilde's

---

[1] This essay contains some material about biographies of Wilde that I have discussed elsewhere (Bristow 2004, 2008). My thanks go to Lucy Baines, archivist at Queen's College, London, for information about Walter Rippmann.

aphorisms, while in 1907 (when Mansfield returned for a visit to New Zealand) she finished three short stories – 'Vignette', 'Silhouettes', and 'In a Café' – that were 'written in the manner of Oscar Wilde with the heavy exoticism of the "nineties"' ('LM' 1971, 24, 35). As Sydney Janet Kaplan recognizes, the imprint of Wilde's style – especially in phrases that Mansfield copied into her journal from *PDG* – is particularly evident in 'Vignettes': 'Strange that these anemones – scarlet, amethyst, and purple – vibrant with colour, always appear to me a trifle dangerous, sinister, seductive, but poisonous' (Kaplan 1991, 24). Such wording clearly echoes not just Wilde's but a more pervasively decadent obsession with transmogrifying flowers into tempting but treacherous blooms that look strikingly unnatural. Even if, in later years, Mansfield worked hard to dissociate the decadent style of her early fiction from that of her *fin-de-siècle* precursors, Wilde's 'traces' (as Vincent O'Sullivan observes) remain visible 'in her work for the rest of her life' (O'Sullivan 1975, 98–99). This point, as Kaplan shows, is true of one of her most famous stories, 'Bliss' (1920), in which the ingenuous woman protagonist, Pearl Fulton, cannot understand her sexual attraction to the woman who (we eventually discover) is involved in an affair with Pearl's husband. By the time Mansfield wrote this story of sexual intrigue, she treated with considerable suspicion the idea that an adulterous spouse might adopt the kind of decadent 'pose' that Wilde made into an art form. As Pearl watches her husband 'enjoy [...] his dinner', she detects that there is something untrustworthy in his eroticized manner of speaking (one that resembles Wilde's) about his 'shameless passion for the white flesh of the lobster' (Mansfield 2002, 181).

As Baker knew, had it not been for the schoolgirls' liberal-minded German teacher, Walter Rippmann, it is unlikely that their adolescent interest would have been aroused in the Irish writer whose stigmatized decadence had become synonymous with the supposedly exotic 1890s. Rippmann, who became well known for his handbooks on modern language teaching, was certainly unusual in introducing his privately educated charges to the works of an author whose name had been almost unspeakable in polite society at the time of his demise on 30 November 1900. The well-respected *Academy*, for instance, could not bring itself to allude to Wilde in person; in its obituary, this literary weekly referred evasively to Wilde as 'the unhappy man who died in Paris the other day' ('The Bookworm' 1900, 542). But such embarrassed muffling of Wilde's identity should not suggest that every notice of his death indulged in censure of this kind. Even if the *Bookman* asserted that Wilde 'gave up all his ideals and accepted mere notoriety as an easy substitute for fame', it nonetheless conceded that he 'was brilliant to the last': 'The records of contemporary literature contain nothing sadder than the story of this gifted, brilliant and unhappy man' ('H.T.P.' 1901, 453). The only commentator who adopted an unapologetic tone when paying his respects to Wilde was the twenty-nine-year-old Max Beerbohm, who had made his earliest mark with the fine satires he published in the first issues of the magazine most closely linked with British decadence, the *Yellow Book* (1894–97). In the *Saturday Review*, where he regularly discussed theatre productions, Beerbohm observed that even if '[a]t the moment of Wilde's downfall, it was natural that the public sentiment should be one of repulsion', it remained the case that after two years

of imprisonment Wilde had 'at least suffered the full penalty': 'now that he is dead', Beerbohm adds, 'they will realise also, fully, what was for them involved in his downfall, how lamentable the loss to dramatic literature' (Beerbohm 1900, 720).

Yet where Beerbohm believed that the greatest sadness of Wilde's death lay in the loss to the theatre, Mansfield sees the Irish author as a figure whose downfall tells a fearsome story that touches on her own troubled sexual identification. 'In New Zealand', Mansfield confides to Baker in her 1909 letter, 'Wilde acted so strongly and terribly upon me that I was constantly subject to the same fits of madness as those which caused his ruin and his mental decay' (Mansfield 1984–2008, 1: 89–90). Two years earlier, in her journal Mansfield had already divulged her erotic attraction to a woman friend: 'O Oscar! am I so susceptible to sexual impulse' (Mansfield 1984–2008, 1: 90). Mansfield's fretful interpretation of Wilde's sexuality is understandable because by the time she was writing to Baker there were a number of dispiriting sources relating to his legendary, if not notorious, career.

In all probability, the biography that told Mansfield of her idol's 'ruin and mental decay' came from the pen of Robert Harborough Sherard: an English writer whose career included several journalistic exposés of child-labour in British cities, a substantial study of Emile Zola's fiction and – from 1902 onward – no less than four somewhat unreliable accounts of Wilde's life. Sherard's forays into recording his intimate knowledge of Wilde stand at the head of a biographical tradition that for many years presented a distorted impression of the writer's career. In *Oscar Wilde: The Story of an Unhappy Friendship* (1902), Sherard creates an admittedly anecdotal account of the increasingly precarious friendship that they developed after their first meeting in Paris in 1882. Even though Sherard worked hard to defend Wilde's reputation during the trials of April and May 1895, he had already run into trouble when Wilde suspected that Sherard might capitalize on a friendship whose former 'splendour', as Sherard puts it, was now 'relaxed' (Sherard 1902, 119). Sherard recounts that during a Christmas lunch held at Wilde's home in 1894 the Irish author's face appeared to 'have lost its spiritual beauty, and was oozing with material prosperity' instead, since the author now earned in excess of £8,000 per annum (Sherard 1902, 120). As he indulged in conversation that was by no means as 'agreeable' as Sherard once found it, Wilde spoke in confidence with him about the circumstances in which Alfred Douglas (together with Reggie Turner and E. F. Benson) had met the writer Robert Hichens at Cairo (Sherard 1902, 120). The meeting was significant because it enabled Hichens, early in his career, to gather the materials that shaped his satirical roman à clef named *The Green Carnation* (1894), in which Wilde and Douglas feature as the two dandyish protagonists, Esmé Amarinth and Lord Reginald Hastings. Besides insinuating that Wilde and Douglas were lovers, Hichens's lightly mocking novel reveals its intimacy with the urban homosexual culture of the 1890s by focusing its title on the artificially coloured boutonnière that signalled – according to increasingly widespread rumours of the time – a man's attraction to his own sex. Once he told Sherard about the background to *The Green Carnation*, Wilde insisted that complete discretion was in order: 'this', he told his friend, 'is not for publication' (Sherard 1902, 121).

To be sure, Sherard took Wilde's admonishment so badly that he contemplated leaving the author's Tite Street home in protest. But this episode reveals that Wilde anticipated Sherard would never cease to reap whatever rewards he could from a friendship destined to come to an abrupt halt three years later. In December 1897, when news reached Sherard that Wilde had reunited with his lover Alfred Douglas at the Villa Giudice outside Naples, the journalist bruited his belief that Wilde had made an 'unfortunate mistake' (Sherard 1902, 258). After Wilde had received word of Sherard's disapproval, he reprimanded his increasingly estranged friend: 'it is easy – far too easy – for you to find an audience that does not contain any friends of mine; before them, play Tartuffe in the style of Termagant to your heart's content; but when you do it in the presence of friends of mine, you expose yourself to rebuke and contempt' (Sherard 1902, 259). Later on, Wilde made some amends by giving Sherard a signed copy of *BRG* 'in memory of our long friendship' (Sherard 1902, 261). But the two men appear not to have spoken to each other again.

If, in his 1902 memoir, Sherard wishes to pass himself off as a truly compassionate and wrongly alienated friend, then in his full-fledged *Life of Oscar Wilde* (1906) he is altogether more ambitious in trying to advance his authority on his subject. For the most part, Sherard adopts a high-minded tone toward an 'unhappy man' whose hereditary misfortunes caused his downfall (Sherard 1906, 2). Sherard seeks to explain his subject's sexual preference in light of theories of cultural and racial degeneration that had been popularized, much to Wilde's detriment, at the time of the trials. The work that provided the definitive gloss on the widely touted concept of degeneration – one that had its roots in writings by the Comte du Buffon, Bénédict Morel, and, most influentially, Cesare Lombroso – was Max Nordau's *Entartung* (1892), which appeared in English as *Degeneration* (1895). Even though, as Stephen Arata has observed, 'Nordau has relatively little to say about Wilde in *Degeneration*', the press reports of the trials quickly followed some of the assumptions that Nordau made about Wilde's early career as an aesthete who was known for both his striking rhetorical flourishes and his flamboyant dress (Arata 1996, 54). In making much of the 'ego-mania' evident in Wilde's apparent predilection for 'strange costume', Nordau promptly characterizes this style as 'a pathological aberration of a racial instinct' (Nordau 1895, 318).

More than ten years after Nordau's pronouncements had such an adverse effect on press reports of Wilde's courtroom appearances, Sherard shows that incoherent beliefs in Wilde's degeneration still enjoyed currency:

> For while in [Wilde's] immediate parentage will be discovered people whose incontestable genius was united, as is so often the case, with pronounced moral degeneracy, his ascending lines, traced back to remote generations, display such solid qualities of sane normality and civic excellence, that this unhappy man's aberration must appear one of those malignant, morbid developments which alarm and confound the psychologist when they unexpectedly produce themselves in a man's mentality, no less than as by the sudden development in the body of malignant and morbid growths the practitioner is confounded and alarmed. (Sherard 1906, 2)

Sherard, it is worth noting, was scarcely alone in appropriating Nordau's rhetoric in order to paint a dismal picture of Wilde's seemingly accursed heredity, even if critics such as George Bernard Shaw found Nordau's reasoning ludicrous (Shaw 1908, 223–24).[2] C. Ranger Gull, writing under the pseudonym Leonard Cresswell Ingleby, explicitly opens his disreputable 1907 critical study by paying homage to 'the merit of absolute detachment and sincerity' that he finds in Nordau's commentary on Wilde (Ingleby 1907, 11). Accordingly, Gull, a popular novelist who had success with the stories he later published as 'Guy Thorne', readily declares: 'That Wilde's *social* downfall was due to a kind of elliptiform insanity is without doubt' (Ingleby 1907, 11). Given that such views still had widespread currency, it is perhaps unsurprising that Sherard opens his study by emphasizing that '[w]hen Oscar was born' his mother's 'disappointment was great': 'She refused to admit that her new child was a boy. She used to treat him, to speak of him as a girl, and as long as it was possible to do so, she dressed him as a girl. To pathologists these facts will appear of importance' (Sherard 1906, 5).

Much of Sherard's study follows in this vein: 'It is possible', he writes, 'that a pathologist would have seen in the extraordinary brilliancy of Oscar Wilde's talk, in its unceasing flow and the apparently inexhaustible resources of wit and knowledge on which he drew, the prodromes of the disease of which he died. The cause of his death was meningitis, which is an inflammation of the brain' (Sherard 1906, 273). Not surprisingly, the *Bookman* responded to such statements by noting that 'Sherard himself [...] is forced to make so many admissions unfavourable to his subject as to demolish the case which he endeavours to present' (Kemp 1906, 365–66). Yet it would be mistaken to conclude that Sherard's biography interprets each detail about Wilde's life as a matter that arises exclusively from his subject's presumed degeneration. Sherard unearthed a wealth of information about Wilde's career, and he took pains to examine the critical reception of many of the works that the author brought before the public. It is to Sherard's credit that he acknowledged the importance of building a comprehensive bibliography of Wilde's writings, although he could have mentioned that Christopher Sclater Millard (who published under the pseudonym Stuart Mason) was responsible for some of his comments.

Sherard, however, is more independent when he reminds readers of the hostility that a number of British publications – including the *Daily Chronicle* and the *Scots Observer* – expressed toward *PDG* when it first appeared in the American *Lippincott's Monthly Magazine* (June 1890). Moreover, he provides a helpful digest of the reception of Wilde's dramas, showing how many members of the press experienced great frustration with the manner in which (as the London *Times* bluntly put it) *IBE* 'bristles with epigram of the now accepted

2   In the *New Age*, Shaw objected to Nordau's false syllogisms, which for Shaw suggested that to Nordau the idea that 'Oscar Wilde was a sexual pervert' could be extrapolated to make the ridiculous proposition that 'the entire population of London during the eighteen-nineties were sexual perverts' (Shaw 1908, 224). The New Age Press published Shaw's sustained polemic against Nordau's assertions, *The Sanity of Art: An Exposure of the Current Nonsense about Artists Being Degenerate* (1908).

pattern' (Sherard 1906, 297; 'St James's Theatre', 5). To strike some balance against such adverse reviews, Sherard states that '[e]ach audience laughed as never an audience laughed before in a theatre where the work of an English writer of comedy has been performed' (Sherard 1906, 298). Unfortunately, the moralist in Sherard returns in his final chapters where he celebrates what he sees as Wilde's purgatorial two-year spell in jail: 'The prison *régime*, the enforced temperance in food, the enforced abstinence from all narcotic drugs and drink, the regular hours, the periodical exercise: the simple life, in one word, had restored to him the splendid heritage that he had received from Nature' (Sherard 1906, 333). If the truth be told, it was the terrible conditions of prison life that led a malnourished Wilde to lose his balance, fall over, and suffer the injury to his ear that most likely made him vulnerable to the attack of meningitis that took his life.

Like many of his contemporaries, Sherard justified his belief that jail-time improved Wilde morally. He formed this view on the basis of the carefully edited extract from the autobiographical document the Irish author completed during the final months of his sentence. In 1905, one of the two friends who attended Wilde at his deathbed, Robert Ross, issued this portion of the document as *DP*. The religious title, taken from Psalm 130, had been suggested by Ross's editor at Methuen, E.V. Lucas. In Sherard's view, *DP* 'describes the road by which' Wilde 'came from hyper-culture and abstract thought to a simplicity and completeness of soul' (Sherard 1906, 335). Doubtless Sherard was impressed by the sentiments Wilde conveyed when contemplating the manner in which the life of Jesus Christ informed his appreciation of what it meant 'to have' on doctor's orders 'white bread to eat instead of the coarse black or brown bread of ordinary prison fare' (Wilde 1905, 101). 'It will sound strange', Wilde continues, 'that dry bread could possibly be a delicacy to anyone' (Wilde 1905, 101). But when Wilde recognizes 'that to Christ imagination was simply a form of love, and that to him love was lord in the fullest meaning of the phrase', then he knows 'that nothing should be wasted of what is given to me' (Wilde 1905, 101, 102). To G. S. Street, whose *Autobiography of a Boy* (1894) counts among the more prominent satires of literary decadence, it was exactly this 'finely-sustained study [...] of the human Christ' that contributed to the impact that *DP* made on him (Beckson 1970, 254).

Since the majority of reviewers agreed with Street that in this work Wilde wisely atoned for his sins, *DP* proved to be an immense aid in lending some respectability to the Irish author. For other readers, *DP* had an equally strong though different appeal. The aspiring poet, Rupert Brooke, had just turned eighteen when he informed his friend James Strachey that he was so 'obsessed by [Wilde's] De Profundis that' he had 'no other views of this subject than those expressed therein. The Perfect Artistic Temperament. − !' (Hale 1998, 23). In capitalizing these words, Brooke most probably had in mind Wilde's declaration that '[t]hose who have the artistic temperament go into exile with Dante and learn how salt is the bread of others, and how steep their stairs' (Wilde 1905, 86). Like Brooke, Beerbohm could see that *DP* remained significant because it was 'the artistic essay of an artist' (Beckson 1970, 249). In many parts of this work, Wilde's interest lies in characterizing the spiritual value derived from the 'sorrow and beauty' of Christ's life in emphatically aesthetic terms. For this reason, Beerbohm asserted that readers were mistaken to think that *DP* was simply a 'heartcry' that appealed to Christ out of religious despair. Instead, it was a document that showed that Wilde made 'no idle boast' when he claimed to be, in a memorable phrase, a 'lord of language' (Beckson 1970, 250; Wilde 1905, 13–14). Beerbohm could see that Wilde, even if physically abased and emotionally troubled by his prison existence, nonetheless maintained full rhetorical control over his written account if it.

Yet, regardless of whether readers believed that *DP* revealed a penitent Wilde who atoned for his sins or an artist who retained his integrity to the last, the 1905 volume was an unqualified success. Not only did it run into many editions; it was also translated into numerous languages. As Sherard recognized, Ross – 'the subject of the glowing eulogy one finds in "De Profundis"' – had 'fought and worked hard to safeguard his friend's interests' (Sherard 1906, 375). Before his death, Wilde had appointed Ross as his literary executor, and he had also given to this loyal friend his instructions that the prison document that became known as *DP* should be typed and copied according to specific instructions, with the implication that the complete document would be ready for publication at some later date. In every way, Ross remained dedicated to preserving Wilde's memory. The excellent sales of *DP* defrayed the remaining debts attached to Wilde's estate. Furthermore, Ross took steps to restore Wilde's copyright over a number of works. More pressingly, he remained aware that he needed to exercise discretion in bringing *DP* to light. Since the much larger document from which he had extracted the 1905 edition contains vindictive, if not incriminating, comments about Douglas, Ross had to protect himself and his publisher from charges of libel.

As a consequence, the reading public in 1905 had no idea that Wilde addresses the 55,000-word manuscript written on blue prison paper to 'Dear Bosie'. In the complete document, Wilde immediately launches into a resentful attack on their relationship: 'Our ill-fated and most lamentable friendship has ended in ruin and infamy for me' (Wilde 2000, 684). From this point on, Wilde lays the burden of blame for his imprisonment not so much on Douglas's capricious behaviour as his willingness to have allowed Douglas to bring 'the entire ethical degradation' that he has suffered upon himself (Wilde 2000, 689). Wilde, for example, reviles Douglas for failing to give up the 'horrible habit of writing offensive letters' to his friends, such as Ross and Sherard, both of whom had visited Wilde in jail when Douglas – for reasons Wilde failed to understand – had not. Since he had no personal contact with Wilde during the prison sentence, Douglas sought to defend his lover in what he assumed would be a sympathetic French press. This was a development, as the following passage shows, which alarmed Wilde: 'When Robert Sherard heard from me that I did not wish you to publish any article on me in the *Mercure de France*, with or without letters, you should have been grateful to him for having ascertained my wishes on the point, and for having saved you from, without intending it, inflicting more pain on me that you had done already' (Wilde 2000, 761).

Since Ross recognized that the temperamental Douglas would take exception if Wilde's antipathy became public knowledge, he reached an agreement in 1909 with the British Library to place the manuscript of *DP* in safekeeping, on the understanding that the document would remain sealed for fifty years. Although Wilde's son, Vyvyan Holland, issued an edition of the complete text in 1949 (some four years after Douglas's death), it was only in 1962, when Rupert Hart-Davis published his impressive volume of Wilde's *Collected Letters*, that readers had access to an authoritative version of this work. Ross, however, did not take enough caution to prevent the German translator, Max Meyerfeld, from disclosing in 1909 that Wilde addressed the lengthy prison document to Douglas (Bristow 2008, 22). Furthermore, Ross appears not to have placed any constraints on the materials he shared with the English novelist Arthur Ransome, who was preparing what became the most informative early critical inquiry into Wilde's achievements. Although Ransome refrains from mentioning Douglas by name, he reveals that the entire 'letter, a manuscript of "eighty close-written pages on twenty folio sheets", is not addressed to Mr. Ross but to a man to whom Wilde felt that he owed some, at least, of the circumstances of his public disgrace' (Ransome 1912, 157). On reading these words, Douglas – whose irritation with Ross's guardianship of Wilde's memory had deepened in the past four years – took out a law suit. In the court case that followed, Douglas suffered considerable humiliation when the most rancorous passages from the complete manuscript were read aloud and reported in newspapers. Until the time of his death in 1918, Ross experienced further legal conflicts with the volatile Douglas, who went defensively into print with *Oscar Wilde and Myself* (1914). This book-length assault on his former lover was largely written by T. W. H. Crosland, a subeditor working under Douglas (then editor at the *Academy*), who despised the influential political circle surrounding the Prime Minister, H. H. Asquith, to which Ross had for some time belonged. Crosland's contempt can be heard in the more flatly written passages that defame Wilde's literary ability: 'Wilde knew himself for a shallow and oblique thinker. The fact that he never did anything really great has been set down to his indolence. It was due really to shallowness rather than indolence' (Douglas 1914, 63).

Douglas's offensive against Wilde's memory proved distracting after the decade-long period when Ross had made staunch efforts to put the literary estate in order. Ross had not only restored the copyright on Wilde's writings but also ensured that the fourteen-volume *Collected Works* appeared from Methuen in 1908. In preparing this fine edition, Ross employed Millard, whose earliest publication on Wilde was an authorized translation of a largely uncomplimentary essay by André Gide that first appeared in the French journal *L'Ermitage* for 1902 (for a full treatment of this, see Victoria Reid's essay in this volume). As Millard implies, the value of Gide's memoir lies in the light it throws on 'the sorrows and sufferings of the last few years' of Wilde's life (Gide 1905, 9). Millard provides useful annotations to some of Gide's asser-tions. Where Gide reports that Wilde said he was 'absolutely without a penny' when residing in Paris (Gide 1905, 85), Millard observes that Douglas had claimed to have provided Wilde with cheques amounting to £600 during the twelve months leading up to the writer's demise. More important still is the scrupulous list of Wilde's works that Millard appends to his 1905 volume. This document forms the basis of Millard's imposing *Bibliography of Oscar Wilde* that

appeared in 1914. In its review of this major work, the *Nation* – if unwilling
to concede much greatness to Wilde's achievement – readily observed that
the bibliography was an 'astonishing and ingenious compilation' (Review
1914, 716). Besides his magisterial *Bibliography*, Millard produced several
other noteworthy volumes, including an essay that looks back at the moralistic
hostility that several journals expressed toward *PDG* (1908, revised 1912), as
well as the *Oscar Wilde Calendar* (1910), a collection of Wilde's *Impressions of
America* (1906) and, perhaps most enlightening of all, an edition of the press
reports of the 1895 trials (1912).

By the time Ross and Millard were working together in the name of
lending accuracy and dignity to Wilde's legacy, there were a number of
publications that provided intelligent critical assessments of Wilde. The most
noteworthy is the *New Age*: the journal with roots in the early nineteenth
century that Holbrook Jackson and A. R. Orage acquired in 1907 and
quickly transformed into one of the most significant weeklies linked with
literary modernism. Orage, however, was not always sympathetic to the
literary Decadence to which Wilde's name was often attached. In particular,
Orage denounced the 'yellow fever' evident in the pages of the *Yellow Book*,
with its cover design by 'Weirdsley wonderful' (i.e. Aubrey Beardsley), whose
illustrations accompanying the English edition of *Salomé* (1894) had already
caused a furore (Gibbons 1973, 102). By 1907, though, the *New Age* showed
little of such prejudice. If anything, the open-mindedness of this periodical
is especially striking when one reads its anonymous assessment of C. Ranger
Gull's incompetent biography. The reviewer dismisses Gull's study as 'an
impertinence' ('Ingleby has no qualifications for writing an appreciation of
a brilliant man of letters') and suggests that 'scientific analysis' may soon
help us to judge 'whether Wilde was falsely accused or not' (Review 1907,
93–94). In one of the earliest uses of the term 'homosexuality' that I have
found in the popular press, the *New Age* refers its readers to the authority
of a German scientist named Professor Semon who 'pushes Samuel Butler's
theory of unconscious memory to its logical extreme' (1907, 94). On this
view, homosexual acts derive 'from a quality which is found slumbering in
every individual' (1907, 94). Such information, the reviewer adds, may not
'influence a mob that still must be supplied with gladiatorial shows' but it
reminds socialists that they 'will scarcely dare to think harshly of the author
of "The Soul of Man"' (1907, 94).

By comparison, L. Haden Guest – the Fabian doctor who regularly reviewed
theatre productions for the earlier numbers of the *New Age* – finds it difficult to
reconcile the ways in which 'the lord of language' creates 'unreal and melodramatic plots' in a play such as *WNI* with the radical tone that the fickle dandy
Lord Illingworth strikes when he declares that the only means of solving the
'problem of slavery' is by 'amusing the slaves' (Guest 1907, 75; Wilde 1908, 4:
22). 'I bitterly resent this', Guest observes, because the predictable 'mechanism'
of Wilde's drama shows a writer who is 'shackling his talents within the mesh
of conventional society restrictions' (Guest 1907, 75). At no point will Guest
concede that Wilde's society comedy implies a critique of the dramatic and
social conventions it depicts. Guest bases his comments on a recent revival
of *WNI* by Herbert Beerbohm Tree, who directed the first production that

opened at the Haymarket Theatre on 19 April 1893. Tree's 1907 production at Her Majesty's Theatre, which received mixed reviews, reveals the enduring public interest in Wilde's society comedies, which had resumed as early as 1901 with performances of *LWF* and *IBE* at the Coronet Theatre, London. The director was George Alexander, who had been responsible for the premieres of both plays in the 1890s. In 1914 Alexander revived *IH* at the fashionable St James's Theatre, where it had premiered nineteen years earlier.

Such information reveals that no matter how much embarrassment might be aroused whenever people mentioned Wilde's name, his presence in literary culture was hardly eclipsed. By 1909, when reviewing a fresh edition of *LASCOS,* the *New Age* observed that the 'interest in Oscar Wilde is perennial' (Review 1909, 400). David Nutt, who published *HPOT* in 1888, issued a third edition of this finely illustrated volume in 1902. This collection, which many later publishers would take up, has remained in print ever since. The same point can be raised in relation to Wilde's French-language drama, *Salomé.* Even if this experimental Symbolist play could not be publicly staged owing to the ban that the Lord Chamberlain's office had put on it in 1892, it became well known through Richard Strauss's imposing operatic adaptation, as well as through Canadian dancer Maud Allan's *Vision of Salomé* (1906). Meanwhile, although two private performances of this drama – by the New Stage Club in 1905 and by the Literary Theatre Club in 1906 – were largely ignored by the national press, they nevertheless attracted strong interest from the literary elite. Wilde's publisher, John Lane, reprinted the 1894 edition (accompanied by Ross's 'Note on "Salome"') on several occasions from 1906 onward; at the time, the *Academy* shrewdly remarked that 'it is a pity that those who dealt the heavy-handed attacks on an extraordinarily beautiful, if unwholesome piece of work, did not realise that the last word of criticism had been said by the illustrator' (i.e. Aubrey Beardsley, who satirized Wilde in some of the 1894 illustrations) (Review 1906, 382).

It was, however, not until 1910 that Strauss's *Salome*, performed by Sir Thomas Beecham's Company, opened at Covent Garden, London. Even then, the Lord Chamberlain at first refused to license the libretto. As Steven Nicholson has pointed out, Beecham protested loudly that it would be a 'national calamity' if 'England alone in the world should be deprived of the opportunity of hearing the finest opera of modern days' (Nicholson 2003, 73). Beecham decided to go over the Lord Chamberlain's head by bringing the matter to Prime Minister Asquith's attention. As a consequence, Beecham had to negotiate emendations that would ensure that there was no unseemly representation of intimacy between Salome and the Iokanaan. More pressingly, his company had to revise the scene in which Salome sings to the prophet's decapitated head. At first, Beecham was told that it would be acceptable for her to sing to a bloodied sword. But after Aino Ackte (whom Strauss had selected to sing Salome) asked instead for the head to be set on a tray covered with a cloth, Beecham had to agree to the Lord Chamberlain's stipulation that the obscured body part should not 'build up a great heap in which it would look suggestive' (Nicholson 2003, 74).

While the *New Age* did not engage with the ongoing censorship of *Salomé* and the growing fame of Strauss's opera, it paid close attention to Wilde's standing in modern culture. Perhaps the *New Age*'s most significant assessment of Wilde's reputation during the *début de siècle* emerges in a commentary by Orage called 'The New Romanticism', which takes the form of a dialogue that reflects on the dinner held in December 1908 in honour of Robert Ross's *Collected Works of Oscar Wilde*, which Methuen had just issued. This dinner, hosted at the Ritz Hotel, was a widely publicized affair, and it helped to reinforce the public's awareness of Wilde's greatness as a writer – as we can see in the remarks that one of Orage's speakers makes: 'Eight years ago nobody but a brilliant speaker dared breathe Wilde's name at a gathering of over half a dozen people. Today his name can be bawled by the dullest speakers and heard with enthusiasm by a crowd of the most timorously obscure' (Orage 1909, 379). Wilde's newfound popularity, it seems, derived from the fact that he was a precursor of the transformations that were taking place in early modernism. 'We are', Orage's speaker asserts, 'standing now where Wilde stood at the opening of his career [...] at the cradle of a second English Renaissance in Art, Literature, and the Drama' (Orage 1909, 379).

From this perspective, since Wilde had the potential to purge the nineteenth century of its 'Victorian sentiment', he emerges for Orage – in a striking phrase – as 'our English Nietzsche' (Orage 1909, 379). Even if Wilde, as James Joyce made clear in a contemporaneous essay discussed by Elisa Bizzotto later in this volume, bore an elaborate name whose 'high-sounding titles' symbolized him as an eminent Irishman, Orage's observation nonetheless heralds a series of historical accounts that identify Wilde's position as a harbinger of the modern (Joyce 2000, 148).[3] Assuredly, this was not a position that Wyndham Lewis shared when in 1915 he dismissed Wilde's belief that 'Nature imitates Art, not Art Nature' (Lewis 1915, 70; Wilde 1908, 8: 33). 'Let us take up this old aesthetic quip', Lewis remonstrates, 'and set ourselves the task of blasting it indolently away' (Lewis 1915, 70). But the idea that nature might be an invented category would be reiterated by 'A.E.R.', who also grasped the contradictory position that Wilde held in the 1890s: 'Wilde's assertion that the public did not concern him was beggared by the fact that he appealed to it'. Thus it follows that 'what Nietzsche said of Wagner is true of Wilde: "He says a thing again and again until one despairs – until one believes it."' In other words, it was Wilde's dislike of English narrow-mindedness that eventually led, with much irony, to the popular view that 'the absence of Morality implied the presence of Art' ('A.E.R.' 1912, 615).

By the middle of World War I, John Cowper Powys implicitly absorbed some of the *New Age*'s wisest observations into what is arguably the most penetrating retrospective on Wilde's career to emerge in the 1910s. Besides following Beerbohm by stating that 'it is a mistake to regard "De Profundis" as a recantation', Powys contends that the Irish writer's symbolic value lies in

---

3   Joyce's point is that Wilde's full name, with which the author signed himself in his early career, was Oscar Fingal O'Flahertie Wills Wilde, whose first three names derive from the *The Poems of Ossian* (1765) by the Scottish poet, James Macpherson, and 'the fierce Irish tribe' of O'Flahertie, respectively (Joyce 2000, 148).

the fact he 'salute[d], in the name of the aesthetic freedom he represented, those enduring elements of human loveliness and beauty in that figure which three hundred years of hypocritical Puritanism have proved unable to tarnish' (Powys 1916, 420, 402). In particular, Powys focuses on the price Wilde had to pay for the defiant manner in which he flaunted his epigrammatic wit 'in the face of the heretical mob' (Powys 1916, 404). For this reason, Wilde bore 'the brunt of the battle for the spiritual liberties of the race', and he therefore stands as a forerunner of 'the sterner and more formidable figure of Nietzsche' – namely, 'the Superman' (Powys 1916, 404). On this basis, Wilde opposed not only 'the impertinence of the artist' to 'the impertinence of society' but also stood well ahead of his time, as one can see in SMUS: an essay that to Powys rightly attacks the so-called 'honourableness of work' that labourers undertake in a degrading capitalist system (Powys 1916, 405, 411). Powys maintains that Wilde's artificial style in making incisive observations of this kind is so powerful that it proves impossible to 'escape from him': 'His influence is everywhere', Powys asserts, in full recognition of Wilde's modernity (Powys 1916, 417).

As both the *New Age* and Powys reveal, in the years leading up to and including World War I the best critics of Wilde had increasingly understood his historical significance as an artist whose views were by no means super-annuated. Unfortunately, some of the well-intentioned attempts to bring his works to new audiences failed, as we can see in the American author G. Constant Lounsbery's clumsy stage adaptation of *PDG*, which opened at the Vaudeville Theatre, London, in the summer of 1913. Lounsbery, a Bryn Mawr graduate who belonged to Gertrude Stein's circle and later established the first Buddhist college in France, tried to update Wilde's novel. Not surprisingly, the London *Times* found the production 'an exasperating bore': 'All the features of Wilde's story [...] for which it is worth reading – his characteristic wit, his intellectual curiosity, his brilliant coruscations of paradox [...] cannot be transferred to the stage' (Anon. 1913, 7). Noticeably, the reviewer makes nothing of the supposed immorality of Wilde's story that inflamed a small but vocal group of critics in 1890. By the time Lounsbery's adaptation appeared, Wilde's novel was available in Britain in an authorized edition from the trade publishers Simpkin, Marshall, Hamilton, Kent and Co. (this publisher also issued Lounsbery's play). As 'A.E.R.' had already emphasized in his review of Millard's *Oscar Wilde: Art and Morality* (1912), *PDG* was essentially a 'book dealing morally with prurient matter', thus showing that the mid–1890s onslaught against the attributed depravity of the novel was the result of moral-istic small-mindedness ('A.E.R.' 1912, 616).

Yet, in a climate where it had become increasingly possible to view Wilde as a figure of enduring significance, it remained hard for those readers to find a biographical source that was untainted either by Sherard's belief that Wilde was congenitally diseased or by the squabbles that had put Ross and Douglas at odds. Even if Powys recognized that Wilde in *DP* was right to claim that he was 'a symbolic figure' and that his genius lay in his life, there were few reliable sources to which readers could turn to gain an informed understanding of Wilde's career (Wilde 1905, 22; Powys 1916, 401). Certainly, Ransome's study, which was reissued in 1913 without the offending allusion to Douglas, had provided a thoughtful critical guide. But Douglas's constant legal threats made it impossible for Wilde's friend, Frank Harris, to issue his two-volume *Oscar Wilde: His Life and Confessions* (1916) in Britain. In some respects, this was no loss because Harris's often slapdash work, even if it does not lapse into Sherard's moralizing about Wilde's degeneration, tends to weave tall tales at the expense of accuracy, especially by repeating Ross's fanciful claim that when Wilde died there was such a 'loud explosion' of 'mucus' from the corpse that '[e]ven the bedding had to be burned' (Harris 1916, 2: 539). Certainly, Harris aimed to elevate Wilde's name in the canons of English literature: 'in kindly, happy humour', Harris writes, 'he is without peer in English literature' (Harris 1916, 2: 416). Moreover, Harris takes pains to emphasize that Wilde's 'kindliness was ingrained' (Harris 1916, 2: 423). But it is clear from Harris's largely anecdotal approach that he aims to depict Wilde as a man whose fundamental weaknesses ensure that he deserves our pity. Harris bases much of his commentary on his not altogether precise recollections of his long friendship with Wilde. While there is no doubt that Harris played an important editorial role in Wilde's career (he published his friend's works in both the *Fortnightly Review* and the *Saturday Review*), he was hardly an intimate who enjoyed at first hand knowledge of the kind he pretends to impart in his biography.

In his undependable account of Wilde's career, Harris seldom refrains from adding a sensational touch. When he is not making Wilde look repulsive, Harris devotes his energy to recounting word-for-word implausible conversations that the two of them supposedly enjoyed with each other. Particularly far-fetched are the melodramatic colloquies that allude to Wilde's intimacy with Douglas: 'He frightened me, Frank', Harris recalls Wilde saying, 'as much as he attracted me, and I held away from him. But he wouldn't have it; he sought me out again and again and I couldn't resist him. That is my only fault. That's what ruined me' (Harris 1916, 1: 149). Harris no doubt toed this line because he presumed that this was what a clamouring public wished to hear about a volatile aristocrat whom Wilde had defamed in the unpublished parts of *DP*. 'There can', Harris states, 'be no doubt that Lord Alfred Douglas's habitual extravagance kept Oscar Wilde hard up' (Harris 1916, 1: 151). Eager to entertain a prurient readership, Harris quickly adds: 'There were other and worse results of the intimacy which need not be exposed here in so many words' (Harris 1916, 1: 151). Implicitly, Harris believes that Douglas should bear the burden of blame for the sexual exploits that led a vulnerable and weak-willed Wilde to his imprisonment. The fact that Harris is overstating his claims, however, catches our attention when he backtracks in a footnote that reprints Douglas's fine poetic tribute to Wilde, a sonnet titled 'The Dead Poet', which appeared in the *Academy* in 1904. 'I am conscious', Harris observes, 'that I may be doing [Douglas] some injustice' (Harris 1916, 2: 522). Predictably, Douglas went into print demanding that Harris retract countless lies, and by 1925 the two men agreed that the biography warranted serious correction. The costs of resetting *Oscar Wilde*, however, were prohibitive, and it took until 1938 – twenty years after Douglas had resolved, once Ross was deceased, not to embark on any further gratuitous attacks on his former lover – before Harris's study appeared in Britain.

Some of the materials that came to light in the interwar period produced a more comprehensive picture of Wilde's busy professional life. But even when the conflict with Germany broke out in 1939 no one in Britain could claim to have completed a reliable biography of an increasingly respected author. In the 1930s, Wilde's plays had long been part of the repertory. Furthermore, a number of his writings, especially *DP* and his fairy tales, had become classics of modern literature. By and large, the fact that no one in England had published an adequate account of Wilde's career derived not only from the tedious disputes that persisted after Ross's death in 1918 between Douglas, Harris and Sherard; the difficulty also arose because of the enduring hostility that British society expressed toward male homosexuality. In 1913–14, for example, E. M. Forster (1879–1970) completed but declined to publish his homophile novel, *Maurice*, which depicts a successful love-affair between a middle-class man and a gamekeeper. The stigma attached to homosexuality remained so palpable for Forster that he was disinclined to bring this courageous novel before the public during his lifetime. Noticeably, at a key moment in *Maurice*, Wilde provides a significant reference-point for the fears that Forster's protagonist, Maurice Hall, experiences in his attraction to other men. During his initial consultation with a doctor about his condition, Hall declares: 'I'm an unspeakable of the Oscar Wilde sort' (Forster 1971, 159). By the 1910s, even if Wilde's works had been restored to some level of respectability, the 'unspeakable' nature of Wilde's sexuality continued to resurface because his name remained entangled in sexual controversy. Although, by World War I, Wilde could stand nobly as 'our English Nietzsche' for intellectuals like Orage, it was still the case that references to the trials that had taken place twenty years earlier could stir up – especially for propagandistic reasons – disquiet in a nation that feared it had lost 'moral fibre' and might suffer defeat at the hands of the Germans.

'This curious perverted brilliant creature': reviving Wilde during the interwar years

In the final year of World War I, the British press could hardly ignore a spectacular legal case that revived Wilde's notoriety as a sexual pervert, in the name of attacking the Liberal Prime Minister, Lloyd George. This highly publicized case arose when an impetuous Independent MP, Noel Pemberton Billing, included the following announcement in his reactionary newspaper, the *Vigilante*, at the prompting of the popular romantic novelist Marie Corelli:

> The Cult of the Clitoris
> To be a member of Maud Allan's private performances in Oscar Wilde's *Salome* one has to apply to a Miss Valetta, of 9, Duke Street, Adelphi, W.C. If Scotland Yard were to seize this list of these members I have no doubt they would secure the names of several thousand of the first 47,000. (Kettle 1977, 18–19)

The allusion to the 'first 47,000' was not cryptic to Billing's readers, though it seems that scarcely anyone who saw the word 'clitoris' – a term that was confined mainly to medical literature and erotic writing – grasped the point that he regarded *Salomé* as a work of masturbatory intent that would in turn arouse the treacherous homosexuals who thronged to see it.

In the earlier incarnation of his paper, the *Imperialist*, Billing informed his readership that '[t]here exists in the *Cabinet noir* of a certain German prince a book compiled by the Secret Service from the reports of German agents' that revealed that thousands of English men and women from all walks of life – 'Privy Councillors, youths of the chorus, wives of Cabinet Ministers, dancing girls' – belonged to a despicable class that 'all decent men thought had perished in Sodom and Lesbia' (Kettle 1977, 8). As part of his campaign against known homosexuals such as Ross (now a trustee of the Tate Gallery), Billing contended that these perverts would betray the nation in order to satisfy their insatiable desires. In his discussion of the furore that surrounded Billing's inflammatory article, Michael Kettle reveals that the belief that homosexuals were susceptible to German seducers had its origins in Arnold White's essay, 'Efficiency and Vice', which appeared in the *English Review* in 1916. ('The urning [i.e. homosexual] population of Germany', White warned, 'is increasing'; thus the enemy was set 'to infect clean nations with Hunnish erotomania' [Kettle 1977].) Corelli, who kept her eyes peeled for violations of moral purity, had been alarmed by an advertisement in the *Sunday Times* that stated that two private performances of *Salomé* were scheduled to take place in London on 7 and 14 April that year. The producer was the well-known businessman, J. T. Grein, who organized the Independent Theatre Society, which had earned respect for its pioneering staging of some of Henrik Ibsen's and George Bernard Shaw's radical dramas. Such was Grein's standing that in March 1918 a government official asked him to organize a programme of English theatrical propaganda in neutral Scandinavia and The Netherlands. Even though the ban on *Salomé* was still in place, Grein – who was in the midst of preparing his private performances of the play – included Wilde's drama as part of the programme he submitted to the government. At the Ministry of Information, Robert Donald expressed no objection. This was a clear sign that *Salomé*, which, as many essays in this volume reveal, enjoyed widespread fame throughout the Continent, could not be viewed as unpatriotic. But when the Canadian dancer Maud Allan decided with Grein to take out suits against Billing for defamatory libel, they could not have anticipated that they would become enmeshed in a complex political plot.

Soon after Grein's *Salomé* went into production at the Court Theatre in April 1918, the case of 'The Cult of the Clitoris' had come before the Bow Street magistrate. Both the production and the proceedings subjected *Salomé* to a critical assault that no other work of Wilde's had experienced since the time of the first trial of 1895, when Edward Carson took the 1890 edition of *PDG* to pieces for its imputed immorality. In court, on 6 April, Billing – who conducted his own defence – asked Grein about Wilde's reputation: 'Are you aware that there is peculiar significance attaching to his name today?' Grein simply replied: 'No longer.' 'Are you aware', Billing persisted, 'that he was a great moral pervert?' (Kettle 1977, 24). This exchange, as Michael Kettle shows, was enough to alarm the Lord Chamberlain, whose office relayed to the press that Grein's private performance of *Salomé* had received no subsidy from the state (Kettle 1977, 24–25). Since Grein's production, in which Allan took her first speaking part on stage, had become a source of controversy, important sections of the press reviewed it. The *Stage* condemned Wilde's play as 'animalism, or worse': 'As a study in decadent expression [...] *Salome* is interesting in the library, but it is not fitted for stage representation' (Kettle 1977, 25). No sooner had Grein's performance been slammed than Billing was back in court asserting that the play's 'presentation of a physical orgasm' in an adolescent was 'calculated to attract moral perverts who [...] seek sexual satisfaction in the watching of this exhibition by others' (Kettle 1977, 25). Even though he declared that he never had read Wilde's drama, Billing stuck firmly to his belief that *Salomé* culminated in a scene of female masturbation. This was his basic defence of his newspaper's reference to a 'cult' of perverts who worshipped at the shrine of the clitoris. More to the point, his focus on clitoral pleasure insinuated that Allan – who had been suspected of having an intimate affair with the former Prime Minister Asquith's spouse, Margot – was lesbian (this was a rumour that Ross's antagonist, T. W. H. Crosland, had mentioned in a satirical poem).

Since Billing's testiness in court earned the magistrate's displeasure, he was committed for trial at the Old Bailey for both obscene and defamatory libel. These were, as Kettle reminds us, criminal charges (Kettle 1977, 30). On the first day of the trial, Billing resumed his critical assault on *Salomé*, asking Allan if she was aware that 'in this play Salome herself admits that Herod has an incestuous passion for her' (Kettle 1977, 76). While Allan denied that this was the case, Billing's line of inquiry managed to identify other patterns of sexual transgression that he wanted Allan to acknowledge: 'Miss Allan, if Salome had [...] cut off that head [i.e. John the Baptist's] herself, she would have committed [...] an act of sadism' (Kettle 1977, 80). 'Do you know what sadism is?' Billing asked, tauntingly (Kettle 1977, 81). Allan's counsel responded tartly: 'that is a very indecent question to ask this lady' (Kettle 1977, 81). To make matters worse, Billing raised this impertinent question again on the fourth day of the case, when he recruited the headstrong Douglas to give testimony. Douglas sympathized with Billing's cause because he realized it would give him another opportunity to defame Ross in court. Already, during proceedings at Bow Street, Billing had stated that any performance of *Salomé* could not go ahead without the permission of Ross, who managed Wilde's literary estate. Part of Billing's plan was to suggest that Ross was a perverted traitor who had declared 'that *Salome* has made the author's name a household word wherever the English language is *not* spoken' (Kettle 1977, 79). In this context, Douglas eagerly asserted that Wilde 'was the greatest force of evil that has appeared in Europe during the last 350 years' (Kettle 1977, 173). Furthermore, he assented to Justice Darling's query that 'Wilde would call spiritual what you call sadism' (Kettle 1977, 178). As they made these extreme claims, Douglas and Billing did not predict that Ross, who died five months later, would become too ill to be cross-examined at the Old Bailey.

In any case, the trial threatened to spin out of control because it touched on government fears about secret intelligence. One of the witnesses whom Billing called on to testify about the German *Cabinet noir* had been hired as an agent provocateur by Lloyd George's government, in an attempt to lure Billing into a brothel where he would be surreptitiously photographed. The person in question, Eileen Villiers-Stuart, soon became Billing's mistress and subsequently undermined Lloyd George's efforts to destroy the maverick

Independent MP. Had the court subjected Villiers-Stuart to too much scrutiny, the authorities would have had to answer some serious questions about their underhand manoeuvrings. In the meantime, Allan's counsel was forced to face up to the fact that Billing's repeated onslaughts against *Salomé* made it impossible to defend the drama from any imputation of sexual transgression. Billing, after all, had called Dr Serrell Cooke (a questionable authority on psychiatry) to declare that 'it would have been impossible' for Wilde' to 'have written' *Salomé* without intimate knowledge of 'sexual perverts': 'The probability is that he had von Krafft-Ebing's *Psychopathia Sexualis* in front of him all the time' (Kettle 1977, 152). At the end of the war, Krafft-Ebing's pioneering study, which circulated in an English translation dating from 1892, was still a recognized authority on sexual perversion, although it was never a work that Wilde consulted. Thus Allan's counsel felt obliged to remark that even if Wilde – 'this curious perverted brilliant creature' – wrote 'some of the best comedies produced in England', he was also the author of 'this [...] very unpleasant tragedy' (Kettle 1977, 238). Since Justice Darling reminded the court that the second medical witness (Dr Leonard Williams) had concluded that *Salomé* was 'an obscene, indecent, sadistic play', it followed that the jury reached a verdict of 'Not Guilty' (Kettle 1977, 261).

While it might seem that Billing's acquittal did much to reinforce the basis on which *Salomé* had been banned in 1892, he succeeded (as William Tydeman and Steven Price observe) 'in exposing something in the play of which many others must have been aware, and no future production could be staged in innocence' (Tydeman and Price 1996, 86). Even though *Salomé* remained censored, it was the case that private performances resumed, under Terence Gray's direction, at the Festival Theatre, Cambridge, in 1929 and 1931. A further production opened at the Gate Theatre Studio, with choreography by Ninette de Valois, also in 1931. Later that year, after the Lord Chamberlain's office decided to lift the ban, the first public performance took place at the Savoy Theatre, directed by Nancy Price. Neither of the two London productions impressed the London *Times*, which believed that the play showed that Wilde was simply a 'verbal decorator' (Review 1931a, 10). Perhaps it was the fact that no one appeared outraged by the drama that resulted in the Lord Chamberlain's willingness to lift the ban on it. (In all probability, the liberal-minded Examiner of Plays, G. S. Street, who had long admired Wilde's works, may have succeeded in exercising influence over his boss, Lord Cromer.) One cannot, however, read too much into the Lord Chamberlain's change of heart. This was hardly an era when literary and theatre censorship was relaxing. In the late 1920s and early 1930s, reactionaries targeted two noteworthy novels – D. H. Lawrence's *Lady Chatterley's Lover* (1928) and Radclyffe Hall's *The Well of Loneliness* (1928) – for obscene libel. At the same time, the Lord Chamberlain refused licenses for various plays that had a glimmer of homosexual content, such as Aimée Stuart and Philip Stuart's *Love of Women* (1934) and Lillian Hellman's *The Children's Hour* (1934). Then again, some dramas that implied desire between members of the same sex – including Mordaunt Sharp's *The Green Bay Tree* (1933) and the English translation of Christa Winsloe's *Mädchen in Uniform* (1930) – managed to pass the censor (on Street's recommendation, it seems) (Shellard and Nicholson 2004, 109–16). Whatever one makes of the vicissitudes of the Lord Chamberlain's office, it is clear that its Examiner of Plays was now reporting on dramas that were far more explicit in their depictions of same-sex desire than *Salomé*.

In 1921, no doubt mindful of 'The Cult of the Clitoris' case, Richard Le Gallienne could detect that even if to modern eyes the 1890s looked outdated, it was still true that those writers who were most closely associated with the period had 'sowed the seed of every kind of freedom of which we are now reaping the whirlwind'. Le Gallienne, who made his earliest literary mark during the *fin de siècle*, presses home his point by declaring that 'Wilde and Shaw, through that medium of innumerable editions, dictate the morals of the very youngest of the young generation' (Le Gallienne 1921a, 3). By the summer of that year, British readers were aware that the interest in editions of Wilde's work had led to the American publication of the 28,000-word manuscript of his PMWH, which had appeared, in a much shorter form, over thirty years earlier in *Blackwood's Edinburgh Magazine*. The bookseller, Mitchell Kennerley, who ran the Anderson Galleries in New York, obtained in 1920 a copy of the manuscript, which consists of Wilde's corrected proofs of his contribution to *Blackwood's* with interleaved folios. As Josephine M. Guy has pointed out, it remains unclear whether this manuscript 'represents Wilde's final thoughts on his essay' or if 'it was in a state which he, or his putative publishers, ever genuinely thought worthy of publication' (Guy 2007, xvii). In April 1920, Kennerley – whose career began as a messenger for Wilde's publisher in London, John Lane – had already overseen the New York sale of John B. Stetson Jr's collection of Wilde's manuscripts. The acquisition of PMWH was perhaps Kennerley's rarest find, and the reasons behind its long-delayed appearance struck Le Gallienne as 'a literary mystery' that had 'an exciting charm almost as great as that of a buried treasure' (Le Gallienne 1921b, 162).

If the Billing trial revived the negative memory of Wilde's sexual criminality, then Kennerley's edition served to emphasize his intellectual brilliance. In their contrasting ways, both events formed part of a more general trend that gave the impression that Wilde's spirit – no matter whether one revered or reviled him – remained very much alive. Several writers did their best to re-embody Wilde by emulating Harris's technique of recording long conversations that had taken place many years before with the author. In *Echo de Paris: A Study from Life* (1923), Laurence Housman – whose fiction and illustrations Wilde had first encountered during the early 1890s in the *Universal Review* – attempts to reconstruct exchanges that he enjoyed with the writer, Ross and other friends in Paris during the autumn of 1899. *Echo de Paris* draws attention to Wilde's critical standpoint on the artistic temperament that readers encountered in the 1905 edition of *DP*: 'You cannot create an artist: you can only invent one – and it always remains a fiction. Artists – like God's last creation, secret recipients of the Word of Life – continue to create themselves' (Housman 1923, 38). There is no question that Housman, a homophile campaigner, had sought to acknowledge the dignity of Wilde's thought at a time when the Irish author found it impossible to contemplate resuming his literary career: 'I told you that I was going to write something; I tell everybody that', Wilde is reported to have said in 1899. 'But in my heart [...] I know that I never shall' (Housman 1923, 34).

Moreover, Housman has another point to impress about Wilde's lasting significance. In a long polemical 'Footnote', he observes that even if 'the name of Oscar Wilde' is still 'likely to carry with it a shadowy implication of that strange pathological trouble that caused his downfall', it is now the case that for those 'men whose tendencies are ineradicably homosexual' it shall be treated in a manner that is 'health-giving in character and purpose, carrying with it no social or moral damnation' (Housman 1923, 56–57). He proceeds to observe that men's desires for their own sex continue to be treated with 'comical ignorance and ineptitude' – such as he discovered in the 'most eminent of British bacteriologists' who claimed that since 'homosexuality came from meat-eating' it followed that 'all homosexuals' should be 'put to death' (Housman 1923, 57). Given that such thoughtlessness persisted in the 1920s, Housman rues 'the strange irony' of the fact that 'the man who tried most to detach himself from the unlovely complications of modern civilization should have become the symbol, or the by-word, of one of its least solved problems' (Housman 1923, 60). In Housman's view, Wilde's downfall paradox-ically 'did at least this great service to humanity, that – by the sheer force of notoriety – it made the "unmentionable" mentionable' (Housman 1923, 56). Since he was a member of both the progressive Society for the Study of Sex Psychology and the homophile Order of Chaeronea (established by George Ives), Housman moved in circles that increasingly acknowledged the place that Wilde's public disgrace held in the struggle for homosexual liberation.

In 1932, a year after his death, the Nonesuch Press issued an equally forth-right and exquisitely printed volume by Charles Ricketts, who had designed and illustrated several of Wilde's books. In a style not dissimilar to Housman's, Ricketts presents his memories of Wilde in a manner than is openly fictional. Noticeably, he situates Wilde's cultural significance in a broadly cosmopolitan context. The opening chapter, set in a small hotel at Tunis, brings together English, French, German and Swedish characters who converse with an elderly man (Ricketts's own persona) who knew Wilde intimately. This worldly-wise character informs the well-educated European company of the reasons why Wilde's libel suit against the Marquess of Queensberry foundered in court:

> The Wilde tragedy culminated in its atrocious verdict out of fear of that popular British bias against art, artists, and even culture. Trusting to his reputation, wit and intellect, Wilde lost his case on a tangle of corrupt evidence, which would have damned no one else. The mere mention of Shakespeare's sonnets was imprudent. (Ricketts 1932, 11)

Ricketts's point is to explain to these mystified Europeans why the English 'believe that art, wit and culture can harm' (Ricketts 1932, 12).

In the remaining chapters, Ricketts devises a series of letters to an imaginary friend, Jean Paul Raymond, whom he depicts as one of Wilde's knowledgeable French readers. Throughout, Ricketts depicts Wilde's intelligence with respect and compassion. 'Had Mr W. H. not made Shakespeare suffer', Ricketts recalls Wilde saying in 1889, 'we should not possess the Sonnets and England would be glad' (Ricketts 1932, 32). He reveals, too, that it was on the day that Wilde received Queensberry's libellous visiting-card (accusing Wilde, in a famous misspelling, of 'posing as a somdomite') that the author wanted him to publish the full-length edition of 'Mr. W. H.'. Finally, Ricketts recounts accompanying Wilde's most loyal friends, Robert Ross and More Adey, to Reading Gaol in the spring of 1897, when he asked the Irish author about his plans for future publications: 'I must return to literature', Wilde said, 'and you must print "A Portrait of Mr W. H."' (Ricketts 1932, 48). When Ricketts replied that he would willingly issue another work – such as the unfinished *SCo* – Wilde wittily responded: 'Yes, perhaps you are right [...]. "Mr W.H." might be imprudent [...] the English public would have to read Shakespeare's sonnets' (Ricketts 1932, 48). The positive spirit of Ricketts's volume finds an echo in the painter and theatre designer W. Graham Robertson's recollections in *Time Was* (1931). Robertson's engaging memoir contains comparable reminiscences of Wilde's sparkling conversation, which for him display his former friend's 'boyish good-humour, the almost child-like love of fun, the irresponsible gaiety and lightness of touch in which lay his unquestionable charm' (Robert 1931, 137–38). Such views concur with Le Gallienne's observation that Wilde's 'poses were self-dramatizations, of which he expected others to see the fun'; 'there was', Le Gallienne adds, 'reality behind them all' – 'a serious philosophy' (Le Gallienne 1926, 256–57).

Although Wilde's relations with Housman, Ricketts, Robertson and Le Gallienne have been documented, little is known about A. H. Cooper-Prichard, who in 1931 brought out *Conversations with Oscar Wilde*: a work comprising eleven fanciful colloquies between the Irish writer and a cast of characters, including Walt Whitman and William Morris. The volume, which counts among a larger body of literature that seeks to bring Wilde's exuberant wit back to life, may have had some basis in Cooper-Prichard's claim that he became acquainted as a boy with Wilde in the late 1880s, around the time when Henry Irving's *Faust* was playing at the Lyceum Theatre. But *Conversations with Oscar Wilde*, no matter how questionable its origins, looks far more honest than works such as J. M. Stuart-Young's fabricated 1905 memoir of the time he spent as a youth in Wilde's company when *WNI* first played at the Haymarket Theatre (see Newell 2006, 63–64; Bristow 2008, 26–27). And Cooper-Prichard's work appears positively sane when compared with the 'automatic writings' that one 'Mr V' recorded in the early 1920s while the psychic medium Hester Travers Smith channelled Wilde's spirit. 'Mr V' (S. G. Soal), a university lecturer later exposed as a fraud, was clearly mindful of Cecily Cardew's memorable aversion to German ('It isn't at all a becoming language') in *IBE* when he recorded the following message from the paranormal: 'But though I have forgiven the world the humiliations that were heaped upon me, and though I can forgive even that last insult of posthumous popularity that has been offered me, I find it hard to forgive them for translating my beautiful prose into German' (Wilde 1908, 6: 67; Smith 1924, 57). Perhaps the hardest thing to forgive in Smith's bizarre *Psychic Messages from Oscar Wilde* (1924) is the ineptitude with which it tries to authenticate Wilde's droll humour.

A much more concerted attempt to re-embody Wilde had been made by a number of European and American playwrights, who represented scenes from his life on stage. The first British dramatic version of Wilde's career was the brothers Leslie Stokes and Sewell Stokes's *Oscar Wilde* (1936), to which the Lord Chamberlain refused to grant a license. Twelve years later, a further application was made, and the Lord Chamberlain's reader, H. C. Game, would still not shift his position: 'We do not', Game added, 'license plays about pederasts and in my opinion, rightly so' (Shellard and Nicholson 2004, 136). The Lord Chamberlain subsequently refused a further application in 1948 because 'the ban on perverts and perversion must be maintained' (Shellard and Nicholson 2004, 138). For this reason, two French plays relating to Wilde – the one by Léon Guillot de Saix, the other by Maurice Rostand – were similarly declined by the Lord Chamberlin in 1954 (the centenary of Wilde's death) (Shellard and Nicholson 2004, 138, 180). It took until 1961, four years after the Wolfenden Report made its recommendations for the decriminali-zation of male homosexuality, before the Lord Chamberlain agreed to lift the prohibition, largely, it seems, because two 1960 films about the trials made such censorship look unreasonable.[4]

Since it was refused a license in 1936, the Stokeses' play opened at the Gate Theatre Studio as a private performance; its lukewarm reception – as one can see from the comments of two influential critics, Harold Hobson and Desmond McCarthy – might suggest that it had greater symbolic than artistic value (Tanitch 1999, 21). But when the production transferred to the Fulton Theatre, New York, reviewers found Robert Morley's performance as Wilde 'extraordinary' (Tanitch 1999, 22). Even though the Stokeses' *Oscar Wilde* hardly passes as a major work of interwar drama, there are several aspects of it that warrant close attention. To begin with, the 1938 American edition carries an approving preface by Alfred Douglas, who observes that even if he has not seen the drama ('it would be too painful for me') he applauds the play-script because 'it is truthful and dramatic in a high degree' (Stokes and Stokes 1938, 11). Moreover, Douglas emphasizes his admiration for the work because it 'has aroused great sympathy for a man whom' he 'consider[s] to have been cruelly and unjustly treated and whose brilliant genius, if he had not been condemned by an ungrateful country to prison and resulting early death, would have enriched the English stage with many more masterpieces of dramatic art' (Stokes and Stokes 1938, 11). Since Douglas (with Crosland's help) poured such vitriol on Wilde's name in *Oscar Wilde and Myself*, it is important to understand what prompted him to reverse his opinion. In large part, the death of Robert Ross in 1918 laid Douglas's enmity toward Wilde to rest. His change of heart informs his celebratory comments in his preface to the Stokeses' play, where he affirms that Wilde was the author of what he considers to be, 'apart from Shakespeare, the finest comedy ever written in the English language' (i.e. *IBE*) (Stokes and Stokes 1938, 12).

The Stokes brothers were certainly testing the water, as were many other writers, when they stretched the truth to accentuate Wilde's unbridled yearning for younger males. As Francesca Coppa observes, from our

---

[4]   The films in question were *Oscar Wilde* (dir. Gregory Ratoff), starring Robert Morley, and *The Trials of Oscar Wilde* (dir. Ken Hughes), starring Peter Finch.

twenty-first-century standpoint 'it is surprising how overt the play is about Wilde's homosexuality, giving Wilde an entourage of two effeminate men: Louis Dijon, who, being French, apparently takes Wilde's behavior as a matter of course; and Eustace, an Englishman who admits to using rouge and was one of the many crowding the boat-trains out of London when Wilde was arrested' (Coppa 2008, 262). But, as Coppa also remarks, most of the Stokeses' drama presents what were by the 1930s fairly familiar stereotypes of Wilde. In the first scene, a seductive Wilde sounds identical to Lord Henry in *PDG*, as if he were inseparable from his fiction: 'I think, perhaps, that Bosie will always be fond of me – if only because I represent to him all the sins he will never have the courage to commit' (Stokes and Stokes 1938, 30). Later, Harris's self-regarding *Oscar Wilde* can be heard when the biographer (who takes a central role in the play) tells the author: 'I think I am right that you should know that the most scandalous things are being said against you, all over London' (Stokes and Stokes 1938, 47). The trial scenes in the drama also depend heavily on Harris, whose report of the courtroom exchanges relies in turn on Millard's 1912 volume. And in the final scene, which focuses on an episode that Harris takes pains to embellish, we witness him talking to Wilde about the scenario for a play that the now impoverished writer had sold to at least half a dozen people, with little or no intention of fulfilling the agreements he had reached with them to finish the work. (Harris transformed the scenario into a full-fledged work, *Mr and Mrs Daventry* [1900], which enjoyed a successful run in London at the time of Wilde's demise.) At the close of the Stokeses' drama, Wilde appears as a deluded, tragic individual: 'Absinthe', he says dreamily to Douglas and Harris, 'helps you to see things as you wish they were' (Stokes and Stokes 1938, 147). While there is no doubt that Wilde was drinking excessively at this time, the idea that he would burst into a '*horrible laugh*' once he hears the orchestra play *See Me Dance the Polka* (a tune that has been heard earlier when Wilde dined, five years earlier, with the prostitute Charlie Parker) makes for a grotesque ending (Stokes and Stokes 1938, 149). This is the dissolute Wilde that Harris had over twenty years before portrayed as an object of pity.

By the 1930s, Harris's condescending version of Wilde's life, despite the ban on it in Britain, was commonly accepted, as we can see in a number of literary works.[5] Take, for example, the ballad that opens the future poet laureate John Betjeman's first collection, *Continual Dew* (1937). Written in brisk common metre, Betjeman's 'The Arrest of Oscar Wilde at the Cadogan Hotel' dramatizes an episode that Harris had vividly recorded more than twenty years before. After his libel suit failed, Wilde repaired with Ross to the Cadogan Hotel, Knightsbridge, where Douglas had been staying for some time, and where another good friend, Reggie Turner, awaited him. Both Ross and Turner, Harris says, 'advised Oscar to go at once to Dover and try to get to France; but he would only say, "the train has gone; it is too late"' (Harris 1916,

---

5   Arthur Symons, who reviewed Wilde's work in the 1890s, quotes Harris on trust in his largely thoughtful 1930 study of Wilde (see, in particular, Symons 1930, 33–34).

239). Wilde could not be persuaded to flee the country: 'he sat', Harris states, 'as if glued to his chair, and drank hock and seltzer steadily in almost unbroken silence' (Harris 1916, 239). In Harris's report, once the two detectives had entered the hotel room, Wilde bewilderedly asked: 'Where shall I be taken?' (Harris 1916, 241). After he learned that he was to be led off to Bow Street, Wilde 'picked up a copy of the Yellow Book and groped for his overcoat'; 'they all noticed', Harris adds, 'that he was very drunk' (Harris 1916, 241). Betjeman elaborates this image of the inebriated writer, who cannot part with his decadent reading, by rendering Harris's mostly dumbfounded Wilde incredibly vocal. Moreover, he adds touches that make the writer's body look aesthetically ornate as well as deficient in sight:

> He sipped at his weak hock and seltzer
>   As he gazed at the London skies
> Through the Nottingham lace of the curtains
>   Or was it his bees-winged eyes. (Betjeman 1937, 1)

'I want some more hock in my seltzer', Wilde petitions. 'More hock, Robbie', he insists, as if alcohol was the only thing that mattered in his world (Betjeman 1937, 1).

The very idea that Wilde might have thought carefully about his decision to accept the consequences of his arrest cannot enter this dismal account of his vacuous drunkenness. In any case, there has been some dispute about the 'Yellow Book' that Wilde happened to be reading. For one thing, it is worth remembering that Beardsley insisted that Wilde should be excluded from the journal, whose provocative contents the American editor Henry Harland knew would shock English readers. Harris's suggestion that Wilde might have taken much interest in this periodical remains open to some question. Yet what is clear is that Harris's dubious portrayal of this episode allows Betjeman to indulge in a number of other distortions. One would never imagine, in Betjeman's carefully concocted account, that the policemen were anything other than typecast Cockney constables; here they gracelessly tell Wilde that they ''ave come tew take' him 'Where felons and criminals dwell' (Betjeman 1937, 2). In such degrading circumstances, all that Betjeman's intoxicated Wilde can do is 'stagger' as he is 'helped to the hansom outside' (Betjeman 1937, 2).

'The Arrest of Oscar Wilde at the Cadogan Hotel' takes to extremes information that was familiar not only to Harris's biography but also to such writings as W. B. Yeats's 'The Tragic Generation' (1922): an influential retrospective essay in which Yeats did much to distance himself from, as well as devalue, the achievements of the group of poets connected with the early 1890s Rhymers' Club, through which Yeats had gained a foothold in London's literary culture. Yeats, however, gives more credence than either Harris or Betjeman to the fact that Wilde refused to escape arrest. 'I have never doubted', Yeats says, 'that he made the right decision'; and yet he undercuts this affirmation by stating that Wilde 'owes to that decision half of his renown' (Yeats 1999, 226). In other words, Yeats suggests that the public would implicitly hold the writer's reputation in somewhat less regard had this pitiable member of the 'tragic generation' not gone through such gruelling humiliation in court. In 1936, Yeats once more claimed that Wilde did not deserve the fame that had by then been bestowed upon him. In that year, when he reprinted *BRG* in *The Oxford Book of Modern Verse*, Yeats wished to make amends for what he believed was Wilde's lack of development as a writer. He took the liberty of excising seventy-one of the 109 stanzas: 'I plucked out even famous lines [...] because, effective in themselves, put into the Ballad they become artificial, trivial, arbitrary.' 'I have', he adds portentously, 'stood in judgement upon Wilde, bringing into the light a great, or almost great poem, as he himself had done had he lived' (Yeats 1936, vii–viii). To Yeats it seemed that Wilde's legendary presence in modern culture could hardly be justified because his compatriot's literary ability had still not ripened at the time of his death.

By the end of the decade, however, there were stirrings of discontent about such discouraging characterizations of Wilde's life and writings. Harris's sensationalist tale-telling may have pleased a growing crowd of readers but it unfairly pushed Wilde into the lower ranks of the literary canon. In 1938 the essayist Hugh Kingsmill began the task of restoring Wilde's dignity by providing a thoughtful critique of Harris's biography, especially in light of George Bernard Shaw's belief that Harris 'was really a frightful liar, writing imaginary conversations in an imaginary character, with odd little bits of actual reminiscence in them' (Kingsmill 1938, 298). Kingsmill, however, remained puzzled by the fact that no matter how low an opinion Shaw may have had of Harris, the senior playwright still put his faith in him. In Shaw's view, Harris was 'an unimpeachable authority on Wilde, but a frightful liar about everyone else' (Kingsmill 1938, 298). To resolve this matter, Kingsmill contacted Shaw and discovered from the revered dramatist that 'Harris's *Wilde* was far more interesting than the real Wilde' (Kingsmill 1938, 299).

Yet when Kingsmill read Shaw's affirmation that the American critic Vincent O'Sullivan's *Aspects of Wilde* (1936) 'would prove a valuable corrective to Frank Harris's' work, he knew that Shaw had in the past been disingenuous about the unreliable 1916 biography. Even though the first British edition of Harris's *Oscar Wilde* (1938) contained a number of unspecified emendations, it remained clear to Kingsmill that the volume (for which Shaw wrote a forty-page preface) was simply an 'authoritative hotch-potch' that had passed little muster with respected reviewers: 'Mr. Desmond MacCarthy suggested the publishers should withdraw it, Mr. Harold Nicolson said that it ought never to have appeared' (Kingsmill 1938, 301). By comparison, even if O'Sullivan's *Aspects of Wilde* pulls together, in non-chronological order, a discontinuous series of apercus about Wilde's life, it presents a more engaging, more accurate and more disinterested explanation of the writer than any work that had appeared before. 'In his peculiar form of wit', O'Sullivan observes, 'Wilde had imitators, but no predecessors', though Wilde's limitations are also evident: he 'kept to the opulent class – which was indeed the only class he knew much about' (O'Sullivan 1936, 7, 16). O'Sullivan's book was one of the first steps in the direction of a more dependable biographical study in the English-language world.

'A towering figure': liberating Wilde in the post-war period

A decade would elapse before the British reading public finally had access to a biography that for the first time offered a comprehensive yet measured account of Wilde's career. In his admirable *Life of Oscar Wilde* (1946), Hesketh Pearson undertook to transform the widespread perception of Wilde as a man fallen from grace who eventually adopted 'the pose of martyr' to a distinguished writer whose greatness exists in his 'invincible gaiety of spirit' (Pearson 1946, 2). Pearson opens his independent-minded biography by commenting that in 1943, when he declared to Shaw that he proposed to write a study of Wilde, he received a most discouraging reply: 'Don't', said the seventy-seven-year-old dramatist (Pearson 1946, 1). In Shaw's view, '[s]o much has been written since' Wilde's 'conviction on the subject of his inverted sexual instinct that the subject' had grown 'stale' (Pearson 1946, 1). Pearson states that he responded to Shaw's reproof by declaring that his intention was to take Wilde 'out of the fog of pathology into the light of comedy, to restore the true perspective of his career, to revive the conversationalist, not the convict' (Pearson 1946, 1). In pursuing this aim, Pearson's account flatly rebuts that of Harris: a former friend about whom, like Kingsmill before him, Pearson had written at length. Pearson deems 'the conversations [Harris] records between Wilde and himself' as 'simply the conversations of Harris with himself' (Pearson 1946, 181). In particular, Pearson remains sceptical of the confidence that Harris presumes to have enjoyed with Wilde. 'Harris', he contends, 'was responsible for the only unkind thing' that the painter William Rothenstein 'ever heard Wilde say' (Pearson 1946, 181).

In his wish to revolutionize received wisdom about Wilde, Pearson turns to the 'wealth of Wildeana' that 'has lain for some years untouched by a biographer', including the important writings by Housman, Ricketts and Robertson (Pearson 1946, 3). Moreover, Pearson's long career, which involved working in the 1910s as an actor alongside Herbert Beerbohm Tree, brought him into contact with several of Wilde's acquaintances and supporters, such as Douglas, Ross and Sherard. Since Pearson refrains from burdening his study with precise documentation on his sources, his discussion – which often relies on transcribed conversations with Wilde's friends – can appear somewhat unscholarly. But, even if he presents much of his material in the form of lively anecdotes, his generally affirmative account provides plenty of information that broadens our knowledge of Wilde's professional life. He tells us, for example, that the publisher William Heinemann approached Wilde to write an introduction to Gérard Harry's translation of Maurice Maeterlinck's highly stylized drama, *La Princess Maleine* (1889) and he instructively adds that Wilde's *Salomé* 'shows the influence of [...] the Belgian Shakespeare' (Pearson 1946, 196, 226). Moreover, as he unfolds details of Wilde's conviviality, Pearson's subject emerges as a courteous, likeable individual.

Overall, Pearson's heartening picture stresses Wilde's 'perennial boyishness': 'Wilde', Pearson comments, 'never experienced a day's unhappiness until he was forty years old; and although he was to know what it felt like to be wretched from his forty-first year onwards, his resilience was such that he could not remain in the depth for many hours at a time' (Pearson 1946,

163). By adopting this positive tone, Pearson relieves as much pressure as he can from the question of Wilde's 'sexual peculiarity' (Pearson 1946, 2). Not surprisingly, his refusal to endorse Harris's belief in Wilde's calamitous intimacy with other men prompted Ian Hunter to remark that 'one could read all but a dozen of Pearson's four hundred pages without realizing that Wilde was a notorious, practising homosexual' (Hunter 1987, 33). Yet, to Harold Nicolson in the *Observer* for 1946, Pearson's reluctance to overstate Wilde's sexual life made for 'the most sensible and the fairest' biographical study to date (Calder 1995, 193). Pearson concludes his narrative by calmly mentioning that, although Wilde 'was dying from cerebral meningitis, perhaps complicated by syphilis', he still managed to retain his 'charm' and 'humour' when discussing his epitaph with Ross (Pearson 1946, 376, 377).

Pearson's study provoked at least one heated response. In *Oscar Wilde: A Present Time Appraisal* (1951), the Irish playwright St John Ervine states that Pearson's belief in Wilde's 'perennial boyishness' suggests that the author was 'mentally deficient or so shallow or egotistical that trouble is not felt for more than a moment or is used for the fires of self-esteem' (Ervine 1951, 160). But Ervine had sharper axes to grind in what turns into a wholehearted assault on Wilde's reputation. In tones far less restrained than anything we find in Sherard's volumes, Ervine lashes out at the 'deliberately sodomistic' Wilde (1951, 41). And when he is not reviling Wilde's erotic intimacy with other men as 'a denial of life, a cult of sterility', Ervine blames the 'small, bunched-up sodomite' Robert Ross for leading Wilde sexually astray (1951, 35, 126). Yet the most troubling aspect of Ervine's study emerges when he accuses Wilde of lying about what happened when the prisoner was moved from one jail to another. In his view, *DP* hardly shows that Wilde had been 'purged by suffering'; it is, instead, a work that reveals a man 'polluted by self-pity' (1951, 312).

One might wonder whether it was simply Pearson's study that motivated Ervine's stubborn attempt to drive Wilde back into disrepute. By the mid–1950s, however, there were at least two other developments that, in related ways, had once again placed Wilde at the centre of contentious legal and political debate. The first was the appearance of H. Montgomery Hyde's *Trials of Oscar Wilde* (1948). In preparing this volume, Hyde, a trained barrister, relied mostly on Millard's substantial *Oscar Wilde: Three Times Tried* (1912), which includes transcripts derived from newspaper reports of the proceedings. To these materials Hyde added his own concise account of Wilde's career, in which he throws light on many technical aspects of the law. Yet even if Hyde acknowledged that Pearson rejects many details that Harris laid out in *Oscar Wilde: His Life and Confessions*, he still quotes plentifully from this questionable source (see, for example, Hyde 1948, 80–81). Although Hyde acknowledged that Harris's account was 'highly coloured and often untrustworthy as regards details', he remained convinced that it was a 'not unfaithful portrait of Wilde' (Hyde 1948, 44). Furthermore, in his revised 1962 edition of the *Trials*, Hyde readily characterizes Wilde as 'a pathological case study', in which the writer's discovery some years into his marriage that his 'youthful malady' (namely, syphilis) had not been 'eradicated from his system' meant that he 'turned towards homosexuality' (Hyde 1973, 50, 55).

Although Hyde does not echo the Russian-American critic Boris Brasol by assuming that 'these sad events' activated in Wilde 'an abnormal interest in crime' and 'a perverted longing for sin', he nonetheless agrees that Sherard is the reliable source for information on Wilde's turn away from sexual intimacy with his spouse (Brasol 1938, 211; Hyde 1973, 55). By invoking Havelock Ellis's pioneering work of sexology, *Sexual Inversion* (1896), Hyde confidently remarks that '[t]he precise mode in which Wilde's peculiar inverted instincts found satisfaction is of interest from the medico-legal standpoint' (Hyde 1973, 60). Where Hyde differs from his predecessors on the question of Wilde's homosexuality lies in his view that '[n]ot everyone today would agree with the fairness of' the 'judicial structure' under which Wilde was tried (Hyde 1973, 19). Until 1967, the eleventh section of the Criminal Law Amendment Act (1885), under which Wilde had been charged for committing acts of 'gross indecency' with other men, remained on the statute books in England and Wales. During the 1950s, Hyde was one of the most vocal parliamentary supporters of homosexual law reform.

By the middle of the 1950s, when Hyde's version of the *Trials* had been reprinted, there was increasing pressure to lift the 1885 law. In particular, the rise in arrests of men for homosexual offences generated impassioned debate. Social historians have remained divided on the reasons behind the escalating number of men taken into custody during this decade, and, in retrospect, it appears that changes in police officers' beats in Central London were more likely to have resulted in the growth of charges for 'gross indecency' than a calculated government witch-hunt against men seeking sex with other men (Houlbrook 2005, 31–37). These arrests came to a head in early 1954 when three prosperous individuals – Edward Montagu (a hereditary peer), Michael Pitt-Rivers (a West Country landowner) and Peter Wildeblood (a diplomatic correspondent at the *Daily Mail*) – appeared at the Magistrate's Office in Lymington, Hampshire, where they were accused of conspiring to commit acts of 'gross indecency' with two Royal Air Force servicemen, John Reynolds and Edward McNally, whose superiors has discovered their activities through incriminating evidence. This case marked the first use of the charge of conspiracy in a homosexual context since the time Wilde was sent down. At the trial at Winchester Assizes, Reynolds and McNally, with full protection from the Director of Public Prosecution, divulged questionable information, which resulted in a twelve-month sentence for Montagu and eighteen-month sentences each for Pitt-Rivers and Wildeblood. Soon afterwards, when articles protesting against these judgments had appeared in the *Sunday Times* and the *New Statesman*, the Home Secretary, David Maxwell Fyfe, agreed to appoint a departmental committee to review the laws covering homosexual offences. The recommendations of this committee, which formed in August that year, were set forth in the Wolfenden Report (1957). Meanwhile, Wildeblood on his release published *Against the Law* (1955): a remarkable account of his sentencing and incarceration in which he presents himself unremorsefully as 'the first homosexual to tell what it felt like to be an exile in one's own country' (Wildeblood 1955, 55). Wildeblood asserts that much of the prejudice against gay men dated from received wisdom about Wilde's supposedly corrupt behaviour. In his eyes, 'an immense amount of harm' had 'been done during the last sixty years by the Wilde legend', not least because the truth was that Wilde could hardly have been thought to have corrupted the male prostitutes with whom he committed homosexual acts (Wildeblood 1955, 5).

These tumultuous events took place in the months leading up to the centenary of Wilde's birth, which was marked by several celebrations and publications. To begin with, Wilde's youngest son, Vyvyan Holland, brought out his thoughtful autobiography, in which he recalls his childhood perplexity on leaving for the Continent with his mother and older brother after the arrest of his father, whom he never saw again. Holland remarks that in 1905 and 1906, when he was studying law at Cambridge, he managed to read editions of only *Intentions* and *PDG*, since 'it was impossible to find copies of any of his other works' – though later contact with Helen Carew (who provided the funds for Jacob Epstein's monument to Wilde in Père Lachaise) gave him access to precious inscribed volumes (Holland 1954, 179). Furthermore, Holland admits that until he was thirty-five he cared little for biographies of his father because he was brought up to believe in the unhappiness that Wilde had imposed upon the family. But over the years he eventually concluded that 'the penalties inflicted upon' his father 'were unnecessarily severe' (Holland 1954, 18). As a consequence, Holland took part, with his spouse and young son, Merlin, in the ceremony where a plaque in Wilde's honour was unveiled at the Tite Street home. The novelist Compton Mackenzie presided over this event, which was attended by T. S. Eliot and H. Montgomery Hyde, as well as distinguished members of the theatre world, including Peggy Ashcroft, Michael Redgrave and Edith Evans (famous for her role as Lady Bracknell in Anthony Asquith's splendid film adaptation of *IBE* [1952]). Representatives from Trinity College Dublin, Magdalen College Oxford and the Douglas family were also there. At the luncheon that followed at the Savoy Hotel, Mackenzie read messages from several old friends such as the elderly Laurence Housman, who stated that Wilde's 'unhappy fate' had 'done the world a signal service in defeating the blind obscurantists: he has made the world think' ('Commemoration' 1954, 8).

In the years following 1954, there were further reasons for the reading public to think more seriously about Wilde. At the end of his memoir, Holland reprinted thirty-three letters that Wilde wrote to close male friends during his undergraduate years at Oxford. This correspondence, which came from Hyde's large personal collection of Wildeana, was included in the imposing *Letters of Oscar Wilde* edited by Rupert Hart-Davis. In his finely detailed 1987 biography, Richard Ellmann readily acknowledged that Hart-Davis's 950-page edition was 'a landmark in modern scholarship' (Ellmann 1988, xi). More than any other work before it, the *Letters* provided a firm foundation upon which notable scholars such as Ellmann could write with considerable authority about Wilde. Moreover, critics could conduct their research in an increasingly liberated environment – one that would, for example, witness both the partial decriminalization of private homosexual acts and, in 1968, the removal of theatre censorship.

In 1967, when the Wolfenden Report's recommendations were finally realized in law, Rupert Croft-Cooke – who had written at length in 1955 about his own jail sentence for committing an act of 'gross indecency' – published *Feasting with Panthers*: a volume that looks at the sexual insubordination associated with the late-Victorian circles in which Algernon Charles Swinburne, John Addington Symonds and Oscar Wilde moved. Croft-Cooke counts among the earliest historians to appreciate that the greatest advance made by Hart-Davis's *Letters* was that it prevented critics from viewing Wilde as 'anything but [...] a promiscuous homosexual who enjoyed slumming with male prostitutes' (Croft-Cooke 1967, 169). Croft-Cooke reveals the extent of Wilde's homosexual milieu at Oxford, which included Lord Ronald Sutherland-Gower and the painter Frank Miles. With such information, Croft-Cooke asserts that '[t]o suggest as some innocent biographers have done that Wilde knew nothing about himself in his early years and suddenly took to homosexuality, as a man might take to stamp collecting, after meeting Robert Ross in 1886 is nonsense' (Croft-Cooke 1967, 197). Even if, like Pearson, Croft-Cooke provides little in the way of precise documentation to verify his insights, his 1967 study – together with his *Unrecorded Life of Oscar Wilde* (1972) – went a long way toward presenting Wilde as a man who had always recognized, if not experienced, his deep-rooted homosexuality.

By the 1980s, Ellmann would take this view one step further by asserting that once Wilde discontinued sexual intimacy with his wife it was homosexuality that at last 'fired his mind': 'It was the major stage', Ellmann insists, 'in his discovery of himself' (Ellmann 1988, 281). More to the point, Ellmann believes that Wilde's sexual self-realization not only 'liberated his art' but also 'liberated his critical faculty' (Ellmann 1988, 286). In the 1980s – an era when British society had benefited from the political activism of Gay Liberation – Ellmann's *Oscar Wilde* presented exactly the kind of emancipated version of the Irish writer that open-minded audiences wished to consume, especially at a time when Margaret Thatcher's moralistic backlash against growing sexual freedoms would lead to retrograde legal rulings that prohibited discussion of homosexuality in state-funded schools.[6] Thatcher, after all, promulgated her version of 'Victorian values'; Ellmann, by contrast, insisted that Wilde belonged 'to our world more than to Victoria's' (Ellmann 1988, 589). Since it flew in the face of Thatcherite philistinism, Ellmann's substantial study was for the most part very well received. Frank Kermode, for example, found much to commend in the 'generous sentence' with which Ellmann ends his discussion of Wilde: 'Now', Ellmann writes of the 1980s, Wilde 'is beyond the reach of scandal, his best writings validated by time, he comes before us, still a towering figure, laughing and weeping, with parables and paradoxes, so generous, so amusing, and so right' (Kermode 1987, 12; Ellmann 1988, 589). Appropriately enough, Kermode declared that the rousing note that concludes *Oscar Wilde* proved particularly satisfying because it was the last word that Ellmann – an esteemed Oxford professor whom Gore Vidal called 'our time's best academic biographer' – put into print before he died in May 1987 (Vidal 1987, 1063).

---

6   Clause 28 of the Local Government Act (1988) prohibited the promotion of homosexuality in schools maintained by the state; it was repealed in Scotland in 2000 and in the rest of the United Kingdom in 2003.

But no sooner had Ellmann's *Oscar Wilde* appeared than scholars detected errors in his documentation and raised questions about his assumptions. To begin with, his reproduction of a photograph from the Guillot de Saix theatre collection bears the caption 'Wilde in costume as Salome' (Ellmann 1988, opposite 429). Nowhere in his study does Ellmann explain anything further about this document. Although there is some plausible resemblance between the heavy-set figure in the photograph and Wilde, the image depicts the Hungarian opera singer, Alice Guszalewicz, in an early production of Strauss's *Salome*. Furthermore, Ellmann was willing to agree with Ross's and Sherard's beliefs that Wilde suffered from syphilis, even if 'the evidence is not decisive' (Ellmann 1988, 92). The reason guiding Ellmann's view on this matter boils down to a question of belief: 'I am convinced that Wilde had syphilis, and that conviction is central to my conception of Wilde's character and my interpretation of many things in his later life' (Ellmann 1988, 92). Such a statement hints that, even if Ellmann sets out to liberate Wilde's sexuality, he is following the life of a man whose actions and behaviour were at times dictated by venereal disease. From this perspective, Ellmann's position is not entirely distinct from that of those biographers, including Sherard and Hyde, who regarded Wilde as a pathological case.

The scholar who quickly identified the greatest number of problems in Ellmann's *Oscar Wilde* was Horst Schroeder. Some of Ellmann's frequent slips, as Schroeder reveals, are factual. Schroeder, for example, reminds us that Ellmann is in error when he claims that Ricketts was responsible for the stage designs of the London production of *Salomé*, which was aborted when the Lord Chamberlain's office declined to issue a license (Ellmann 1988, 371; Schroeder 2002, 1280). Ricketts provided his assistance to the Literary Theatre Society's private performance of the play in 1906. At times, Ellmann readily reproduces disputed anecdotes. Moreover, he offers unreasonable speculations about Wilde's private life: 'Wilde and [John] Gray were assumed to be lovers, and there seems no reason to doubt it' (Ellmann 1988, 308). As Schroeder observes, it is in the full text of *DP* that Wilde states that when he compared his friendship with Douglas 'with such still younger men as John Gray and Pierre Louÿs' he felt 'ashamed' – 'My high life', Wilde adds, 'was with them' (Schroeder 2002, 109; Wilde 2000, 686). The upshot of Schroeder's sedulous research is that the devil is so much in the details of Ellmann's scholarship that one cannot recommend *Oscar Wilde* as an altogether dependable source.

Despite its shortcomings, however, Ellmann's *Oscar Wilde* – which his publishers have not as yet taken any steps to correct – remains, in its own right, the most complete account of Wilde's career that we have to date, and its influence has been phenomenal. Practically each and every subsequent representation of Wilde's life and writings has found Ellmann's volume indispensable. Consequently, Ellmann's biases (as well as his numerous errors) have guided such dramas about Wilde's career as Tom Stoppard's *The Invention of Love* (1997) and David Hare's *The Judas Kiss* (1998). Coppa, in her discussion of English plays about Wilde, remarks that these late twentieth-century works tend to draw uncritically on Ellmann's negative portrait of Douglas (Coppa 2008, 274–79). Assuredly, Douglas was no saint. But Ellmann's view of him largely derives from the misunderstandings that fuelled much of Wilde's vitriol against his lover in *DP*. In the end, Ellmann's preferences and partialities – not to say his inattention to matters of detail – suggest that time has come for another scholar to produce a more accurate picture of Wilde. Perhaps some day we will finally have what Katherine Mansfield wanted in 1909: a source that will go further still in helping us picture, with greater accuracy, Wilde's 'exact decadence'.

2 Performance and Place: Oscar Wilde and the Irish National Interest

Noreen Doody

Dublin is a city that commends itself on its native wit and expressive use of the English language, and it considers Oscar Wilde as belonging within its community, as being 'one of its own'. On a recent visit to Dublin, Merlin Holland, Wilde's grandson, was struck by the near familial response of a taxi driver to his grandfather: 'Poor Oscar', he said, 'he had his troubles'.[1] Wilde's reception in Ireland has been marked from the outset by familiarity and a partisan interest in the progress of his personal and professional life. Wilde figures strongly both in the popular imagination and in the creative imagination of Irish writers.

Wilde, who once lamented that not being talked about was a far worse thing than being talked about, would have no reason to complain on this account in relation to his current reception in Ireland: he is regularly quoted, his plays are continually in performance on the amateur and professional stage and he is endlessly discussed in the print and digital media. His name has appeared at least once a week during the past forty years in the *Irish Times*, one of Ireland's foremost national daily newspapers, and almost as frequently in this paper in the preceding two decades. In earlier years (1907–1950) mention of Wilde was a consistent occurrence in the *Irish Times* and during his lifetime his exploits were regularly reported. The years 1896–1906, however, saw little mention of Wilde's name in the Irish media; these were the silent years that followed from the trials.

In this essay I use the evidence of the *Irish Times* in order to analyse how Wilde was generally perceived over time in Ireland. Before moving to the newspaper records, however, it is necessary to consider the historical and social context into which Wilde was born, in 1854, into a Protestant

---

[1]   A remark made by Merlin Holland in his speech to mark the occasion of a plaque being placed on the Wilde family grave in Mount Jerome, Dublin, to commemorate the centenary of the death of Lady Wilde. The American College, No. 1 Merrion Square, Dublin, 3 February 1996.

Anglo-Irish family. By the time of Wilde's birth, Ireland had been a British colony for some 700 years. In the nineteenth century the country was ruled from London through a legislative executive situated in Dublin Castle and presided over by a Lord Lieutenant. During the 700 years of occupation many discriminatory laws were passed and the majority religion of the people, Catholicism, was suppressed through various statutes. As far back as the seventeenth century Catholics had endured violations and privations levied against them on grounds of their religion, including the confiscation of land and its redistribution amongst Protestant people from Scotland and England. Irish Protestants continued to enjoy greater privileges than Irish Catholics up until the nineteenth century, even though by this time the harsher laws pertaining to Catholics had been relaxed. Even so, Anglo-Irish Protestant people in nineteenth-century Ireland had fuller employment and greater legislative authority than their Catholic neighbours and enjoyed a higher standard of living. This inequitable circumstance, coupled with the memory of historical discrimination, ensured a psychological barrier between the two denominations and a real sense of difference.

With the Act of Union of 1801, Ireland lost its status as a 'self-governing' colony of the British Empire. This Act had devastating effects on the Irish economy and society in general and calls for its repeal were loud and immediate. With the closure of the Irish Parliament and the centralization of government in London, many MPs, titled people and the upper echelons of Irish society moved to England. Dublin, which had once been known as one of the foremost capitals in Europe, became something of a social backwater. Houses became vacant in many of the affluent locations in the city and were bought by the rising professional classes who filled the social vacuum left by those departing. Later in the century (1855), the Wildes would move from their relatively modest house in Westland Row to take up residence on one of the city's choicest Georgian squares, taking their place amid the upper reaches of the professional classes of Irish society. George Bernard Shaw in later years would accuse Wilde of snobbishness because of his having been brought up at an address on Merrion Square.

The Wildes were a distinguished Irish Protestant family but were well respected by both the Irish and Anglo-Irish communities in Ireland. W. B. Yeats wrote of Lady Wilde: 'She came out of the tradition of her own class and joined herself to the people of Ireland' (Yeats n.d.). Her son's boast in *DP* was in no way an empty one: 'She [his mother] and my father had bequeathed me a name they had made noble and honoured, not merely in literature, art, archaeology, and science, but in the public history of my own country, in its evolution as a nation' (Wilde 1922, 23). Wilde's father, Sir William Wilde, was a celebrated surgeon who was remembered after his death for his scholarship, his importance to the Royal Irish Academy and to the cultural life of the city and for having at the age of twenty-nine built a hospital with his own money, later handing it over to a Board of Trustees for the treatment of the poor of the city. Wilde's mother was a nationalist poet who wrote under the pen-name Speranza. During the Great Famine of 1845–48 she composed outraged verse about England's mishandling of the situation for the popular nationalist paper, *The Nation*, and urged her countrymen to rise up and confront 'the enemy'.

Indeed, Lady Wilde was celebrated all of her life as an eminent and much respected poet and patriot. People cheered her carriage whenever it was recognized on the streets of Dublin (Coakley 1994, 11). And, in 1896, at a time when her son's name was seldom mentioned in the Irish media, a deferential notice of her death appeared in the nationalist newspaper, the *Freeman's Journal*. Given the high national profile of his parents, interest in Wilde's activities by the general Irish public was ensured throughout his lifetime. The familiar approach to him as a topic of interest and object of national pride had its beginnings in this early relationship between the Irish public and his immediate family.

The *Irish Times* was one of the main national newspapers that followed Wilde's career from his early youth. During Wilde's lifetime the *Irish Times* was a moderate, conservative paper; it was Protestant owned and in the 1870s swapped its pro-Home Rule stance for a Unionist one. Some commentators see the paper's stance as wholly expressive of a Protestant Unionist outlook but as Fintan O'Toole points out 'its self-image was never quite that stable [...]. Its own early descriptions of its political identity range from that of its founder Lawrence E. Knox in 1860 (the Protestant and Conservative daily newspaper) to Moderate-Conservative (1882), Independent (1887) and Unionist (1895)' (O'Toole 2008, 3). The paper, by and large, reported fairly on Protestant and Catholic concerns and had a wide readership among Protestants and the rising Catholic middle and professional classes. By 1873 it was firmly established as Ireland's leading newspaper and boasted to possess 'a wide readership among members of all classes' (James 2008, 2, 18, 20, 25, 29). One of the first mentions of Wilde in the *Irish Times* is as a scholar. In 1871 his name appears in the list of successful students to gain entry to Trinity College Dublin. A few years later, on 25 May 1877, when Wilde was already at Oxford, his name was also listed among the Catholic students and Jesuit staff in attendance at the Catholic University's Literary and Historical Society student meeting on the 'Formation of an Irish National Literature'. Wilde's name again appears in the *Freeman's Journal* as a contributor to the funds of a Catholic Children's Hospital in the city; the citation reads: 'Oscar Wilde, Esq., and some friends in Magdalen College, Oxford: £5.00' (8 January 1878, 8). The *Freeman's Journal* was the largest Catholic nationalist paper until challenged for this position by the *Irish Independent* in 1900. When Wilde won the Newdigate Prize in 1878 the *Irish Times* boasted of his intellectual prowess in terms of a national triumph, writing that the 'literary achievement of carrying off the Newdigate prize for English Verse at Oxford was performed this year – and for the first time in the history of this ancient academic trophy, by an Irishman [...] the distinguished demy of Magdalen, who bore away the prize from many competitors, is a son of our great Irish specialist, the late Sir William Wilde' (17 June 1878, 4). Notices in the *Freeman's Journal* in 1877 record his various poetic contributions to the *Illustrated Monitor*, while his article on the Grosvenor Gallery in the *Dublin University Magazine* is recommended as being an article 'worth reading' (5 July 1877, 5).

The presence of Wilde and his brother Willie at the Mayor's home in the Mansion House, Dublin, is duly noted in the *Irish Times* on 5 March 1879, but most of the reportage on Wilde in the 1880s has to do with his tour of

America. Reports of the early part of his tour, January and February, tell of Wilde's failure to engage the American audiences. A short article appeared in March stating that Wilde had been bested in a witticism by a niece of Oliver Wendell Holmes in Boston. Although the tone of the piece is ironic and there is no doubt that the author is gently poking fun at his fellow countryman, the idea of Wilde as a public representative of his country continues to be the point of view from which his activities are reported: 'For the honour of Ireland I'm sorry to say Mr. Wilde was unable to churn up a reply, and left soon after in a great huff, leaving in the circle a decided impression of failure' (1882a).

News of Wilde in the *Irish Times* was often given in a column entitled 'Our London Letter', which contained items about what was happening in London that might be of special interest to Irish readers. In the reports of Wilde's activities during the 1880s, pride in his achievements becomes somewhat tempered by a tone of mockery. In one such article the columnist gleefully relates how Wilde, disguised in worn-out clothes, opened the door of Sarah Bernhardt's carriage and received a coin in payment which he then put to his lips and kissed (1882b). Wilde immediately denied the story and demanded a retraction. Six days later a rather tongue-in-cheek retraction appeared: 'I have to express my abject and profound contrition for having taken the aesthetic name of Oscar Wilde in vain respecting that Bernhardt business'. The journalist continues, a malign suggestiveness in his comments: 'That may be, but I heard the singer of the sunflower and the worm of corruption distinctly named in connection with the romantic incident' (1882c). A snide account of Wilde in America appears in a follow-up column of 'Our London Letter' in which Wilde's stance as an aesthete and Irishman is called into question: 'The ornamental Oscar having come out last St. Patrick's Day in a suit of shamrocks before an American audience they are asking here why he has not paraded his patriotism in London?' The writer is being disingenuous here and knows well that the career-minded Irishman in nineteenth-century London did well to blend in some way with the denizens of that city. The article persists in a heavily sarcastic tone mocking Wilde's assertion of Irishness in a place where it can do him no harm: 'I am not able to say but as an Irishman myself I admire and applaud Mr. Wilde's exhibition in the backwoods, which is noticed here chiefly because it must have been very imposing and picturesque. The lecturer was not arrayed in leaves only. He added to that wardrobe a swallow tail coat covered in round towers, wolf dogs, harps sunburst and other symbols of an ancient and glorious nationality' (1882d). These emblems are of course the symbols associated with Irish nationalism. The article evidences personal spite and the columnist points up Wilde to his fellow countrymen as a hypocrite: either toadying up to the English by not displaying his nationality or playing the bogus stage Irishman to the Americans for personal gain. The writer would have been aware that these types of allegations would have been most effective slurs in discrediting Wilde among his own people given the politically charged atmosphere of the time. Ireland was engaged in pursuing a resolute quest for political autonomy from Britain and its foremost political leader of the time, Charles Stewart Parnell, was currently in Kilmainham Gaol from where he was negotiating the Kilmainham Treaty on land reform with the

British Prime Minister Gladstone. Matters of national dignity and identity were issues of acute sensitivity and Wilde, as a high-profile Irishman, would have been quickly judged by his fellow citizens in this regard. A month following the appearance of this article the precarious situation was evidenced in the murder of the Lord Lieutenant of Ireland, Britain's chief official representative in the country, by a group of insurgents in Dublin's Phoenix Park. In an interview with the American press Wilde roundly denounced the murder but added that England was reaping the fruits of 700 years of injustice and misrule in Ireland (Ellmann 1987, 186).

Although Wilde is still considered in terms of his national identity in later reporting of his activities, there is a growing interest in his professional progress as a writer. His editorship of the *Woman's World* during the years 1887–89 meets with critical approval and a short review of *Intentions* appears in the *Irish Times* in May 1891 (1891a). The writer is of the opinion that '[t]he volume contains some excellent criticism, but too many words'. In December 1891, *HOP* is commended for its ornamentation and illustrations (1891b).

In 1883 Wilde returned to Dublin to give two lectures at the Gaiety Theatre on 22 and 23 November: 'The House Beautiful' and 'Personal Impressions of America'. Public interest in Wilde was high and the lectures, given to packed houses, were very well received. The eighteen-year-old Yeats was among the audience at the Gaiety Theatre. Two years later, Wilde lectured again in the same venue (5 and 6 January 1885) on 'Dress' and 'The Value of Art in Modern Life'. The review of the lectures in the *Irish Times* says that the attendance was 'scanty' but those who were there seemed to enjoy themselves (1885).

In 1893, the *Irish Times* reported on the huge audiences packing the houses for performances of *WNI* in London and Glasgow, where 'business is phenomenal'. Continued pride in the author's national identity is evident in the journalist's remarks: 'Dublin playgoers will probably soon have an opportunity of witnessing their distinguished fellow citizen's latest work' (1893a). And, indeed, in November of that year, *WNI* opened in Dublin to a large audience. Irish critics for the most part favourably reviewed *WNI* and *LWF*, although the morality of each was questioned. The reviewer for the *Irish Times*, while objecting to aspects of *WNI* as immoral, contends that the last two acts have 'a touch of genius, just as though the author had been poking fun at his audience' (1893c). Fellow Irish playwrights Yeats and Shaw fully believed that this was the case; in 1891 Yeats had written that Wilde was continually stinging John Bull with his peashooter of wit, and that every pea found its mark and left the recipient feeling stung but wondering what exactly had befallen him (Yeats 1970, 204). The review of *LWF* in October 1893 objects to Wilde's apparent attack on the corruption of British society. The reviewer insists that the British are 'a people animated as a rule by wholesome thoughts' but nevertheless concludes that Wilde is teaching good lessons in morality and that the play is 'really brilliant' (1893b). It is difficult to determine whether the journalist is being serious or subversive. What can be said is that in both these reviews there is an awareness of Wilde as an Irish author who dealt in his works with the mores of a separate country. His attack on English society in *LWF* is noted by the Irish reviewer who, if being sincere, runs to the defence of English society or, if being sarcastic, agrees with Wilde. In either case the reviewer perceives that Wilde's play has serious undertones and is not simply a comic play built about a set of characters and funny situations.

The tone of derisive familiarity noted in some earlier newspaper articles surfaces again in a piece written in September 1894 for the amusement of Wilde's 'people back home' by a London Correspondent. The article begins: 'There is a delightfully pungent little letter from Mr. Oscar Wilde this evening. The apostle of the cult of the sunflower'. The journalist goes on to describe Wilde's vexation at a piece of doggerel verse, 'The Shamrock', which had been ascribed to him by T. P. O'Connor's London newspaper, *Sunday Sun*, and at the accusation that he had plagiarized the verse in the first instance (1894a). In a follow-up article some days later the true author of the poem is revealed to be a 'modest' lady living in the 'Asylum for the Blind' in County Cork. The writer feels certain Wilde would not have been so harsh in his critique of the poem had he but known by whom it had been written (1894b). There is definitely a lot of fun being had here at the expense of Wilde; mischief is afoot and Wilde is being sent up by his fellow countrymen. Perhaps O'Connor's paper was reminding him of his roots and cautioning him not to get above himself; certainly, it can be no accident that the London correspondent of the *Irish Times* juxtaposes Wilde's association with the cult of the flamboyant sunflower with the modest little shamrock, symbol of Wilde's homeland.

Some months after the appearance of the 'shamrock' article the *Irish Times* announced the Queensberry trial. The author notes this 'sensational trial' and relates that Queensberry must 'answer the charge of criminally libelling Mr. Oscar Wilde', but there is no mention as to what the libel consists of. The report talks of the 'crammed' courtroom and of people 'clamoring at the doors for admission', and gives Edward Clarke's opening remarks, in which he states that Wilde 'was the son of Sir William Wilde and had had a brilliant career both at Dublin and at Oxford' and that his poetic works represented 'the thoughts of a man of high culture' (1895a).

The subsequent coverage of the trials in the *Irish Times* is sparse. The arrest of 'Mr. Oscar Wilde' is reported briefly and concisely on 6 April (1895b) and, in the record of his being criminally charged on 8 April, 'Mr. Wilde' becomes, for the first time in all the reporting of his activities, simply 'Wilde' (1895c). The substance of the charge is not stated. Also, for the first time in this paper, Wilde's full name, Oscar Fingal O'Flahertie Wills Wilde, is cited in the opening paragraph of this account. This may be done to emphasize the serious nature of his predicament or it may be to instil in the readers that this was indeed, and no mistake about it, the Oscar Wilde whom they all knew, the recently successful playwright and sometime aesthete from Merrion Square, now the key player in these 'unspeakable' events. The paragraph goes: 'On Saturday Oscar Fingal O'Flaherty Wills Wilde was brought up before Sir John Bridge of Bow Street Police Court. For half an hour before the doors opened a huge crowd had gathered in front of the court'.

There is no coverage of the final trial in the *Irish Times*, no mention of it even. The hung jury of the first trial is briefly noted, as is Wilde's release on bail and his appearance at the Bankruptcy Court in September 1895. Most other Irish newspapers were equally reticent. If anything there is a strain of sympathy for the man within the meagre, inadequate reportage of his charge: it is noted that Wilde had been 'very depressed and almost hysterical' and had been heard to say that 'he should be obliged to commit suicide if he had a chance' (1895c). Similarly, in a review article in the *Westmeath Examiner*, Wilde is designated as the 'unfortunate, poor Oscar Wilde' (28 September 1895, 3). There were some exceptions to this style of response, notably in the *Freeman's Journal,* which carried a detailed and strongly vindictive account of the trials (Walshe 2005, 47–51).

The lack of media coverage of the Wilde trials is puzzling. It may be a reticence that springs from prudery or Victorian squeamishness. This, however, seems unlikely as eleven years previously, in 1884, the trials of Gustavus Cornwall and others for sodomy and associated 'crimes' were fully reported in the Irish press. Éibhear Walshe suggests that the lack of acknowledgement by the Irish media of the nature of Wilde's offence and its refusal to engage with his homosexuality were bound up with strong nationalist attitudes (Walshe 2005, 38–57). Walshe cites the Castle Scandals, which involved the trial of the Chief Secretary of the General Post Office and other Dublin Castle Government officials, as pertinent to nationalist feeling in relation to any highlighting of the Wilde trials. Much nationalist propaganda had been made of the Castle Scandals and those involved were seen as having imported the 'vice' from abroad; contrasts were drawn between an implied English depravity and an Irish 'innocence' or 'purity'. The 1884 scandal caused huge political upheaval in Ireland and England and newspapers in both countries divided along national lines (Cocks 2003, 142–43). The imputation of 'sodomitical vice' which had been used so successfully during the 1884 trials by Irish nationalists to undermine the English establishment in Ireland had ricocheted and was now being laid against an Irishman who for so long had been viewed in Ireland as a public representative of his country. The history of Irish patriots being tried in English courts and the concomitant distrust of that system may also have played a part in keeping quiet in relation to the accused, no matter how unrelated to patriotic activities his purported crime. It may be that the Irish media had no wish to collude or in any way aid the Crown in the prosecution of a fellow Irishman at a moment of polarized cultural outlook, sharp political division and intense endeavour towards Home Rule for Ireland.

The great respect and admiration of the country for Wilde's parents, also noted by Walshe, and their centrality to Irish national life would undoubtedly have inhibited graphic reporting of Wilde's situation. A sense of compassion and long familiarity in relation to Wilde himself, whose activities had been a feature of newspaper reports since his college days, cannot be ruled out as a possible contributory reason for the reluctance to publish details of his very public fall from grace. Although the full proceedings of the trials were not reported in most Irish newspapers, judging by the published un-contextualized fragments of Wilde's story at this time, there was a tacit understanding that the facts of the case were somehow finding their way to the reader. Of course, British newspapers were widely available in Ireland at the time.

Wilde's name is seldom mentioned in the Irish media during the following ten years and not at all in the *Irish Times* until 1905, five years following his death, when he is referred to by the writer, George Moore, in a letter about J. M. Synge on the Letters page of the paper. George Moore writes: 'I have not forgotten Oscar Wilde's plays – that delicious comedy *The Importance of Being Earnest*, but however much I admire them I cannot forget that their style is derived from that of the Restoration comedy'. He then goes on to praise the originality of Synge. Moore's use of the words 'forgotten' and 'forget' resonates with the absence of Wilde during the preceding years. This letter, published almost exactly 10 years since the opening night of Wilde's play in 1895, seems to have lifted the moratorium on Wilde that had been in place since his trials. From this point onwards, references to and comments on Wilde begin to creep back into the pages of the *Irish Times*. In December 1906 an article claims that the 'late Oscar Wilde' and George Bernard Shaw are celebrated writers in Germany (1906a). The following week a review praising the publication of *Echoes from Kottabos*, selected writings from the University of Dublin's Classics magazine, *Kottabos*, declared: 'A great part of it comes from the pen of that unhappy genius, Oscar Wilde, whose translations from Aeschylus and Euripides are inspired models in, perhaps, the most difficult of arts' (1906b).

In July 1907 the Gaiety Theatre announced that 'Oscar Wilde's brilliant plays' would be playing for one week at the theatre in matinee and evening performances. *LWF* and *IBE*, which had been performed in Ireland in 1901 by the visiting company of George Alexander at the Theatre Royal Dublin and the Grand Opera House Belfast, were welcomed to the Dublin stage in the week of 2 September 1907 (Leahy and Rose 2008). The plays were well received and played to a full house. A review of *LWF* published in the *Irish Times* on 3 September judges it 'one of the most brilliant plays written in the 19th century'. The writer discusses Wilde and his work in glowing terms, notes the playwright's wit, his 'powerful genius' and his sharp criticism of English society, and at the same time makes subtle suggestions to the initiated of a darker side to Wilde's life: 'Wilde knew life thoroughly, as all students of his works know. He reveals the faults, foibles and tragedies which occasionally convulse Mayfair society with no unsparing hand'. The reviewer does not address Wilde's downfall but his late absence is noted. It seems that, although Wilde could now be spoken about, any overt discussion of the reasons for his long absence was still taboo. The theatre critic hails the performance before a full capacity house as 'a revival of Oscar Wilde plays' and designates Wilde as 'second only among Irish playwrights to Sheridan himself' (1907). This is high praise indeed given Sheridan's long-held popularity on the Irish and English stage at the time. Wilde is once again claimed in print as a source of national pride. The following year he is included in another article with Wharton and Shaw in the assertion that 'the three men who have exercised the profoundest influence on the English stage in our generation, have all been Dublin men' (1908a).

From the 1930s onwards, Wilde's plays continued to be performed in Irish theatres by professional companies and by the flourishing network of vibrant amateur dramatic societies. *IBE* featured prominently in Dublin's first International Theatre Festival (1957) with Margaret Rutherford playing Lady Bracknell. But one theatre more than any other in Ireland became synonymous with Wilde's work: the Gate Theatre. The Gate Theatre was founded by Micheál MacLiammóir and Hilton Edwards and was the first theatre in the world to show the full canon of Wilde's works. It opened in Dublin in 1928 in the premises of the Abbey's Peacock Theatre with performances of *Peer Gynt* and the first public staging in Britain and Ireland of Wilde's *Salomé*. MacLiammóir, who, as Walshe contends, was 'the most important figure for the transformation of Wilde's reputation in Ireland' (Walshe, forthcoming), wrote a very successful one-man show, *The Importance of Being Oscar,* based on the writings of Wilde and first performed in the Gate Theatre in 1960. The show subsequently moved to Broadway and other venues worldwide. In the eighty years since its founding the Gate Theatre has staged over forty separate productions of Wilde's work.

In contrast, the National Theatre of Ireland, the Abbey Theatre, has paid sporadic attention to Wilde's work. *IBE* was first seen on the Abbey's stage in 1922 in a production by the repertory company of Madam Kirkwood Hackett. This was followed by the Abbey's own production of the play in 1926. In more recent times the Abbey Theatre has been responsible for a strikingly innovative rendition of *IBE*, directed by Conall Morrison, in 2005 and 2006. Morrison's production opened with a prologue, written by Morrison himself, set in a Parisian café, where Wilde, who is now in his later days and seems broke and lonely, is in the company of some young men. His old friend, Frank Harris, enters the scene and lends Wilde some money. Although impecunious, Wilde proceeds to buy drinks for all; then each one departs and leaves him alone on the stage. The scene is powerful. What might have been mawkish and sentimental is confounded by the acuity of the writing and the heroic quality in Wilde's demeanour: his humility, generosity and sense of joy even in dire adversity. The prologue is brought seamlessly to an end as the character of Wilde falls into a reverie of things past. He then adopts a hat and shawl, which has been posing as a tablecloth, and becomes before our eyes Lady Bracknell. The lights dim and Wilde's *IBE* unfolds on the stage, played by the rent boys who have earlier appeared with Wilde in the café. Although there was an all-male cast, the production purposely avoided high camp. Alan Stanford in the dual role of Wilde and his creation was manifestly brilliant. The set of the *Art Nouveau* Parisian café was created from coloured stained glass windows (Sabine Dargent) and suffused with subtly toned lighting by Ben Ormerod. The set reinforced the sense of artifice and cleverly reflected the images of the characters in motion.

Morrison and MacLiammóir have not been the only Irish writers influenced by Wilde. During his lifetime Wilde commanded the respect and often the admiration of his fellow Irish authors. Yeats admired Wilde's stance and style and, although he often denied it, his creative work was profoundly affected by Wilde. Wilde's contribution to Yeats's developing metaphysical doctrine is central to his imaginative impact on the poet (see Doody 2001 and 2002). This can be seen, for instance, in the imaginative understanding of life that Yeats systematizes in philosophical writings such as *A Vision* or *Per Amica Silentia Lunae*, which is crucially important as the dynamic underpinning of his creative work. Yeats's system of interrelated symbols is infiltrated by symbols and images that originated with Wilde and, although Yeats develops and intensifies each one of these symbols, re-imagining and re-setting them within a new context, they still retain their primary signification, ensuring that Wilde's thought inflects Yeats's creative language.

Yeats met Wilde in London in 1888 and became friendly with him, visiting his home in Chelsea and exchanging conversation with him on Irish politics and other matters. Later that year he spent Christmas day with the Wilde family and, together with Wilde's wife, Constance, listened attentively to Wilde as he read out the proofs of DL. Yeats was a shy, if forthright young man, who found in Wilde a kind and encouraging role model. Yeats, who subscribed strongly to cultural nationalism, considered Wilde a radical critic of English society. Indeed, he believed that in order fully to understand Wilde it was necessary to read him through his national identity (see Doody 2000 and 2001). During Wilde's trials Yeats collected letters of encouragement for him from many Irish men of letters, among them Douglas Hyde, who would later become the first President of Ireland. When asked by a journalist why he thought Wilde had not made his escape before his arrest, Yeats responded that, Wilde being an Irish gentleman, 'it was with him a point of honour to face the trial' (Kingsmill 1977, 295). George Bernard Shaw also believed that Wilde's nationality contributed to his reaction at his arrest and imprisonment (Shaw 1962, 30). Shaw recalls that, although they liked one another, he and Wilde had a somewhat strained relationship: they seemed to embarrass one another and a reciprocal shyness prevented them from becoming good friends.

Another Dubliner, James Joyce, greatly admired Wilde. In the article he wrote on Wilde in Trieste, 'The Author of *Salomé*', discussed by Elisa Bizzotto in this volume, Joyce finds Wilde to be a deeply spiritual writer but declares that he cannot approve of Wilde's deathbed conversion to the Catholic Church. In recent years critics have attempted to assess Joyce's creative debt to Wilde: Franklin Walton, for instance, sees Wilde as 'a paradigm for the fallen father' in *Finnegan's Wake* and, while Sam Slote complicates and interrogates this image, he finds that Wilde is a dynamic creative presence in Joyce's work (Slote 1995). Walshe quotes Margot Backus's contention that references to the Wilde trials inform Joyce's epic novel, *Ulysses*. Walshe asserts that 'Joyce saw Wilde as an exemplar, refashioned in his own likeness as a subversive and a rebel, affording him both a counter-tradition of Irish dissent and also an attack against Ireland and Britain' (Walshe, forthcoming).

Contemporary Irish writers such as Colm Tóibín, Frank McGuinness, Thomas Kilroy and John Banville are greatly indebted to Wilde as their precursor; and, in view of the unambiguous reception of Wilde as Irish by his fellow countrymen and literary peers during his lifetime, it is surprising to find that for some part of the twentieth century Wilde was considered English by many of his Irish counterparts. Throughout the first half of the century Wilde's Irish identity was non-negotiable: Douglas Hyde claimed that Wilde's grandfather was a hedge schoolmaster from Connacht (1938b) and the newspaper notice of the sale of Moytura House, the one-time summer-house of the Wilde family in Galway/Mayo, designates the property as 'Oscar Wilde's *home*' (1949). The confusion over Wilde's identity seems to have occurred somewhere around the 1950s and persisted as late as 1984 when one of Ireland's foremost literary critics, Seamus Deane, labelled Wilde an English writer. In order to understand this we should consider some factors that might help to throw light upon it: Wilde's image in the literature and film of the period; the wide dissemination of his works through translation; language and location; and the complex Irish political situation.

Wilde's Englishness is, of course, a myth to whose invention Wilde contributed in his lifestyle and in his plays. But later writers such as Somerset Maugham, P. G. Wodehouse and Noel Coward retrospectively implicated Wilde as a quintessential Englishman in their derivative writings. This seemingly clear-cut image was accepted and propagated by their readers (Kiberd, personal communication). As early as 1908 Maugham is being compared to Wilde in the Irish media (1908b). Similarly, the image of Wilde projected through the many cinematic depictions of him and his work in the 1940s and '50s, figuring such actors as George Sanders who played superbly the ultra English Englishman, would have bolstered the idea of Wilde as English, further distancing him from his previously unquestioned Irish identity.

Irish literature has reached most of the world through translation and Wilde's works have been translated not only from English but also from French and German into various other languages. Somewhere along the way of this complex journey of reception it is possible that Wilde's roots may have become unhitched from their origins. A number of articles in the *Irish Times* address the question that Wilde was being conceived of as English by non-Irish nationals (see for instance 1938a). The fact that Wilde did not write explicitly about Ireland, that he set his plays and most of his fictional writings in England, and that he gained a reputation as the finest talker of his time in the English language would have encouraged people outside of Ireland to believe in his 'Englishness'. The fact that he left Ireland in his early twenties (his last letter addressed from Merrion Square Dublin is dated 1878) and lived for about twenty years in England and that his public trials took place there would have added to this perception. This external misapprehension may have contributed to the corrosion of his purchase on Irish identity at home and made it more possible for people to doubt his true Irishness – a sentiment which may have its roots in the bifurcated nature of Ireland's history and politics and the wider issue of Irish identity.

At the turn of the twentieth century hot debates raged in the pages of the Irish newspapers as to what constituted 'Irishness'. Parties such as newspaper owner D. P. Moran were of the opinion that Anglo-Irish writers like Congreve and Sheridan were not Irish as they were seen as writing in English for an English audience about English subjects. It was sometimes questioned whether it was possible for Anglo-Irish people to be fully Irish given their many connections with England. These were times of cultural revival and the remaking of a national identity. As the Irish Republic came into being these identity wars moved off centre stage but did not disappear. In the change from the old regime to a new order, Anglo-Ireland lost its central position of power and its people became more marginalized. To the new generations of middle-class Catholics, the Anglo-Irish were marked off by their tendency to live, work and socialize in particular areas and locations of the country. The accents and religion of the Anglo-Irish would also have been perceived as aligning them with the English neighbours. These attitudes towards Anglo-Ireland surfaced again in a discussion that arose in the pages of the *Irish Times* in 1954, the centenary of Wilde's birth. The debate on the question of Wilde's identity seems to have been started by Miles Na Gopaleen, aka the writer Flann O'Brien. O'Brien, who wrote a satirical column for the paper and was renowned for his mischievous wit and anarchic views, suggested, in jest or seriousness, that Wilde's birth in Ireland was but a geographical error (1954a). This allegation was met with a quick response from the paper's Letters Page: one correspondent cited an article written by Wilde in his youth in praise of Irish patriotism and the patriot William Smith O'Brien in particular, finishing the letter with the conviction that 'the spirit of the true Irishman was in the son of Speranza of the *Nation*' (1954b).

The identity controversy arose in response to the intention of Hilton Edwards and Micheál MacLiammóir to erect a plaque on Wilde's birthplace at number 21 Westland Row. Although relevant public bodies were contacted by them, no money was donated by official sources towards the project and the plaque was eventually erected by means of public subscription. Meanwhile in London a similar ceremony was planned to take place at Wilde's former home in Tite Street. At both of these ceremonies great emphasis was put on the fact that Wilde was an Irishman, presumably to counter the allegations being made in the national media. Lennox Robinson, who unveiled the plaque in Dublin, said that he 'wanted to stress Wilde's Irishness' and 'emphatically claim Wilde as a great Irish writer'. The Irish Ambassador attending the London event was reported by the *Irish Independent* to be 'appreciative of the references to his country, which were many and flattering' (18 October 1954, 8). One journalist, however, suggested that the two ceremonies marked the difference in national temperament, claiming that the occasion in England lacked humour and was like a memorial service; he observed that the Irish guests present looked on in some surprise as their hosts gravely mourned the passing of 'one of the funniest men who ever lived' (1954c). This columnist reports that the only humour in evidence at the dinner that followed the ceremony was directed at Wilde's national identity. This uneasy relationship between England and its former colony is reflected in a number of reports in the twentieth-century press of England's dismissal of the national identity of Irish dramatists, including Wilde, in favour of a British one.

The full reclamation of Wilde's Irish identity came with the advent of post-colonial theory and the publication of a number of books dealing with Wilde's Irishness, notably Richard Pine's pioneering work in the *Gill's Irish Lives* series, *Oscar Wilde* (1983) and, most crucially, Declan Kiberd's *Inventing Ireland* (1995) and Davis Coakley's biography, *Oscar Wilde: the Importance of Being Irish* (1995). Following these and several recent other studies, critics in Ireland and elsewhere have found many ways of engaging with the question of Wilde's Irishness (for an overview see Doody 2004). In a speech given to the Joint Houses of Parliament in Westminster on 15 May 2007, the then Irish Prime Minister, Taoiseach Bertie Ahern, expounded on the cultural interaction between Ireland and England describing the 'meeting between the English language and the Irish people' as 'one of the most creative moments in human history'; he cited writers such as Swift, Joyce, Wilde and Yeats, and declared that 'they all found their genius in the English language, but they drew on a perspective that was uniquely Irish'.

Dublin commemorates its writes by erecting monuments and statues to them and christening them anew: Brendan Behan's image sits on the banks of the Royal Canal on the north side of the city while the poet, Patrick Kavanagh, dubbed by Dublin wags 'The Crank on the Bank', gazes into the Grand Canal on Dublin's south side. James Joyce leans on his walking cane on Earl Street, just off Dublin's main thoroughfare, O'Connell Street, and is affectionately known as 'The Prick with the Stick'. Wilde's monument, which reclines on a large granite rock on Merrion Square, has been christened twice – in keeping with the intentions of the protagonists of *IBE* – and is named 'The Quare on the Square' and 'The Fag on the Crag'. This monument is often the recipient of floral tributes left by admirers at its side.

Wilde remains something of a national icon in Ireland and is very much a presence in the current cultural landscape. His various public commemorations include the monument by Danny Osborne on Merrion Square and, in the hallway of Wilde's former home on the Square, a stained glass window of the Happy Prince by artist Peadar Lamb, commissioned by Dublin's Oscar Wilde Society in 1995. In Galway a monument depicting Wilde in conversation with Eduard Vilde stands in the centre of the city. This sculpture was presented to the people of Galway by the people of Tartu, Estonia, in celebration of the Day of Welcome for the new accession states to the EU. The original of the monument is situated in Tartu outside *The Wilde Irish Pub*. The summer season is peak time for tourism and Wilde, along with other Irish writers, has been co-opted on to the cultural consumerism trail. Tales of Wilde feature hugely in the popular Dublin Pub Crawl while it is possible to eat at restaurants around the country named for Wilde: *Oscar's* in Enniskillen, the neighbourhood of Wilde's boyhood school, Portora Royal College, or *Wilde Oscar's* in Listowel, County Kerry. In 2007, in line with their policy of naming their ships for Irish literary figures, Irish Ferries christened their most recently acquired luxury cruise ship, which sails between Ireland and France, the *Oscar Wilde*. Images of Danny Osborne's Wilde Monument decorate the sides of Dublin tour buses, and this particular image of Wilde is also to be seen on the Government's official website. *The Oscar Wilde House*, Number 1, Merrion Square, is owned by the American College; it is open to the public on certain days of the week but operates full time as an institute of third-level education. A few kilometres down the street from Merrion Square, in Wilde's birthplace on Westland Row, *The Oscar Wilde Centre for Irish Writing* of Trinity College Dublin is also in use as a full-time establishment of learning for postgraduate students. These high-profile landmarks in the centre of the city fittingly commemorate Wilde's keen intellect and scholarship. Generations of secondary-level students have left Irish schools with a knowledge of Wilde's drama, as *IBE* has featured on the National Curriculum for secondary schools since the 1970s.

Wilde continues to inhabit theatrical circles: the sixth International Dublin Gay Theatre Festival, whose logo depicts Oscar Wilde with a green carnation held between his teeth, took place in 2009. Further afield, in Los Angeles, 'Oscar Wilde: Honouring the Irish in Film', the Irish-US Alliance's award, is presented annually at a pre-Oscars event. Wilde's popular appeal is such that his name, image and work are continuously employed in present-day Ireland to illustrate current problems and depict contemporary situations: he is rarely absent from the media but is alluded to and quoted on topics as diverse as climate change, fashion, property sales, literature and economics. In a recent report in the *Irish Times* on the current economic depression, in a practice established from his first appearance in the newspaper columns in Ireland, Wilde is aligned with his countrymen:

> The total lack of movement within the property market at the moment has resulted in fewer snippets of gossip and fewer tales to tell. But as a nation of professional talkers, if there isn't anything in particular to say, we'll just invent something. Perhaps Oscar Wilde was correct when he said, 'There is only one thing in the world worse than being talked about, and that is not being talked about'. There is no doubt that he was Irish. (2008)

3   The Artist as Aesthete:
The French Creation of Wilde

Richard Hibbitt

Before the month of December 1891, when Mr Wilde came to Paris, the English, his compatriots, did not know how to appreciate him. (Wyzewa 1892, 423)[1]

From our twenty-first-century perspective, the reception of Oscar Wilde in France seems remarkably modern. Wilde was a well-known figure in France before most people there had read any of his work; he was fêted by the mass media; he was adept at public relations. One might even advance the case for Wilde's being a celebrity *avant la lettre*, famous partly for being famous, albeit for more than fifteen minutes. Wilde's celebrity status in France can be attributed initially to two factors: he went to Paris with the specific aim of cultivating literary relationships, and he became a newsworthy figure for the vast number of daily newspapers and literary periodicals during the late nineteenth century.[2] The French creation of Wilde's persona as the archetypal English aesthete stems therefore both from his own self-publicizing and from the media's construction of this image. But the situation is of course more complex. The existential dimension of aestheticism inevitably encouraged an interest in his life as well as in his work. This interest was accentuated by

---

[1]   'Avant le mois de décembre 1891, où M. Wilde est venu à Paris, les Anglais, ses compatriotes, ne savaient pas l'apprécier.'

[2]   The number of daily newspapers published in Paris rose considerably during the late nineteenth century, encouraged by improved technology and the 1881 law which freed the press from state control. Often they consisted of only four pages and would contain serialized literary works alongside domestic and foreign current affairs, financial reports and advertisements. The reports on Wilde are frequently found in the society columns of papers such as *Le Figaro* or *L'Echo de Paris*, demonstrating both that he was known initially as a socialite rather than a writer and that readers were interested in the latest gossip. The reports on Wilde's writing tend to be found in monthly literary journals such as *La Plume* or *La Revue bleue*, although it will be shown here that many pieces combine references to his life and to his work. Many of the Parisian dailies had correspondents based in London: Jacques St.-Cere of *Le Figaro* was actually called to be a juror for Wilde and Taylor's second trial (Erber 1996, 563).

the fact that Wilde was renowned in France before most of his works had been translated into French, so the person preceded the work. In this respect the social reception of Wilde in France influenced the literary reception by creating the predominant image of Wilde as an artist of life.

The above claim by the critic Téodor de Wyzewa accords a particular significance to the French reception of Wilde: not only did the French appreciate Wilde before the English did, but it took the French reception to enlighten them. Wilde's own Francophilia and his knowledge of French literature are well known, as are the specific French influences on his own work.[3] The reciprocal influence of Wilde on French culture has also been explored in various studies, notably in Jacques de Langlade's *Oscar Wilde: Ecrivain français* (Oscar Wilde: French writer) (1975), whose title suggests that Wilde can be seen primarily as a French writer rather than an Irish or English one. Although Wilde is obviously not a French writer in the ways that, for example, either Samuel Beckett or Milan Kundera can be seen as French writers, this argument does not rest on the original language and production of *Salomé*, or on the fact that Wilde chose to live in France after his release from prison. For Langlade, the affinities between Wilde's aestheticism and the artistic currents of Symbolism and Decadence point to a shared conception of art which both transcends the national and simultaneously privileges French culture. If Wilde can be seen as a French writer in spirit, this can be attributed both to his Francophilia and to the role that France played in creating his reputation.

The reception of Wilde in France is partly due to the personal contacts he made during his various visits there, initially in 1883 but predominantly between 1891 and 1893. The roll-call of writers, painters, composers, actors, critics and journalists whom he met during the periods he spent in Paris reads like a *who's who* of *fin-de-siècle* French culture: Sarah Bernhardt, Claude Debussy, Edgar Degas, André Gide, Edmond de Goncourt, Victor Hugo, Joris-Karl Huysmans, Stéphane Mallarmé, Camille Pissarro, Marcel Proust, Henri de Toulouse-Lautrec, Paul Verlaine, Emile Zola. However, Gide aside, the most important contributions to his reception are provided by a host of less famous writers, translators and critics, of whom many were his junior, including Henry Bauër, Henry Davray, Ernest La Jeunesse, Jean Lorrain, Pierre Louÿs, Stuart Merrill, Octave Mirbeau, Hugues Rebell, Henri de Régnier, Marcel Schwob and Robert Sherard. Wilde's relationship to France has already been discussed in several biographies and critical works (Acquien 2006, Ellmann 1987, Erber 1996, Jullian 1971, Langlade 1975, Lemonnier

---

3   The French writers whom Wilde particularly admired included Honoré de Balzac, Charles Baudelaire, Gustave Flaubert, Théophile Gautier and George Sand, but he was of course familiar with contemporary *fin-de-siècle* writers such as Joris-Karl Huysmans and Rachilde. The combination of humorous dialogue between fictional characters and theoretical discussion employed in DL and CA also suggests a particular affinity with Denis Diderot's *Paradoxe sur le comédien* (1830). See Hartley 1935; cf. Wright 2008 for a recent discussion of some of the French books in Wilde's collection.

1931). The present essay explores how writers, critics and journalists created the French image of Wilde as an aesthete, focusing particularly on his visits to France in 1883 and 1891 and on the response to his trials and imprisonment in 1895.

2

In January 1883 Wilde went to Paris with the dual aim of writing and self-promotion (Ellmann 1985, 202–18). Although he was unknown there and his poetry had not been translated into French, he soon set about cultivating literary relationships by sending elegantly bound copies of *Poems* to several well-known writers, including Hugo, Mallarmé, Edmond de Goncourt, Catulle Mendès and Maurice Rollinat (Jullian 1971, 99). Wilde made the acquaintance of the American author and journalist Robert Sherard, who introduced him to a number of writers including Hugo, by then aged eighty-one; unfortunately Hugo fell asleep at the dinner table, thereby missing Wilde's discussions of Swinburne and other English poets (Langlade 1975, 20). He also met Stuart Merrill, an American-born poet who wrote in French, who was to become one of Wilde's friends and staunchest advocates. One of the earliest records of his reception in French artistic circles comes in the entry in Edmond de Goncourt's diary for 21 April 1883:

> The English poet Oscar Wilde told me this evening that the only Englishman who had read Balzac up to now was Swinburne. And this Swinburne, he portrays him to me as a braggart of vice, who had done everything to convince his fellow citizens of his pederasty and bestiality without being in the slightest way either a pederast or a bestialist. (Goncourt 1957, XIII, 28)[4]

Goncourt's comments show how Wilde's theatricality and love of the anecdote made an obvious impression. In his entry for 5 May 1883, Goncourt refers to him again as 'this poet and teller of implausible tales [...] this individual of doubtful gender, speaking the language of a ham actor, regaling us with his banter' (1957, XIII, 32).[5] Although the one evening he spent with Verlaine failed to make a good impression on either of them, Sarah Bernhardt was impressed by the fact that, unlike most men, his acts of friendship did not conceal a desire to seduce her (Langlade 1975, 21). He also forged friendships with the actor, Coquelin, and the painter, Jacques-Emile Blanche. However, the excessive cost of this lifestyle eventually forced Wilde to return

---

4   'Le Poète anglais Oscar Wilde me disait, ce soir, que le seul Anglais qui avait lu Balzac à l'heure actuelle était Swinburne. Et ce Swinburne, il me le montre comme un fanfaron de vice, qui avait tout fait pour faire croire ses concitoyens à sa pédérastie, à sa bestialité, sans être le moins du monde pédéraste ni bestialitaire.'
5   'ce poète aux récits invraisemblables [...] cet individu au sexe douteux, au langage de cabotin, aux récits blagueurs.' In the same entry Goncourt relates a tale Wilde told about an American theatre company engaging a recently freed poisoner to play Lady Macbeth.

to England, where he gave lectures on his impressions of America. There is little evidence of further French reception in the 1880s except for one of the first recorded translations of Wilde's works, an unsigned French version of BI entitled 'L'Anniversaire de la petite infante', translated by Stuart Merrill and published alongside the original English version in the journal *Paris Illustré* on 30 March 1889.

3

When Wilde returned to Paris in 1891 he was now an established writer whose reputation had spread to France, although his actual works were still relatively unknown there and no further translations had appeared (Ellmann 1987, 316–41). The vast amount of literary contacts which Wilde made testifies to a crucial change in his social and literary position: the overtures that he made to other writers were now gradually reciprocated. On 24 February 1891 he attended for the first time one of Mallarmé's famous *mardis*, the Tuesday evening soirées renowned for their discussions of art (Clive 1970). The following day Wilde wrote to thank him for his hospitality and to congratulate him on his translation of Poe's 'The Raven' ('Le Corbeau'). Later that year Wilde gave him an inscribed copy of *PDG*, which Mallarmé discussed in a letter to Wilde dated 10 November:

> I am finishing the book, one of the few that has the capacity to move, given that its turmoil is composed of an essential reverie and the strangest perfumes of the soul. That it again becomes poignant, thanks to the unprecedented intellectual refinement, and human, in such a perverse atmosphere of beauty, is a miracle that you have accomplished, and with what use of all the writer's arts!
> 'It was the portrait that had done everything.' This full-length portrait, troubling, of Dorian Gray, will haunt, but in written form, having become a book itself. (Mallarmé 1973, 327–28) [6]

Wilde's own admiration for Mallarmé's work is of course particularly evident in the preface to *PDG*, which shows a clear debt to Mallarmé's views of poetry and to related ideas common to Symbolism. However, although Mallarmé's appreciation of *PDG* is a rare example of a reception of the work rather than the person, the characteristically private nature of his appraisal meant that it would not exert a great influence on Wilde's public status.

Wilde also became acquainted with a younger generation of French writers and began to acquire potential translators for his works. Marcel Schwob

---

6   'J'achève le livre, un des seuls qui puissent émouvoir, vu que d'une rêverie essen-
tielle et des parfums d'âme les plus étranges s'est fait son orage. Redevenir poignant
à travers l'inouï raffinement d'intellect, et humain, en une pareille perverse atmos-
phère de beauté, est un miracle que vous accomplissez et selon quel emploi de tous
les arts de l'écrivain!
   "It was the portrait that had done everything." Ce portrait en pied, inquiétant,
d'un Dorian Gray, hantera, mais écrit, étant devenu livre lui-même.'

translated SG, published as 'Le Géant égoïste' in the daily newspaper *L'Echo de Paris* (The Paris echo) on 27 December 1891; Schwob and Jean Lorrain both dedicated tales to Wilde (Erber 1996, 554; Langlade 1975, 31). He was also invited into some of the fashionable salons of the day and consequently his reputation spread beyond the literary world into the society pages of the newspapers, transforming him into a public figure. On 2 December 1891 a piece by the journalist Hugues Le Roux entitled 'Oscar Wilde' appeared in *Le Figaro*, introducing Wilde as an Irish writer renowned in the Anglophone world. Le Roux states that Wilde's popularity is associated with his person as much as his works, setting the tone for the subsequent French reception. Although Wilde is introduced by the salon hostess in hushed tones as the author of *PDG*, the novel itself remains a somewhat mystical tome which very few people in France have actually read. Le Roux then gives a short biographical sketch of Wilde, explaining how he swiftly gained a reputation in London due to his aesthetic philosophy, his brilliant conversation and his curiously masculine-cum-feminine appearance. This is followed by a translation of a paragraph from DL on art and reality and by a discussion of the poem 'Charimydis' (*sic.*), which Le Roux considers to encapsulate Wilde's aesthetic theory with regard to the worship of Beauty. He explains how this theory influences life as a whole rather than art alone, citing the tale of Wilde's appearance in Piccadilly dressed in medieval costume and holding a sunflower. The piece ends by contrasting Wilde's admirable ability to 'live out his dream in its entirety' ('vivre tout son rêve') with the sad conditions faced by contemporary French artists, who are sterilized by the fear of prejudice, indifference or ridicule.

Le Roux's favourable portrayal was followed by an interview with Wilde by the journalist Jacques Daurelle, published in *L'Echo de Paris* on 6 December 1891. Daurelle's piece describes meeting Wilde with Stuart Merrill and the young French poet Henri de Régnier. Merrill explains to the journalist that Wilde is an English writer who is virtually unknown in France due to the paucity of translated works, describing *Poems* as a masterpiece and HP and *HOP* as 'delicious' ('délicieux') (1891, 2). Merrill then relates some anecdotes about Wilde's life (his appearance, his witty remarks, his eccentricities, his penchant for exotic objects), insisting that this behaviour is not a 'pose' but is motivated by sincerity, and emphasizing Wilde's credentials as both writer and aesthete by aligning him with Gautier rather than with the Sar Péladan.[7] Daurelle recounts how this initial meeting led to an interview with Wilde in his hotel, in which Wilde spoke of how much he loved Paris, French courtly romances and contemporary French poetry. Daurelle asks Wilde whether the anecdotes one hears about him are true, to which he replies that what is true about a man is not what he does, but 'the legend which is created around him';[8] Wilde illustrates the point by stating that he had never actually paraded

---

[7]   The Sar Péladan (1859–1918), best known as the founder of the Rosicrucian Order and author of the fourteen-volume novel *La Décadence latine*, was widely regarded as a self-publicist.

[8]   'la légende qui se crée autour de lui'.

in the streets of London holding a lily, but that this myth revealed his character more than if it had been true (1891, 2).

This burgeoning interest in Wilde was intensified by the coincidental publication in *L'Echo de Paris* of Edmond de Goncourt's aforementioned diary entry from 21 April 1883, which was part of the ongoing serialization of his *Journal* (Goncourt 1891). Anxious to rectify the impression that he had referred to Swinburne as 'a braggart of vice', Wilde wrote an open letter to Goncourt which was published in *L'Echo de Paris* on 19 December (Wilde 1891a).[9] In the letter Wilde hastens to correct what he perceives to be a misunderstanding due to his own poor command of French, lavishing praise on both Goncourt and Swinburne and explaining that he was referring to the reception of Swinburne by the ignorant English public rather than to his own opinion. Interestingly, Wilde begins the letter by stating that 'the intellectual basis of my aesthetic is the Philosophy of Unreality', jokingly confirming the impression that he is a fantasist, although it is clear from his tone that he is serious about rectifying the mistake (1891, 2).[10] The editor introduces Wilde as '[o]ne of the greatest personalities of contemporary English literature, the aesthete Oscar Wilde, who is at present our guest and the *Great Event* of the Parisian literary salons' (Wilde 1891, 2).[11] Wilde is perceived here primarily as an aesthete and thereafter as a literary personality or 'Great Event'; there is no mention of his works, to the extent that the uninitiated reader might conclude that he was simply a society figure and literary raconteur rather than a published critic, novelist, playwright and poet. This emphasis on the element of performance – of life as the work of art – epitomizes the French reception.

The closing weeks of December 1891 saw the apogee of the initial French interest in Wilde (Ellmann 1987, 326–41). On 15 December, Maurice Barrès gave a dinner in his honour; Wilde met Léon Daudet, Anatole France, Huysmans and Jean Moréas *inter alios*; he was invited by Zola, but the two men did not find much common ground for discussion (Langlade 175, 31–32).[12] Wilde was also introduced to Proust, who impressed him with his knowledge of English literature, especially Ruskin. Although they did not develop their acquaintance, Proust was to refer to Wilde again in his later work (see the chapter by Emily Eells in this volume).[13] He had also made the acquaintance of two other young writers, Pierre Louÿs and André Gide. Gide's subsequent writings on Wilde would play a central role in his posthumous reception in France, as Victoria Reid's chapter in this volume shows. While working on *Salomé* during

---

[9]   The letter, written in French and dated 17 December 1891, is reprinted in Hart-Davis 1979, 100–01.

[10] '[quoique] la base intellectuelle de mon esthétique soit La Philosophie de l'Irréalité'.

[11] 'Une des plus grandes personnalités de la littérature anglaise contemporaine, l'esthète Oscar Wilde, qui est en ce moment notre hôte et le *Great Event* des salons littéraires parisiens.'

[12] Moréas, best known as the writer of the Symbolist manifesto, did not take kindly to a rival writer and raconteur on his home territory, remarking that 'this Englishman [*sic.*] is a pain in the arse' ('cet Anglais est emmerdant') (Ellmann 1987, 328).

[13] For an account of Proust's comically failed attempt to have Wilde dine with his family, see Ellmann 1987, 327–28.

November and December 1891, Wilde sent Louÿs a draft version, asking him to correct any mistakes in the French. In February 1892 Wilde invited him to London to see *LWF*, which was being performed for the first time. However, although Louÿs appreciated the artistic value of both *PDG* and *Salomé*, his letters to his brother from London show that his apprehension of homosexuality meant that he was unsure about Wilde's character and the influence of his company (Clive 1969; Langlade 1975, 34–39). Wilde's letters to Louÿs show how his initial pleasure in his company was gradually replaced by disappointment, particularly at the younger man's muted response to having *Salomé* dedicated to him.[14] Louÿs's decision to distance himself from Wilde represents a new tendency in the reception, marking the point where fear of being associated with a homosexual influenced those who might otherwise have championed his work in public.

In April 1892 the first extensive critical assessment of Wilde's work was published, a six-page article in *La Revue bleue* (Blue review) entitled 'M. Oscar Wilde et les jeunes littérateurs anglais' (Mr Oscar Wilde and the young English writers) by the critic Téodor de Wyzewa (1892), co-editor of the Symbolist journal *La Revue wagnérienne* (Wagnerian review). The article begins with the claim that forms the epigraph to the present essay, namely that the French had revealed Wilde's genius to the English three months earlier (Wyzewa 1892, 423). But this apparent praise is immediately tempered by the assertion that the English had hitherto considered Wilde to be a mediocre novelist, poet and critic, whose only outstanding feature is a heightened predilection for paradox concerning the choice of his ties and his ideas. Wyzewa's sardonic zeugma sets the tone for the rest of his piece, in which he comments that the only work of Wilde's that the French have seen is a little moral tale without great importance, presumably referring to Schwob's translation of SG. However, since Wilde was introduced to them as 'the prince of the mysterious tribe of English *aesthetes*' ('le prince de la mystérieuse tribu des *esthètes* anglais'), the French were still happy to embrace him with open arms. Wyzewa sees this uncritical reception as part of a wider trend of recent French Anglophilia centred around the alluring terms *esthète* and *préraphaélite*, citing the names of Shelley, Keats and Rossetti as other examples. On Wilde's arrival in France in 1891, as a result of the media interest, the French public soon considered Wilde to be England's national young poet (1892, 424). Wyzewa then argues that the English were initially mystified by the French reception of Wilde, but eventually assumed that it was because he possessed an eminently Parisian talent, which is automatically equated with elegance. Wilde's subsequent reception in England therefore rested on a similar acceptance (and confusion) of national stereotypes: 'And this is how Mr Wilde, who became famous in France as an English aesthete, has become famous in his country as a Parisian entertainer' (Wyzewa 1892, 424).[15]

---

14 See Wilde's letters to Louÿs dated 28 November 1891, December 1891 and 27 February 1893, in Hart-Davis 1979, 96–97, 101 and 110–11.

15 'Et voila comment M. Wilde, devenu fameux chez nous en qualité d'esthète anglais, est devenu fameux dans son pays en qualité de fantaisiste parisien.' The word 'fantaisiste' has several meanings, including 'variety artist', 'entertainer' and 'eccentric', with pejorative connotations of shallowness.

Wyzewa's hypothesis is unsubstantiated and his conflation of aestheticism and Pre-Raphaelitism reveals the limitations of his knowledge of Wilde. Moreover, his evaluation of Wilde's French reception in 1891 seems largely to be based on the pieces by Daurelle and Le Roux discussed above. As for Wilde's works, he claims that the success of *LWF* in London is due to this impression that it is 'Parisian' – a term understood by its audience as synonymous with a disregard for verisimilitude and a penchant for word play. For Wyzewa however, Wilde is no more than 'a banal copyist' ('un banal polygraphe') (1892, 425). He claims that Wilde's poems are decent imitations of Swinburne and Rossetti, or reminiscent of translations of Baudelaire, suggesting that not even their author considered them to be of great value. As for the moral tales (he lists HP, NR, SG and DF), they are prettily written and illustrated, but no more than agreeable trifles which conceal Wilde's personality rather than revealing it. Wyzewa dismisses *PDG* as simply 'a bad novel' ('un mauvais roman'), comparing it to an adventure novel which supports Wilde's theories by suppressing emotion; the one exception is the description of the character of Sibyl Vane, which he considers to be a decent chapter in the style of Dickens (Wyzewa 1892, 426).

The one work that Wyzewa deems worthy of keeping is *Intentions*, which he believes is able to give a clear idea of the author's personality. He argues that Wilde's aim of surprising his reader is laudable if it is linked to an interesting critical purpose; however, he criticizes Wilde for merely affirming and repeating the tenets of his aesthetic theory rather than developing them. Wyzewa also claims that Wilde's theories are in essence no more than the doctrine of *l'art pour l'art* pushed to the extreme; although these are already familiar to the French, Wilde has now become the spokesman for a new generation of writers because he was the first to affirm them so openly in England (1892, 427). In this respect, Wyzewa argues, *Intentions* is interesting because it portrays a particular contemporary English perspective on literature, centred on Oxford and characterized by the tendency to reject conventional views of art and morality. Wyzewa claims that the current English interest in Mallarmé and Verlaine is based on a desire to imitate the French vogue for Symbolism, a literary movement whose principles and works are hard enough for the French to understand, let alone the English; consequently they gain their knowledge from 'easier' writers such as Baudelaire, Flaubert and Gautier. Wyzewa concludes his discussion by asserting that all of Wilde's aesthetic theories derive from Gautier, referring in particular to Gautier's preface to the posthumous third edition of Baudelaire's *Les Fleurs du Mal* (*Flowers of Evil*) (1892, 427). The article ends with the claim that none of the young people who venerated Wilde during his visit to Paris would agree with his outmoded theories; unlike Mallarmé, Verlaine or Dickens, Wilde's view of literature remains focused on artificiality and is devoid of philosophical, moral and emotional engagement (1892, 428).

It is easy to find flaws in Wyzewa's argument. Like many polemics, it rests on a dogmatic perspective which ignores exception or relativism, such as the possibility that some English writers might be able to understand Symbolism (there is no reference to Wilde's preface to *PDG*). However, his points about the role that self-publicity and media interest played in the French reception of Wilde are astute. Moreover, his praise for Dickens in the article shows that his criticism is not merely jingoistic. Wyzewa's dismissal of Wilde can mainly be attributed to his specific conception of literature: when he writes that Wilde and his young compatriots believe that 'these paradoxes and this way of repeating them are the latest fashion in French dilettantism today' (1892, 428),[16] he is locating Wilde within a particular sphere of contemporary French discourse where dilettantism refers to a critical disposition that embraces contradiction and paradox and refuses to take a specific position. This dilettantism, initially identified as a positive quality by Paul Bourget in an 1882 essay on Ernest Renan, prefigures to some extent Wilde's own disposition and places him in a French tradition that Wyzewa rejects.[17]

Wilde's celebrity status in France began to wane after 1892, partly because rumours concerning his homosexuality exerted a detrimental influence and many of his acquaintances avoided him.[18] There are however two examples of individual reception before the watershed year of 1895 which provide an interesting counterweight to Wyzewa's article. In March 1893, Stuart Merrill published a three-page portrait of him in the new literary magazine *La Plume*, which would play a central role in supporting Wilde during his trials and imprisonment. Merrill introduces Wilde as the master of the aesthetic school in England, explaining how he had been influenced by Pre-Raphaelitism as a student (1893, 116). After a synopsis of English aestheticism, Merrill turns his attention to Wilde's works, commenting approvingly on *Poems*, defending him from accusations of being merely an imitator of Keats and Gautier and emphasizing the authenticity of his masterpieces. He praises both *PDG* and *Intentions*, referring to Wilde's skilful employment of the maieutic method and to his use of the paradox as an aesthete rather than as a sophist (1893, 117). The summary of Wilde's work ends with a reference to the sharp social satire of *LWF* and to Merrill's hope that Sarah Bernhardt might one day be able to play the lead role in *Salomé*. However, the piece is not an unconditional panegyric, as Merrill distinguishes between Wilde and the 'demi-gods' ('demi-dieux') of Tennyson, Rossetti and Swinburne, claiming that the modest Wilde himself refuses to be ranked alongside them. This reservation notwithstanding, Merrill affirms the certainty of Wilde's posterity and concludes by emphasizing his 'mysterious gift of illusion' ('mystérieux don d'illusion') (1893, 118).

Another positive response to Wilde's work was given by Anatole France, who met him at a society lunch given in Wilde's honour named 'le déjeuner mauve' (the purple luncheon). In a piece published in *L'Univers illustré* (The illustrated universe) on 10 June 1893, France recounts his experience of the

---

[16]   'ces paradoxes et cette manière de les répéter sont la dernière expression du dilet-tantisme français d'aujourd'hui'.

[17]   It is possible that Wyzewa's article also exerted a direct influence on Hermann Bahr's 1894 essay 'Décadence' (Bahr 1968), where Bahr dismisses Wilde and Robert de Montesquiou-Fezensac as dilettantes whose works are limited by their sterility.

[18]   Edmond de Goncourt's diary entry for 30 April 1893 (1956, IXX, 107), unpublished at the time, shows that Wilde's 'pederasty' was already discussed in France, albeit in private circles.

purple-themed event, which included a reading from one of Wilde's works. France introduces Wilde as an 'English symbolist' ('symboliste anglais'), describing him as the founder of a new aesthetic and speaking of his attempt 'to draw his compatriots and contemporaries towards the exclusive worship of the Beautiful' ('ramener ses compatriotes et ses contemporains au culte exclusif du Beau') (1893, 318). France's appraisal serves as a direct riposte to Wyzewa's dismissal of Wilde's aesthetic theories on the grounds of unoriginality, portraying him as a Symbolist writer who has invented a new aesthetic based on the principal tenet of *l'art pour l'art*. One can surmise that Wilde would have been delighted by such praise. The remainder of the piece serves once more as a biographical introduction to Wilde, which is then illustrated by a long passage from CA translated into French (France 1893, 318). France doubtlessly recognized in Wilde's writing his own belief in the essentially personal nature of criticism: France's own earlier dictum that 'the good critic is the one who relates the adventures of his soul among masterpieces' shows a clear affinity with Wilde's ideas (France, 1888, iii–iv).[19]

The debate about the moral responsibility of art catalyzed by *l'art pour l'art* and again by Decadence was revived in the early 1890s by an exchange between Anatole France and the conservative critic Ferdinand Brunetière regarding the artist's freedom. Brunetière (1892) criticized the moral relativism of the so-called 'impressionist criticism' favoured by France and Jules Lemaître. Wilde's own view of the critic as artist clearly corresponds to the notion of impressionist criticism, and these affinities between Wilde and contemporary French views on criticism and literature complicate Wyzewa's claim that Wilde's art was merely derivative. For Merrill and Anatole France, as for Mallarmé before, Wilde's art possessed particular qualities which transcended imitation, posing and sophistry. These conflicting views of Wilde *qua* artist and aesthete would become part of the moral debate which would bring him once more under the French media's spotlight.

4

If 1891 can be viewed as the birth of Wilde's reception in France, 1895 and 1896 can be seen as the time of its simultaneous maturity and decline. This is due to the fact that Wilde's trials and imprisonment coincided with the publication of the first French translation of *PDG* in June 1895 and the first performance of *Salomé* in Paris, in February 1896. As Emily Eells shows in the following chapter, the French reception of these two works is inseparable from Wilde's personal circumstances at the time; as in England, the reception of Wilde in France was indelibly marked by the scandal. The court cases and sentence generated an enormous amount of press coverage in France, polarizing opinion and eliciting comments on British morality and parallels with the ongoing Dreyfus case (Erber 1996, Langlade 1994). Many of the pieces

---

[19] 'Le bon critique est celui qui raconte les aventures de son âme au milieu des chefs-d'œuvre'.

published in defence of Wilde have now been collected in the volume *Pour Oscar Wilde: Des écrivains français au secours du condamné* (For Oscar Wilde: French writers in support of the convict) (Brunet 1994). For our purposes the most interesting aspect of the French reaction to Wilde's imprisonment concerns the ways in which the issue of homosexuality was linked to Wilde's image as the quintessential English aesthete.

Before news of the first trial broke, Wilde had virtually disappeared off the radar of the French press. One exception is a review on 20 February 1895 in *Le Petit Temps* of the concurrent first performances of *IH* and *IBE*, written by the paper's London correspondent and signed by the initials F. O. The review begins by describing how the English had managed to prevent their prodigal son from carrying out his threat to leave them and to live in Paris. As for the two comedies, the author suggests that the audience's laughter showed that Wilde was a good judge of his public; although the content is not particularly new or original, it is at least funny (F. O. 1895, 1). The news of Wilde's libel suit and the Marquis of Queensberry's acquittal on 4 April was quickly reported in France: the following day a report appeared in *Le Figaro*, commenting on Wilde's performance in the court (Villars 1895a). The trial was excitedly described as 'the London scandal' ('le scandale de Londres'), presented as if it were a piece of theatre itself (Villars 1895b). The French press covered the events with great interest and for a while it was suggested that Wilde might try to flee the country and take refuge in France (Ellmann 1987, 426–28). On 6 April, Wilde's friend Henry Bauër, a journalist, critic and dramatist, published a front-page article in *L'Echo de Paris*, emphasizing Wilde's qualities as both writer and raconteur, whilst referring to England as his 'ungrateful homeland' and lambasting its 'profound moral hypocrisy' (Bauër 1895a, 1).[20] On the same day Wilde was arrested, charged with 'committing indecent acts' and refused bail. The following morning (7 April) the case was on the front page of *Le Figaro* under the sub-heading of 'Esthètes' ('Echos: Esthètes' 1895, 1), where the anonymous writer proposed a clear if implicit link between aestheticism and homosexuality. Beginning by mentioning the instructive 'lessons in aestheticism' ('des leçons d'esthétisme') which the English are now providing, the article suggests that the 'deviation of certain literary faculties towards a refined sensualism' ('la déviation de certaines facultés littéraires vers un sensualisme raffiné') can exert an influence on personal morals. Preferring not to draw any conclusions about specifically English morals, the writer then claims that the moral well-being of Europe as a whole is at stake:

> The most significant factor, as far as the right direction for the public spirit throughout Europe is concerned, is to determine how an aesthetic movement can collapse into the mud, and in this respect the case of Mr Oscar Wilde is fairly convincing. ('Echos: Esthètes' 1895, 1)[21]

---

20 'son ingrate patrie [...] profondément hypocrite dans toutes les questions de morale'.
21 'Il importe seulement à la bonne direction de l'esprit public dans toute l'Europe

The remainder of the piece traces this moral decline back through the Pre-Raphaelites to Carlyle, ending by asking aesthetes to moderate their behaviour in order to safeguard French morals and the French spirit. The article is characteristic of the popular reactionary outlook in France during the 1890s, which conflated literary Decadence with moral decadence and eschewed foreign cosmopolitan influences in favour of nationalism and Catholicism. It shows how Wilde's case became part of the ongoing debate about morals and aesthetics that divided French opinion, overlapping with the questions of national security, integrity and anti-Semitism that instigated the Dreyfus affair. Elements of homophobia, jingoism and inverted snobbery can be found in a number of French reports of the trial (Langlade 1975, 43–45).[22] A portrait entitled 'Pastel Cruel' (Cruel sketch), signed George Bec and published in *L'Echo de Paris* on 11 April, excoriates Wilde as a vain, rich and talentless vaudevillian who is admired by the snobs from *La Revue blanche* (White review); the author revels in Wilde's downfall, referring to his fondness for 'little boys' ('petits garçons') and suggesting that he must now explain to the judge why he walked down Piccadilly holding a lily (Bec 1895). Here aestheticism itself is in the dock and Wilde becomes the scapegoat for its perceived decadence.

The opprobrium facing Wilde was swiftly directed at his Parisian friends and acquaintances: on 13 April the journalist Jules Huret (1895, 59) wrote in *Le Figaro* that the writers Jean Lorrain, Catulle Mendès and Marcel Schwob had been among Wilde's close acquaintances ('familiers'). Mendès denied the accusation and fought a duel with Huret; Schwob also denied it and challenged Huret to a duel which was not fought (Ellmann 1987, 430 and 577–79). Although he denied being close to Wilde, the novelist and journalist Lorrain (himself gay) published an article in *L'Echo de Paris* on 27 April, a day after Wilde's first trial had opened, in which he denounced the English legal system for accusing Wilde and Alfred Taylor whilst allowing the evidence of unreliable witnesses. Wilde was visited in Pentonville jail by the London-based journalist Ange Goldemar, who reported on the difficulty of the forced labour in a front-page article in *Le Gaulois* on 13 June 1895.[23] The report provoked

---

de déterminer comment un mouvement esthétique peut s'effondrer dans la boue; et sur ce point le cas de M. Oscar Wilde est assez probant.'

22 Homosexuality was not technically illegal in France at the time: the Revolution had abolished the crime of sodomy in 1791 and the Napoleonic Code of 1810 did not reintroduce it, although it did establish offences of 'affronts to public decency' and 'incitement to debauchery and corruption of young persons under the age of twenty-one', both of which could be used against homosexuals (Robinson 1995, 2). The terms 'homosexuel' and 'homosexualité' themselves are rarely found before 1891(Robinson 1995, 7). Publishing offences could however be punished by trial by jury, so writers and editors were forced to find a balance between clarity and euphemism in their references to Wilde's trials in order to avoid possible charges of indecency or inciting corruption. In other words, a form of self-censorship influenced both the attacks on Wilde and the articles in support of him.

23 After his transfer to Wandsworth jail Wilde was observed in the exercise yard by a

immediate outrage from some quarters: on 15 June, Henry Bauër published a piece in *L'Echo de Paris* entitled 'Oscar Wilde en prison' (Oscar Wilde in gaol), calling on the French to protest against the severity of the sentence (1895b); on 16 June, Octave Mirbeau published 'A propos du "Hard Labour"' (On 'Hard Labour') in *Le Journal*, criticizing the barbarity of the English legal system *tout court* (1895). Although Gide and Louÿs remained silent, other writers also defended Wilde in public and criticized the English attitude towards his 'crime', including the novelist and dramatist Paul Adam (1895), the critic and editor Louis Lormel (1895), the poet and novelist Hugues Rebell (1895), the poet, novelist and essayist Henri de Régnier (1895) and the poet and pamphleteer Laurent Tailhade (1895a). The support for Wilde proved that certain writers and critics refused to let the conservative critique of his actions lead to a blanket rejection of his work. The parallels with the support in the British press for Alfred Dreyfus, who was imprisoned on Devil's Island at the same time, show that Wilde's case had become a similar *cause célèbre* which raised interesting questions of national characteristics and double standards (Langlade 1994).

In October, Robert Sherard visited Wilde in the prison infirmary at Wandsworth, describing his poor health in a letter to Stuart Merrill. Moved by Wilde's plight, Merrill wrote an open letter to Léon Deschamps, editor of *La Plume*, calling on writers in France and England to sign a petition demanding Wilde's release. Merrill claims that a great artist is being slowly killed by the authorities not because of his alleged vice, but 'because of hatred of that Beauty of which he was the apostle, in his life as in his work, and of which he is now the martyr, like Byron and Shelley before him' (1895, 508).[24] He condemns the hypocritical bourgeois society for punishing Wilde while covering up for others and argues that the petition needs names that are familiar to the European public, suggesting Zola, Goncourt, José-Maria Hérédia, Alphonse Daudet, François Coppée, Swinburne, Thomas Hardy and Henry James *inter alios* (1895, 509). On 1 December, Deschamps and Merrill (1895, 559) launched the petition in *La Plume* under the name 'L'Affaire Oscar Wilde' (The case of Oscar Wilde), addressing it to 'Her Most Excellent Majesty the Queen' and pleading for clemency 'in the name of art and humanity' ('au nom de l'humanité et de l'art').

The petition was not a success. Although writers including Maurice Barrès and Paul Bourget agreed to sign, Zola, Goncourt, Alphonse Daudet and others refused (Langlade 1975, 49–50). Merrill and Deschamps initially addressed the petition to twenty named prominent writers, but Wilde's supporters also asked to sign it.[25] The following day François Coppée, a well-known poet and

---

group of journalists including Gaston Routier (1895), who commented in *L'Echo de Paris* on 31 July that the shaven-headed Wilde was barely recognizable.

[24] 'par haine de cette Beauté dont il fut, dans sa vie comme dans ses écrits, l'apôtre, et dont il est, après Byron et Shelley, le martyr'.

[25] Henry Bauër (1895c) wrote an article in support of the petition, asking to be allowed to sign it; Laurent Tailhade (1895b) urged other writers to sign; Henri de Régnier (1895) wrote a piece in which he defended Wilde's character. Ellmann (1987, 463) states that Gide signed the petition, although I can find no evidence to support this.

dramatist, wrote a front-page article in *Le Journal* in which he remembered Wilde simply as an 'insufferable poser' ('un insupportable poseur'); despite his disdain for Wilde's person and work Coppée criticizes the barbarity of the sentence, caustically joking that he will sign the petition 'as a member of the Society for Prevention of Cruelty to Animals' ('Membre de la Société protectrice des Animaux') (1895, 1). In an article published in *La Plume* on 1 January 1896, Merrill expressed his surprise and regret at the mixed reaction, claiming that the late Victor Hugo would not have refused to sign because of fears of association with Wilde (1896, 10). Merrill also attributes to Coppée the damning anonymous statement that 'a writer pig is no less a pig' ('un cochon artiste n'en est pas moins un cochon') (1896, 9). In the end the petition was not sent because of the lukewarm response, a fate that was also to befall the two London petitions (Ellmann 1987, 463).[26] Despite the best intentions of Wilde's supporters, the failure of the French petition proved that he remained ostracized by mainstream opinion and that the reception of Wilde in France was not as radically different as some might have believed.

5

The premiere of *Salomé* in Paris, on 11 February 1896, enabled Wilde to be discussed for his work once more. In the September 1896 edition of *La Revue blanche*, Rachilde, novelist and chief literary critic for *Le Mercure de France*, wrote in support of Wilde and Douglas in the context of wider reflections on male and female homosexuality and gender equality.[27] When Edmond de Goncourt died on 15 July 1896, his will stipulated that the Académie Goncourt should be created in his memory (it was eventually established in 1902). Although Mirbeau thought at the time that Wilde should be considered for one of the vacant places, his seemed to be a lone voice (Langlade 1975, 53). One can only hypothesize about the effect that such an acceptance might have had on Wilde's status in France and the bleak years preceding his death, had he returned there after his release from prison to be welcomed into the French literary establishment as one of their own.

Although Wilde spent most of the period between May 1897 and his death in November 1900 in France, he was no longer front-page news. Several former acquaintances now shunned him because of his reputation, although Merrill, Gide, Henry Davray and the young critic Ernest La Jeunesse continued to see him, and he met Jarry, Rachilde and Maeterlinck. He also enjoyed some literary recognition: after its original publication on 13 February 1898, Henry Davray's French translation of *BRG* (*Ballade de la geôle de Reading*) appeared later that year with the prestigious Mercure de France publishing

---

[26] Erber refers to a similar petition organized by Belgian writers (1996, 552).

[27] Douglas (1896) had published a frank article entitled 'Une introduction à mes poèmes, avec quelques considérations sur l'affaire Oscar Wilde' (An introduction to my poems, with some thoughts on the Oscar Wilde affair), which accompanied the publication of some of his poems in the May edition of *La Revue blanche*.

house. The critic Léon Souguenet reviewed the book favourably in *La Plume* on 1 February 1899, commenting that Wilde had replaced the exasperating paradoxes of his earlier works with a new sincerity: 'A man shows himself here to be simply human: a soul reveals itself *in its beauty*' (Souguenet 1899, 86).[28] But Wilde was largely a forgotten man; the years 1897–99 were the height of the Dreyfus affair (Zola's article 'J'accuse' appeared on 13 January 1898), and the public interest had moved on from debates over aestheticism.[29]

Wilde's death merited far fewer column inches than his trials. Jean Lorrain wrote a front-page obituary for *Le Journal* on 6 December 1900; the novelist Lucien Muhlfeld another piece for *Le Journal* on 21 December. Ernest La Jeunesse published a melancholy eulogy in *La Revue blanche* on 15 December; Stuart Merrill wrote a characteristically sympathetic obituary for *La Plume*, reaffirming the value of Wilde's work while condemning his treatment. The journalists of *Le Figaro* were no longer interested in Wilde but his old and new supporters ensured that he was commemorated. Whilst Wilde was still alive, Octave Mirbeau (1983) presented a fictional portrait of him in *Le Journal d'une femme de chambre* (*The Diary of a Chambermaid*), his critique of the Dreyfus era, which was serialized in *La Revue blanche* in 1900. Wilde is the model for the character of Sir Harry Kimberly, introduced as a 'Symbolist musician [and] fervent pederast' accompanied by 'his young friend Lucien Sartorys, as beautiful as a woman' (Mirbeau 1983, 206).[30] In an analeptic chapter the eponymous chambermaid describes a society dinner held by one of her previous employers, in which Kimberly recounts a dinner given in London by the well-known poet John-Giotto Farfadetti (a somewhat unconvincing pseudonym for Dante Gabriel Rossetti). Kimberly's anecdote enables Mirbeau to depict Wilde's flair as a raconteur, culminating in a characteristic epigram: 'The soul does not have a gender' ('Les âmes n'ont pas de sexe') (1983, 218). This thinly veiled portrait confirms the prevalent image of Wilde as gay aesthete and wit. Jean Lorrain also used him as the model for the characters Lord Ethal in *Monsieur de Phocas* (1901) and Filde in *Le Vice errant* (1902) (The errant vice). However, the posthumous reception by Gide, Cocteau, Proust, Raymond Laurent, Léon Guillot de Saix and others discussed elsewhere in this volume – not to mention later examples by Camus, Sartre and Yourcenar *inter alios* – prove that the artist as writer would not be forgotten.

---

[28] 'Un homme s'y montre simplement humain; une âme s'y révèle *en beauté*.'

[29] It is of tangential interest here that although Commandant Ferdinand Esterhazy allegedly confessed his guilt regarding Dreyfus to Wilde and the journalist Rowland Strong at a dinner in March 1898, Wilde did not make the information public (Ellmann 1987, 529–30; cf. Langlade 1975, 61–62).

[30] 'musicien symboliste, fervent pédéraste, et son jeune ami Lucien Sartorys, beau comme une femme'.

4 Naturalizing Oscar Wilde as an *homme de lettres*: The French Reception of *Dorian Gray* and *Salomé* (1895–1922)

Emily Eells

'I shall leave England and settle in France, where I will take out letters of naturalization.' (Wilde cited in the *Pall Mall Gazette,* 29 June 1892, 1)

Oscar Wilde's retort when faced with the imminent banning of *Salomé* from the London stage reveals just how at home he felt in France. Although Wilde never acquired French citizenship, the dynamics of intertextual exchange at work both in the creation of his *œuvre* and its early reception in France engaged him in a process of naturalization as a French man of letters. His particular affinity with contemporary French aesthetic movements of Decadence and art for art's sake prompted Arthur Ransome to hail *PDG* as 'one of the first French novels to be written in English' (1912, 95). Jacques de Langlade went even further when he dubbed Wilde an 'écrivain français' (French writer) in the subtitle of his monograph (1975). This study of the reception of Wilde in France will concentrate on the two works which make the most extensive use of French language and literature: *PDG* and *Salomé*. Their reception is inextricably linked to Wilde's social reception in France, as the translation of *PDG* was published immediately following the coverage of the trials in 1895 and the premiere of *Salomé* in Paris, in 1896, coincided with reports of Wilde's imprisonment. The open, prominent reception Wilde received in the French press was paralleled by covert underground reception, especially rife in gay literary circles. They adopted 'Dorian Gray' as an antonomastic code-name and French writers with an agenda to portray homosexuality in their works turned to Wilde as a model. Jean Cocteau and Marcel Proust paid tribute to Wilde with sealed lips, using his work as building blocks in the construction of their own literary representation of same-sex love.

The critics who introduced *PDG* to French readers before it was translated were ambivalent in their emphasis on the novel's affiliation with French literature. While comparisons with writers such as Huysmans implicitly raised Wilde to the status of a French man of letters, they also backfired when they were turned into charges of plagiarism. Willy, in an issue of *L'Echo de Paris* (The Paris echo) dated 17 April 1895, was scathing about how Wilde 'boisterously served British stomachs heated up left-overs – which had already gone off – of works by doddering French pen-pushers'.[1] In the same newspaper the following month, Laurent Tailhade, under his pen-name Tybalt, categorically dismissed Wilde's art as derivative: 'he didn't leave either a page or a word which was really his own' ('[il] n'a pas laissé une page, un mot vraiment à lui'). Such out-spoken accusations were counterbalanced by Wilde's defenders, who argued that he surpassed the French intertext in his work, with Adolphe Retté in *La Plume* even rating Wilde's novel as 'far superior to that grotesque *Against the Grain*' ('fort supérieur à ce grotesque *A Rebours*') (1895, 474). An article by Henry Bauër prompted by the banning of *Salomé* in London in 1892 pointed to the novel's homosexual subtext and established the parallel with Balzac's portrayal of the Vautrin – Lucien de Rubempré relationship (1892).

The French press came back to *PDG* in their daily reports of the Wilde trials, which made them into a kind of sensational soap-opera (see Richard Hibbitt's chapter in this volume). Coverage of the second day of the hearings in *Le Temps* (The time) of 6 April 1895 related how the prosecutor confused the personal and the literary when he cited *PDG* as evidence of Wilde's homosexuality: 'isn't it the story of a man who has an unhealthy passion for another man?' ('n'est-ce pas l'histoire d'un homme qui éprouve pour un autre homme une passion contre nature ?') In a front page article in *Le Journal* on the same day, an anonymous journalist amalgamates the man and his work, and ironically associates Wilde's homosexuality with Christian love in his pun on the word 'cheek': '[in *PDG*], the author describes, with loving refinement, the delights of the affection of a man for another like himself in a way which is completely different from the love of one's neighbour as extolled in the parable of the *Good Samaritan,* notwithstanding Mr Oscar Wilde's Christian tendency to turn the other cheeks' (*Le Journal* 1895).[2] The literary supplement of *La Lanterne* (The lantern) of 16 June 1895 was equally derisive in a parody of *PDG* entitled 'Métamorphoses d'Oscar Wilde' (Oscar Wilde's metamorphoses), which plays on the slang use of the French word 'tante' (aunt) to mean homosexual ('Two Vavass Sisters' 1895): '"My aunt Aurora" is eighteen years old. She's a pretty, pretty queen of a young man!' ('"Ma tante Aurore" a dix-huit ans, c'est un joli [...] joli jeune homme!') Indeed, *PDG* had made such a bad name for itself in the weeks immediately before it appeared as a translation that Wilde's defenders were landed with the particularly tough task of reinstating the work in their reviews of *Le portrait de Dorian Gray.*

---

[1] 'ce bruyant accommodeur de restes réchauffait, pour les estomacs britanniques, nos vieilles Scribouillies tournées à l'aigre.'

[2] '*Dorian Grey* [*sic.*], dont l'auteur décrit, avec un raffinement amoureux, les délices de la tendresse d'un homme pour un de ses semblables d'une façon tout à fait étrangère à l'amour du prochain tel que le recommande la parabole du *Bon Samaritain,* quelle que soit d'ailleurs la chrétienne tendance de M. Oscar Wilde à tendre les autres joues.'

Wilde's novel was his first major work to appear in French bookstores, where it came on sale on 21 June 1895. The publication of the French *PDG* was enveloped in mystery and scandal. To start with, the translators were not named in the first edition, though they were subsequently identified as Eugène Tardieu and Georges Maurevert (see Mason 1908, 157). Secondly, shortly after the French translation was issued, its publisher, Albert Savine, was declared bankrupt, due to incompetent management and heavy fines incurred by his editions of Anti-Semitic literature. When he was forced to close shop, he sold the Tardieu-Mauvert translation of *PDG* to the publisher P.-V. Stock. Despite losing his status as the publisher of *PDG*, Tardieu remained prominent in the reception of Wilde in France as he went on to translate all of Wilde's other works, which were also published by Stock. The novel's popularity in France is evident in the fact that by 1911 the translation was already in its fifth edition. In addition, the first illustrated edition of the novel was printed in Paris: although it contains the original English text, the artwork was done by Frenchmen. The seven drawings by Paul Thiriat, engraved by Eugène Dété, appeared in Charles Carrington's edition of the novel dated 1908, but not issued until 1910. Although Carrington can be credited with being the first to publish an illustrated edition of *PDG,* his dubious reputation as editor of pornographic literature raises doubts about his motives. All the more so as Carrington had already unscrupulously exploited the publicity surrounding Wilde when he used his French pseudonym – Sebastian Melmoth – followed by the initials 'O. W.' to identify the alleged translator of his English edition of Barbey d'Aurevilly's *Ce qui ne meurt pas* (*What Never Dies*), which he published in 1902. Nevertheless, the French can claim to be amongst the first to illustrate *PDG* as Tardieu and Mauvert's translation and accompanying woodcuts by Fernand Siméon, published by Mornay in 1920, predated the illustrated editions published in England. Although Tardieu and Mauvert were praised as 'faithful and informed' ('avisés et fidèles traducteurs') (Mirbeau 1895b, 1), the shelf-life of their translation expired in 1924, when Stock published a second French translation of the novel, again a collaboration, this time by Edmond Jaloux and Félix Frapereau.

As *Le Portrait de Dorian Gray* was published in the wake of the Wilde trials, the reviews in the press coincided with articles about Wilde's imprisonment. Octave Mirbeau's lengthy report of the hard labour inflicted on Wilde appeared on the front page of *Le Journal* on 16 June 1895 – just a few days before the French translation of *PDG* went on sale. Images of the author's suffering would therefore have been fresh in French readers' minds. The August 1895 issue of *Le Mercure de France* illustrates how the press coverage of Wilde the man overlapped with assessments of Wilde's work, as it contains Hugues Rebell's long 'Défense d'Oscar Wilde' (1895) as well as a review of the translation of *PDG* (Mauclair 1895). Predictably, Wilde's staunch supporters used their reviews of the translation as a means of reviving Wilde's reputation as a writer who, to quote Jean Lorrain writing under his pseudonym of 'Raitif de la Bretonne', was 'buried alive in prudish, Puritan oblivion' ('enfoui vivant dans un pudique et puritain oubli') (1895). Lorrain praised *PDG*, admitting that he took great pleasure in reading it and lamenting that extracts were used in the trials as evidence against Wilde. Camille Mauclair in the *Mercure de France* echoes Lorrain's image of Wilde buried alive when he refers to the translation as a voice from beyond the grave. He is ambivalent in his praise of Wilde's 'unquestionable talent' ('incontestable talent') which proves that he is 'a stylist of great value, with a noble soul' ('un styliste de haute valeur et d'âme noble') even if this soul is sometimes irritatingly light and exasperatingly paradoxical (1895, 237). Adolpe Retté in *La Plume* also took Wilde's defence, branding the journalists who allowed their negative image of Wilde the man to colour their appreciation of his work as 'damned Puritans' ('putains hypocrites'). He nuanced his appreciation of Wilde's work, calling him 'an artist of quality' ('un artiste de valeur') but criticizing the novel's excessively romantic and fantastic dimensions (1895, 474). Retté espoused Wilde's cause, which transpires clearly in the conclusion of his review of *PDG*, where he declares that he 'will continue to militate in favour of Free Art and Justice' ('je continuerai d'œuvrer pour l'Art libre et pour la Justice') (1895, 475).

As for Octave Mirbeau, he uses his article in *Le Journal* on the hard labour inflicted on Oscar Wilde to lament the way the trials affected the reception of Wilde's work in England:

> His plays were shamefully driven out of the theatre, where they had been applauded enthusiastically as recently as the previous evening. What they might possess of impersonal and immaculate beauty was not taken into consideration. All that was seen in that idiotic sentence was the need to dissociate from a man whose personal corruption 'could cast an entire country in a glaringly dubious light'. (1895a, 1) [3]

Mirbeau transcends his own negative opinion of Wilde the man in a long review of *PDG* in which criticism is offset by praise. He recommends indulgence towards the plot, which is 'beautiful in parts, but often without interest and hackneyed in its romanticism' ('belle quelquefois, mais souvent indifférente et d'un romantisme banal'). Mirbeau anticipates that the novel will be dismissed as immoral, and frames a definition of immorality with a Wildean ring to it: 'Immorality is anything which offends intelligence and beauty' ('L'immoralité, c'est tout ce qui offense l'intelligence et la beauté'). He nevertheless cautions that the book is not for general readership, admitting that it is 'not written for young ladies' ('n'est point écrit pour les jeunes filles') (Mirbeau 1895b, 1).

Wilde's novel was appropriated by French sexologists who transformed the literary into the scientific by making *PDG* into a case study in same-sex love. Their work followed in the footsteps of the pioneering treatises in German by Karl Heinrich Ulrichs (1864–65) and Richard von Krafft-Ebing (1886), which were published before Wilde's name had been inscribed in the history of homosexuality. In *Uranisme et unisexualité : Etude sur différentes manifestations*

---

[3] 'Ses pièces furent chassées honteusement du théâtre, où, la veille encore, elles étaient applaudi avec enthousiasme. On ne considéra pas ce qu'elles pouvaient contenir d'impersonnelle et inviolable beauté ; on ne vit dans cette exécution imbécile, que le besoin de se désolidariser d'un homme, dont la corruption individuelle "pouvait jeter, sur tout un pays, un éclat louche".'

de l'instinct sexuel (Uranism and unisexuality: study on different manifestations of the sexual instinct), Marc André Raffalovich castigated the literary dimension of *PDG* as 'far from original [...], artificial, superficial, effeminate' ('peu original [...] artificiel, superficiel, efféminé') (1896, 246). Georges Saint-Paul (1896) picked up on Raffalovich in his *Perversion et perversité sexuelle* (Sexual perversion and perversity), reading the novel from a psychological and autobiographical point of view. Although he finds the work interesting, Saint-Paul criticizes its unevenness and its pervasive sense of morbidity.

The homosexual associations of Dorian Gray's name are anchored in French culture, as is illustrated in the title of Jacques-Emile Blanche's portrait of Sir Coleridge Kennard. It was commissioned by the model's mother – Mrs Carew – who had commissioned the Epstein funeral monument for Wilde's tomb in the Père Lachaise cemetery in Paris. The portrait of the tall, slender Sir Coleridge (or Roy) Kennard with his long tapered fingers caused a life-long rift between Mrs Carew and Blanche, as it revealed his sexual proclivities to her. Roy Kennard agreed to exhibit the painting on condition that his name was not disclosed, which led the organizer of an exhibition of Blanche's work in 1924 to present it under the title *Le portrait de Dorian Gray*. A French artist's portrait of a peer of the realm is thus known under the French title of Wilde's novel and serves as proof of how 'Dorian Gray' circulated in initiated circles as a code-name for homosexuality.

★ ★ ★

Salomé is of paramount importance in the study of Wilde's reception in France, as the play was first printed and performed in Paris. French journalists aroused curiosity about the play by reporting on its composition before it was actually published. In the article already cited in which Henry Bauër introduces Wilde's work, he announces that Wilde had written *Salomé* directly in French, inspired by Flaubert's short story 'Hérodias' (1892, 1). The original French version of Wilde's play was first published in 1893, by the Librairie d'Art Indepéndant in Paris. When the script 'pictured' by Aubrey Beardsley was published in London the following year, its status as a translation from the French was made clear on the title page: '*Salome, A Tragedy in One Act: Translated from the French of Oscar Wilde*' (Wilde 1894).

Salomé's Parisian premiere was reported to have been instigated by Wilde's supporters Camille Mauclair and Henry Bauër (*Le Journal* 1896, 2). Aurélien Lugné-Poe, the director of the recently founded *Théâtre de l'Œuvre*, agreed to stage the play, casting himself in the role of Herod. That production of *Salomé* was performed only once, on 11 February 1896. The event was heralded by Jean Lorrain in a long article in *Le Journal* on the artistic representations of 'Salomé', which reads as an introduction to Wilde's play (1896a, 1–2). Like *PDG,* the reception of *Salomé* cannot be dissociated from events in Wilde's life, as he was serving his term in prison at the time of its first performance. The premiere was conceived as a means of gaining support for him, with an aim to petition to reduce his prison sentence. Although it was unsuccessful on that score, it did succeed in keeping Wilde on the French scene. For example, the journalists writing for the *Grand Journal* under the collective pseudonym 'Les

Treize' (The thirteen) used *Salomé* as a pretext for reviewing Wilde's *œuvre* and concluded by expressing confidence that the Parisian public would rise above biographical considerations to judge it on its literary merits ('Les Treize' 1896).

All the major French daily papers reported on *Salomé*'s 'one night stand', though opinions about the play's literary qualities diverged. Nevertheless, critics were unanimous in their praise of Lina Munte's performance in the title role: in the words of Henry Céard in *Le Matin* (The morning), she was 'absolutely remarkable with her ferocious sensuality' ('tout à fait remarquable de férocité sensuelle') (1896, 3). According to Francisque Sarcey (1896) – the prominent Parisian theatre critic for *Le Temps* – her acting compensated for the play's lack of dramatic art. He particularly appreciated how her diction imitated Sarah Bernhardt, with whom Wilde had started the aborted rehearsals in London.

The reviews conflate the literary and the biographical, as comments on Wilde's imprisonment punctuate appreciation of his play. Most of the reviewers take the motivations for staging the play into account, with Georges Boyer in *L'Evénement* (The event) terming it a protest against English morality (1896, 3). According to Henry Céard (1896), Wilde's extra-literary brush with the law had aroused enough curiosity to justify staging one of his plays, but *Salomé* was of little interest beyond the fact that it was written in French. On 13 February, the review in the *Journal des débats* went so far as to suggest that Wilde was applauded because of his name, and not because of his work:

> When the curtain fell, the audience responded to the name of the playwright with rapturous applause. Does it mean that the base adventure and its much publicized sentence were a necessary prerequisite for Oscar Wilde's talent to be recognized as genius? ([H. F.-C.] 1896, 3)[4]

Camille Le Senne in *Le Siècle* dubs Wilde 'the dubious pontiff of the aesthetes' ('équivoque pontife des esthètes') and expresses reservations about the appropriateness of staging Wilde's play immediately following his trial, which was 'just as repulsive as it was sensational' ('aussi répugnant que retentissant') (1896, 3). Jacques du Tillet in the *Revue bleue* (Blue review) is not optimistic that *Salomé* will be rewarded with Wilde's release from prison, and proposes to consider only the artistic qualities of the work. He admits that he is perplexed about how to define the work, questioning whether it is a play, a poem or a reverie. He is critical of Wilde's excessive rhetoric, which he even qualifies as bestial: 'I am not completely convinced that those long lists, those grunts of an animal in heat, and also those philosophical "summaries" make good poetry' (1896, 219).[5] Given that *Salomé* received such discordant reviews in the press, Henry Bauër's claim in *L'Echo de Paris* that Wilde had found a 'haven of glory

---

4   'Le public, à la chute du rideau, a souligné d'une formidable ovation le nom de l'auteur. Il a donc fallu l'ignoble aventure et la condamnation que l'on sait pour que le talent d'Oscar Wilde devînt du génie ?'

5   'je ne suis pas bien convaincu que ces énumérations, ces rugissements de bête en rut, et aussi ces « résumés » philosophiques soient de bonne poésie.'

in Paris' ('asile de gloire à Paris') sounds like an overstatement (1896, 3). In an article in the same newspaper a few months later, he expressed his regret that revelations made by Alfred Douglas in the *Revue blanche* (White review) in June 1896 had dashed any hope of Wilde's being welcomed into the fold of French letters upon release from prison (1896, 1).

Periodicals partisan to Wilde's cause reviewed the play favourably, though few expressed as unalloyed praise as Jean de Tinan's article in the March issue of the *Mercure de France* (1896). Even Wilde's defenders tainted their reviews with criticism of the play's derivative use of French sources. For example, Jacques de Gachons in *L'Ermitage* begins his assessment of this 'powerful work' ('œuvre puissante') on a resoundingly positive note: 'Mr Wilde's *Salomé* moved and enchanted with its dazzling poetry unfurled like some rich drapery, evoking a terrible moment';[6] but he goes on to condemn the work as plagiarism (203). Paul Marrot in *La Lanterne* is just as ambivalent: he anticipates Achille Segard's appreciation of the musicality of Wilde's prose (1 March 1896), when he terms the play 'moonlight poetry' ('poème de clair de lune'), but at the same time he recognizes that the language is 'full of faded images and excessive repetitions' ('pleine d'images défraîchies et de répétitions abusives') (1896, 2). Critics tended to mark their distance from Wilde, faulting him for his reliance on French sources but also because they found the play tedious and repetitive. George Vanor in *La Paix* (Peace) (1896) gave a positive spin to its Flaubertian intertext, suggesting that using Flaubert as a principal source was Wilde's way of paying homage to the French hospitality he had received. Vanor remained steadfast in his support of Wilde, and later in 1896 delivered a lecture on his plays before the performance of a revival of *Salomé* in a programme which also included a French adaptation of *LWF*. The review of *Salomé* in the *Journal des débats* taxed the play as 'excruciatingly boring' ('cruellement ennuyeux') and dismissed it as 'a mediocre work' ('œuvre médiocre') (1896, 3). Francisque Sarcey is even more forthright in his criticism: 'the boredom it instils is unbearable' ('L'ennui qui s'en dégage est insupportable') (1896, 2). Léon Bernard-Derosne in *Gil Blas* finds Salomé's enumerations 'monotonous' and suggests that she is like a spoilt child in the way she repeats her desire for Iokannan's body – 'J'en veux ! J'en veux !' ('I want it, I want it') – only to change her mind when she hears how he has insulted her (1896, 3).

Most of the critics are disparaging about Wilde's use of French sources, underscoring his lack of originality. Gustave Geffroy in the periodical *Paris* uses litotes when he writes that the play 'rings lots of bells' ('parcourue de réminiscences') (1896, 3). Catulle Mendès in *Le Journal* is more explicit in his use of the word 'pastiche', which he justifies by listing all of Wilde's sources:

Clearly, the very beautiful talent expressed in Mr Oscar Wilde's *Salomé* is debased by a total lack of personality. Mr Oscar Wilde borrowed the majestic images from Leconte de Lisle, the pompous speeches from Gustave Flaubert, the luxurious

---

6   'Poésie éclatante comme quelque déploiement d'une riche draperie, terrible évocation d'une heure terrible, la *Salomé* de M. Wilde a ému et charmé.'

epithets from Théodore de Banville, and the remote mystery in the splendid transparency of the Word from Villiers de l'Isle Adam. He took from Maurice Maeterlinck that slightly distraught and dazed way of rambling on, repeating the same word or the same sentence, as a means – which was always easy and will become banal – of expressing uncertainty, fearful childishness and the groping thought of souls troubled by the Chimera. (1896, 2)[7]

Criticism turned to derision, for example when Tristan Bernard's review in the *Grand Journal* classed *Salomé* as a comedy, arguing that Wilde's ironic streak precluded his being serious: 'I really took pleasure in the barbaric Virgin's aside to the bloody head, when the dish she had ordered was sent up on the funereal dumb-waiter' (1896).[8] The review signed by the 'pompier de service' ('the fireman on duty') in *La Paix* is equally ironic: he writes that Salomé is as stubborn as a mule and uses the common slang term for head – 'une poire' ('a pear') – in a sardonic reference to John the Baptist's beheading. He highlights a discrepancy in the production – the actor playing St John the Baptist had brown hair, whereas the head presented to Salomé had fair hair – marvelling at how grief can make hair change colour ('Le Pompier de service' 1896, 3).

The mixed reviews of the first production did not augur well for the revival of *Salomé* in Paris several months later, with Lina Munte again in the title role. It opened at the *Nouveau Théâtre* (New theatre) on 28 October 1896, coupled with an adaptation of *LWF* by G. Bertal entitled *La Passante* (The Passer-by). According to Jean Lorrain (1896b), the evening was a complete failure: the double bill played to an empty house and neither play succeeded in raising interest, as both were recognized as second-hand literature. Wilde vied for status as a French writer, but his gift as literary chameleon was frowned upon by Jean Lorrain who even indulged in the cruel pleasure of reporting one of the spectator's remarks: 'It's a good thing that Wilde isn't here to see himself dying on stage; for the first time I'm glad to know he's in prison' (1896b, 1).[9] The first performance of *LWF* in Paris did not augur well for the reception of Wilde's comedies in France. There was a lapse of thirteen years before *LWF* was staged again, in a translation by Maurice Rémond and J. Chalençon which opened at the *Théâtre des arts* (Arts theatre), on the boulevard des Batignolles, on 7 May 1909. The event was intended to reinstate Wilde's literary reputation

---

[7] 'Manifestement, le très beau talent dont témoigne la *Salomé* de M. Oscar Wilde se dégrade par un manque total de personnalité. M. Oscar Wilde emprunta à Leconte de Lisle la majesté des images, à Gustave Flaubert la pompe du discours, à Théodore de Banville le luxe des épithètes, à Villiers de l'Isle Adam le lointain du mystère sous la splendide transparence du Verbe ; et il tient de Maurice Maeterlinck cette façon, comme un peu hagarde et hébétée, de dire plusieurs fois la même parole, de radoter la même phrase, moyen, qui fut toujours facile et qui va devenir banal, d'exprimer l'incertitude, la puérilité peureuse, la pensée à tâtons des âmes troublées par la Chimère.'

[8] 'j'ai tout à fait goûté l'apostrophe de la vierge barbare à la tête sanglante, quand le plat commandé lui arrive par le funèbre monte-plats.'

[9] 'Il est heureux que Wilde ne soit pas là pour se voir enterré vivant; c'est la première fois que je suis heureux de le savoir en prison.'

but it was far from successful. The reviews were equivocal about the play's literary qualities, with Léon Blum (1909) following his statement of fact in *Comœdia* – 'the Parisians only know the Wilde legend' ('le public parisien ne connaît guère Oscar Wilde que par sa légende') – with a cutting comment to the effect that he was not sure that it was better to know him through his writing. Wilde's comedies did not figure on the billboards of Parisian theatres until decades after his death. Their success dates from the fervent support of Guillot de Saix, who translated and promoted Wilde's work. He was responsible for the first French performance of *WNI*, which was staged in his translation at the Parisian theatre *La Petite Scène*, in February 1935.

The rare theatrical productions of *Salomé* staged in Paris after 1896 have all echoed the tone set by the premiere. The initial casting included a telling twist of cross-dressing, as the male page was played by Suzanne Després. Her delivery of the lines lamenting the young Syrian's death thus provoked a confused reaction: as Jean de Tinan points out in the *Mercure de France*, the actress recited them so movingly that she masked their homosexual significance:

> Miss Suzanne Després, Herodias's page, was marvellously moving in the lament over the young Syrian's death – *He was my brother and more than a brother to me!* [...] – so that everyone was so enchanted that they did not realize that it was the risqué passage – the passage when devotees of the play are poised to stop their neighbours from blowing their noses. That little page might well have saved everything, with his pretty voice and his shy beauty. (1896, 416)[10]

However, the homosexual subtext of Wilde's play became a recognized element of its reception in France. Not surprisingly, it is the focus of an article on *Salomé* by Jacques d'Adelswärd-Fersen in his journal *Akademos* (1909), known for its open support of homosexuality. Years later, Francis Sourbié's production of the play at the small *Théâtre du Globe* (Globe theatre) in Paris, in the early spring of 1973, foregrounded homosexuality by using an all-male cast: Salomé and her mother were played by transvestites. The production, which targeted an audience of 'non-standard couples and militants of the Homosexual Front of Revolutionary Action' (Matzneff, 1973)[11] resonated with homoeroticism, not only because its aestheticism was reminiscent of Cocteau (Review 1973), but also because its black and white costumes were inspired by Beardsley's drawings ('M. P.' 1973).

Although *Salomé* as a play was not a box-office hit, Wilde's script quickly became known through various transpositions into other artistic genres, including a film produced by Gaumont in 1907. Most notably, as Chris Walton explores in this volume, a German translation of Wilde's *Salomé* was used as

---

10   'Mlle Suzanne Després, page d'Héroidas, s'est trop exquisément lamentée sur la mort du jeune Syrien – *Il était mon frère et plus qu'un frère!* [...] - pour que personne ait songé, charmé que l'on était, que c'était le passage dangereux, – il a peut-être tout sauvé, ce petit page, avec sa jolie voix et sa beauté timide – le passage où les amis de la pièce sont tout prêts à interdire à leurs voisins de se moucher.'

11   'couples irréguliers [et] militants du F.H.A.R. [*front homosexuel d'action révolutionnaire*].'

the libretto of Richard Strauss's opera. Vain attempts were made to maintain *Salomé*'s status as a French work of art, with Strauss himself adapting his score to a French libretto for a production at the *Théâtre de la Monnaie* in Brussels, on 25 March 1907. However, when he conducted the first performance of *Salomé* in Paris just a few weeks later, on 8 May 1907, he reverted to the German libretto. That has remained the standard version in France – and elsewhere –, which has meant that Wilde's text became known to the French through a double displacement: as a German translation and as a musical transposition.

The French composer Antoine Mariotte also strove to preserve *Salomé*'s French identity. Struck by the musical qualities of Wilde's text, he started the composition of his *Salomé* as early as 1895, in other words well before Strauss. Performance of Mariotte's opera was thwarted by Strauss's editor, who claimed to own the copyright for the libretto. The French were divided over this issue: Romain Rolland was stalwart in his support of Strauss, but Mariotte was vehemently defended in the press – notably by Pierre Lalo in *Le Temps* (1908) – and there were even accusations that Strauss had stolen the subject from him. Strauss's editor yielded by granting permission for the premiere of Mariotte's opera, which took place in Lyon on 30 October 1908. It was favourably reviewed in several major newspapers, which welcomed this 'French *Salomé*' (Berr 1908) as an enriching contribution to French culture. It is also a reflection of the contemporary political context in France, as it deletes the Jewish element from Wilde's script, undoubtedly because it premiered in the midst of the Dreyfus affair. Mariotte's opera was first performed in Paris, in April 1910, to great acclaim, with reviews in no fewer than twelve Parisian newspapers, thus rivalling – if not surpassing – critical response to Wilde's play. One of the reviews was by Proust's lover, Reynaldo Hahn, whose interest in the opera may have been prompted by the homosexual subtext of the libretto.

Mariotte's *Salomé* belongs to the French school of composition and resonates with echoes of Vincent d'Indy and Debussy. It is also anchored in the contemporary musical trend of spiritualism, particularly evident in the way Mariotte displaces some of Iokanaan's lines so that his disembodied voice comments on Salomé's dance. Spiritualism also marks the end of the opera, when the choir 'sings' with their mouths closed, humming a litany of prayers, producing a sound which creates the impression that the spirit has departed from the body. Their humming also abolishes linguistic boundaries, thus transposing Wilde's text into a kind of universal language.

The French composer restructured Wilde's work as a series of seven tableaux linked together by orchestral commentary. His opera develops the laconic stage directions pertaining to Salomé's dance, orchestrating it with music and adding scent and light to the scene. Mariotte's opera thus realizes Wilde's initial project to stage *Salomé* using burning braziers of incense to convey emotion (see Ellmann 1987, 351). Mariotte's work might be closer to Wilde's intentions, but his musical achievement has been overshadowed by Strauss's. Sporadic revivals of Mariotte's *Salomé* have failed to establish its precedence over Strauss: the 1910 Paris production was also performed in Marseilles with a rerun the following year in Paris; Mariotte's *Salomé* was staged again at the Paris Opera in 1919 and revived in concert version at the festival of Radio-France in Montpellier in July 2004, recorded on CD in 2006 by Accord, with Friedemann Layer conducting and Kate Aldrich in the title role (a production of Mariotte's opera in French was staged at the Prinzregententheater in Munich in March 2014). Despite these French productions, Strauss's is the better-known opera – and arguably the best-known version of Wilde's text.

The two rival operatic versions of *Salomé* illustrate how Wilde's text was adopted as a pre-text by other artists who used it as a springboard for their own creations. One prominent example is the musical adaptation of *Salomé* which figured as the last piece in Gabriel Astruc's programme for the *Théâtre du Châtelet*'s 1912 season. The performances on 13–14 June 1912 were a major cultural event in Paris and were extensively reviewed in the press. The music by the Russian composer Aleksandr Glazounov comprised a long orchestral overture and a sequence to accompany the dance of the seven veils. The review in *Comœdia* dismissed the music as 'completely without interest' ('aucune espèce d'intérêt') but commended the director, Alexandre Sanine, and Léon Bakst, who had designed the scenery and the costumes ('L. V.' 1912). Critics also focused on the performances of Ida Rubinstein as Salomé: although her diction and Russian accent did not serve Wilde's text well, her dance was more favorably received, especially by *Comœdia*, which praised it as 'one of Mme Ida Rubinstein's most admirable performances' ('une des plus admirables créations de Mme Ida Rubinstein') (Review 1912). However, Pierre Mille in the *Petit Marseillais* of 22 June 1912 deflated any tragic grace in her performance by reporting that it sent a ripple of laughter through the audience and that her limbs were so long that she looked like a folding ladder!

Salomé epitomizes the reception of Wilde's work in France, because it both derives from and contributes to its French heritage. Wilde's *Salomé* may be indebted to such French sources as Flaubert's *Hérodias*, Mallarmé's 'Hérodiade', Gustave Moreau's numerous paintings and Huysmans's descriptions of them in *A Rebours*, but the return has been paid off – and bettered – through the numerous art works it has inspired, and which exist in their own right. An eloquent illustration of this point is when Proust's narrator refers to *Salomé* as an opera by Strauss, and not as a play by Wilde (Proust 1988a, 740–41).

★ ★ ★

Following the publication of *Le portrait de Dorian Gray* in 1895 and the premiere of Wilde's *Salomé* in Paris in 1896, the reception of Wilde in France grew exponentially with the translation of his other works, in particular his comedies. Although the comedies were very rarely performed in the first decades of the history of Wilde's reception in France, various French translators produced their versions of the texts. Gaston Bonnefont (1892) proposed the first translation of *LWF*, which he insisted was literal and not intended for performance. It was followed by Arnelle's volume of three comedies (1906) which contained the second French translation of *LWF* and the first French translations of *IH* and *WNI*. Four years later, Albert Savine (1910–11) published the third French translation of *LWF* and the second of *WNI*. They were followed the next year by his translation of *IH* and the first French translation of *IBE*. The difficulties of translating the title of Wilde's 'trivial comedy for serious people' might well explain why it was the last comedy to be published in French. Savine's title – 'De l'importance d'être sérieux' – is too earnestly literal, as it deletes the pun. An astute play on a French word was not found until 1942, when Guillot de Saix – after considering 'Modeste', 'Sévère' and 'Prudent' – realized that 'Constant' functions both as an adjective suggesting 'earnestness' and as a proper name. His title – *Il importe d'être constant* – has been adopted as the standard French version (Guillot de Saix 1950), although the French playwright Jean Anouilh replaced it with 'Aimé' when he collaborated with Claude Vincent in an adaptation of the play for performance at the *Comédie des Champs-Elysées* in 1954.

Parallel to the open reception, Wilde's work also elicited closet response in the French homosexual literary underground. The complexities of Gide's mediation of Wilde are the subject of Victoria Reid's chapter in this volume. Before concluding on how Proust invisibly inscribed Wilde's name in *A la recherche du temps perdu* (*Remembrance of Things Past*), I will consider the impact Wilde had on two other gay writers who embarked on their literary careers in the early twentieth century: the obscure poet and literary critic, Raymond Laurent, and the jack-of-all-trades, Jean Cocteau, who wrote an almost totally neglected theatrical adaptation of *PDG*, which was published posthumously in 1978 by the small Parisian publishing house Olivier Orban (see also Eells 2010).

Cocteau was eleven years old when Wilde died and thus grew up in the aftermath of the scandal he had provoked. His early admiration of Wilde's work dates from the period when his own sexual inclinations were becoming evident. He was clearly inspired by Wilde's representation of homosexuality and, at the age of twenty, published a series of four poems based on *Salomé*.[12] Two poems in *Le Prince Frivole* (The frivolous prince) (1910) clearly associate Wilde with homosexuality: Cocteau's 'Mr W. H.' echoes the title and theme of Wilde's short story recounting Shakespeare's homosexual love, and in 'Le Dieu Nu' (the naked god), Cocteau cites Alfred Douglas's famous definition of homosexuality – 'I am the Love that dare not speak its name' – as the epigraph, before translating it as the last line of the poem.

Cocteau's theatrical adaptation of *PDG* reveals an ambivalent attitude towards Wilde's work, as it is both a tribute to it and an expression of Cocteau's desire to find a voice of his own. The play, whose title, *Le Portrait surnaturel de Dorian Gray*, spells out the supernatural dimension of the plot, was written in collaboration with Jacques Renaud, a friend whose name Cocteau's mother cites as proof of her son's homosexuality. It is evident from the manuscript of the play, now in the Lilly Library in Bloomington, Indiana, that Cocteau is responsible for the creative work involved in the adaptation. Renaud was left to fill in the dialogues, which mostly meant simply copying out lines from the first French translation of the novel published by Savine in 1895. Cocteau restructured the narrative for the stage, relocating all the scenes indoors and heightening suspense by concentrating the action in one place.

---

12   They were first recited at a reading of his poetry in April 1908 and published the following year in *La Lampe d'Aladin* (1909) (Aladin's lamp).

He updated Wilde's work by introducing the telephone as a means of communication with a character off-stage and by using electrical lighting to achieve
dramatic effect. He also changed Sibyl's nickname for Dorian Gray from
Wilde's original 'Prince Charming' to the more prosaic Jack. Cocteau used
the English spelling of the name, which may hint at an identification between
Jacques Renaud and Wilde's ephebic dandy, as 'Jack' was Cocteau's nickname
for his friend. Cocteau also corrected the manuscript version of the play to
mute its homosexual overtones. The first draft respects Wilde's original text
and refers to Lord Henry's aunt as 'tante Agathe', but Cocteau then changes
her relationship from 'aunt' to 'cousin', perhaps because of the associations of
the French word 'tante' ('queen') mentioned above.

Le portrait surnaturel de Dorian Gray is positioned on the threshold of reception
and creation, as Cocteau both reworks Wilde's text and creates a work of his
own, which contains his future *œuvre* in embryonic form. It has been more
or less neglected in secondary literature on both Cocteau and Wilde.[13] It is
surprising that the play was not published until over sixty year after it was
written, and that it has never been performed, especially as Cocteau and
Renaud corresponded enthusiastically about both publication and performance
when they were writing the play during the summer of 1908. At that time
Cocteau was in Venice, where he and Grace Constant Lounsbery discussed
plans to produce the play at the *Théâtre des arts* in Paris (where *LWF* was
performed the following year in the translation by Rémond and Chalençon).
Given that the script is a finished text (it exists as both a professional fair copy
and a typescript), and that Lounsbery seemed interested in having it performed,
it is a mystery why the project was abandoned when Cocteau returned from
Venice at the end of September 1908 and why the text of the play remained in
his closet until after his death. All the more so as throughout his life Cocteau
frequently referred to the way he had been enthralled by Wilde's novel, and
he reminisced that, when he was sixteen, his friends were all devouring *PDG*
(Cocteau 1950, 237). Cocteau's play was produced for the first time by the
theatre company *Crocs en Scène*, in Reims, 2013.

One of those friends was Cocteau's class-mate at the lycée Condorcet,
Raymond Laurent, a little-known critic of nineteenth-century English art
and literature. The chapter on Oscar Wilde in his *Etudes Anglaises* (English
studies), published by Grasset in 1910, has been overlooked by critics, though
it merits the succinct annotation in Thomas Mikolyzk's bibliography: 'an
excellent scholarly essay on Wilde's life and work' (1993). It is likely that
Laurent's essays – like Cocteau's play – have remained unknown as a result of
the homosexual complexities of the authors' biographies. They intersect in
Venice in September 1908, where Laurent committed suicide in the presence
of Jean Cocteau and Wilde's son, Vyvyan Holland. That dramatic, moonlit
'death in Venice' is discussed in my study of Walter Pater's occult influence in
France (Eells 2004). It cast a pall over the underground reception of Wilde
in France, not only shrouding Laurent's work in oblivion, but also putting an
abrupt end to all plans to have Cocteau's *Dorian Gray* performed in Paris.

---

[13]   Only two articles have been written on it: see Magnan 1979 and Christensen 1986.

The publication of Laurent's volume of *Etudes Anglaises* in November 1910 went all but unnoticed in France. The 'but' refers to Henry-D. Davray (1910), the critic for the English literature section of the *Mercure de France* who always had his finger on the pulse. Davray figures large in the reception of Wilde in France as he worked with Wilde on the first French translation of *BRG*, published in the *Mercure de France* of September 1898, followed the next year by his translation of PP in *La revue blanche*. Davray's short paragraph on Laurent's volume summarizes its introduction and outlines Laurent's argument which names Coleridge as the precursor of the Pre-Raphaelite movement, and Pater and Wilde as its inheritors. Even though Davray praised Laurent's work as 'ingenious' and 'backed by a wealth of arguments' ('la thèse est ingénieuse, et soutenue avec une abondance d'arguments') the volume has barely circu-lated (1910, 173). The only copy in the whole of the French library network belongs to the Maurice Barrès bequest in the *Bibliothèque nationale de France* (French national library) and its pages were uncut until an obliging librarian revealed their secrets to me. [14]

Laurent's sixty-page essay on Wilde views his works as a whole, citing the witticisms of the comedies alongside aesthetic tenets from the essays. He presents Wilde as the culminating figure of a movement which he refers to, borrowing Wilde's title, as 'The English Renaissance'. Laurent sees Wilde as a disciple of Matthew Arnold, sharing with him the conviction that culture instils inner harmony. He reads Wilde's work as a hymn to life, most poign-antly in *DP* and *BRG*, which express an intense appreciation of life precisely because it is under threat. Laurent boldly welcomes Wilde as a salutary figure after a long period of aestheticism, revelling in his sense of corporal vitality after all the insipid superficiality of the art for art's sake movement.

Although Laurent's suicide silenced his voice and plunged Cocteau's *Dorian Gray* into neglect, Grace Lounsbery pursued plans for a theatrical adaptation of *Dorian Gray*, authoring her own version which opened at the Vaudeville Theatre in London on 28 August 1913 with Lou-Tellegen in the title role. The French connection was maintained, as the role of Dorian's valet – Victor – was scripted in French and played by the French actor, André Cernay. Nine years after Grace Lounsbery's English adaptation was published (1913), she collaborated with Fernand Nozière in a very different French adaptation which premiered at the *Comédie des Champs-Elysées* on 20 December 1922, in a production directed by Georges Pitoëff. The script, comprising eight *tableaux*, makes *PDG* suitable for a general audience by attenuating the ambiguous sexual overtones in Wilde's original and adding a heterosexual subplot involving a romance between Dorian and Lady Gwendoline.

Coincidentally, 1922 also saw the publication of Suzanne Mercey's adaptation of *PDG* in French. In the introduction to her play, Mercey uses an image from alchemy to explain that Wilde's text lent itself to dramatization,

---

[14] According to the 'Worldcat' database, a small number of American libraries possess a copy. The only listing in COPAC is the British Library's copy. Their catalogue confuses the Raymond Laurent discussed here with his homonym, a president of the Parisian town council.

obviously because it bears the hallmark of a talented playwright: 'This play is not an adaptation, it's a transmutation of the pure gold of Oscar Wilde's novel into the stuff of drama which is as precious and as shiny, because he had unconsciously prepared it' (Mercey 1922).[15]

1922 can be seen as the closure of the early reception of Wilde in France, as it was also the year of Proust's death and the date of publication of the volumes of his novel explicitly devoted to homosexuality: *Sodome et Gomorrhe*. By that time, Wilde's life story and work were so well-known in France that any allusion to them would have been recognized. *A la recherche du temps perdu* refers twice to Wilde: first of all, in the following passage from *Sodome et Gomorrhe I* on the homosexual as social outcast:

> Their honour precarious, their liberty provisional, lasting only until the discovery of their crime; their position unstable, like that of the poet one day fêted in every drawing-room and applauded in every theatre in London, and the next driven from every lodging unable to find a pillow upon which to lay his head, turning the mill like Samson and saying like him: 'The two sexes shall die, each in a place apart.' (Proust 1988b, 17)[16]

The terms Proust uses to trace the poet's downfall here – from 'applaudi la veille' to 'chassé le lendemain' – echo Octave Mirbeau's reaction to Wilde's imprisonment and suggest that Proust is citing from his article (Mirbeau 1895a). Wilde thus figures in Proust's novel thanks to his biography, and not his bibliography. The way Proust puts the line from de Vigny's *Les Destinées* into the mouth of the poet ostracized from London theatres deliberately confuses the question of authorship. The underlying identification with Wilde seems to suggest that he had written the line of French poetry, in other words that he had become a French man of letters.

Wilde's integration into French culture is also reflected in the way Proust works another allusion to Wilde into his novel. In the manuscript version of an essay he wrote on Balzac, Proust explicitly names Wilde in a reference to the passage in DL in which Vivian voices the opinion that art is superior to reality. Proust equates Vivian to Wilde when he cites Vivian's claim that the most moving experience in his life was reading about Lucien de Rubempré's death:

> There is something peculiarly dramatic moreover about this predilection and compassion in Oscar Wilde, at the height of his success, for Lucien de Rubempré's

---

[15] 'Cette pièce n'est pas une adaptation, c'est une transmutation de l'or pur du roman d'Oscar Wilde en une matière dramatique aussi précieuse et aussi brillante, puisqu'il l'avait inconsciemment préparée.'

[16] 'Sans honneur que précaire, sans liberté que provisoire jusqu'à la découverte du crime ; sans situation qu'instable, comme pour le poète la veille fêté dans tous les salons, applaudi dans tous les théâtres de Londres, chassé le lendemain de tous les garnis sans pouvoir trouver un oreiller où reposer sa tête, tournant la meule comme Samson et disant comme lui : 'Les deux sexes mourront chacun de son côté'. English citation from Proust 1992, vol. 4, 18.

death [...]. [O]ne cannot help reflecting that a few years later he was himself to be Lucien de Rubempré. The end of Lucien de Rubempré in the Conciergerie, when he has seen his brilliant career in the world come crashing down after it has been proved he had been living on intimate terms with a convict, was merely the anticipation – as yet unknown to Wilde, it is true – of exactly what was to happen to Wilde. (Proust 1971, 273)[17]

This extract from one of Proust's manuscripts is persuasive proof that he had read Wilde's essay in Renaud's translation of *Intentions* (1905) – and not in the version by Hugues Rebell (1906) even though Davray rated the latter as superior (1905)[18] – because it echoes the translator's footnote on Rubempré's death: 'Did Wilde foresee his own death?'[19] The paratext of the French translation thus feeds Proust the line in his manuscript version where he reflects on the irony that Wilde would experience in real life what had so moved him in literature. Significantly, when Proust gives the line to the Baron de Charlus in his novel, he deletes Wilde's name and cites his words as if they had been pronounced by a Frenchman:

And the death of Lucien! I forget who the man of taste was who, when he was asked what event in his life had grieved him most, replied: 'The death of Lucien de Rubempré in *Splendeurs et Misères*'. (Proust 1988b, 437–38)[20]

Even though Wilde's voice is only heard in anonymous, displaced remarks, the two allusions Proust makes to him in *A la recherche du temps perdu* serve as a conclusive indication that his presence was indelibly imprinted on French literature. Thirty years after exclaiming that he would take out letters of French naturalization if his art was not well received in England, Wilde had succeeded – albeit posthumously – in being naturalized as a French *homme de lettres*.

---

[17] Il y a d'ailleurs quelque chose de particulièrement dramatique dans cette prédilection et cet attendrissement d'Oscar Wilde, au temps de sa vie brillante, pour la mort de Lucien de Rubempré [...]. [O]n ne peut s'empêcher de penser que, quelques années plus tard, il devait être Lucien de Rubempré lui-même. Et la fin de Lucien de Rubempré à la Conciergerie, voyant toute sa brillante existence mondaine écroulée sur la preuve qui est faite qu'il vivait dans l'intimité d'un forçat, n'était que l'anticipation – inconnue encore de Wilde il est vrai – de ce que devait précisément arriver à Wilde.' Cited in English from Proust 1988d, 65.

[18] Davray's comparative review of the two French translations of *Intentions* (1905) appears to predate the publication of Rebell's translation (1906).

[19] 'Prévoyait-il la sienne?', Wilde 1904, trans. Renaud, 19.

[20] 'Et la mort de Lucien ! je ne me rappelle plus quel homme de goût avait eu cette réponse, à qui lui demandait quel événement l'avait le plus affligé dans sa vie : "La mort de Lucien de Rubempré dans *Splendeurs et misères.*"' English citation from Proust 1992, vol. 4, 520.

5 André Gide's 'Hommage à Oscar Wilde' or 'The Tale of Judas'

Victoria Reid

Significance and Writings

From 1891 to 1933, André Gide (1869–1951) wrote often and in a range of genres on Oscar Wilde. Wilde inspired aesthetic ideas and characters in Gide's fictional *œuvre*, namely *Le Traité du Narcisse* (1891) (*The Treatise of Narcissus*), *Les Norritures terrestres* (1897) (*Fruits of the Earth*), *El Hadj ou le traité du faux prophète* (1899) (The Hadj or the treatise of a false prophet), *L'Immoraliste* (1902) (*The Immoralist*), *La Porte étroite* (1909) (*Straight is the Gate*) and *Les Caves du Vatican* (1914) (*The Vatican Cellars*).[1] Gide's biblical drama *Saül* (1903) (*Saul*) is shaped in part by Wilde's *Salomé* (Brown Downey 2004). His 'Hommage à Oscar Wilde' (Homage to Oscar Wilde), first published in *L'Ermitage* in June 1902, was revised, sometimes under the title of 'In memoriam', in 1903, 1910, 1921 and 1933. His appreciation of *DP*, 'Le "De Profundis" d'Oscar Wilde', came out in 1905, with revised editions in 1910 and 1933. Wilde features in Gide's 1926 autobiography, *Si le grain ne meurt* (1926) (*If It Die*) (Gide 2001, 266 and 298–312) and is cited in Gide's defence of pederasty, *Corydon* (Gide 1924, 19). Gide functioned as repository and disseminator, in France and throughout Europe, of now famous quotations by Wilde. His recollections supplied Léon Guillot de Saix with several *contes parlés* (oral tales) by Wilde, which Saix collected in *Le Chant du cygne* (Swan song) (Wilde 1942), as well as material for a series of radio plays broadcast in the late 1950s on the regional antennae of France II; Guillot de Saix's archives contain draft scripts of these programmes, including notes comprising a mosaic of Gide's writings on Wilde from the *Journal*, 'Hommage' and the autobiography (Guillot de Saix n.d., 4°-COL–31/301). Gide's writings played a crucial role in the European diffusion and understanding of Wilde's works. As several of the essays in this collection make clear, his 1902 essay, translated into German in 1903, had a substantial impact on Wilde's critical reputation (Kohlmayer

---

[1] See, for example, Masson 1998 and 2002 and Segal 1998, 139–40, 180–81 & 292.

1996, ch. 3). Select writings of Gide about Wilde were translated early into German, English and Czech amongst others (Gide 1903a, 1904, 1905b, 1918, 1929) and were sometimes included in editions of Wilde's works. This practice continues to this day: for instance, *DP* was recently translated from French into Romanian and accompanied by Gide's recollections (Wilde 1996).

Meetings

The milieu of the Paris salons in which Wilde and Gide circulated and met is lucidly set out by Richard Hibbitt in this volume. Pierre Louÿs introduced Gide to Wilde at the home of Henri de Régnier on 27 November 1891. Gide was dazzled by the Irish aesthete, then at his apogee (Gide 1955, 139), and saw him at least six times in December (1996, 1389 note; Masson 1978); his appointments diary has 'Wilde' scrawled in giant letters across an entire page (Delay 1957, 133). Jules Renard, who had seen Gide at Marcel Schwob's home, observed him to be 'in love with Oscar Wilde' ('amoureux d'Oscar Wilde') (Renard 1960, 107).

After this first meeting, Gide's fascination soon morphed into terror: he destroyed the pages of his *Journal* which referred to their meetings (Delay 1957, 134) and sought refuge with his paternal family, austere Protestants from Uzès. In the *Journal* of 29–31 December he beseeches God to protect him from evil and lead him towards sincerity and on 1 January 1892 he writes: 'Wilde, I believe, did me only harm. With him I had unlearned to think' (Gide 1996, 148).[2] Directly before his first meeting with Wilde, Paul Valéry had suggested to Gide the possibility of his encountering a double (Gide 1955, 139). There is reason to believe that Gide may have construed Wilde precisely as this. The first noteworthy tale Wilde recounts to Gide features two narcissists locked in mutual fascination (Gide 1999, 838–39), and Delay uses this image as a metaphor for the relationship between Gide and Wilde (Delay 1957, 136). Gide's *Journal* of 27 November 1892, a year to the day after his first meeting with Wilde, reads cryptically: 'This evening, having understood that I must die, I was terror-stricken' (Gide 1996, 156).[3] According to superstition, the man who catches sight of his double will die within a year (Rank 1971, 50).

Gide met Wilde again in Florence, in May 1894. Wilde and Alfred Douglas, who were leaving Florence precipitately, invited Gide to take over their apartment. Gide, who had heard from Louÿs of the camp manners of Wilde's London friends (Gide 2001, 300 and 1187 note) wrote to Régnier: 'It took little to persuade me to occupy the bed of Oscar Wilde' (1997a, 140).[4] The third meeting took place in Blida, Algeria, on 27 January 1895. Three days later, in Algiers, Wilde procured for Gide a pubescent Arab named Mohammed, who was 'Bosie's' (Gide 2001, 307; but see Sherard and Renier

---

[2] 'Wilde ne m'a fait, je crois, que du mal. Avec lui j'avais désappris de penser.'
[3] 'Ce soir, ayant compris qu'il me fallait mourir, je fus effrayé.'
[4] 'Il s'en est fallu de peu que je n'occupe la couche d'Oscar Wilde.'

1933). Gide's autobiography is equivocal on the question of sexual initiation since he had, at that point, already enjoyed fleeting homosexual encounters (278–80), but the narrator can only declare to have found 'ma normale' – that is, his normality, understood as his sexual identity as a homosexual – following the Algiers experience (310). On 31 January, Wilde returned to London for his first trial and Gide and Douglas set off separately to the oasis of Biskra (Gide 1988, 597) where they spent a fortnight together (Gide 2001, 1190 note; Gide 1997b, 90). Their subsequent correspondence stopped in March 1897 (Mouret 1975), Douglas apparently having served his purpose for Gide as a point of contact to Wilde in prison (Reid 2009, 87–89).

Gide visited the freed Wilde in Berneval-sur-Mer, outside Dieppe, on 19 June 1897 (Gide 1999, 852). Afterwards, the two men saw each other infrequently in Paris, Gide lending Wilde money once at least (Wilde 2000, 1108 and 1111), and their last meeting probably took place in 1898. Gide was in Biskra in December 1900 when he learned of Wilde's death.

Treacherous waters

> Like the Greek philosophers, Wilde did not write but spoke and lived his wisdom, conferring it imprudently upon the fluid memory of men, as though he were writing it on water. (Gide 1999, 837)[5]

Accessing Wilde through Gide's 'fluid memory' is a dangerous business. In the *Journal* for 3 July 1913, Gide, triggered by his reading of Arthur Ransome's *Oscar Wilde, a Critical Study* (1912), expresses his ambition to be an explicator of Wilde. The passage is worth quoting in full.

> Ransome's book strikes me as good – and even very good in places. Perhaps he admires a little too much the ornamentation in which Wilde loved to drape his thought and which I continue to find quite artificial. Yet he does not show to what extent the plays *An Ideal Husband* and *A Woman of No Importance* are revealing – and, I would almost say, confidential, despite their apparent objectivity.
>
> Certainly, in my little book on Wilde, I was unjust towards his *œuvre* and criticized it too readily, that is to say, without knowing it sufficiently well. Thinking back, I admire how Wilde listened to me with such equanimity when, in Algiers, I made judgments on his plays (quite impertinently, it strikes me now). There was no hint of impatience in the tone of his response, nor even any protest; it was this that led him to tell me – almost as an excuse – that extraordinary sentence, which I have quoted and which has since been quoted everywhere: 'I put all my genius into my life; I put only my talent into my works.' I would be interested to know if he ever uttered that sentence to anyone else.
>
> At a later point I truly hope to be able to return to that and recount all that I didn't dare say at the outset. I would thereby [or 'also'] like to *explain* Wilde's œuvre

---

5   'Pareil aux philosophes de la Grèce, Wilde n'écrivait pas mais causait et vivait sa sagesse, la confiant imprudemment à la mémoire fluide des hommes, et comme l'écrivant sur de l'eau.'

in my own way, and, in particular, his theatre, of which the greatest interest lies between the lines. (1996, 746–47)[6]

When he shows how his own interrogations elicited Wilde's sentence, "'I put all my genius into my life [...]'", Gide presents himself as catalyst for, chosen repository for and disseminator of, Wilde's wit. The *tête-à-tête* nature of the conversation and its exotic setting allow Gide to pull rank on other commentators by emphasizing his privileged contact with Wilde, as he would again do in 1927 with André Maurois's *Etudes anglaises* (English studies) (Gide 1997b, 43). By contrasting artifice and authenticity, Gide shows that he sees the Wilde beneath the mask and is thus better-placed to interpret his work; at the same time, he signals his own self-assertive departure from Wilde's tenets. The interrelation of life and work, reflected in Wilde's memorable quotation, is a concept which Gide learned from Wilde and which he made an enduring bedrock of his aesthetic: the closing phrase of his final work of fiction, *Thésée* (Theseus, 1946), will read: 'j'ai fait mon œuvre. J'ai vécu' (I created my *œuvre*. I lived) (1958, 1453). On 3 January 1892, Gide writes that the artist is not duty-bound to recount his life as he lived it, but to live it as he plans to recount it (1996, 149).[7] According to an entry of 16 January 1896, Gide considers Wilde's life to be 'more important than his works' (1996, 213),[8] and by 'life' Gide is surely also referring to sexuality, as his comments on Wilde's aestheticism in 1927 suggest: 'Here, as always, and sometimes without the artist even

---

6   'Le livre de Ransome me paraît bon – et même très bon par endroits. Peut-être admire-t-il un peu trop les parures dont Wilde aimait à recouvrir sa pensée, et qui continuent à m'apparaître assez factices – et par contre ne montre-t-il pas à quel point les pièces *Un mari idéal* et *La Femme de peu d'importance* sons révélatrices – et j'allais dire: confidentielles, – malgré leur apparente objectivité. / Certainement, dans mon petit livre sur Wilde, je me suis montré peu juste pour son œuvre et j'en ai fait fi trop à la légère, je veux dire: avant de l'avoir connue suffisamment. J'admire, en y repensant, la bonne grâce avec laquelle Wilde m'écoutait lorsque, à Alger, je faisais le procès de ses pièces (fort impertinemment, à ce qu'il me paraît aujourd'hui). Aucune impatience dans le ton de sa réponse, et même pas une protestation; c'est alors qu'il fut amené à me dire, et presque en manière d'excuse, cette extraordinaire phrase, que j'ai citée et que depuis on a citée partout: 'J'ai mis tout mon génie dans ma vie; je n'ai mis que mon talent dans mes œuvres.' Je serais curieux de savoir s'il a jamais dit cette phrase à quelque autre que moi. / Plus tard j'espère bien pouvoir revenir là-dessus et raconter alors tout ce que je n'ai pas osé dire d'abord. Je voudrais aussi expliquer à ma façon l'œuvre de Wilde, et en particulier son théâtre – dont le plus grand intérêt gît entre les lignes.'

7   Cf. Wilde's comment, cited by Gide: '*Je ne peux pas* penser autrement qu'en contes' (*I cannot* but think in tales) (Gide 1999, 842), and his words in *DP*: 'I knew art as the supreme reality, and life as a mere mode of fiction' (Wilde 2005, 123, note from 1908 edition).

8   'plus importante que ses œuvres'. This diary entry, published for the first time in its entirety in 1996, is very revealing of Wilde's influence on Gide's aesthetic. See Gide 1996 (1893), 170–71.

being aware, it is the secret of the depths of the flesh which dictates, inspires and decides' (1997b, 43).[9]

In the extract Gide reprimands himself for having been too harsh in his criticism of Wilde's works in his book, *Oscar Wilde* (1910). This admission is slippery, since the book in question is a republication of two texts Gide had revised already (1902 and 1905a). Moreover, in *Oscar Wilde*, Gide declares that his accounts are 'simply and strictly exact' ('simplement et strictement exact') (1910a, 51), a view he holds again in 1926 (2001, 299). These shifts in attitude illustrate Gide's ever-changing relation to Wilde. The young Gide of 1902 and 1905 is presented as arrogant, unduly critical and impudent (albeit skilled at eliciting quotations of genius), while his wiser self of 1913 is humble ('my little book'), contrite, self-critical and tender towards the established artist. A partial explanation for these developments can be sought in Harold Bloom's well-known theory of the anxiety of influence, whereby the young poet assimilates the influence of the older poet in a process involving denigration of the precursor in order to extol his/her own merits, before creating an imaginative space in which the older poet can return in the new poet's colours, speaking in his/her voice (Bloom 1973, 141); this last phase would accord with Gide's almost proprietorial desire to explain Wilde's *œuvre*. But Gide's changing depictions of Wilde also depend on the degree of progress towards his own coming-out: in 1926, Gide became the first French author to write about his homosexuality in autobiography, while simultaneously writing of Wilde's. Prior to this, references to the homosexuality of the historical Wilde and his fictional avatars are almost invariably covert.

In the 1913 *Journal* entry, Gide describes Wilde's plays as 'confidential' ('confidentiel') – a term he uses here and elsewhere to denote the homosexual subtext in Wilde's life and his own status as an initiated and knowing listener, reader and critic (e.g. 1999, 147 and 838; 2001, 302–05). When Gide states his wish to be more daring in future accounts of Wilde, the contemporary reader may infer a proleptic allusion to his sexually explicit texts of the 1920s, and yet the quotation immediately swerves to Wilde's *œuvre* and his theatre. If we draw on material from across Gide's works, he seems to be setting up a parallel between Wilde's 'lacking' written output (in comparison to his spoken genius witnessed by only a select few) and his 'lacking' admission to homosexuality. For instance, in *Corydon*, Wilde is berated for denying homosexuality in public (Gide 1924, 19), while in 'Le "De Profundis"' he is shown in private to voice his '"perverse pleasures"' ('"plaisirs pervers"') to an unsuspecting friend (Gide 1999, 147). Thus, in Gide's early texts on Wilde, writing may function as a code for 'outed' homosexuality, whereas speaking signifies its transient practice.

For Gide, the best of Wilde's theatre 'lies between the lines' ('gît entre les lignes'). *Gît* (from the infinitive, *gésir*) evokes buried bodies, *ci-gît* meaning 'here lies'. Gide was, it seems, preoccupied by Wilde's death, as is further suggested by the fact that the memorial texts 'Hommage' and 'Le "De Profundis"' were presented respectively as 'a wreath on a neglected grave' (1999, 837) and

---

[9]   'Ici, comme presque toujours, et parfois à l'insu même de l'artiste, c'est le secret du profond de sa chair qui dicte, inspire et décide.'

a gesture intended to 'pay homage to a sad site of memory' (1999, 149).[10] Elsewhere, Gide intimates that he feels haunted by Wilde (Gide 1968, vol. 1, 67; Langlade 1975, 155), a state which may have motivated his prolonged efforts to represent and re-represent Wilde in terms that right unjust or overly discrete portrayals.

The *Journal* entry of July 1913 alerts us to some of the most important features in Gide's wider presentation of Wilde, namely Gide's belief in his own exceptional ability to penetrate Wilde's artifice; the interrelating of the artist's life and work; Gide's changeable and sometimes equivocal relation to Wilde during his life-time and after; and the role of confidentiality and guilt regarding Wilde in Gide's homotextuality (Apter 1987). In this unstable, coded and spooked context, I wish to put forward a reading of Gide's 'Hommage à Oscar Wilde' as his appropriation of Wilde's 'Tale of Judas'.

'Hommage à Oscar Wilde' or 'The Tale of Judas'

In a letter of March 1910 Wilde's literary executor, Robert Ross, congratulates Gide on his re-edition of the homage, which he considers 'not only the best account of Oscar Wilde at the different stages of his career, but the only true and accurate impression of him that I have ever read' (Gide 2001, 299). If, as Wilde is recorded as having said, '[e]very great man has his disciples, but it is always Judas who writes his biography' (Wilde 1942, 112),[11] we may speculate that Gide, author of the 'best account' of Wilde, may have assumed the role of Judas.

The homage was published in June 1902, fifteen months after Wilde's death, although Gide had been working on it from June 1901. In the original version, place names and people are designated by initials alone. The text is considerably longer than the other thirty-four homages he penned from 1898 to 1951 (to Mallarmé, Conrad, Rilke, Arnold Bennett and others), and is structured around Gide's personal memories. Part 1 presents Wilde in all his glory in Paris, in 1891, and contains six tales he recounted to Gide. Part 2 marks the beginning of Wilde's downfall and describes elliptically Gide's Algerian meeting with Wilde in January 1895. Part 3 relates Gide's visit to Wilde in Berneval–sur–Mer immediately after the latter's release from prison and documents Wilde's vow to complete his writing projects before returning to Paris. Part 4 is a direct quotation from Douglas reiterating Wilde's vow. Part 5 marks Wilde's return to Paris without having written the work he had set out to complete.

Recent critics consider the homage a disservice to Wilde. Daniel Durosay writes of the paradoxical balance of praise and criticism of the pariah (2000, 158). Pierre Masson calls the piece a lament verging on an indictment due to Gide's stress on Wilde's failure to make his writing commensurate with

---

[10] 'une couronne sur une tombe délaissée'; 'servir une triste mémoire'. The 1933 version of this second line in Gide's *Œuvres complètes*, modified after Gide resurrects Wilde in Apollonian terms in *Si le grain ne meurt*, reads 'triste et glorieuse mémoire' (sad and glorious site of memory) (Gide 1999, 1013, variant).

[11] 'Tout grand homme a ses disciples, mais c'est toujours Judas qui écrit la biographie.'

his spoken, lived genius (1988, 115). Richard Ellmann comments that Gide, in this homage and 'Le "De Profundis"', 'achieves a supremacy not attained during their early acquaintance by depicting Wilde as talking away a talent which Gide could husband in books' (Wilde 1969, 4). So, in ostensibly paying tribute to Wilde, Gide is in fact engaged in a game of artistic one-upmanship. Granted, by insisting that Wilde's genius was orally conveyed, not written, and by emphasizing in the homage the acuity of his own ear ('one of those who listened to him most avidly' [Gide 1999, 837]; 'Wilde's words are present in my spirit, I would almost say, in my ear' [1999, 846 note]),[12] Gide shows his own significance as a store for Wilde's evanescent genius. But Gide's privileging of Wilde's orality over his writing could also be viewed as part of his strategy in creating the Christ–Judas relationship: on the one hand, Gide's disparaging of Wilde, from whom he learned so much, may be viewed as a betrayal of sorts; while, on the other, it leaves the disciple (and biographer) behind to record the events of the martyr's life and take up his teaching.[13]

Further textual clues posit Gide as Judas. Wilde's *œuvre* was perceived by some critics as prophetic and open-ended. In the preface of *Etudes anglaises*, Raymond Laurent's neglected study of Wilde and others which Emily Eells brings to our attention in this volume, R. J. E. Tiddy asserts that Wilde's writing will remain an enigma for years to come (Laurent 1910, vii–viii); while Laurent himself writes that Wilde's expression of his apprehension of beauty is 'eternally incomplete' ('éternellement incomplète') (Laurent 1910, 318; see also Gide 1999, 843–44). In this open-ended mode, Gide's and Wilde's tales of Judas are prescient of an archaeological find made in Egypt in the mid–1970s and made public by the *National Geographic* in April 2006: a papyrus entitled *Gospel of Judas* – which appears to be a pseudopigraphy since it is dated at AD150 (Pagels and King 2007, xi note) – which paints Judas as Jesus's closest confidant in contrast to the canonical gospels which lambast Judas as the betrayer.[14] The complex relation of discipleship emerges already from Gide's account of his first meaningful encounter with Wilde, which uncannily resembles verse 2, line 25 of the *Gospel of Judas*, where Jesus urges Judas to '"Separate from them. I will tell you the mysteries of the kingdom"' (Pagals and King 2007, 111). The scene takes place as Wilde, Gide and two other acquaintances had just left a restaurant in Paris, after dining.

> Wilde took me aside: 'You listen with your eyes,' he said to me quite abruptly; 'that is why I shall tell you this story:
> "When Narcissus died, the fields' flowers were saddened and asked the river for droplets of water with which to mourn him [*the tale continues*]."'

---

[12] 'un de ceux qui l'auront le plus avidement écoute' and 'les paroles de Wilde sont présentes à mon esprit, j'allais dire à mon oreille'.

[13] Indeed, in a 1943 *Journal* entry, in which speaking wisely is presented as something to which established worthies ought to aspire, the septuagenarian Gide contrasts his sense of oral impotence to Wilde's admirable ability to talk (Gide 1997b, 892).

[14] Many thanks to Gregory Platten for signalling these sources to me.

Then Wilde, clearing his throat with a strange burst of laughter, added: 'That is called: *The Disciple.*' (Gide 1999, 838–39)[15]

Wilde's choice of Narcissus as his subject matter is particularly timely as Gide was, at that time, finishing *Le Traité du Narcisse*, which he probably modified as a result of their encounter.[16] In the homage Gide sets himself out as a privileged follower of Wilde by quoting Wilde's declaration that the tale is titled 'Le Disciple' and implying that he alone was chosen to listen to it. Other accounts of Wilde contest this exclusivity. Henri de Régnier, for instance, recalls that Wilde recounted tales as though nobody after you 'could possibly merit hearing these wonderful stories which the guileful charmer gave out with such royal profusion' (Wilde 1942, 25–26);[17] and Henry D. Davray remembers how the listener could believe the tales to have been improvised for him or her alone, adding that 'the parable of *The Disciple* was one of his favourites' (Wilde 1942, 48).[18] These bathetic accounts make Gide's self-depiction as disciple appear even more reliant on myth.

Gide's claim that in 1891 and 1892 he saw Wilde 'often and everywhere' ('je le vis souvent et partout') (Gide 1999, 839) is certainly a historical exaggeration, as the Pléiade editor notes (Gide 1999, 1215 note); but, in keeping with the mystical tone of his reminiscences, Gide could also be implying that he saw Wilde everywhere in spirit, as a marker of his haunting quality or even, conceivably, of his divinity. In his 1926 autobiographical account of the period, Gide reports taking Wilde to a dinner at which the Princess Ouroussoff loudly interjected that she had just seen 'around the face of the Irishman, a halo' ('autour du visage de l'Irlandais, une auréole') (Gide 2001, 266). He further relates Wilde to Christ in the homage when he recounts Wilde's biblical tales, evokes his 'representative mission' ('mission représentative') (Gide 1999, 841), observes his ambition to revise established Christian idealism and presents him after prison preaching humility and pity. Interestingly, in the one mention of Gide in Wilde's *DP*, Gide is evoked in conjunction with a conversation on Christ: 'I remember saying once to André Gide [...], that [...] there was nothing that either Plato or Christ had said that could not be transferred immediately into the sphere of Art, and there find its complete fulfilment' (Wilde 2005a, 173). This paragraph marks the beginning of the long section in *DP* in which the post-prison

---

[15] 'Wilde me prit à part: "Vous écoutez avec les yeux," me dit-il assez brusquement; "voilà pourquoi je vous raconterai cette histoire: 'Quand Narcisse fut mort les fleurs des champs se désolèrent et demandèrent à la rivière des gouttes d'eau pour le pleurer [...]'. / Puis Wilde, se rengorgeant avec un bizarre éclat de rire, ajoutait: "Cela s'appelle: *Le Disciple*."' 'The Disciple' was first published in the *Spirit Lamp* 4 (6 June 1893), 49–50, then revised for the *Fortnightly Review* (July 1894), 23–24.

[16] Gide's correspondence with Valéry of November and December 1891 presents a treatise finished before the first meeting with Wilde and unfinished after (Gide 1955, 133–34, 136–37, 141).

[17] 'n'eût été digne d'entendre ces admirables histoires que l'astucieux charmeur répandait avec une si royale profusion.'

[18] 'l'apologue du *Disciple* était un de ses favoris.'

Wilde mythologizes himself as Christ (Wilde 2005a, 173–85). It is likely that Gide responded to this inclusion by espousing Wilde's self-mythologization as Christ in his rereading of their exchanges – Gide's decision in 1910 to republish revised versions of the homage and 'Le "De Profundis" d'Oscar Wilde' together in *Oscar Wilde* certainly points towards this. A similar mythology of Wilde as Christ also emerges in the Italian, Russian and Greek receptions.

Although the 'Hommage' contains no sexual references, intimacy between Wilde and Gide is nevertheless created through emotional, intellectual and physical contact. Gide insists that to most people the Wilde of 1891 appeared as an amusing ghost, the entertainer wearing a carnival mask (1999, 838–39); but as soon as they were alone, he was authentic, enquiring, fascinated by the Gospels and tutelary towards the young Gide. When Gide encounters by chance Wilde's name on the hotel register in Blida, Algeria, he writes of their names touching on the page (1999, 844) (in the later autobiographical version, their names are apart). In their final meeting, their hands touch also: Wilde interrupts Gide's scolding of him for returning to Paris before completing his play by laying his hand on Gide's and telling him that '"one mustn't hold anything against [...] *someone who has been struck*"' ('"il ne faut pas en vouloir [...] à *quelqu'un qui a été frappé*"') (1999, 854). Gide wants to be the first of Wilde's French friends to see him on his release from prison, just as he was the last one to see him before the trial. This intimacy reminds readers of Wilde's 'John and Judas', a sensuous tale mentioned in passing in Gide's homage, in which Judas's betrayal is motivated partly by his jealousy of John for having become Christ's most loved disciple and partly by his faith that Jesus is the messiah and must therefore be betrayed in order to make the prophecy come true: 'because we always end up killing the things we love' ('car on finit toujours par tuer ce qu'on aime') (Wilde 1942, 114). Wilde is also recorded as having commented that Christ should have been betrayed by John, his most beloved disciple, because it is always the person you love most who betrays you, with a kiss (Wilde 1942, 112).

The sensual, expressive image of lips alludes to both the sexual subtext and spoken language. In Paris, in 1891, Wilde tells Gide:

> I don't like your lips; they are straight like those of someone who has never lied. I want to teach you to lie, so that your lips become beautiful and twisted, like those of an antique mask. (Gide 1999, 840)[19]

In Berneval, Wilde tells Gide how you could tell those new to prison because they had not yet learned how to 'speak without moving their lips' ('parler sans remuer les lèvres') (Gide 1999, 850), an image which resonates with Douglas's famous poetic description of male homosexuality as 'the Love that dare not speak its name'. The implication is that if Gide, like Judas, lies or is treacherous

---

[19] 'Je n'aime pas vos lèvres; elles sont droites comme celles de quelqu'un qui n'a jamais menti. Je veux vous apprendre à mentir, pour que vos lèvres deviennent belles et tordues comme celles d'un masque antique.'

in his expression, he is merely doing Wilde's bidding. If, however, he rejects Wilde's teaching in favour of authenticity, at least the reader can be assured that the homage-biography is 'a true and accurate impression' (Robert Ross, cited in English in Gide 2001, 299 note). Showing Wilde after prison to be deft at speaking without moving his lips – still a skilled story-teller but a defeated writer – again puts Gide in the disciple's position, duty-bound to disseminate in text Wilde's teachings delivered confidentially to him.

Wilde explains that he cannot return to Paris before writing a play; otherwise the public will see in him only the convict (Gide 1999, 848). Four pages later, offset by two blank lines, Gide writes: 'That same evening [Wilde] told me his project of a play on Pharaoh and a tale about Judas' ('Ce même soir [Wilde] me raconte son projet de drame sur Pharaon et un conte sur Judas') (1999, 852). The phrasing is deceptive since a cursory reading suggests that Wilde was planning to write a play on Pharaoh as well as a tale of Judas. But grammatically this is impossible since no 'de' precedes 'un conte', meaning that 'raconter' (to recount or to tell) is really being employed zeugmatically: Wilde told Gide of his project of the play on Pharaoh, *then* recounted to him the tale of Judas. Yet the rhetorical trick creates momentarily the impression that Wilde's failure to complete his writing projects by the time of his arrival in Paris involves his failure to write a tale of Judas. Gide, keen to husband in books the talent which Wilde talks away, as Ellmann observes, can therefore pen 'The Tale of Judas' in Wilde's stead.

There are various precedents for Gide's technique of echoing Wilde's work. Philippe Delaveau remarks on the tendentious order in which Gide presents Wilde's tales in the homage, their subject matter following the subject matter of Gide's own publications (1985, 61); and Masson identifies in Gide's play *El Hadj* (1899) a reworking of Wilde's tale of the story-teller (Masson 1998, 116–17; Gide 1999, 839–40). Additionally, Gide's description of Wilde after prison in the homage is a reworking of the image of the dead Dorian Gray which closes Wilde's 1890 novella: Dorian Gray 'was withered, wrinkled, and loathsome of visage. It was not till they had examined the rings that they recognized who it was' (Wilde 2005b, 164). Gide relates of Wilde:

> I note [...] that the skin of his face has become red and rough; that of his hands even more so, yet they are wearing again the same rings; one, to which he is particularly attached, carries in a swivel-top setting a lapis-lazuli Egyptian scarab. (1999, 847–48)[20]

Gide had a penchant for appropriation, in particular with regard to Dostoevsky, upon whose works he comments in order to elucidate his own (Gide 1999, 637 and 559; Gide 1996, 1184). Langlade has argued that Gide found in Dostoevsky's work the same elements that drew him to Wilde's, namely individualism, Christ's humanity and humility (1975, 173–76). When Gide

---

[20] 'Je remarque [...] que la peau du visage est devenue rouge et commune; celle des mains encore plus, qui pourtant ont repris les mêmes bagues; une, à laquelle il tient beaucoup, porte en chaton mobile un scarabée d'Egypte en lapis-lazuli.'

writes, in relation to André Maurois's text on Wilde, that 'one feels that Maurois does not *possess* his subject' ('on sent qu[e Maurois] ne *possède* pas son sujet') (1997b, 43), the implication is that Gide, by contrast, does. The final pages of his homage read like a tale of Judas, which is not so much an echo but rather an appropriation of Wilde's oral tale, which Gide tantalizingly mentions but, unlike the other tales related to him, does not cite (1999, 839–44; 852). Gide recalls:

> One evening on the boulevards where I was strolling with G★★★, I heard someone calling out my name. I turned around to see Wilde. Ah! he was so transformed! [...] 'Were I to leave before writing my play, the world would see in me only the convict', he had told me. He had come back without the play and, since a number of doors had been closed to him, he no longer tried to enter anywhere; he prowled [...]. I was a little embarrassed, I must admit, to see him, especially in a place where so many people might pass by. Wilde was sitting at a table on a café terrace. He ordered for G★★★ and me two cocktails [...]. I made to sit opposite him, that is, so that I would have my back to the passers-by, but Wilde was hurt by this gesture, which he took for a show of absurd shame (alas, he was not far wrong):
> [...] 'Oh! do sit there, next to me' he said, pointing to a chair beside him, 'I am so alone at present!' (1999, 853–54)[21]

By documenting his shame at being seen with Wilde, Gide opens himself to accusations of cowardice and, crucially, betrayal. This passage thus becomes a *mise-en-abyme* for the wider betrayal of the homage's indictment of Wilde's 'deficient' writings, which Ellmann, Durosay and Masson underscore. Simultaneously, Gide's 'Tale of Judas' corresponds to what Bloom calls '*Apophrades*', the final stage of his model of anxiety of influence: it can be read as Gide writing Wilde's 'characteristic work' (Bloom 1973, 16) and, in so doing, fulfilling 'his precursor's prophecies by fundamentally re-creating those prophecies in his own unmistakeable idiom' (Bloom 1973, 152). Bloom's description of '*Apophrades*' resonates with the argument that it was Judas's responsibility to fulfil the prophesy of betrayal.

Why might Gide have wished to play Judas to Wilde's Christ? It seems that exorcizing his guilt *vis-à-vis* Wilde was a necessary part of the process of working towards publicly legitimizing the homosexuality that Wilde had privately legitimized for him in Algiers in 1895. Observing how Gide, 'fully

---

21   'Un soir, sur les boulevards, où je me promenais avec G★★★, je m'entendis appeler par mon nom. Je me retournai: c'était Wilde. Ah! combien il était changé! [...]. "Si je repartais avant d'avoir écrit mon drame, le monde ne voudra voir en moi que le forçat", m'avait-il dit. Il était reparu sans drame et, comme devant lui quelques portes s'étaient fermées, il ne cherchait plus à rentrer nulle part; il rôdait [...] je fus un peu gêné, je l'avoue, de le revoir et dans un lieu où pouvait passer tant de monde. – Wilde était attablé sur la terrasse d'un café. Il commanda pour G★★★ et pour moi deux cocktails [...]. J'allais m'asseoir en face de lui, c'est-à-dire de manière à tourner le dos aux passants, mais Wilde, s'affectant de ce geste, qu'il prit pour un élan d'absurde honte (il ne se trompait, hélas! pas tout à fait): [...] "Oh ! mettez-vous donc là, près de moi, dit-il, en m'indiquant, à côté de lui, une chaise; je suis tellement seul à présent!"'

aware of the anomaly of his impunity', 'spoke of discomfiture at the contrast between his fate and Wilde's', Naomi Segal has argued that Gide fantasized of 'being attacked and surviving with courage' (Segal 1998, 220–22). Illustration of this is provided by Gide's *Journal* of 1917:

> I am not writing these Memoirs [*Si le grain ne meurt*] to defend myself. I don't need to defend myself because I have not been accused. I'm writing them before I am accused. I'm writing them in order to be accused. (Gide 1996, 1019)[22]

This 'writing to be accused' is also behind Gide's self-presentation as Judas in 'Hommage à Oscar Wilde'.

Masson identifies in Gide's *Les Caves du Vatican* (1914) a cluster of Wildean signifiers surrounding the fictional character Fabien Taylor, Lord Gravensdale, in whose name 'Cravan' (as in 'Arthur') and 'Dorian Gray' are inscribed anagrammatically (Masson 2002, 72–73). Significantly, Taylor is an English-looking gentleman who is *très accusé* – that is, he has 'very accentuated features' or rather he is 'very accused' (Gide 1958, 715). Recall the fleeting intimation in 1891–92 that Gide perceived Wilde as his double and Gide's decision in his 1926 autobiography to expose his own homosexuality next to Wilde's. Gide's own soliciting of accusation in the 'Hommage' may well be intended to align himself to the 'very accused' Wilde, the disciple's desire to imitate the master's experience.

---

22 'Je n'écris pas ces Mémoires pour me défendre. Je n'ai point à me défendre, puisque je ne suis pas accusé. Je les écris avant d'être accusé. Je les écris pour qu'on m'accuse'.

6 'Astonishing in my Italian': Oscar Wilde's First Italian Editions 1890–1952

Rita Severi

'The Italian papers assign [Wilde] a much higher place than that which he held in London society.' (Ouida)

Introducing the aesthete

The reception and fame of most great authors partly rely on the work of their translators. Oscar Wilde was keenly aware of this and, when possible, befriended and kept in close contact with his translators throughout his life. He was on friendly terms with Henry D. Davray, who translated *BRG* into French in 1898 (just after its first English edition) and then PP in 1899. In his *Oscar Wilde, la tragédie finale* (Oscar Wilde, the final tragedy) (1928), Davray also gave resonance to Wildean aesthetics in France. Wilde exchanged ideas about literary and artistic issues with Enrique Gomez Carrillo (Ellmann 1987, 322–24 and Richard Cardwell in this volume), a young poet from Guatemala who contributed to Wilde's fame in South America with his versions of *Salomé*: *El triunfo de Salomé* (The triumph of *Salomé*) (1900) and *El origen de la Salomé de Wilde* (The origin of Wilde' *Salomé*) (1902). He often confided his thoughts to the French translator of *Intentions* (1905), Jean Joseph Renaud, a sharp observer of the writer's mannerisms and witticisms in his own social milieu (Ellmann 1987, 251 and 261) and a friend whom Wilde trusted even in his darkest moments. Some critics consider Renaud Wilde's first biographer because of the anecdotes and striking episodes told by him, which have come down to us as part of an authentic Wildean lore.

Since English was not widely studied or spoken in Italy, most translators relied on French editions. French was the language of culture and mediation throughout the nineteenth century and its associations with refinement and sophistication endured through the first half of the twentieth century. As a consequence most Italian translations of English authors of the time follow the French versions. This is also true in the case of Wilde, with a few exceptions. Wilde had met his first Italian translators in Naples in 1897; but he did not live to see their translations published. All Italian translations of his literary and dramatic works, save the script for the first Italian performance of *VN*, appeared after Wilde's death. *VN* was staged at the Teatro Diana in Milan by Andrea Maggi and Clara Della Guardia's theatre company in 1890. It was a fiasco, running for only three nights, and was never revived (Wilde 1994, 283).

SMUS, by contrast, enjoyed great acclaim and became popular throughout Italy. First published by the *Fortnightly Review* in February 1890, this essay appeared in book form just a year later, published in New York by Humboldt. It was reprinted in London in 1895 by Arthur Humphreys (Holland 2003, 253), while the Hebrew translation was issued on the pages of the London magazine, *The Worker's Friend*. It is somewhat surprising, therefore, to discover that in 1892 a few paragraphs of Wilde's essay made up a booklet entitled 'L'individualismo' (Individualism) that was sold with the periodical *L'Uguaglianza Sociale* (Social equality), distributed in the Sicilian city of Marsala. This Italian anarchist paper, along with similar publications across Europe – *La Révolte* (Rebellion) in Paris, *Productor* in Barcelona and the German periodical *Die Autonomie* (Autonomy) in London, all of which printed the same extracts from *SMUS* – kept up-to-date about current avant-garde ideas alongside its social criticism (Wilde 1913a, 219–220).

Another striking exception to the posthumous publication of Wilde's work in Italy is a review of the French translation of *BRG* by the young writer, journalist and art critic Ugo Ojetti (1871–1946). Ojetti's review appeared in the literary magazine *Il Marzocco* on 4 December 1898 under an elaborate *fin-de-siècle* frieze drawn by the Venetian artist Mariano Fortuny. Considering *BRG* a modern Dantesque Inferno, Ojetti paraphrases the poem and translates a number of stanzas into Italian. Like subsequent translations of *BRG*, the excerpt was rendered directly from the French version by Davray; it was full of Gallicisms and adopted a prose periphrasis that prevents the Italian reader from inferring anything about its musicality, at a time when poetical translations were published without the original on the opposite page. Nonetheless, *La ballata del carcere di Reading* soon acquired a wide readership (D'Amico and Severi 2001, 73–85).

During his last trip to Italy, Wilde stayed in Palermo between 2 and 10 April 1900. In a letter dated 16 April 1900 and sent from Rome, he tells Robert Ross how enthralled he had been by the sight of the city, praising it as one of the most wonderful places in the world: 'it dreams away its life in the Conca d'Oro, the exquisite valley that lies between two seas' (Wilde 2000, 1178–81). On 10 April 1900, the newspaper *Giornale di Sicilia* (Sicilian journal) notes Wilde's time in Palermo under the heading 'Note Mondane' (Worldly notes): 'Oscar Wilde, the aesthete, professes the principle that life is worthless if we live it like everybody else',[1] and quotes (in a terrible translation) a few aphorisms and some lines from the 'ballata dell'ergastolo' ('ballad of the death ward', *sic!*), defined as 'an example of macabre lyrical verse' ('uno squarcio di lirica macabra') (D'Amico and Severi 2001, 179–209).

---

[1] 'Oscar Wilde, l'esteta, professa questo principio: che la vita non ha alcun valore se la si vive come tutti gli altri'.

His letters make it clear that Wilde wanted his works to be circulated more widely in Italy. However, he was well aware that few Italians could read English and that most Italian translators relied on French versions. This may have accounted for his eagerness to see his Symbolist play *Salomé*, originally written in French, translated into Italian before his other works.

Translating *Salomé* in Naples

After his release from prison, Wilde joined Alfred Douglas in Naples (D'Amico 1994, 76–81). It was here that he met the men who would become his first Italian translators: Biagio Chiara and Giuseppe Garibaldi Rocco. A young poet and the first Italian translator of *Salomé*, Rocco is mentioned twice in Wilde's letters from within a week of arriving in the city as providing 'lessons in Italian conversation' three times a week (Wilde 2000, 950 and 966). On 19 October 1897, when he was deeply engrossed in composing *BRG*, Wilde wrote from the Villa del Giudice (now 37 via Posillipo) to More Adey: 'I am getting rather astonishing in my Italian conversation. I believe I talk a mixture of Dante and the worst modern slang' (Wilde 2000, 967).

Very little is known about Rocco. His parents must have admired the Risorgimento general Giuseppe Garibaldi; he was evidently striving to make a living by his pen; and he enjoyed a modest success as the editor of the magazine *Strenna Margherita* in 1894, securing contributions by such well-known writers as Matilde Serao,[2] Alphonse Allais, Roberto Bracco, Salvatore Di Giacomo, Olindo Guerrini, Paolo Borrelli and Neera (Anna Radius Zuccari). He was most probably a socialist and a homosexual. Rocco published an articulate defense of Alfred Dreyfus and seems to have been the author of a gay novel, set in Naples, entitled *L'uomo femmina* (The female man, ca. 1899). He was also confident enough to propose to Wilde that he should translate *Salomé* into Italian. It is likely that Wilde saw that, if his first Italian translation were carried out on his only French work, he would stand a good chance of obtaining a fair deal and an accurate edition of the play that would begin to establish his fame in Italy. As soon as Rocco suggested the translation, Wilde began planning a Neapolitan performance (Wilde 2000, 948 and 959). However, it appears that no text of *Salomé* was available in Naples at this time. So Ada Leverson sent Wilde her copy, which arrived around the time of Wilde's birthday, on 16 October 1897 (Wilde 2000, 961). Rocco probably started work on his translation immediately, possibly with the aid of Wilde himself (Wilde 2000, 967: 'I am also supervising an Italian version of *Salomé*, which is being made here by a young Neapolitan poet'). The first draft of the translation must have been completed just two months later because Wilde returned the book and thanked the Sphinx in a letter dated 16 November 1897 (Wilde 2000, 981).

---

2   Serao announced Wilde's presence in Naples as a calamity in the local paper, *Il Mattino* (The morning), on 7 October 1897. A literary portrait of Serao, illustrated with her photograph, had appeared in *The Woman's World*, where she was compared to Madame De Staël (Sylvester 1889).

A note deposited in the office of the Neapolitan notary, Sodano, on 25 October 1897 shows that Wilde wanted the whole transaction to be legally conducted: 'Dear Mr Rocco, I authorize you with great pleasure to translate and arrange for the performance of my play *Salomé* on the Italian stage. Oscar Wilde'.[3] The original note, a copy of which is preserved in the archives of the publisher Bideri, is presumably still stored in the notary's office. It was Ferdinando Bideri (1851–1930) who printed the first Italian edition of *Salomé* in a volume of 1906 (Bideri Archive 1906; Gerra 1978, 87). Bideri, poet, journalist, musician and publisher, was one of the leading figures of the literary avant-garde in Naples. In 1891 he founded the literary journal *La Tavola Rotonda* (The round table), which published articles by the leading Neapolitan writers of the time and translations of works by important European poets and novelists. For instance, Bideri was the first in Italy to publish works by Emile Zola and Maxim Gorky. He also published works by Gabriele D'Annunzio – including the first edition of *L'Innocente* (1892) (*The Intruder*, trans. A. Hornblow, 1898) and the poems *Intermezzo di Rime* (1894) (Rhymed intermezzo) – and, for Pierro editions, the definitive version of *Giovanni Episcopo* (1892), a book that Wilde owned and may have bought in Naples (in the Eccles Bequest, British Library). Bideri collaborated with Pierro and the two publishers monopolized the editorial activity in Naples, ranging from magazines to poems, novels, music scores and song books (D'Ambrosio, 1990).

Wilde evidently felt that, after the 1896 Parisian performance, *Salomé* should have an Italian debut in Naples; but his plans were thwarted. It seems that Rocco and the poet Biagio Chiara (1880?–1918) held a private reading of the Italian version of *Salomé* in the literary salon of the socialist MP Giovanni Bovio (1838?–1903). Bovio, one of the most outstanding political figures of the time, was also a writer and playwright, whose *Cristo alla festa di Purim* (Christ at the feast of Purim) had been performed while Wilde was in Naples (D'Amico and Severi 2001, 73–85). One of Bovio's guests, the lawyer Luigi Conforti, was so struck by the poetical energy of Wilde's writing that he tried to organize a public reading in the Circolo Filologico di Napoli, but nothing came of it. Towards the end of November, the actor-manager Cesare Rossi was in Naples with his theatre company, which included Eleonora Duse. Wilde had Rossi read *Salomé* and, after his favourable response, approached Duse through her friends. She turned him down. In his long introduction to the Italian translation of *LASC*, Rocco (writing under the pseudonym Arnaldo De Lisle) explains that Duse would have been more than happy to perform the play, 'if only the bad reputation of its author hadn't prevented it' (Wilde 1908, 7–51).[4] It is interesting to note that in that period Duse had begun her affair with Gabriele D'Annunzio, who might well have been informed of Wilde's proposal. After she had proffered her verdict, many of the players in the company agreed with her, considering that Wilde had just come out of

---

[3]   'Caro signor Rocco, vi autorizzo con molto piacere a tradurre e far rappresentare il mio dramma *Salomé* sulla scena italiana. Oscar Wilde.'

[4]   'se la cattiva reputazione dell'autore non l'avesse impedito'.

prison, that he was a 'pervertito' – a homosexual, a man banned from good society – and concluded that his work likewise had to be banned. A decade later, when Wilde had become an acclaimed author in Europe and America, De Lisle lamented this missed opportunity of lending *Salomé* an Italian voice during the author's lifetime. In the end, Rocco's translation of *Salomé* was first published in the Neapolitan journal *Rassegna Italiana* (Italian review) in 1901.

The play was first performed at the *Teatro dei Filodrammatici* in Milan on 30 December 1904, with Mario Fumagalli as Herod and Edvige Reinach as Salomé. The troupe, however, did not use Rocco's translation, which was unknown outside Naples, but relied on a translation by G. Bonaspetti and Sem Benelli. Benelli (1877–1949) was a journalist and playwright who would soon become one of D'Annunzio's rivals, especially with his play *La Cena delle Beffe* (1909) (*The Jest*, performed in New York in 1919 by the Barrymore brothers). He was also well known as a friend of the founder of Italian Futurism, Filippo Tommaso Marinetti (Antonini 2008; D'Ambrosio 1990, 1–24). The leading actor of the first production of the play, Fumagalli, had worked in Germany, where he had been exposed to experimental techniques of directing and had even been compared to Max Reinhardt. As stage manager, or artistic director of *Salomé*, he established a new approach to the text by attempting a complete adherence to its meaning – a sort of philological representation of the words as synaesthetic images. Moreover, Fumagalli laid down that the theatre audience should sit in complete darkness in order to devote all their attention to what was going on before their eyes. It was the first time that an Italian audience had sat in a dark theatre to watch a play (Livio 1992, 111). In the same year, 1904, D'Annunzio was enjoying a theatrical triumph with his tragedy *La figlia di Iorio* (The daughter of Jorio), which had premièred on 2 March at the *Teatro Lirico*, also in Milan. D'Annunzio was so taken with Fumagalli's direction of *Salomé* that he asked the actor to direct his next play, *La fiaccola sotto il moggio* (1905) (The torch under the bushel). Thus, only a year before the great *Salomé* craze launched by Richard Strauss's operatic masterpiece, Italian audiences enjoyed a performance of Wilde's play which was reminiscent in its style of the new lyrical drama introduced by D'Annunzio in early plays such as *La città morta* (1896) (*The Dead City*, trans. Arthur Symons, 1900) and *Sogno di un mattino di primavera* (1897) (Dream of a spring morning), both performed by Duse to great acclaim.

Salomé began touring Northern Italy soon after its first performance. A typewritten receipt for the rights of performance of the play, held at the Fondazione Bideri, Naples, dated 28 October 1911, shows that *Salomé* was performed at the *Teatro Apollo* in Rome by the *Compagnia Drammatica Italiana Ruggieri*; and in Venice and Verona respectively on 12 and 24 March 1912. The young princess had become a legendary figure (Vitaletti 1908, 45–56). The play must also have been popular in book form because in 1908 Bideri issued a new edition with a preface by Chiara, who is best remembered as Wilde's first Italian translator and editor. Chiara was also a friend of the poet Giovanni Pascoli as well as being one of Marinetti's early collaborators and a skilful poet, whose work was deeply influenced by the French Parnassians and Symbolists, the English Pre-Raphaelites and especially by Wilde (D'Ambrosio 1990, 1–24; Rovito 1922 and *Index Bibliographicus Notorum Hominum*, 1985). He edited translations of Baudelaire and works by several contemporary Neapolitan writers as well as textbooks for school children by means of which he was able to gain a small livelihood. Chiara was deeply influenced by Wilde, especially in his homosexual tales, *L'Umano Convito* (The human banquet) of 1903. In 1906 he published a translation of Wilde's prose-poem HJ in Bideri's journal *Tavola Rotonda*, in which he also issued the preface to his translation of *HOP* (Chiara 1906) and, in 1907, a few choice pieces of criticism.

Doriano Gray Dipinto

Chiara is recognizable in Wilde's description, in a letter dated 10 [?] December 1897, of a 'Neapolitan poet and good English scholar' who wanted to translate *PDG* (Wilde 2000, 1005). Wilde again alludes to the young Neapolitan in a letter addressed to Smithers written in the same month, in which he asks his publisher to forward a copy of the novel for a potential Italian translation (D'Amico 1994, 76–81). Wilde, as was often the case, trusted Chiara and relied on his linguistic skills. Chiara probably started translating *PDG* immediately, taking advantage of Wilde's stay in Naples and relying heavily on the French translation of the novel by Eugène Tardieu, which had been published in Paris by Albert Savine in 1895. However, his efforts must have been frustrated. Chiara had to wait until 1905 before his translation was finally published, and this only after he financed the publication himself, omitting the name of the translator and giving a misleading place of publication. The first edition of *Doriano Gray Dipinto* (an awkward title: 'Dorian Gray painted') appeared to have been published in Palermo, but it was actually printed by Bideri in Naples and dedicated by Chiara to his friend, the painter Nino Brusa.

The first Italian translation of HP, *Il principe felice*, appeared in 1904 on the pages of the Florentine cultural journal *Il Marzocco*, edited by Angelo and Adolfo Orvieto. It was signed by F. Bianco. Bianco perfectly understood the bond of friendship between the prince and the little swallow in Wilde's original: most contemporary versions of the tale render the English bird 'swallow' as the feminine 'rondine', but Bianco opted for the masculine dimitutive 'rondinino', thereby underlining the strong Platonic relationship between the two male creatures, the prince and his helper.

De Profundis

In February 1905, Robert Ross published with Methuen a few excerpts of the famous long letter addressed to Alfred Douglas that the playwright had composed in jail. *DP* was brought out in Italian in May of the same year by Rosen in Venice, in an edition by Olga Bicchierai (Wilde 1905). In her preface Bicchierai strenuously defended her choice of publishing an author whose notorious reputation had condemned him to oblivion:

> If his name used to have the ring of evil for the most chaste and puritanical ears when newspapers and gossip mongers vied to weave around it a legend of shame,

the echo of those scandalous events in which he acted the part of a hero is now so weak that the fame of the writer shines forth and imposes its stature again as it had never done before. (Wilde 1905, 5–6)[5]

Reviewing the book, Giuseppe Lipparini noted that 'the Italian translation is so literal and close to the English original that some pages are almost incomprehensible' (Lipparini 1905);[6] so much so that he recommended reading it in the original. Wilde's disguise as Job in the book does little to convince the reviewer, who paraphrases Henri De Régnier's statement that Wilde had been condemnned to a harsh jail sentence because he thought he was still living in classical antiquity whereas he was, in fact, a British subject.

Bicchierai disagreed with critics who considered Wilde 'a fashionable author, even among those affected by angelic "pruderie"'.[7] She was proud that early twentieth-century Italian theatre-goers could enjoy *Salomé* in the staging by Fumagalli which was triumphantly touring the North of the country. The year 1905 was undoubtedly the *annus mirabilis* for *Salomé*. In his opera based on Wilde's tragedy, Richard Strauss turned the fate of the young princess into a modern myth (Severi 1985, 53–64). In Italy, the two important publishing houses Ricordi and Sonzogno printed the libretto of the musical drama, translated by Alex Leawington.

During the same season, Wilde's fame grew as new editions of his works began to flood the market: in 1906 there was a second edition of *Doriano Gray Dipinto* and *LWF* was published in a translation by Carlo Castelli and Ferruccio Bernardini. The play had been successfully staged in 1905 by Fumagalli and the actresses Teresa Franchini, Evelina Poli and Elisa Berti Masi, with stage design by Rovescalli and costumes by Caramba. Later on the performances of the *Compagnia Città di Roma* and a legendary interpretation by Emma Grammatica would be considered memorable (Wilde 1994, 383). *BRG* appeared in the pages of the first issue of the cultural magazine *Prose* (Proses) (December 1906-January 1907) in a prose translation by Giuseppe Vannicola (Horodisch 1954, 23 and D'Amico and Severi 2001, 81).

Intentions

In 1906 Raffaello Piccoli, a prominent literary figure and friend of Giuseppe Prezzolini and Antonio Gramsci, translated the essays in *Intentions*, which included 'La decadenza del mentire' (DL), 'Penna, matita e veleno' (PPP),

---

5   'Se il suo nome potè suonar male agli orecchi più castigati e più pudichi allorché la cronaca e il pettegolezzo andarono a gara per tessergli intorno una leggenda di ludibrio, l'eco dei fatti scandalosi dei quali fu l'eroe s'è così assopita che la fama del letterato ritorna a risplendere e ad imporsi nuovamente come prima non aveva brillato mai, come mai prima s'era imposta.'

6   'la versione italiana segue così da presso il testo inglese, che certe pagine riescono quasi incomprensibili'.

7   'autore in voga, non ostico neppure all'angelica "pruderie!"'

'Il critico come artista' (CA) and 'La verità delle maschere' (TM) (Limentani 1997, 877–892 and Giammattei 2003, 302). Piccoli added a long critical introduction that analyzed Wilde's works and their reception in Italy for the first time. He defined Wilde as 'a fascinating conversationalist, a marvellous teller of tales [who] thought and talked in a fashion that the English admirably convey with one simple word: *fiction*'.[8] Although Wilde was well-known for his affectation, Piccoli considered this trait simply a form of 'sprezzatura' – the studied effortlessness described by Baldassarre Castiglione in his *Book of the Courtier* (1528) – as if Wilde were one of Castiglione's characters and his life an example of sincerity to the very end (xi). In his introduction to the essays Piccoli quotes several paragraphs from *DP*, which he re-translates because he finds Bicchierai's edition unreliable. He also adds translations of a number of Wilde's poems: 'Requiescat', 'Sonetto in avvicinarsi all'Italia', 'San Miniato', 'E Tenebris' and 'Sull'Arno', as well as a few stanzas from 'Sfinge' and 'Ballata del Carcere di Reading' (*BRG*). His aim is to make readers acquainted with some of Wilde's minor poems. To these he adds some free translations of Wilde's prose poems: 'Il Discepolo' ('The Disciple'), 'Il Poeta' ('The Poet') and 'L'Artista' ('The Artist'), the last of which Gide recollects Wilde reciting with a musical intonation. Piccoli also summarizes two of Wilde's other writings: the 'Envoi', which Wilde had composed as an introduction to the poems of his friend Rennell Rodd, and his lecture on the English Renaissance delivered on the American tour. Piccoli goes on to discuss Wilde's early drama, revealing the complex plot of *DOP*, first staged in London in 1905. In conclusion, Piccoli guides the reader through the topics of the essays of *Intentions* and, curiously, compares Wilde's aesthetics with those of the Italian poet Giacomo Leopardi:

> The love of paradox is really what spoils Wilde's works: his novel, his plays, even these essays. Some of us surely remember that Leopardi states that 'truth is in fact the complete opposite of beauty' [...]. This aphorism had given us pause; but here comes Wilde who, in his *Decay of Lying*, turns it into a sytem, develops, demonstrates and summarizes it so that, in the end, its profound fascination vanishes, its subtle enchantment is broken (Wilde 1906, xxxv).[9]

Piccoli displays a wide knowledge of the full range of Wilde's works and an uncommon sensitivity, compared to other Italian intellectuals of that period, to what he calls the 'sad tale' of the man. He has an unrelenting curiosity about the writer and his myth: he reports, for instance, that 'in the spring of

---

[8]   'un conversatore affascinante, un favoleggiatore meraviglioso [...] che pensava e parlava in quella maniera che gli inglesi indicano ammirabilmente con una parola sola: *fiction*'.

[9]   'L'amore del paradosso, è anzi quel che guasta molto dell'opera dell'Wilde [*sic!*]; del suo romanzo, dei drammi, di questi saggi. Di noi alcuni avran pur letto Leopardi, che, "del bello, il maggior contrario è propriamente il vero"; [...] questo aforisma ci aveva fatto meditare; ma ecco, nella *Decadenza del Mentire*, l'Wilde [*sic!*] ne fa un sistema, lo sviluppa, lo dimostra, lo riassume, e il fascino profondo è svanito, spezzato l'incanto sottile'.

1905 an idle gazetteer announced to the nations of Europe that Oscar Wilde was still alive and living as a recluse in a Spanish convent' (Wilde 1906, lxix; Muret 1904).[10]

Piccoli never neglects his critical task, however: his introduction is full of detailed notes that help us reconstruct Wilde's early reception. We learn, for instance, that the Italian translation of *DP* utterly fails to suggest the force of the original and that *Salomé* and *Doriano Gray Dipinto* are hardly known in Italy because they have not received adequate circulation. The translator has clearly researched Wilde's bibliography and he tries to be exhaustive by quoting from relatively recent publications, such as Robert Sherard's *The Story of an Unhappy Friendship* (1902), and various periodical articles including M. Muret's essay in *Journal des Débats*, 9 March 1904 (lxix). Piccoli was also a collector of Wildeiana and rarely misses an opportunity to tell about his most recent discoveries. Shortly before going to print, he added a brief note informing the reader that, on 1 August 1906, *Il Corriere della Sera* (The Evening Courier) had reported that the Literary Theatre Club in London was staging FT. Not everyone appreciated his exhaustive explanations. In the copy of *Intenzioni* that I consulted at the Biblioteca Nazionale Centrale in Florence, an indignant reader had glossed the pages with invectives against the editor, whom he or she judged to be excessively academic.[11]

The plays

Wilde's comedies made their debut on the Italian publishing scene in 1907. That year Carlo Castelli and Ferruccio Bernardini translated *WNI* as *Una donna qualunque* for the popular Roman publisher Voghera, reducing the play's four acts to three. Also in 1907, the Bolognese printer Brugnoli published *Un marito ideale* (*IH*) in a reduced version, freely adapted for the Italian stage by Giovanni Battista Palmieri. The previous year, in Naples, Rocco had published a full version of *Salomé* with black and white 'Pompeian' illustrations by F. Galante. In his long preface to the play, Rocco alternates hyperbolic praise for this Symbolist drama with anecdotes from Wilde's life, derived mostly from the memoirs of the poet Henri de Régnier. Rocco was infatuated with Wilde's play:

> Salomé! Salomé! And the eyes of the fatal poet, which his vision had made large and bright and which shone because of the dream that sweltered in his mind like a last day of spring – these eyes were full of desire when they saw the emeralds green like seaweed, the pearls iridescent like the sky at dawn, the rubies vermilion like blood, the amethysts languid like regret, the saffron-coloured topaz, the diamonds which were like tangible rays of light [...]. Every gem was both a different desire

---

[10]   'Nella primavera del 1905 un gazzettiere ozioso annunciò all'Europa che Oscar Wilde viveva ancora, viveva chiuso in un convento spagnolo'.

[11]   *Intenzioni*, Biblioteca Nazionale Centrale di Firenze, 5.80.2.123.

and a symbol for a new work of art, just as every rhyme lends both ornament and harmony to the poem. (1907, v–vi)[12]

As the previous passage shows, Rocco's translation reflects the emphatic style that was then considered most effective on stage. It interprets the play's misogynist undercurrent with some linguistic sophistication. For instance, Rocco found an admirable solution for the ending: Herod's expression of disgust in his order to 'Kill that *woman!*', when he sees Salomé kissing the lips of the dead head of the Baptist, is translated by the Neapolitan as 'Uccidete quella *femmina!*' Rocco, who understands how Herod despises the *woman* in Salomé in that moment, aptly chooses, instead of the more common 'donna', the word 'femmina' (female), which is an idiomatic expression of traditional Southern Italian, chauvinistic male attitudes to women (1907, 80).

The edition has a long Appendix, *Un ritratto meraviglioso* (A marvellous portrait), written by the translator, dramatist and early follower of the Naples Futurist movement Achille Macchia. Macchia, who deals with other translations of Wilde's works, notes that *Una donna di nessun conto* (*WNI*) had been performed at the *Teatro Argentina* in Rome in the winter of 1906, and that 'the path to Oscar Wilde's novels [*sic.*] and plays was opened by a book full of anguish, humiliation and decadence: *De Profundis*'.[13] He adds that in 'a brilliant preface to *Doriano Gray Dipinto*, Biagio Chiara, who is a sincere admirer and subtle and deep interpreter of Oscar Wilde, is pleased to see that the rehabilitation of the great English [*sic.*] poet is by now beginning everywhere.'[14] But Macchia is neither naive nor so easily deceived:

> Curiosity is ephemeral: all the Italian citizens who are over twenty-one years of age and can read and write, are not only able to vote and be elected, but they approach Oscar Wilde as a crowd is drawn to peer through the windows of a *morgue* to gaze at a mangled corpse from which they had initially turned away with a sense of dread. (1907)[15]

---

[12] 'Salomé! Salomé! E gli occhi del poeta fatale, grandi, luminosi della visione, accesi del sogno, che ferveva nella mente come una primavera ultima, spasimavano di desiderio alla vista degli smeraldi verdi come alghe marine, delle perle iridate come il cielo dell'alba, dei rubini vermigli come il sangue, degli ametisti [*sic.*] languidi come un rimpianto, dei topazi dal croco d'autunno, dei diamanti, raggi tangibili di luce [...]. Ogni gemma era un desiderio e un simbolo per l'opera d'arte, come ogni rima è ornamento e armonia per il poema.'

[13] 'la via ai romanzi ed ai drammi di Oscar Wilde l'ha aperta un libro di angoscia, di umiliazione e di decadimento: il *De Profundis*'.

[14] 'In una smagliante prefazione al "Doriano Gray dipinto" Biagio Chiara, che dell'opera di Oscar Wilde è ammiratore sincero ed interprete profondo e sottile, si compiace che cominci dovunque il periodo di riabilitazione del grande poeta inglese [*sic.*]'.

[15] 'La curiosità è efimera [*sic.*]: i cittadini italiani che abbiano compiuto ventun'anni e sappiano leggere e scrivere non solo sono elettori ed eletti, ma si accostano a Oscar Wilde come la folla si sente attratta a guardar fisso attraverso i vetri di una *morgue* il cadavere sbrindellato di qualche vittima, dopo che se n'era ritratta con un moto istintivo di spavento, in principio.'

In 1907 Chiara also introduced the Italian public to Wilde's fairy tales with his translation of *La Casa dei Melograni* (*HOP*). The translated collection includes 'L'adolescente re' (YK), 'Il genetliaco dell'Infanta' (BI), 'Il pescatore e la sua anima' (FHS) and 'L'astro fanciullo' (SC) from the original collection. To these stories he added 'L'usignolo e la rosa' (NR) from *HPOT* and the prose poem 'Il maestro di sapienza' (MW). Chiara dedicated his literary labour to the Countess Giulia Tornielli Bellini di Borgolavezzaro, a gentlewoman from Novara who probably helped him meet the costs of publication.

BRG and SMUS

In 1907 another well-known popular publisher, the Roman Bernardo Lux, launched Wilde's most famous poem, *La Ballata della Prigione di Reading* (*BRG*). It had been translated and edited by the poet and musician Giuseppe Vannicola (1876–1915). Vannicola is the only Italian translator of Wilde who had achieved prominence in Florentine cultural and literary circles and was also respected among Roman publishers. Between 1904 and 1908, he founded and directed two cosmopolitan journals based in Florence: *Prose* and *Revue du Nord* (Northern review), which published articles that either dealt with Symbolist literature or were influenced by it. Especially influential was the example of Jules Laforgue, a writer with whom Vannicola shared many literary traits and whom he openly imitated. But he also imitated Wilde, attempting to apply his wit and dandified style both to his writing and to his life. Giovanni Papini, who met Vannicola in 1903, describes him as an eccentric: half *bohémien*, half dandy writer (Gerra 1978 and Falchi Picchinesi 1985, 45–48). In Rome, where the intellectual milieu was more hostile, Vannicola created his own literary community by gravitating to the publisher Lux, for whom he also edited *Salomé* in 1908.

In 1914, Vannicola completed what would become for some time the authoritative editions of *Il fantasma di Canterville* and *Il delitto di Lord Savile* (CG and LASC). Vannicola was devastated by repeated attacks of chronic polyarthritis which would eventually lead him to a premature death. From the correspondence between him and his publisher, Formiggini, which takes place between 1913 and 1915 and is made up of postcards and brief letters, the translator's difficulties are almost tangible:[16] he complains about his health (high fevers and fits which rarely leave him free to work) and lack of money, a sad and frequent note that haunts his entire short life. Formiggini, who was convinced of Wilde's great literary merit, asked Vannicola to add the translation of 'Sfinge senza segreto' (*SWS*), to pad the otherwise rather slim volume that was to be published in the acclaimed series 'Classici del Ridere' (Comic classics). When the volume came out, however, the short story had been omitted for no apparent reason. Vannicola had translated it and published it in the literary pages of the newspaper *Il Resto del Carlino-La Patria* on 20 October

---

[16] Biblioteca Estense di Modena, *Archivio Editoriale Formiggini*, file: Vannicola, Giuseppe.

1912. When the proofs reached him, Vannicola seemed satisfied and appreciative of the illustrations by G. Mazzoni: he found them original and in tune with Wilde's taste. On a small undated sheet of paper he wrote to Formiggini: 'I'm in bed with a slight temperature. I was able to dictate the Wilde translation to my good friend Bruni. I'm sending you part of it through the same Bruni. The rest will arrive tomorrow night or on Monday at the latest. Could you please add ten more *lire* to my advance payment and let me have it by the same messenger?'[17] Vannicola died young, after struggling thoughout his short life against poverty and the illness which had also cut short his chosen career as a violinist.

In 1912 the Palermo publisher Sandron published the complete collection of the tales of *Il principe felice* (*HPOT*), with the original drawings by Crane and Hood from the English edition of 1888. The stories were translated by Misa, a pseudonym that appears only in the 1919 reissue. In the same year another popular publisher, Carabba of Lanciano issued the first Italian translation of SMUS, entitled *L'anima dell'uomo e Sebastiano Melmoth* and edited by A. Agresti. A collection of aphorisms chosen from Wilde's works followed the pamphlet. The following year Luigi Fabbri (1888–1966), a well-known trade union leader from Romagna (Andreucci and Detti 1976, 270–71), published his own political version of Wilde's essay, which soon became one of the standard texts of Italian socialism. In the 'Preface', Fabbri explains to his readers how Wilde's individualism is not only compatible with, but an integral and important part of socialism:

> In this essay the author develops the following idea: the establishment of a Socialist regime, that is of an economic order in which property has become socialized, is the actual and necessary condition for the development of individualism. This is the same as the idea manifested by the socialist anarchists who avoid mentioning individualism simply because they do not want to introduce new terms and thus add to the confusion that currently reigns in the field of social doctrines; but their concept is the same: socialism should be understood as the foundation and warranty of individual freedom. (8–9)[18]

Fabbri compares Wilde to the Russian anarchist Peter Kropotkin, claiming that the two thinkers reach the same conclusions, even though Wilde never mentions the word 'anarchy' and his original point of view and motivations

---

[17] 'Sono a letto con un poco di febbre. Ho potuto dettare al mio buon amico Bruni la traduzione inglese di Wilde: Le mando per lo stesso Bruni, parte di essa. Il resto a domani sera, o al più tardi lunedì. Abbia la cortesia di aggiungere, per mezzo del latore, ancora dieci lire a titolo di anticipo.'

[18] 'L'idea sviluppata dall'autore è questa: lo stabilirsi di un regime socialista e cioè di una organizzazione economica in cui la proprietà sia socializzata, è la condizione di fatto necessaria per lo svilupparsi dell'individualismo. È la medesima idea degli anarchici socialisti, i quali, se evitano di parlare d'individualismo, è solo per non aumentare con terminologie nuove l'attuale confusione che regna nel campo delle dottrine sociali; ma il loro concetto è il medesimo: il socialismo considerato come base e garanzia della libertà individuale.'

are 'mostly artistic and exclusively individualistic' ('prevalentemente artistiche ed esclusivamente individualiste').

In 1913, Chiara, who was an active admirer of Wilde's aestheticism and a follower of his Hellenism, published his translation of PA (*Il prete e l'accolito*, Napoli, Bideri). The tale, which was clearly produced within a homosexual environment, was attributed to Wilde when it first appeared in the Oxford journal *Chameleon* in December 1894, but it was later discovered to have been written by a student called John Bloxam. In his preface, Chiara used cryptic, obscure language to praise the secret sect of those faithful lovers with whom he feels a close affinity: 'The tale tells of a religion with its commandments, its sacraments, its ritual, its celebrations, its consummation, its confessors. In front of the pale Christ who raises his bony visage with majestic calm to testify to the misunderstood cult of love, the celebrants prevail over the idolatry of convention' (10).[19] Chiara, whom the young poet Corrado Govoni (1894–1965) remembered as a 'poet aesthete and the first in Italy to introduce some of the works and habits of Oscar Wilde' ('poeta estetizzante e il primo traduttore in Italia di alcune opere e dei costumi di Oscar Wilde'), was no novice in challenging conventional moral standards (Govoni 1943). In 1903, for instance, he published a volume titled *L'Umano Convito* (The human banquet), a scabrous book made up of three stories which dealt with homosexual themes inspired by Wilde's works.

An ornate edition of *Poemi in Prosa* (PP) was published in 1914, in a translation by Franz W. Von Tigerström, with a preface by Marco Slonim and decorations by Francesco Chiappelli. This volume contained the prose poems which had been published by Gide in French and four stories from *HPOT*. There was nothing new about this collection consisting of unremarkable renditions of Wilde's works. Certainly more noteworthy is a musical version of FT (*Una tragedia fiorentina*), composed by Carlo Ravasenga (1891–1964) and with a libretto by Ettore Moschino (1887–1941). In 1919, Moschino reprinted the musical tragedy of FT along with the translation of SCo (*La santa cortigiana*), with a warning to his readers that he had cut the dialogue betweeen Bianca and Guido in the first play because of its 'unsustainable prolixity' ('prolissità insostenibile'), and that what remained of the second play was a mere fragment 'which has never been translated into any language' ('mai tradotto in nessun idioma') (Wilde 1919, i–vi and 49).

In the meantime, the first collection of Wilde's aphorisms had appeared in 1916. From the copy of this book held at the *Biblioteca Nazionale Centrale* in Florence, it is difficult to tell whether the editor, F. Stocchetti, compiled his somewhat jumbled selection after having read Wilde's complete *ouevre* or if he chose material at random from Constance Wilde's edition of *Oscariana*, which she had published privately in January 1895 and which was re-printed for the

---

[19] 'Il racconto è una religione con i suoi comandamenti, con i suoi sacramenti, con il suo rito, con le sue celebrazioni, con la sua consumazione, con i suoi confessori. Dinanzi al pallore del Cristo che il volto ossuto erge in maestosa calma a testimoniare l'incompreso culto d'amore, i celebranti prevalgono sulla idolatria della convenzione.'

New York edition of Wilde's *Works* in 1909 and then again, a year later, by Humphreys in London.

The popular writer

In the years after the end of World War I, Wilde had become a well-known popular writer in Italy: his fame was such that, on 25 January 1925, the daily paper *Il Resto del Carlino-La Patria*, published a short story attributed to Wilde in which an Irish drunkard named Patsy O'Neill accepts a wager to let his face be bitten by a gutter rat while a small crowd assembles to bet on the winner. Patsy withstands his ordeal and wins, and is bought a drink by a member of the crowd. The drunkard is so grateful that he decides to spend all his hard-earned money on a round of drinks for everyone. This apocryphal story is signed with Wilde's name and followed by a note that forbids its reproduction, suggesting that, by this date, Wilde's name was not only famous but it also sold well.

It comes as no surprise then that, during and just after World War I, translations of Wilde's works were being printed and re-printed. It was only in 1922, however, that Wilde's major dramatic success, *IBE*, became accessible to an Italian audience as *L'importanza di far sul serio* (The importance of being serious), an altogether unsatisfactory translation of its original title. In a brief preface, Carlo Pellegrini commends the play for 'a series of original and new, if not always realistic, concoctions – such as, for instance, the ending, which seems to have been invented to *épater* the well-meaning audience or naive reader.'[20] The translator, Irene Nori Giambastiani, however, fails to render the witty, ambiguous language and the irony of the situations, and even the correct spelling of the characters' names. Lady Bracknell becomes Lady Brachnell, and with her impoverished language she never manages to capture Wilde's brilliant criticism of Victorian institutions and conventions. The play was first performed in 1941 under the title *L'importanza di essere Onesto* (The importance of being Honest, in which Honest functions as a first name in Italian), directed by Corrado Pavolini. The year was unfavourable, the acting improbable and the play a flop. It fared much better in 1949 at the *Teatro Quirino* in Rome, under the direction of Lucio Chiavarelli. In this performace, actors such as Marcello Mastroianni, Paolo Panelli and Mario Scaccia played minor roles (Lane, Chasuble and Merriman, respectively). The best performance of the period, however, was staged in 1954 at the Teatro Olympia in Milan. It was directed by Mario Ferrero and had stage settings by Pier Luigi Pizzi; its outstanding cast included Ernesto Calindri (Moncrieff), Lia Zoppelli, Lauretta Masiero and Franco Volpi (D'Amico 1994, 515–16).

In the 1920s, during the Fascist regime, Wilde's readers multiplied and the book market responded with frequent reprints and cheap editions of his

---

[20] 'una serie di trovate originali e sempre nuove, anche se non tutte verosimili – quale ad esempio l'epilogo, che sembra in realtà fatto per épater un po' il buon pubblico o il benigno lettore'.

works. These were mainly published by Facchi, Sonzogno, Bietti, Bolla and others. The year 1928 marks the first Italian translation of *DOP* (*La Duchessa di Padova*), edited by the popular adventure writer Luigi Motta (1881–1956). Motta was the author of comedies, libretti and over a hundred novels, many of which were translated into various languages, including two into English (Gallo and Tiloca 2007). He dedicated his edition of the play to the actresses Maria Melato and Tatiana Pavlova, 'possible interpreters' ('possibili creatrici'). The play was already known in Italy but there are no records of productions, except for one staged by Maria Melato at the Teatro Manzoni in Milan in 1942, under the direction of Alessandro Brissoni, with costumes by Titina Rota and musical accompaniment by Guido Soresina (Wilde 1994, 318–19).

During a regime that promoted autarchy, not least in cultural matters, it may come as a surprise that the Anglo-Irish Wilde, by now considered an author with a philosophical vision and a 'moralizing' influence, was being taught in Italian schools in 1931. In that year, Luigi Pratesi introduced and annotated the first edition of *HPOT* for the publisher Giusti (Livorno) as a school primer for children who were learning English. The edition was successful enough to be reprinted in 1934, 1938 and 1946. It became the first required English reading for more than one generation of Italian students before and after World War II. In 1964 it was reissued by La Nuova Italia (Florence).

With the end of World War II, the book market interpreted the change in the political scene as more than twenty years of dictatorship came to an end. Different translations of Wilde's most famous political pamphlet, *L'anima dell'uomo sotto il socialismo* (SMUS) were issued in Turin, Spoleto, Florence, Rome and Bologna (Wilde 1945a, 1945b, 1945c, 1946, 1947). In Brescia, the Socialist Guglielmo Zatti published a curious translation of Wilde's essay with the title *Individualismo e Socialismo* (Individualism and socialism), with the declared objective of 'contrasting the squalor of present-day Italian culture, after twenty years of Mandarin Fascist rule and four centuries of spiritual decay, with an example of an active culture, which is critical and scientific at the same time'.[21]

In 1948, Carlo Franzero and Lorenzo Gigli published Wilde's dramatic works as part of a publisher's series dedicated to works by world-famous writers. They described Wilde as the greatest playwright of the Victorian era and an immortal author worthy of figuring among the popular classics of all times. The following year a new translation appeared: Longino Valbia introduced Italian readers to *Il mistero del Signor W. H.* (PMWH), published with other tales from *LASCOS*. In 1951–52 Wilde's works were collected in two volumes in the prestigious series 'I Grandi Maestri' (Great masters) that Aldo Camerini published for Casini in Rome. This would be the standard

---

21 'opporre allo squallore della cultura italiana quale oggi si presenta, dopo vent'anni di mandarinato fascista e quattro secoli di decadenza spirituale, una viva cultura critica e scientifica'. The preface is anonymous, but it is probably to be ascribed to Zatti. The cover bears a drawing of a serpent biting its own tail and the inscription 'do not fear to swim against the stream' ('non temete nuotare contro il torrente').

edition for the next quarter of a century, until Masolino D'Amico's masterly translations of the late 1970s made Wilde a household name in Italy.

Wilde had, by now, conquered the Italian public at large. Having started out as a controversial and scandalous author, known for his hedonistic lifestyle, witty aphorisms and paradoxical and sexually ambiguous works such as the Symbolist *Salomé*, FT and SCo, he gradually came to be known and loved in Italy as a popular writer, capable of speaking to children and the ordinary people who hoped for a revolution in Italian politics, social rescue and equality. His wide reception was due not so much to the transformation of Italian society, but rather to the enchantment of his words, which even the (often unfaithful) translations were able to communicate. Today Wilde's stature in Italy is that of a cultural authority, often quoted even in forms of popular culture such as advertisements, and a classic. Anyone who enters an Italian bookshop and sees the many editions of his novel, plays, tales, critical essays, poems and collections of aphorisms will have to admit that, after Shakespeare, Wilde is the most loved 'English' author in Italy.

7   'Children of Pleasure': Oscar Wilde and Italian Decadence

Elisa Bizzotto

In a little-known volume of memoirs published in 1956, the French translator André Doderet relates Gabriele D'Annunzio's laconic account of a meeting with Oscar Wilde in Italy, after Wilde's release from Reading Gaol:

> D'Annunzio enters a Neapolitan restaurant in Rome [...] and, as a timid young man, advances towards [Wilde] and greets him saying,
> – Sir, would you allow me to shake your hand?
> Without answering, Wilde put his hand in the hand that was offered to him and D'Annunzio went to his usual table to have lunch.
> When Wilde had finished his meal, before leaving, he stopped in front of the unknown young man,
> – Excuse me, there's no doubt that you are a man of letters, sir.
> – Yes, I am, sir.
> – What's your name?
> – Gabriele D'Annunzio.
> – Goodbye, sir.
> – Goodbye, sir.
> [...]
> I asked D'Annunzio: Have you seen Oscar Wilde again?
> He answered: 'Never.' (Doderet 1956, 142–43)[1]

---

[1] D'Annunzio entre dans un restaurant napolitain de Rome [...] et, jeune homme timide, s'avance vers lui, le salue en disant:
– Monsieur, voulez-vous me permettre de vous serrer la main?
Wilde, sans rien répondre, mit sa main dans la main offerte et D'Annunzio alla déjeuner à sa place habituelle. Quand Wilde eut terminé son repas, il s'arrêta avant de sortir devant le jeune inconnu:
– Pardon, dit-il, vous êtes sans doute littérateur, Monsieur.
– Oui, Monsieur.
– Comment vous nomme-t-on?
– Gabriele D'Annunzio.
– Au revoir, Monsieur.
– Au revoir, Monsieur.
[...]
Je demandai à D'Annunzio: Avez-vous revu Oscar Wilde?
Il me répondit: 'Jamais.'

With D'Annunzio, even more than with Wilde, self-fabulation is always a strong possibility. But whether or not this meeting actually took place, Doderet's anecdote testifies to a bond of sympathy and intellectual kinship between the two writers, at least on D'Annunzio's part. However, the story appears to be the only available evidence for such a bond. While it has become a critical common-place to associate Wilde with Italy's most flamboyant and charismatic author of the *fin de siècle* – generally by referring to analogies between D'Annunzio's *Il piacere* (*The Child of Pleasure*) (1889) and *PDG* – there is in fact no further record of exchange between the two writers, who never mention each other in their writings (Weiss 1968, 466 and Marabini Moevs 2001, 92). This is especially striking in the case of D'Annunzio, who often drew not only on British and European aestheticism but specifically on Wilde (see Marabini Moevs 1976, 127–29, and 2001; Slawinski 1990; 48–53; and Veronesi 2004). D'Annunzio's novels, plays and criticism make frequent yet often oblique and unacknowledged reference to Wilde. The same is true of the works of his followers and acolytes. Wilde's influence on the D'Annunzio circle, and on Italian Decadent culture more broadly, was widespread and long-lasting. It started in the early 1890s with D'Annunzio's rise as Italy's most notable aesthete and continued well after World War I and the advent of Fascism, only to end with D'Annunzio's death shortly before the outbreak of World War II.

The D'Annunzio circle

In order to consider the impact of Wilde on D'Annunzio and his circle, it is useful to investigate some of the *fin-de-siècle* magazines that became a major vehicle for the diffusion of European aestheticism in Italy. Common to these publications was the presence of D'Annunzio himself, whose life and art had been shaped by the principles of the Aesthetic Movement ever since his literary debut in the 1880s. Under the cover of anonymity – which was quite unusual for him – D'Annunzio wrote the 'Proemio' (Proem) for one of those journals, *Convito*, issued in Rome on 1 January 1895. *Convito* was momentous though short-lived (it only ran for one year). It was part of a movement to renew art in order to establish the cultural foundations for a new nation, combining aesthetic credo and militancy in a way that anticipated D'Annunzio's evolution from dandy and priest of beauty to bard of national glory and, eventually, 'poet laureate' of Fascism. 'Proemio' represents a crucial step in the reception of the Aesthetic Movement in Italy – a process which had arguably been started by D'Annunzio himself in his earlier article 'Cronaca Bizantina: Un poeta d'autunno' (Byzantine chronicle: an autumn poet), published in the Roman daily *La Tribuna* on 8 October 1887. Although no British author is mentioned in 'Proemio', the doctrines of the Pre-Raphaelites, Ruskin and Pater inform the manifesto of these Italian 'artists, writers and painters, who share the same fervent and sincere cult for the noblest forms of Art' (D'Annunzio 1895, 1).[2]

---

2   'artisti, scrittori e pittori, accomunati da uno stesso culto sincero e fervente per tutte le più nobili forme dell'Arte.'

'Proemio' is the earliest Italian attempt at a programmatic re-formulation of the doctrines of the Aesthetic Movement. The first published reference to Wilde in Italy, however, appeared in a later *Convito* article on contemporary English painting by the artist Giulio Aristide Sartorio (1860–1932). 'Esposizione di Venezia: Nota sulla pittura in Inghilterra' (Venice exhibition: a note on painting in England) was published in the seventh issue of the magazine (July 1895), after the clamour of Wilde's trials. In the article Sartorio formulates a negative criticism of the hybrid concoction of European and Oriental sources displayed by Wilde and Beardsley in the illustrated *Salomé* of 1894.

Although Sartorio's mention of Wilde by name remained an isolated instance for some years, Wilde's presence permeated Italian aesthetic culture. Another important literary and artistic magazine, *Il Marzocco*, first issued on 2 February 1896, provides a case in point. Based in Florence, then the centre of Italian cosmopolitanism and anglophilia, *Il Marzocco* set out to spread the fashionable European cult of Beauty. Alongside D'Annunzio, its contributors included some of the most progressive Italian intellectuals of the time: the well-known poet Giovanni Pascoli (1855–1912), the journalist, minor poet and Decadent Giuseppe Saverio Gargano (1859–1930) and the young journalist Ugo Ojetti (1871–1946), the last of whom was to make an important contribution to Wilde's reception in Italy in the second year of the journal's run. Jointly signed by D'Annunzio and Gargano, the 'Prologo' (Prologue) to *Il Marzocco* represented a mature manifesto of Italian aestheticism, consciously placing the magazine in the midst of the contemporary European (primarily British) debate. The 'Prologo' not only subscribed to Pater's defence of impressionistic criticism in *The Renaissance* (1873), but also to Wilde's more sensational doctrines laid out in 'Preface' to *PDG* and *Intentions*. Wilde's influence is unmistakable though it remained undeclared, possibly as a result of the trials:

> We believe that every single manifestation of individual genius has in itself, and only by virtue of its being an artwork, a precise sociological and moral value. We shall therefore never use the objects of our analysis to find support for our ideals in everyday life, nor shall we use these ideals to ostracize any work of beauty. (D'Annunzio 1896, 1)[3]

Matteo Veronesi has suggested CA as a source for D'Annunzio and Gargano's view of criticism as artistic creation, noting that these theories would then be mediated into the twentieth century by the work of a number of minor critics, first and foremost Angelo Conti (Veronesi 2000b, 191). Conti (1860–1930), who was immortalized as Daniele Glauro in D'Annunzio's novel *Il fuoco* (*The Flame of Life*) (1900), was one of D'Annunzio's closest friends and main interlocutors on matters relating to aestheticism (Zanetti 1996, 40–42, 68–73,

---

[3]   'Noi pensiamo che ogni alta manifestazione dell'ingegno ha di per sé stessa, per il solo fatto di essere un'opera d'arte, un valore sociologico e morale ben definito, e quindi non ci proporremo di trovar mai in tutto ciò che sarà oggetto del nostro esame un sostegno alle nostre idee sulla vita civile, né in nome di queste daremo l'ostracismo alle opere belle.'

147–53). He was also the author of an influential essay on art, *Giorgione: Studio* (Giorgione: a study) (1894), clearly inspired by Pater. Pater, however, was not the only English source that Conti drew on: as Ricciarda Ricorda has suggested, Conti borrowed from Wilde the crucial principle of the critic as artist (Ricorda 1993, 49).

Despite his profound debt to Wilde, towards the end of the 1890s Conti distanced himself from the idea of the amorality of art, as it clashed with his religious convictions (cf. Ricorda 1993, 49n). This change of perspective might also have been due to the rumours that accompanied Wilde's Italian sojourns after his release from prison: first in Naples between September 1897 and February 1898, then in Genoa in April and May 1899 and finally in Palermo and Rome in the spring of 1900 (when the meeting related in Doderet's anecdote may have taken place). It was Wilde's Neapolitan stay which proved particularly controversial, as is testified by several articles in the local press. Among the most explicit of these was 'C'è o non c'è?' (Is he there or isn't he?), a piece by writer and bluestocking Matilde Serao (1856–1927), who, together with her journalist husband Edoardo Scarfoglio, was a member of D'Annunzio's circle. Serao's article appeared in the local daily *Il mattino* (The morning) on 7 October 1897. The answer to the question was soon made clear: not only had Wilde established friendships with the town's intellectuals in order to have his works translated, but he had also indulged in the company of Neapolitan youths along with his fellow traveller, Alfred Douglas (Miracco 1998, 39).

Such a gossipy, unsympathetic atmosphere might have contributed to exacerbate the tone of two articles Conti wrote for *Il Marzocco* over the next couple of years. In 'Il poeta' (The poet) (1899) and 'Le vicende dell'arte' (The facts of art) (1899), Conti declares his opposition to Wilde's views on art and morality. The articles, however, also betray an inescapable anxiety of influence that emerges in Conti's descriptions of Wilde as a figure of Romantic and Decadent derivation. In 'Il poeta', Conti distances himself from Wilde's definition of the artist as 'the creator of beautiful things' by characterizing the poet as 'one who is able to show men what is most alive and true – the flower of truth and the essence of life' (Conti 1911, 17).[4] In 'Le vicende dell'arte' Conti is equally critical. Here he launches a general attack on European aestheticism by arguing against three of its most important formulae: Verlaine's '*de la musique avant toute chose*' (music above all), Pater's 'wisest [...] among the children of this world' and Wilde's 'There is no such thing as a moral or an immoral book'. These very tenets had formed the basis of Conti's own aesthetic system just a few years earlier. More surprisingly still, in this article Conti rejects what had previously been a central notion in his own criticism: Wilde's idea of the critic as creator. Conti now attacks professional critics as 'people who live by ransacking' ('gente che vive di rapina') and ridicules their 'endless lucubrations' ('interminabili elucubrazioni') and ambitions (Conti 1911, 32–34). Conti's change of heart, however, was an exception in the contemporary reception of Wilde in Italy, and it did not

---

4   'Il poeta è uno che sa rappresentare agli uomini ciò che è più vivo e più vero, il fiore della verità e l'essenza della vita.'

succeed in preventing the spread of his popularity, especially among other members of the D'Annunzio circle. The extent of Wilde's influence is shown, for instance, in an article by Ojetti published in *Il Marzocco* during Wilde's stay in Naples: 'Dialoghi dei vivi: della critica e dell'entusiasmo' (Dialogues of the living: on criticism and enthusiasm) drew heavily on CA both in its choice of the dialogue form and in its argument. Despite its borrowings, or perhaps just because of them, Ojetti's piece raised interest for Wilde's essay in Italy well before its Italian translation and publication in 1906.

Ojetti played a major part in Italian *fin-de-siècle* culture and his influence continued to grow, culminating in his editorship of the national daily *Corriere della Sera* (Evening courier) from 1925 to 1927 and, in 1930, his appointment to Fascist Italy's most prestigious cultural institution, the Accademia d'Italia (Italian Academy). Ojetti also exerted his influence as the founder of three alternative art magazines: *Dedalo* (Daedalus) (1920–33), *Pegaso* (Pegasus) (1929–33) and *Pan* (1933–46). Like many Italian intellectuals at this time, he managed his multiple interests and engagements within a position of enlightened adherence to Fascism. D'Annunzio was another such non-conformist Fascist (cf. Andreoli 2000, 594–98). It was therefore no accident that the two enjoyed an intense friendship. Throughout their lively correspondence over many years, however, Wilde's name never appears (Ceccuti 1979). Undeclared though it was, Wilde's influence pervades Ojetti's 'Dialoghi dei vivi'. Veronesi goes as far as to argue that Ojetti's 'plagiaristic piece' mediated between CA and Conti's important essay on aesthetics, *Beata riva* (Blessed shore) of 1900. Despite Conti's criticism of Wilde at the time of writing, *Beata riva* draws heavily on Wilde's ideas and literary techniques in order to promote Italy's participation in European Symbolism (Veronesi 2000a, 54–55). D'Annunzio, on the other hand, had already drawn on the combined influences of Pater and Wilde in the Dedicatory Letter to the painter Francesco Paolo Michetti (1851–1929), which prefaced his novel *Trionfo della morte* (1894) (*Triumph of Death*). Here D'Annunzio traces his 'philosophy of composition' of fiction to Wagner's theory of the *Gesamtkunstwerk* (total work of art) and Pater's idea (drawn from Schelling) of the *Anders-streben* (aspiration to be other) of the arts towards the condition of music, both of which also reverberate in the 'Preface' to *PDG*:

> We had many times discussed together the issue of an ideal modern book of prose which – being as varied in sound and rhythm as a poem and combining in its style the most diverse virtues of the written word – would harmonize all modes of knowledge and modes of mystery; which would alternate the precision of science with the seduction of dream; which would seem to be not just an imitation but a *continuation* of Nature [...]. [T]he principal aim is to create a work of beauty and poetry, and a plastic and symphonic prose rich in images and music. (D'Annunzio 1988, vol. 1, 639–40)[5]

---

5   'Avevamo più volte insieme ragionato d'un ideal libro di prosa moderno che – essendo vario di suoni e di ritmi come un poema, riunendo nel suo stile le più diverse virtù della parola scritta – armonizzasse tutte le varietà del conoscimento e tutte le varietà del mistero; alternasse le precisioni della scienza alle seduzioni del sogno; sembrasse non imitare ma *continuare* la Natura [...]. [V]'è, sopra tutto,

Although Wilde's novel was not translated into Italian until 1905, D'Annunzio's Dedicatory Letter suggests familiarity with Wilde's preface. Indeed, D'Annunzio owned and annotated a copy of the first 1895 French edition of *PDG*, now housed at Il Vittoriale, his hideaway on Lake Garda. For all its influence on D'Annunzio and on some of his circle, *PDG* did not enjoy widespread success in Italy. After the French edition had been circulating in Italy for ten years, the belated 1905 Italian translation never met with the interest generated by other works by Wilde. The tepid reception may well have been a result of *PDG*'s many analogies and parallelisms with the golden book of Italian aestheticism, D'Annunzio's *Il piacere* of 1889, which functioned as the Italian compendium of aesthetic practices.

A more enthusiastic response awaited *BRG*, a work which time would prove to be particularly appealing to Italian readers. *BRG* was introduced by Ojetti in *Il Marzocco* a year after 'Dialoghi dei vivi', in an article that emphasized the poem's redemptive quality in comparison with Wilde's earlier work. By giving relevance to such features in the text, Ojetti abandoned a Wildean exegesis strictly based on the principles of aestheticism in favour of one founded on thematic and cross-cultural criticism *avant la lettre*. Thus Ojetti inaugurated a major, most vital trend in Wilde's Italian reception which would, from then on, largely concentrate on the conflict between guilt and the possibility of expiation and salvation (Ojetti 1898, 1–2). Ojetti's piece paved the way for the great Italian success of the poem, which increased considerably after the first translation in 1906–07 (see De Michelis 1979, 69; Severi 1998, 25; Audoli 2002, 27 and Rita Severi's essay in this volume).

BRG came to attract even greater attention in two subsequent translations by G. Frasca De Naro (1914) and Adelina Manzotti-Bignone (1919), both of whom associated the ballad with *DP* as Wilde's other significant text about guilt, repentance and atonement. Enclosed within a suffocating Catholic environment that created an obsession with sin and redemption, even the most progressive Italian intellectuals must have found Wilde's letter intriguing. Its extensive and varied impact on early twentieth-century Italy bears evidence to Wilde's recognition not only in aesthetic circles, but in culture at large. The first translation of *DP*, by Olga Bicchierai, appeared soon after the original 1905 edition by Robbie Ross, making the text immediately available to Italian readers. The potential appeal to a wider public emerges in an advertisement in *Il Marzocco*, which recommended *DP* as 'the book which contains the interesting moral and artistic confession of the wretched author of *Salomé*' (anon. 1905).[6]

D'Annunzio himself owned two copies of the first Italian version of *DP* – today at Il Vittoriale – one of which has been copiously annotated. He also possessed three other copies of the text, in English, German and French. The fact that only the French edition is glossed confirms the assumption

---

il proposito di fare opera di bellezza e di poesia, prosa plastica e sinfonica, ricca d'imagini e di musiche.'

6   'il libro che contiene l'interessante confessione morale ed artistica del disgraziato autore di *Salomé*.' One month later, on 4 June 1905, half a page of the magazine was assigned to advertising its translation.

that D'Annunzio avoided reading English while alternating between Italian and French. D'Annunzio's penchant for *DP* reflects the centrality of the sin-repentance-atonement motif in his own work. Morbid attraction to Catholicism is a recurrent theme in his novels, particularly in *L'innocente* (*The Intruder*) (1891) and *Trionfo della morte*, and in his most controversial drama, *Le Martyre de Saint Sébastien* (The martyrdom of Saint Sebastian) of 1911, which blends Christian elements with erotic allusions and fantasies. Composed in archaic French during D'Annunzio's Parisian exile in 1910–15, and put to music by Claude Debussy, *Le Martyre* was intended to be 'mimed, danced and played' by the *prima donna* Ida Rubinstein (Andreoli 2000, 459). The parallels with *Salomé* are striking: Wilde's play had originally been written in French for the diva Sarah Bernhardt and later became a libretto for Richard Strauss's homonymous opera (see also Re 2002, 129). The plays also share the themes of temptation, sanctity and sensuality linked to a typically Decadent idea of religion. The sadomasochist overtones of *Le Martyre* also come close to *BRG*: Wilde's famous adage, 'each man kills the thing he loves', is echoed in the line by Renaissance poetess Veronica Gambara, 'He that loves me most, wounds me most' ('Chi più m'ama, più mi ferisce'), which D'Annunzio indicated as the main inspiration for his play (Andreoli 2000, 460).

The wide circulation of *DP* that followed Bicchierai's translation also elicited responses from more lukewarm currents of Italian aestheticism, sensitive to the theme of guilt in the text. In the summer of 1905, Giuseppe Lipparini (1877–1951), a lesser Decadent poet in the classicist vein, published an article on Wilde's *epistola* in *Il Marzocco*. Although Lipparini reproves Wilde for his human frailty, he commends his poetic talent and expresses sympathy for Wilde's prison experience, formulating an analogy between Wilde and Job that was to be later expanded by James Joyce. Lipparini highlights Wilde's classical legacy both by obliquely relating his homosexuality to common practices in the ancient world and, especially, by showing the influence of classical models on *DP*. Lipparini's response to Wilde is a rare example coming from that important pocket of *fin-de-siècle* Italian culture that surrounded D'Annunzio's rival poet Giovanni Pascoli, whose Symbolism was rooted in the Greek and Latin traditions. The Italian translator Luigi Gamberale (1840–1929), who was close to Pascoli, provided another prompt response to *DP* in the Roman magazine *Rivista d'Italia* (Italian magazine). In 'Un più reale Oscar Wilde' (A more real Oscar Wilde) (1905), Gamberale pursued an unoriginal attempt to rehabilitate Wilde in the light of his prison experience (Gamberale 1912b). Only one year before Gamberale had published 'Il processo e l'estetica di Oscar Wilde' (The trial and aesthetics of Oscar Wilde), an introduction to the author in the form of an imaginary dialogue between Wilde and Edward Carson during the trials (Gamberale 1912b).

In the first decade of the twentieth century, several of the new avant-garde magazines brought out a number of more penetrating pieces, which testified to a wide knowledge of the Wilde corpus and to the desire to understand its specificity. A case in point was *Leonardo*, a Florentine periodical professing aesthetic and irrationalistic principles. In an article of 1903 entitled 'Arte e democrazia' (Art and democracy), the philosopher Emilio Bodrero (1874–1949), writing under the pseudonym Alastor, threw light on Wilde's notion of social justice as linked to Beauty. In 1905, the unsigned article 'La psicologia di Cristo' (The psychology of Christ) analysed Christ's personality according to Fichte, Nietzsche and Wilde. Despite the religious scepticism of these unorthodox nineteenth-century thinkers, the anonymous author highlighted in them a shared will to stress the extraordinariness of the figure of Christ. In order to grasp Wilde's move towards religious orthodoxy, the author cites passages from DP rather than from the otherwise equally relevant SMUS.

Contemporary critics also offered readings in defence of others of Wilde's works, thus indicating the necessity to investigate the complexities of his multi-faceted corpus. The revision of previous critical notions on Wilde was once again induced by translations that circulated texts otherwise unavailable to the Italian readership, whose *lingua franca*, as exemplified by D'Annunzio, was French rather than English. In February 1912, *Il Marzocco* reported on a recent publication by Wilde's jailer which lay emphasis on Wilde's longing for redemption. Excerpts from the volume substantiated the image of Wilde as a deeply repentant man, comparing him to Bunyan in his imprisonment and even to St Francis – a favourite icon of the Italian *fin de siècle*. St Francis remains an unexplored link between Italian and British late nineteenth-century culture. First introduced by Matthew Arnold in *Essays in Criticism* (1875) and, later, a recurring figure in Pater's theoretical and creative writing (the most evident example being the imaginary portrait 'Denys l'Auxerrois'), the saint fascinated Wilde in his post-prison years.[7] For English aesthetic writers, St Francis became either an emblem for the aspiration to asceticism which often accompanied and balanced Decadent excess, or the expression of a yearning for Panic communion with nature. Within Italian *fin-de-siècle* culture, however, the saint acquired an even more emphatic symbolism, retaining strong political connotations as the patron saint of a new nation in search of common identity and cultural cohesion. Conti's last work – a spiritual testament posthumously published in 1931 – was entitled *San Francesco*, while D'Annunzio made frequent reference to the saint in many of his writings (Mariano 1978, 89–103). In 1898 D'Annunzio had been much absorbed by the project of a Franciscan tragedy to be entitled *Frate Sole* (Brother Sun) (Andreoli 2000, 326). Favoured by this mystical atmosphere, the sanctification of Wilde continued in *Il Marzocco* with a 1911 review by Aldo Sorani (1883–1945). The anglophile Sorani, who was among the founders of the British Institute in Florence in 1917, was a journalist whose intellectual affiliations are evident in his active collaboration with aestheti-cally-oriented magazines such as Ojetti's *Pan*. Sorani saw Anna de Brémond's *Oscar Wilde and his Mother* as the engine behind a thorough rehabilitation of the writer. He went as far as to declare that 'death and faith and glory have now purified Oscar Wilde, who has entered the infinite reign of spirit'

---

7   Ellmann (1987, 508–09) reports a dialogue between Wilde and Gide in which the former declared in 1897 that his path was 'that of St Francis of Assisi'. Then, 'when Gide proved to be knowledgeable about St Francis, Wilde asked him to send the best book he knew on the saint'.

(Sorani 1911, 3–4)[8] – an assertion that paved the way for the growth of the Wilde myth in Italy. Some years later, again in *Il Marzocco*, Sorani argued that Wilde's early journalism anticipated his ultimate artistic and human evolution epitomized by *DP* (Sorani 1920, 5).

Sorani's articles threw new light on Wilde's work and continued to increase his reception in Italy. They also show us how, in the first two decades of the new century, the debate on Wilde prospered while D'Annunzio was still dictating the canons of literary taste. Assessments which tried to gauge the intrinsic value of his oeuvre, rather than inscribing it within categories of 'morality' and 'normality', began to come more often to the fore. Gargano – the co-author, with D'Annunzio, of the 'Prologo' to *Il Marzocco* – re-entered the debate with 'Precetti di estetica wildiana' (1906) (Precepts of Wildean aesthetics), an article probably prompted by the first Italian edition of *Intentions*, translated by the poet and critic Raffaello Piccoli (1886–1933) (Marjanovic 2005). Another innovative approach, prefiguring reader-response criticism, is present in an unsigned piece for *Il Marzocco* entitled 'Oscar Wilde e il pubblico' (Oscar Wilde and the public), published in 1914. The article reports the view of the Swedish critic Ernst Bendz in *Vie des Lettres* (Life of letters), according to which Wilde had never been fully understood in Britain because of what would today be called his marginality. If from a biographical perspective this was due to his Irish roots, artistically it depended on his unconventional hybridization of literary genres and modes. The latter aspect showed that Wilde was neither an ironist nor a sentimentalist and it accounted for the impossibility of pigeon-holing his writings and, following from this, the misunderstanding they encountered. 'Oscar Wilde e il pubblico' is significant because it focused, albeit somewhat superficially, on the unusual topic of Wilde's liminality. In doing so, it not only followed, as will be seen, Joyce's much deeper analysis of the implications of Wilde's Irishness, but it also hinted at the necessity of a comprehensive exploration of the categories of difference and dissent in his work.

Homosexuality, masculinity, Fascism

Wilde's marginalization due to his sexual dissidence was not often mentioned by Italian critics. Where such references occurred, they were usually in the form of periphrasis or euphemism. A famous exception is Filippo Tommaso Marinetti's *Futurist Speech to the English*, which was, however, delivered at a safe distance from Italy, in London's Lyceum Club for Women in December 1910:

> Do you remember the dismal, ridiculous condemnation of Oscar Wilde, which Europe has never forgiven you for? Didn't all your newspapers cry out then that it was time to throw open every window because the plague was over? [...] Naturally in such an atmosphere of habitual and hypocritical formality, your young women

---

8   'la morte e la fede e la gloria hanno purificato ormai Oscar Wilde entrato nell'infinito regno dello spirito.'

are skilled in the use of their naïve elegance to carry on the most audaciously lascivious games, to prepare themselves well for marriage: the intangible domain of the conjugal police. As for your twenty-year-old young men, almost all of them are homosexuals for a time, which, after all, is absolutely respectable. This taste of theirs evolves through a kind of intensification of the camaraderie and friendship found in athletic sports during the years before they turn thirty, the time for work and good order, when they show their heels to Sodom in order to marry a young woman whose gown is shamelessly décolleté. Then they hasten to condemn the born invert severely, the counterfeit man, the half-woman who fails to conform. (Marinetti 2005, 7)

In Italy, open references to Wilde's homosexuality tended to come from scholars with a scientific or sociological approach, most often to emphasize (sometimes morbidly) the abnormality of his sexual inclinations, and not rarely – one suspects – in order to exorcize them. A precursor outside of Italy was the aesthetic poet, art patron and one-time friend of Wilde's, Marc-André Raffalovich (1864–1934). Raffalovich published his influential sexological study *Uranisme et Unisexualité* (Uranism and unisexuality) in 1896. One of the chapters of this volume, previously published in *Archives d'Anthropologie criminelle* (Archives of criminal anthropology), was translated into Italian by G. Bruni in 1896 as *L'uranismo, inversione sessuale congenita* (Uranism, congenital sexual inversion). This edition included Raffalovich's 'L'affaire Oscar Wilde' (1895) as 'Il processo di Oscar Wilde' (Oscar Wilde's trial) – the first account of Wilde's court case in Italy. Bruni's note to 'Il processo di Oscar Wilde' shows the emergence of an interpretation of Wilde as a case study, centring on his scientific interest rather than his artistic greatness. Wilde is defined as 'the depraved poet whose fame is precisely due to the facts that led him to court and to the punishment that many judged severe rather than to his comedies and his extravagant and trifling novels [*sic*.]' (Raffalovich 1896, 4).[9]

Paolo Valera (1850–1926) was more explicit in his book about Wilde's trials, which he had observed at first hand: *I gentiluomini invertiti: Echi dello scandalo di Milano. Il capo-scuola Oscar Wilde al processo con i suoi giovanotti* (The inverted gentlemen: echoes of the Milan scandal. The precursor Oscar Wilde on trial with his young men) (1909). Valera takes his cue from a recent homosexual scandal involving members of Milanese high society and fire fighters (Miracco 1985) in order to stigmatize Wilde as the initiator and divulger of the most horrible of contemporary evils, which he names 'oscarwildismo' and describes in apocalyptic terms and with bestial imagery (Benadusi 2005, 41–42 and 327 n. 37). An analogous example can be found in an article published in *Nuova Antologia* in 1911, 'Oscar Wilde in carcere' (Oscar Wilde in jail), by the Florentine jurist and deputy Giovanni Rosadi (1862–1925). Rosadi betrays his enthusiasm for the methodology of the case study by insisting on Wilde's 'perverted instincts', 'immorality', 'really abnormal nature', 'amalgamation of genius and insanity', 'perverted conscience', 'sexual [...] psychopathology',

---

9   'il poeta vizioso, la cui fama è dovuta precisamente ai fatti che lo trassero dinanzi al giurì inglese, alla pena che molti dissero severa, piuttosto ché alle sue commedie ed a' suoi romanzi [*sic*.] stravaganti ed insulsi'.

etc., only finally to describe Wilde as, quite predictably, a victim to hysteria (Rosadi 1911, 407–418).[10] Ultimately, however, the author rehabilitates Wilde on account of his deathbed conversion and praises the twin texts *BRG* and *DP*. *DP* is also extensively quoted in the introductory essay by Arnaldo de Lisle (*nom de plume* of Giuseppe Garibaldi Rocco) to the 1908 edition of LASC translated by Federigo Verdinois. Here, *DP* is brought as evidence of Wilde's 'penitence and [...] expiation' ('penitenza e [...] espiazione') after an irregular life caused – in the terms of Lombroso and Nordau – by his 'degeneration' (de Lisle 1908, 36 and 39). This theory presents yet another emblematic coalescence of Positivism and Christian faith.

More spontaneous discussions of Wilde's homosexuality were, of course, carried out in letters and private papers. In May 1913, in the wake of World War I and of new proto-fascist models of masculinity, the painter-poet Ardengo Soffici (1879–1964), a collaborator of *Leonardo* and other avant-garde magazines, harshly commented in his diary on the hypocrisy of British society towards Wilde and Douglas and called for 'a little more penetration, intelligence and tact' ('un po' più di penetrazione, d'intelligenza e di tatto') in the discussion of this topic. He adds: 'Shall we ever understand that morals, virtue and philistinism must melt down and disappear in front of the gushing power of life and instinct, which are always victorious and legitimate?' (Soffici 1918, 89)[11]

Around the same time, another Italian painter and poet, Filippo de Pisis (1896–1956), recognized a soul mate in Wilde during his struggle to liberate himself from a rigid Catholic upbringing. De Pisis's early prose writings – partially published only after his death – are haunted by Wilde's persona and bear witness to what De Pisis believed to be their shared artistic dedication and private dilemmas (Zanotto 1996, 107 and 111). De Pisis's close reading of Wilde in the late 1910s, during his university years in Bologna, was to culminate in the manuscript notes entitled 'Wildismo' (Wildism), which are dominated by the contemplation of androgynous Apollonian beauty and the longing for the ephebic ideal (Zanotto 1996, 111 and 140).

More pruriently, Emilio Cecchi (1884–1966), who would soon emerge as a crucial figure in Wilde studies in Italy, made ironical reference to the writer's homosexuality in a 1921 letter to Mario Praz (Crucitti Ullrich 1985, 92). Strangely enough, this is the only allusion to the writer in the correspondence between these two Wilde scholars. This seems even more surprising when one considers the homosocial sentiments their correspondence repeatedly evoked, with Cecchi and the young Praz relishing each other's friendship. On the other hand, the form and essence of Cecchi's reference are typical of a certain aspect of Italian culture, which, at this time, rested firmly on political, intellectual and emotional modes of male bonding which fully banned the female

---

[10] 'istinti pervertiti', 'immoralità', 'natura veramente anormale', 'impasto di genio e insania', 'coscienza pervertita', 'psicopatia [...] sessuale'.

[11] 'Si capirà mai che l'etica, la virtù, il filisteismo debbono squagliarsi e sparire davanti all'irruenza della vita e dell'istinto vittoriosi sempre e sempre legittimi?'

subject, and considered such brotherhood as normative and exclusive of the sexual sphere. Fascism itself, which was then on the rise (the March on Rome would take place the following year), laid its foundations on such types of relationships. The word chosen to designate a militant fascist, *camerata*, carried homosocial overtones that strangely mirrored the late-Victorian use of *comrade* as code for 'homosexual'. D'Annunzio, himself a *camerata*, had been steeped in the Fascist cult of male friendships since his school days, and later cherished a circle of close male friends. This did not prevent him from becoming a notorious, hyper-masculine womanizer. Although Wilde's homosocial leanings had something in common with the Italian hegemonic culture of the early twentieth century, we can account for the widespread reticence about his sexual orientation by considering the form of *machista* masculinity generally shared by D'Annunzio and Italian Decadent culture. Within Fascism, such gender stereotypes were exalted in strikingly anti-Wildean terms: 'Fascism is, in one word, an instigator of virility against any feminisation and softening of the spirit. [...] [I]t is against [...] the foppishness of social customs [...]. Can one be more male than that?' (Maggiore 1929, 141)[12] The obsession with virility was driven by Fascism's imperative to preserve the race, combined with the Catholic Church's determination to restrain sexual practices that clashed with its incitement to 'go forth and multiply'. It comes as no surprise, then, that Fascism and the Church worked together to reinforce their common positions through a rigid control of people's habits (Benadusi 2005, 88). Along the same lines, Giovanni Dall'Orto (2000, 524) emphasizes the joint aims of the Fascist regime and the Church, though he also argues that the Fascist power tended to disregard the repression of homosexuality in the knowledge that the Church was already embroiled in that particular battle. Dall'Orto's observation indirectly points to reticence as one of Fascism's privileged strategies in its crusade against the spreading of non-normative behaviour – a point with which Benadusi agrees (2005, 122–23). Such a policy of silence came to affect Wilde's Italian reception, as revealed by an anonymous 1926 article in *Il popolo d'Italia* (The Italian people) – the official organ of the Fascist Party, founded by Benito Mussolini and edited at the time by his brother Arnaldo. The article cites Wilde's case as representative of what ought and ought not to be said about homosexuality and why. The article – significantly entitled 'Perversioni' (Perversions) – is one of the very few references to Wilde to come from the Fascist intellectual elite:

> Our intent is to keep pure and vigilant the fortunate sanity of our people. Therefore, even though we enjoy *LWF* in the theatre or take pleasure in HOP or *BRG*, where this mediocre and derivative writer touches certain profound human chords, in Italian newspapers – which end up in the hands of everybody – we ought to be silent about the epistolary evidence of shameful diseases, thrown to the public under cover of vaguely literary pretexts. Silence is the only form of respectful

---

12 'Il Fascismo è, in una parola, suscitatore di virilità contro ogni infemminimento e infrollimento dello spirito. [...] [È] contro [...] il cicisbeismo del costume [...]. Si può essere più maschi di così?'

pity for the dead man and the only form of preserving the living from contagion. ('Perversioni' 1926)[13]

Despite the censorious tone, the passage leaves some space for the appreciation of Wilde's works, which in fact enjoyed a certain amount of success in the 1920s. At this time there was a considerable demand for popular editions of his writings, especially the comedies: *IBE, LWF, WNI, IH* but also *Salomé* and even *DOP* were all issued during the first seven years of Fascist rule, between 1922 and 1929 (Severi 1998, 20 and 24–29). Wilde's dramas were possibly considered less threatening to hegemonic culture than the rest of his output. Besides, the dramas were seen as an innocent form of entertainment, distinct from such challenging and resistant texts as *Intentions* and, especially, SMUS. The latter two were never reprinted during the Fascist period. Significantly enough, SMUS was issued immediately after the end of the Second World War in 1945 (Severi 1998, 24 and 27). Wilde's children's stories also enjoyed great favour under the Fascist regime, during which there were several editions of *HPOT* and the first schoolboy version of the text, released in 1931 (Severi 1998, 20 and 28).

The Decadent legacy

Wilde's partial inclusion in the Fascist literary canon can be seen to depend on his popularity with avant-garde figures of pre-war Italian culture – Marinetti, Soffici and de Pisis are cases in point – who had come out of a tradition of *fin-de-siècle* poetics, but whose aesthetic ideologies contributed to the creation of Fascist mythologies. In 1913, for instance, Wilde appears to have indirectly inspired the foundation of *Lacerba* – a militant Florentine magazine, close in spirit to *Leonardo* – that soon became the mouthpiece for the Futurists. The sixteen-point 'Introibo' (an irreverent title that adopts the name of the initial rite of the Catholic mass) that prefaced the journal looked back to the manifesto structure of *Convito* and *Il Marzocco* and, through them, to the 'Preface' to *PDG*. Obvious Wildean traits in the 'Introibo' included the glorification of the aesthetic moment, the taste for witty and provocative aphorisms and, in the words of Romano Luperini, 'the exaltation of individualism, of artistic genius, of aesthetic strangeness' (1976, 30).[14] These are two significant passages:

---

[13] 'Curiamo di mantenere pura e vigile la fortunata sanità del nostro popolo, e se ascoltiamo con piacere a teatro *Il ventaglio di Lady Windermere*, o ci compiacciamo per *La casa del melograno* o *La ballata del prigioniero*, dove questo mediocre poeta e scrittore di derivazione pur tocca certe note umane profonde, nei giornali italiani – che vanno per le mani di tutti – si faccia il silenzio intorno alle documentazioni epistolari di vergognose malattie, abbandonate al pubblico sotto pretesti vagamente letterarii. Il silenzio è l'unica forma di rispettosa pietà per il morto e di preservazione del contagio per i vivi.' For a detailed analysis of the article, see Dall'Orto 2000, 526–27.

[14] 'l'esaltazione dell'individualismo, del genio artistico, della stranezza estetica.'

7. Art: justification of the world – counterbalance on life's tragic scales. Our reason for being, for accepting everything with joy. [...] 11. We love truth up to (and including) paradox – life up to (and including) evil – and art up to (and including) strangeness. (Papini 1913, 1)[15]

In the meantime, Wilde mainly continued to be discussed from an ethical perspective. Such was the case with Giorgio Barini's 'La morale nelle opere di Oscar Wilde (con un ritratto)' (Morality in Oscar Wilde's works (with a portrait)) (1908), which was released in the authoritative Florentine magazine, *Nuova Antologia* (New anthology). In order to rehabilitate *Salomé* – both the tragedy and the opera – from the charges of immorality, Barini (1864–1944), a foremost music critic of the Decadent and post-Decadent ages, provided a cursory survey of Wilde's works that attested their morality.

A more perceptive contribution to Wilde studies in Italy came from James Joyce, who was living in Trieste at the time. Joyce, who was an admirer of D'Annunzio's aesthetic novels, belongs among the critics who saw strong ethical interests in Wilde's work.[16] Unlike D'Annunzio's followers, however, Joyce stressed the centrality of Wilde's Irish identity, thus offering a highly modern analysis of his life and *oeuvre*. Joyce's contribution appeared in the Triestine daily *Il Piccolo della Sera*, in which he published a series of articles on Irish topics between 1907 and 1912. These were often complex and ambivalent pieces, written as they were by a colonized subject from a peripheral area of the British Empire to other colonized subjects from a peripheral area of another Empire – Trieste formed part of Austro-Hungary at the time and its struggle for independence would be among the reasons for Italy's entry into World War I.

Joyce's article on Wilde, which was issued on 24 March 1909 to coincide with the Triestine premiere of Strauss's *Salome*, represents the first Italian response to Wilde's Irishness and to his Irish anti-colonial dissidence. After a detailed biographical account, Joyce uses Wilde's fall as a vantage point from which to assess him, ultimately, as an orthodox figure. Joyce portrays Wilde as the incarnation of the redemptive value of guilt, which he sees, in clear Catholic terms, as a bequest of Wilde's origins. In Joyce's eyes, the values associated with Irishness and Catholicism redeem Wilde, while the English educational system is to blame for his errors, which, as Joyce observes, were shared by his fiercest accusers. Wilde thus emerges as both a creature and a victim of English culture: 'far from being a perverted monster who sprang in

---

[15] '7. Arte: giustificazione del mondo – contrappeso nella bilancia tragica dell'esistenza. Nostra ragione di essere, di accettar tutto con gioia. [...] 11. Noi amiamo la verità fino al paradosso (incluso) – la vita fino al male (incluso) – e l'arte fino alla stranezza (inclusa).'

[16] Joyce's juvenile essay 'The Day of the Rabblement' (1901) was actually rejected by *St Stephen's* magazine, an undergraduate journal at University College, Dublin, because of its reference to D'Annunzio's *Il fuoco*, then listed in the Vatican Index of Prohibited Books. Joyce's admiration for the Italian author is confirmed by his claim that Tolstoy, Kipling and D'Annunzio were the 'three writers of the nineteenth century who had the greatest natural talents' (Ellmann 1982, 661).

some inexplicable way from the civilization of modern England, [Wilde] is the logical and inescapable product of the Anglo-Saxon college and university system, with its secrecy and restrictions' (Joyce 1959b, 204). For Joyce, Wilde was able to achieve his finest artistic inspiration only after rejecting mimicry and refusing assimilation into English society:

> Here we touch the pulse of Wilde's art – sin. He deceived himself into believing that he was the bearer of good news of neo-paganism to an enslaved people. His own distinctive qualities, the qualities, perhaps, of his race – keenness, generosity, and a sexless intellect – he placed at the service of a theory of beauty which, according to him, was to bring back the Golden Age and the joy of the world's youth. But, if some truth adheres to his subjective interpretations of Aristotle, to his restless thought that proceeds by sophisms rather than syllogisms, to his assimilations of natures as foreign as the delinquent is to the humble, at its very base is the truth inherent in the soul of Catholicism: that man cannot reach the divine heart except through that sense of separation and loss called sin. (Joyce 1959b, 204–05)

Joyce develops his interpretation within this problematic vision of Wilde as a victim of colonialism who at last finds his identity by approaching the Catholic faith of his countrymen. For Joyce, the final word on Wilde can be found in *DP*, which is most evidently shaped by the ethos of Catholicism. It is again possible to see D'Annunzio's influence in Joyce's insistence on binary oppositions such as temptation *versus* atonement and pagan extravagance *versus* Franciscan simplicity, as well as in his use of redundant and evocative prose:

> In his last book, *De Profundis*, he kneels before a gnostic Christ, resurrected from the apocryphal pages of *The House of Pomegranates*, and then his true soul, trembling, timid, and saddened, shines through the mantle of Heliogabalus. His fantastic legend, his opera – a polyphonic variation on the rapport of art and nature, but at the same time a revelation of his own psyche – his brilliant books sparkling with epigrams (which made him, in the view of some people, the most penetrating speaker of the last century), these are now divided booty.
>
> A verse from the book of Job is cut on the tombstone in the impoverished cemetery at Bagneux. It praises his facility, 'eloquium suum', – the great legendary mantle which is now divided booty. Perhaps the future will also carve there another verse, less proud but more pious:
>
> *Partiti sunt sibi vestimenta mea et super*
> *vestem meam miserunt sortis.* (Joyce 1959b, 205)[17]

Joyce's response to Wilde is, in many ways, representative of a younger generation of children of pleasure, who are still galvanized by D'Annunzio's personality a couple of decades after his aesthetic heyday, and who still draw on him to open new hermeneutic paths in Wilde criticism.

---

[17]   The Latin quotation comes from John 19:24. It refers to Christ's crucifixion and translates as 'they parted my raiment among them, and for my vesture did they cast lots.'

A most gifted member of this circle was Emilio Cecchi, one of the fathers of English studies in Italy. Cecchi's education and literary models were predicated on the aesthetic canons of the *fin de siècle*. It seems appropriate to end this survey of Wilde's reception with Cecchi's 1928 essay 'Il mito di O. Wilde' (The myth of O. Wilde). This piece may be taken as the Italian Decadents' final statement on Wilde, although it simultaneously shows a continuity in Italian Wilde scholarship that stretches from its outset in the 1890s up to the interwar period and beyond, well into the second half of the twentieth century. Typically, Cecchi lays the emphasis on morality as the privileged category with which to judge Wilde's work. Cecchi finds 'a type of honesty and sanity' in Wilde's writings, 'which, in the moral order, correspond to the pugnacious frankness with which he lived and defended his paradoxes and sins' (1976, 181).[18] Cecchi's debt to Joyce, of whom he was one of the first Italian critics, emerges in his insistence on Wilde's origins:

> Wilde's Irishness is seldom sufficiently noted. What in other Irishmen had been a clear and harsh impulse of political revolt against English ideas and priorities, becomes anti-puritan paradox in Wilde [...]. In his comedies of manners and in the dialogues of *Intentions* we find a less choice but more convincing aspect of him, that somehow confirms and reproduces the contrast between Wilde and his public and shows us at its fullest the struggle, which is far less innocuous than it might seem, between this 'drawing-room leviathan' and his middle-class enemies. (1976, 181–82)[19]

In contrast to Joyce's praise for *DP*, Cecchi privileges Wilde's other cathartic text, *BRG*, as Wilde's major achievement (1976, 182). Ojetti had done precisely the same thirty years earlier in his juvenile article in *Il Marzocco*. Cecchi, influenced by D'Annunzio and Decadent aesthetics, exemplifies the vitality of an interpretation of Wilde that fluctuates between attempts to justify his behaviour, acknowledgements of his uniqueness and, finally, a recognition of 'perversion'. Such categories – artistic greatness, morality and deviation – are more famously employed in the critique of Wilde formulated by Cecchi's major disciple, Mario Praz – a 'grandchild' of pleasure or, in Franco Marucci's words, 'a Decadent of sorts' (1996, 15) – in his classic *La carne, la morte, e il diavolo nella letteratura romantica* (*The Romantic Agony*) (1930).

The vision of the Decadent children of pleasure would only be supplanted half a century later, by which time Structuralism had eclipsed the impressionistic,

---

18 'una salute e un'onestà [...] che corrispondono, nell'ordine morale, alla pugnace franchezza con la quale egli visse e difese i suoi paradossi e i suoi peccati'.

19 'non si dà, per solito, sufficiente rilievo al carattere irlandese del Wilde. Ciò che in altri irlandesi fu, nettamente e duramente, impulso di rivolta politica alle idee e prevalenze inglesi, nel Wilde si trasforma in paradosso antipuritano [...]. Nelle commedie mondane e nei dialoghi di *Intentions*, se ne ritrova un aspetto meno prelibato e più convincente, che in qualche modo conferma e riproduce il contrasto fra Wilde e il suo pubblico: e ci mostra in pieno sviluppo la lotta, assai meno innocua di quanto alla superficie potesse sembrare, fra questo "leviatano da salotto" e i borghesi avversari.'

pre-theory criticism of Romantic and Decadent legacy. This change took place in the 1970s, through the works of critics Masolino D'Amico and Giovanna Franci. The analytic approach is exemplified in D'Amico's *Oscar Wilde: Il critico e le sue maschere* (Oscar Wilde: the critic and his masks) (1973), soon followed by his biographical study *Vita di Oscar Wilde attraverso le lettere* (Oscar Wilde's life through his letters) (1977) and by his Meridiani Mondadori edition (1979), which included new translations, unpublished letters and articles by Wilde as well as a comprehensive critical apparatus. D'Amico's studies ran parallel to Franci's scholarly criticism in *Il sistema del dandy: Wilde-Beardsley-Beerbohm* (The system of the dandy: Wilde-Beardsley-Beerbohm) (1977). It is not coincidental that the latest reprint of Cecchi's collected essays, containing 'Il mito di O. Wilde', was released in 1976, in the midst of these new developments in Wilde studies. It must be taken as a final statement of the most durable and influential, though bygone phase of Wilde's Italian reception.

8 The Strange Adventures of Oscar Wilde in Spain (1892–1912)

Richard A. Cardwell

No literary period is a cocoon, separated from the extra-literary obsessions, concerns, debates and discourses of its age.[1] And this is particularly true in the context of the reception of Oscar Wilde in *fin-de-siècle* Spain. Even as late as the 1890s the literary scene in Spain was dominated by Realism and Naturalism in the novel and by civic and national concerns in poetry. While poetic tastes were changing with the impact of the new aesthetics of Gustavo Adolfo Bécquer in the 1870s and the new lyrical and musical tone of writers like Ricardo Gil and Francisco A. de Icaza in the late 1890s,[2] traditionalist Spain had yet to catch up with European artistic developments, especially French ones. The young writers born in the late 1870s and early 1880s, with their deep concerns over national political and social decline, felt powerless to effect any radical or concrete change. Thus they challenged the bourgeois establishment in an indirect way: through a new art and culture. After 1903 their work offered a programme of spiritual reform through Art – a radical programme to which we shall return. But the means to such a literary programme, initially, was wanting to the new generation and, thus, they looked abroad for inspiration. Some, like the Machado brothers, spent a year in Paris in 1899 where both turned to Symbolism; Juan Ramón Jiménez spent five months in a sanatorium near Bordeaux in 1901, where he read the new poets and the *Mercure de France*; José Martínez Ruiz, future novelist and essayist, was reading French texts in the mid–1890s.

France was far from *terra incognita* to some young writers, as the intemperate essays of the establishment critics against them and, more broadly, against the deleterious effects of French culture at the turn of the century demonstrate. But no Spanish writer (as against Latin American writers) took up the new French trends seriously until the new century. The major source of positive

---

[1] Parts of this essay appeared in another form in Cardwell 2003. The present author thanks Legenda for permission to re-use some of this material.

[2] For an overview see Cardwell 1972, 1984, 1998a, 1999, 2004.

assessment of these trends and the 'discovery' of Wilde therefore fell to Latin American writers resident in Paris and Madrid. As established artists, they had been sent by their respective governments as diplomatic representatives to the two cities, where they rapidly became part of the progressive literary coteries. They were among the first to record, through expatriate newspaper columns in Paris and the press in Madrid, their impressions of the new literary scene. Avid readers of all new ideas, including scientific advances, in their essays we find an extraordinary interplay of discourses. And this admixture of Positivism and Idealism is nowhere more evident than in the elaboration of the character and identity of the modern artist as set out by the Guatemalan essayist Enrique Gómez Carrillo and the Nicaraguan poet Rubén Darío in their reception of Wilde. Yet despite all their promotion of Wilde's aesthetics, translations of his works into Spanish were tardy. The earliest translation is of *Salomé* in 1902; but no translation of the major plays, the tales or the more important critical essays appeared until the second decade of the twentieth century.[3] The essays of Gómez Carrillo and Darío therefore played a key role in creating knowledge of Wilde's work among Spanish readers.

The earliest reference belongs to 1891, the year of *Intentions*, a book which enshrines the core beliefs of Wilde's aestheticism. The French translation did not appear until 1905. It must therefore be supposed that Gómez Carrillo had a reading knowledge of English or that Wilde spoke *in extenso* of his book in French, a language which Gómez Carrillo also spoke. In the second chapter of *Sensaciones de arte* (Artistic sensations) Gómez Carrillo presented to his Hispanic readers the modern aesthete *par excellence*: Oscar Wilde (Gómez Carrillo 1891). The essay offered an informed portrait and assessment of Wilde's work up to that date. It contains a précis of an interview Wilde gave *Le Figaro* and various statements by Wilde and anecdotes concerning him, including a (probably fictitious) account of Wilde's lectures in the United States and his insulting remarks to his audiences. The inclusion of Wilde's comments served, of course, as a veiled attack on an out-dated Spanish culture. Gómez Carrillo praises *Intentions* and, through one of Wilde's well-known epigrams and an attempt at Wildean wit of his own, he once more throws the new aesthetic in the face of its detractors:

> In this book [*Intentions*], in effect an admirable work, we find outlined nearly all the author's aesthetic ideas. 'Modern novelists claim that art should imitate nature, when, on the contrary, it is nature which should imitate art.' And this odd comment [...] contains more artistic substance than the whole of Zola's 'Le Roman Experimental'. What, in reality, is nature without adornment? An immense space always the same, always monotonous and almost always ghastly. For me a mountain of stone is only beautiful when the hand of man has converted it into a column or an obelisk [...]. And the same for the rest [...]. Oscar Wilde's ideas have this advantage. From a single one of his statements one could form a book, while from a book by Zola one could hardly make a phrase. Oscar Wilde is a great critic, and

---

3   French versions, which many young Spaniards could read, appeared earlier: *LWF* was published in 1892, followed by translations of *PDG* (1895), *BRG* (1902) and *HOP* (1902).

thanks to his influence French Naturalism has not made serious inroads on the young literature of England. (1891, 45–46)[4]

In this paragraph we find all the call signs of the resistance to establishment norms by young literary critics like Gómez Carrillo, which were to emerge more fully at the turn of the new century. Wilde's inversion of the nature/culture binary seemed scandalous to a public nurtured on the Romantic vision of picturesque nature and the prettified evocations in the Spanish conservative *costumbrista* novel and Restoration poetry. Gómez Carrillo 'urbanizes', that is, aestheticizes nature by converting it into a metropolitan monument. He aligns himself unconditionally with the new aesthetic. In *Esquisses* he reprints the same article and adds some new material returning to Wilde's desire to subvert nature (and shock the bourgeoisie) by recording that Wilde 'blasphemes frequently; for in his strange manner of thought he would always seek to put God right' (Gómez Carrillo 1892, 14).[5] The poet has usurped God. Art is a new revelation.

The homage to Wilde in *Sensaciones* [6] begins, however, with the following autobiographical memoir: 'It was in Stuart Merrill's house, the admired poet of *Les Fastes,* where, one wintry night, I first met the celebrated author of *Salomé* and *PDG*' (Gómez Carrillo 1891, 41).[7] Again, his knowledge of these works pre-dates the French translations.[8] Gómez Carrillo establishes his literary credentials with the mention of his friendship with Stuart Merrill and his knowledge of Wilde's most recent book identifies Wilde conspiratorially by his works. In so doing, he assumes his readers will know of whom he writes. Yet, in spite of this self-serving, he is recalling an accredited gathering (Ellmann 1987, 324). We know from Yvanhoe Rambasson, an acquaintance

---

4   'En ese libro [*Intentions*], efectivamente admirable, se encuentran resumidas casi todas las ideas estéticas del autor. "Los novelistas modernos pretenden que el arte debe imitar a la naturaleza, cuando, al contrario, es la naturaleza quien debe imitar al arte." Y esta frase [...] contiene más substancia artística que toda *La novela experimental* de Zola. ¿Qué es, en realidad la naturaleza sin adornos? Una inmensidad siempre igual, siempre monótona y casi siempre horrible. Para mí, una montaña de piedra no es bella sino cuando la mano del hombre la ha convertido en columna o obelisco [...]. Y así todo lo demás [...]. Las ideas escritas de Oscar Wilde tienen esa ventaja. De una sola de sus frases podría hacerse un libro, mientras que un libro de Zola apenas podría hacerse una frase. Oscar Wilde es un gran crítico, gracias a cuya influencia el naturalismo francés no ha hecho muchos estragos en la joven literatura de Inglaterra'.

5   'blasfema con frecuencia; porque en su modo raro de pensar querría, a cada momento, enmendarle a Dios la plana'.

6   It is possible that this title is meant to recall the English aesthetic tradition of impressionistic criticism that includes Pater's *Appreciations* and Wilde's *Intentions*.

7   'Fue en casa de Stuart Merrill, el poeta adorable de *Los fastos*, donde encontré por primera vez, una noche de crudo invierno, al autor ilustre de *Salomé* y del *Retrato de Dorian Gray*.'

8   *Salomé* appeared in 1893; *Le Portrait de Dorian Gray* in 1895, with further editions in 1904 and 1920 (see Emily Eell's essay in this volume for a full treatment of the French reception of these two works).

of Wilde in Paris in the early 1890s, that, in the winter of 1891, he and Wilde retired to the Café d'Harcourt where they were joined by Gómez Carrillo and Verlaine. Wilde, disgusted by the appearance of the latter, addressed his conversation to the Guatemalan and spoke of his life, travels and art. The two became close friends and Gómez Carrillo a confidant (Ellmann 1987, 324). The supper with Stuart Merrill followed that first meeting.

PDG had been presented in serial form in the July issue of *Lippincott's Monthly Magazine* in 1890 and published in book form by Stoddart in the April of 1891. The final part of Gómez Carrillo's essay, published only months later, deals in some detail with this novel, arguing that Wilde is a greater stylist than theoretician. The commentary on Dorian's story stresses the protagonist's struggle between the spirit and the fleshly impulse and the brilliance of Wilde's evocations. *Salomé*, though, remained unfinished at the time of the article in 1891. Clearly, Gómez Carrillo knew of the play and may even have heard Wilde reading parts in literary *salons*. In London, *Salomé* was violently attacked in the conservative press. Such had also been the case with *PDG* in 1891, when W. H. Smith refused to market the book on the grounds of its 'filth'. As Richard Hibbitt and Emily Eells document in this volume, in Paris the reaction was different. In Gómez Carrillo's article we learn that *PDG* provoked a letter from Mallarmé on the receipt of a signed copy. This letter, quoted verbatim in French, was not re-published until the 1960s in the Pléiade edition of Mallarmé's complete works. Wilde, presumably, had lent Mallarmé's letter to his Guatemalan friend.

In an essay written at a later date (1920?), Gómez Carrillo relates that Wilde was obsessed with the figure of Salome. He recalls the same dinner party at Stuart Merrill's house in late 1891 where Wilde and Remy de Gourmont argued about the play. The young Guatemalan was evidently a principal witness and *habitué* of the Wilde circle. But the essay in *Sensaciones* is addressed specifically to *Intentions*. Gómez Carrillo is able to gloss Wilde's theories on art: his rejection of nature, the necessary function of art in improving nature, the artist in splendid isolation from mundane preoccupations, the artist as a subversive. However, the direct quotations offered, which are intended to highlight Wilde's skill as an epigrammatist, are not to be found among the essays of *Intentions*. Possibly inspired by DL or, as I suspect, taken down verbatim from Wilde's own mouth in conversation, these epigrams nevertheless express the principal sentiments of Wilde's revolutionary aestheticism. Gómez Carrillo presents Wilde, in the main, as a profoundly subversive theorist while not overlooking his power as a creative writer.

Most surprising, however, is the pen portrait with which the essay begins. Gómez Carrillo is struck by Wilde's 'singular and insinuating manner of speaking French' (Gómez Carrillo 1891, 41). [9] He records his fascination with Wilde's 'enormous face of a sad and dreamy adolescent' and comments on

---

[9]   'manera singular e insinuante de hablar francés'. One might compare the same fascination with Wilde's style of speaking in Helen Potter's *Impersonations* of 1891, which offers a detailed account of how Wilde accented and paused for dramatic effect in his American lectures (Potter, 23).

his 'athletic frame of a certain special distinction which draws feminine gazes' (41),[10] avoiding any mention of Wilde's homosexuality, of which he was all too aware. Gómez Carrillo had no such tendencies (nor did Darío) so that the praise for Wilde's physique and looks was inspired elsewhere as we shall see. He closes this section with a description of Wilde's attire. On a visit to Wilde's flat he notes his 'robust fighter's torso [which] made me think of the immortal figures of Rubens [...]. And when I come upon him in any literary café in the Latin Quarter, dressed in that studied *tenue* of the English, his gigantic frame recalls an old portrait of Tourgénief [*sic.*], which I saw some time ago and cannot recall where' (41–42).[11] The references to Rubens and Turgenev betray, incidentally, Gómez Carrillo's obsession with Decadent artifice and the conversion of nature into art. He is reminded of another artistic creation when he describes Wilde's 'huge eyes, humid and slanted, [which] had a certain expression in the pupils which neither the word sadness nor melancholy can quite express; they were pale eyes, as was pale the smile of Catulle Mendès's heroine, with the paleness in the description and not in the colour' (42).[12] The reference is probably to Mendès's collection of poetry *Philoméla* of 1863, a further sign of the underlying Decadent cast of this evocation. The terms used in this passage – 'ojos melancólicos', 'palidez' –, like the adjective 'soñador' employed in the previous description, are soon to recur in the critical writings and poetic evocations of young Spanish writers by the late 1890s, especially Francisco Villaespesa and Juan Ramón Jiménez in their 1900 collections of verses. In essence, then, Wilde is evoked as the very model of the aesthete, the refined spirit, the soulful, aloof, feminine and Decadent dreamer and yet as a man of robust and attractive physique. We note again the aestheticism of the evocation and the gendering, where reality (Wilde's torso) is transmuted into art (Rubens, Turgenev, Mendès's heroine): the very picture of Dorian Gray and the artist as described by Théophile Gautier, Charles Baudelaire and Barbey d'Aurevilly. Even Wilde's 'blonde, fine and silky hair' ('cabellera blonda, fina y sedeña'), with its arranged central parting covering his 'fine ears' ('finas orejas'), the aquiline nose and the 'sensual mouth' ('boca sensual') confirm the portrait of the artist as dreamer and aesthete.

While the Spanish reader of this enthusiastic essay might be tempted to read Wilde's works, the stress on his physique and personality creates a problem of performance. In emphasizing temperament and physical characteristics as much as creative genius, Gómez Carrillo is clearly seduced by the former.

---

[10] 'su enorme rostro de adolescente triste y soñador' ; 'envoltura atlética, de cierta distinción especial que atrae las miradas femeninas'.

[11] 'su robusto torso de luchador [que] me hace pensar en las figuras inmortales de Rubens [...]. Y cuando trajeado ya con esa cuidadosa *tenue* de los ingleses, le encuentro en cualquier café literario del barrio latino, su talle gigantesco me trae a la memoria un viejo retrato de Tourgénief, que vi hace ya bastante tiempo y ni aun recuerdo donde'.

[12] 'ojos largos, húmedos y oblicuos [que] tienen cierta expresión en las pupilas que ni la voz tristeza, ni la voz melancolía alcanzan a denotar; son ojos pálidos, como era pálida la sonrisa de aquella heroina de Catulle Mendès, con la palidez en el dibujo, y no en el color'.

The Parisian intimacy with a kindred spirit is powerfully evoked but it does not carry the same performative message as the literary critical commentary. Readers can enjoy Wilde's writings but they cannot share Gómez Carrillo's personal experience. The account of Wilde's wit and charm cannot be fully communicated to his readers who have had no such personal acquaintance. So why does Gómez Carrillo indulge in this emphasis on Wilde's physical bearing? Such a description is not an isolated example. Similar portraits of other contemporary artists appear both in *Esquisses* and in later essays. They can also be found in Darío's *Los raros* (The rare ones) (1896). Pen-portraits of this type, however, are neither unique nor original. If we look at a whole range of essays dedicated to Edgar Allan Poe – arguably the most inspiring and enduring icon of the personal sacrifice to art and the spiritually troubled life of the artist at the end of the century (Quinn 1957) – we shall perceive the similarities, even though Gómez Carrillo's picture is more detailed in his evocation.

In the second half of the nineteenth century, the artistic and literary vogue for Poe was strong among French writers. From 1851 with Baudelaire and then after 1873 with Mallarmé and many others, the task of translating and paying homage to Poe became a major feature of the French poetic scene. Both writers penned idealized portraits of their tragic poet-hero who, for Baudelaire in *L'Art Romantique* (Romantic art), was 'the most powerful artist of the epoch' ('l'artiste le plus puissant de l'époque') (Baudelaire 1961, 57). In Baudelaire's 'Edgar Allan Poe, sa vie et ses ouvrages' (Edgar Allan Poe, his life and works) of 1852 and 'Edgar Poe, sa vie et ses oeuvres' (Edgar Poe, his life and works) of 1856, Poe is reincarnated as the sensitive artist crushed by an uncomprehending public, the visionary poet simultaneously blessed and cursed by his visions and insights. The descriptions of Poe's dress and physiognomy simply confirm the theme. Mallarmé's portrait in 'Quelques médaillons et portraits en pied' (Some lockets and full-length portraits), though published in 1894, had been widely discussed in the Mallarmé circle which Gómez Carrillo frequented. The Guatemalan is drawing, then, from an existing literary tradition and working in an established archive. He is depicting Wilde as the true artist, a fitting companion of Edgar Allan Poe. Wilde, as an admirer of Poe, would have recognized the conscious (or unconscious) frame of reference. This portrait of the artist was to be further enriched, three years later, in *Les Poètes maudits* (Accursed poets) of Paul Verlaine, friend and companion of both Wilde and Gómez Carrillo. In the latter's evocation of Verlaine in his hospital bed in *Esquisses* we find, once more, the formulaic image of the artist as dreamer and melancholic. We also discover the same aestheticizing tendency and the same mixture of the sublime and the subversive, the serious and the ironic – aspects which Darío will note later in his own essays on Wilde. What is striking about Gómez Carrillo's pen portraits of his artist contemporaries is the strong emphasis on physical features: eyes, nose, hair, complexion, physical strength and body contour. This interest in physiognomy partly reflects the paradigms set down by Poe's biographer John Henry Ingram and other precursors. It is also, however, a response to a number of significant departures in art criticism which were to have the most profound effects on the discourses of literary writing – departures which were far from aesthetic in origin.

In 1864, Cesare Lombroso, Professor of Mental Diseases in the University of Pavia, published the first of a series of studies on mental degeneration and the relationship between madness and genius: *Genio e follia* (Genius and madness). Twelve years later, in 1876, he published a more substantial and pioneering study on the relationship between mental disease and criminality: *L'uomo delinquente* (The criminal man).[13] His findings were shaped in part by the clinical observations as an army surgeon and prison inspector that he had gathered before accepting the Chair in Pavia. His researches lacked, however, a purely scientific rigour in that he allowed personal obsessions and prejudices to intrude upon his conclusions. The work of earlier European clinicians converged in his training and experience to shape his insights regarding the nature and causes of criminal behaviour (Wolfgang 1960, 168–277). Lombroso came to believe that certain individuals were born criminals or were atavistic criminals, biological throwbacks from a primitive stage of evolution. Thus his patients unfailingly demonstrated an inherited disposition to criminal behaviour, evidenced in recognizable physical characteristics, and his reports reflected his preoccupation with eliminating from society those elements which might inhibit or hinder the evolutionary development of man to his highest potential. Lombroso's major contribution to the debates of the time was to link physical characteristics and mental degeneration, generally found, in his view, in the 'criminal type'. Such 'types', argued Lombroso, showed specific physical attributes (shape of the head and jaw, posture, alignment of eyes, nose and mouth, etc.) which marked out what he termed 'degener-ates'.[14] What was significant in his work, however, was that he introduced a discourse which had no proper place in scientific experimentation and research. Lombroso's contribution was blemished by his insistence that physi-cally 'degenerate' types were also morally irresponsible and/or corrupting of 'healthy' society. Thus, the binaries healthy/sick, good/evil and moral/immoral entered scientific experimentation, debate and writing.

Lombroso's work was to have an enormous impact on literature, notably the Naturalist novel. In Spain his influence was profound (Maristany 1973; Fernández 1995). But his greatest influence was to be on the discourses of literary criticism, especially after the publication of his *L'uomo di genio* (The man of genius) in 1889. The Spanish translation appeared in 1891 (the same year as the English translation), the very year of Gómez Carrillo's *Sensaciones de arte* and the essay on Wilde. In this work Lombroso proposed that the artist-genius

---

13   The French translation, *L'Homme criminel* appeared in 1887, with a second edition in 1888. It was probably these translations with which Gómez Carrillo was acquainted.

14   In one report Lombroso describes his analysis of a skull where he 'seemed to see of a sudden [...] the problem of the nature of the criminal – an atavistic being who reproduces in his person the ferocious instincts of primitive humanity and the inferior animals'. He goes on to describe the jaws, cheek-bones, eye orbits, ears, all features 'found in criminals, savages and apes', which demonstrate 'the irresistible craving for evil for its own sake [...] to mutilate the corpse, tear its flesh, and drink its blood'. Quoted in Lombroso-Ferrero 1911, xiv–xvi.

was not the 'hierophant of the future' and the 'seer' that Shelley and Hugo had proposed in the heady days of Romantic heroism and imaginative excess when the artist was identified with a special madness. In reality, Lombroso is not concerned with 'genius' as the hallmark of outstanding or mould-breaking intellectual prowess. In the context of the evidence it is clear that he restricts the term 'genius' to artists and thinkers, applying it ironically. He coins the term *mattoide* (pseudo-madman) to describe his subjects since they exhibit symptoms of instability, see-sawing between geniality and delirium, altruism and madness. While they are, in all respects, apparently physically healthy, their ideas are absurd and dangerous, unlike the genuine genius. Applying the same flawed model of *L'uomo delinquente,* Lombroso linked moral and physical characteristics with artistic creativity and mental powers to conclude that the modern artist demonstrated 'degenerative psychosis of the epileptic category' (Lombroso-Ferrero 1911, 42). Inspiration was nothing more than a rare form of epilepsy. Thus the modern artist was a spurious 'genius' and, through his eccentric behaviour, remained a danger to society. His moral corruption, his subversive attitudes, his introspection, his alienation from his fellows and other unsocial patterns of behaviour made him a social misfit. Lombroso then proposed methods for his control and marginalization.

It seems more than coincidental that Gómez Carrillo should emphasize physical characteristics and describe them in such a way as to invert the binary construct of Lombroso's design. Those features that Lombroso perceives of as pointers to moral corruption, social peril and subversion, Gómez Carrillo evokes as the necessary and appropriate features and characteristics of the modern artist. Science, tainted with moral, legal and social concerns ends up serving a literary response of superiority and new ideals. In this way, the reversal of the binary constructs of healthy/sick, sane/mad and good/evil was a token of subversion and revolt against the controlling centre of the original Lombrosian discourse. Gómez Carrillo was in touch, as ever, with the latest trends. For him, Wilde is a true artist of the age: only artistic criteria can influence the conception of a work of art. While he might argue that the artist bears no obligation to established codes, moral or ethical, that he is as noble in his tribulations as he is in his creative work and in his person, the very language he employs betrays his own assertion that art is distinct from life. His use of the same discourses of the sciences unwittingly vitiates his claim, the more so when he also employs discourses which belong to another powerful entity in the society of the Spain of the 1890s: religion.

In many ways, as with Rubén Darío's essay on Verlaine in *Los raros,* we discover, in these pen portraits, a type of displaced theology in that the artist is re-created as a Christ-like figure – a man of vision who preaches a new redemptive religion and who is martyr to his faith. As such, the portrait was at the same time deeply shocking to a conservative and Catholic audience and exhilarating for young Spanish writers eager for any sign that the stranglehold of Restoration civic, religious and moral ideals had begun to weaken. It was this outlook which made Wilde appear subversive and dangerous and this aspect almost certainly lies in the traces and supplements from medicine, evolutionism, degeneration, the law and criminality, and Christian teaching embedded in Gómez Carrillo's evocation of his friend. Indeed, it is specifically to the subversive aspects of Wilde that his next Hispanic commentator responds.

Rubén Darío also knew Wilde. He was drawn into the Wilde circle through his friend Gómez Carrillo. In his essay 'Purificaciones de la piedad' (Purifications of piety), written on 8 December 1900, shortly after Wilde's death on 30 November, Darío depicts his late-lamented friend as a *poète maudit,* martyr to his artistic ideals. The essay reviews Wilde's life and achievements and shows a close acquaintance with *Intentions* and *PDG*. Darío also quotes Mallarmé's letter to Wilde from which Gómez Carrillo had first cited in 1892 in *Sensaciones de arte* (Darío 1950, III: 468–74). But it is in *Los raros,* a study widely read by the young Spanish writers after Darío's visit to Madrid in 1899, that we discover more clearly the means by which Wilde was acculturized into the progressive artistic scene of Hispanic letters. *Los raros* was to exercise a profound impression on Villaespesa and Jiménez. The book marks a phase of Wilde's Spanish reception which both confirms and extends the process so far examined, especially since it is heavily influenced by the pen portraits of *Sensaciones de arte* and *Esquisses.*

Los raros comprises an introductory essay on the new artistic trends and twenty further essays dedicated to specific artists, mostly French and today mostly forgotten. Several stand out: Poe, Paul Verlaine, Henrik Ibsen. But one figure fails to conform to the pattern: Max Nordau, author of *Entartung* (*Degeneration*) (1892–93). Even more strangely, Darío specifically mentions Wilde in the essay on Nordau. *Degeneration* represented a major contribution to the moral offensive which had begun in the 1870s in the work of Lombroso against the new styles of writing which we know as Symbolism and Decadence. Nordau was one of the most enthusiastic of Lombroso's supporters and applied Lombroso's theories to specific modern artists, including Wilde. Both Lombroso and Nordau thus employed the discourses of the new medical sciences of heredity, degeneration and psychopathology as literary-critical tools to marginalize and control artistic trends which they felt to be deeply subversive, even injurious, to society. In a sense, with the added application of ethical and moral criteria and judgements, they sought to criminalize the new writers. The man of genius, for Lombroso, was not far from the criminal man in that both were a threat to society. Nordau took up Lombroso's theme and added to it evolutionary theory and some half-baked psychological theories of his own to argue that the modern artist was a 'degenerate', an evolutionary failure, an introverted and alienated obsessive and a danger to himself and his fellows.

In *Degeneration* the discourses of power of the establishment work through a system of binaries where the hegemonic centre appropriates to itself the positive aspects of a series of binary forms of specific social and scientific discourses and relegates to the margins the object of judgement in entirely negative terms. Those terms (or variants of the powerful discourses at play) are drawn from disciplines quite inappropriate to the matter at hand, such as literary criticism, and have no place in an assessment of artistic or aesthetic merit or value. Discourses of the law, medicine, sexual morality and of Christian teaching and religious morals are brought into play to stigmatize and criminalize and, thus, marginalize the modern artist. It was to this complex interplay of discursive controls, especially in their application to Wilde's person and writings, that Darío and, later, the young writers in Spain responded. And their response was to play Nordau at his own game by the simple process of subverting the discursive pattern, by inverting the binary constructs.

Degeneration was translated into French in 1894 (*Dégénéréscence*), soon after its original publication in German. Like other Latin American writers based in Paris and Madrid, Darío was soon to respond. The effect of *Los raros* is to ironize Nordau's position and to offer a riposte in a very special way (Cardwell 1998b). Wilde, notes Darío, 'in [Nordau's] ambush of the aesthetes and decadents, bears the badge of captain of the first line' (Darío 1950, II: 461).[15] But from direct quotation of Nordau's assessment of Wilde, Darío moves to the offensive in a revision of the discourse employed by Nordau. 'Indeed', notes Darío with evident irony, 'Dorian Gray is a raving lunatic, and so Dorian Gray goes to his cell. *Intentions* cannot be written with a completely sane cerebral mass' (Darío 1950, II: 462).[16] We might note in passing Darío's emphasis on madness, a condition frequently alleged against the modern artist. He then attacks Nordau, rejecting his therapies for the degenerate artist who suffers from a 'morbid egotism' ('egoísmo morboso'), his advice to suppress thoughts concerning 'the mystery of life' and 'the unknown' ('el misterio de la vida'; 'lo desconocido'), his recommendation that certain works should not be read. He scoffs at Nordau's aetiology of the artist's 'degeneration as a result of the weakness of the centres of perception and sensitive nerves'[17] and his suggestion that the modern artist should be quarantined on the margins of society (Darío 1950, II: 462).

Increasingly, from the late 1870s onwards, we find the appropriation of the discourses of medicine in debates concerning the nature and role of the artist and, especially, in literary criticism. Thus, when Nordau stigmatizes Wilde for his 'queer costumes' (perhaps most apt in the present semantic of the word), 'anti-social megalomania', 'pathological aberration' and 'perversion' (Nordau 1968, 316–18), he employs a medical discourse. But he also, principally, employs moral categories to condemn and marginalize. The two forms of control, in these finisecular literary debates and confrontations, are often inseparable. Wilde's apparent deviation from 'normal' behaviour demands that he be controlled not only through the powerful discourse of establishment morality but also through the authority of medicine, especially that branch of the discipline (note again the coercive aspect of these discourses) that is concerned with mental health and disease. We note, however, that the criterion for acceptance is physical, social and moral 'health'. Since Nordau finds Wilde wanting, he is quarantined and incarcerated as a 'madman'. This is the archive which Darío employs in his presentation of Wilde, as becomes

---

[15] 'al paso [de Nordau] de los estetas y decadentes, lleva la insignia de capitán de los primeros'.

[16] 'Sí, Dorian Gray es un loco rematado, y allá va Dorian Gray a su celda. No puede escribirse con la masa cerebral completamente sana el libro *Intentions*'.

[17] 'degeneración como un resultado de la debilidad de los centros de percepción y de los nervios sensitivos'.

very clear in Darío's reply to the accusation of Wilde as a subversive. In Wilde's necrology of 1900, a chastened Darío, with no little irony amidst the seriousness of his comment, wrote the following:

> This martyr to his own eccentricity and to honourable England learned to his cost in *hard labour* that life is serious, that the *pose* is dangerous; that literature, whatever one thinks, cannot be separated from life; that times change, that Ancient Greece is not modern Great Britain, that psychopathologies are treated in clinics […] and that society, while it may be destroyed […], must be held, if not in respect, then in fear […]. The bourgeois whom you want to *épater* has fearsome coarseness and cruel refinements of revenge. (Darío 1950, III: 471)[18]

And, as Darío knew full well,

> But one cannot play with words, and even less with acts […]. The unfortunate Wilde fell from on high for having wished to abuse the smile. The public proclamation and praise of things held to be infamous, the exaggerated pose of a Brummell; the desire at each moment to *épater les bourgeois* – and what *bourgeois* are those of incomparable Albion! –, the taking of central ideas as a matter for comedy; going out into the world in which one lives and rudely rubbing up that same world […] they all brought him to sink into shame, to the prison cell, to misery, to death. (Darío 1950, III: 469–70)[19]

Wilde's (and the modern artist's) ludic attitude to art and the game of upsetting a bourgeois public by eccentric gestures and outrageous proclamations are, insists Darío, a two-edged sword. Like the discourses with their binary versions and reversions, the artistic *pose* can, all too quickly, rebound on itself. By 1900, when the initial euphoria for Symbolism was being challenged, Darío was all too aware that the ironic pose and the mocking laughter which concealed the tragic sense of life, as it had earlier been for Byron and others, would be misconstrued. In a Positivist and mercantile age levity is a sign of anti-social behaviour. Moreover, for others art was not a game but a sacred mission. Thus Darío's descriptions of Wilde, like those of Gómez Carrillo before him, are a defence of the tragic condition of the artist's life and genius

---

[18] 'Este mártir de su propia excentricidad y de la honorable Inglaterra aprendió duramente en el *hard labour* que la vida es seria, que la *pose* es peligrosa; que la literatura, por más que se suene, no puede separarse de la vida; que los tiempos cambian, que Grecia antigua no es la Gran Bretaña moderna, que las psicopatías se tratan en las clínicas […] y que a la sociedad, mientras la destruya […] hay que tenerle, ya que no respeto, siquiera temor […]. El burgués a quien queréis *épater* tiene rudezas espantosas y refinamientos crueles de venganza.'

[19] 'Pero no se puede jugar con las palabras, y menos con los actos […]. El desventurado Wilde cayó desde muy alto por haber querido abusar de la sonrisa. La proclamación y alabanza de cosas tenidas por infames; el brummelismo exagerado; el querer a toda costa *épater les bourgeois* –¡y qué *bourgeois* los de la incomparable Albión!–, el tomar las ideas primordiales como asunto comediable; el salirse del mundo en que se vive rozando ásperamente a ese mismo mundo […], le hizo bajar hasta la vergüenza, hasta la cárcel, hasta la miseria, hasta la muerte.'

as much as an attempt to reverse the binary construction of Nordau's claim that Wilde was a degenerate.

In the context of Darío's decision to include Nordau in his gallery of *raros*, his friendship with Gómez Carrillo, as much as his reading of *Degeneration,* is arguably an important feature of the reception of Wilde in Spain. Gómez Carrillo had met Nordau in 1893 or 1894, at the time of the French translation of *Degeneration*. He had also discussed Decadent literature with him in 1891 and, thus, one might reasonably suppose, had learned something of Nordau's attitude to modern art and culture, as is testified by his essay 'Notas sobre las enfermedades de la sensación, desde el punto de vista de la literatura' (Notes on the infirmities of sensations, from the point of view of literature) of 1894 (Gómez Carrrillo [1920?], XI: 83–145). Any discourse, however powerful, is incapable of resisting revisions and reversals. So, too, with the portraits of Wilde by Gómez Carrillo and Darío. Thus, against the degenerate figure of Wilde depicted by Nordau and against the attacks of Lombroso on the artist-genius, the two Latin American writers evoke a positive picture of the artist-genius. For Darío the Wilde of 1899 had the mien of an abbot with an air of perfect distinction. In conversation he found Wilde's dexterity in framing phrases to be singular. Wilde also spoke of matters of high moment, of pure ideas and questions of beauty. His vocabulary was picturesque, fine and subtle (Darío 1950, III: 473). In the same way Darío's account of *PDG* and *Intentions* is positive – a view underlined by the reproduction of the letter from Mallarmé. In his *Autobiografía* (Autobiography) of 1912, Darío recalls the same meeting described in the 1900 article and repeats, with minor differences of detail, the same picture of Wilde. But he adds: '[b]ut rarely have I encountered a greater distinction, a more elegant culture and a more refined urbanity' (Darío 1950, I: 149).[20]

In their assessments, both Gómez Carrillo and Darío seem to have relied either on a knowledge of English originals or on Wilde's own words. In the early history of Wilde's Spanish reception, before the first translations, it seems that the two Latin Americans were the major propagandists of Wilde. The artistic establishment, both conservative and progressive, consciously and unconsciously responded to the archive of the contending discourses of power concerning the nature of the artist-genius raised by Lombroso and subsequently given notoriety in Nordau's *Degeneration*. In these debates, Wilde became an object of revulsion or a rallying point. Yet it was the paradoxical state of art within the existing social order that brought another reaction to Wilde. While the modern artist seemed to stand apart from the concerns of the age, he was also profoundly preoccupied with the mysteries of life and with the more degenerate aspects of society. Wilde's SMUS, published in 1891, was well known in Spain though not then available in Spanish. The French version appeared in 1906; the Spanish one in 1919. Yet, for all of Wilde's attempt to incorporate the spell of art into an age made ugly by the pursuit of materialism and the inroads of industrialism, certain liberal elements in the new century

---

[20] 'Rara vez he encontrado una distinción mayor, una cultura más elegante y una urbanidad más gentil'.

reacted negatively to his work. Nordau's attack on Wilde's immorality, his want of decorum and his anti-social poses conditioned opinion, especially after the publication of the Spanish version of *Degeneration* (*Degeneración*) in 1902. Gómez Carrillo and Darío were lone voices who inspired, albeit briefly, the first phase of the new aestheticizing art in Spain marked by Villaespesa's *La copa del rey de Thule* (The cup of the King of Thule), which took up the idea of the artist as a martyred Nazarene, and Juan Ramón Jiménez's *Ninfeas* (Nymphs/ Water Lilies), both of 1900, which portray the poet as dreamer and martyr.

But it was also the reaction against the idea of Decadence (in the sense of evolutionary paralysis or the reversal of progress) and the attempt to arrest what was considered to be a rapid national decline and a failure of the national will (fed now by the writings of Nietzsche and Schopenhauer), that prevented any widespread admiration for the views put forward by Wilde. Aestheticism seemed to have no positive role to play in the process of national regeneration along the lines suggested in the works of Lucas Mallada, Rafael Altamira, Pompeyo Gener, Macías Picavea and Joaquín Costa. The journal *Vida Nueva* (New life), arguably the most progressive and militant review of the time, was fervently anti-establishment in its Republican politics and its commitment to a more open society. Yet it had little time for aestheticism and gave its support to Zola (especially after his essay 'J'accuse') and Tolstoy's essays on the role of art in a modern society. In October 1898, only months following Spain's national humiliation after the twin naval defeats at the hands of the United States and the loss of the last of its overseas colonies, an article, under the title, 'Los estetas' (Aesthetes) appeared in *Vida Nueva*. 'This noun [aestheticism]', the anonymous editor wrote,

> which at first served to describe an artistic school, today has fallen not into the stream but into the sewer. If it appears in the columns of *Vida Nueva,* it is to name what our unfortunate politics have placed in shameful evidence. In copying what has been said of the aesthetes by such famous men as Max Nordau and Zola, we aspire to contribute to the erasure from our society of this sickness whose name only sullies the paper on which it is printed.[21]

Underneath the editor reproduced Nordau's section on 'Aestheticism', including the passage on Wilde. To this he appended Zola's description of Wilde as a moral and physical degenerate. The binaries are reversed again. Aestheticism is, once more, a sewer to be disinfected and a disease to be eradicated in contrast to the morality of *Vida Nueva*, which upholds the crystalline spring of Zola and Nordau. *Vida Nueva* must act as a reluctant but necessary sanitary inspector to cleanse society of a highly infectious disease rather than

---

[21] 'Este nombre [estetismo] que en un principio sirvió para designar una escuela artística, ha caído hoy no en el arroyo sino en la cloaca. Si hoy aparece en las columnas de *Vida Nueva*, es para nombrar lo que nuestra desventurada política ha puesto en vergonzosa evidencia. Al copiar lo que acerca de los estetas han descrito autores tan ilustres como Max Nordau y Zola, aspiramos a contribuir a que se borre de nuestra sociedad esa lepra cuyo nombre sólo mancha el papel en que se estampa.'

as an arbiter of aesthetic taste and judgement. The article is not about literary and aesthetic issues; it is about public health. It does not employ the lexicon of literary criticism but the discourse of medicine and pathology.

The young generation of poets who had initially been inspired by Darío and the critical work of Gómez Carrillo in the late 1890s had, by 1903, under the idealistic banner of the *Helios* group and its eponymous magazine, turned away from the extreme aestheticism of the Decadence to espouse a new form of artistic practice. Influenced by the Krausist circles and the Institución Libre de Enseñanza (Free school of learning) and under the inspirational leadership of Giner de los Ríos, writers such as Juan Ramón Jiménez and Antonio Machado had begun to create a poetry which sought to 'redeem' and 'regenerate' the national spirit. Poetry, now inspired by the messianic belief that art could change the spiritual temper of Spain – a belief fostered by the reception of Coleridge and Shelley[22] – was seen as a programme for the political and moral improvement of the nation in crisis. Thus, the *Helios* magazine never refers to Wilde. Jiménez and Machado, the two major poets of the group, barely give him a mention.[23]

It was not until the end of the first decade of the new century, long after the victory of a more moderate and more spiritually and morally idealistic aestheticism over conservatism, more than a decade after the scandal of Wilde's impeachment and imprisonment, that Wilde's fame finally began to grow in Spain. In 1908, within months of the first English edition of Wilde's collected works, a review appeared in the quality *avant-garde* Spanish literary journal *Prometeo* (Prometheus), soon to be followed by the first of a series of translations. From then on Wilde was not only influential, especially for his plays, but bankable. He became fashionable and popular with the theatre-going public. *WNI* and *BRG* appeared in 1911; *DL* in 1912. *HOP* was translated in 1909, possibly provoked by Gregorio Martínez Sierra's *Teatro de ensueño* (Theatre of dreams) of 1905 and a series of fairy stories by Martínez Sierra, Gómez Carrillo and others, with their emphasis on fantasy. The Spanish translation of *Intentions* finally appeared in 1919. Wilde's works became a part of the currency of the early *avant-garde*, represented by Ricardo Baeza (who, as Marta Mateo shows in this volume, was to become the major translator of the plays) and the brothers Julio and Ramón Gómez de la Serna, the latter of whom was the editor of *Prometeo* and author of the vanguardist *Greguerías*. In a manuscript note of Jiménez we perceive the gulf that separated the *Helios* group, influenced by Giner de los Ríos and the Institución Libre de Enseñanza, and those unconnected with these shaping forces. When Jiménez finally met Ramón Gómez

---

[22]   See the volumes on the reception of Shelley and Coleridge in this series.

[23]   Jiménez compares one of the characters, El Pájaro Verde, in *Platero y yo* (1914) (*Platero and I*) to Wilde and refers again to him in a manuscript note quoted below. Antonio Machado, in the preface to the re-issue of his poems, *Páginas escogidas* (Selected pages), in 1913 notes the following, with no further information or comment: 'From Madrid to Paris at the age of 24 [1899]. I knew Oscar Wilde personally and Jean Moréas' ('De Madrid a París a los veinticuatro años [...]. Conocí personalmente a Oscar Wilde y a Jean Moréas').

de la Serna in December 1912, after a long correspondence, he was appalled by the latter's dress and his Madrid provincialism, and disagreeably surprised by his stubby, corpulent stature and his chequered tie, all of which he associated with Wilde. Jiménez recalled that his friend censured the asceticism of the Residencia (the University branch of the Institución) and advised him to 'put on a tie like this'; '[h]e was flashy. The pretentious seek to call attention with external signs [...] dressed in black, enormous overcoat, sideburns, clown, elegant'.[24] The want of interest in Wilde between 1902 and 1912 among the young progressive writers is similarly a question of ascetic temperament and of outlook. The true 'spiritual' and 'ethical' artist is, as Jiménez observed in the note quoted above, 'a man like everyone else, who shares their thoughts and feelings. I believed that one should dress in public like everyone else'.[25] By 1912, as new artistic goals were being sought, this attitude only remained in the major writers. By the 1920s the first biographies began to appear. This second phase of Wilde's Spanish reception is studied in the following chapter, which reveals the continued process of cultural transfer.[26]

---

[24] 'Me quería dar consejos. "Ponte una corbata así" [...] Cursi es el que pretende llamar la atención con aparatos externos [...] vestido de negro, levitón gigante, patillas, payaso, elegante'. I am indebted for this information to Professor Javier Blasco of the University of Valladolid.

[25] 'Yo creí siempre, desde muchacho, que un poeta, un pintor, un músico, era un hombre como todo lo demás, que tenían su pensamiento y su sentimiento. Creí que debían vestir en la vida como [word missing], vivir y morir como todo lo demás'.

[26] I am indebted to Davis 1973 for some details in this essay.

9 The Reception of Wilde's Works in Spain through Theatre Performances at the Turn of the Twentieth and Twenty-first Centuries

Marta Mateo

The initial reception of Oscar Wilde in Spain, in the early twentieth century, was surrounded by considerable controversy, despite the fact that most of his major works – with some rare exceptions, such as *Salomé* – actually had to wait until the second decade of the century to be rendered into Spanish. The controversy, then, was mainly connected with his personality and his theoretical works, which were the first of his writings to be known to Spanish and Spanish-American writers (Davis 1973, 137–39). Considered as the leading English aesthete, Wilde was at the centre of debates about the role of art and the artist in a social context. He soon became the object of critical reviews, articles and books by renowned writers of the time such as Azorín (José Martínez Ruiz), Alcalá Galiano, Ramiro de Maeztu, Gómez Carrillo, Manuel Machado, Pérez de Ayala, Eugenio d'Ors, Pío Baroja, Miguel de Unamuno, Rubén Darío and Ramón Gómez de la Serna, 'the principal spokesman for Oscar Wilde in the Spain of his generation' (Davis 1973, 144).

This article will focus on the reception of Wilde's dramatic works in Spain at the turn of the twentieth and twenty-first centuries – the two periods in which the stage reception of his works was at its richest. Wilde's plays were first introduced through the translations and theatre productions by Ricardo Baeza, an influential figure in the literary circles of the time, who contributed substantially to the Spanish theatre world as translator, impresario, director and critic. By examining reviews of those early productions and by looking briefly at Baeza's target texts, we may deepen our understanding of the factors that triggered the performance history of Wilde in Spain and determined his continuous presence in the country's theatre repertories. Turning our attention to performances in the 1990s and the early twenty-first century, we may then compare the earliest and the most recent reception: the writer is now part of the country's literary canon and recent productions, which do not confine themselves to his dramas but often include his narrative and poetic works, reflect the political and social changes the country has undergone over the last century. Besides, the centenary of Wilde's death in 2000 sparked a renewed interest in the writer's work, which could also be seen in the country's theatres. With this analysis of the Spanish performances of each period, I intend to throw light on the reception of Wilde's dramatic works and on his contribution to the theatre world in Spain.

First publications of Wilde's plays in Spanish: Ricardo Baeza's translations

Wilde's comedies had to wait until World War I to become known to Spanish audiences. However, his presence could already be noted in 1902, when his one-act tragedy *Salomé* was translated and published in Madrid three years before the play's first London staging (see Joseph Bristow's essay in this volume). *Salomé* had been translated by J. Pérez Jorba and B. Rodríguez and published in Madrid by Rodríguez Serra around 1902 (Palau y Dulcet 1990, 228). Pérez Jorba would later publish a 'direct translation' of his own in Barcelona in 1910. Wilde's poetic play was also serialized in Spanish in the newspaper *El nuevo mercurio* (The new Mercury) from July 1907 (Rodríguez Fonseca 1997, 105).[1] Other translations soon followed on both sides of the Atlantic: Lisa Davis, for instance, mentions a translation by Miguel Guerra-Mondragón which appeared in the *Revista de las Antillas* (Review of the Antilles) in November 1914, which she finds 'a model for excellence in style and accuracy' (1973, 139). *Salomé* proved seminal for many Spanish and Spanish-American writers who elaborated on its theme in the first decades of the twentieth century: Delfina Rodríguez Fonseca (1997) traces the subtle but powerful influence that the play exerted on Spanish texts of different genres, published by writers such as Rubén Darío, José Ortega y Gasset, Ramón del Valle-Inclán and Francisco Villaespesa, all of whom drew on the play's characters, atmosphere and language, and particularly on Wilde's reinterpretation of the myth. A remarkable example is Valle-Inclán's *esperpento* play,[2] *La cabeza del Bautista* (The Baptist's head), which some interpret as a clear parody of Wilde's play (Davis 1973: 142, see also Rodríguez Fonseca 1997, 190–201).[3]

Ricardo Baeza would also make his own translation of *Salomé*, included in one of the volumes which came out in 1927 as part of his edition of Wilde's

---

[1]   There is another early translation of *Salomé* by the writer Gregorio Martínez Sierra, which I have not been able to date exactly.

[2]   A type of grotesque play created by Valle-Inclán, in which reality is systematically deformed by highlighting its grotesque and absurd features, and conventional literary values are subverted through an unexpected use of language.

[3]   The Modernist writer Ramón Gómez de la Serna was also influenced by *Salomé*. According to Soldevilla-Durante, his one-act play *Beatriz*, published in *Prometeo* in 1909, can be seen as a sequel to Wilde's work: the positive model of femininity advanced by Gómez de la Serna creates a deliberate contrast with Wilde's degenerate heroine (1992, 74).

Spanish *Obras completas* (Complete works), which he had started to publish in 1923 (see below). But Baeza first came into contact with Wilde's drama in the 1910s, when he translated the comedies. Cuban-born Baeza was in most cases the first to render Wilde's plays into Spanish, thus inaugurating a long succession of translations of Wilde which has continued till the present day. As a theatre director and impresario, he was also a distinguished contributor to the performance of Wilde's plays in Spanish theatres. Baeza translated an impressive range of novelists, poets, philosophers and, above all, playwrights, including Gabriele D'Annunzio, Christian Friedrich Hebbel, Henrik Ibsen, Maurice Maeterlinck, William Somerset Maugham, Eugene O'Neill, Luigi Pirandello and Wilde – D'Annunzio and Wilde being his favourites (Anderson 1994a, 231–32). His Spanish renditions of Wilde's comedies were published in the second decade of the twentieth century. *Una mujer sin importancia* (*WNI*) was the first to come out, in 1911. It was serialized in the prestigious literary review *Prometeo*, edited by Ramón Gómez de la Serna. From 1909 onwards *Prometeo* also published Baeza's translations of HP (*El príncipe feliz*), BRG (*Balada de la cárcel de Reading*), PP (*Poemas en prosa*) and PPUY (*Frases y filosofías para el uso de los jóvenes*).[4] *Un marido ideal* (*IH*) came out in 1918,[5] with *El abanico de Lady Windermere* (*LWF*) and *La importancia de llamarse Ernesto* (*IBE*) both appearing in 1920.

Baeza translated all of Wilde's major works, some of them as independent publications (like the comedies mentioned above), the rest either in *Prometeo* or as part of his edition of Wilde's collected works, which was the first canonical Spanish translation of the writer's entire production. Julio Gómez de la Serna's *Obras completas* (1991 [1943]), which followed Baeza's twenty years later, is regarded as the other canonical edition of Wilde's complete works in Spanish. These two translations, however, show distinctly different approaches: Gómez de la Serna's *Obras completas* seems to have been conceived as a reader-oriented target text; Baeza's translations, on the other hand, are clearly performance-oriented, despite the fact that they are presented as 'translated' rather than as 'adapted', thus implying that he did not conceive his translations as deviating significantly from the original.

In his role as the London correspondent for *El Sol* (The sun), Baeza was the author of various articles on topics such as British and European drama, the new Russian theatre and the 'conflict' between theatre and cinema, including a long series of articles under the title 'En torno al problema del teatro' (on the theatre problem), which appeared in the newspaper in the late 1920s.[6] His translations and articles on foreign drama become all the more important when

---

[4]   These translations were published together with those of other eminent foreign writers still unknown in Spain, such as Colette, Bernard Shaw, D'Annunzio, Marinetti, Marcel Schwob, A. C. Swinburne and Walt Whitman, indicating the prominent place Wilde held for the elder Gómez de la Serna, the representative of the Spanish Modernists (see Julio Gómez de la Serna 1991[1943], 66).

[5]   An earlier translation of this play, by Román Jori, was published in Barcelona in 1914.

[6]   For this other sphere of interest of Baeza's, see Anderson (1994a, 234–35).

one considers that many Spanish writers of the time had a limited knowledge of foreign languages (Anderson 1994a, 230). Baeza published his translations of Wilde's works in his own publishing house, Atenea, which he had founded in 1916 and which was to thrive throughout the 1920s (Anderson 1994b, 30). As was his usual practice, he rendered directly from the original source texts, showing an excellent command of English. His target texts reflect the orality of the English plays, always including idiomatic turns of phrase in Spanish. He also exploits the language, as Wilde does, both for social characterization and to create the effect of artificiality, central both to the theme and humour of the plays. He inserted footnotes indicating the correct pronunciation of the characters' names, by means of an interesting and very approximate transcription.[7] This signals once again that Baeza conceived his target texts as scripts for performance, which is also confirmed by a footnote below the *dramatis personae* of *Un marido ideal* (*IH*) specifying that 'To make it easier for the actor, the figurative pronunciation of foreign names is given in brackets'.[8]

While Baeza's translations frequently entailed a degree of adaptation to the Spanish theatrical context, they did not replace English cultural references with Spanish ones: his changes, deletions and reductions seem always to have been intended to make the source texts succeed on the stage, facilitating the actors' performance as well as aiding the Spanish audiences' understanding and enjoyment of Wilde's plays. His most frequent deletions concern extra-linguistic references which are too culture-specific, but the context always remains markedly English. He did, however, suppress some ironical comments on certain social and moral issues which may have been too harsh for Spanish audiences.[9] But the essence of Wilde's comedy is always there. The Irish playwright's reversal of discursive, linguistic, social and even moral expectations (see Mateo 1995) are practically always recreated in these translations. His cynical remarks are all turned into Spanish with the same devices of humour: subverting the audience's values, language use and/or common sense. The dramatic irony strongly present in all Wilde's comedies occupies an equally important place in these target texts by Baeza, who showed a special concern with the main moral stance of each play.

The beginnings of Wilde's performance history in Spain: early theatre productions

Thanks to Baeza's translations, Spanish theatre audiences became acquainted with Wilde's comedies practically at the same time as the translations were

---

[7] For example, in *Un marido ideal* (*IH*), 'Harlock: ★Pronúnciese: Járlock'; 'Jane Barford: ★Pronúnciese: Yein Barford', etc.

[8] 'Para facilidad del actor, se pone entre paréntesis la pronunciación figurada de los nombres extranjeros.'

[9] For instance, certain cynical references to the poor or to women in *WNI* as well as a typically Wildean comment on the futility of telling the truth in *IH*.

published, sometimes before.[10] The very first Spanish performance of a play by Wilde, however, did not take place in a theatre: according to Julio Gómez de la Serna (1991[1943], 83), it was a reading performance of *Una mujer sin importancia* (*WNI*) in Baeza's translation, organized by Ramón Gómez de la Serna for a select audience at one of Madrid's important cultural centres, the *Ateneo*. Gómez de la Serna Junior cannot recall the exact date of this reading, which was given by Spanish writers and artists and enjoyed a well-deserved success, but he places it around 1910 or 1911.

The first play by Wilde actually to go on stage in Spain, then, was *Salomé*, albeit not in Baeza's translation, which, it must be remembered, came much later than his renderings of the comedies. If Wilde seems to have intended his original Salomé for the great Sarah Bernhardt (Ellmann 1988, 371), the first enactment of this Wildean character in Spain came from one of the greatest Spanish actresses of all times, Margarita Xirgu, the Catalan artist particularly talented for verse plays whom García Lorca would engage for his most important productions. This first staging of *Salomé* was in fact a Catalan version by Joaquim Pena (1908), performed in 1910 at Barcelona's *Teatro Principal* – a theatre that aimed to acquaint Catalan audiences with foreign plays of the greatest renown. According to a review of the first night, the production was warmly welcomed by the audience (Portusach, 1910). The reviewer commends the 'immaculate' Catalan version by Pena, the 'very beautiful and appropriate' ('muy bella y apropiada') scenery and the cast's felicitous performances, particularly by Margarita Xirgu and by the actors playing the leading male roles (Herod and Jokanaan), one of whom was also the director of the company. It is worth mentioning here that this was common practice in Spain in the early twentieth century: great actors or actresses would have their own company, which was linked to a theatre, a certain type of play and a performing style. Many dramatists would write their plays specifically for a certain actor or actress, so audiences knew what type of show to expect in each theatre (Amorós 1988, 8).

Xirgu would also take the leading role in the first Castilian Spanish stage version of *Salomé*, in Madrid, c. 1913 (the exact date is difficult to establish, according to Davis [1973, 147]). This production, described as 'bizarre' by Davis, seems to have been an adaptation into Castilian of the earlier Catalan version; its language Ruiz Contreras termed an 'absurd tongue-twister' ('tan absurdo trabalenguas') rather than real Spanish (1930, 278–79). Alcalá-Galiano did not like Xirgu's acting and described it as a lacklustre, affected and monotonous performance (1919, 158). This Spanish *Salomé* followed the same problematic path of the first English production of Wilde's play, for it was closed down by the authorities immediately after its premiere (Davis 1973, 147). Richard Strauss's operatic adaptation seems to have been more fortunate

---

10   I would like to express my gratitude to Dr Antonio Fernández Insuela, from the Departamento de Filología Española at the Universidad de Oviedo, for providing me with much of the material I have needed for this section and guiding me to the relevant sources. The excellent theatre library of the Fundación Juan March in Madrid, and the help provided by its staff, have also been invaluable.

in Spain, however, since it enjoyed a successful production in 1910, which encouraged Luis París to translate the libretto that same year (Davis 1973, 137). Opinions about the opera differed, but the negative comments seem to have centred around the music, which appeared to some as 'a dangerous drug' ('una droga peligrosa') and 'more harmful and unhealthy than the libretto itself' ('más dañina y malsana que el mismo libreto'), as José Subira would recall in 1949 (Coletes 1985, 20). As I have suggested in a study on the different versions of Wilde's tragedy (Mateo 2005, 231–32), the diverse fortunes of the play and the opera in Spain are probably closely linked to the linguistic issue: since the translation norm governing the production of foreign operas then was that of non-translation, Strauss's text, performed in German, was much less accessible and, thus, less dangerous than Wilde's work, which necessarily had to be translated into Spanish in order to be performed.

The first of Wilde's comedies to be produced in a theatre in Spain was *Una mujer sin importancia* (*WNI*), in October 1917. This production did not use the version by Baeza which had been read out at the *Ateneo*, but rather a Spanish translation done by Antonio Plañiol.[11] It was put on at the Teatro de la Princesa (Princess's theatre) in Madrid by a company directed by Francisco García Ortega, who also took the leading role (Lord Illingworth) while Mrs Arbuthnot was played by Ana Adamuz. Although not many people attended the first night, the reviewer for the influential Madrid daily *ABC* described it as splendid and as 'perhaps the most generous and important' of all Wilde's plays. He compared Rachel to Ibsen's Nora in *A Doll's House* and praised Ana Adamuz's elegance and García Ortega's impressive performance. This reviewer attributed the small audience partly to the fact that Wilde was then mostly known in Spain for his scandalous trial, and he regretted that so many people should have missed 'one of the most beautiful, vigorous and intense plays of modern theatre'. He finally encouraged the whole of Madrid to see it 'if there is still any good taste left'.[12]

Only one month later, the *Príncipe Alfonso* theatre in Madrid staged *Un marido ideal*, also performed by Adamuz and García Ortega's company, this time in Baeza's version. This Spanish production and translation of *IH* were the object of a lawsuit between Antonio Plañiol, who claimed he was the only person authorized by Wilde's heirs to translate and stage the play, and Baeza, who maintained he had documentary proof of his copyright permission. Eventually, Plañiol decided to drop his lawsuit. According to the reviewer for the *ABC*, the audience seemed to like the play but did not show great enthusiasm on that first night of 17 November 1917. Although the anonymous

---

[11] According to Anderson (1994a, 236), a production of this comedy in Baeza's translation was also put on in the same theatre in November 1917. If this is correct, it would mean that Plañiol's text was replaced by Baeza's only one month after it had gone on stage.

[12] 'acaso la más generosa y fundamental de cuantas escribió'; 'una de las obras más bellas, más fuertes y más intensas del teatro moderno'; '¡Y ahora es de suponer que todo Madrid irá a ver tan estupenda comedia, si es que queda un poco de buen gusto!' ('Notas teatrales' 1917a).

reviewer does not count the play among the select group of Wilde's best creations, he does think that this production was a brilliant choice with which to open the winter season of the *Teatro Alfonso* and praises the universal character of its moral and social stance ('Notas teatrales' 1917b). Some cartoon strips appeared in the same paper two days later (on 20 November), by way of a visual introduction to the production; the caricatures, though, do not seem to do justice to the main actress, Ana Adamuz (who must have been thirty-one years old then), for she certainly looks much older in them than Wilde's description of Lady Chiltern as a woman 'about twenty seven years of age'.

Despite these favourable reviews, Alcalá Galiano must have disliked the productions for, in his articles on Wilde published in *La Revista Quincenal* (The bimonthly review) in 1918, he complained of the 'dreadful scenic presentation' ('deplorable presentación escénica') and poor performances by means of which Wilde's plays had been conveyed to Spanish audiences up until then (1919, 155–56). Nevertheless, as Coletes argues (1985, 22), these productions would certainly contribute to Wilde's popularity in Spain more than the Spanish editions of his works which had regularly been coming out from 1902. Baeza's translation of *IH* would go back on stage eight years later, on 20 October 1925, with another theatre company of repute, Ernesto Vilches's, at the *Teatro Infanta Beatriz* in Madrid.

IBE and *LWF* were also performed for the first time in Spain in Baeza's versions during a theatre season (1919–1920) in which productions of contemporary plays consisted mostly of Spanish writers' works rather than of translations of foreign plays (Dougherty and Vilches 1990, 68). This made the presence of these two Wilde comedies even more noteworthy. *La importancia de llamarse Ernesto* (*IBE*) was presented by Baeza's own theatre company, Atenea, which he founded in 1919 with the aim of challenging established theatrical norms (Dougherty and Vilches 1990, 50). What moved Baeza to set up his own theatre company was, on the one hand, his interest in modern European drama and, on the other, his wish to see his translations performed under his own control (see Anderson 1994b, 30). With Atenea, he would no longer have to put up with the constant delays in performances or with the equally constant modifications of his translations suggested by actors and actresses. *IBE* was the second production by the company, which had made their debut with Ibsen's *John Gabriel Borkman*: Baeza's *IBE* was put on at the *Teatro de la Princesa* in October 1919 and it had the largest number of performances (33) of all six shows the company gave during their two-month period at the theatre that season. Although most critics saw little substance in the comedy, the company's performance of this production was considered much better than was the case in the Ibsen (Anderson 1994b, 35). According to a review, this first Spanish version of *IBE* was unquestionably the most successful of Atenea's productions (in Anderson 1994b, 35).

El abanico de Lady Windermere (*LWF*), however, had to be performed by a different theatre group, as Baeza's had already broken up when this play came to be put on: his translation was therefore produced by one of the most popular companies of the time, the Guerrero-Díaz de Mendoza, who were the real holders of the *Teatro de la Princesa*, where this play was put on in February 1920 (Anderson 1994b, 33 and 37). According to Julio Gómez de la

Serna, this production marked the first time a play by Wilde was staged with the greatest dignity and performed with remarkable skill, thanks to the actress María Guerrero (1991[1943], 83). It went through twenty-four performances. The company would stage the play again in the same theatre two years later, in the 1922–23 season, when there were few productions of foreign plays and the staging of Wilde's comedy – together with plays by Shaw, D'Annunzio, Ibsen and Dario Niccodemi – stood out from the others (Dougherty & Vilches 1990, 77).

Thanks to Baeza's translations, then, Wilde's plays were all performed with notable success in the main Madrid theatres during the second and the third decades of the twentieth century. Davis (1973, 147) and Dougherty and Vilches (1990 and 1997) register several productions of Wilde's plays by different companies, most of them in Baeza's versions, during the interwar years: *Una mujer sin importancia* (*WNI*) was included in the repertory in 1917, 1919, 1924 and 1928;[13] *Un marido ideal* (*IH*) in 1917 and 1928 (and, according to an edition of the play in the literary review *El teatro* [November 1925], also in 1925); *La importancia de llamarse Ernesto* (*IBE*) was performed in 1919 and 1924; and *El abanico de Lady Windermere* (*LWF*) was on stage in 1920, 1922, 1924, 1929 and 1931.[14] It is interesting to note that in many of the seasons when, according to Dougherty and Vilches's registers, productions of translations of foreign plays were comparatively rare, there was frequently a play by Wilde on stage (*cf.* 1919–20, 1922–23, 1923–24 and 1927–28). In 1919, the critic Rafael Urbina could write in *Cosmópolis* that 'Wilde is still in fashion. All publishers want him, all writers translate him, all audiences request his plays' (in Coletes 1985, 28).[15] Baeza's Compañía Dramática Atenea only lasted one year due to financial difficulties (Anderson 1994 a/b). But its break-up, early in 1920, did not put an end to the performances of Baeza's translations of Wilde. These now became part of other companies' repertoires.

Despite a general feeling of crisis in the Spanish theatre – due to the maintainance of stagnating conventions and the prevalence of comedies with no critical intention – theatre journals brought news of theatrical events and innovations that took place all over the world. This encouraged some companies to take the risk of introducing changes and experimentation into Spanish theatres, particularly in Madrid and Barcelona (Dougherty and Vilches 1990, 45–46). A need for reform was widely acknowledged, not just regarding the themes of the plays but also the elements of performance. As regards *mise-en-scène* and acting, the main reformers were the playwright and theatre director Gregorio Martínez Sierra (who, as I have mentioned,

---

[13] An adaptation with the title *Una mujer que no miente* (A woman who does not lie) was rendered by José Andrés Prada and Miguel Mihura and performed, by different companies, at the Teatro Infanta Isabel in 1919 and at the Coliseo Imperial in 1920.

[14] Another adaptation by Tomás Luceño and R. Moya Rico, with the title *El abanico de su majestad* (His Majesty's fan), was staged at the Teatro Calderón in Madrid in June 1930.

[15] 'Sigue la moda de Wilde. Todos los editores lo quieren, todos los escritores lo traducen, todos los públicos lo solicitan.'

also translated Wilde's *Salomé*), the actress Margarita Xirgu and the theatre director and critic Cipriano Rivas Cherif (Aszyk, 1986, 79). In Barcelona, Adrià Gual and his *Teatre Íntim* were also important exponents of this spirit of renewal, performing plays by writers such as Ibsen, Hauptmann, Maeterlink and D'Annunzio (ibid, 80–81). Moreover, foreign companies (mostly South American, French and Italian) could often be seen in Madrid theatres and were usually enthusiastically welcomed by both audiences and critics despite the language barrier. This brought news not just of new playwrights and revolutionary texts from abroad but also of the most modern *mise-en-scène* elements (Vilches & Dougherty 1997, 275, 306).

In the late 1920s, then, well-known theatre companies took pride in staging internationally acclaimed masterpieces or new plays by renowned foreign playwrights. In the 1928–29 season, for instance, three of Wilde's plays – *El abanico de Lady Windermere* (*LWF*), *El fantasma de Canterville* (*CG*) and *Un marido ideal* (*IH*) – featured in the repertory of two different companies, the Argentinian Lola Membrives and the Spanish company directed by Irene López Heredia, together with works by Pirandello, Ibsen, Edward Sheldon, Bernard Shaw and Somerset Maugham (Vilches & Dougherty 1997, 315 & 359–60).

In December 1927, Baeza started collaborating with the renowned actress Irene López Heredia, becoming artistic director of her company. Their aim was to bring about gradual but continuous reform, rather than a hasty revolution (Anderson 2000, 137), by combining conventional plays with more ground-breaking ones. Great attention was to be paid to the translations of foreign plays, many of them by Baeza, and to the quality of both the set designs – which should be modern and synthetic – and the actors (Anderson 2000, 138). Unfortunately, the collaboration only lasted for five months, during which Baeza and López Heredia gave an extraordinary 261 performances of nineteen plays, both by Spanish and foreign writers, one of which was *IH*, which occupied the fourth position in the number of performances (28: considerably more than, for instance, Bernard Shaw's *Candida*, which had 6). It is interesting to note that Wilde's comedy was already considered a 'safe' play – indeed, it took over from Somerset Maugham's *Our Betters* (*Entre gente bien*), which was withdrawn only two days after its first night due to the audiences' disapproval and negative reviews (Anderson 2000, 147).

By the late 1920s Wilde's works were already very popular among Spanish theatre audiences. Wilde's presence on Spanish stages stretched beyond his dramas: a three-act Spanish theatre adaptation of *CG* by Ceferino Palencia Tubau, *El fantasma de Canterville*, opened at the *Teatro Infanta Beatriz* in Madrid in January 1929, with Irene López Heredia's company, enjoying 26 performances; and an adaptation of Wilde's tale *LASC* (*El crimen de lord Arturo*) by playwright Alejandro Casona, was premiered in Saragossa in February 1929. His dramas also reached the Spanish public of the early twentieth century in adaptations into other media: a silent film of *LWF*, made in the USA, was shown in Madrid around 1918 and another cinema adaptation of the same play, a sound film this time, would be seen in Spain twenty years later, in 1938 (for Gómez de la Serna's comments on these two films, see 1991[1943], 84).

If, in the 1918–19 theatre season, Wilde was counted among 'the contemporary European writers whose names were heard everywhere', he was already referred to as 'a classic' in 1923–24, together with Alexandre Dumas, Victor Hugo, Guy de Maupassant, Ivan Turgenieff and Shakespeare (Dougherty and Vilches 1990, 66 & 79). After the Spanish translation of *DP* in 1925, critics' interest in Wilde's works declined. By then he was generally perceived to be a writer of the past, albeit firmly established among the Spanish reading public (Coletes 1985, 31). Yet, in 1929, the theatre critic Manuel Abril mentioned Wilde, together with Ibsen, D'Annunzio, Maeterlinck and Strindberg, as one of the pillars of modern theatre – although with the quali-fication that Bernard Shaw, Pirandello and Henri-René Lenormand stood out from them (Vilches & Dougherty 1997, 277). And in 1934, after more than twenty years of Wilde's presence in Spanish theatres, Antonio de Obregón described the Irish playwright as 'the writer whose life and work have most fascinated audiences so far this century, and who has exerted the greatest influence on new literary generations' (in Davis 1973, 136).[16]

Wilde's plays in Spain at the turn of the twenty-first century

Since Baeza's translations and the early performances, new published versions and stage productions of Wilde's plays have never ceased to appear.[17] All of his works have now been translated into Spanish, his comedies having been rendered several times by different translators and published in various editions of either performance-oriented versions or reader-oriented texts, as well as in bilingual editions. Baeza's and Gómez de la Serna's respective translations of Wilde's complete works have both been re-edited and reprinted. Wilde has certainly been part of the literary canon in Spain for a long time now. This is clear from his inclusion in Espasa Calpe's collection devoted to writers such as Shakespeare, Calderón and Chekhov, and in Aguilar's 'Grandes Clásicos' (Great classics) or, in earlier editions, in its 'Obras eternas' (Eternal works).

Indeed, in the requests for publication submitted for Government sanction (necessary because of the censorship imposed during the Franco years, 1939–1975) – which are exhaustively recorded today in the Archivo General de la Administración (AGA) in Alcalá de Henares[18] – Wilde features, in various files, in series such as 'clásicos de la lengua inglesa' (English language classics), 'colección de joyas literarias' (literary gems), 'grandes maestros de la literatura clásica' (great masters of classic literature) or 'obras inmortales' (immortal

---

[16] 'el escritor cuya vida y cuya obra han apasionado más a los públicos en lo que va de siglo y que más influencia ha tenido en las nuevas generaciones literarias.'

[17] For instance, *Una mujer sin importancia* was performed again soon after the Spanish Civil War, in October 1941, by López Heredia's company with Baeza's translation, once more achieving a remarkable success (Gómez de la Serna 1991 [1943], 83).

[18] I am grateful to Dr. Raquel Merino, from the Universidad del País Vasco, for her generosity in providing me with all the data they have collected on Wilde and sharing her general impressions about the history of Wilde's works under the censorship in Franco regime and the issue of homosexuality.

works). The TRACE research group on censorship – a joint project between the Universidad de León and the Universidad del País Vasco – has recorded all the AGA files on Wilde, consisting of requests for both publication and performance, in their database (http://www.ehu.es/trace). Although Wilde has not as yet been the object of a specific study by the group, the director of the theatre section of the Project, Raquel Merino, is convinced that Wilde was not representative of the patterns of theatre censorship during Franco's regime. This is due to the fact that he was considered a classic and, therefore, was likely to have been given a different treatment by the authorities than that received by Spanish playwrights. The database also reveals that, between 1939 and 1983, the number of published editions and reprints of Wilde's works was greater than that of performances. This conclusion is based on the number of files per work registered (each file containing, at least, one request). These are highly reliable data since absolutely everything had to be submitted to the censorship authorities and all requests were filed. For theatre productions, the obligation continued even after Franco's death, until 1978 (and the registering inertia remained until 1985).

The files in the theatre section at the AGA comprise requests for performances not only of Wilde's plays but also of some of his narrative fiction and poetry, including *El retrato de Dorian Gray* (PDG), *El príncipe feliz* (HP), *El gigante egoísta* (SG) and *Balada de la cárcel de Reading* (BRG). *Salomé* has the highest number of files (8)[19] while, in the Books section, it is *LWF*, with 37 files, and *IBE*, with 33, that seem to have been published most frequently during those years. The low number of requests to perform Wilde's plays probably implies that his dramas were not often seen in the theatres. But we cannot assume that this was a question of censorship, for they were repeatedly published and reprinted. A more thorough study would be required in order to know the reasons for this decline.

At the end of the twentieth century, however, with the celebrations of the centenary of Wilde's death in 2000, there was a revival of interest in all spheres. Works by and about Wilde were re-edited. His letters were translated into Spanish in 1992 and his collected poetry appeared for the first time in an edition including poems so far unpublished in Spanish (1999). There have been new stage versions, based both on his dramatic and non-dramatic works as well as on his life. In 2002, a series of lectures on Wilde took place in Madrid (*Ciclo de conferencias en torno a Oscar Wilde*), in which writers, translators and theatre directors, together with the actress Núria Espert, discussed aspects of his life and writings. Various articles published in newspapers around 2000 noted that Wilde's life still sparks more interest than his works: 'Isn't it high time we stopped dealing with the affairs of his life and started reading his tales, novels and plays; poetry and essays?', one critic complained in a cultural supplement to the Spanish daily *El País* (The country) in 2000, even though

---

[19]   This does not necessarily mean that the play was only produced on eight occasions over all those years since subsequent requests for performance were sometimes registered in a previous file of the same play.

he also admitted that 'it is hard to imagine an English [*sic.*] writer who is more widely read' (de Juan 2000, 9).[20]

As regards theatre productions of his works at the turn of this century, we may start with an extraordinary production of *Salomé* of 1985, adapted into Spanish by the popular Catalan writer Terenci Moix, directed by one of the most acclaimed Spanish theatre directors, Mario Gas, and performed by the celebrated actress Núria Espert. This production, which opened the *Festival de Teatro Clásico* at Mérida, was a landmark in the history of the festival. It was later performed in Catalan – Núria Espert's very first performance in this language – after the public silence the Catalan language had been subjected to during the Franco regime. The 1990s saw at least three other versions of *Salomé*: two different amateur productions in southern Spain in 1996 and a dance version in 1997. The latter, which mixed flamenco and contemporary ballet, was directed by Gerardo Vera and performed by the flamenco dancer Carmen Cortés and contemporary ballet dancer Toni Fabré, and also opened the Mérida Festival. The show included a sadomasochistic scene between the Nubian soldier and Jokanaan.

The new millenium opened with yet another theatre production of Wilde's play: *Salomé: La Hija de Herodías* (Salomé: Herodias's daughter), translated and directed by Luis González Carreño and performed at the *Teatro Galileo* in Madrid in 2000. This version of *Salomé* presented the Biblical story on a modern note: it was described as a rite of initiation into fatality and a stage representation of the relationship between the mysteries of death and love. It was warmly welcomed as a good way to celebrate the centenary of Wilde's death (Víllora 2000, 72). The year 2002 saw another flamenco version of Salomé's story, this time in a musical film by director Carlos Saura, who combined the filmed ballet and documentary formats to create a production that won an award at the Montreal Festival. This is not really a version of Wilde's play but a reinterpretation of the myth; however, Saura's version in his film clearly draws on Wilde's. Finally, the season 2005–06 brought us a modern adaptation of *Salomé*, translated by Mauro Armiño and directed by the renowned playwright, theatre and cinema director, Miguel Narros. This was Narros's first contact with Wilde on the stage. It was premiered in Seville, moved on to the *Teatro Álbeniz* in Madrid and later started a sell-out tour around the country. The production combined the poetic essence of the original text with a present-day look: the stage design took the audience to the Near East and the USA, using the oil crisis as its historical background; the dialogues, as Narros explained, used a modern urban language 'in order to achieve a direct communication with today's audiences'.[21] The performance included a dance choreographed by celebrated Spanish ballet dancer Víctor

---

[20]   '¿No va siendo hora de que dejemos de ocuparnos del enredo de su vida y leamos sus relatos, novelas y obras dramáticas; su poesía y sus ensayos? [...] Resulta difícil imaginar un autor inglés más leído'.

[21]   'para lograr una comunicación directa con el espectador que se desenvuelve en el mundo de hoy' ('Palabras de Miguel Narros', in *Salomé*, http://es.geocities.com/ Kanaria1973/salome, last accessed 23 September 2008).

Ullate, set to a mixture of hip-hop and oriental music. The director chose two popular television actors for the main roles, who cast their respective parts as a ruthless and lubricious, half-cruel half-innocent Lolita in the case of Salomé, and as a histrionic and paranoid killer in that of Herod. The result was a production marked by a frenetic rhythm and sexual tension, enhanced by the seductive element of dance.

Of the comedies, *IH, WNI* and *LWF* enjoyed fewer productions than *IBE*, as might be expected. But they have all been performed in recent years. I have gathered evidence of at least one important production of *Un marido ideal* (*IH*), in 1996, translated by writer Juan José de Arteche from a French version by Pierre Laville and directed by Alfonso Zurro. It was produced at the *Teatro Alcázar* in Madrid and later toured around the country. The programme stated that Wilde's comic dramas were now no longer regarded simply as comedies of manners but rather as classics. Nevertheless, one of the most respected theatre critics of the second half of the twentieth century, the late Eduardo Haro Tecglen, wondered, in his review for *El País* (1996), why *IH* had not been directly translated from the English. He criticized, as he did on several other occasions, the way Spanish actors have always performed English high comedy by Wilde, Bernard Shaw, Somerset Maugham and Noel Coward, wrongly assuming that London elegance is equivalent to Spanish affectation, thus making the acting too precious and marked by 'extravagant manners' ('extravagantes maneras') (Haro Tecglen 1996).[22] This comedy also had an amateur production by a university theatre group in Madrid in 2007.

Similarly, *Una mujer sin importancia* (*WNI*) has had at least two productions: a performance directed by Tomás Gayo and Julio Escalada, with well-known theatre actors, during the season 1999–2000, and a more local, probably amateur, production in 2004. Interestingly, though, this comedy was also chosen for publication by the Dirección de la Mujer (Women's issues board) of Madrid's autonomous government in a series of translated dramas published as part of an awareness campaign in connection with women's rights in the region's secondary schools. It came out, together with Strindberg's *Miss Julie*, among other plays, in 2008.

I have only been able to trace one production of *LWF* in Spanish in the last two decades, albeit one that stands out: *El abanico de Lady Windermere... o la importancia de llamarse Wilde* (Lady Windermere's fan... or the importance of being Wilde), a free version by actress and writer Ana Diosdado, directed by a young but experienced director, Juan Carlos Pérez de la Fuente, and performed by an important cast with the celebrated actress Amparo Rivelles in the main role. It was first staged at the *Teatro Alcázar* in Madrid in 1992 and then toured around the country. The production was intended to pay homage to Wilde, as the translator-adaptor explains in the programme and in the published edition of the version in question, which came out in 1993: the 'real' Wilde is made to step into his own play, mixing with his characters and appearing as a worldly, bold, eccentric and brilliant man. Sometimes he

---

22 For a study of the effect of this type of acting on conveying Wilde's humour, see Mateo (2009).

acts as narrator, incorporating passages from his other works; at other times he replaces a character in the play, superimposing his own figure. Wilde's part was played by the British actor James Duggan, who had previously been cast as Wilde in Britain and who now impersonated him in Spanish with a strong English accent. Both Haro Tecglen, in *El País* (1992), and the writer Francisco Umbral, in *El Mundo* (The world) (1992), found that this contributed to the playful novelty of the production, adding to its unorthodox presentation of the comedy. Haro Tecglen, however, regretted Wilde's portrayal as 'a queen' ('una loca'), since he had never pictured him that way but as 'a refined, decadent dandy, of jocular aestheticism' ('un dandy refinado, decadente, de un esteticismo burlón'). Both these critics condemned the slow pace of the dramaturgy but praised the stage design and the production.

IBE opened the last decade of the twentieth century with a Spanish edition by a well-known man of the theatre, Alfonso Sastre, who worked on a translation made by his brother José Sastre, in order to create an operetta libretto, adding rhymed and rhythmical ballades and duets to the dialogues, which the actors were meant to sing and dance to. It was entitled *Bunbury: Comedia con alguna música escrita sobre la obra de Oscar Wilde 'La importancia de llamarse Ernesto' (o de ser formal según se mire)* (Bunbury: A comedy with a little music inspired by Oscar Wilde's play 'The Importance of Being Ernest' [or being serious, if you prefer]) and was published in 1990. Sastre hoped that a composer would set it to music so that it could be performed on the centenary of the original play's first performance in 1895. This production never took place, but Wilde's play would enjoy several interesting performances in the course of the 1990s.

La importancia de llamarse Ernesto: Siendo formal y moderadamente ambiguo (The importance of being Ernest: Being earnest and moderately ambiguous), an unabridged version by the Spanish poet and fervent admirer of Wilde, Luis Antonio de Villena, directed by Pedro Miguel Martínez, was premiered at the *Teatro Reina Victoria* in Madrid in September 1995. For his translation, Villena used the very first four-act version produced by Wilde, which the playwright had reduced to three acts before the play's first night. Villena decided to be faithful to the primitive structure of the full version, cutting each of the four acts slightly so that the performance would not be too long. Opinions were mixed on this decision to use the full version: some critics considered it wise while others thought that 'correcting' the playwright did not add anything to the success of the performance. Everybody agreed, however, on the excellent quality of Villena's translation. Unfortunately, many critics also agreed on the poor quality of the production: most actors were criticized for overacting, some for giving a mistaken, strident or even 'embarrasing' performance. The director's work was also severely condemned as inexperienced, imposing an extremely slow rhythm which made the final scenes tedious. All in all, this production was said to have shown that, but for Villena, nobody in it had clearly understood Wilde, whose high comedy had been turned into a coarse farce (see Centeno 1995, Haro Tecglen 1995, López Sancho 1995, Pérez-Rasilla 1995 and Villán 1995). Surprisingly, though, the show seems to have been relatively successful with the audiences, both in Madrid and in its tour around several Spanish towns (probably because of the popularity of some of the young members of the cast).

Another successful production of *IBE* came from *Teatro de Papel*, a company directed by Claudio Martín. This staging, which was seen in a few Spanish towns in 2005, 2006 and 2008, included changes in the *dramatis personae* of the play and made its language 'simpler' in order to reach a wider audience. 2007 brought another adapted version of Wilde's comedy, directed by Gabriel Olivares and translated by Daniel Pérez and Eduardo Galán, who together decided to modernize the text by setting the plot on a golf course. This production opened at the *Teatro Cervantes* in Valladolid in the autumn of 2007 and toured around Spain in 2008. It was presented as a light-hearted version of the play: it kept the most witty dialogues but did away with certain minor characters and scenes and 'modernized' the language (surprisingly making Lady Bracknell use some outright vulgar expressions). It also introduced a number of other changes, such as making the characters address the audience with some of Wilde's aphorisms not in the original play, incorporating some explicit sexual content (Algernon trying to kiss Jack, for instance) and giving the female roles, particularly Lady Bracknell, much more weight in the plot. The performance, which the director described as 'Oscar Wilde in jeans', seems to have been enjoyed by the audiences (see Cortina 2008 and Moreno 2008).

In 2007, *IBE* was also made visible through a performance of the British playwright Mark Ravenhill's *Handbag: The Importance of Being Someone*. This was the result of a joint project between producers from Madrid and Barcelona. Ravenhill's play, in which couples of gay and lesbian characters wanting to be parents mix with junkies, prostitutes and Teletubbies – Wilde's famous handbag being linked with the Teletubby Tinky Winky's red bag –, is marked by harsh language and disturbing images of sex and violence. The translator was Joan Sellent and the director of both the Catalan and the Castilian Spanish performances was Josep Maria Mestres.

The turn of the twenty-first century has also seen theatre productions of Wilde's non-dramatic works. *DP* was the object of two of them: *Oscar Wilde no tiene nombre* (Oscar Wilde has no name), a Spanish play by Jose Antonio Vitoria performed by the Compañía Tanttaka in the Basque country in 1992; and *El amor que no osa decir su nombre* (The love that dare not speak its name), a theatre adaptation by María Cereijo performed by Jesús Calvo and directed by Fernando Calatrava at the *Teatro de las Aguas* in Madrid in March 2008.

For its part, *PDG* was translated and adapted for the stage by the writer and philosopher Fernando Savater, and performed by well-known actors in a production directed by María Ruiz. It opened at the *Teatro Lope de Vega* in Seville in May 2004 and then toured around Spain for more than a year. The idea of adapting Wilde's novel came from the producers, who had first contemplated having John Osborne's theatre version translated; but Savater preferred to translate and adapt himself the story of this character who, as the Spanish philosopher states in the theatre programme, is already part of our cultural imagery. According to several reviewers, including Haro Tecglen (2005), Savater's version fell short of the quality of the original text. Another adaptation of Wilde's novel was produced in Valencia in 2006 by the Chilean company La Factoría Teatro, who included it as part of their work *Sinfonía para Goethe, Poe y Wilde* (A Symphony for Goethe, Poe and Wilde), for which they won an award.

Wilde's life has also provided material for stage productions in Spanish: an opera with the title *El secreto enamorado* (The secret in love), with a libretto by the poet Ana Rossetti and music by Manuel Balboa, was performed at the *Sala Olimpia* in Madrid in 1993. In 1994 the actor James Duggan performed *Oscar Wilde*, a one-actor performance based on Terry Eagleton's *Saint Oscar* and on works by Wilde himself, with Patsy Maguire's translation into Spanish, at Madrid's *Sala Triángulo*. *El beso de Judas* (*The Judas Kiss*), a translation of David Hare's play by the experienced theatre translator, adaptor and director Nacho Artime, was performed in 2007 and 2008.

As can be observed in some of the productions mentioned in this section, Wilde now reaches Spanish audiences in the different languages spoken, and officially recognized, in the country today – after having been either politically silenced, as Catalan was in Franco's times, or socially marginalized and confined to the home and mostly rural use, as in the case of Basque and Galician. In this context it is worth mentioning a Galician production of *Salomé* in 1989, adapted by Roberto Vidal and John Eastham for the *Centro Dramático Galego* in Santiago de Compostela, as well as two amateur performances by university theatre groups in the same language: one of *IH* by a group from Vigo, in 2002, and *O abanico de lady Windermere* (*LWF*) at the Universidade de Santiago de Compostela in 2008. Non-dramatic works by Wilde or connected with him have also inspired plays in Galician: the company Matarile Teatro performed *O cumpreaños da infanta* (BI) in 1986; and Teatro Quartoescuro, from Pontevedra, produced Joan Schenkar's *A importancia de chamarse Dolly Wilde* (The importance of being called Dolly Wilde), the story of a strong woman who suffers the stigma of being Wilde's niece, which was staged in 2005. A recent example of a Catalan production is *El ventall de Lady Windermere*, translated by Joan Sellent and directed by Josep María Mestres (see Ravenhill's play above), which was put on at the *Teatre Nacional de Catalunya* in Barcelona in 2007. This was in fact the first of Wilde's works ever to have been staged at Catalonia's national theatre and the production, a remarkable success, earned Mestres the Director of the Year Award given by the National Association of Theatre Directors in Spain (ADE). Wilde's works have also started to be performed in Basque: for instance, CG was translated into the language and adapted by Begoña Bilbao, who herself directed the Hankatxo company in their performance of *Cantervilleko mamua* in Irún in May 2006. A reading performance of *IBE* in Basque was given in Pamplona in May 2008.

Concluding remarks

At the turn of the twenty-first century, there still appears to be some confusion in Spain regarding Wilde's national identity: in the most serious theatre criticism he is usually referred to as 'the Irish playwright', while in newspaper articles he is often presented as 'English' (not 'British'). This 'Englishness' slips into theatre programmes and, occasionally, into reviews published in the quality press (de Juan 2000, 9). Wilde is clearly popularly associated more readily with his language or with English (metropolitan) society than with his country of origin. Wilde's life and persona still have a strong presence in his reception: they may be said to attract at least the same attention as his works – if not more. Indeed, his trial, imprisonment, exile and, occasionally, his homosexuality, are often mentioned in theatre programmes. The issue of homosexuality has actually become more and more visible in recent productions. Homosexuals were persecuted under Franco's regime[23] and homosexuality was a taboo topic for censors; however, as Merino has studied in an enlightening article (2007), homosexuality gradually and unexpectedly made its way onto Spanish stages long before Franco's death, leaving other dangerous topics like sexual morality, religion and politics behind. It was through translated and censored foreign plays that this process started around 1955, homosexuality becoming a fairly well-established topic in Spanish theatres in the 1960s, albeit in an indirect manner (Merino 2007, 262). Nevertheless, Wilde does not seem to have been associated with homosexuality during the Franco years: according to Merino,[24] Wilde is not generally regarded as an influence on the open treatment of homosexuality on the Spanish stage (whereas Tennessee Williams's and Peter Shaffer's works often are), probably, once more, because he was received as 'a classic'. Today, however, the 'gay myth' of Wilde is strongly present in the staging of his works.

Wilde now enjoys a multiple reception across the different languages spoken in the country. Various critics, though, have complained that his plays have often been let down by the quality of the actors' performances and of some of the productions. Even so, the plays have generally been warmly welcomed by audiences, who seem ever eager to see a work by Wilde or, more recently, on Wilde. We may, therefore, conclude that the plays have probably enjoyed better fortune with the quality of their translations, which have allowed Spanish audiences and readers to savour what the poet Luis Antonio de Villena once described as 'that rare gift of dazzling joy and beauty which constitutes Oscar Wilde's style and world' (1983: xiii).[25]

---

[23] Under the *Ley de Vagos y Maleantes* (the Vagrants and Malefactors' Act) or Article 431 of the Penal Code (Merino 2007, 243).

[24] Personal communication.

[25] 'ese raro don de deslumbradora alegría y de belleza [que] constituye el estilo y el mundo de Oscar Wilde'.

10 Tragedy and the Apostle of Beauty: The Early Literary Reception of Oscar Wilde in Germany and Austria

Robert Vilain

It is ironic, given how central the primacy of art over life was in Oscar Wilde's writings, that his reception in the German-speaking lands usually testifies to the greater attractiveness of his life than his art. Wilde was enormously well-known in Germany and Austria in the late nineteenth and early twentieth centuries, enjoying an unstable mixture of fame and notoriety. An early bibliography of translations of English literature into German lists no fewer than 250 translations of Wilde published between 1900 and 1934 (Schlösser 1937, 87–120). The majority appeared after 1905, with the onset of what Arthur Roeßler at the time called 'Wilde-mania',[1] the first publication (in German rather than English) of DP and the appearance of an edition of the complete works in Vienna and Leipzig (Wilde 1906–08). There had already been significant interest after Max Reinhardt's famous first German production of Salomé in private at the Kleines Theater in Berlin on 15 November 1902 (treated by Rainer Kohlmayer and Lucia Krämer in this volume) and after the first wave of translations which began in that year.

The reviews of this performance are mostly characteristic of the main trends of Wilde's reception in the German-speaking lands, since many critics failed to 'separate Wilde's life story from consideration of the play' (Davis 2001, 160–61), as one of them, Max Meyerfeld, noted a few years later (1905, 986). Even those critics who took a more balanced line, attempting a serious critique of the aesthetic value of the play, tended to find its merits – richness, splendour, suggestiveness, intensity – counterbalanced or even outweighed by its doubtful moral implications and overblown eroticism (Davis 2001, 163). One even went so far as to see in the character of Salomé a figuration of Wilde himself (Ernstmann 1906, 20).

---

[1] In the preface to his 1905 translation of Intentions; quoted by Bridgwater 1999, 55.

With some notable exceptions – Franz Kafka, for example, had no time at all for him[2] – Wilde came to be seen in Germany and Austria as the very embodiment of one of the most fascinating aspects of the intellectual and aesthetic temper of his age, the aesthetic movement. Not only was he seen as 'the Apostle of Beauty' ('der Apostel der Schönheit'), to use a phrase coined by Meyerfeld (1903, 407), he was received as the champion of the vibrant, expressive individual in his battle against the dusty repressiveness of Victorian mores and morality. Early critics focused on Wilde's essays – Hermann Bahr on DL in 1894 and Johannes Gaulke on SMUS in 1893[3] – and it was not until the early 1900s that Wilde's comedies began to be scrutinized, initially by Ernst Mayer (1901–02), but above all in the numerous essays published by Meyerfeld, the Berlin critic of the *Neue Zürcher Zeitung* (New Zurich newspaper) and a friend and translator of several important English and Irish writers, most notably John Galsworthy, George Moore and J. M. Synge.

In the early twentieth century Wilde was translated into German by a variety of different hands, including Gustav Landauer, Franz Blei, Felix Paul Greve, Hedwig Lachmann, Isidore Leo Pavia, Hermann Freiherr von Teschenberg and Carl Hagemann. Their versions met with varying degrees of success, as Kohlmayer demonstrates (1996, passim). The first performance of *Salomé* in a translation by Lachmann (Wilde 1900 and 1902f) was much lauded, but Greve's (initially anonymous) version of *IBE* (Wilde 1903a) was slated by the Wilde expert Max Meyerfeld (see Kohlmayer 1996, 25) as being marred by Greve's only modest command of English. Three publishers dominated the field: Max Spohr in Leipzig (a firm that specialized in works on homosexuality and anarchism), with translations by Isidore Leo Pavia and Hermann Freiherr von Teschenberg; Greve's publisher J. C. C. Bruns in Minden (specializing in anti-Naturalist writing and with links to the George circle and Rilke); and Lachmann's publisher, Insel, also in Leipzig. The most interesting figure amongst the translators is Greve, who was imprisoned for fraud in 1903, staged a fake suicide in 1909 and emigrated to Canada, where he eventually emerged as the novelist Frederick Philip Grove. He was a hugely prolific translator (partly so as to repay the large sums he had defrauded), encompassing Cervantes, Alexandre Dumas, Honoré de Balzac, Gustave Flaubert, André Gide, Robert Browning, Thomas De Quincey, Ernest Dowson, George Meredith and A. C. Swinburne (amongst many others), but his early efforts were focused on Wilde. His first venture into translating Wilde was a 1902 pamphlet in an edition of 150 copies entitled *Lehren und Sprüche für die reifere Jugend* (Teachings and sayings for grown youths), an anthology of aphorisms culled from PPUY, *IBE* and *IH* (see Knoenagel 1986). Between 1902 and 1904, Greve translated *Intentions*, the anonymous 'Apologia pro Oscar Wilde', *PDG*, PMWH and LASC for Bruns, and wrote a long essay

---

[2] 'Für Meyrink hatte er [Kafka] nichts übrig. Ebenso wenig für Wedekind, Oscar Wilde' (Brod 1937, 59).

[3] Gaulke's stress on Wilde's social utopianism was an approach that, via Gustav Landauer, was to last until, and culminate in, Arnold Zweig's introduction to his 1930 two-volume edition of Wilde's works.

entitled *Randarabesken zu Oscar Wilde* (Marginal arabesques on Oscar Wilde) (Greve 1903). *HOP* appeared in 1905 with Insel.

However, the earliest reception of Wilde in German pre-dates even the first of these translations by some years. The journalist, novelist and playwright Hermann Bahr is usually cited as one of those principally responsible for bringing the message of aestheticism to Vienna. The Viennese weekly paper of which he was literary editor, *Die Zeit* (Time), published DL in German in November 1894. Bahr had read it in English in the summer of that year, as his diary notes reveal: here he quotes Vivian's words – 'Enjoy Nature! I am glad to say that I have entirely lost that faculty' – as a definition of English Decadence (Bahr 1996, 77) and notes a number of aphorisms from the essay, mostly about the superiority of art in its relationship to life. Later on in the same notebook he also quotes Vivian's dictum that 'it is style that makes us believe in a thing – nothing but style' (91). It is hard to judge from the somewhat disjointed form of these notes but they seem to be quoted with a degree of fascination if not exactly approval. Vivian's comment on Balzac, an author somewhat unexpectedly dragooned as an ally of the aesthetes, is that he 'created life, he did not copy it' (77): such pronouncements are likely to have given someone as energetic and larger-than-life as Bahr grounds for admiration. In his essay 'Décadence', also published in *Die Zeit* in November 1894, he writes positively of 'the English [Robert de] Montesquiou' (referring to the inspiration for Marcel Proust's Baron de Charlus and Joris-Karl Huysmans' Des Esseintes): Wilde's adventurousness, his hostility to the banal and to bourgeois sensibilities and his lustful chasing after chimeras are all sources of excited fascination (Bahr 1894, 88).

However, later in the same essay (indeed, later in the same paragraph) Bahr is less than generous to the movement and to Wilde as its chief representative. He claims that Wilde is more famous for his 'fairy-tale' life than for his works and thus identifies very early the key trend in Wilde's German-language reception. In Bahr's view, the works 'have a winsome gift for pretty décor [...]. Here the eye is flattered, there the ear, all one's senses are debauched; but true emotion is silent. [...] They are profligate with the noblest of seasonings; but they lack the essence that will produce real intoxication'.[4] He quotes from DL but damns it with faint praise when he calls it 'a delectable document' ('ein köstliches Dokument'), recording the temporary fashion of the Decadent style. For Bahr, Wilde is superficial and transient, not even powerful enough to be dangerous. A similar view is expressed ten years later by the critic Alfred Polgar: writing in *Die Schaubühne* (The stage), he finds the comedies rather faded, seeing what were formerly splendid pyrotechnic displays of wit and irony as 'ghostly' ('gespenstisch') and 'melancholy' ('melancholisch') (1905, 458).

Hermann Bahr's 1894 jottings on DL are immediately followed by some notes on his friend, the precocious Austrian poet, essayist and dramatist Hugo

---

4   'Diese haben [...] eine gefällige Gabe, schön zu tapezieren [...]. Jetzt schmeicheln sie dem Auge, jetzt dem Ohre, alle Sinne schwelgen; aber es schweigt das Gefühl. [...] Sie verschwenden die edelsten Würzen; aber es fehlt der Saft, der den großen Rausch gibt.'

von Hofmannsthal, who by that year had also developed views on Wilde that diverged somewhat from Bahr's. Comparisons have been drawn between Wilde and Hofmannsthal for many years – at least since the essay 'Drei Dramen und ihre Richter' (Three dramas and their judges) (1906) by the utopian Socialist Gustav Landauer and his ensuing debate with Fritz Mauthner (see Altenhofer 1978). More recently, in one of the very few extended analyses of this relationship, Alexander Stillmark has observed: '[b]oth first realized their gifts as lyrical poets [...]; both were essayists of the first order and used the form liberally to include the dialogue [...]; both commanded the tragedy as well as the social comedy [...]; both were strongly attracted to the allegorical fairy-tale and the short story; both wrote one novel in a highly personal, self-exploratory vein; both published collections of aphorisms' (1981, 9).

Hofmannsthal was certainly aware of, and interested in, Wilde as one of the most important representatives of what he called, unusually, 'Ästhetismus' ('aesthetism', his translation of the French 'esthétisme'). He was initially spell-bound by Wilde, writing to Bahr that he had subconsciously been longing to read *Intentions* for five-and-a-half years! In a letter to Carl August Klein, the publisher of Stefan George's elitist periodical *Blätter für die Kunst* (Pages for art), he includes Wilde in a series of essays he plans to write: 'incidentally, I intend to attempt to discuss in the daily papers the manifestations of foreign literature that are related to our work (Verlaine, Swinburne, Oscar Wilde, the Pre-Raphaelites, etc.) and, quite naturally, what will emerge will be my own personal view on these and hints of a similar tendency present in Germany, too' (19 December 1892; George/Hofmannsthal 1953, 53).[5] Hofmannsthal was reading *Intentions* at about this time (see Hofmannsthal 1935, 69) and imitated Wilde's aphoristic style, even going so far as to adapt some of the formulations of DL in his essay 'Algernon Charles Swinburne' (January 1893): 'for them [the English Pre-Raphaelites] life only becomes a living thing when it has been filtered through art of some kind and received a style and a mood' (Hofmannsthal 1979b, 143).[6] Steve Rizza summarizes Hofmannsthal's early attitudes to Wilde thus: 'Hofmannsthal's equivocal formulation of this aspect of the elusive art/life relationship [...] has marked affinities with Oscar Wilde's paradoxical contention that life imitates art. Wilde's deliberately provocative assertion of the primacy of art over immediate experience, a central tenet of his aestheticism, is a radical inversion of the traditional mimetic relationship between art and nature' (1997, 38).

There are a few embarrassing examples in Hofmannsthal's early works of the corollary of this attitude, an extreme form of Wildean snobbery. The short poem 'Tobt der Pöbel in den Gassen' (The rabble are revolting in the

---

5   'Ich werde übrigens nächstens versuchen, in Tagesblättern die uns verwandten Erscheinungen fremder Litteraturen (Verlaine, Swinburne, Oscar Wilde, die Praeraphaeliten etc.) zu besprechen, dabei kommt ja ganz naturgemäß eine persönliche Stellungnahme und Andeutungen eines auch in Deutschland vorhandenen Programmes heraus.'

6   'Ihnen wird das Leben erst lebendig, wenn es durch irgendeine Kunst hindurchgegangen ist, Stil und Stimmung empfangen hat.'

streets) was written on a visiting card in a moment of youthful conceitedness on the occasion of an Austrian Workers' Movement demonstration in Vienna on 1 May 1890. It ends 'Leave the rabble in the streets: rhetoric, rapture, lies, pretence, / These will disappear, they are fading away, only *beautiful* truth can *live*' (Hofmannsthal 1988, 22).[7] It is true that many of Hofmannsthal's early works do register a degree of attraction to the beauty and opulence of the aesthete's world, and for decades this dominated the critical view of Hofmannsthal, who was seen primarily as the German-language representative of the aesthetic movement *par excellence*. Richard Alewyn puts the date of Hofmannsthal's 'Wandlung' (conversion) away from aestheticism at 1895 and specifically links it to Wilde (1967, 168–70). In late May of that year the Austrian press carried reports of Wilde's sentence of two years' hard labour after a conviction for gross indecency.[8] It may be that this most public of come-uppances for one of Europe's most conspicuous aesthetes had some effect on the composition of Hofmannsthal's 'Das Märchen der 672. Nacht' (Tale of the 672nd night), first published in November of that year.[9] This is the tale of a wealthy merchant's son who is lured out of his ivory tower of aesthetic refinement and material luxury by an anonymous letter accusing one of his servants of an unspecified offence, which he interprets as a threat to his security and well-being. A series of unsettling reminders of this man and his three other servants – who are all in some respects mirrors or symbols of aspects of the protagonist himself – entices him through squalid city streets to a barracks, where he is robbed by the soldiers and fatally wounded by a kick from an angry horse. Hofmannsthal himself described the story as 'the Day of Judgement for aestheticism raised to the level of a fairy-tale' (Hofmannsthal 1979a, 666).[10] In a letter written to Hermann Bahr between July and November 1896, Hofmannsthal is just as forceful and even more direct: he considers writing about 'the "cul-de-sac of aestheticism" (in connection with peculiar deep-rooted affinities between "Aphrodite" by [Pierre] Louÿs and "Dorian Gray" by Oscar Wilde)' (1935, 206).[11] The symbol of the golden lily in Hofmannsthal's play *Der Kaiser und die Hexe* (The Emperor and the sorceress) (1897), can also be seen as consciously bound up with his knowledge of the English aesthetes and of Wilde in particular: here the lily symbolizes insubstantiality and deception (not the purity of art as in Wilde's work) and it is intended as a warning against everything that Hofmannsthal felt Wilde stood for (see Dormer 1977).

Clear though the message of these examples from after 1895 may be, the seeds of Hofmannsthal's dissatisfaction were sown somewhat earlier. In his

---

[7] 'Lass den Pöbel in den Gassen: Phrasen, Taumel, Lügen, Schein, / Sie verschwinden, sie verblassen[,] *schöne* Wahrheit *lebt* allein.'

[8] For details of the press response to the trial see Weber 1971.

[9] Weber notes some textual echoes of *PDG* in Hofmannsthal's tale (1971, 104); for echoes of Wilde's YK in 'Das Märchen', see Arlaud 2000, 115–20.

[10] 'Ein ins Märchen gehobener Gerichtstag des Ästhetizismus.'

[11] '"die Sackgasse des Ästhetismus" (anläßlich sonderbarer tiefliegender Zusammenhänge zwischen der "Aphrodite" von Louÿs und "Dorian Gray" von Oscar Wilde).'

notebook for 1894 he records his view of English 'aesthetism' in German-language culture: 'I. First encounter: as a peculiarity, probably a kind of affectation, dressing up, etc.; II. Oscar Wilde, *Intentions*: strong narcotic magic, sophistically seductive, inelegantly paradoxical, a reaction against English utilitarianism' (1979c, 386).[12] He then contrasts Wilde unfavourably with John Ruskin, Walter Pater, Ford Madox Brown, Dante Gabriel Rossetti and Edward Burne-Jones, who more genuinely seek to develop spirituality. The language employed by Hofmannsthal is fairly strong: he sees Wilde as an intoxicant, a sophistical thinker and – almost uniquely in Germany and Austria – as inelegant.[13] But even this is a late manifestation of Hofmannsthal's dissatis-faction with what Wilde represented. There are in fact barely any published works, from his very beginnings and throughout the 1890s, that do not distance themselves from aestheticism. Claudio, the Wilde-like protagonist of the lyrical drama *Der Tor und der Tod* (Death and the fool) (1893), has tried to live of art alone, spurning or selfishly exploiting the human relationships (with his mother, his lover and his best friend) that should by rights have been the substance of his life; but death exposes the utter emptiness of his existence and the folly of the aestheticist lifestyle. Earlier still, in 1891, there may be a direct reference to Wilde's DL in *Gestern* (Yesterday), in which the chief character, Andrea, voices a paean to the sensuous pleasures of mendacity: 'We all lie, I do as well – most willingly! / O golden lies, growing without foundations, / An impulse of art in the mouths of those blissfully unaware! / O wise lies, painstakingly woven, [...] How sweet it is to enjoy lies consciously / Until lies and truth merge gently into one another' (1982, 19).[14] Andrea's aim is to enjoy today for its own sake, not worrying about yesterday or tomorrow and systematically closing his eyes to moral and social responsibility. His preten-sions to the perfect aesthetic existence are punctured when his lover, Arlette, confesses to a brief liaison with his friend and he is unable to put into practice his belief that actions have no consequences, hammering another nail into the coffin of the Wildean credo.

The obituary is Hofmannsthal's essay 'Sebastian Melmoth', which appeared not in a Viennese paper but in Berlin's *Der Tag* (The day), in March 1905, as a review of the German book publication of *DP*. The essay is full of images of death, from that of the mask in the opening line (referring to Wilde's use of a pseudonym after his release from gaol), via references to ghosts and spirits, coffins and burials, to the quotation at the end of Jalal ad-Din Muhammad Rumi's aphorism, 'Whosoever knows the power of the round-dance does not

---

12 'I. Erstes Entgegentreten: als Sonderbarkeit, wohl etwa Affektation, Kostümtragen etc. II. Oscar Wilde, "Intentions": starker narkotischer Zauber, sophistisch verführerisch, unelegant paradoxal, Reaktion gegen englischen Utilitarismus.'

13 The motif of intoxication to describe Wilde's effects is a recurrent one: see, for example, Efraim Frisch's description of *Salomé* (Frisch 1903–04, 30).

14 'Wir lügen alle und ich selbst – wie gern! / O goldne Lügen, werdend ohne Grund, / Ein Trieb der Kunst, im unbewußten Mund! / O weise Lügen, mühevoll gewebt, / Wo eins das andre färbt und hält und hebt! / Wie süß, die Lüge wissend zu genießen, / Bis Lüg und Wahrheit sanft zusammenfließen.'

fear death, for he knows that love can kill' (Hofmannsthal 1979b, 341–44).[15]
Hofmannsthal objects to the current tendency (represented by Meyerfeld
amongst many others) to distinguish between 'the early Wilde' and 'the
other Wilde' – the aesthete on the one hand and the Catholic convert on
the other – and to regard him as a victim or a martyr: 'It makes no sense
to speak as if Oscar Wilde's fate and Oscar Wilde's character were two
different things and as if fate had attacked him from behind like a snapping
cur leaping on an unsuspecting peasant child carrying a basket of eggs on its
head'.[16] On the contrary, he says, the aesthete and the dandy were already
no less tragic than Prisoner C33. Hofmannsthal even wants to deny Wilde
the dignity of the term 'aesthete' by comparing him with Pater, a man 'who
lived from the enjoyment and recreation of beauty and was full of reserve
and restraint in the face of life, full of discipline'. These are the natural
attributes of the aesthete. 'But Oscar Wilde was full of indiscipline, full of
tragic indiscipline. His aestheticism was a kind of paroxysm. The precious
stones that he pretended to rummage in with so much pleasure were like
damaged eyes, frozen because they had not withstood the sight of life'.[17] The
essay is a fascinating combination of sympathy and frustration. Hofmannsthal
regards Wilde's fate as a genuine tragedy in that it was inevitable; but he is
manifestly frustrated with Wilde for continually provoking and defying life,
for insulting reality instead of respecting it, and he is therefore not wholly
able to regret life's final revenge on Wilde. He clearly has little patience with
Wilde's own judgement on himself in *DP*, which reads like a version of the
fate of Dorian Gray – 'I would sooner say, or hear it said of me, that I was
so typical a child of my age, that in my perversity, and for that perversity's
sake, I turned the good things of my life to evil, and the evil things of life
to good' (Wilde 1962, 469) – for in truth Wilde had always had been little
else than an aberration.[18] There are grounds for suspecting that the reasons
for such ambivalence lie partly in Hofmannsthal's shame about his own
homosexual desires, which were sometimes linked to his reception of Wilde.
In a letter written nearly a decade before to Hans Schlesinger, for example,
he recommends *PDG* in the context of a full-length young male nude that

---

[15] 'Wer die Gewalt des Reigens kennt, fürchtet nicht den Tod. Denn er weiß, daß
die Liebe tötet.'

[16] 'Es hat gar keinen Sinn so zu sprechen, als ob Oscar Wildes Schicksal und Oscar
Wildes Wesen zweierlei gewesen wären und als ob das Schicksal ihn so angefallen
hätte wie ein bissiger Köter ein ahnungsloses Bauernkind, das einen Korb mit
Eiern auf dem Kopf trägt.'

[17] 'ein Mensch, der vom Genießen und Nachschaffen der Schönheit lebte, und er
war dem Leben gegenüber voll Scheu und Zurückhaltung, voll Zucht [...]. Oscar
Wilde aber war voll Unzucht, voll tragischer Unzucht. Sein Ästhetismus war etwas
wie ein Krampf. Die Edelsteine, in denen er vorgab mit Lust zu wühlen, waren
wie gebrochene Augen, die erstarrt waren, weil sie den Anblick des Lebens nicht
ertragen hatten.' On Hofmannsthal's reception of Pater, see Vilain 2002, 63–66,
and Vilain 2000a, 265–66.

[18] 'Hofmannsthal kann den erotischen Eskapismus Wildes nur als Flucht vor dem
Opfer deuten' (Brittnacher 1996, 40).

Schlesinger was painting. To add another layer of guilt, Schlesinger later became his brother-in-law.[19]

There is altogether less tension in the obituary proper that another Vienna-based writer composed a few days after Wilde's death in 1900, Rudolf Kassner's 'Zum Tode Oskar Wildes. Einiges über das Paradoxe' (On the death of Oscar Wilde. Some thoughts on the paradoxical). Kassner had actually been in Paris when Wilde died. In the obituary he anticipates Hofmannsthal's insistence on the integrity of Wilde's life: he suggests that 'Oscar Wilde was himself truly paradoxical, not merely sections of his life' and, drawing on DL, he explains that 'paradox is the image of lying just as truth is the image of reality, paradox is the conscious lie, the free lie, lies as art' (Kassner [1901] 1969, II: 381 and 383).[20] Like many of his contemporaries before 1905, Kassner is familiar with the prose works and essays but not the comedies. He expresses here his admiration for *Intentions* and Wilde's prose poems, two of which he appends to the essay in his own translation, and goes to great lengths to give Wilde's aesthetics a proper cultural and intellectual pedigree, locating them as the modern manifestation of Keats's famous claim that 'the poet has no identity' (Keats 1987, 157). Elsewhere Kassner even went so far as to suggest that Wilde was one of the avatars of Keats, who 'lived life as a model for others' with 'the tragedy of his life in the writings of poets to come', including Pater's *Marius the Epicurean* and Wilde's paradoxes (Kassner 1969, I, 118–19).[21] Where others will claim that parallels or similarities with other writers render Wilde derivative or unoriginal, Kassner sees such creative and intellectual overlaps as proof of his representative genius.

Kassner's obituary concludes with his translations of two of Wilde's prose poems, 'Der Schüler' ('The Disciple') and 'Der Meister' ('The Master'). The first is a variant on the myth of Narcissus, in which traditionally Narcissus is consumed by love for his own reflection in a pool of water. In Wilde's version the pool loves Narcissus 'because, as he lay on my banks and looked down at me, in the mirror of his eyes I saw ever my own beauty mirrored'. Richard Ellmann links the parable to Gide, whose *Traité du Narcisse* had appeared in 1891, shortly before he met Wilde in Paris, and sees its message as 'a lesson to one of Mallarmé's disciples from a rival master', namely 'there are no disciples' (Ellmann 1988, 337). As Victoria Reid explains in her essay in this volume, Gide's essay on Wilde, which picked up the polarity of life and art to devastating effect, demonstrates a form of revenge for having been intellectually seduced by this rival master. It is relevant in this context because it is now widely regarded as being amongst the earliest and most influential contributions to the reception of Wilde in German. First appearing in French in 1902

---

[19] On Hofmannsthal's homosexuality, see Weinzierl 2005, 103–230 (on Schlesinger, p. 131).

[20] 'Denn Oskar Wilde war wirklich paradox und nicht nur ein Theil seines Lebens war es'; 'die Paradoxie ist das Bild der Lüge, wie die Wahrheit das Bild der Wirklichkeit ist.'

[21] 'Keats […] lebte das Leben den anderen vor, und die Tragödie seines Lebens ist die Dichtung kommender Dichter.'

in *L'Ermitage*, it was translated by Bertha Franzos for publication in three parts in the *Rheinisch-Westfälische Zeitung* (Rhenish-Westphalian newspaper) in July 1903 before being revised and edited by Franz Blei to open *In Memoriam Oscar Wilde* (Blei 1904, 1–31). Gide's first impressions of Wilde in Paris in 1891 had been overwhelmingly positive: he described him as 'radiant', praising his French, his wit and his conversation. But, like many others before and after him, he had quickly realized that Wilde was potentially more destructive than inspirational. Gide cleverly structures and stylizes Wilde's personal fate in terms of a Greek tragedy (his five-part structure resembles the five-act drama) but he is devastatingly negative about Wilde as a writer. His talent, he says, was for life and his wisdom was dispensed in conversation; 'grand écrivain non pas, mais grand viveur' (not a great writer but a great exponent of life) (Gide 1947, 222). Even Wilde's much-vaunted gift for form is thought to have been exaggerated, since Gide feels that Wilde was unable to prevent the proliferation of witticisms from strangling any genuine emotional content.

Aspects of Gide's critique were toned down by Franz Blei for the 1904 *In Memoriam* publication: for example, Gide's introduction, the most censorious part of the essay, was omitted. Nonetheless, Gide's negative judgement was shared by many others: Felix Paul Greve paraphrased aspects of it in an essay that appeared later in 1903; another influential critic and theatre practitioner, Carl Hagemann, used it as the basis for his own interpretations of Wilde (see Kohlmayer 1996, 119–26 and Kohlmayer and Krämer in this volume). Whether directly influenced by Gide or not, Alfred Polgar, a writer and critic living and working in Vienna, makes the same telling attack on the most famous of Wilde's talents two years later: 'It is precisely the paradox, precisely the thing that the exclusive Oscar thought kept him furthest away from vulgarity, precisely that has fallen prey – to vulgarity. No sooner had the poet lighted on his first aperçu than there were thousands of them. You can catalogue them according to the way they are generated: the apodosis that negates the protasis; the inverted proverb; the switching of premise and conclusion; [...] the treatment of a moral question as an aesthetic one' (1905, 458).[22] Empty of spirit and essence, Wilde has fallen victim to his own facility with words.

The editor of the volume in which Gide's essay became best known, Franz Blei, Viennese journalist, biographer and playwright, was also another of Wilde's translators. He modified Teschenberg's 1903 version of *Bunbury* (*IBE*), for example, to make it slicker, more elegant and more theatrically practical, published versions of Wilde's poems and aphorisms, as well as translations of HP and many other stories that are still currently available.[23] He had known

---

[22] 'Grade die Pardoxie, grade das, wodurch der exklusive Oscar von Vulgarität sich am weitesten zu entfernen glaubte, grade das wurde Beute – der Vulgarität. Mit dem ersten Aperçu, zu dem der Dichter sich entschloß, hatter er tausende. Man kann sie nach Herstellungsmethoden ordnen: der den Vordersatz aufhebende Nachsatz; das verkehrte Sprichwort; der Tausch von Schluß und Prämisse; [...] die Behandlung einer moralischen Frage als ästhetische'.

[23] For a thorough list of Blei's translations and reviews, see Mitterbauer 2003, 22.

Wilde personally, too, which may account for the stress of his own essay in that volume on the character of the man rather than the value, or otherwise, of the works. There is an amusing entry on Wilde in Blei's *Das große Bestiarium der Literatur* (The great bestiary of modern literature) (1922) that puns on the fact that his name and the German for 'wildness' are homographs. 'Das Wilde' is described as a beautiful beast of prey, who loved to parade around in human costume before the snobs of his age; in other words, he is the epitome of the posing, self-stylizing dandy. There is a sharp and not unsympathetic *pointe* to this little satire as we learn how 'Das Wilde' became the futile victim of the very caste to which he belonged (Blei 1995, 123).

Blei wrote several other essays on Wilde, the most extensive and penetrating of which appeared in the collection *Männer und Masken* (Men and masks) (1930). Like so many others, the essay opens with a claim that Wilde's works could hardly have generated as much interest as his conviction for crimes of a sexual nature. Blei is dismissive of the early works, most of which he feels are derivative of Baudelaire, De Quincey, Huysmans, Mallarmé, de l'Isle-Adam and Flaubert: these ingredients are stirred up to make a dish consisting of 'the critical prose of Walter Pater's aestheticism with a dash of French art for art's sake' (Blei 1930, 173).[24] Only in the later works did Wilde achieve the combination of 'pain and sympathetic love' ('Schmerz und mitleidige Liebe') (179) that allow him to construct a personal mythology of Christ that both integrates Him into the ancient pagan world that Wilde used to inhabit and simultaneously transcends this world.

Most significantly, however, this essay demonstrates how Blei shared with Wilde a desire to shake up social attitudes to eroticism and sexuality. Blei uses Wilde's attitudes and experience to develop a model of life as 'ethical play' ('ethisches Spiel'). The ethical, he suggests, is not a goal to be striven for and not a solution to anything; it is instead a means or an instrument, just as love, money and art are instruments. The goal is form and its variations (186). Social conventions are only taken to represent reality because the ethical has been mistaken for the ultimate purpose rather than a means to an end. The 'game' of life only works if everyone pretends not to see that it is a game – not to see that the opposition of 'truth' and 'beauty' is an aesthetic instrument like any other, not an existential absolute; those who see through the game too publicly must be punished equally publicly. Life and art are not distinguished except by being governed by different conventions. What makes Blei's somewhat tenuously spun argument something other than a simple repetition of an old *plaidoyer* for the superiority of art over life is the fact that it moves ever more forcefully at the end towards a call for a psycho-social revolution. Within himself Wilde was able to accomplish what society had taken a hundred years to dismantle, the construct that matched love with sexual activity and dual-gendered life-partnerships:

> This is the case with Wilde, which has to be considered not in the medical laboratory but in a psycho-social context. Prepared by a high level of aesthetic

---

[24] 'Die kritische Prosa von Walter Paters Ästhetizismus mit einem Schuß von franzö-
sischem art pour art.'

hyperaesthesia, as the first renegade from the previously prevailing erotic idolatry of women, he defected from this kind of veneration because, despite being a man, he could no longer fall into the category of 'the male of the species' (198).[25]

Sexuality is one of the main issues for another Viennese author and critic who seized upon Wilde in the early years of the twentieth century, Karl Kraus. The other is anti-Semitism. The Viennese première of *Salomé* at the *Volkstheater* (People's theatre) on 12 December 1903 caused a scandal that was amplified and exacerbated by the critique of Friedrich Schütz in the *Neue Freie Presse* (New free press) which suggested that the works of a homosexual author would necessarily be morally and aesthetically tainted, Wilde's own beliefs in the amoral status of art notwithstanding. Kraus retorts that Schütz's motivation in attacking Wilde for his sexuality is merely to make it clear to others that he, Schütz, is not one of *them* (Kraus 1903, 2). But Schütz also suggests that Wilde was anti-Semitic since all the Jews in the production were felt to have been portrayed 'in a very unflattering light: Herod as an incestuous father, Herodias as an unnatural mother, Salome a hysterical girl, and the Jews in general as sexual perverts, or just grotesque' (Le Rider 1993, 264). Moreover, the Jews spoke in the Galician accents of the *Ostjuden* – unassimilated, and thus negatively regarded Eastern European Jews. It is possible that this decision (not Wilde's but that of the play's director) was an artistic decision aimed, consciously or otherwise, at appealing to the latent anti-Semitism of Austrian audiences. Indeed, it proved to be the case that *Salomé* in Germany and Austria often did exaggerate Jewish stereotypes (Gilman 1988, 155–81), but Kraus saw the complaint as evidence of paranoia on the part of Schütz and his paper. In print, in the pages of his own paper *Die Fackel* (The torch), Kraus was coruscating in his anger towards Schütz:

> If the *Neue Freie Presse* praises Sudermann's trash and spits on Wilde's play then it must be that anti-Semitism has a hand in it somewhere. How on earth can that be the case? Art for art's sake, aestheticism, English Decadence and – anti-Semitism? A glance at Herr Schütz's way of thinking explains everything. This man of progress, who observes modern art from the perspective of Prague's *Kleinseite* [Lesser Quarter], has for years and years been propagating one single idea. It isn't a very profound one, but it is firmly lodged: every work of literature that is exposed to him for review must somewhere and somehow give some indication of the attitude of its author to the Jewish question.[26] (Kraus 1903, 7)

---

25 'Dieses ist der Fall Wilde, der nicht im medizinischen Laboratorium zu diskutieren ist, sondern im sozial-psychologischen. Er fiel, vorbereitet darauf durch eine hohe ästhetische Hyperästhesie, als erster Abtrünniger von der bisherigen erotischen Idolatrie des Weibes, von dieser Verehrung ab, weil er, männlich wie er war, nicht mehr ins Männchenhafte fallen konnte.'

26 'Wenn die "Neue Freie Presse" Sudermann's Theaterschmarren preist und Wilde's Dichtung bespeit, dann, ja dann muß – der Antisemitismus seine Hand im Spiele haben. Wie das? L'art pour l'art, Ästhetentum, englische Dekadence und – Antisemitismus? Ein Blick in das Gemütsleben des Herrn Schütz macht alles erklärlich. Dieser Fortschrittsmann, der die moderne Kunst aus dem Gesichtswinkel der Prager Kleinseite betrachtet, propagiert seit Jahr und Tag eine

Kraus's commitment to sexual freedom went hand in hand with another stage in his complex exploration of his own Jewish identity.

Wilde has more mentions in *Die Fackel* than any other English author with the exception of Shakespeare (Timms 1986, 188). In the wake of his intervention in the *Salomé* controversy, Kraus made positive comments on, and provided long quotations from, *PDG* (Kraus 1904a) and *BRG*, although the hyperbolic manner in which he expresses himself may well be affected by the polemic stance. Between October 1904 and March 1905, *Die Fackel* devotes much attention to SMUS, which it describes as 'the deepest, most noble and most beautiful thing that this genius murdered by philistinism ever created [...] the true gospel of modern thought' (Kraus 1904b, 10).[27] Kraus's enthusiasm is doubtless generated in part by Wilde's attitudes to the press, which, as Kraus points out, are not so far from his own. Wilde becomes one of the instruments by which Kraus establishes the key distinction between public and private life, but the 'gospel' of individualism that he found in the essay was also music to his ears. Edward Timms shows the direct influence of Wilde on Kraus's thinking on a number of key issues including the nature of the artist (art being a way of life rather than a series of cultural productions) and the importance of adopting masks in life (1986, 189–92).

This time marked the height of 'Wilde-mania'. In Germany, Thea Sternheim, the wife of the comic playwright Carl Sternheim, recommended *DP* to her husband in March 1905, almost immediately after its publication: '[d]as ist schön sage ich Dir, wunderbar' ('It is beautiful, let me tell you, wonderful'). Like Blei, she particularly appreciated Wilde's understanding of the person of Christ (Sternheim 1988, I: 203 and 213). An incomplete German edition of *DP* had been published in January and February of that year in *Die neue Rundschau* (The new review). The translation was by Max Meyerfeld from a manuscript sent to him by Robert Ross and with decorative initials by the *art nouveau* illustrator Emil Rudolf Weiss. It appeared in book form on 11 February 1905 (thus about two weeks earlier than the English edition).[28] Meyerfeld's introduction again emphasizes the tragic nature of the letter, referring explicitly to the three years that Wilde lived after his incarceration as 'the last act of the tragedy'. In increasingly heart-wrenching terms he describes the 'medieval barbarity' of the English penal system: Wilde's cell is 'a kind of rabbit hutch with a wire frame nailed over it', his only possessions the four Gospels in Greek. 'The mighty fist of life smashed to pieces the

---

Idee. Sie ist zwar nicht tief, aber fix: Jedes Dichterwerk, das seiner Besprechung ausgeliefert ist, muß irgendwo und irgendwie über die Stellung seines Autors zur Judenfrage Aufschluß geben können.'

[27] 'das Tiefste, Adeligste und Schönste, das der vom Philistersinn gemordete Genius geschaffen [...] das wahre Evangelium modernen Denkens.'

[28] The book version ran to eight editions by the end of 1905 and thirteen by 1907. A new German edition appeared in 1909: this was an enlarged and revised version of the 1905 publication and it identified the addressee of the letter as Lord Alfred Douglas (information not made public in Britain until the Ransome trial of 1912). For details see Schroeder (n.d.).

intentions of that poor mortal [...]. His pose had almost reached the point of becoming part of his nature, but then the tornado of life swept it away like autumn leaves' (Wilde 1905a, 86–87).[29]

Sternheim may have been affected in her views of Wilde by Meyerfeld, since she describes Wilde in another letter of 13 September 1905 as 'a martyr' (I: 278), but she was most effusive when discussing the works. A performance of *Salomé* in November 1905 prompted a long and enthusiastic account (I: 377). 'The play was performed brilliantly, staged brilliantly', she gushed, 'and is beautiful, beautiful'.[30] She praises Wilde's simplicity, the precision of his language and the dignity of the characters, but the most poignant aspect of the letter is the way she weaves her huge enthusiasm for Wilde together with her powerful feelings for her beloved husband – who in response was rather less excited about Wilde's play. He granted that Wilde was a 'Künstler', an artist who understood his craft, but complained that 'there is lots of rhetoric in it [*Salomé*], and lots of Decadence, but not much force' (I: 385).[31] Despite Thea's renewed attempts to convince him, Carl remained firm: 'Wilde's goodness, his inferno, this snivelling I find intolerable. And in any case, the man *wasn't* good, it was just posturing. That's what they all do if they have no *force*, they turn it into goodness, into something feminine' (I: 392).[32] It was another year until he had anything good to say about Wilde. After watching a performance of *LWF*, he was impressed by his wit and above all by his grasp of the craft of drama (I: 774). Grudgingly he describes the moment where Lady Windermere sees Mrs Erlynne arrive, lifts and then drops her fan, as 'not great, not earth-shattering, not definitive – but dramatic'.[33]

Something happened between 1906 and 1924 to change Sternheim's view of Wilde, most probably the translation of Frank Harris's biography that appeared in 1923. He was gripped by it, read deep into the night and seized every daylight moment to carry on until completion. 'More than Wilde's fate, it is the density of the way he depicts the conditions of the age that seizes me. But even after this insight into England's inadequacies I am struck by the fact that in no country in Europe is the level of human cooperation as undeveloped as in Germany' (II: 825).[34] He came to see Wilde as a dramatic

---

[29] 'diese[r] letzte Akt der Tragödie [...] mittelalterliche Barbarei [...] eine Art Kaninchenstall, [...] über dem ein Drahtgitter genagelt war. [...] Das Leben mit seiner Riesenfaust zerbröckelte alle Vorsätze des armen Sterblichen [...]. Die Pose war fast auf dem Punkt angelangt, zur Natur zu werden: da fegte sie der Wirbelwind des Lebens wie herbstliches Laub hinweg.'

[30] 'Das Stück war glänzend gespielt, glänzend inszeniert – und ist auch schön, schön.'

[31] 'Es ist viel Phrase und Dekadence drin, wenig Kraft, freilich ist Wilde *Künstler.*'

[32] 'Die Güte an Wilde, sein Inferno, diese Jammerlappigkeit ist mir unausstehlich. Und nämlich: der Mann *war* gar nicht gut, er posiert darauf. Das thun sie alle, die nicht die *Kraft* haben, sie führen's auf die Güte hin. Auf etwas Weibliches.'

[33] 'nicht groß – nicht weltbewegend – nicht begriffbildend – aber dramatisch.' Shortly afterwards, on 28 December 1906, Thea saw *IBE* in Munich and was predictably impressed (II: 8).

[34] 'Mehr als das Wildesche Schicksal packt mich Dichte des mit vollendeter Kunst geschilderten Zeitzustands. Aber selbst nach diesem Einblick in die

figure in himself (II: 297) and began a play about him that was to see its first performance a year later on 31 March 1925 in Berlin as *Oskar Wilde. Sein Drama* (Oscar Wilde. His drama), which is discussed elsewhere in this volume. The bitingly sarcastic tone of his response to negative public criticism of the play resembles the polemic that Kraus directed against Schütz, in this case with Sternheim's ire aimed at the pioneer of Expressionism, Kurt Pinthus.

Sternheim's view of Wilde ultimately contributed strongly to the conception of him that stressed the courageous, responsible artist in revolt against a society that was too rigid or blinkered to accommodate his insights. Thomas Mann falls into the same tradition. He made the somewhat exaggerated claim that many of Wilde's aphorisms might be imagined in the mouth of Friedrich Nietzsche, and vice versa (Mann 1997, 72),[35] which as Stillmark notes (1981, 10), is indicative of the degree of earnestness with which Wilde was regarded in Germany.[36] Mann was indeed serious about the comparison, for later in the same essay he links the two even more firmly: 'as men in revolt, indeed in revolt in the name of beauty, they belong together': aestheticism is the first form taken by revolt against the whole moral structure of the bourgeois age (Mann 1997, 87).[37] Patrick Bridgwater has succinctly suggested a number of telling parallels between Nietzsche and Wilde, concluding that their 'ideas correspond [...] on a range of issues including hypocrisy, convention, the Victorian / Wilhelmine attitude towards sex [...], pain, creative passion, lying, altruism, art and [...] the mask-motif'. Underpinning them all is the two writers' shared sense of the importance of the individual: 'Wilde's pronouncement in [SMUS] that "Over the portal of the new world, 'Be Thyself' shall be written" is identical with Nietzsche's motto in the third of his *Thoughts out of Season* [*Unzeitgemäße Betrachtungen*]' (1999, 243). Nietzsche's text reads thus: 'The man who wishes not to belong to the mass of humanity only needs to stop being comfortable; let him follow his conscience when it calls to him "be yourself!"' (Nietzsche 1954–56, I: 287–8).[38] (It may be the echo of Nietzsche that caused Peter Altenberg to single out this phrase in his review, too; 1905, 15). And individuality in turn lies behind both writers' insight into the close relationship of art and lying, where the aesthetic value of an utterance trumps its traditional 'moral' status.

Mann's remarks on Wilde as a revolutionary quoted above stem from an

---

Unzulänglichkeiten Englands drängt sich dennoch die Feststellung auf, daß in keinem Land Europas das mitmenschliche Niveau so unentwickelt blieb wie in Deutschland' (from Sternheim's diary of 2 February 1924).

[35] 'Es ist überraschend, die nahe Verwandschaft mancher Aperçus von Nietzsche mit den keineswegs nur eitlen Attacken auf die Moral festzustellen, mit denen ungefähr gleichzeitig Oscar Wilde, der englische Ästhet, sein Publikum schockierte und zum Lachen brachte'.

[36] Gide makes a similar remark in his essay on Wilde (see Kassner 1969, II: 809).

[37] 'als Revoltierende und zwar im Namen der Schönheit Revoltierende gehören sie zusammen'.

[38] 'Der Mensch, welcher nicht zur Masse gehören will, braucht nur aufzuhören, gegen sich bequem zu sein; er folge seinem Gewissen, welches ihm zuruft: "sei du selbst!"'.

essay written in 1949, but his enthusiasm for the English aesthete dates back to his earliest years when he was himself most intimately concerned with the apparent mutual exclusivity of art and life. He read *PDG* in 1901, as soon as it appeared in German, which in the longer term may well have influenced aspects of his own late novel *Die Bekenntnisse des Hochstaplers Felix Krull* (*Confessions of Felix Krull, Confidence Man*) (1954) and even *Der Tod in Venedig* (*Death in Venice*) (1912). Earlier, less well-known works such as the short story 'Gerächt' (Avenged) (1899) already show an interest in cognate themes. It is unsurprising that in his copy of Blei's *In Memoriam* volume he underlined the phrase 'The Dandy is an artist, he is equally egocentric; like the artist he likes to relate to the public, yet prefers his own company' (quoted by Bridgwater 1999, 245). It might also be plausible to see in the fatal deal that Adrian Leverkühn seals in *Doktor Faustus* (1947) an echo of Dorian Gray's no less lethal pact.

Mann's homosexuality, largely suppressed throughout his life, may have been a factor in the fascination that Wilde exercised over him; he may have seen and admired a degree of courage in the face of public approbation that he could not himself muster. But what seems most to have attracted Mann – the epitome of the self-disciplined, self-abnegating *praeceptor Germaniae* – to the hedonistic outsider Wilde, nicely described by a late nineteenth-century critic as '[ein] genießender Dilettant' (literally 'a relishing dilettante', Herzfeld 1898, 187), was the consistent intensity of his stance. In his wartime polemic *Betrachtungen eines Unpolitischen* (*Reflections of a Non-Political Man*) (1918), he defends both Baudelaire and Wilde as representatives of a 'pure aestheticism capable of the most intense effects'. *Salomé*, he says, 'is a work of immortal pithiness and power; the uncompromising artificiality of his unaffected and uninhibited aestheticism epitomizes the beauty and the vice of life' (Mann 1960, 548).[39]

With respect to Wilde's reception in the German-speaking lands, there is something to be learned from Kassner's casual observation, namely that 'we should not forget that he was an Englishman, and in London the aesthete is just as natural as he is superfluous in Paris, comic in Berlin and miserable in Vienna' (Kassner 1969, II: 386).[40] Wilde was not, of course, English, which almost all his German-speaking critics and admirers seem not to have known or to have ignored. There is little evidence that Berlin found the 'Englishman' comic; on the contrary, Sternheim and Mann, who stand here as representatives of the German reception, are enthralled by his political implications and by his artistic rigour, finding very little that might be amusing, indeed little that one might even describe as incongruous. Kraus, although Austrian,

---

[39] 'Der reine Ästhetizismus ist intensivster Wirkungen fähig. Oskar Wilde's "Salome" etwa ist ein Werk von unsterblicher Prägnanz und Kraft; die harte Künstlichkeit dieses aufrichtigen und aufrechten Ästhetizismus hat die Wahrheit des bösen und schönen Lebens.' The translation in the text is Bridgwater's (2002, 238).

[40] 'Man vergesse auch nicht, dass er Engländer war und in London ist der Ästhet ebenso natürlich, wie er in Paris überflüssig, in Berlin komisch und in Wien unglücklich ist.'

fits alongside them, as does Blei to an extent. As Sternheim's interest was slowly ignited, the prejudices mediated by popular clichés giving way both to admiration of Wilde's dramatic skill and artistic integrity, at almost the same time Wilde's comedies were being found wanting by Alfred Polgar in Vienna. Of a performance of *WNI* in December 1925 he wrote that, whilst the human emotions depicted are still breathtakingly beautiful, the spirit of the age has not survived: 'The scent has faded, what remains is wishy-washy; it carries now only the faintest of memories that here there was once a fragrance. The *bons mots* fly out of the dialogue like moths; meagre and sad, like rain-soaked paper chains, the paradoxes reel' (1925, 954).[41] This sentiment is certainly aptly described as melancholy. It marks a late development of a trend initiated by Bahr and Hofmannsthal, that of admiration for what might have been mixed with disappointment and frustration at Wilde's failure to live up to his promise.

---

[41]   Das Aroma ist fort, das Wässerige geblieben; nur leise Erinnerung, daß da einmal was geduftet hat, hängt noch an ihm. Wie Motten fliegen die Mots aus dem Dialog, arm und traurig, zerregnete Papiergirlanden, schwankt die Paradoxie.'

11 *Bunbury* in Germany: Alive and Kicking

Rainer Kohlmayer and Lucia Krämer

Oscar Wilde may have made fun of Germany and its reputation for seriousness in *IBE*, where the country and its language are primarily associated with plainness, arid respectability and boredom. Yet the posthumous reception of his works in Germany – together with that in France – became the main catalyst of the spread of Wilde's literary fame in the rest of Europe and, as such, it was decisive for his literary afterlife. At the time of Wilde's greatest triumphs in England, he was still relatively unknown in Germany (Schlösser 1937, 78), where awareness of him first broadened in the wake of his spectacular trials. However, Wilde's German renown was to grow 'almost in inverse proportion to its decline in Britain' (Gilman 1988, 158), so that the publication of the first edition of his complete works in German (1906–08) by Wiener actually began two years before the first volume of Robert Ross's *Works* came on the British market. Schlösser's detailed overview of English literature in Germany shows that no less than 225 editions of works by Wilde, the large majority of which were made up by his narrative prose texts, were published in Germany between 1900 and 1934 (1937, 173, 328–39). This made Wilde by far the most widely published contemporary British author of 'serious' literature and naturally spawned a large number of critical writings. Max Meyerfeld, probably the foremost early German Wilde specialist, thus revised his earlier scepticism about Wilde's potential to reach a wide German audience (1903) and claimed in 1905 that the literature on Wilde in German had 'taken on alarming proportions' ('eine schier beängstigende Ausdehnung […] angenommen') (1905, col. 985).

Not little of this interest was due to *Salomé*, which, following the success of Max Reinhardt's production of the play in 1902, became by far Wilde's most widely performed play on German stages until it was superseded by Strauss's operatic version. After this, Wilde the playwright came to be associated predominantly with his four society comedies, which have been performed thousands of times in Germany's bigger cities and provincial theatres. During Germany's changeable history in the twentieth century the plays underwent remarkable ideological transformations and were staged under the reign of Germany's last *Kaiser* and during World War I as well as in the Roaring Twenties and, even more successfully, throughout the Third Reich. They were performed time and again in the after-war years and were successful both in capitalist West Germany and communist East Germany. Today, *IBE* and *IH* continue to thrive on German stages in productions that range from flat boulevardizations to experimental appropriations by the German *Regietheater* (director's theatre). There are thus dozens of German Oscar Wildes, each one the result of some German translator, writer, editor or theatre director creating an Oscar of his or her own fashion, in response to a specific socio-cultural context. This essay will sketch a tentative history of how German theatre has responded to the consciously cultivated ambiguities and contradictions in Wilde's comedies (cf. Höfele 1999, Kohl 1980) and their consequent inter-pretative potential.

While *IBE*, whose German title has been *Bunbury* from the very beginning of its stage history, is Wilde's most popular play on German stages today, its career began with a classic false start, brought about by a combination of circumstances that was to hamper the reception of Wilde's comedies for several years. The main reason for this development was the overshadowing presence of *Salomé*, which was such a resounding success that in comparison everything else Wilde had written for the theatre seemed to shrink into insignificance. The first German translation of *Salomé* by Hedwig Lachmann appeared in the art journal *Wiener Rundschau* (Vienna review) in June 1900. The play's triumphal career on German stages began on 15 November 1902 with a performance produced by visionary actor and theatre director Max Reinhardt at the *Kleines Theater* (Small Theatre) in Berlin, whose significance for the reception of Wilde as a modernist classic as well as for the development of German theatre '[i]t would be difficult to overestimate' (Davis 2001, 154). Since an official performance of the play was impossible because Prussian censorship laws forbade the representation of biblical characters on stage (Davis 2001, 152), the play was presented in a private *matinée* performance to a hand-picked audience. Reinhardt, the shooting star of the German theatre world, had invited 300 leading German critics and artists, including, among others, Stefan George and his circle, painter Lovis Corinth and composer Richard Strauss, to see a programme consisting of the unlikely combination of *Salomé* and *IBE*.

Salome (the German version is spelled without the accent) was performed first and turned out to be an enormous success. Realizing that 'the chamber art of the modern poets' ('die Kammerkunst der modernen Dichter') (Reinhardt 1987, 31) such as Frank Wedekind, Hugo von Hofmannsthal and Wilde, required different types of acting and staging than the naturalistic theatre or the pathos-laden performances at the court theatres (Fiedler 1975, 37), Reinhardt deliberately produced *Salome* as a demonstration of his post-naturalistic theatre aesthetics. The result was a theatre of atmosphere and moods, nuances and colours, of music and splendid visual imagination, which subordinated Wilde's text to the overall atmospheric effect. *Salome*, which transferred in 1903 for a very successful run at Reinhardt's *Neues Theater* (New Theatre), can thus be considered the first striking manifestation of a new *Regietheater* and the first of Reinhardt's productions where all elements combined successfully to create a stylized theatrical *Gesamtkunstwerk* (Epstein 1984, 60). All aspects of the production were designed to contribute to its experiential quality. For example, indirect lighting instead of ramp lights enhanced the atmospheric intensity of the production, and the use of a semi-circular backdrop, instead of normal flat ones, created a new illusion of the stage as a three-dimensional space (cf. Niessen 1984). Most importantly, the great actress Gertrud Eysoldt, who would go on to play roles such as Wedekind's Lulu and Hofmannsthal's Elektra, perfectly captured the characterization of Salome as a *femme fatale* implied in Lachmann's powerful translation by stressing the archaic and animalistic traits of the character and providing her with an almost predatory sexuality (cf. Kohlmayer 1996b, 174, 178–79). Eysoldt's interpretation must be considered a key step in the process of the increasing radicalization and brutalization of the Salome character in early German adaptations, which took their inspiration from Beardsley's illustrations, and via Lachmann's translation and Eysoldt's interpretation in Reinhardt's production, would culminate in Richard Strauss's opera (Kohlmayer 1996b, 181).

The *matinée* performance of *Salome* at the *Kleines Theater* left the audience and reviewers deeply impressed. Arthur Eloesser, for example, was fascinated by 'the glowing splendour of colours; heavy with exotic odours [the play] breathes passion and putrefaction, a black mood of despair' (1902);[1] and Siegfried Jacobsohn was enthusiastic: '[t]he single performance of [...] 'Salome' resulted in a harmony of words, sounds, gestures, colours and forms, which Berlin has not experienced before and which will remain unforgettable' (quoted in Fiedler 1975, 37).[2]

After this *Salomé*, the spectators found it hard to switch emotionally to the completely different *IBE*. The critic Isidor Landau, for example, complained of the double bill as '[t]oo odd a couple: Pegasus and a cute, capering ape!' ('Ein zu ungleiches Gespann. Pegasus und ein possierlicher, Capriolen machender Affe!') (1902). The overall picture emerging from the reviews is that of a performance marked by speed and caricature, which left many spectators at a loss. Several critics attributed the play's alleged incomprehensibility to the specificity of its cultural setting: 'It is hard to say what the point of the whole thing is. Maybe only an Englishman can understand it completely' (Mahn 1902).[3] At this early stage Wilde therefore seems to have been received as a quintessentially English writer regardless of his Irishness. Even Meyerfeld labelled him an 'Engländer' (Englishman) (1903, col. 458), a term that Schlösser was still using to designate both Wilde and Shaw in 1937 (45). Due to Wilde's critical stance towards British society and his victimization

---

[1]   'von einer glühenden Pracht der Farben; von exotischen Düften schwer, haucht er Leidenschaft und Verwesung, eine Weltuntergangsstimmung'.

[2]   'Die Einzelaufführung seiner 'Salome' ergab eine Harmonie von Worten, Tönen, Gesten, Farben und Formen, die in Berlin noch nicht erlebt worden ist und unvergeßlich bleibt.'

[3]   'Es ist schwer genau zu sagen, worauf das Ganze hinauswill. Vielleicht ist es völlig nur für einen Engländer verständlich.' In a similar vein, Meyerfeld claimed in his essay 'Oscar Wilde in Deutschland' (Oscar Wilde in Germany) that in Germany there was too little knowledge of the life of London society for the nuances of Wilde's comedies to be appreciated according to their merit (1903, col. 458).

by it, his case could be used in the service of anti-British propaganda in the
context of the mounting tensions between Germany and Britain in the years
leading up to World War I. In the light of the intense appreciation Wilde
received in Germany, he fulfilled the role of a 'famous "English" writer who
had fallen foul of all the least attractive features of English society and justice,
and whose case provided opportunity alike for denigration of England and the
satisfying conviction of German cultural superiority' (Bridgwater 2002, 243).[4]
Even the fact that Wilde himself could have been considered an example of
British cultural decline (ibid.) or of 'degeneracy', as Nordau had suggested
in *Entartung* (*Degeneration*), was no obstacle for this instrumentalization: 'It is
logical that the aversion against everything English did not affect him, whom
British "cant" had made a martyr' (Schlösser 1937, 80).[5]

After Reinhardt's triumphant production, Wilde's comedies were quite
simply eclipsed by *Salomé* for several years, even though 'it was Strauss's operatic
version, a single act lasting 1 ¾ hours, which ensured Wilde's permanent entry
into the mainstream of German culture' (Blackburn 1995, 32). The first
night of Strauss's opera on 9 December 1905 in Dresden has gone down into
operatic history as one of its most outstanding successes. This contributed
to the general perception that, at this early stage, Wilde the playwright was
primarily identified as the author of *Salomé*. Another reason that strengthened
this image was the quality of the early translations of Wilde's society comedies,
which in comparison with Lachmann's monumental achievement must be
considered disappointingly poor. Felix Paul Greve, the translator of the text
of *IBE* performed alongside Reinhardt's memorable *Salomé* (cf. Kohlmayer
1996a, 24–27) and published in the first German edition of Wilde's complete
works, was a very prolific translator, who would go on to tackle several more
works by Wilde. Yet his knowledge of English was totally inadequate even
to recognize the various nuances in Wilde's virtuoso text. Greve's translation,
based on the three-act version of *IBE*, was flat and lacked the aphoristic wit
and verbal eccentricity of the original.

Unfortunately for Wilde's German career, the translations by Freiherr von
Teschenberg and Isidore Leo Pavia, which had the German stage rights in the
years after Wilde's death, were little better. The texts were first published in
1902 and 1903 by the Leipzig publishing house Max Spohr, which specialized
in homoerotic literature. Although the translators' English, in contrast to
Greve's, seems to have been good enough, their German was stilted and
wooden. Moreover, Teschenberg's translation of *IBE*, the only one he
produced without Pavia, aims at utmost literalness, which results in a bureaucratic kind of German that may be suitable for Lady Brancaster – Teschenberg
probably translated the lost four-act manuscript version that Wilde originally
delivered to George Alexander (cf. Kohlmayer 1996a, 128) – but robs the four
young lovers of their verbal elegance.

---

[4]   See also Pfister's remarks on the anti-British impulse of the early German Wilde
      reception (1986, 13f.).
[5]   'Es leuchtet ein, daß sich der Widerwille gegen alles Englische nicht auch auf ihn
      auswirkte, den der britische 'cant' zum Märtyrer hatte werden lassen.'

The insufficiencies of the Pavia/Teschenberg translations provided producers of the plays with a good excuse for changing more than mere stylistic niceties. Thus in the first German productions of *IH* in Munich (1905, *Residenztheater*) and Hamburg (1906, *Thalia Theater*) the vital letter scene in the last act was simply cut out. Entirely new reading versions of the four comedies appeared in 1908 as part of the Wiener edition of Wilde's complete works. Although these translations by Alfred Brieger (*LWF*), Greve (*WNI* and *IBE*) and Alfred Neumann (*IH*) were superior to the Pavia/Teschenberg text, they were barred from theatrical production for copyright reasons. They could, however, be used as a source of inspiration by theatre producers and directors.

Yet another reason for the initial denigration of Wilde's comedies lay in André Gide's biographical essay 'Oscar Wilde' (1902), which was first published in German in 1903. It contained Wilde's famous dictum that he had put his genius into his life and only his talent into his works and quoted Wilde as saying that his comedies were not quality work but potboilers and written almost exclusively as the consequence of bets. Gide's footnote anecdote about the literary worthlessness of Wilde's comedies did enormous harm to their reception in Germany, where the essay was read as an authentic document. Moreover, Carl Hagemann based his own criticism of the plays on Gide's in his influential *Oscar Wilde* (1904), the first comprehensive study of Wilde in German, and consequently presented them as mere 'Schwankfutter' (low burlesque) (83). Wilde's early reception in Germany thus developed in a completely opposite direction to that in Britain, since the German Wilde began as a great tragic poet whereas his comedies had to overcome several obstacles before they were accepted.

In the case of *IBE*, one important stepping stone in this process was a production by Richard Vallentin, Reinhardt's former rival in Berlin, at the *Deutsches Volkstheater* in Vienna (see also Sandra Mayer's essay in this volume). Vallentin considerably shortened Teschenberg's four-act version, cutting it down to three acts, and corrected many shortcomings in the translation. The remaining verbal inadequacies were put to good ironical use since all the actors were made to speak with an English accent. This device stressed the play's Englishness and created a comic impression of linguistic snobbery. In another effort to overcome the lack of verbal comedy of Teschenberg's text, Vallentin emphasized the play's situation comedy and replaced dialogue with visual humour, thus turning the dandiacal couples into Harlequin-like puppets in the local Viennese tradition.

1906 saw another successful revision of Teschenberg's text, fabricated by German writer Franz Blei together with Carl Zeiß, director of the Dresden *Königliches Schauspielhaus* (Royal Playhouse). Probably with the help of an English three-act version of the play (cf. Kohlmayer 1996a, 190), Blei and Zeiß produced a *Bunbury* in three acts, in which the eccentricities of the characters were toned down and anything that could be considered too British was radically cut from the text. The Dresden production was the first to focus on the aestheticist and dandiacal qualities of Wilde's play. Its celebration of the social elegance of aristocratic life, however, meant the excision of most of its satirical aspects. Vallentin's rather burlesque Viennese adaptation and Blei and Zeiß's Dresden version, which presented *IBE* as a highly elegant social game, were to become the main two models of *Bunbury* available for the German stage after 1906.

In the following years, all of Wilde's society comedies saw several successful individual productions. Yet World War I, partly coinciding with German expressionism, was no fertile ground for the plays. The so-called *Wedekindjahrzehnt* (Wedekind's decade) of German theatre favoured a more ecstatic, radical and brutal kind of play and acting. Among Wilde's plays, especially *Bunbury*, the most contested and least understood of the society comedies, seems to have gone stale: for the period from 1908 to 1919 only two productions of *IBE* are documented in important German theatre cities: 1913–14 in Frankfurt a. M. (*Neues Theater*) and 1917–18 in Munich (*Kammerspiele*).

In the 1920s, however, the play saw an astonishing renaissance, due to one of the greatest German actresses of the *fin de siècle*. Adele Sandrock had been the most famous tragic actress around 1900 and had been celebrated for her interpretation of roles such as Medea and Phedre. After being ruined by the end of World War I, with her face wrinkled beyond recognition and her voice changed into a masculine-sounding bass, Sandrock saw herself obliged to perform in Berlin cabarets. When she accepted to play the role of Lady Brancaster in a Berlin production of *Bunbury* of 1920, however, she embarked on an entirely new career as one of Germany's greatest comic actresses and became even more famous in her old age than she had been in her prime as a tragedienne. Sandrock's overwhelming stage presence even made some critics claim that it was only due to her acting that Wilde's plays were still alive in Germany. Monty Jacobs (1929), for example, opined that 'Adele Sandrock is worth the resurrection of *Bunbury*' ('Adele Sandrock ist wert, daß *Bunbury* […] aufersteht'). For fourteen years, Sandrock played Lady Brancaster hundreds of times, mainly in Berlin and Vienna. Her influence on the German reception of *IBE* cannot be overestimated, since she virtually put the character of Lady Brancaster on the critical map. Before 1920, due to the deficiencies of Teschenberg's text, most dramaturges had radically cut down the character, who was then interpreted as a conventional society lady and to whom the critics paid little attention. Yet in Sandrock's interpretation Lady Brancaster became the central figure of the play, as was reflected in the theatre programmes, where the sequence of the cast was modified accordingly.

On the one hand, Sandrock's performance was highly self-reflexive, since she drew on her former fame as a tragic actress to undermine her own stature and thus increase the comic potential of her performance. On the other hand, she also perfectly captured the comically grotesque nature of Lady Bracknell and turned her into an 'aristocratic monster-aunt' ('aristokratisches Tantenungetüm') (Servaes 1929). Sandrock's deep voice, her old-fashioned costumes, which put her into deliberately anachronistic contrast with her fellow-actors, and her pseudo-heroic gestures (cf. Pinthus 1929) as well as her steely authority and domineering presence of mind and body resulted in an almost masculine performance that perfectly conveyed the character's function as a caricature of conservative authority and Darwinist social elitism.

Such an interpretation fitted well into the context of the 1920s and the Weimar Republic, as Wilde came to be associated with the political Left. Thus when the Wiener edition of the complete works was reprinted in a popular two-volume version in 1930, its editor, Arnold Zweig, one of the later founding fathers of the German Democratic Republic, located Wilde firmly in a Socialist tradition. In his introductory essay he declared Georg Büchner and Heinrich Mann to be Wilde's closest spiritual allies and presented Wilde's essay SMUS as the central and lasting statement of his world-view.

The message of individualism projected by Wilde's life and oeuvre was also central for the interpretation of Wilde in the biographical drama *Oskar Wilde* (*sic.*) by Carl Sternheim, which was first performed on 31 March 1925 at the *Deutsches Theater* (German Theatre) in Berlin. With this play Sternheim, who is best known for his satirical comedy cycle 'Aus dem bürgerlichen Heldenleben' (From the heroic life of the bourgeoisie), created one of the earliest fictional biographies of Wilde in a deliberate attempt to complement the biographical writings already in existence (cf. Sternheim 1964, 269–70).

Sternheim's drama is a perfect example of fictional biography as appropriation, since, both stylistically and ideologically, Wilde as an artist is modelled in Sternheim's image. The play alludes to *IBE*, for example, and its Wilde character tells the story of 'The Disciple', yet linguistically the style is pure Sternheim. Moreover, Wilde is used as a symbol of individualism and rebelliousness, in keeping with the author's concept of the outstanding artist as innovator and rebel. Thus in his preface to the play, which bears the motto 'Was nottut ist Individualismus!' (There's a need for individualism), Sternheim presents Wilde as a prime representative of what he called 'Privatkurage', the courage to stand up against the establishment and to challenge the upper classes with an independent spirit.

The idiosyncrasy of Sternheim's drama lies in his explanation of Wilde's behaviour, which goes beyond former attempts at excusing or justifying him. According to Sternheim, the true motivation for Wilde's erotic relationships with men was that Wilde wanted to turn away from 'the ugly' as represented by women, towards man as the embodiment of 'beauty'. This interpretation is based on the author's misogynist view of woman as an incarnation of waste, who makes no contribution to the nation or to the private property of her family, but instead abuses through her whims all the male righteousness that she is offered (271).

Sternheim thus transcended the individual case of the historical Wilde to appropriate him as a representative and carrier of (his own) ideas. In keeping with earlier German texts on Wilde, Sternheim combined this appropriation with a decidedly anti-British stance and unequivocally represented France as a safe haven where Wilde could escape English Puritanism, hypocrisy, stupidity and mediocrity (314, 322). Sternheim even went so far as to imply that the deficiencies in English society stemmed from essential faults in the character of the English people to whom he ascribed qualities such as 'idiocy' ('Stumpfsinn', 335), barbarity, maliciousness and a thirst for blood (357).

Despite Wilde's celebration as a champion of individualism by writers as different as Sternheim and Arnold Zweig, his comedies went on to become perfectly integrated into the theatre world of the Third Reich; Wilde even became the most frequently performed author of the theatre season 1936–37 (Pitsch 1952, 245). This was mainly an achievement of the German translator and dramaturge Karl Lerbs, who managed to safeguard Wilde's presence in the hostile context of the Third Reich, but paid for it by transforming Wilde into a champion of collectivism and moral conformism.

The tenor of Lerbs's versions of *LWF*, *WNI* and *IH* – he did not tackle the more subversive *IBE* – can be gleaned from two short essays by Lerbs which were regularly printed in theatre programmes. In 'Warum spielen wir heute Oscar Wilde?' (Why do we perform Oscar Wilde today?) and 'Der zeitnahe Wilde' (The contemporary Wilde) Wilde's individualism is roundly turned on its head. Thus Lerbs claims that in Wilde's plays 'the mockers, the cynics, the shameless egomaniacs are annihilated' (1935).[6] He also practically declares Wilde to be a forerunner of National Socialism since in his plays 'the coming great conflict of the irresponsible with the responsible is foreseen and solved in favour of a future-oriented responsibility' (1935).[7] Lerbs's justification for this interpretation of Wilde and for his translations lies in the claim that he is recovering an authentic Wilde whose 'image has been put in a completely false light by almost four decades of interpretation' (1935).[8]

Possibly the two most striking tendencies in Lerbs's translations are the heroification of man and woman and the adaptation of the ethnic-nationalist (*völkisch*) social model of National Socialism. In *IH*, for example, Wilde's dandies are made to display soldierly self-discipline and Nietzschean will-power. Thus Lerbs adds stage directions ordering the characters to speak 'strongly', 'with fanatical resolve' or 'with a steely tension of will'[9], and he describes Lord Goring as a 'spotless dandy of best breeding' (Wilde 1935a, 19)[10] – the word *breeding* connoting biological and military selection and discipline.

Lerbs's ideal women, in contrast, are more independent and emancipated than in Wilde's texts and thus closer to Lerbs's male ideal. In his translation of *WNI*, for example, Lerbs thoroughly re-wrote the climax scene, in which Hester storms into the room after Lord Illingworth has tried to kiss her. In Wilde's text, Hester is running from Illingworth in almost neurotic panic and seeks protection from Gerald. In Lerbs's text, in contrast, she appears much more independent, even claiming 'I can protect myself against insults' ('Ich kann mich allein schützen, wenn man mich beleidigt') (Wilde 1934a, 107), and distances herself contemptuously from Illingworth. The psychological contrast between the two characters has been changed into an ideological one, where Illingworth, the prototypical Decadent, is overcome by the emancipated yet ideologically orthodox Hester.

---

6   'In ihnen werden die Spötter, die Zyniker, die hemmungslosen Ichmenschen vernichtend geschlagen.'

7   'die kommende große Auseinandersetzung der Verantwortungslosen mit den Verantwortungsbewußten vorgeahnt und zugunsten zukunftstragender Verantwortung entschieden.'

8   'Bild [...] durch eine Überlieferung von fast vier Jahrzehnten für uns Heutige in ein völlig falsches Licht gerückt ist.'

9   'stark', 'mit fanatischer Entschlossenheit', 'mit stählerner Gespanntheit des Willens'.

10 'makellose Dandy bester Zucht'.

Subordination is the reverse side of the coin of Lerbs's transformation of the positive male and female characters in Wilde's plays into heroes. Thus, in his *LWF* and *WNI* the females-as-heroes, Mrs Erlynne and Mrs Arbuthnot, are portrayed chiefly as mothers prepared for sacrifice and struggle, while their other character traits are suppressed. Lerbs's manipulations are most obvious, however, in his version of *IH*, where he fundamentally changed the moral balance between the dandy Lord Goring and Robert Chiltern. Goring's dandy's mask now conceals an authoritarian officer, while Wilde's psychologically damaged Chiltern, whose 'passion for power' led to a fatal mistake in his youth, becomes a charismatic politician gifted with a 'will for power and achievement' (Wilde 1935a, 54).[11] In the last act, Lord Goring even becomes a propagandist for Robert Chiltern: in contrast to Wilde's original, where Goring asks Gertrude to love and forgive her husband, Lerbs's dandy charges her with 'the great duty of carrying the work of her husband to completion' (151).[12] In the context of the year of composition, Goring's advice to Gertrude sounds like instructions for the audience concerning the ideologically correct attitude of heroic subordination to the goals of a charismatic political *Führer*.

Stage performances of Lerbs's translations were not always as soldierly as the texts suggested, and the critics were not unanimous in their reaction to Lerbs's morality lessons. One reviewer of the 1936 Mannheim production of *WNI* wrote that '[t]he performance remained a hybrid, as most actors were not Wilde's, but seemed removed from him and his spirit. The adaptation may be partly to blame for this' (C. O. E. 1936).[13] Otto Küster reacted to a Hamburg performance of *IH* in 1935 in a similar vein:

> So Wilde the mocker is turned into a prosecutor and world-improver. One can see Wilde like that, but it is not necessary, and hardly an improvement [...]. The result: three hours of lecturing, seriously meant by Lerbs, delivered to the people via Lord Goring-Wilde [...]. During it one frequently finds oneself recalling – and not without a certain fondness, it has to be said – the times when he still walked through life breezily and merrily.[14]

Reviewing a Berlin performance, the official party paper *Völkischer Beobachter* (National observer), in contrast, praised Lerbs's black-and-white depiction: 'The woman with her purity, with her authenticity and honesty, with her

---

11 'Willen [...] zur Macht und zur Leistung'– thus Lerbs's ideologizing translation of the original 'passion for power'.
12 'die grosse Pflicht, die Arbeit des Mannes ans Ziel zu tragen.'
13 'Die Aufführung blieb ein Zwitter, weil die meisten Darsteller nicht bei Wilde standen, sondern ihm und seinem Geist entfremdet schienen. Daran mag die Bearbeitung einen Teil der Schuld tragen.'
14 'Der Spötter Wilde wird bei Lerbs also zum Ankläger und Weltverbesserer. Man kann Wilde so sehen, notwendig ist es nicht und besser – kaum [...]. Ergebnis: drei Stunden einer von Lerbs ernst gemeinten Belehrung des Volkes durch Lord Goring-Wilde [...]. Man denkt dabei – und nicht einmal ungern – öfter an die Zeiten zurück, da er noch hurtig und lustig durch das Leben lief.'

belief and her passion, defeats Lord Illingworth who is representative of a whole caste, the epitome of the salon' (Rainalter 1936).[15]

Lerbs's ideological conformism was the main reason for the strong presence of Wilde on German stages during the years of the Third Reich. Yet there was another important strategy that made Wilde performable in the context of National Socialist censorship: aesthetic escapism. In the case of the subversive *IBE*, the text of choice for such an approach was Blei and Zeiß's elegant version that cut the social criticism from the play and left only its playful and fairy-tale qualities. This was also the text used in the production by Paul Bildt, which premiered in Gustaf Gründgens's Berlin *Staatstheater* (State Theatre) on 10 April 1937. According to the critics, the costumes were 'inimitably elegant' ('von unnachahmlicher Eleganz') (Otte 1937) and the stage designs ravishingly beautiful (cf. Krünes 1937). The magnificent production design and the splendid performances, with Hermine Körner creating a highly elegant counter-version to Sandrock's Lady Brancaster, were a demonstration of the schizophrenic state of the arts during the Third Reich: art could provide an aesthetic legitimation of the power of the Nazis, while, to the artists remaining in Germany, it could serve as a utopian escape from reality. In the Berlin production, whose first night was attended by Hermann Göhring and his wife, Wilde's most subversive play was transformed into a perfectly harmless operetta or elegant fairy-tale, in which moral conformism and aesthetic escapism coincided, in accordance with Gründgens's attempt to hold on to a strictly non-political, purely aesthetic interpretation of art.

Despite the strictures of Nazi censorship, Ernst Sander managed to create a remarkable version of *IBE* in 1935, which dared to make fun of Nazi ideology. Even more pointedly than Lerbs, in *Vor allem Ernst! (Bunbury)* he transposed the play right into the present and the cultural context of Nazi Germany. He modernized Wilde's play through references to, for example, telephones, the radio, the League of Nations or Hindemith's music, and provided his dandies with dashing and sometimes colloquial present-day language. Sander went even further in making the play topical, however, by including ironic allusions to central institutions and ideologemes of Nazism, most importantly its policies concerning 'racial purity'. He cut the most obviously authoritarian and proto-fascist traits in Wilde's Lady Bracknell, and therefore for example deleted her speech against 'the modern sympathy with invalids. I consider it morbid. Illness of any kind is hardly a thing to be encouraged in others. Health is the primary duty of life' (Wilde 1990, 19). Such a speech would have sounded too much like a comically grotesque affirmation of the Law for the Prevention of Hereditarily Diseased Offspring of 1933 and thus like a monumental caricature of National Socialism. Yet Sander bravely included several more covertly ironical allusions. For example, when Jack assures Lady Bracknell of Cecily's immaculate background, he enumerates her 'certificates of birth and baptism, those of the parents, the four grandparents and

---

15   'Die Frau siegt mit ihrer Reinheit, mit ihrer Echtheit und Ehrlichkeit, mit ihrem Glauben und ihrer Leidenschaft über Lord Illingworth, der eine ganze Kaste, der den Salon schlechthin repräsentiert.'

eight great-grandparents' (Wilde 1935b, 143),[16] thus alluding to the 1935 Nuremberg Race Laws and ridiculing the Nazis' bureaucratic perfectionism.

Sander's Lady Bracknell has individualistic character traits that transcend her role as the comic representative of orthodox ideology. She may express a dislike of Marxism, yet she occasionally expresses the same subversive individualism as Wilde's dandies, for example when she claims that 'clever people do not have to be good. They can pretend' (1935b, 147).[17] Moreover, Sander introduced various aphorisms of his own into the text, such as '[e]ven the most exalted principles do not give anybody the right to sacrifice anybody but oneself' (1935b, 136).[18] Through these devices Sander effectually created a text with the liberating message that art and private life can represent reserves of individual freedom even in the face of the overwhelming presence of Nazism.

When this subversive text was first performed on 31 October 1935 at the Hamburg *Neues Theater* (New Theatre), about half the critics, and the audience, were delighted:

> He has turned the comedy into a piece about the present, which all members of the audience with a sense of humour will find 'suitable'. One can feel the humour, the hint of acerbity just as much as the literary elegance of the journalist and novelist Ernst Sander, and therefore he was able to register a splendid success at the *Neues Theater* – especially with his small topical allusions [...]. (A. 1935)[19]

Others were rather put off or, like the *Völkischer Beobachter*, disgusted: 'We cannot agree with Ernst Sander's adaptation [...]. Oscar Wilde has nothing to say to us today. His little flashes of wit could delight an audience thirty years ago' (ze. 1935).[20] More explicitly, Wolf Schramm criticized a lack of 'subordination under an idea and the sense of community' (1935).[21]

When Sander's text was staged again at the Vienna *Burgtheater* (Palace Theatre) in October 1938, half a year after Austria's *Anschluß* into Greater Germany, most of the ironical allusions that Sander had smuggled into the text were removed and the performance reduced to a 'fashion show of the Burgtheater's great tradition of diction' ('Modeschau des guten Burgtheatertons') (Barcata

---

16 'Geburtsschein und Taufschein, die der Eltern, der vier Großeltern und acht Urgroßeltern.'

17 'kluge Menschen brauchen nicht gut zu sein. Die können simulieren.'

18 'Auch um der erhabensten Grundsätze willen hat niemand das Recht, jemand anders als sich selbst zu opfern.'

19 'Er hat aus der [...] Komödie [...] ein Gegenwartsstück gemacht, das allen humorigen Hörern 'passend' vorkommen dürfte. Man spürt den Humor, die kleine Bissigkeit, genau so wie die schriftstellerische Eleganz des [...] Journalisten und Romanschriftstellers Ernst Sander, und so konnte er im *Neuen Theater* – besonders mit seinen kleinen aktuellen Anspielungen – einen vollen Erfolg buchen.'

20 'Mit der Bearbeitung Ernst Sanders können wir uns nicht einverstanden erklären [...]. Oscar Wilde hat uns heute nichts mehr zu sagen. Seine Geistreicheleien konnten ein Publikum vor 30 Jahren begeistern.'

21 'Unterordnung unter eine Idee und den Gemeinschaftssinn'.

1938). The same kind of domestication occurred when the *Complete Works* were reprinted in 1937 and Arnold Zweig's introduction was replaced by another of exactly the same length by Wolfgang Goetz, which assured the reader of Wilde's political harmlessness.

During the Third Reich, the prevailing approach to Wilde was thus to reduce the openness of the texts of Wilde's works and life to a specific meaning in accordance with the dominant ideology.[22] Unsurprisingly, the same mechanism applied to Wilde's reception in the German Democratic Republic, where Wilde could be published if he was presented to fit into the current cultural policies, although his personal attitudes, aestheticist view of art and homosexuality contrasted starkly with the prevailing ideology of Socialism (cf. Giovanopoulos 2002, 275). As Giovanopoulos has shown, the censorship system in the GDR, where publishers, academics and government and party censors negotiated the meaning of texts in a complex web of evaluations, was flexible enough to accommodate Wilde if he was presented from a Marxist perspective, which basically meant that editions of any of his works had to present Wilde himself as a representative of the decadent bourgeoisie and point out instances of social criticism in his work (2002, 278). Wilde's life-style and his aestheticism had to be neglected (2002, 281). This ideological reduction of Wilde could be conveyed either in texts accompanying the actual translation, such as prefaces or postscripts, or in the translation itself. Kurt Jung-Alsen's 1973 version of *IH*, for example, contained several deliberate changes of the original to make Wilde subservient to the aesthetics of socialist realism. Most importantly, Jung-Alsen presents the characters as determined by their class and guides the sympathy against the individualistic dandy Lord Goring, who appears as a representative of imperialist class interests and as an ideological enemy of the people (cf. Kohlmayer 1991, 452–55).

It was in Christine Hoeppener's more neutral translations from 1975 however, that Wilde's plays would rise to the top of the list of best-selling books in the GDR in 1976. Hoeppener was one of several translators along with Paul Baudisch, Siegfried Schmitz, Rainer Kohlmayer and Hans Wollschläger who in the seventies and eighties produced new and reliable translations that drove back the use of secondary and tertiary texts – often updated or plagiarized Teschenberg versions – on the basis of which Wilde's comedies had usually been staged in the years after World War II. Further continuities with pre-war interpretations of Wilde had been visible in the continued use of Lerbs's versions of Wilde's 'serious' comedies, at least in the German provinces, throughout the 1950s. The most obvious tendency in the German reception of Wilde's comedies after World War II, however, was the reduction of the plays to the level of boulevard theatre. In the tradition of Hagemann's characterization of Wilde's comedies as 'Schwankfutter', the plays were predominantly presented as one-dimensional entertainment. There was a general tendency not to recognize or systematically to reduce the aggressive

---

[22] For information about the less ideologically orthodox film adaptations of Wilde's plays during the Nazi period see Kohlmayer 1996a, 236–38.

subtext of Wilde's humour and the anarchical hostility against authorities inherent especially in *IBE* (Kohlmayer 1993, 384).

In this de-politicized shape, Wilde did obviously not fit into the politically conscious climate of the 1960s, during which his comedies practically disappeared from the programmes of the larger German theatres. *WNI* and, to a lesser degree, *LWF*, whose sentimental mother figures had appealed strongly to the German public from 1934 to about 1960, have fared worse than Wilde's last two comedies and, apart from rare productions, have today largely disappeared from the German stage. Yet *IH* and *IBE* are still regularly performed, with *IBE* clearly taking the lion share of the new Wilde productions, in particular those at important theatres.

Even today, the notion of Wilde as an author of harmless entertainment theatre keeps haunting his German reception. Renowned theatre critic Joachim Kaiser, for example, found it imperative to emphasize in his review of a non-experimental, historicizing production of *IBE* in the *Kleine Komödie* (Small Comedy) in Munich in 1984 that the play 'is neither a divine comic entertainment nor an event of infernal burlesque, but takes a moderate place in the middle.'[23] Ulrich Deuter showed a similar abhorrence of the boulevardized Wilde in his review of Thirza Bruncken's 1998 production of *IBE* in Bonn, praising the performance for not stooping to 'the most awful thing that Wilde can be turned into: the boulevard.'[24] Yet, in her review of Bettina Bruinier's 2006 production of the same play at the Berlin *Deutsches Theater*, *Tagesspiegel* (Daily mirror) critic Christine Wahl called Wilde's play a 'witty drawing-room burlesque' ('wortwitzige Salonklamotte'), despite Bruinier's constant use of alienating devices, which in accordance with Wilde's own meta-theatrical exaggeration of the conventions of melodrama, break through the imaginary fourth wall between the audience and the fictional world of the play and thus emphasize the performative nature of both theatre and real life.

The view of *IBE* as a burlesque is one variation of the notion of Wilde as an entertainer, and it has even fed into productions by some of the more renowned representatives of the German *Regietheater* such as Leander Haußmann, whose 1994 interpretation of *Bunbury* in Munich introduced various slapstick elements into the play. Peter Zadek assaulted the audience's pre-conceptions in his 1980 production at the *Freie Volksbühne* (Free People's Stage) in Berlin with the off-stage defloration of a very child-like Cecily who appeared as a symbol of idyllic innocence. However, though it was variously praised (e.g. Göpfert 1980), this production too was accused of 'roughening up Wilde's play into a burlesque' ('bis zur Burleske auf[ge]rauht') (Wirsing 1980).

This tendency is not all-pervasive. For example, the minimalist production of *Bunbury* by Werner Düggelin, which premiered at the *Züricher Schauspielhaus* (Zurich Playhouse) on 30 September 2006, cut Wilde's text so radically that

---

[23] 'Es ist weder ein himmlisches Komödien-Vergnügen noch eine höllische Klamotten-Veranstaltung, sondern liegt hübsch bescheiden in der Mitte'.

[24] 'Kurz, wir sehen das Furchtbarste, was man aus Wilde machen kann, nicht: den Boulevard.'

the play assumed an enigmatic air reminiscent of the theatre of the absurd. Due to a consistent strategy of reduction on the levels of dialogue and production design, it gave the impression of an elegant celebration of the anarchical acerbity of Wilde's language and his modernity. In contrast, Elfriede Jelinek's version of the play, *Ernst ist das Leben (Bunbury)* (Life is earnest – Bunbury), which was first produced at the Vienna *Akademietheater* (Academy Theatre) in 2005, might be interpreted as yet a step further in the process of the re-invention of *IBE* as a burlesque, due to Jelinek's in-yer-face sexualization of Wilde's language and characters and her aggressively low-brow approach to Wilde's wit.[25] Yet Jelinek's device of bringing Wilde's high-flying style down to earth can also be regarded as a deliberate reflection on the conventions of comedy, and her over-fulfilment of the idea of Wilde as a jokester effectively problematizes this very perception of the writer. Despite the almost unanimously negative reviews of this production in the German press and accusations that both Jelinek and director Falk Richter were unfair or unfaithful towards Wilde's original (e.g. cf. Krug 2005), several recent German productions of *IBE* have already been based on Jelinek's version. After the many re-inventions of Wilde in Germany during the twentieth century, Jelinek's *Ernst ist das Leben* thus represents yet another appropriation of Wilde to the artistic and ideological universe of a translator or adaptor, which in turn spawns its own adaptations that add to the ever increasing multitude of conceptualizations of Wilde and his most famous comedy.

---

[25]　For a fuller analysis of this production see Sandra Mayer's essay in this volume.

12 When Critics Disagree, the Artist Survives: Oscar Wilde, an All-Time Favourite of the Viennese Stage in the Twentieth Century

Sandra Mayer

Setting the scene: Wilde enters the Viennese stage

In an article that appeared in the Viennese newspaper *Neue Freie Presse* (New free press) on 23 April 1905, Bernard Shaw offered a characteristically double-edged explanation for his Irish compatriot and fellow dramatist Oscar Wilde's popularity in Vienna:

> In Vienna, I will not be understood for at least another one hundred years, because I am part of the twentieth century [...]. But Vienna will more easily get used to the style of Oscar Wilde, for not only did Oscar Wilde embody the artistic culture of the eighteenth century, but he also showed a very mundane inclination towards wealth, luxury and elegance [...]. Seeing that Vienna, apart from Paris, is the most regressive city in Europe, though it still considers itself an 'enfant de son siècle par excellence', it ought to appreciate Oscar Wilde far more greatly than he will ever be appreciated anywhere in Germany or England (38).[1]

Indeed, the data compiled by the University of Vienna research project *Weltbühne Wien – World Stage Vienna* on the reception of Anglophone plays

---

[1] 'In Wien werde ich zumindest noch weitere hundert Jahre nicht verstanden werden, denn ich gehöre dem zwanzigsten Jahrhundert an [...]. Aber mit der Art Oskar Wildes wird sich Wien viel leichter befreunden, denn Oskar Wilde besaß nicht nur die künstlerische Kultur des achtzehnten Jahrhunderts, sondern auch eine sehr weltliche Vorliebe für Reichtum, Luxus und Eleganz [...]. Und da Wien nach Paris die unmodernste Stadt Europas ist und sich dabei doch für ein "enfant de son siècle par excellence" hält, so sollte Wien Oskar Wilde besser zu schätzen wissen, als er jemals irgendwo in Deutschland oder in England geschätzt werden wird'.

on twentieth-century Viennese stages reveal that, throughout the twentieth century and up to the present, on average every two to three years one of Wilde's plays has been produced by some major Viennese theatre. The society comedies, which reflect the author's attempt to strike a fragile balance between accomplished self-invention, professional recognition and commercial success, have found prevailing favour with Viennese audiences. However, it is intriguing to observe that the early reception and discussion of Wilde and his works already constituted a common denominator among the close-knit and dynamically interacting network of Viennese intellectuals, long before the 'flying Irishman' ('fliegender Irländer'), as Wilde is commendatorily referred to by Anton Lindner in an early journalistic evaluation of 1903 (12), produced a lasting imprint on the Austro-Hungarian capital's theatrical landscape. Notably, almost one decade prior to Wilde's introduction to Viennese theatre audiences with the premiere of *Salomé* on 12 December 1903, Hermann Bahr, one of the main catalysts and agents of European Modernism within the 'Young Vienna' movement (Daviau 2001, 13), dedicated a lengthy essay to the Anglo-Irish writer in the liberal weekly *Die Zeit* (The time). Suggesting that Wilde's fame rested on his notorious public persona to a greater extent than on the literary merits of his writings, it laid the foundation of one of the major currents in the German and Austrian reception (Bahr 1894, 87–89).

In Vienna as elsewhere, interest in Wilde's work and personal life was fuelled by the broad coverage of the author's spectacular court case, subsequent prison sentence and untimely death (Bridgwater 1999, 48). Wilde became subject to much public curiosity, lurid sensationalism and ideological instrumentalization. The Viennese *fin-de-siècle* reception of Wilde's writings (including, to a lesser extent, his society comedies) was thus dominated by a sense of inseparable interdependence of the writer's life and work.

However, it seems as if Wilde's aesthetic theories, influenced by French Symbolism, 'found considerably more resonance in Francophile Vienna (and Munich) than in Francophobe Berlin' (Bridgwater 1999, 47), more naturally harmonizing with and fertilizing the local artistic avant-garde. Thus, the Viennese *fin-de-siècle* affinity with Parisian Symbolism and basic orientation towards the aesthetic theories of French Decadence may have eased the transfer of *Salomé* into the Austrian theatre scene, even though, as censorship records and contemporary press reviews imply, the play was read and perceived within a context of disease, sexual aberration and pathological degeneration (Gilman 1988, 55).[2] While in Berlin *Salomé* had initially been banned from public performance, the Viennese authorities, not without prescribing a host of textual amendments and modifications, eventually licensed the play for

---

[2]   The recommendations delivered by the Austrian censorship authorities reveal that *Salomé* was regarded as essentially indicative of Wilde's public image of moral degeneracy. In a statement issued by the police official in charge of theatre censorship, following the submission of the play's textbook in March 1903, objections are raised on account of the fact that the author had been publicly designated a sexual pervert, and therefore traces of his morbid inclinations were to be detected in his work (Mayer and Pfeifer 2007, 63).

production at the *Deutsches Volkstheater* (German People's Theatre), which had developed a reputation for its artistically ambitious repertory, particularly focussing on contemporary English drama (Weiss 1999, 346). Entirely in tune with the scandal-tainted history of the play, the Viennese production met with a mixed reception: as the police report on the performance notes, violent protest alternated with roaring applause (Mayer and Pfeifer 2007, 65).

In this context, it appears that Wilde's Symbolist one-act tragedy did not generate much interest beyond its pan-European *fin-de-siècle* craze, which attracted the attention, among others, of the Canadian-born dancer Maud Allan. Before touring other European capitals, her legendary performance act entitled 'Visions of Salome' had its public premiere in Vienna on 30 December 1906, and was primarily noted on account of Allan's rather revealing costume. Eventually eclipsed in fame and popularity by Richard Strauss's operatic version, *Salomé* more or less disappeared from the Viennese theatres. A 1906 revival of the original production was followed by two smaller-scale productions – again at the *Deutsches Volkstheater* and the *Neue Wiener Bühne* (New Viennese Stage) in 1913 – and a widely-noted guest performance of Alexander Tairov's Moscow Chamber Theatre in 1925. It was to take almost eighty years for Wilde's play, then in its German adaptation by the Austrian poet Gerhard Rühm, to reappear on the stage of one of the major Viennese theatres in 2004.

1905. *Eine triviale Komödie für seriöse Leute*: shares of aphoristic wit on the Viennese theatre stock market

Oscar Wilde's society comedies quickly established themselves as periodically revived all-time classics on the Viennese stages, where they were largely perceived as apolitical farces toying with social gesture and convention. From the very beginning they invited a broad spectrum of reactions, frequently revealing a striking gap between critical and audience reception. In the case of Wilde, critics and audience were unaccustomed to his paradoxical humour and they were mildly puzzled by the novelty of the dramatist's comic inversions of norms, social conventions and traditions. It has been convincingly argued that the early reception of Wilde's comedies in Vienna was influenced by the reverse chronological sequencing of their first Viennese productions in relation to the plays' London premieres (Weiss 1999, 379). Thus, it was Wilde's final comedy and commonly acknowledged masterpiece *IBE* that was to follow *Salomé*, first entering the Viennese theatre scene under its translated subtitle *Eine triviale Komödie für seriöse Leute* (A trivial comedy for serious people) on 9 December 1905. Coincidentally, this was the day of the Dresden premiere of Strauss's opera. *IBE* was soon followed, in November 1906, by the unprecedented box-office success of *Ein idealer Gatte* (*IH*), the most frequently performed English play in the first decade of the twentieth century (Weiss 1999, 347), and almost simultaneously, in early 1907, by *Lady Windermeres Fächer* (*LWF*) and *Eine Frau ohne Bedeutung* (*WNI*).[3]

---

[3]   In addition to these, *Eine florentinische Tragödie* (FT) enjoyed only a brief spell of interest between 1907 and 1910.

The Viennese reactions to *IBE*'s first production at the *Deutsches Volkstheater*, directed by Richard Vallentin,[4] followed the pattern of the critical reception of the London premiere of the play ten years earlier: they present a mixed array of eloquent praise, downright perplexity and evident misconception. Wilde's 'comic anarchy' (Gordon 1998, 132) came as a startling novelty and some critics failed to warm to his subversive concept of 'comedy for comedy's sake'. Others conceived the comedy as what it was: a satire on upper-class manners bordering on the farcical and surreal, geared at undermining social as well as theatrical conventions, concepts of dramatic genre and Victorian ideals of moral and intellectual seriousness. Ludwig Hevesi of the *Fremden-Blatt* (Foreigners' paper) commends Wilde's sparkling dialogue and notes his satirical intertextual citation of popular literature and conventional dramatic motifs and devices:

> He does not forge a plot of his own creative invention but, with a significant measure of smart parody, knocks one together from the plots of familiar comedies and novels. He builds a framework out of inane and well-worn elements to be found in mediocre literary works but crowns it with the most colourful floral wreaths of his arabesque whims. (1905, 17)[5]

For the anonymous critic of the *Illustrirtes Wiener Extrablatt* (Illustrated Viennese supplement), Wilde's verbal darts are primarily aimed at the London upper-class social microcosm, rendering the play a

> parody on everything good and precious to London society, which really means everything bad and worthless, a parody on English virgins displaying their hollow masks of propriety, on education and marriage, on bigotry and social prudery [...] and, eventually, on wantonly proliferating melodrama. ('Theaterzeitung: Deutsches Volkstheater' 1905, 9)[6]

Similarly, the critic of the *Deutsches Volksblatt* (German people's paper) comments on the author's tendency to make fun of himself, his play and its audience, who, in turn, is expected to derive great amusement from the caricature of English society depicted on stage ('Deutsches Volkstheater' 1905, 9). While the reviewer in the liberal daily newspaper *Neue Freie Presse*,

---

4   One of the most influential early twentieth-century Berlin directors, Vallentin had directed the German premiere of *Eine Frau ohne Bedeutung* (*WNI*) at Max Reinhardt's *Neues Theater* (New theatre) in Berlin in September 1903.

5   'Er schafft keine Handlung aus Eigenem, sondern kombiniert eine mit viel parodistischem Schick aus den Handlungen der landläufigen Lustspiele und Romane. Er baut ein Gerüst aus blöden und abgedroschenen Elementen der Durchschnitts-Machwerke, behängt es aber mit den buntesten Blumengewinden seiner eigenen Arabeskenlaune.'

6   'Es handelt sich um eine Parodie auf Alles, was in der Londoner Gesellschaft gut und theuer, das heißt schlecht und billig ist, um eine Parodie auf die englischen Jungfrauen mit ihrer hohlen Maske des Anstandes, auf Erziehung und Eheschließung, auf religiöse Heuchelei und gesellschaftliche Prüderie [...] und zu guterletzt auf das üppig wuchernde Melodrama.'

recording a rather reserved audience reception, appears to be puzzled by the issue of generic categorization posed by *IBE*, which blends satire, comedy and farce, and playfully subverts both English social mores and dramatic traditions (1905b, 13).

Critics disagreed over the director's decision to let the actors deliver their lines in a monotonous English accent, which was intended to evoke an artificial milieu and was thus an attempt to broach the crucial issue of the successful linguistic and cultural transfer of Wilde's comedies (Kohlmayer 1996, 162). This was broadly perceived as (over)emphasizing the satirical quality of the play, or even misconceived as lending it local colouring and thereby allowing insights into a specifically English society, its manners and habits. Thus, Stefan Grossmann of the *Arbeiter-Zeitung* (Workers' newspaper) indicates that the performance suffered from an immoderate quantity of stylized mannerisms, whose comic effects wore off quickly (1905, 7). In the review quoted above, his colleague of the *Fremden-Blatt* is even more scathing of the linguistic inadequacies of Vallentin's production, where the characters 'move like automatons and speak German like English governesses' ('die sich wie Automaten bewegen und das Deutsch von englischen Gouvernanten sprechen') (Hevesi 1905, 17).

Rounding off his critical appraisal of the Viennese premiere of *Eine triviale Komödie*, the Austrian writer and critic Rudolph Lothar predicted that '[i]f the Viennese audiences show any kind of taste, then this Wildean comedy is destined to play to packed houses for a long time to come' (1905, 1206).[7] Indeed, henceforth Vienna proved to be a particularly fertile soil for the production of Wilde's society comedies, all of them experiencing their Viennese stage debut within fourteen months of the premiere of *IBE*, which went on to become the most frequently produced Wildean drama in the Austrian capital. The critics were decidedly less enthusiastic about Wilde's earlier comedies, such as *LWF*, with its seemingly far-fetched plot which, as one anonymous critic put it, had been showily dressed up for the occasion with glittering verbal trinkets ('Wiener Bürgertheater' 1907, 9). Even though the other comedies must have presented something of an anti-climax after *Eine triviale Komödie*, the demand for new dramatic works by Wilde even resulted in a highly peculiar race for the simultaneous premieres of two hastily-produced boulevard versions of *PDG*.[8] This incident reflects the extent to which Wilde had been transformed into a popular theatrical commodity, on whose success translators, theatre managers and directors were eager to cash in.

The Viennese Wilde-vogue was perceptively analysed by Rudolph Lothar on the occasion of the fiftieth performance of *Ein idealer Gatte* (*IH*) at the *Josefstadt* theatre:

---

[7] 'Wenn das Wiener Publikum Geschmack hat, dann wird die Wildesche Komödie lange Zeit ausverkaufte Häuser machen.'

[8] *Dorian Gray, Comedy in Five Acts* in a stage adaptation by George Bentley and German translation by Ludwig Wolff, premiered in the *Theater in der Josefstadt* (Theatre in the Josefstadt) on 18 September 1907. *Dorian Grays Bildnis* (Dorian Gray's picture), play in three acts by Otto Stockhausen, opened the same day at the *Kleines Schauspielhaus* (Small playhouse).

Nowadays, Oscar Wilde has become a theatrical trump card in Vienna [...]. Vienna has always been a place where the elegant way of life has played an important, perhaps even unduly important role. The Viennese take particular pleasure in seeing the epitome of elegant living displayed before them on stage [...]. If the Viennese snobs now get drunk on Wilde, it is because they regard him as a man of the world of sophisticated culture and refinement. (1907, 389)[9]

As Theodor Antropp accurately − even if a trifle irreverently − observed in a review of *Eine Frau ohne Bedeutung* (*WNI*), the 'English stage gabbler' ('der englische Bühnenplauderer') had become fashionable, and the shares of his aphoristic wit were rising rapidly on the Viennese theatre stock market (1907, 311).

1955. *Bunbury*: pretence survives purpose: a comedy classic for Viennese stage legends

When Ernst Lothar's production of *IBE*, *Bunbury, oder die Komödie des Ernst-Seins* (Bunbury, or the comedy of being Earnest), opened on 29 January 1955 at the former vaudeville theatre *Ronacher* − then serving as 'exile' venue to the bombed out *Burgtheater* (Palace Theatre) − the critic Edwin Rollett of the *Wiener Zeitung* (Viennese newspaper) was not the only one to perceive the play as slightly dust-covered entertainment drama. The sharp edges of Wilde's social criticism had apparently lost their poignancy and had been transformed instead into kind-hearted pinpricks of harmless banter: 'satire has been deprived of its object. What remains is a playful treatment of eternal human superficiality, the grotesque fate experienced by those without purpose − merely wit for wit's sake' (1955, 3).[10] For Herta Singer of *Der Abend* (The evening), the play had been stripped of its 'satirical headdress' ('satirischer Kopfschmuck'), its pretence had survived the original purpose and earnestness had been transformed into cheerfulness (1955, [n.p.]).

To be sure, in the fifty years that had elapsed since the introduction of *IBE* to Viennese theatre audiences, the Austrians had witnessed at least three major political and socio-economic *caesuras*, which affected the course of the nation's cultural life and policy. From the collapse of the Habsburg Monarchy in 1918, the First Republic emerged as a small independent Austrian rump state. Twenty years later, this was absorbed into the Third Reich, before it regained nominal independence as the Second Republic in 1945. After a

---

9   'Denn heute ist Oskar Wilde in Wien Trumpf [...]. Wien war immer eine Stadt, wo elegante Lebensart nach Gebühr, vielleicht über Gebühr geschätzt wurde. Der Wiener hat ein besonderes Vergnügen daran, auf der Bühne die Blüte der feinsten Lebensart zu bewundern [...]. Wenn nun Wilde auf einmal alle Wiener Snobs berauscht, so kommt das daher, weil man in ihm einen Weltmann von raffinierter Kultur sieht und hört.'

10   'die Satire findet kein Ziel mehr. Was übrigblieb, ist Spiel um die anhaltende menschliche Oberflächlichkeit, Groteske des Schicksals der Schwerpunktlosen, Witz um des Witzes willen.'

decade of Allied occupation, Austria was then re-established as a sovereign state with the signing of the State Treaty in May 1955. And yet, it is significant that with the end of hostilities and Nazi rule in late April 1945, Vienna, as 'the heart of the theatrical life in central Europe until the First World War' (Yates, Fiddler and Warren 2001, 9), experienced a veritable 'renaissance of theatre' (O'Brien 1982, 134). Fuelled by the existence of over thirty theatres and troupes and the gradual return of actors, writers and directors from exile, a need was felt to 'express the best in the nation's heritage' by once more producing the works of authors banned under the Nazi regime, coupled with 'the hunger to see classical and contemporary plays from other cultures' (O'Brien 1982, 134). Therefore, the popular Viennese actor and director Hans Thimig's production of *LWF*, which opened on 23 December 1945 at the *Volkstheater* after a six-year intermission during which Wilde's plays had been banned from stage production, undoubtedly presented a return to well-loved classical comedy repertory. Presumably intended to provide light-hearted comedy entertainment to those who sought escape from the dire conditions of the immediate post-war situation, the production, which was framed by lavishly designed decorative period sets, nevertheless alienated many critics, who were struck by the remoteness of the characters portrayed on stage. Thus, the anonymous critic of the *Kleines Volksblatt* (Little people's paper) considers the audience's applause merely a symptom of an instinctive desire to escape into a period fortunate enough not to be burdened with existential concerns ('Volkstheater' 1945, [n.p.]).

Ten years later, only a few months prior to the ceremonious reopening of the *Burgtheater* – Austria's famed national theatre, which had been severely damaged by bombs and shelling in 1945 – Ernst Lothar's meek period production of *Bunbury* was greeted with nearly unanimous praise for presenting the English comedy classic as an integral part of timeless literary theatre (Basil 1955, 5). Even though the pointed edges of the play's social satire may have become obsolete, its central philosophy endowed it with a highly contemporary appeal. The play was described as a 'parable of life as tomfoolery, the triumph of the surreal over the real' ('Gleichnis für das Leben als Närrischkeit, für den Triumph des Unwirklichen über das Wirkliche') (Fontana 1955, 4). Director Ernst Lothar[11] was complimented on his German stage version, which, according to Herta Singer, was conspicuously characterized by 'elegant wit and polished irony' ('elegante[r] Witz und geschliffene[] Ironie') (1955, [n.p.]). Only the critic of the *Volksstimme* (People's voice) deemed Lothar's new German version already dated at its premiere (Kauer 1955, [n.p.]). An interesting point was raised by Otto Basil, cultural editor of

---

[11]   The writer, director and theatre critic Ernst Lothar was one of the central figures in Austrian cultural politics before Hitler's annexation of Austria forced him into American exile on account of his Jewish origins. After the war, Lothar returned as US cultural officer responsible for denazification, the reconstruction of cultural life in the US-zone of occupation and the transfer and dissemination of US theatre and music (Rathkolb 2006, 288). Lothar produced German stage versions of *IBE*, *WNI* and *IH*.

Neues Österreich (New Austria), who considered Wilde's comedies inseparable from the author's post-prison works *BRG* and *DP*, as they were perceived to offer profound insights into Wilde's tragic fate and the human condition in general (1955, 5). Convinced of the essential interdependence of the author's life and work, Basil suggests that in their paradoxical wisdom Wilde's comedies appear like 'the gaping mouth of a Greek theatre mask or the thickly painted lips of a clown, and one never knows whether it expresses pleasure or pain' ('sie wirken wie der aufgerissene Mund einer griechischen Theatermaske oder der dickgeschminkte eines Clowns, und man weiß nicht, ob sie Lust oder Schmerz ausdrücken'). For him it is the directors' responsibility to approach Wilde's works in their multi-layered entirety, taking into account their ethical as well as their aesthetic implications, so as not to render them mere antiquated exhibits in a 'museum of humour' ('Humor-Museum') (1955, 5). Basil reasserts his argument three years later in a review of Ernst Lothar's production of *WNI*, in which he claims that modern stagings of Wilde's society comedies needed to be aware of the cultural historicity of Wildean theatre if they wanted to avoid being reduced to antiquated and implausible plots (1958, 6). He argues that Wilde the dandy and aesthete, the cynic and brilliant conversationalist, has become largely inaccessible to modern audiences, who may be able to relate much better to the author's personal tragedy. Basil's explanation is worth recording, as it hints at the specifically local historical background that influenced the playwright's reception:

> The 'no man's land generation', scorched by the furnace heat of two world wars and several social and political transformations, stands in awe and sympathy for the poet bearing the prisoner's number C.3.3, who, after his release from jail [...], lived a sorry existence in Paris as a pale, bloated spectre, a living corpse. (1958, 6)[12]

In the context of Lothar's 1955 *Bunbury* production, it is worth noting that the part of Lady Bracknell, played by Alma Seidler, one of the *grandes dames* of Viennese theatre, was expressly singled out by most critics as the chief attraction of the performance (see for instance Rollett 1955, 3). In Vienna as in England, where Edith Evans had set nigh inimitable standards for any subsequent interpretation of Wilde's 'greatest comical creation' (Pfister 1990, 128), '[i]t took time for Lady Bracknell to become everybody's favourite joke' (Stokes 1994, 169). It was not until 1931 that a production of *IBE* was noted by the critics mainly on account of the appearance of one of Vienna's most revered star actresses as Lady Bracknell (or Lady Brancaster, in the German translation).[13] The hitherto scarcely noticed part was now transformed into a so-called 'star role'. Adele Sandrock played Lady Brancaster as an 'imposing, typically

---

12 'Die "Generation im Niemandsland", die durch den Feuerofen von zwei Weltkriegen und etlichen Umbrüchen gegangen ist, bekennt sich in Ehrfurcht und Mitleid zu dem Dichter, der die Sträflingsnummer C.3.3. trug und nach verbüßter Zuchthausstrafe [...] als ein bleiches, gedunsenes Gespenst, als lebender Leichnam in Paris dahinvegetierte.'

13 *Bunbury*, directed by Herbert Furreg, opened on 2 May 1931 at the *Deutsches Volkstheater*.

English *grande dame*, with stiff distinction, as grotesque as she is grandiose' ('Adele Sandrock' 1931, 5).[14] It has been argued that *Bunbury's* transformation into one of the great German comedy classics in the 1920s is inseparably tied up with the name of Sandrock, since German theatre distinctly lacks a model for Lady Brancaster's comically threatening and imposing demeanour (Kohlmayer 1996, 169–71; see also the fuller treatment of this topic in Rainer Kohlmayer and Lucia Krämer's essay in this volume). Incidentally, this is in tune with the proverbial Viennese 'star cult', which manifests itself as the passionate idolization of theatrical heroes who would frequently guarantee the audience success of an otherwise mediocre production. 'Theatre in Vienna is synonymous with actors' theatre' (O'Brien 1982, 134) or, in another fifty years' time, adaptationers' theatre.

2005. *Ernst ist das Leben*: between trash operetta, 'popmodern' parody and punch-line pornography: Jelinek goes Wilde

Whereas in the English context *IBE* largely appears to have remained hostage to the phenomenal success of John Gielgud's legendary revivals of the 1930s and 1940s, as well as the parameters of expectation set by Anthony Asquith's 1952 film (Kaplan 1997, 270), a recent German translation of the play has become subject to radically idiosyncratic rewriting by the Nobel Prize-winning Austrian feminist novelist and playwright Elfriede Jelinek (b. 1946). Employing a linguistic method that is abrupt, disruptive and characterized by cynical humour (Honegger 2006, 5), the author's eclectic oeuvre, ranging from prose, stage texts and radio plays to libretti, translations and stage adaptations, is highly influenced by her political activism. Her works are dominated by the prevalent themes of female sexuality, power relations between the sexes and, more recently, Austria's ambivalent approach to its National Socialist past. Following her previous adaptations of such stage classics as Christopher Marlowe's *The Jew of Malta*, or Georges Feydeau's *A Flea in Her Ear*, Jelinek feels especially attracted by Wilde's quick and sophisticated repartee, which she considers rare in German-language literature (Augustin 2004, 105). 'Dialogues in theatre I find banal and useless', she claims, 'unless they are by Oscar Wilde'. Jelinek freely admits to the unbridled 'Jelinekization' of Wilde's comedy:

> I love Oscar Wilde [...], especially his comedies. I have translated French farces, Labiche and Feydeau, and now I am translating – together with Karin Rausch – Oscar Wilde, who, unfortunately, is more and more turning into Jelinek, unless somebody will save him. In comedies, social conflicts grow more acute [...]. They are the outlets through which social pressure noisily escapes. (2005, 6)[15]

---

14   'Adele Sandrock [...] spielte eine imposante altenglische, große Dame in gestraffter Vornehmheit so grotesk wie grandios.'

15   'Dialoge im Theater finde ich banal und sinnlos, außer sie sind von Oscar Wilde. Ich liebe Oscar Wilde [...], überhaupt seine Komödien. Ich habe französische Farcen übersetzt, Labiche und Feydeau, und jetzt übersetze ich, gemeinsam mit Karin Rausch, Oscar Wilde, der leider immer mehr zu Jelinek wird, wenn ihn

Jelinek's eccentric adaptation, titled *Ernst ist das Leben* (Life is earnest), '"nuzzles up to the original like a lamb to the wolf"' (Augustin 2004, 101),[16] and does not shy away from the artificial, the flat and platitudinous, the sexually explicit and, at times, even the coarsely vulgar. It deliberately employs the 'punch-line pornography' ('Pointenporno') (Richter 2005, 66) of conventional slapstick comedy in order to exploit and foreground the elements of sexual ambivalence and social criticism contained in Wilde's play. In fact, Jelinek conspicuously attributes the subtle ambivalence of Wilde's language to his 'existence in clandestine double life and secrecy', sensing a common denominator that links the author's life and work (Hirschmann–Altzinger 2005, 33).[17]

Jelinek's 'practically rewritten [...] and sexually reoriented' adaptation (Schneeberger 2005, 122),[18] was premiered on 18 February 2005 at the Vienna *Akademietheater* (Academy theatre) in a production by Falk Richter. Wilde's Victorian dandy protagonists are transformed into two worn-out party-animals, whose excessive life-styles have taken their toll. In Act One, Jelinek's modern dandies, whose friendship is unmistakably characterized by a rather more intimate quality, begin to feel severely troubled by their pasts as they lethargically lounge by a swimming-pool within glamorous surroundings. Eventually, they reach the sobering conclusion that their hitherto carefree lives, solely dedicated to maximizing pleasure, have become blighted by somewhat dire financial circumstances. Inconveniently, this appears to necessitate the (at least temporary) renunciation of their comfortable arrangements, for 'when the money runs out, the dandy becomes a tragic case' (Pohl 2005a).[19] Roland Koch defines his own and his co-star Michael Maertens's individual approach to the central characters in the following terms: '"Wondering how these characters could be translated into the here and now, we arrived at the image of pop stars who haven't been able to land a hit single in a long time. As the dandies run out of money, they need to give up their double lives and become part of respectable society"' (Lohs 2005, 34).[20] It becomes obvious that Jack is eager to escape an arrangement that apparently has reached its irreversible sell-by date, while Algernon is visibly indignant over his lover's defection. As he considers the acquisition of a considerable fortune as the sole compensation for getting involved with a woman, the institution of marriage is exposed as a calculated business transaction. Stripped of any trace of romantic quality, the dispassionate trade-off becomes a revealing symptom of a hollow and depraved

---

nicht jemand vorher rettet. Komödien spitzen gesellschaftliche Konflikte immer zu [...]. Sie sind die Ventile, durch die der gesellschaftliche Druck zischend entweichen kann.'

16   'Die Übersetzung schmiegt sich an das Original wie das Lamm an den Wolf.'
17   'Dieses Leben der Klandestinität, der Heimlichkeit [...] hat bei ihm diese Doppelbödigkeit der Sprache hervorgebracht [...].'
18   'praktisch neu geschrieben – und sexuell umgepolt.'
19   'wenn das Geld ausgeht, wird es für den Dandy tragisch.'
20   'Wir sind bei unseren Überlegungen, wer diesen Figuren heute entsprechen könnte, bei Popstars gelandet, die schon länger keinen Hit mehr verbuchen konnten. Weil den Dandys die Finanzen versiegen, müssen sie auf das Doppelleben verzichten und sich in die Gesellschaft einklinken.'

social world where perpetual mask-switching and the mix-up of identities are even further complicated by the confusion over ethical standards.

Under Jelinek's treatment, *IBE* is deprived of its inherent sexual and moral ambiguity. Her aim in doing so may be to exploit the political implications of Wilde's works, which, when it comes to audience interest, these days have successfully superseded notions of literary merit: 'Wilde's writings have tended to be of interest principally insofar as they can be subsumed into this larger political narrative: put crudely, insofar as they can be interpreted as interrogating or subverting the values and attitudes of the culture which criminalized him' (Guy and Small 2006, 23). Jelinek's version unmistakably interprets the nature of 'bunburying' as homosexual double existence: Jack and Algernon are two happily queer dowry hunters in eccentric dress, Gwendolen an iron-willed, latex-clad dominatrix and Canon Chasuble a barely contained letch performing an act of zoophilia on an unsuspecting stuffed sheep.

Katrin Hoffmann's stage design was noted for replacing 'Victorian grandeur with yuppie decadence' (Villiger Heilig 2005, 18).[21] Employing crystal chandeliers as gigantic swings, violently rotating mirror-glass doors, as well as a substantial herd of stuffed farm-animals grouped around an idyllic country pond, it was meant to accentuate Jelinek's frequent intertextual citations of popular trash and consumer culture. Thus, Cousin Cecily not only reminds Algernon of a pink rose but something (or rather, someone) else too, as he adds meaningfully: 'Good bye, England's rose!' (Wilde 2005, 31).[22]

Considering Jelinek's fascination with Wilde's brilliant stage dialogues, it is hardly surprising that language assumes a central position in *Ernst ist das Leben*, finding vivid expression in the author's remarkable linguistic dexterity, which brims with feckless word-play and puns, ingenious improvisation and frivolous innuendo. Language becomes a slippery terrain, inhibiting the characters' communication and offering them endless opportunities for shrewd manoeu-vring. Frequently the characters display a stammer, hopelessly stumbling over a host of heavily sexually-connoted Freudian slips, thereby giving away their hidden selves.

> Algernon: Bunbury. I would never ever part with my Bunny. And if you really should get married, which seems to me extremely problematic, you will be very glad to know my Bun. I shall gladly lend him to you. A man, especially when he carries the weight on both shoulders, always ought to take along his Burberry, I mean, his Bunbury. Otherwise, he will get bored to death. (Wilde 2005, 15)[23]

---

[21] 'Katrin Hoffmann hat den originalviktorianischen Pomp durch Yuppie-Dekadenz ersetzt.'

[22] 'Algernon: Weil Sie mich an eine rosa Rose gemahnen, Cousine Cecily. Good bye, England's rose!'

[23] 'Algernon: Bunbury. Nie im Leben würde ich mich von meinem Bunny trennen. Und wenn du wirklich heiraten solltest, was mir mehr als problematisch vorkäme, wirst du noch froh sein, meinen Bun zu kennen. Ich leihe ihn dir gern. Ein Mann, besonders wenn er auf beiden Schultern trägt, muß immer seinen Burberry, ich meine seinen Bunbury bei sich haben. Sonst langweilt er sich zu Tode.'

In this context, it is another noteworthy feature of Falk Richter's production that the expressions of emotionally charged or sensitive subjects are usually cloaked in a melancholy chanson, introduced as an additional level of commentary and interpretation.[24]

For the director, Jelinek's postmodern rewriting of *IBE* presents an 'explosion of humour – too much of everything – no well-tempered comedy, but always too much, tasteless, a comedy exorcism' (Richter 2005, 74).[25] On a linguistic level, this represents a claim to amplify what Wilde would have expressed more candidly if he had not faced immediate social ostracism. Needless to say, this bold assumption was fiercely contested by a number of critics who, in turn, felt that the Nobel Prize-winner's adaptation conspicuously failed to do justice to Wilde's comedy. 'Jelinek turns Wilde from head to bottom, from brain to bowels, from punch-line to penis': thus Gerhard Stadelmaier of the *Frankfurter Allgemeine Zeitung* gives vent to his disapproval of the perceived vulgarity of Jelinek's humour and Richter's production, judging that 'Oscar Wilde's head is placed under the director's guillotine' (2005, 39).[26] Others strive to offer more differentiated criticism, acknowledging the transformation of Wilde's comedy into a Jelinek-text, only to re-emerge as a 'bourgeois fantasy of adventurous aestheticism and camp decadence' ('eine Kleinbürgerphantasie von verwegenem Ästhetentum und schwuler Dekadenz') (Michalzik 2005, 16) or a 'cheap trash operetta', a 'popmodern parody of an aging celebrity in-crowd' ('eine billige Trash-Operette'; 'popmoderne Persiflage einer haltlosen Bussi-Bussi-Mosi-Promi-Gesellschaft') (Dössel 2005, 17). Moreover, the perceived violation of the sphere of ambiguity and multiple interpretation so central to Wilde's play is considered by some critics as highly problematic. Thus, Ronald Pohl in *Der Standard* (The Standard) feels that, where the inherent sphere of ambiguity does not allow for specification, a concept which translates every form of escapism into acts of fornication is consigned to failure (2005b). Even though many reviewers point out the fun factor of Jelinek's verbal play, it is frequently felt that in the end the comedy's sense of boulevardesque clownery and light-heartedness becomes slightly overbearing. Comical explosions appear to be replaced by routine, as if Jelinek had embarked on a rampage aimed at killing off the comedy with an overdose of bawdy witticisms. In this context, Barbara Petsch's balanced assessment probably captures most succinctly the diverse reactions to the production:

> Conservative minds hardly will be pleased about this thoroughly tossed and shaken *Bunbury*-cocktail. Open-minded theatre-goers, however, will derive great pleasure from the production, especially those prepared to overlook graciously a few

---

[24] Lyrics by Falk Richter and 'post-punk entertainer' Rocko Schamoni, who, together with Jonas Landerschier, also wrote the music.

[25] 'humor explosion – von allem zu viel – keine wohltemperierte komödie, sondern immerzu too much, geschmacklos, die komödienaustreibung.'

[26] 'Die Jelinek bringt den Wilde vom Kopf auf den Po, vom Hirn auf den Unterleib, von der Pointe auf den Pimmel [...]. Unter [dem] Regiefallbeil liegt der Kopf des Oscar Wilde.'

exaggerations, vulgarisms – and a few dragging parts. In the wake of this version it will be more difficult to stage *Bunbury* as meek British society comedy. (2005, 15)[27]

The success of the 2005 production of Jelinek's adaptation of *IBE* has set new standards for modern stagings of Wilde's most popular comedy. What is more, it has, in part, answered the eternal question, repeatedly posed by commentators ever since the 1920s and 1930s, of how Wilde's society plays, perceived to be so firmly anchored in the specific social and cultural milieu of their times, will stand their ground in contemporary theatre. This was to be observed particularly well when Hans Hollmann's production of *Bunbury* opened barely one year later, on 26 January 2006, at the *Theater in der Josefstadt*. Despite employing an all-male cast, including two well-loved Austrian veteran star actors, the director's concept of comical subversion was decidedly lost on the critics. Strikingly, the production was generally considered tame and conventional, a 'return to the old, dust-covered Wilde all dressed in plush' ('Rückkehr zum alten, staubigen Plüsch-Wilde') (Petsch 2006, [n.p.]), and was frequently compared unfavourably to the *Akademietheater* production. It is worth quoting Guido Tartarotti of the *Kurier* (Courier), who poses the central question of how Wilde's comedy classic should be played in the twenty-first century: 'First option: not at all. Second option: the text will become subject to modernization, as it is done at the *Akademietheater*, where Elfriede Jelinek's crude version is shown as a grim satire on an exhausted and worn-out hedonistic society' (2006, 33).[28] In view of the unbroken popularity of Wilde's plays on Vienna's stages, option number one appears hardly applicable – certainly not as long as Jelinek keeps up her fascination with Wilde.[29]

Conclusion: curtain call

Wilde's society comedies are profoundly rooted in the socio-cultural framework of *fin-de-siècle* England and, for this reason, have often faced charges of being outmoded and difficult to adapt for the modern stage. In spite of this, Wilde's

---

[27] 'Konservative Gemüter dürften wenig erbaut sein über diesen wahrhaft durch gerüttelten und geschüttelten Bunbury-Cocktail. Aufgeschlossene Theaterfreunde dafür um so mehr, vor allem jene, die bereit sind, über manche Überzogenheiten, Ungezogenheiten, hinweg zu sehen – und über einige Längen. Den "Bunbury" als braves britisches Lustspiel aufführen, das wird nach dieser Version in Zukunft schwerer sein.'

[28] 'Erste Möglichkeit: Gar nicht. Zweite Möglichkeit: Man holt den Text ins heute, wie das Akademietheater, wo Elfriede Jelineks brachiale Fassung als Abrechnung mit einer ermüdeten Spaßgesellschaft gezeigt wird.'

[29] Jelinek's adaptation of Oscar Wilde's *IH*, retitled *Der ideale Mann* (The ideal man), premiered at Vienna's Akademietheater on 23 November 2011. In her version, Wilde's play about a morally upright, up-and-coming politician with a shady past contains unmistakable references to the Austrian political landscape and the corruption and banking scandals during the Conservative coalition government in the early and mid 2000s.

sustained presence as a periodically revived all-time favourite of Viennese theatre has been a remarkable success story. In this context, the three productions of Wilde's acclaimed comedy masterpiece singled out for discussion in this essay function as crucial signposts demarcating two intervals of fifty years, and sketch out a panorama of the comedies' Viennese reception in the course of one full century. Not unlike their English counterparts, early twentieth-century Austrian commentators were uncertain about the generic categorization of Wilde's society plays and were occasionally prone to pronouncing the author an insubstantial playwright, whose comedies had emerged purely as a well-calculated commercial enterprise. The comedies' enormous popularity with the audience was secured by the author's humour and generous deployment of the paradox as 'a truth seen round a corner' (Newman 1970, 204), which were certainly perceived as a novel and striking feature of his dramatic art.

However, the society plays also appeared to evoke a sense of nostalgia for a lost world of elegance and splendour, promoted by the specific local colouring of period productions that offered a considerable quantity of rewarding star roles to the most popular Austrian actors of the day. At the same time they allowed Viennese audiences to draw satisfaction from their observations of weaknesses attributed to 'the others'. In general, Wilde's comedies, in which the author successfully treads the thin line of pleasing and teasing the audience, delivering his pinpricks of social satire on a silver plate of dazzling fireworks of epigrammatic wit, were considered to be apolitical entertainment drama. Wilde's success in Vienna seems to have been facilitated by the *genius loci* of the Austrian comic tradition, which has been seen to derive from Baroque theatre but is also to be found in the satirically witty, darkly comic, and faintly anarchic work of Johann Nestroy, Arthur Schnitzler, Karl Kraus, Ödön von Horvath, Jura Soyfer and Thomas Bernhard (Huish 1998, 3).

As the discussion of Jelinek's adaptation of *IBE* ought to have illustrated, at the beginning of the twenty-first century the popularity of Wilde's plays on the contemporary stage is motivated, to a significant degree, by the lively interest in the author as a 'pop-cultural icon, a multiform signifier of youth, rebelliousness, individualism, sexual freedom, modernity' (Sammells 2004, 109). Ever since Wilde was introduced to the Viennese context, the author's biographical details have engendered enormous interest, attested, for example, by a successful guest performance of Leslie and Sewell Stokes's play *Oscar Wilde (His Life and Trial)* by Edward Stirling and the English Players in 1937.[30] Nowadays, in many respects, Wilde seems to have become even more 'our contemporary', certainly on the Viennese stage, where the 2005 production of *Ernst ist das Leben* utilized 'a quality endemic to the plays: an interplay between performance, audience, and outside world that was already active in the conditions of late Victorian theatre, though taken to new extremes by Wilde – from the very start of his career' (Stokes 1994, 171).

---

[30] The play, which later became the basis of Gregory Ratoff's 1960 film *Oscar Wilde*, starring Robert Morley, was performed twice on 1 and 6 December 1937 at the theatre *Scala*.

13 Composing Oscar: Settings of Wilde for the German Stage

Chris Walton

There are several reasons why a writer might appeal to composers. The obvious one is the nature of his poetry or prose: its rhythms, its melodies, metaphors and similes. In the case of a dramatist, the plot can be the thing. But many of the obvious reasons why a composer would want to set a writer to music disappear when that writing has been translated into another language. To be true, there have been fads for setting, say, East Asian poetry in translation (as in the case of Mahler with his *Lied von der Erde*, the *Quatre poèmes hindous* by Maurice Delage or Igor Stravinsky's *Three Japanese Lyrics*, all roughly contemporaneous). But it is uncommon for a writer to appeal to composers after he has been translated.

Oscar Wilde thus forms a remarkable exception, for the best-known musical settings of his work are in German. The prime example is Richard Strauss's *Salome* (the title of the opera is spelt without the accent), which is one of the most-often performed operas of the past century. But operatic settings by Alexander Zemlinsky have also entered the repertory in recent years, and Wilde's popularity among composers has proven particularly durable in German Switzerland. As we shall observe, however, the composers in question seem to have had very varied reasons for choosing to put his works on the operatic stage.

Strauss first saw *Salomé* in Max Reinhardt's Berlin production of 1902, with Gertrud Eysoldt in the title role. While this made an immense impression on him, he later recalled that his attention had already been drawn to the play's musical possibilities by the Viennese poet Anton Lindner (whose 'Hochzeitlich Lied' he had set as his Op. 37 No. 6). 'With my agreement, he sent me a few cleverly versified opening scenes, but I could not decide to set them until it occurred to me one day: Why not compose without further ado "How beautiful is the Princess Salome tonight!"' (Strauss 1989, 224).[1] So Strauss

---

[1] 'Auf meine Zustimmung hin schickte er mir ein Paar geschickt versifizierte Anfangsszenen, ohne daß ich mich zur Komposition entschließen konnte, bis es mir eines Tages aufstieg: Warum komponiere ich nicht gleich ohne weiteres "Wie schön ist die Prinzessin Salome heute Nacht!"'

himself set about cutting down Hedwig Lachmann's German translation to make a suitable libretto. He began work on the music in August 1903, completed the sketch in September 1904 and the scoring nine months later. This was not the first time that a composer had set a play directly to music instead of having it versified into a libretto, for Debussy had done the same to *Pelléas et Mélisande* by Maurice Maeterlinck just a few years earlier (the fact that Wilde had himself been influenced by Maeterlinck when writing *Salomé* nicely closes the circle). But the phenomenal success of Strauss's *Salome* made it arguably the real progenitor of the widespread twentieth-century vogue for *Literaturoper*, the genre to which some of the finest operas of the century belong, ranging from Strauss's own *Elektra* to Alban Berg's *Wozzeck* and *Lulu* and Bernd Alois Zimmermann's *Die Soldaten* (The soldiers).

Salome represented a turning-point in Strauss's career. Whereas his reputation had hitherto rested on his symphonic poems and his songs, *Salome* now confirmed him as both a leading music dramatist and the foremost modernist in music. Within two years it had received fifty different productions and its success at the box office has never waned since. As several of the essays in this volume demonstrate, Strauss's *Salome*, with its extensive record of performances in several European countries, played a fundamental role in the transmission of Wilde's works (see for instance Beran, Grubica, Kohlmayer and Krämer, Mayer). The effects of *Salome* are well documented: for Strauss, its success meant financial wealth and eventual freedom from the conductor's daily round; while for music history in general the opera marked the birth of musical Expressionism and a major step on the path towards atonality. Strauss's reasons for choosing Wilde's play as the basis for an opera have thus far been sought primarily in the *fin-de-siècle* shock appeal of the play itself, in the pariah status of its author and in the emergence of sexuality as an accepted, if controversial, subject of modern drama. Indeed, there is no doubt that Strauss understood what every Hollywood producer knows today: sex sells, and sells all the more when it shocks. But this was a lesson that he had already learnt well before *Salome*.

Strauss's first opera, the neo-Wagnerian *Guntram*, had not been well received, and was largely forgotten after its première in Weimar in 1894. His next opera, *Feuersnot* (*Fire Famine*), to a libretto by Ernst von Wolzogen based on an old Dutch tale, was an attack on his native city of Munich for having supposedly failed to recognize both Wagner's genius and his own (Strauss had left the Munich Opera in 1898 under a cloud to become instead the First Capellmeister at the Berlin Court Opera). But it is the sexual directness of *Feuersnot* that is its most surprising aspect. Kunrad, a magician, casts a spell that puts out all the fires in the town. At the close of the opera, the townspeople as one urge the heroine to lose her 'Lirumlarumlei' to Kunrad in order to placate him. She acquiesces, and as she does so (offstage), the orchestra winds up to a climax with whooping horns and all. The fires appropriately spurt into life across the town while the people roar their approval in raucous celebration of the heroine's near-public defloration. As both composer and librettist knew, the authorities would hardly allow such 'obscenities' on stage, and changes had to be made before the world premiere in Dresden on 21 November 1901, under Ernst von Schuch. Strauss's correspondence of the day leaves little doubt that he hoped for a scandal in order to increase his returns (see Blaukopf 1988, 230).

Strauss's decision to take Wilde's *Salomé* for his next opera text should be seen in the light of his experiences with *Feuersnot*. For Wilde's play is heavily determined by forms of 'deviant' sexual desire, ranging from homosexuality to necrophilia. Strauss's eagerness for financial profit is well documented, so there can be little doubt that the choice was made with the intent to create a yet bigger scandal and to turn this shock value into box office returns. Given the recent introduction of new copyright laws in Germany – largely on the initiative of Strauss himself – he knew that any major operatic success would pay him substantial royalties for years to come.

Strauss's score itself is rightly regarded as one of the most virtuosic feats of orchestration of the twentieth century, not least because it achieves a transparency often reminiscent of chamber music, despite being written for an orchestra of a hundred musicians. It also pushed tonality to its very boundaries (only in *Elektra* would Strauss ever venture any further). Although here, as elsewhere, Strauss refrains from embarking on the kind of leitmotivic web that we encounter in Wagner, the two main characters are assigned reminiscence motives that are developed and combined as the plot suggests it, as in Wagner's music dramas. It was also Wagner's example of placing the main musical argument in the orchestra that allowed later composers like Strauss to set prose texts such as Wilde's *Salomé* to music. Salomé's final monologue, a love paean sung to the Prophet's severed head culminating in the kissing of it, is a musical study in psychological breakdown whose most obvious precursor was Kundry's seduction scene in the second act of Wagner's *Parsifal*. But the scene in Strauss's *Salome* was also obviously intended as a reference to Isolde's 'Liebestod' (love death) in Wagner's *Tristan und Isolde*, where the enraptured heroine sings before the corpse of her beloved. Strauss followed Isolde's example by providing his lone princess with a climax both musical and obviously sexual, and it should not surprise us that some opera producers today prefer to substitute one set of lips for another in a below-the-belt, Freudian slip of the tongue, presumably prompted too by Salomé's words 'es war ein bitterer Geschmack auf deinen Lippen' (There was a bitter taste on thy lips). Salomé's monologue is one of several latently operatic aspects of Wilde's play that Strauss retained when cutting down the text to form his libretto. The most obvious are perhaps Salomé's threefold declaration of love to Jokanaan (to his hair, his body and his lips) and Herod's threefold call to Salomé to dance, which have countless operatic precursors in the nineteenth century, such as the threefold condemnation of Radames in Verdi's *Aida* or the three trials of Pamina and Tamino in Mozart's *Zauberflöte* (*Magic Flute*). Strauss did not, however, shy away from changing whatever seemed musically necessary, even down to the word order, as in the opening pages, when he rearranged Lachmann's 'die aus dem Grab aufsteigt' (rising from the tomb) in order to place 'Grab' on a low note at the very end of the sentence.

Strauss might however have been drawn to Wilde's *Salomé* for reasons beyond its immediate shock appeal.[2] Its action takes place at the court of Herod: a trumped-up, highly superstitious monarch with a short attention

---

[2]   I deal with these issues at much greater length in Walton 2005. I am grateful to

span, rapid mood swings and a love of lavish display, but mindful of his own dubious origins and of the greater splendours of Caesar's court in Rome – in his late reminiscences, Strauss referred specifically to this last trait of Herod's (Strauss 1989, 226). Here we have an odd correlation with circumstances close to the composer; for his employer, Kaiser Wilhelm II, was notoriously fond of pomp, though as a member of the Hohenzollern dynasty he had no real historical claim to the title of 'Kaiser' of all Germany, and was for ever in awe of the greater glamour surrounding his grandmother, Queen Victoria. Wilhelm's closest friend, Philipp von Eulenburg, prompted him to take a peripheral interest in spiritism (Röhl 1994, 64–68). Moreover, like Herod, the Kaiser was well known for his mood swings and short attention span (Röhl 1994, 21–26). These traits find musical expression in Strauss's depiction of the vacillating Herod, who is not assigned any specific motif of his own and who, thus Tethys Carpenter, is 'depicted more by the sonority of his accompaniment than by its tonality which, though static, is deliberately weak [...]. Throughout the scene he continues to appropriate keys apparently at random or to reflect those of Jochanaan or Salome' (Carpenter 1989, 94).

Also pertinent here is the fact that although Wilde's well-known criminal transgression, his homosexuality, was also illegal in Wilhelmine Germany, it was in fact common in the circles closest to the Kaiser (see Sombart 1982). The influence of Philipp von Eulenburg on Wilhelm only ceased completely after the former was openly accused of homosexuality in 1907 by Maximilian Harden, the editor of the periodical *Die Zukunft* (The future). Eulenburg – a married father of eight children, though by all accounts bisexual – was accordingly arrested the following year. 'Philine' Eulenburg – his close friends called him by this feminine diminutive – was a highly cultivated man and an acquaintance of Cosima Wagner, the Wolzogens and many others in artistic circles. But he was also given to absurd intrigues (Röhl 1983, 3: 2040–49; von Bülow 1930, 1: 604–05), while his country seat of Liebenberg was for many years the meeting point of a circle of influential yet frivolous aristocrats that even included Strauss's employer, Georg von Hülsen, one of the Kaiser's close childhood friends. The Liebenberg circle disintegrated from late 1906 in the wake of public scandal surrounding the indeterminate sexuality of its host and his guests.

We can safely assume that Strauss was aware of the stories, both true and rumoured, of the 'depravities' taking place in the aristocratic milieu around him in Berlin. And while it would be unwise to assume that Strauss intended in *Salome*, as he had in *Feuersnot*, to draw direct parallels between real life and the characters and situations of his opera, we must surely consider to what extent similar parodic intentions determined his choice and treatment of Wilde's play. The Kaiser and Strauss's Herod share numerous character traits, just as the sexual goings-on at the Wilhelmine court found a resonance in the various forms of perverse desire depicted in the opera. It is thus tempting to think that *Salome*, which was originally intended to form a double bill

the editor of *The Musical Times*, Antony Bye, for permission to re-use some of that material here.

with *Feuersnot*, can be read on one level as a parody of Berlin, just as the earlier opera had parodied Munich (one could then even postulate the later *Rosenkavalier* as a third city portrait in opera, with its stylized depiction of Vienna). The fact that Strauss never mentions any such parallels in the case of *Salome* does not mean that they were not in some way intentional. Any kind of open declaration would naturally have resulted in a blanket ban on the opera. Not only would Strauss have lost his job, but he could conceivably have been prosecuted and convicted (as were other critics of the Kaiser) of the crime of 'Majestätsbeleidigung' (slander of the Emperor). In the event, the Kaiser's reaction to the opera seems just to have been one of general distaste. As Strauss related in his memoirs, His Majesty had only allowed it to be performed in Berlin after Hülsen had suggested a depiction of the Star of Bethlehem at the close, signalling the change from the Old-Testament to the New-Testament regime, this being somehow deemed to lessen the horrors to be found in the remainder of the opera (Strauss 1989, 227).

Given Strauss's rip-roaring success with *Salome*, it is surprising that there was no flood of Wilde settings intended to cash in on the flavour of the moment. Indeed, the next 'setting' of Wilde in the German-speaking world was not really a setting at all, but a dance pantomime for chamber orchestra by the Austrian composer Franz Schreker (1878–1934) entitled *Der Geburtstag der Infantin* (The birthday of the Infanta). It was commissioned for Grete and Elsa Wiesenthal to dance at the official opening of the Viennese 'Kunstschau' in June 1908, organized by Gustav Klimt and his fellow Secessionists (at which were exhibited some of the paintings for which Klimt is today most famous, such as 'The Kiss'). Schreker's dozen numbers follow Wilde's BI closely. He later arranged the music for large orchestra, independent of the ballet, and in this guise it attained a considerable degree of popularity in the 1920s. Schreker's late-Romantic idiom has similar forerunners as Strauss. His early operas, especially *Der ferne Klang* (*The Distant Sound*), on which he was working at the time of the commission for the *Infantin*, enjoyed immense success, though his star soon waned and he was for a long time thereafter regarded essentially as a stylistic stepping stone from Strauss to Berg, from *Salome* to *Wozzeck*. A well-deserved reassessment of Schreker's art in the late twentieth century has since succeeded in bringing him finally, firmly out of the shadows. What is perhaps most striking about his ballet music for the *Infantin* is its frequent stylistic proximity to Igor Stravinsky's ballet *Petrushka* of three years later, both in its use of *ostinati* (as at the very beginning), orchestration (as in its prominent use of solo trumpet) and even in its tendency towards a montage manner of composition – something that Stravinsky employed extensively in *Petrushka* and which later became a defining characteristic of his compositional technique. There are even certain similarities in the respective subject matters of the *Infantin* and *Petrushka*, the (anti)hero in each case being a clumsy figure of fun, a perpetual outsider whose amorous ambitions appear absurd to others and are thus doomed from the start.

There is no proof that Stravinsky heard Schreker's pantomime before writing *Petrushka*, and while it is unlikely that he saw its score, it is not wholly impossible. But we can be reasonably sure that it won admiration on the part of at least one of Schreker's fellow composers in Vienna, for it seems to have prompted him to a project of his own (Beaumont 2005, 440). Alexander von Zemlinsky (1871–1942) was at the turn of the century regarded as one of the city's most promising composing talents, though his achievements were later eclipsed by those of his brother-in-law Arnold Schoenberg and his pupils. Zemlinsky was dogged by bad luck, not least in love, and suffered continually on account of his outward appearance. His composition pupils included Alma Schindler, who left a decidedly unappealing physical description of him in her memoirs (Mahler-Werfel 1963, 29) and yet who began an affair with him that ended only when she abandoned him for Gustav Mahler.

Zemlinsky took years to get over his rejection by Alma. This was a fate he shared with others, most notably Oskar Kokoschka, and the two men endeavoured – independently of each other – to overcome it by artistic means. Whereas the ditched Kokoschka had a life-sized, anatomically faithful Alma-doll fabricated for his pleasure, Zemlinsky was consumed by a self-loathing that he subsequently composed out in operatic form. He first asked Franz Schreker in 1909 to write him a libretto on the 'tragedy of an ugly man' (in the wake, it seems, of his seeing Schreker's *Infantin* ballet). Schreker complied, but found that the result – the text for *Die Gezeichneten* (*The Branded*) – so stimulated his own musical muse that he asked to be able to set it himself. Zemlinsky acquiesced, though it can only have depressed him further, as he had in effect been rejected now not just by Alma but by the very story of his rejection.

For whatever reason, Zemlinsky refrained for the moment from turning directly to Wilde's BI (perhaps the proximity to Schreker prevented him). Independently of either, it seems, the German composer Bernhard Sekles (1872–1934) wrote a 'Tanzspiel' (dance play) in two scenes in 1913 entitled *Der Zwerg und die Infantin* (The dwarf and the infanta) to a scenario adapted from Wilde by Karlheinz Martin. It was Sekles's first work for the theatre. While Hugo Schlemüller in the *Signale für die musikalische Welt* (Signals for the musical world) hailed it as a great success and praised the modernity of the music, it seems never to have been performed whole again, surviving instead briefly, in fragmentary form, as a concert suite (Tschiedel 2005, 41–43). Sekles had begun in a late-Romantic idiom, as had so many others, and moved during the second and third decades of the century towards a more neo-classical aesthetic not too far removed from the *Neue Sachlichkeit* (new objectivity) of his most famous student, Paul Hindemith. It is as a teacher that Sekles is remembered today – his other students included Hans Rosbaud and Theodor W. Adorno – while his oeuvre as a whole has suffered more or less the same fate as his early Wilde ballet.

Whether or not Zemlinsky heard of Sekles's ballet, he was soon afterwards drawn back to Wilde – though still leaving BI well alone. From 1914 to 1916 he composed a one-act opera based on FT. The play, although a fragment, had begun to attract the interest of composers soon after its first performance in 1906. Giacomo Puccini pondered making it into an opera but decided against it on the advice of his publisher, Ricordi. Ferruccio Busoni read it in 1913 but found it left him cold. Zemlinsky seems to have been drawn to it because he found Alma in it again: it reminded him of the love triangle of Alma, her husband Gustav and Walter Gropius, with whom Alma had begun an affair in

1910 that reputedly exacerbated Mahler's heart condition (he died just months later). But Zemlinsky also seems to have found it resonant of yet another love triangle: that of Arnold Schoenberg, his wife Mathilde (Zemlinsky's sister) and the painter Richard Gerstl. In 1908, after Mathilde had terminated the affair she was having with Gerstl, he committed suicide (Beaumont 2005, 353).

Zemlinsky set Wilde's play largely intact, in the translation by Max Meyerfeld. The first performance took place in Stuttgart on 30 January 1917. The missing opening scene that Wilde never wrote is replaced here by an overture in which the principal motives are heard, while the close, with its astonishing reversal of the main characters' affections, is thanks to the music no longer so abrupt, but gains in emotional and dramatic intensity. As the contemporary critic Felix Adler remarked in 1917, Zemlinsky 'has through motivic clarification succeeded [...] in making palpable and visible the connections that had lain hidden beneath the surface' (Adler 1917). Five weeks after its world premiere, Zemlinsky's *Florentine Tragedy* was given in Prague under the composer's baton, and it enjoyed several productions in and around Germany over the next decade. It then disappeared into obscurity for half a century until its composer was resurrected along with many others in the late twentieth-century's vogue for 'forgotten' late-Romantics.

A year after the première of his *Florentine Tragedy*, Zemlinsky was contacted by the young writer Georg Klaren with a view to their writing an opera together. One of the topics that Zemlinsky himself proposed was Wilde's BI, the same that had so occupied his thoughts a decade before. Klaren delivered a libretto based closely on Wilde, but with several important changes. His Princess is an eighteen-year-old woman, not the pre-pubertal character of Wilde's tale, and she here speaks directly with the dwarf, which does not happen in Wilde. The dwarf's love for her is also obviously sexual. The princess's taunting rejection of him is thus more an act of sadism than the semi-innocent callousness of a child that we find in the original story. Klaren intentionally modelled the Dwarf on Zemlinsky, even making of him a composer/singer, while Zemlinsky responded by weaving into the fabric of his opera innumerable musical motives from works that he associated with Alma. Most of the music was sketched in mid–1919, the composition was finished by early 1921 and the world premiere took place on 28 May 1922 in Cologne under Otto Klemperer. While Gustav Mahler is the composer perhaps most obviously evoked in the love music, the Dwarf's subsequent discovery of his mirror image prompts orchestral squeals and squawks that are in their impact most reminiscent of the final scene of Strauss's *Salome*.

Various friends had tried to dissuade Zemlinsky from writing the opera, which was so cringingly autobiographical. The incongruity of casting the dwarf as a *Heldentenor* (heroic tenor) can perhaps only be explained as an act of wish-fulfilment on the part of the composer. Zemlinsky simply found the topic too compelling to resist, and there is no denying the intensity of the love music sung by the dwarf as he waits expectantly for his night of love with the Princess. Zemlinsky seems not even to have been embarrassed by the fetishistic tendencies of his vertically challenged *alter ego*, who resorts in his erotic reverie to kissing the cushion of the chair upon which the Princess has been sitting (could Klaren perhaps have known how Alma Mahler had prompted at least one man to fetishism, in the shape of Kokoschka's sex doll?). Several critics, such as Julius Korngold, seem to have found the whole thing simply too embarrassing (Beaumont 2005, 445–46). After an initial success and further productions in Prague, Vienna, Karlsruhe and Berlin, *Der Zwerg* disappeared from the repertoire for half a century.

Despite Zemlinsky's debt to Strauss, the influence of *Salome* made itself felt most strongly in operas that were not themselves settings of Wilde. While the character of Salome herself was descended in part from Kundry in Wagner's *Parsifal* (as already noted above), she herself spawned a whole host of blood-thirsty anti-heroines. One can even trace a graph of increasing horror in the wicked women of the operatic stage who are to some extent modelled on her. Salome demands the death of the man she loves, descends into madness and does unspeakable things with his severed head. The Woman in Schoenberg's *Erwartung* (*Expectation*) (1909) is deranged from the start, and after she stumbles upon her lover's body as she wanders through the woods, it becomes clear that she has killed him herself; while Penthesilea, the Amazon queen in the opera of the same name by the Swiss composer Othmar Schoeck (1886–1957), goes one step further by killing *her* lover and half-devouring his body. Schoeck was in fact at one time also attracted by FT, though that attraction never reached a point of serious operatic interest.

Wilde became immensely popular in Germany in the 1920s and, as Rainer Kohlmayer and Lucia Krämer observe elsewhere in this volume, his critical stance towards English society played a considerable role in allowing his subsequent appropriation by the Nazis. By comparison, his popularity in neutral, democratic Switzerland was diminishing, even among the many emigrant actors from Nazi Germany. The Zurich *Schauspielhaus* (Playhouse), for example, which was a home to many emigrants, brought nothing in the 1933–34 season, *Bunbury* (the German-language version of *IBE*) in September 1934, *LWF* in September 1935, *Bunbury* again in May 1941, but nothing of Wilde's again until long after the end of World War II (Wolfer 1988). It is thus an odd fact that interest in Wilde among German composers dwindled, while it was in German-speaking Switzerland that Wilde received the most musical attention over the coming decades.

The first German-Swiss opera on a topic by Wilde was by Richard Flury (1896–1961). Luckily for him, Max Meyerfeld had refused to grant Zemlinsky the sole rights to use his translation of FT and he now willingly allowed Flury to use it as a libretto. Flury had studied with Hans Huber in Basle, Ernst Kurth in Berne and Joseph Marx in Vienna before returning to spend his career teaching and conducting in his native canton of Solothurn. His *Eine florentinische Tragödie* – in fact his first-ever opera – was composed in 1926 and performed three years later at the theatre of Bienne/Solothurn (Flury 1950, 203–04). Like Zemlinsky's opera, it is cast in one act, though it is somewhat less expansive (the only extant recording lasts less than forty-five minutes). It has taken Zemlinsky's work over a half a century to enter the repertoire, albeit hesitantly, and, while Flury's work is unlikely to follow, it would deserve an occasional airing; in his day, his music was performed by topflight interpreters such as the violinist Georg Kulenkampff and the conductor Felix Weingartner. In his public statements Flury was avowedly conservative in his aesthetic: he regarded atonality as a modernist horror, though in fact this opera proves that he did not always shy away from dissonance and was in full command of a late-Romantic musical language not dissimilar to that of Zemlinsky, Erich Wolfgang Korngold and their peers.

The first opera to be based on *PDG* seems to have been by the German composer Hans Leger. His *Das Bildnis des Dorian Gray*, to a libretto by Caroline Creutzer, was cast in five acts and had its world premiere in Karlsruhe on 24 March 1939. The only reference to it in the secondary literature seems to be a single sentence in *The Musical Times* of July 1939 that it 'was produced with moderate success' ('Musical notes from abroad' 1939, 548). *PDG* hardly seems the kind of topic that would have proven popular in Germany on the cusp of World War II. The next composition to be based on Wilde was apparently by Richard Flury's Swiss compatriot Franz Tischhauser (b. 1921), though, as in the case of Schreker and Sekles three decades before, it was BI to which he was drawn on account of its balletic possibilities. His twenty-five-minute *Tanzspiel* on the topic was composed in 1941 while he was still a composition student at the Zurich Conservatory. It was first performed in Zurich in that same year. Stylistically, it displays the neoclassical tendencies that would remain in evidence throughout Tischhauser's later *oeuvre*, though its indebtedness to the Parisian music of the years before World War I is also apparent (from the Stravinsky of *Petrushka* to Ravel, Debussy and Satie). Nevertheless, it must be counted among the more successful works based on Wilde and is hardly less deserving of performance than Schreker's ballet on the same topic. Since it has recently been published in both full score and piano reduction, perhaps it might yet reach the stage again. This decade also saw yet another ballet based on BI, this time by Wolfgang Fortner (1907–1987), one of the more prominent German composers of the immediate post-war years. It was entitled *Die weisse Rose* (The white rose), in reference to the flower given to the dwarf by the princess. It was premiered in Baden-Baden in 1950.

In 1947–48, *PDG* was once more taken as the topic for an opera, this time by the Swiss composer Hans Schaeuble (1906–1988). Schaeuble had studied at the Leipzig Conservatory in the late 1920s under Hermann Grabner. He had then spent most of the next decade in Berlin until he returned to Switzerland for his compulsory military service in mid–1939. He went again to Berlin two years later but stayed only a year before travelling back to Switzerland for good. Schaeuble was a man of immense contradictions: he was gay but married in 1938 (his wife in fact died of cancer within a year); he did not care for the Nazis but found himself attracted to the superficial rigour of their totalitarian society; and while he was extremely wealthy, he remained somehow convinced that a genuine composer ought to be eking out a living in a lonely garret. Schaeuble enjoyed considerable success in the 1930s, with his works taken up by Bote & Bock and by conductors such as Hermann Scherchen, Carl Schuricht and Ernest Ansermet. But after World War II he found himself accused (if mostly behind his back) of having been too friendly towards the Nazis, and his diaries record with depressing candour his descent into self-loathing and creative sterility.

Dorian Gray op. 32 was Schaeuble's only mature opera. He sketched both the libretto and the music in 1947 and scored the opera the following year.

It follows Wilde closely, though Schaeuble also readily admitted to having been inspired by the 1945 Hollywood film, directed by Albert Lewin. Over the next forty years, Schaeuble invested much time and energy in trying to interest opera houses and singers in the work. It was all to no avail, which merely reinforced his increasingly intense feelings of inadequacy. In the manner in which he recorded in his diaries his tirades of self-disgust, yet donated those same diaries (along with his works) to the *Zentralbibliothek Zürich* (Zurich central library) for future generations of scholars to peruse, we find a disturbing parallel to the tale of Dorian Gray himself: hiding the true picture of himself away, and yet unable to stifle completely the urge to reveal it. *Dorian Gray* did not receive its premiere until 2004, when it was performed at the Opera School of the University of North Texas in Denton. It proved itself thoroughly worthy of occasional performance, though the score is hampered by Schaeuble's refusal (or inability) to allow his music to bloom properly. He seems always to be reining it in – though given his obvious identification with Wilde, coupled with his own fear of the world 'finding out' his real nature, this is hardly surprising. Schaeuble's diaries over many years make evident his notion that creativity was somehow an expression of masculine sexuality (only men could be creative, of that he was sure), while at the same time laying bare his fears of his own 'strong feminine element'.[3] His incessant revisions to his music, carried out in his later years when he could compose no longer, were thus perhaps a result of an innate fear that his lack of inspiration – and thus his perceived lack of masculinity – might become evident to the listening public and therefore had to be covered up at all costs. In fact, Zurich society, despite its supposedly Zwinglian morals, was in the mid-twentieth century relatively tolerant of homosexuality (at least when compared to other European cities) and even saw the publication of a gay journal, *Der Kreis* (The circle) from 1940 to 1968. In this context Schaeuble's gayness was an open secret that seems to have bothered no one in particular.

Perhaps as a result of the gradual relaxation of attitudes towards homosexuality in Europe after World War II, there were a few more *PDG* settings in the decades after Schaeuble. The ballet *Dorian Gray* op. 35 by Paul Walter Fürst (b. 1926), composed in 1963 to a scenario by Ernst Jandl, has still not been performed (Heindl 2002, 4) and a two-act chamber opera on the topic by Eberhard Eyser (b. 1932), composed in 1985–87, would appear to have shared its fate thus far. Two other settings have had a little more success in that they have at least taken to the stage: *Dorian Gray*, an opera by Robert Hansell to his own libretto, was first performed on 9 June 1962 at the Dresden State Opera. Born in Czechoslovakia in 1925 but active in Germany from an early age, Hansell was in 1955 appointed by Walter Felsenstein to the post of First Kapellmeister at the *Komische Oper* (Comic opera) in East Berlin. Another ballet: *Dorian Gray – Today* by the Swiss composer Max Lang (1917–1987), scored for women's chorus and orchestra, was premiered in Basle in 1966 to choreography by Vaslav Orlikowsky. Neither Hansell's opera nor Lang's ballet seems to have been performed since, however.

---

[3]   See entries for 18 December 1951 and 21 November 1928.

The only known setting of Wilde's CG is another Swiss work, this time by Heinrich Sutermeister (1910–1995). Sutermeister had been one of the first composers to write a radio opera – *Die schwarze Spinne* (The black spider) of 1936, after Gotthelf – and in the early 1960s he turned to the newer medium of television as well. His *Das Gespenst von Canterville* was the first TV opera commissioned by the German second programme, ZDF, and was broadcast on 6 September 1964 to generally good reviews (von Lewinski 1964, W. P. 1964). Sutermeister had first come to prominence with an opera based on Shakespeare's *Romeo and Juliet*, which enjoyed almost unprecedented success in the opera houses of Germany after its world premiere under Karl Böhm in Dresden in 1940. All of Sutermeister's operas testify to his fine literary sensibility and the libretto to his *Canterville* – by the composer himself – is no exception, offering a succinct and well-structured retelling of the tale. Within the framework of its sixty minutes, the opera covers a broad spectrum of forms and genres ranging from a little 'madness' aria for Mrs Otis to an interlude based on the Westminster chimes, assorted combinations of spoken and sung speech and even a chorus of American tourists. The fact that the composer's moderate, essentially neoclassical musical language was rapidly becoming out of date in the mid–1960s probably hindered the opera from achieving a more than fleeting success (though it should be mentioned that of all the television operas written from the 1950s onwards, only Menotti's sugary *Amahl and the Night Visitors* has retained any real popularity. Not even Benjamin Britten's essay in the genre, *Owen Wingrave*, was a real success).

Bunbury remained the most popular of Wilde's plays in Germany, though it seems to have attracted far less musical attention than BI or *PDG*. Two musical comedies based on it appeared at roughly the same time as Sutermeister's CG was on the air. *Mein Freund Bunbury* (My friend Bunbury) by East Germany's most successful musical composer, Gerd Natschinski (b. 1928), a former student of Hanns Eisler, was first performed in Berlin in 1964 and is still to be seen in Germany today (the latest production was in 2008 in Leipzig). The song texts were by Jürgen Degenhardt, the book by Degenhardt and Helmut Bez. *Bunbury*, a musical comedy by the Swiss composer Paul Burkhard (1911–1977) to a text by Hans Weigel, was first performed in Basle on 7 October 1965. Burkhard was trained at the Zurich Conservatory under Paul Müller–Zürich and Volkmar Andreae, and enjoyed huge success with a number of musicals and light operas. His song 'O mein Papa' even made him famous throughout the English-speaking world in the 1950s and it is undeniably catchy despite being devoid of any real melodic, rhythmic or harmonic interest. On a larger scale, however, such as in the through-composed *Bunbury*, the composer's limited musical imagination becomes all-too evident. Its manuscript vocal score is almost 400 pages long, though a perusal of it suggests that in performance it could well seem far longer still. Not even the presence of rapid patter passages (similar at times to those the English know from Gilbert and Sullivan) can do much to lighten things up. Its early reviews were positive, though the work's indebtedness to an array of models from Rossini to Verdi and Strauss did not go unnoticed (Flury and Kaufmann 1979, 162–64) and it thereafter disappeared more or less without a trace until a modern revival of the work, with piano accompaniment, in 2004 in Zurich. This also received good local reviews (see Zoppi 2004), though in fact it had been heavily cut, precisely in an attempt to avoid its many *longueurs*. The conductor of the revival, Karl Scheuber, is of the opinion that while Burkhard's own gayness had obviously prompted him to a close identification with the plight of *Bunbury*'s author, this had in the end been more of a hindrance than a help to the work itself.[4]

The late twentieth and early twenty-first centuries have seen a number of Wilde settings of very different sorts, from *Das Salome-Prinzip* (The Salome principle) by Enjott Schneider (b. 1950), first performed in Gelsenkirchen in 2002 (though admittedly composed already in 1983) to settings for speaker and piano of HP and for speaker and orchestra of SG by Stefan Heucke (b. 1959) and an 'orchestral radio play' by Henrik Albrecht (b. 1969) on CG.[5] There has even been *Dorian Gray – The Musical*, composed by the Hungarian composer Mátyás Várkonyi (b. 1950) to a libretto by the German Gunar Braunke and collaborators. It was first performed in Budapest in 1990 and thereafter enjoyed an extended run in the German-speaking world. Its British premiere at the Bloomsbury Theatre in London in May 1995 was apparently less successful (see Engelbert 2003), though its composer who, according to his own website, was in Hungary responsible for 'numerous popular tunes in the 60s' has gone on to write numerous stage works since.[6]

If there is a common denominator among most of the settings of Wilde's texts in the German-speaking lands in the first two-thirds of the twentieth century, then it seems to lie in the self-identification of the composers with either Wilde or his subject matter. Wilde's homosexuality, coupled with the fact that he was made a pariah for it, undoubtedly drew gay composers such as Schaeuble and Burkhard to his writing, either out of empathy for his fate or from a desire to use his work to express in musical terms their own predicament. Zemlinsky's personal involvement in the topics of his two operas had other causes, but was no less intense for it. Even Strauss, who first claimed Wilde for the musical stage, seems to have seen in the characters of *Salomé* a reflection of those around him. Those works based on Wilde since the latter third of the twentieth century, however, seem far more concerned with the literature itself than with any autobiographical aspects of it, latent or real. This should hardly surprise us, given that it was the student revolts and the anti-Vietnam protests of the 1960s that helped to create today's Western liberal society in which the stigma of homosexuality has all but vanished. Today's composers, perhaps, are at last more concerned with setting Wilde for what he said, rather than why they think he said it.

---

[4]   Email from Karl Scheuber, 31 December 2008.

[5]   Produced by the Südwestfunk and published on CD: Cologne: Headroom Sound Production, 2006.

[6]   See <http://3rdproof.com/matyasvarkonyi/navi.php?lang=en&page=cv> [accessed 22 December 2008].

14 From Continental Discourse to 'A Breath from a Better World': Oscar Wilde and Denmark

Lene Østermark-Johansen

Shortly before Lady Bracknell leaves Gwendolen alone with Jack in Act One of *IBE*, she outlines her theory of how morals relate to language: 'French songs I cannot possibly allow. People always seem to think that they are improper, and either look shocked, which is vulgar, or laugh, which is worse. But German sounds a thoroughly respectable language, and, indeed I believe is so.' She has just been ringing the doorbell in a Wagnerian manner, and this dichotomy between everything French as morally risky and enjoyable, and everything German as plain, sensible and dull runs through the entire play, from its title pun on Schiller's 'Ernst ist das Leben, heiter ist die Kunst' (life is earnest, art is light-hearted), over Cecily's angry outbursts about German grammar, to the wicked brother Ernest's having been carried off by a severe chill in Paris.

Oscar Wilde's way to the Danish audience went through both France and Germany, and a Teutonic earnestness – far more restrictive than in Germany where Wilde was well received from quite early on – prevented the Danes from embracing the full range and complexity of Wilde's works and genius until after World War II. It took two World Wars, including five years of German occupation, to undermine that earnestness and pave the way for an enjoyment of Wildean wit, style and paradox. In 1944, during the last year of the German occupation, Wilde obtained a new popularity through the first performance of *IBE* at the Royal Theatre in Copenhagen. This was intended as a clear manifestation of sympathy with the Allied Forces and, paradoxically, as a representation on the stage of something quintessentially English. Wilde the Irishman would have been turning in his grave, and yet the subversive aspect of that performance at that specific time would undoubtedly have pleased another side of him immensely.

The fact that French and German, rather than English, were the foreign languages mastered by well-educated Danes until the 1930s, as well as the fact that Paris and Berlin, rather than London and New York, were the cultural centres towards which bohemian and intellectual Danes gravitated before

World War II, contributed to Wilde's detours to his Danish audience. The new orientation towards Anglo-American culture after the War changed this distortion radically: with English as by far the predominant foreign language, Danes soon became aware of how much of Wilde was lost in translation, with the result that few new translations and very few critical studies in Danish appeared. It is questionable whether it makes much sense to speak of a specifically Danish reception of Wilde after World War II, since it was soon blurred by internationalization. The focus of the present essay therefore is almost exclusively on the first decades of the twentieth century.

In the course of the 1880s, when the English satirical journal *Punch* was caricaturing Wilde in almost every issue as, among others, 'Oscuro Wildgoose', 'the Wilde Eyed Poet', 'Our own Aesthetic Bard' and 'Ossian Wilderness' (see Mikhail 1978, 227–31, for a full list of the caricatures in *Punch*), the Danish equivalent journal, likewise entitled *Punch,* was running a similar campaign against Wilde's Danish contemporary – the novelist, critic and playwright Herman Bang (1857–1912) – demonstrating an equal degree of inventiveness in its vitriolic attacks on Bang's dandyism and aesthetic ideals. The nicknames applied to Bang frequently ridiculed his effeminacy ('Frøken Hermine Bang') (Miss Hermine Bang), his homosexuality ('Hr. Manbang') and his cosmopolitan sympathies ('Ermano de Bang', 'Hermann von Bangemachen' and 'Armand de Bangenét'). Cartoons continued this line, as in an image of him as Narcissus, requesting a kiss from a female marble statue posed as Bang, or in Georg Brandes's exercise in literary phrenology in which he concluded that there was a dead spot on the inside of Bang's brain, which reduced his intellect to that of the average woman (see Heede 2007). Already in 1880 Bang had caused a major scandal with his first novel *Haabløse Slægter* (Hopeless generations), which was about a diseased family which had reached the last of its line in the form of a hypersensitive male protagonist with thinly veiled homoerotic tendencies. Bang's first book brought French Decadence to a very unwelcoming Danish audience. He continued his prolific output in prose, fiction, poetry and drama, moved to Paris as a theatre director in 1893–94, was involved in a major homosexual scandal in 1906 and went into exile in Berlin, before suddenly dying during a lecture trip to America in 1912.

In many respects the lives of Wilde and Bang are parallel lives: they follow one another from the 1880s until Bang's death, sometimes intersecting and interweaving, sometimes as parallel manifestations of the late nineteenth-century dandy and litterateur. The relatively late arrival and popularity of Wilde's works in Denmark may well be related to the overwhelming presence of Bang as the homosexual dandy above all others. The Danes had their own Wilde, who fulfilled the role as the local aesthete with cosmopolitan leanings, a strange flower in the provincial garden. By 1904, when Bang's most explicitly Wildean text, his novel *Mikaël*, was first published, the only text by Wilde to have appeared in Danish was *Salomé*, translated by Paul Sarauw. The Swedes were far more advanced when it came to embracing Wilde at an early stage, with translations of *Intentions* in 1893 and of *Salomé* in 1895, a translation and production of *LWF* in 1897 and a translation of 59 stanzas of *BRG* in 1900. To this should be added several reviews and shorter critical articles about Wilde in Swedish newspapers and journals (Nelson 1966, 1–37).

There is little doubt that Bang was highly instrumental in introducing Wilde into Denmark in the years between 1903 and 1910. His ongoing dialogue with Wilde was one of plagiarism, denial, subtle allusion and appropriation, on both a personal and a professional level, in a complex manner befitting an aesthete almost as obsessed with mirrors and their reflections as Wilde was. Wilde's route to Denmark went through Bang and the French and German theatres. Both Bang and Wilde were friends and admirers of Sarah Bernhardt. In 1893–94, Bang had worked in Paris with Aurélien Lugné-Poë, directing Henrik Ibsen and Bjørnstjerne Bjørnson at the Théâtre de l'Oeuvre. In 1896, Lugné-Poë was the first theatre director to put on a complete performance of Wilde's *Salomé*, some four years after it had been banned in London and less than a year after the Wilde trials (Tydeman and Price 1996, 25–31; see also Emily Eells's essay in this volume). Bang's former lover, the German actor Max Eisfeldt, had played the part of Jokanaan in the first public performance of Max Reinhardt's production of *Salomé* at the Neues Theater in Berlin on 29 September 1903 (Tydeman and Price 1996, 33). When, only some two months later, the play was staged at the Dagmar Theatre in Copenhagen, Bang was not officially directing the play, but he was carrying out his own private theatre direction in the evenings: Anna Larsen, the *grande dame* of Danish theatre, who took the part of Salomé, used to come to his flat after her rehearsals at the theatre, thickly veiled, to study her role with him. Larsen, who had been working with Bang for years and owed much of her theatrical success to him, complained to Bang in a letter of 13 October 1904 that she found the directing at the theatre 'inartistic' by comparison with the 'sacred flame' of the art of acting which was kindled during her private rehearsals (Borg 1986, 144).

Salomé was performed twelve times between 10 December 1903 and 11 February 1904. According to the liberal daily *Politiken* of 11 December 1903, the opening night was not a success: '*Salomé* was booed at the Dagmar Theatre last night, and for once the audience was right: the failure was fully deserved' (Review 1903).[1] The reviewer commented on the 'perverted fantasy' ('pervers Fantasi') behind the play as an outlet for the playwright's 'diseased imagination' ('betændte Fantasi'), praised the aesthetic stage design and the choice of colours for the costumes – black and deep red – but came down very heavily on the hysterical, dilettantish acting ('Komedianteri').

Photographs of the production confirm this description of a somewhat melodramatic mode of acting against a setting of lush Oriental rugs, pieces of Assyrian architecture and a suggestive backdrop with a full moon and stars. The reviewer in *Politiken* had applied the term 'hysterical' to Anna Larsen's performance; in the decade after Joseph Breuer, Sigmund Freud and Jean-Martin Charcot's studies in hysteria, their writings provided a framework for the figure of Salomé. In the journal *Teateret* (The theatre), Albert Gnudtzmann stressed the obsession with death in the play and praised the artfulness of Anna Larsen's performance as 'a study of a hysterical woman,

---

[1] 'Salome blev hysset ud paa Dagmarteatret i aftes, og for én Gangs Skyld kan man give Publikum Ret: Nederlaget var fuldkomment fortjent.'

pathologically correct although – like Wilde's figure – it had nothing Biblical or historical about it' (Gnudtzmann 1903, 32).[2]

Bang explored this element of latent hysteria in *Salomé* when in 1907 he published his last volume of fiction, a Poe-inspired collection entitled *Sælsomme Fortællinger* (Strange tales), which dealt with the return of the repressed in several ways. *Salomé* functions as leitmotif in the last of the tales, entitled 'Stærkest' (Strongest), in which a cosmopolitan group of men meets in a zoo. Bang takes the first soldier's opening line in *Salomé* – 'What an uproar! Who are those wild beasts howling?' – very literally by setting the conversation against a background of shrieking vultures, roaring tigers and trumpeting elephants. A thunderstorm breaks out and produces fear and anxiety among beasts and men. Interrupting the nervous animal and human sounds are the tunes from the local brass band, playing Richard Strauss's opera *Salome*. The Frenchman asks twice 'What are they playing' and is given the same answer, 'They are playing *Salome*'. The Rumanian urges the other characters to 'listen to *Salome*', and the conversation then turns to the power of the human will, exemplified in the story of one of the characters, a theatre director who, through sheer will and strange mesmeric powers, caused the death of an ethereal young male actor on the stage. Their relationship, based on sexual desire coupled with both physical and mental power, forms an obvious parallel to the relationship between Salomé and Jokanaan. Wilde's tragic fate is hinted at in the connection between the shrieking animals and the five effeminate men, emblematic of the homosexuals of Europe, caged like animals by their sexuality – a sexuality often referred to in the jargon of the day as 'beastlike'.

The date of publication of Bang's short story coincided with the scandal known in Danish as 'Den store sædelighedsskandale' (the big public decency scandal), a series of trials against homosexuals in Copenhagen, which began in late 1906 and ran until the autumn of 1907, by which date fifteen men had been arrested and some fifty homosexuals had been called to the witness bar. Nine men were sentenced to punishments between one month and two years (von Rosen 1993, II: 712–50). The media took an active part in the scandal: thus the tabloid newspaper *Middagsposten* (Midday post) produced over 300 articles relating to the trials. Bang had been publicly accused of homosexuality by his fellow writer Johannes V. Jensen in *Politiken* on 30 November 1906 and decided to go into exile in Berlin. Jensen had placed himself between two stools. He was a great admirer and promoter of Walt Whitman: in his novel *Hjulet* (The wheel) of 1905, he had translated several poems from *Leaves of Grass*, among them two of the Calamus poems; yet he also had to take a position on Whitman's homosexuality. He did so in another article on American literature in *Politiken*, when again Bang was implied as his favourite target:

As far as Whitman is concerned, it is relevant to notice that, with a fine term, he was a homosexualist [*sic.*], but that he was so in the ordinary low manner. Yet it

---

[2]   'Det var et Studie af et hysterisk Kvindemenneske, der sikkert var patologisk rigtig, selv om den ikke – saa lidt som iøvrigt Wildes Skildring – havde noget bibelsk eller historisk ved sig.'

has to be said that Whitman was a great and strange thinker, first of all abnormal – contrary to the cases in this country where you start out as a dirty sexual criminal and from then, with the passionate approval of all the other decadent aesthetes and bastards, advance to the status of a poet. (Jensen 1906)[3]

The intellectual climate in Copenhagen in the first decade of the twentieth century was strongly homophobic. Most of the serious discourse on homosexuality, involving Danish readers and contributors, took place south of the border in such German periodicals as Magnus Hirschfeld's *Jahrbuch für sexuelle Zwischenstufen* (Journal of sexual abnormalities). The first volume of this journal (1899) included a discussion of the Wilde trials and the third volume of 1901 placed Hans Christian Andersen and Wilde side by side with the essays 'H. C. Andersen: Beweis seiner Homosexualität' (H. C. Andersen: Proof of his homosexuality) by the Dane Albert Hansen (pseudonym for Carl Albert Hansen Fahlberg), followed by 'Oskar Wilde: Ein Bericht von Dr. jur. Numa Prätorius' (Oscar Wilde: A report by Numa Praetorius LLD) and 'Oskar Wildes *Dorian Gray*' by Johannes Gaulke. The essay on Andersen introduced a new conception of Andersen as homosexual, which had its followers mainly outside Denmark (von Rosen 1993, 2: 621). As for Wilde, neither the first reading of his life nor the second of his novel questioned his sexuality. In the seventh volume of 1905 Whitman joined the ranks (Bertz 1905). German was also the language adopted by Bang himself when in 1911 he wrote his own treatise on his sexuality, *Gedanken zum Sexualitätsproblem* (Thoughts on the problem of sexuality), published posthumously by his friend the Berlin physician Max Wasbutzki in 1922. Bang does not himself mention Wilde, but Siegfried Placzek (1866–1946), the noted German neurologist and sexologist who wrote the preface to the treatise after Bang's death, compared Bang's works, especially his novel *Mikaël*, with Wilde's *DP* (Bang 1922, 12). Georg Brandes's dismissal in 1913 – 'As for Walt Whitman and Oscar Wilde, I don't see much in them. They are all the same to me' (Schyberg 1933, 15)[4] – testifies to the limited scope of vision of one of the leading Danish literary critics, but it may also explain why Bang was so anxious to dissociate himself from Wilde. A couple of anecdotes reflect this 'Wildeophobia', for example the one narrated by Bang's journalist friend Christian Houmark (1869–1950):

One day I was alone in Bang's flat while he was attending a rehearsal at the Casino Theatre. I saw Wilde's *Dorian Gray* lying open on a table in the room. When Bang returned, he said, looking at the book,
'Oh, I see you have not been bored.'
'I read the book a while ago. Wilde is a great artist.'

---

3 'For Whitmans Vedkommende er det aktuelt at bemærke, at han med et fint Ord var Homoseksualist, men at han iøvrigt var det paa den almindelige gemene Maade. Dog skal det siges, at Whitman var en stor og mærkelig Tænker, først og fremmest abnorm, i Modsætning til Eksempler herhjemmefra, hvor man begynder med at være en snavset Sædelighedsforbryder og derfra med alle de andre forfaldne Skønaanders og Bastarders lidenskabelige Billigelse avancerer til Digter.'
4 'Jeg ser ikke meget i Walt Whitman eller Oscar Wilde, jeg tager dem under ét.'

'No, he is a brilliant artist, everything he produced was done with great virtuosity. That I don't like him may be because I used to know him. In Art I cannot ignore sympathies and antipathies. Possibly with my shoemaker, but certainly not with my tailor.'

'This sounds like Wilde.'

'Thank you.'

'Many people think you resemble him.'

'Please don't offend me.'

'People say that you copy him.'

'As a poet I – no, I resemble no one.'

'As a man, I mean, in your dress, your hair style, in your behaviour – in your eccentricity.'

'No, I do not copy him, but there are certain points of resemblance – sadly, for me.'

He paced up and down the floor, stopped for a moment and resumed his pacing. Then he took up *Dorian Gray*, tore it to bits and flung the pieces into the wastepaper basket.

I wanted to take up the shreds to throw them into the stove.

'No, no – leave them. They belong in the wastepaper basket, I do not want them devoured by the pure fire.'

Pacing up and down he continued in broken sentences:

'When Wilde had served his sentence, that unfortunate, barbarous sentence, he moved to Paris, he stayed in the same hotel as I, we spoke to one another, always about the same thing, about the friends who had all deserted him.' [...] Bang continued:

'When Wilde died, Lord Douglas came to me in my hotel, imploring me to be part of the train of followers after Wilde's coffin, since he feared that the train would consist of nothing but the pimps and gamblers of Parisian nightlife. I answered him – he was still a very handsome man – that I had told Oscar when we met in Paris how I despised him for, as I said to him, the married man, the family man has duties towards society which the single man never has, not even today.' (Houmark 1950, 89–91)[5]

---

5   'En Dag sad jeg oppe hos Bang, jeg var alene, han var til Prøve på Casino. Jeg saa, at Wilde's "Dorian Gray" laa opslaaet paa et Bord. Da han kom, sagde han, seende paa Bogen: "Naa, De har da ikke kedet Dem."

"Jeg har læst den før, Wilde er en stor Kunstner."

"Nej, en blændende Artist, det er Virtuoseri alt, hvad han har frembragt. Det, at jeg ikke kan lide ham, skyldes maaske, at jeg har kendt ham; i kunsten kan jeg ikke se bort fra Sympathi og Antipathi, hos min Skomager muligvis, men slet ikke hos min Skrædder."

"Det lyder af Wilde."

"Tak."

"Der er mange, som synes, at De ligner ham."

"De behøver ikke at fornærme mig."

"Der siges, at De kopierer ham."

"Som Digter, jeg – nej, jeg ligner Ingen."

"Som Menneske, mener jeg, i Klæder og i Frisurer og i Væsen – i Eccentricitet."

"Nej, jeg kopierer ham ikke, men der er Lighedspunkter – desværre for mig."

Han gik op og ned ad Gulvet, standsede og gik igen. Saa tog han "Dorian Gray", splittede den ad og slængte den i papirkurven.

Jeg ville tage Stumperne for at kaste dem i kakkelovnen.

I have not been able to verify Houmark's anecdote,[6] but it is an interesting comment on the dialogue between the two writers, revolving around the Wildean dichotomies of art and life, original and copy. The constant comparisons with Wilde must have distressed Bang immensely. Bang's need to assert his own originality rises to almost grotesque proportions when he commits the atrocious act of tearing to shreds Wilde's only novel, without even allowing it to end up as a 'hard gemlike flame'. The poisonous book has been reduced to pure materiality and Bang emerges from the story as the moralizing writer who, despite external resemblances to Wilde, has guarded his talent and his sexuality carefully and therefore has survived, both as a man and as an artist. Wilde, on the other hand, ends up in the wastepaper basket, a solitary outcast followed to the grave by the scum of Paris. The anecdote functions as Bang's final revenge on Wilde, the copy turns against the original, not unlike the way the portrait assumes a life of its own in *PDG*. As men and artists, Bang and Wilde, especially before the fall, relate to one another as the tragic and the comic mask: they are two sides of the same coin, and Bang saw Wilde's wit and reckless lifestyle as utterly inappropriate attitudes to the tragic fate of being born a homosexual. Bang's public persona as the tragic aesthete may well have had a determining influence on the parts of Wilde's oeuvre which first gained public recognition in Denmark.

The rivalry with Wilde was not only a figment of Houmark's brain. Bang's friend Albrecht Schmidt recounted how in 1904 he had confronted Bang with the many similarities between *PDG* and Bang's own novel *Mikaël*. Bang's facial expression changed dramatically at the accusation of plagiarism, he denied it vehemently, but Schmidt was convinced he had struck him to the core (Schmidt 1937, 121). The overall parallels between *PDG* and *Mikaël* must have been obvious to anyone familiar with Wilde's novel. It remains uncertain whether Bang had read it in English, in some of the early German translations or possibly in the French 1895 translation. His own novel preceded both the Danish and the Swedish translations by a year. It may even have paved the way for Sten Drewsen's Danish translation of 1905, reprinted in 1918 and 1930 and

---

"Nej, nej, lad dem ligge, de skal i Skralde-Spanden, de skal ikke fortæres af den rene Ild."

Medens han blev ved at gaa, sagde han i afbrudte Sætninger:

"Da Wilde havde udstaaet sin Straf, den Ulykkelige, sin barbariske Straf, flyttede han til Paris, han boede paa samme Hotel som jeg, vi talte med hinanden, han altid kun om det samme, om Vennerne, som alle havde forladt ham. [...] Bang fortsatte: "Da Wilde døde, kom Lord Douglas op til mig paa mit Hotel og bad mig indtrængende om at følge efter Wildes kiste, da han frygtede, at Følget ellers ville komme til at bestaa af Nattens og Gadens Soutenører og Spillefugle og Alfonser. Jeg svarede ham – han var endnu en uhyre smuk Mand – at jeg havde sagt Oscar, da vi mødtes i Paris, at jeg foragtede ham, for, sagde jeg til ham, den gifte Mand og Familie-Faderen har Pligter overfor Samfundet, som den Ensomme aldrig har, det mener jeg – ogsaa i dag.'"

6   Bang's meeting with Wilde and his participation in Wilde's funeral are questioned by his biographer (Jacobsen 1966, 50–51). According to Heede, Houmark was notoriously unreliable at times.

only replaced by a new translation by Grethe Juel Jørgensen in 1953. Bang's novel is set in contemporary Paris and develops around a *ménage-à-quatre* that involves the celebrated history painter Claude Zoret, his handsome adoptive son Eugène Mikaël, Zoret's friend, the art critic Charles Schwitt, and Lucia de Zamikoff, an impecunious Russian aristocrat who becomes the young man's exploitative lover. Despite the romance between Mikaël and Lucia, the real love triangle plays itself out between the three men, just as in Wilde's novel the Sybil Vane plot is subordinate to the main plot. The face and body of Mikaël are an obsessive presence in Zoret's art: he is his favourite model, appearing as Alcibiades in Zoret's grand painting entitled *Sejren* (The victory), which, like Dorian's portrait, reveals the model's beauty to himself and functions as a lover's gift between painter and model. The painting is moved to Mikaël's private apartments, sold to pay Lucia's debts, but eventually it is bought back by Zoret and placed demonstratively in Mikaël's bedroom. When Zoret first meets Mikaël, the youth is a cold marble statue which the artist gradually brings to life through his love and his art. As a painter of 'the Hellenistic myth' ('den hellenistiske myte') Zoret thus becomes a Pygmalion; his male Galatea becomes a selfish monster who eventually slays his Master by not reciprocating his love. Zoret's other great painting of Mikaël as *The German Wounding Caesar* is a clear allusion to the filial ingratitude and emotional patricide experienced by the great artist. Zoret is celebrated by all of Paris as the 'Master of suffering', revealing himself to the world in his self-portraits as Job and generously leaving all his belongings to Mikaël before dying from a broken heart.

Despite Bang's denials, his novel is packed with Wildean references. His study of the generous artistic genius, who must die at the height of his career for his art and his love of a younger ungrateful man, has clear parallels with Wilde. Bang issued his novel with epigrams echoing *DP*: 'Now I can die in peace; I have seen a great passion' ('Nu kan jeg dø roligt: Jeg har set en stor lidenskab') and 'We suffer and we cause suffering in others. That is all we know' ('Vi lider og bereder Lidelser. – Mere véd vi ikke'). Although the first edition of *DP* was not published until 1905, Bang must have been familiar with the fallen Wilde through his friend, the Norwegian landscape painter Fritz Thaulow (1847–1906), who spent the last fourteen years of his life in Paris and the years 1894–98 in Dieppe where he became a close friend of Wilde after the latter's release from prison. The Norwegian writer Christian Krohg gave an account of his visit to the Thaulows at Dieppe in 1897 when Wilde was staying with them (Mikhail 1979, 2: 346–51, and Krohg 1999), and Bang visited the Thaulows in Paris in 1902 during his very brief stay to make studies for the Parisian setting of *Mikaël* (Krohg 1999).

The statuesque beauty of the young men in Wilde and Bang's novels is compared with and eventually defeated by the warm, complex and revealing power of the paintings, which serve as mirrors, revealing artist, spectator and model to each other. In a dramatic episode Zoret discovers that Mikaël has two faces, a discovery which marks the first breach of trust and intimacy between painter and model, father and son. As with Wilde, the artist must die in the course of the novel, while his love and his art survive, merged in the painting, which triumphs over the sordidness of human life. Unlike Dorian, Mikaël is curiously referred to by his surname only – the archangel with the flaming sword, the vanquisher – a name which by the early twentieth century implied a reference to one of the greatest homosexual artists, Michelangelo Buonarroti. Michelangelo figures in several of Wilde's catalogues of famous lovers, in the expanded version of PMWH, in *PDG* and in his own definition of 'the love that dare not speak its name' pronounced in the Old Bailey in 1895 (see Østermark-Johansen 1998, 205–37).

Bang toured Danish and European theatres with his public readings of *Mikaël*, which more than anything became vivid and moving dramatizations of his text, most frequently of the final scene in which the artist dies in a grand heroic manner (see Bang and Lange 2008, 14–17). He clearly found it difficult to let go of this book, and in 1910 he turned it into a theatre script together with his fellow critic Sven Lange. The play was never performed: Bang died suddenly in 1912 and the script encountered harsh criticism from the censorship at the Royal Theatre, but Bang made one significant alteration in the stage directions which brought it yet closer to *PDG*. In the first scene of the fourth act, Mikaël is left alone with Zoret's painting of him as the German wounding Caesar, and in the brief epiphanic moment when he is confronted with the painting, he realizes its autobiographical impact, fetches a knife and is just about to slash the painting when he is interrupted by Zoret (Bang and Lange 2008, 115–16).

The scene has all the high tension of melodrama or silent film, and this is no coincidence, as 1910 was also the year of the first ever film version of *PDG*, *Dorian Grays Portræt*, directed by Alex Strøm for Regia Kunstfilm, and shown on 6 October 1910 at the Panoptikon Theatre in Copenhagen. The 35 mm film, now lost, had a total playing time of 24 minutes. It became the great breakthrough for one of the earliest stars of Danish silent film, Valdemar Psilander, who was himself described as a Dorian by his biographer in 1942 – as one loved by the gods, who died young (Psilander died in 1917 aged 33). Psilander's biography gives us some idea of the low-budget film. It was partly shot in a tiny attic in central Copenhagen which served both as Basil's studio and the theatre in which Sybil Vane acted; the scenes in London's East End were filmed in the seedy area of Copenhagen known as Christianshavn. The reviewers complained that the film did not capture the eerie atmosphere of the novel and that the mysterious portrait, partly due to its vague appearance in the film, never caught the spectators' interest fully. The actors were, however, all praised for their highly dramatic acting, which held the audience breathless (Hending 1942, 43–46).

The reviewers all expected their readers to be familiar with Wilde's novel. When Sten Drewsen had translated the book in 1905, it received by far its lengthiest review on 7 April in *Politiken*, where Poul Levin took the opportunity to give a survey of Wilde's career and complain about the current chaos in the world of publishing in Denmark. A random range of novels in translation was, he argued, thrust upon Danish readers, and while he saw no reason to translate H. G. Wells's *The Food of the Gods*, likewise up for review, he did see some sense in publishing a Danish *PDG*. The novel was a distillation of everything great in Wilde: his sense of paradox and witty conversation, his gift for hedonistic enjoyment coupled with the horror of a gothic tale, which was given full poignancy by the tragic and moralizing ending. Levin was highly dismissive of Wilde the playwright: neither *Salomé* nor the comedies received any praise, but Wilde nevertheless emerged from the review as a great modern international writer, in league with the French Decadents and Gabriele D'Annunzio.

Two months later, in June 1905, the first Swedish translation of Wilde's novel appeared, but although the Swedes were far more appreciative of Wilde, it was the serious Wilde of *Salomé, PDG, BRG* and *DP* which dominated. Shortly after Ross had published his expurgated version of Wilde's letter in February 1905, Swedish reviewers took note of it, for instance on 1 March in the Swedish-Finnish journal *Euterpe* and on 26 March in *Svenska Dagbladet* (Swedish daily paper). Already by the early autumn of that year a Swedish translation of Ross's text was produced, giving rise to a whole new series of reviews in October and November (Nelson 1966, 13–15). In 1908 the text was subjected to a lengthy study by Nathan Söderblom, Swedish archbishop, in *Ord och billedar* (Words and images). Söderblom concentrated on the representation of the figure of Christ in *DP* and, although he was critical of Wilde's paradoxes, he nevertheless placed him in the select company of St Paul, St Augustine, Lev Tolstoy and Søren Kierkegaard, sometimes to Wilde's advantage (Nelson 1966, 16–17). A Danish translation of *DP* did not appear until Marguérite Gamél's of 1927. Only in 1962 did a new Danish translation by Ingeborg Buhl appear on the basis of the complete 1949 text, even though this was severely abbreviated in many places.

The Finnish theatre in Helsinki paved the way for the reception Wilde's dramas in Scandinavia with productions in Finnish of *IH* and *Salomé* in October and November of 1905. These were followed by Swedish performances of *IH* in Stockholm in September 1906, of *IBE* at the Swedish Theatre in Helsinki likewise in September of 1906 and again of *IBE* at the Vasa Theatre in Stockholm in January 1907. The comedies received negative reviews from the Swedish critics who found them superficial and without much dramatic power. This was also the case when the comedies eventually reached the Danish fringe theatres. *IH* was first performed at Det Ny Teater (The new theatre) on 2 January 1910 (Gregaard 1959, 15) and *IBE* – whose untranslatable title had now become *Hvad hedder han?* (What is his name?) – at Frederiksberg Theatre on 4 October of that same year. On 3 January the anonymous reviewer in *Politiken* praised the wit and literary sophistication of Wilde's *IH* but was highly critical of the translator, Edgard Høyer, who only rarely managed to capture Wilde's stylistic elegance. But, when *IBE* was reviewed in the same newspaper, the critic 'Hj. C.' saw Wilde's play as shallow and quite foreign. After a brief summary of the plot the critic concluded: 'There is nothing more to say about this comedy, at least not on a Danish stage. English eyes may be able to find a certain satire over certain aspects of English society' (Hj. C. 1910, [n.p.]).[7]

The overall picture of Wilde in Denmark was, however, gradually becoming more nuanced. Likewise in the autumn of 1910, *BRG* received

---

7   'Mere er der ikke i dette Lystspil, i hvert Fald ikke paa en dansk Scene. Engelske Øjne vil maaske nok kunne finde en Del Satire over visse Sider af engelsk Samfundsliv.'

its first Danish translation by Oskar V. Andersen. This was greeted with much approval from the Symbolist poet Johannes Jørgensen, who praised the metrics of the translation and recommended Wilde's poem as a powerful antidote to the saccharine tone of much modern poetry (Jørgensen 1910). His colleague in *Politiken* commented with admiration on how 'the Danish verses have cadences like the English; grand and simple; the unique pathos has been preserved, it cuts through the heart with a merciless power, but the words are plain and very quiet, with an ominous quietness, a voice half-choked by its own excessive emotion' (Christian R. 1910).[8] Andersen was a professional translator, translating from German, Dutch, Provençal and Spanish, and his rendering of Wilde's poem has become the classic one, with reprints in 1928, 1944 and as recently as 1994. In 1911 Andersen translated the four tales from *HPOT* closest in spirit to the national bard, Hans Christian Andersen, namely HP, NR, SG and DF. He thus left out RR with its Whistlerian references and the somewhat problematic PMWH. Unlike the comedies, which pose almost insurmountable challenges for the translator with their puns and paradoxes, Wilde's fairy tales fall into a very national diction. Although Paul Levin had complained in 1905 of the absence of good literary introductions to the many volumes of English literature in translation, neither of these new translations was issued with a critical introduction.

Wilde-wise, the second decade of the twentieth century was uneventful. World War I put an end to the proliferation of Wilde's texts. Strauss's opera *Salome* had its first performance in Denmark at the Royal Theatre in the season of 1918–19, and two decades after the 1903 failure of *Salomé*, the Dagmar Theatre had the courage to put on first *IBE* (1922–23) and then *WNI* (1924–25). To my knowledge there have been no further Danish productions of Wilde's *Salomé* since the 1903 production, whereas Strauss's opera has been performed repeatedly. Wilde's afterlife in Denmark in the 1920s was inextricably connected to a Niels Th. Thomsen. Thomsen had obtained an MA in mid-life, worked as a professional interpreter and translated both *IBE* and *WNI*. He was thus responsible for finding a Danish title for Wilde's untranslatable *IBE*: ever since the 1922–23 production the play has been performed, following the German model, under the (in many ways unsatisfactory) title *Bunbury*. Thomsen was of even greater importance as the author of the first monographic study of Wilde of 1920: *Oscar Wilde: Literaturbilleder fra det Moderne England* (Oscar Wilde: Literary pictures from modern England). Based on his MA thesis, the book was printed privately at his own expense in 250 copies. In his bitter and angry preface, Thomsen accused Danish publishers of thinking of profit only, happily publishing translations of light-hearted English literature while turning down scholarly studies of Wilde and George Bernard Shaw.

---

8   'de danske Vers falder som de engelske: storladent og enkelt; den særegne Pathos er bevaret, den skærer igennem Hjertet med en ubarmhjertig Kraft, men Ordene er jævne og meget stille, en Stilhed, der er uvejrssvanger, en Stemme, der er halvkvalt af sin egen Følelses Overmaal.'

Thomsen's study, subdivided into one section on Wilde the dramatist and another on Wilde the critic, was based on his reading of Alfred Douglas, Frank Harris, Leonard Ingleby, Halfdan Langgaard and Robert Sherard. Refreshingly free of anecdote and biographical material, the book references works both inside and outside Wilde's oeuvre and takes a marked critical stance. Thomsen considered *Salomé* Wilde's best dramatic work and suspected that British censorship had prevented his writings from taking a more serious turn. He included discussions of *VN* and *DOP* and achieved a far more nuanced view on Wilde as a dramatist than most of his contemporaries. Thomsen launched a fierce attack on British theatre as far more controlled by censorship than continental theatre (Thomsen 1920, 20–21); this polemical note may well be related to Thomsen's contact with Shaw. The Shaw Collection in the British Library holds a copy of Thomsen's book with the author's dedication to the Irish playwright (BL shelfmark Shaw 25).

The second half of Thomsen's book deals mostly with *Intentions*, which was translated into Danish by Henning Kehler in 1953 as *Kritikeren som Kunstner* (The critic as artist). Thomsen stresses Wilde's indebtedness to Walter Pater, and in his discussion of CA he concludes provocatively that 'Wilde's literary criticism makes you feel like reading more – of PATER' (Thomsen 1920, 81).[9] He saw Wilde as essentially un-English, as Gallic rather, in his love of wit and paradox and thus positioned him as an outsider in British society from beginning to end (88–89). Even this work is haunted by the spectre of Bang: when speaking of Wilde as a public lecturer, Thomsen drew comparisons with Bang, suggesting many similarities between the two and mentioning his own personal conversations with Bang (61) which may well have planted the seed of Thomsen's interest in Wilde.

For a couple of decades Thomsen became the Danish expert on Wilde. He wrote the entry on Wilde in the great Danish encyclopaedia, *Salmonsens Konversationsleksikon* of 1928, and an English introduction to *IBE* for Danish drama students in connection with a visiting English production of the play (Thomsen 1932). Another English production of *IBE* by Westminster Productions gave a single performance at Copenhagen's Det Ny Teater in 1938 (Gregaard 1959, 31). It would seem that despite Thomsen's comprehensive discussion of the full range of Wilde's dramatic oeuvre, the picture that was consolidating itself of Wilde the playwright in the interwar years was centred almost exclusively on *IBE*.

On 14 November 1936, Kelvin Lindemann and Kai Normann Andersen's vaudeville version of *IBE* was produced in Copenhagen at the Apollo Theatre. The title had been changed to *Musen paa Bordet* (The mouse on the table), presumably in allusion to the proverb 'when the cat's away, the mice will play'. A string of lyrics had been added to Wilde's text: the duet 'What a weather!' between Jack and Algernon, another between Gwendolen and Jack with the telling title 'One kiss too little', Cecily's great solo at the beginning of Act Two entitled 'German Grammar' followed by Jack's 'My brother's dead in Paris', Algernon and Cecily's duet 'A little hot something' and another one on 'A

---

9   'Wildes literære Kritik giver En Lyst til at læse mere – af PATER.'

quick little lie', before Lady Bracknell's moving solo on love in the third act as
she realizes that she is the only character who is alone on the stage:

> Come take me along
> Before it's too late
> Love!
> Sinful and blissful
> Wonderful
> Honi soit qui mal y …
> God save the King!
> Vive l'amour!
> It's the only thing that works! (Lindemann and Andersen 1936a, 103)[10]

The monster has been transformed into a fairy godmother. Unlike Thomsen's
1922 translation, which in most cases was faithful but plodding and devoid of
puns, this new translation is very free, full of 1930s jargon, and great effort
has been taken to make the text as modern and topical as possible. Thus Lady
Bracknell rings in 'that Armstrongian manner' – one would love to hear that
doorbell – carriages have been replaced by cars, Jack telephones his secretary
to get his ancestry sorted out, the French Revolution has been replaced by
the Russian and the fall of the rupee has been altered to the fall of the dollar.
The topicality had various political undertones, as in Cecily's song on German
grammar. In Wilde's text her observations on how German is not at all a
becoming language culminate in her outburst, 'Horrid political Economy!
Horrid Geography! Horrid, horrid German!', and by 1936 these lines could
not have been spoken with complete innocence. Her solo is remarkably explicit
in its strange mixture of cheekiness and sentimentality, using 'Heil' as a rhyming
word, an effect which sadly cannot be rendered, even in my free translation:

> 'Ich bin, Du bist, er ist –,' 'Famos' and 'wunderschön' and 'Heil!'
> The blemishes of German all on file.
> I know them all by heart
> But I don't care a fart
> 'bout all those horrors in a row
> 'Ich liebe Dich' and 'Küsse mich' – now there's a language for you!
> It's been deleted in my book!
> 'Ich liebe' I can conjugate,
> I'll have to keep an eye on it
> – till I find one to conjugate it with!
> But what to do with grammar? (Lindemann and Andersen 1936a, 51–52)[11]

---

[10] 'Kom og tag mig med!/ Men før det blir for sent!/ Kærlighed!/ Syndefuld og salig,/
Vidunderlig …/Honi soit qui mal y …/God save the King!/Vive l'amour!/D'er
det eneste, der du'r!' The script for the vaudeville is housed in the Royal Library
in Copenhagen.

[11] 'Ich bin, Du bist, er ist –,' 'Famos' og 'wunderschön' og 'Heil!'/ Hvor er det Sprog
dog fuldt af Skønhedsfejl./Jeg kan dem udenad/Men jeg er ligeglad/Med alle disse
Rædsler paa en Rad!/'Ich liebe Dich' og 'Küsse mich' – se det er vel et Sprog!/
Men det er strøget i min Skolebog!/'Ich liebe' kan jeg bøje,/Det skal jeg holde Øje
med/ – til jeg engang faar en at bøje med!/Men hvad skal jeg med Grammatik?'

In the published musical score, the satirical text has been tamed considerably, the references to 'Heil' and the blemishes of the German language have been left out altogether, and one wonders which version was performed on the stage (Lindemann 1936b, 16–17). The review in *Berlingske Tidende* (Berling's gazette) of 15 November 1936 makes no mention of the political satire in the play but, as it appears on the page in between headlines such as 'Growing tension between Germany and Russia' and 'Shower of Bombs over Central Madrid', the modern reader is inevitably reminded of the sinister political climate in which the vaudeville appeared. While describing the production as 'harmless', the condescending anonymous reviewer blamed Lindemann for ambitiously aiming at an international audience while using impossible and constrained rhymes (Review 1936). Lindemann (1911–2004) continued his politically subversive activities during the German occupation (9 April 1940 – 5 May 1945), when he was deeply involved in the resistance movement, in charge of illegal transport of Jews to Sweden and eventually had to flee to Sweden in February of 1944. In 1943 he published the novel *Den kan vel Frihed bære* (He who carries freedom), ostensibly about the Swedish occupation of the Danish island of Bornholm in 1658 but with obvious parallels to the German occupation. The first edition of 35,000 copies was sold out in a couple of days before the book was banned. Although *Musen paa Bordet* is in many ways a silly, sentimental and not particularly profound rewriting of Wilde's play, Lindemann's modernization of it testified to his instinctive awareness of the potential in the Wildean tension between surface and depth.

The Royal Theatre, as the Danish national stage, was subjected to strict censorship during the German occupation, yet statistics of the productions during those five dark years reveal quite clearly how, in the choice of *repertoire* at least, a certain freedom was allowed. Thus, during the entire occupation, only 4 per cent of all productions (drama, ballet and opera) were by German authors or composers and in 1945–47 there was absolutely none. By comparison, 65 per cent were of Danish origin, 4 of other Nordic origin and 27 per cent of allied origin. Immediately after the war, from 1945–47, the figures were reversed, testifying to the explosive interest in Anglo-American culture: now 60 per cent of all productions originated from the countries of the Allied Forces, whereas only 27 per cent were Danish (Thomsen 1948, 281).

When, on 10 November 1944, *IBE* was first played at the Royal Theatre, Wilde had already figured quite prominently that year on the publishers' lists with a re-issue of Andersen's translation of *BRG*, a new translation by A. C. Normann of four tales from *HPOT* and the first Danish translation of CG and LASC by K. Robert Adamsen. In the weeks before the opening night, the newspapers were full of preview articles, many of which asked the question: 'why does the Royal Theatre put on a production like *IBE* at a serious time like this?' The director, Holger Gabrielsen, came up with two different answers: one was that a little comic relief was needed between such serious plays as Ibsen's *Peer Gynt*, Bjørnson's *En Fallit* (A bankruptcy) and Carl Erik Soya's *Parasitterne* (The Parasites), all in the autumn repertory; another was that the theatre had a particularly brilliant set of actors who could perform Wilde's play with all the wit, style and elegance required. Gabrielsen may well have had in mind the celebrated Gielgud productions in London at the Globe Theatre in 1939, with Edith Evans and Margaret Rutherford, and at the Phoenix Theatre in 1942, with Edith Evans again and Peggy Ashcroft. The 1944 Copenhagen production – with Ebbe Rohde, Mogens Wieth, Karin Nellemose, Bodil Kjer and Clara Pontoppidan – became likewise legendary in Danish theatre history, with its 105 performances between 1944 and 1947. The critics' anxieties about the timeliness of such a production were clearly unfounded. On 7 November, Poul Lindeballe had written a lengthy article on Wilde in *Berlingske Aftenavis* (Berling's evening paper) under the headline 'Klunketidens sorte Faar' (The black sheep of the Victorian age) in which he had aired his concerns that the Royal Theatre was developing into a museum by playing nothing but nineteenth-century plays. Actuality was being replaced by the patina of history, and he imagined that the chief interest of Wilde's play to a modern audience would be a historical one for the connoisseurs.

Some reviewers spotted the topical relevance of *IBE*. Soya, himself the author of *Parasitterne* – a play about moral double standards –, immediately put Wildean dialogue into contemporary use. Writing in *Ekstra Bladet* he complained about the mechanical aspect of Wilde's wit:

> You simply say the opposite of what is generally assumed, and you motivate your statement in a cheeky, saucy or rude manner. An example: 'We must hope that the war will not end too soon. Just imagine how we shall miss something to talk about, once it is over.' (Soya 1944)[12]

Soya was himself balancing on a tight rope: in 1942 he had spent sixty days in prison for his thinly veiled allegory of the German occupation in his novel *En Gæst* (A visitor) of 1941; and in 1943 he had been briefly interned and the Germans had tried to liquidate him. By 1945 he had to flee to Sweden. The reviewer in *Børsen* (The exchange) adopted a different tone when he spoke of how blissful it was 'at a time so dark as this in every respect to see infectious Anglo-Saxon humour interpreted in such a spirited, elegant and civilized way.' He concluded that 'Oscar Wilde's frivolous wit came as a liberating breath from a better world, releasing the need for a moment's abandonment in the harmless delight over prejudice ridiculed' (Hauch 1944).[13] The reviewers in the right-wing and Christian papers, however, found the play utterly infantile and silly and could see no reason to perform it during the war (see Geismar 1944 and Barfod 1944).

---

[12] 'Man siger det modsatte af, hvad der er gængs Anskuelse, og motiverer sin Udtalelse paa en fræk, flabet eller uforskammet Maade. For Eksempel: Man maa jo haabe, Krigen ikke slutter foreløbig. For tænk, hvor vi kommer til at savne Konversationsstof, naar den engang er forbi.'

[13] 'men hvor er det velgørende i en Mørketid paa alle Omraader at se den smittende angelsaksiske Humor tolket saa spirituelt, saa elegant, saa gennemkultiveret. [...] Oscar Wildes løsslupne Vid kom som et befriende Pust fra en bedre Verden, der udløste trangen til et Øjebliks Hengivelse i harmløs Fryd over latterliggjort Fordom.'

The Danish nation obviously passed its own judgement on the play by attending so many performances of it. In 1946, Mogens Lind's translation came out in book form as the first published translation of Wilde's play into Danish; in 1953 it was transferred to the Radio Theatre and in 1959 to the television. A glance at the director's copy of the script from 1944 in the Royal Theatre archives shows, however, how carefully Holger Gabrielsen had gone through the text. Indentations from pencil marks in the paper reveal how every reference to anything German was pencilled over at first, but the pencil cross-outs were subsequently erased. He altered Lady Bracknell's reference to German as 'a respectable language' to 'a solid and decent language' ('Tysk klinger derimod absolut solidt og anstændigt') and at first substituted 'grammar' for 'German' in Cecily's list of hateful subjects. In the end it would appear that she was allowed to speak the original line, leaving German as the most detestable of all subjects: 'Horrid political economy! Horrid Geography! Horrid, horrid German!'

In the course of his first forty years in Denmark, Wilde had moved from Continental Symbolist theatre, performed as melodrama in a production never repeated, to becoming 'the liberating breath from a better world'. It would appear that he had eventually rid himself of the chains of Reading Gaol and his status as martyr to his sexuality, which cast such long shadows over the first decades of the twentieth century. Wilde kept his status as a subversive writer, but where the subversive character of his literature was intrinsically tied up with his sexuality at the beginning of the century, it gained political overtones during the decades dominated by Nazism. The Wildean tension between surface and depth guarantees his works a continuing presence, yet after the recent 2007–08 production of *IBE* at the Royal Theatre, a piece of postmodern clowning which completely took the elegance out of Wilde, one wonders whether the time has not come for a revival of *Salomé*.

15 An Ideal Situation? The Importance of Oscar Wilde's Dramatic Work in Hungary

Mária Kurdi

Paradoxically, the life of Oscar Wilde in Hungarian culture began only after his untimely death. The steady rise of an explicit if rather varied and uneven interest in Wilde's personality and work in Hungary from 1902 onwards can be illustrated by several facts. 1902 was the year when the journal *Magyar Géniusz* (Hungarian genius), which targeted a comparatively small and well-educated reading public, brought out the first two articles on Wilde. One of these, from June 1902, was by the Decadent poet Géza Szilágyi, whose own work is remembered today for its eccentricity. At the age of twenty-one, in 1896, Szilágyi had been summoned to court and accused of immorality following the appearance of his volume *Tristia*, which had shocked the public with its poems celebrating carnal love. The parallel with Wilde's fate speaks for itself. In *Géniusz* the Hungarian poet admires Wilde for daring to value chaos at the expense of order and to condemn prescribed sexual mores for their rigid universalizing ethos. He also praises Wilde for choosing to live his life as if it had been a luscious, colourful tale. This enthusiastic piece ends with an impressive selection of Wildean aphorisms which illustrate the transforming power that art and beauty implied for Szilágyi (Szilágyi 1902, 419–20). In August 1902, *Géniusz* published its second article on Wilde, authored by Gyula Szini, a writer on whom Wilde had a lasting impact. Szini's own work used lyrical prose and displayed a sense of strange dreaminess, portraying characters lost in the realm of the imagination. In the article for *Géniusz*, Szini claims that Wilde, an exotic butterfly destined to an early death, cultivated beauty as existing 'beyond good and evil', thereby implying the presence of echoes of Friedrich Nietzsche in Wilde's aesthetics (1902, 583). Szini would return to Wilde in his 1908 essay, 'A mese alkonya' (The twilight of fable). Here, as Gabriella Vöő has argued, he 'calls for the return of our capacity for enchantment by pure art. To argue his point he cites Wilde as an authority on the ontological difference between the real world and the world of art' (Vöő 2009, 145).

The early twentieth century saw the translation of three books on Wilde, originally authored by Halfdan Langgaard, Alfred Douglas and André Gide.[1] These are dominated by a subjective tone in their approach to Wilde as person and artist, and the decision to translate these works into Hungarian seems to be symptomatic of the general view of the author in early twentieth-century Hungary. It was the anti-Victorian attitude and sensational features of Wilde that attracted most attention, launching the vogue for an almost limitless admiration for the writer's dandyism and the provocative display of his belief in personal autonomy. Nevertheless, the critical fate of Wilde in Hungary defies easy generalizations from the start. This essay will map the trends evolving in the cultural history of the writer's reception by sampling theatre productions and the responses to these, primarily with regard to the social and ideological changes that underpinned Wilde's reception. I intend to pay special attention to the role of major representatives of Hungarian literature, criticism and philosophy in this history. Firstly I will focus on the period before 1949, the year when the communist system secured its one-party power in Hungary; I will then consider the decades under authoritarian rule until the political change in 1989; my investigation will finish by examining the last two decades up to the 2008 revival of *IBE*.

Wilde in Hungary before 1949

In the early twentieth century productions of Wilde's plays followed one another on the Hungarian stage as part of the vivid contemporary theatre life of Budapest, a fast developing cultural metropolis. The very first production, the January 1903 premiere of *LWF* at the *Nemzeti Színház* (National theatre) had a mixed reception. Critics hesitated on how to handle the novelties Wilde brought to the Hungarian stage. Among those who responded to this performance was Ernő Osvát, a literary critic of rising fame, who claimed that it was not the improbable plot but the lyrical qualities of the work that sustained the audience's interest, while the general tone of the play conveyed a measure of apathy instead of a fresh outlook on life (1945 [1903], 200–01). The Marxist philosopher and literary critic, György Lukács, commenting on the same premiere, wrote that Hungary merely followed the German example when starting to produce Wilde's plays. Lukács does not elaborate further, but his silence, rendered ironical by three dots in the text, elliptically hints at the country's history as part of the Austro-Hungarian Monarchy and at the influence of German-speaking culture throughout its semi-colonial history. However, Lukács concedes that, on this occasion, the urge to imitate proved to be rewarding because of the choice itself, and he goes on with an intense appreciation of *LWF* for its questioning of the boundary between good and evil. The production itself, as Lukács saw it, was largely carried by Mari Jászai as Mrs Erlynne. Jászai was a famous Hungarian actress who excelled in several great classical roles, from Antigone to Lady Macbeth (Lukács 1977 [1903],

---

[1]   Langgaard (1907) *Wilde Oszkár*; Douglas (1919) *Wilde és én* (Oscar Wilde and Myself); Gide (1925) *Oscar Wilde*.

61). Three year later (1906), *WNI* had its premiere at the *Nemzeti Színház*. The Hungarian reading public had just become familiar with Wilde's fairy tales (Wilde 1904), the success of which might explain the choice of this play with a fairy-tale ending and an expressed belief in the redeeming power of love. Praising it with moderation, a review of the production takes the trouble to trace Wilde's models and emphasizes the echoes of Victorien Sardou (P. 1906, 306), perhaps to reassure the audience that they would not have to face anything too unexpected or shocking.

1907 proved to be an *annus mirabilis* for Wilde's stage journey in Hungary, with productions of *IH* at the *Nemzeti Színház*, *Salomé* and *Bunbury* (*IBE*) at the Vígszínház (Comedy Theatre), and the production of a dramatized version of *PDG* at the *Magyar Színház* (Hungarian Theatre). Dezső Kosztolányi wrote about each of the productions in *Budapesti Napló* (Budapest diary). Kosztolányi was an eminent poet and author of lyrical fiction; he was a sharp-eyed critic as well as the translator of many canonical works, including *PDG*. For him, *IH* offered a study of the demonic in the figure of Mrs Cheveley. However, he considered the production itself a failure, owing both to the weaknesses of the translation and to the miscasting of the main character, the ideal husband, who was played by an actor incapable of uniting the opposites the role involved (Kosztolányi 1978 [1907], 238). *IBE* was premiered at the *Vígszínház* under the title *Bunbury*, as the pun in the original title would not work in Hungarian. Kosztolányi was fascinated by the play and its visible success on its first night. He claims that the production's careful attention to style would have appealed to the writer himself. The play also inspired him to write a Wildean dialogue between Ő (He) and Én (I) on the aesthetics of this production and modern drama in general, which highlights Én's view that realism and naturalism were dead and irretrievably gone from the stage (Kosztolányi 1978 [1907], 244–46).

Early twentieth-century intellectual life in Hungary was characterized by heated debates and controversies which resulted from the increasing polarization of progressive versus conservative attitudes to Western Modernism and its possible and desirable influence on the national culture and home-bred writers. In this context, Wilde's work tended to be either condemned for its moral dangers or admired for its daring originality. This division reflected the clash of opinions on the national stage. Not surprisingly, the early Hungarian reception of *Salomé* was a contentious matter. The play first reached Budapest in May 1903, two years before its English premiere, as the memorable guest co-production of the *Neues und Kleines Theater* (New and Small Theatres) in Berlin, directed by Max Reinhardt. On this occasion Lukács had no longer any reservations about the German influence on Hungarian art but was thoroughly impressed by the production and called Wilde a poet of the stage. In this staging of *Salomé*, Wilde's poetic sensibility was united with the colours of Sándor Bródy – a contemporary Hungarian playwright and novelist – Gerhart Hauptmann's plasticity, the beauty of Maurice Maeterlinck's poetic language and the spectacular scenic designs of Richard Wagner (quoted in Gajdó 2001, 571). Some years later, in his book about the history of modern drama (1911), Lukács would stress the superiority of *Salomé* to Wilde's comedies (1911, 465–67).

The year 1907 saw the Hungarian premiere of *Salomé*, which used a poetic translation by Szini. Kosztolányi gave an enthusiastic account, reporting on the solemn yet celebratory atmosphere in the theatre and underscoring the production's fusion of the Biblical story with passion characteristic of modernity to create a sense of eternal human tragedy (1978, 240–41). A review in *Budapesti Hírlap* (Budapest news), however, questioned not only the play's transgressive morals but also the aesthetic qualities of *Salomé* and its usefulness for the Hungarian audience, predicting that its bizarre and perverse scenes would bring no lasting success for the *Vígszínház* (Sn. 1907, 12). Voices of more weight could also be heard: for instance, Béla Tóth, a widely-known ultra-conservative journalist, used the occasion of *Salomé's* Hungarian premiere to publish a disparaging critique of Wilde which, in its turn, provoked an invective answer by the major Symbolist poet, Endre Ady. In his article Ady condemned Tóth's attack on Wilde as grossly outdated when set against the awakening of a new Hungarian cultural spirit which, for Ady, anticipating the notions of Joyce's Stephen Dedalus, was also European (Ady 1987, 483). In the words of László Kontler, Ady himself embodied the 'quintessential voice of Hungarian modernism', whose '"new songs of a new age", sung in the idiom of Baudelaire and Verlaine [were] grafted on to that of rebellious Protestant preachers and the destitute "outlaws" of Thököly and Rákóczi' (1999, 318). Through his achievement, Ady demonstrated that the impact of modern literature could serve as a catalyzing rather than overwhelming ingredient in the shaping of an entirely new and modern voice in contemporary Hungarian literature.

Wilde's early reception in Hungary had its superficial features as well. These were summed up by Kosztolányi in 1919 when, looking back on the earlier years of the century, he recalled that, during the five years when the Wilde fever was at its height (1904–09), fashion-crazy youngsters took up the habits of parting their hair in the middle and wearing a buttonhole and chipped a monocle on their left eye. The cult of Wilde, he continued, soon gave way to that of Sigmund Freud as his astonishing discoveries about the unconscious became known. However, neither of these cults, Kosztolányi added sardonically, flourished because of a widespread interest in and under-standing of innovative developments in the arts and sciences. Their persistence had far more to do with the fact that both Wilde and Freud focused on intense subjectivity, psychological difference and asocial forms of behaviour, something which appealed to many snobs as a source of moral self-justification (Kosztolányi 1978, 61). An outstanding exception to this phenomenon was *A gólyakalifa* (The stork caliph) (1916), a novel by the poet and leading literary authority Mihály Babits, which successfully united the influence of Wilde and Freud to explore the working of the subconscious.

Apart from the whims of fashion, it remains a fact that, by the mid 1920s, when the years of Wilde's sensational novelty were over, two prestigious publishing houses (Lampel R. T. and Genius Könyvkiadó R. T) brought out most of the Wilde canon in Hungarian translation. This clearly suggests that interest in his work did not slacken. In the meantime, the critical reception of Wilde had developed a more mature perspective and analytical treatment. The outstanding literary journal *Nyugat* (West), which ran between 1908 and 1941, assumed a conspicuous role in familiarizing Hungarian readers with the aesthetic and intellectual novelties of Western Europe. As a forum for leading

Hungarian literati and artists, *Nyugat* also became an epitome of modernist principles, endorsing a cosmopolitan orientation balanced by respect for the national culture. Its first editor-in-chief was Hugo Veigelsberg, a versatile literary man from a German-speaking family who used the pen-name Ignotus. His editorial policy was tolerance for widely differing trends in literature and, while 'acknowledging the validity of national literature, Ignotus did not regard it as an end in itself as the traditionalists did; in his view the assertion of national values could not be a policy, an aim, or a standard in literature' (Czigány 2000). Babits followed Ignotus as editor-in-chief of the journal between 1917 and 1941.

Nyugat welcomed the expression of contentious views and Wilde's reception provided a good case in point. Early in the journal's life, Zoltán Szász published the first article of considerable length surveying the full spectrum of Wilde's *oeuvre*. Szász made a serious attempt to engage with the works critically: regarding Wilde's dramatic achievement he contends that, although the plays abound in sparkling remarks and witty paradoxes, they remain superficial. Despite these criticisms, Szász's discussion tips the scale in favour of Wilde as it hints at his ability to unsettle his audience and inspire them to reflect seriously on what they see (1908, 650–78). The largely conventional outlook of this article was counterbalanced by the fact that leading literati such as Babits and Kosztolányi were dedicated translators of Wilde's poetry, and *Nyugat* often provided a forum for exchanging ideas concerning the problems of translation. Readers' interest in Wilde's work was sustained through reviews of different Hungarian versions of, for example, *BRG* and 'Charmides', written by first-rate poets. For instance, *Nyugat* published the essay 'Tóth Árpád Wilde-fordítása' (Árpád Tóth's translation of Wilde) in 1921, in which the poet Lőrinc Szabó discussed Tóth's rendering of *BRG*. It was again in *Nyugat* that playwright and Hollywood film-script writer Menyhért Lengyel, author of the international success *The Typhoon* (1909), reviewed the 1909 Hungarian premiere of *DOP* at the *Magyar Színház*. Lengyel noticed the hallmark of Wilde's genius even in this perhaps deservedly neglected work. Discussing the playful and clever juxtaposition of Shakespearean motifs in *DOP*, he nonetheless points to a lack of dramaturgical skill in interweaving them (1909, 386–87).

The intellectual ambience of *Nyugat* did not remain unaffected by the major changes the country suffered due to the peace treaty of Trianon (1920), according to which Hungary lost two-thirds of its former territory, with millions of Hungarians left outside the borders of the mother country suffering minority status abroad. Because of the Hungarians' enhanced sensitivity to the troubled historical experience of other small nations, literary criticism after this date tended to identify Irish-born authors as different from English writers in attitudes and aesthetics. A 1929 article by Ignotus is a good example: he points to the defining presence of 'Irish blood' in authors such as Thomas Moore, Jonathan Swift, Wilde and George Bernard Shaw (716). Reviews of the new Hungarian theatre productions of Wilde's plays attempted both to measure the subtleties of the dramas according to their own merits and to deal with the demands of performing them adequately. In the interwar period Aladár Schöpflin, an immensely influential and prolific critic, wrote important commentaries on new performances of Wilde's plays. About the 1926 production of *IH* at the *Nemzeti Színház*, Schöpflin wrote that Wilde's elegant, witty conversations were rendered unevenly since only some of the actors were able to speak their lines with the necessary ease and verve – a shortcoming which Schöpflin deplored as more and more discernable in contemporary Hungarian theatre (1926, 842–43). *Bunbury* had three revivals before World War II: in 1924 at the *Vígszínház*, in 1928 at the *Kamaraszínház* (Chamber Theatre) and in 1939 as an exam production put on by drama students. The 1928 production proved to be most memorable: it was performed altogether forty-six times in front of enthusiastic audiences. Schöpflin was of the opinion that the play itself thrived on parody and the grotesque – qualities which this production aimed to underscore through, for instance, the marionette-like acting style of the love couples in Act Three. The main merits of the venture, in Schöpflin's summary, were that it breathed new life into a fading play thanks to the director's fresh interpretation and that it gave a good opportunity for actors to experiment with a range of styles (1928, 495).

From 1949 to 1989

Wilde's drama, like most theatre activities, was silenced in Hungary during the war. Following the end of the war, in the so-called Coalition Period (1945–48), literary life quickly recovered and a number of periodicals with distinctive profiles were put into circulation; among these was *Új hold* (New moon), which ran from 1946 to 1948 and attracted young authors with ideals shaped by *Nyugat* (Czigány 2000). The May 1949 staging of *IH* at the *Művész Színház* (Arts Theatre) can be seen as a remnant of the post-war ambition to revitalize Hungarian cultural activities. However, 1949 was the year in which the communist power gained a political monopoly over the country and the play only went through three performances, after which the theatre was closed down. Surprisingly, several reviews of the production have survived: these oscillate between aesthetic appraisal in the vein of pre-war theatre criticism and ideologically-driven judgement, illustrating that it was a period of political transition. Szilárd Darvas praised the production for rendering the true Wilde by bringing out the satire in the play, while László Vass highlighted the vibrant acting of the main characters, especially that of Mrs Cheveley (Darvas 1949; Vass 1949). Other reviews appreciated the revival of the play on account of the social message it carried, criticizing as it does the aristocratic class that the new Hungarian political leadership was determined to punish severely. One of these articles was by the poet György Faludy, who later turned against the regime and left the country in 1956. In the 1949 review, however, he welcomed the timely staging of the play just after a successful performance in Moscow, the imperial centre of the Soviet Bloc countries.

From 1950, an ideologically controlled form of literary dictatorship was introduced, which expected writers and cultural life in general to follow the strict principles of socialist realism, the chief doctrine of communist aesthetics. A playwright such as Wilde was considered too bourgeois to serve the goals of the new cultural politics, and was deemed to have no place in the theatre programmes. The end of Stalinism, in 1953, marked the onset of a slow thaw, 'particularly perceptible in the ideological and in the intellectual sphere', which enabled silenced writers (and silenced plays) to re-enter the literary scene (Kontler 1999, 423). In early 1956, Wilde's FT (*Firenzei tragédia*) had its Hungarian premiere at the *Déryné Színház*, in Miskolc. After the 1956 revolution and its ruthless crushing by Soviet forces, with the execution of Imre Nagy to follow in June 1958, the Communist Party under the leadership of János Kádár declared the onset of a revised cultural policy. As part of this, the party was willing to acknowledge the humanist merits of the best of bourgeois literature in order to win the support of intellectuals (Kontler 1999, 436). Wilde was rehabilitated during this process. Between 1959 and 1989, the year of the political change that ended communist rule, there were fifteen new productions of Wilde's dramas, played not only in Budapest but also in provincial theatres and thus reaching a wider audience than before. Although most of them earned only moderate success and elicited mixed reactions, they tended to raise contentious issues such as the attitude to the bohemian figure and to Wilde's transgressive work in a socialist country.[2] These productions also stirred interest in the potential of Hungarian theatres to improve their work through stylistic experimentation. Reviews reflect the state of theatre criticism in a political milieu which, after 1968, was labelled as a 'soft' dictatorship, a state of affairs that brought some dubious advantages but also engendered uncertainty about the tolerance of the regime toward voices of dissent.

In 1959, *LWF* was revived at the *Madách Kamara Színház* (Madách Chamber Theatre) in Budapest. On this occasion, Marxist philosopher and literary historian István Hermann published a review in the daily *Magyar Nemzet* (Hungarian nation), which meditated on the secret of Wilde's unceasing popularity in spite of the weaknesses of his work. Hermann concluded that Wilde's plays have a quality that invites directors and actors to shape their own style, and that this stylistic experiment was achieved with partial success by the production under review (1959). After FT had had two more unremarkable revivals, Wilde's most experimental theatre piece, *Salomé*, reappeared on stage twice during the Kádárist period. The venues, however, counted as marginal: one of the productions was staged at the Summer Theatre of Pécs in 1978, with the participation of the local ballet company; the other was performed in 1981 at the *Ódry Színpad* (Ódry Stage), a venue used by drama students for their exam performances. According to one review, the open-air summer production was a failure because Imre Eck, the director of the ballet company, separated the dance scenes from the others too sharply, thus violating the homogenous artistic wholeness of the drama. The reviewer also reminds us of the success that Lindsay Kemp's dance theatre group had earned in England by staging the play not long before Eck, providing a source of inspiration

---

2   Wilde's SMUS was translated into Hungarian as early as 1912 by Anna Winkler, but it never received a critical analysis. Interestingly, the translator omitted the word 'socialism' from the title, which appeared as *Az ember lelke* (The soul of man).

for the Hungarian production (Mészáros 1978, 6). *IH* was revived by the *Veszprém* Theatre in 1981. It was an unusually fresh and vibrant production, reflecting the director's talent and admiration for the writer. However, it failed to convince that Wilde's plays should be more frequently staged in Hungary because of their lasting value (Ézsaiás 1981, 20).

IBE enjoyed nine revivals between 1959 and 1989. Four of these productions used the title *Bunbury*, whereas the other five used a new name, *Hazudj igazat* (Lie to me the truth), attempting to convey some sense of the paradox so brilliantly at work in the original. One of the most important productions of *Bunbury* was undertaken by the *Nemzeti Színház* of Pécs in 1959. Reflecting the official ideological approach to literature characteristic of the times, one critic argued that the strength of the enterprise was in offering a critique of capitalism, even though Wilde's social criticism was deemed inferior to that of Shaw and J. B. Priestley (Lemle 1959). In a similar way, the 1960 production of *Hazudj igazat* in Szeged was blamed for not bringing out all the critical potential of the drama, which, in the words of one reviewer, wittily handles the petty-bourgeois interpretation of certain social concepts and phenomena (Simon 1960). András Rajk's report of a 1968 staging of *Bunbury* at the *Ódry Színpad* describes an interesting experiment of playing Wilde in operetta-fashion, with music by Emil Petrovics (1968). Lady Bracknell was acted by Hanna Honthy, a versatile actress and singer who earned herself lasting fame both at home and abroad in the title role of *Csárdás Queen*, Imre Kálmán's grand operetta composed early in the twentieth century. Dedicated experimentation, however, did not always work. A 1971 staging of *Hazudj igazat* by the *Szigligeti Színház* of Szolnok also used music, more of the popular kind this time. While a reviewer celebrated the Szolnok production for enhancing the ironic and satirical effects of the play, he complained that the music and dance scenes broke the rhythm of action and criticized the eagerness to present something new by changing Wilde's original so thoroughly (Csík 1971, 5).

In the Hungarian reception of Wilde, the pre–1990 period saw, at last, the appearance of longer studies of the writer. In his 1983 book, which adopts the principles of drama analysis as theorized by Lukács, literary historian Péter Egri offers a broad picture of the playwriting practices that flourished across different countries between the politically-charged dates of 1871 and 1917. It is a survey of authors whose dramaturgical innovations Egri sees as milestones of the revolution taking place in modern European theatre. A chapter entitled 'The Paradox of Aestheticism' treats Wilde's dramatic work, interspersing the analysis with ample reference to his essays. The sole existing book-length monograph on Wilde by a Hungarian author was written by András Török and published in the year of political transition, 1989. Written for the wider public, the book provides ample information about the circumstances of Wilde's career and includes bibliographical details as well as the dates of the English and Hungarian premieres of his plays.[3] The individual works by Wilde are introduced relying on international research findings. The book contains

---

[3]   The bibliographical material provided in this book has been an important source for the present study.

an original analysis of *IBE* as an inverted absurd drama that exhibits optimism instead of despair in a perfect form (Török 1989, 226–27).

1990 to the present

Between 1990 and 2008, only three of Wilde's plays were revived in Hungarian theatres: *Salomé* (three times), *IH* (once) and *IBE* (nine times). The selection of these plays seems to have been governed by assumptions about the adaptability of the works in performance to the needs of the contemporary Hungarian audience, rather than by any conscious plan to re-evaluate Wilde's dramatic *oeuvre*. Among the new stagings, the 1995 *Salomé* by the *Nemzeti Színház* in Miskolc, directed by film-director Zoltán Kamondi, proved to be noteworthy as a multilevel re-interpretation. A review in Hungary's most prestigious forum of theatre criticism, *Színház* (Theatre), begins its commentary by assessing the use of time and space in this version of *Salomé*. The performance set three temporal levels against each other: the ancient story; World War II, dominated by the horrors of Fascism; and the 1990s, with their increasingly widespread manifestations of brutality. The quickly-changing scenes within this expanded time frame took place on a stage that looked very much unlike the bright colours Wilde once imagined for the setting (Kállai 1995, 15): it was a tunnel with black walls, the end of which was out of sight, as if representing the twentieth century itself in black and white. Besides the traditional title role, Salomé was alternately transformed into a female doctor of a Nazi concentration camp who feels unbridled desire for the body of a handsome Jewish boy, and into an ugly old hag who tries to seduce a yuppie-looking youth. This inventive production stays true to the original by presenting the frustration of Salomé's desire in each of her roles. Tamás Koltai, however, noted that, in our era devoid of myths, the ritual story had lost all its dignity, and concluded his analysis with the image of the dirty-hag version of Salomé throwing the withered head of Jokanaan into a ragged plastic bag (1995, 16). In 1996, the theatre of Kaposvár staged a production of *Salomé* conceived in terms of the Wildean idea of total theatre. The result, to borrow Péter P. Müller's terms, was an updated version, which replaced the *fin-de-siècle* ornamentation of the original design with postmodern stylistic effects (1996, 43).

The only revival of *IH* after 1990 took place in late 2003; it was put on by the *Radnóti Színház* in Budapest. In an interview director Péter Valló was asked about his motivations for choosing this play over twenty years after its last performance in Hungary. As a significant reason for his decision he mentioned the timeliness of the work on account of its resonance with the increasingly aggressive features of political life in contemporary Hungary (Vámos 2004). Critics, however, found that the production went too far in trying to foreground this timeliness. Judit Szántó, while discontented with the new title, *Az ideális férj*, for being less rhythmic than the one used earlier (*Az eszményi férj*), argued that the director gave up too much of the original without the support of a well-established governing concept of how to modernize the play's subtle details (2004, 34). The firm structure Wilde once created became fragmented in this version of *IH*, resulting in a sense of artificiality which alienated the audience.

Working out a new approach to staging *IBE* apparently put directors and actors to the test. The play's first revival during the period, by the theatre of Nyíregyháza in 1990, was soon forgotten, as its sole aim was to entertain an audience grateful to see their favourite actors in a fine comedy. In early 1995, the exceptionally talented Hungarian actor Miklós Gábor, who had become famous nationwide for his memorable interpretation of several classic roles including Hamlet, undertook the direction of a new version of *IBE*. In an interview during rehearsals, Gábor told the critic Gabriella Lőcsei that his work had a strong conceptual basis. Although the year 1994 witnessed celebrations of Wilde in Hungary on the occasion of the 150th anniversary of his birth, Gábor lamented that there had been no revival of the author's dramatic work on stage or screen. What fascinated him personally, he said, was the text of *IBE*, a carefully chiselled work of art achieved by an author for whom finding the *mot juste* was of paramount importance (Lőcsei 1995, 19). In accordance, the production directed by Gábor used the early twentieth-century 'classical' translation by Frigyes Karinthy, a writer noted, amongst other things, for his Hungarian renderings of such popular masterpieces as *Gulliver's Travels* and *Winnie the Pooh*. The revival of *IBE*, with Gábor as director of the *Józsefvárosi Színház*, impressed an audience used to the simplifications and even vulgarities of contemporary life, which they could forget about in the theatre while enjoying Wilde's complex aesthetics and elegance of language and style (Koltai 1995, 16). All in all, Gábor's new stage version succeeded in re-creating Wilde's masterful verbal artfulness, holding the audience's interest in an age that had largely lost the penchant for eloquence which did not serve propagandistic goals.

Subsequent revivals of *IBE* were mostly staged in view of more conventional expectations than Gábor's, devoting attention to casting rather than innovation. Critics' appraisals were sometimes misleading as well, especially when they highlighted the timeliness of Wilde for reasons alien to the play. The 2003 performance of *IBE* in Győr ambitiously presented a comedy of intrigue and miscomprehensions which, a critic noted, concluded in the errant characters' finding their way back to the right path. This kind of moralizing attitude on the part of the reviewer derived from the misplaced urge to compare the world of the play with the loss of values by the twenty-first century, stressing that the former at least knew the distinction between right and wrong, which the audience was pleased to recall while watching the performance (V. L. 2003). Another 2003 staging of the play, by the *József Attila Színház* in Budapest, aimed at bringing out the comic effects of the original as fully as possible, incorporating musical accompaniment to this end. Both this and the most recent, early 2008 production of *IBE* at the *Radnóti Miklós Színház* in Budapest, used a new translation of the play by Ádám Nádasdy, a poet known for his renderings of Shakespeare and Synge. His version found an equivalent for the name Earnest in the Hungarian name Szilárd, which is also an adjective meaning 'firm'. Playing with words in the manner of Wilde, the most recent production of *IBE* offered a smoothly working interpretation of the text, relying on the world-wide fame of the play and its potential for being staged with a heightened amount of theatricality.

On the centenary of Wilde's death in 2000, some old but mostly new translations of the major works (poetry, prose and drama) were published in two large, hard-bound volumes, soon to be followed by a Hungarian translation of Jörg W. Rademacher's book on Wilde (2001). Kosztolányi's standard translation of *PDG* (*Dorian Gray arcképe*) was also reprinted in new editions in 2006 and 2007. The most recent collection of texts by Wilde is the form of an elegant, slender volume that offers a selection of what the editor-translator Miklós Molnár has found most valuable in the treasury of the writer's ideas about art and life (Wilde 2008). In 2002 Krisztina Lajosi published the first article on Wilde in Hungary under the title 'The Reception of Oscar Wilde in Hungary: Translator as Critic – Critic as Artist – Translator as Artist', which deals mainly with questions of translation and concludes that 'Wilde had a strong influence on Hungarian literature' (Lajosi 2002, 266).

Judging from the ups and downs of the rich variety of Wilde stagings that the above assessment has revealed, the story of Wilde in Hungarian theatres appears to be a seamless one, in which the early years, influenced by the international theatrical milieu and the discovery of Wilde by the Hungarian Modernists, form a cornerstone. Taken as a whole, the Hungarian reception of Wilde's plays invites, in keeping with their semantic ambiguities, the description 'an ideal situation' because of its steady continuity and constant self-renewal against the backdrop of the extreme political and socio-cultural changes the country faced throughout the last century. Although Wilde himself would probably dispute and challenge the designation in a shower of brilliant paradoxes, his dramatic *oeuvre* has by now established itself as a classic in modern world theatre. For its part, the Hungarian theatre world has become well aware of the need to redefine its relation to the classics again and again by using new translations and revised concepts in order to explore how Wilde's works can speak to audiences more than a century after their inception. 'Tho' much is taken, much abides', one is tempted to say with Alfred Tennyson, a poet Wilde respected and cited in his own poetry: like the vast lands in front of Tennyson's old hero, Ulysses, Wilde's dramatic *oeuvre* has remained an inexhaustible source of material for Hungarian theatres on account of its intrinsic value and adaptability.

16 Oscar Wilde and the Czech Decadence

Zdeněk Beran

For more than a century Oscar Wilde has been one of the most popular figures among Czech readers and theatre-goers. The list of his published works in Czech translation, which were issued in book form as well as in magazines, exceeds two hundred items and the list of different productions of his plays in the Czech and Moravian theatres includes almost the same number. Wilde's life and work have inspired writers, poets and artists at different times; some of his texts have been adapted for radio or television, and a few years ago a musical based on *PDG* was staged in Prague.[1] Yet it is obvious that, although his popularity has never abated, the focus has changed. The role of Wilde in the Czech culture of the first two decades of the twentieth century was considerably different from the one he played in the post-war period. The present article attempts to define the place Wilde held in those early years, and especially his position in the formation of the Czech Decadent movement. In his essay 'Oscar Wilde a české písemnictví' (Oscar Wilde and Czech literature), Jan Reichman points out that the first noteworthy mention of Wilde in Czech criticism was made in 1890 by Hubert Gordon Schauer, in his article 'O úkolech naší kritiky' (The aims of our criticism) (*Národní listy*, 31 October). Schauer (1862–92) was a young, vigorous and often rather controversial critic, who, unlike most of his contemporaries, preferred modern literature to the traditional literary canon and who saw in Wilde one of the most important critics of the day.[2] Although he slightly alters the title of Wilde's essay, calling it 'The Functions of Criticism' (CA was originally entitled 'The True Function

---

1   Written by Michal Pavlíček (music) and Jan Sahara Hedl (libretto), the musical *Obraz Doriana Graye* was premiered in February 2006.

2   Jan Herben, a journalist, novelist and supporter of Professor Masaryk's programme of Czech national and political independence, remembers Schauer as a highly individualistic person: 'He derided both Czech science and Czech literature with cruelty. He loathed reading contemporary Czech fiction [...]. He would be sarcastic, impolite, contemptuous, and he also liked to show off his knowledge of the great writers of the world with a kind of vanity.' ('O vědě i krásném písemnictví českém měl pojem posměšně krutý. Beletrii tehdejší hnusilo se mu čísti [...].

and Value of Criticism'), he supports his views of the supremacy of the critical mind in the development of art and literature by paraphrasing Wilde's words. The whole article (six full pages in the book edition of Schauer's works, cf. Schauer 1917, 262–67) sounds like Wilde turned serious and hectoring, but at least, in this way, some of Wilde's ideas were introduced to the Czech reading public. At that time Schauer's was a lone voice (Reichmann 1919, 113) and it is hard to predict what his attitude to the Czech Decadent movement and the *Moderní revue* (Modern review) would have been, had he not died prematurely. The cultural cosmopolitanism of the movement's major representatives would have appealed to him but their extreme political nationalism and anti-German attitudes would have been unacceptable to a man whose father was German and who – rather scandalously – suggested that Czech literature and culture should become part of a broader German cultural context (in 'Naše dvě otázky', *Čas*, 1886).

The real history of Wilde's presence in the Czech cultural context begins five years later, with a fierce polemic provoked by the sensational news of the writer's conviction and imprisonment. The key role in this altercation was played by the *Moderní revue*, a new magazine 'for literature, art and life', founded in 1894 by two young Decadent artists and critics, Arnošt Procházka (1869–1925) and Jiří Karásek ze Lvovic (1871–1951). On 4 May 1895 the *Čas*, a prestigious liberal weekly, reported the first Wilde trial. Here, in an article entitled simply 'Oscar Wilde', an anonymous author called Wilde a man with 'a beast living inside him' ('žila v něm však bestie') and pointed out that his unnatural perversity had already transpired through his essay DL, in which he expressed his loathing for all that was natural ('Oscar Wilde' 1895). The *Moderní revue* reacted immediately: in the May number of its second volume, a writer who signed himself as (-C-) protested vehemently against the insulting words and objected to the public prying into any artist's private life. This prompted a response in several periodicals: the *Čas* replied briefly and ironically; *Naše Doba* (Our time), in an article signed by 'Sursum' (a collective pseudonym of three leading representatives of the realist movement in philosophy and literature, T. G. Masaryk, J. S. Machar and F. V. Krejčí), argued against the alleged lack of traditional moral principles in those who did not believe in God (an idea expressed in the *Moderní revue* article) and, in the following issue, presented Krafft-Ebing's new scientific understanding of pederasty; the *Studentský sborník* (Students' yearbook) violently defended morals in general and the public's right to know the private lives of artists in particular ('Rozhledy časopisecké' 1895); whereas the *Niva*, to which Karásek was a contributor, resorted to what may be understood as a middle ground (*Niva* 1895). The *Moderní revue*, in its June number, defended its position in two shorter pieces ([Procházka & Karásek ze Lvovic] 1895). The first, signed -A- (Procházka), argued that 'we are not impudent enough or stupid enough or cruel enough to condemn a man for an act that is pathological [...], to see him destroyed and to participate in destroying him, as the deceitful bourgeois

---

Mluvil sarkasticky, drsně, pohrdlivě a jaksi marnivě blýskal se autory všeho světa.')
(Herben 1936, 279)

prudery and its institutions do in England and elsewhere.'[3] The second, signed -K- (Karásek), urged the papers 'not to be ashamed to pillory the cruel and beastly way in which prurient England handles a man who should be treated by doctors and psychologists'.[4]

Forty years later Karásek recalled the situation in his memoirs:

> All the Czech magazines that informed about the Oscar Wilde trial did so accusing Wilde in the worst way possible [...]. I could hardly withstand these attacks, much as I sympathized with Oscar Wilde, a great artist, then absolutely unknown to the Czech reading public. My attitude was also shared by Arnošt Procházka, who saw mere psychic pathology in Wilde's case [...]. The worst of all were private attacks against the *Moderní revue* for its Wilde number. We were accused of defending homosexuality [...]. I was told at the Topič's and Srdce's [publishers and booksellers] that a woman writer had come in demanding that the number of the *Moderní revue* propagating Oscar Wilde be removed from the shop window. (Karásek 1994, 130–33)[5]

Procházka was the owner and publisher of the review, whereas Karásek held the position of literary editor. In the following thirty years they were to become the major figures of the Czech Decadence (or 'synthetic art', as they sometimes preferred to call it) and the *Moderní revue* its principal organ. During the three decades of its existence (the review ended with Procházka's death in 1925), the *Moderní revue* attracted a number of young writers, poets, critics and artists, some talented, some less so, some of them staying for years, some of them leaving soon after joining. Procházka was the *spiritus agens* of the project, having contacts with other Decadent and Symbolist artists abroad (especially Stanisław Przybyszewski in Berlin) and being able to get access to foreign literature and art. Karásek, who, unlike Procházka, did not come from a well-off family and for many years had to depend on his employment at the Prague GPO (first as a clerk, later as a director of the Prague Postal Museum), supplied the magazine with his own poetry, short stories, novels and, most

---

3　'Nejsme ani dosti drzi ani dosti omezeni ani dosti surovi, abychom soudili člověka pro případ pathologický [...], abychom jej pokládali za zničeného a sami jej ničili, jako lhářská pruderie bourgeoisná a její vnucované instituce, nejen v Anglii, i jinde.' Besides the *Moderní revue*, Karásek also defended his stance in the *Literární listy* (cf. Karásek 1895b).

4　'neostýchaly se na pranýř postaviti surový a bestiální způsob, jakým se jedná v cudné Anglii s člověkem, jenž patří nejvýše lékaři a psychologu'.

5　'Všechny české časopisy, které referovaly o procesu Oscara Wilda, psaly proti Wildovi nejhorším způsobem [...]. Nesl jsem těžce tyto útoky, čím více jsem sympatizoval s velikým umělcem, jako byl Oscar Wilde, tehdejšímu českému čtenářstvu ovšem zcela neznámý. Mé stanovisko sdílel i Arnošt Procházka, jenž v případě Wildově viděl jen psychickou patologii [...]. Proti Moderní revui pro číslo věnované Oscaru Wildovi byly nejhorší útoky soukromé. Zazlívalo se nám, že obhajujeme homosexualitu [...] u Topičů a Srdců [mi] říkali, že tam byla zmíněná spisovatelka a intervenovala, aby z výkladu odstranili ono číslo Moderní revue, v němž se propaguje Oscar Wilde.'

of all, critical essays. Luboš Merhaut characterizes Procházka and his idea of Decadence in the following way:

> Procházka, the central theorist and defender of Decadence, gradually matured to the concept of Anti-Positivism, *Aestheticism*: the autonomy of pure and absolute art. From the second half of the 1890s [...] he held to the exclusivity of the world of art, rejected its influencing by everyday reality and even its influence on reality. He created the cult of the Individual and of Beauty as the antithesis of run-of-the-mill reality. He was seeking after and interpreting (mostly foreign) poets and artists who were provocative, doubting established values, programmatically opposing themselves to their surroundings and to fashion, poets and artists who were misunderstood, condemned and suppressed. He was concerned with mystery and dreams, the polarity of evil and good, death, Satanism, erotic instinct, perversity, exoticism, Narcissism – in connection with the research of the time into the subconscious as domains and essences of the spiritual life. (Merhaut 2006, 53)

In the first volume of the *Moderní revue* the programme of the new art is presented in ways similar to this, be it in Procházka's essay 'Immoralita v umění' (Immorality in art), Bohuslav Chaloupka's manifesto 'Budoucí umění' (Future art) or Karásek's 'O kritice jako žánru uměleckém' (Criticism as a genre of art). None of these early texts mentions Wilde by name but the ideas expressed are close to his. Procházka writes that the 'supreme products of the human spirit, the most splendid achievements of art, have always been in opposition to the view and habits of the crowd' (1895, 117);[6] the core of Chaloupka's argument is that the *'synthesis of beauty and life is the aim of the art of the future'* (1895, 123);[7] and Karásek defends the 'life of criticism that is individual, personal, independent, rich, creative; criticism as a *new genre of art'* (1895a, 133).[8] All these are Wildean echoes. Although the founders of the magazine were oriented principally towards modern French literature and art, Wilde had been an iconic figure for them from the very beginning, as Karásek was to confess later (Karásek 1994, 185).

The controversy surrounding Wilde's imprisonment became an impulse for introducing his works to Czech readers. The first text to appear in the *Moderní revue* was DL, translated by Hugo Kosterka in four instalments (1895). Two related articles appeared with the first instalment: Dr Oskar Panizza's 'Bayreuth a homosexualita' (Bayreuth and homosexuality), translated by Procházka, and Karásek's own 'Afféra p. Panizzova' (An affair of Mr Panizza), about the confiscation by the German authorities of Panizza's book *Das*

---

6   'Co největšího kdy lidský duch, co nejskvělejšího umění zrodilo, bylo vždy v odporu s názorem a zvyklostmi davu.'

7   *'Synthese krásy a života je metou umění budoucnosti.'*

8   'život kritiky individuálné, personelní, kritiky samostatné, bohaté, tvůrčí; kritiky jako *nového genru umění'*. It is perhaps not without interest to note that Chaloupka sees Decadence as a synthesis of all the modern (i.e. nineteenth-century) tendencies in art and literature (Chaloupka 1895, 122). Chaloupka's words sound like a misapplication of F. X. Šalda's ideas, formed principally under the influence of Emile Hennequin and expressed in his youthful essay 'Synthetism v novém umění' (Synthetism in New Art).

Liebeskonzil (The love council). The reason for including these was apparently to warn the public that even Czech culture might face similar intolerance. Karásek, himself a homosexual, felt that the danger might be quite imminent, and indeed the Austrian authorities were soon to confiscate his own book, the collection of homoerotic poetry *Sodoma* (Sodom).[9] Karásek's initial idea was to devote Number 3 of the *Moderní revue* entirely to Wilde, in order 'to give the abused poet full satisfaction, for the sake of young people at least' ('abychom poplivanému básníkovi zjednali satisfakci aspoň u mládeže') (Karásek 1994, 130). But it is more than evident that the aim was wider and more personal, definitely for Karásek if not for others: 'This whole number of the *Moderní revue* is the first defence in Czech literature of the problem of the sexually inverted' ('Celé toto číslo *Moderní revue* je první obhajobou problému pohlavně invertovaných v české literatuře') (Karásek 1994, 131; cf. also Vévoda 1999, 221–22). Over the following years, the *Moderní revue* continued to publish short texts by Wilde, all in translations by Procházka (Wilde 1896, 1899, 1900).

A fresh stimulus came with the news of Wilde's death five years later. Volume 12 of the *Moderní revue* is dedicated to the deceased artist: Karásek opens the January 1901 number with a short study of Wilde; Jiří Živný's translation of *BRG* runs through the January, February and March numbers; the March issue brings Albert C. Sterner's portrait of Wilde in pen and ink; and the July number Procházka's translation of Stuart Merrill's sketch, 'written at the moment of Wilde's death'. The hard cover issued for the twelve numbers of the volume was accordingly adorned with a profile drawing of Wilde's face. From this moment on, Wilde's name never disappeared from the pages of the magazine, though its presence became less intense. We find fewer translations, but there are reviews of editions and theatrical productions, written by new contributors such as Miloš Marten, Kamil Fiala or Jarmil Krecar. Wilde's name and quotations from his works function in many articles as a kind of reference point. His iconic status among the Decadents who gathered around the *Moderní revue* was indisputable.

One of the reasons why translations of Wilde did not appear more frequently in the review later on was that, after 1901, it was much easier to publish his texts in book form. To be exact, a turning point in this respect came at the very beginning of 1904 when Václav Tille, soon to become Professor of Comparative Literature at Prague University, published an essay on Wilde in the January issue of the *Nová česká revue* (New Czech review).[10]

---

9   In September 1895 the police confiscated not only all the 200 copies of *Sodoma*, prepared for distribution in the printer's shop, but also no. 6 of *Moderní revue*, which contained two poems from the prohibited book ('Sodoma' and 'Venus masculinus') as well as the last installment of Kosterka's translation of DL. Alfred Thomas's suggestion that the magazine was confiscated also because of the Wilde text can hardly apply since the earlier parts of the essay had appeared in the preceding three numbers without any intervention of the authorities (cf. Thomas 1999, 172).

10   Tille's favourable attitude to Wilde's art may have been influenced by his sustained

Tille's text is for the most part a reproduction of Robert Harborough Sherard's book on Wilde, then just published in Germany, but it is more than clear that Tille shares Sherard's view of Wilde as a pure and moral man. The essay ends with an open defence of Wilde and a sincere endorsement of his work. What Tille appreciates most is Wilde's ability to present 'a synthesis of fascinating, fragile forms, delightful tales full of the innocence and purity of a child's soul, splendid images, as colourful and emotional as Japanese art, [...] paradoxes as well as profound philosophical and critical ideas' ('synthesi úchvatných, křehkých forem, líbezné pohádky dýchající nevinností a čistotou dětských duší, skvělé obrazy, barevné a vycítěné jako japonské umění, [...] paradoxa i hluboké filozofické i kritické myšlenky') (Tille 1904, 275). The last sentence of the article expresses yet another hope: 'The time is not too far when his disease, like Dostoevsky's epilepsy, will no longer prevent an assessment of his works according to their value' ('Není daleko doba, kdy jeho nemoc nebude, jako epilepsie Dostojevského, závadou, aby jeho díla byla posuzována dle své hodnoty') (Tille 1904, 276). It was Tille's authority that helped to launch Wilde to a broader reading public.

Paradoxically, or perhaps symptomatically, now that Wilde was safely dead, he became much more popular among publishers, critics and readers of diverse persuasions – a modern classic in fact. The *Moderní revue* itself launched an exquisite series of books, *Knihovna Moderní revue* (Modern Review library), and included some of Wilde's shorter texts (1908 and 1918). In addition, Procházka was preparing new titles for Kamilla Neumannová's series *Knihy dobrých autorů* (Books by good authors) and published not only his own translations of Wilde's essays and stories (1909), but also other people's renderings, such as Antonín Starý's *DP* (1906, 1908) or Jiří Živný's *BRG* (1909a). However, it was more than clear that Wilde ceased to be an exclusive possession of the Decadents and became public property, in the best sense of the word. Within the first two decades of the new century Czech readers could have read almost everything he had written and even some texts of dubious authorship, such as the infamous PA, translated as *Kněz a ministrant* by Jan Rey. Jan Reichmann, in the bibliography attached to the essay mentioned above, lists about fifty titles published up to 1919, covering eight plays, selections of poetry, stories, essays, *PDG* and fairy tales, some of them in more than one translation.

In this sudden upsurge of general interest in Wilde, the Decadents maintained a specific position. Unlike more academic critics, such as Josef Bartoš or Václav Tille who, in an attempt to present a relatively complex picture, made their readers acquainted with the circumstances of Wilde's life and work (often depending on unreliable sources),[11] the critics affiliated with the *Moderní revue* resorted mostly to what may be called 'imaginary portraits'. Thus Karásek, in his sketch written after Wilde's death and later included in

---

interest in modern French literature and life-long passion for collecting folk tales (Blümlová 1999, 73–74).

[11] Bartoš wrote an introduction for Marie Jesenská's translation of Wilde's fairy tales (1904); Tille introduced Otakar Theer's translation of *Salomé* (1905).

a collection of critical studies called *Renaissanční touhy v umění* (Renaissance desires in art), dramatizes Wilde as a tragic hero – an Icarus, whose dream was crushed by hard reality and whose fall was fatal. Karásek sees the paradox of Wilde's life in the fact that his light, colourful French spirit could live in materialist, pedantic, commerce-oriented Britain, and concludes that art does not depend on reality itself but on a dream of reality (Karásek 1926, 66–68). This idea, though it hardly captures all the aspects of Wilde's conception of art, is very close to Karásek's own aesthetic ideal, as is apparent from many of his works, most of all from his 'Chinese' drama *Sen o říši krásy* (Dream of the empire of beauty), inspired perhaps more by Maurice Maeterlinck than Wilde. Characteristically, Wilde helps Karásek define his own position as a writer and poet, and the picture we receive is thus very subjective.

In this sense Karásek's text, full of purple prose as it is, can be taken as a preparatory ground for his own works of fiction. All his Decadent novels, from *Gotická duše* (The Gothic soul) to *Ganymedes* (Ganymede), contain a hero who, in different ways, does not belong to the setting in which he lives. Three novels especially seem resonant of Wildean motifs. *Román Manfreda Macmillena* (The novel of Manfred Macmillen) (1907), the first volume of a trilogy called *Romány tří mágů* (The novels of three magicians), presents a mysterious aristocratic hero – outwardly a typical dandy but in private a man harrowed by the problems of duality. Not only does he bear an uncanny physical resemblance to an eighteenth-century portrait of Cagliostro, an Italian magician and alchemist, but he is also haunted by a living double, the dramatist Walter Mora, whose play about Cagliostro is a huge success. The novel culminates in a fatal confrontation between the two men, perhaps no more than Narcissistic projections of the painting, during which both disappear, leaving the young narrator in doubt of their existence. The story takes place in Prague – not modern Prague, however, but an evocation of the hypothetic *Praga magica* of old churches, palaces, magicians and alchemists, which seems more authentic to the narrator-hero than reality.

If *Manfred Macmillen* reflects the Wildean questions of the relationship between art and reality, duality and fluid identity, the third novel of the series, *Ganymedes* (1925), brings the central triangle (represented by Manfred, Walter Mora and Cagliostro in the previous novel) even closer to the model of *PDG*. Set again in the mystic atmosphere of Prague, the story now takes the readers to the Jewish ghetto, reviving its old tales and legends. In the old Jewish cemetery, the hero, Radovan, a young homosexual (or even androgynous) boy emotionally attached to an acquaintance of his mother, Adrian, meets the mysterious figure of Jorn Möller. Möller is a Danish sculptor whose ambition is to create a new Golem, the legendary android from the times of Emperor Rudolph II. The artist finally succeeds in making a statue of Radovan and, using his art of sorcery, endows it with life. The outcome is tragic: the statue strangles its original, Radovan, to death. Hana Bednaříková rightly argues that the triangular pattern derives directly from Wilde's novel: Jorn Möller as a creator of an aesthetic object is based on Basil Hallward; Adrian, whose role is to be Radovan's guide in the process of initiation, on Lord Henry Wotton; and Radovan, a perfect object of art and initiation, on Dorian (Bednaříková 2000, 61). Yet the theme is different: while in Karásek there is an attempt to overcome the imperfections of physical existence by creating a perfect piece of art even at the expense of one's life, *PDG* rather exposes the destructive illusion of substituting life for art.

The hero of *Zastřený obraz* (The hidden painting) (1923) similarly holds a complex attitude to the facts of life. His Prague consists of baroque palaces, the old Lesser-Town cemetery (a Christian one this time) and a nearby church. Nonetheless, the crucial theme of the novel is hidden mystery, or better, 'hiddenness' itself. The protagonist, solitary artist Jiljí (Giles), enters a curious intimate relationship with a long dead aristocrat, René-Alexander, whose grave he discovers in the cemetery. By accident, he finds himself in the country house where René lived and there, in a secret chamber, he discovers René's painting of his sister and learns about their incestuous relationship. The greater secret hidden behind this inconspicuous representation of René's sin, however, is the fact of Jiljí's homosexuality and his struggle to recognize and accept it. The hidden painting is thus hidden in more than one sense: it is hidden from the eyes of spectators, like Dorian Gray's picture, and it is also hidden (or covered) as a mirror in which one dares not look.[12] If in his early sketch Karásek drew a parallel between the history of Wilde and that of his Dorian Gray (death was for both the only solution to the romantic interference of life into art), then in his novels he develops the impulses taken from Wilde's work in new, unexpected directions, combining his intense love of late-Renaissance and baroque Prague with the modern issues of aesthetic representation. Nor are Karásek's plays free of Wilde's influence. This is especially true about his one-act dramatic poem *Apollonius z Tyany* (Apollonius of Tyana), where the former courtesan Tarsia dances twice, as she takes off the veils of her robe, first to express her love for Apollonius and then, at the end of the play, over his body which had been crushed to death by an angry crowd.

Critics have especially emphasized the influence of Wilde's work on Karásek's later development (cf. e.g. Novák 1946, 468). This was not always seen as a positive feature. For instance, the influential literary critic F. X. Šalda rather invidiously said of Karásek that 'even a blind man can see how he has sweated to learn Wilde's art of lightness and paradox' (Šalda 1963, 26);[13] while Fedor Soldan presented the influence of Wilde upon Karásek in more moderate terms, drawing attention to questions of sexual perversion and to the philosophy of lying (Soldan 1941, 22).

Jarmil Krecar (1884–1959) began publishing in the *Moderní revue* in 1914, first as translator, then, from 1917, as critic. He translated three of Wilde's plays: *Salomé*, FT (*Florencká tragédie*) and SCo (*Svatá kurtizána neb Žena pokrytá drahokamy*). Miloš Klincman praised the book editions of these plays

---

[12] The Czech word *zastřený* suggests not only that the painting is covered with cloth but also that its meaning is obscure and difficult to reconstruct.

[13] 'I slepec vidí, jak se v potu tváře učil lehkosti a paradoxnosti wildovské.' Šalda himself translated Wilde's CA in 1903–04 (one of the first translations from Wilde outside the *Moderní revue*) and wrote an entry on Wilde for *Ottův slovník naučný* (Otto's general encyclopaedia), the most comprehensive encyclopaedia of the period (1908).

from the point of view of typography and design (Klincman 1918, 294). As a typical advocate of exquisite, high-brow, Decadent art, Krecar ignored Wilde's comedies and also, apparently, did not primarily intend to have his translations staged. Indeed it seems that Krecar's translations have never been performed. In this respect he was especially unfortunate with *Salomé*. The play was translated for the Prague National Theatre by Otakar Theer, a poet who occasionally published in the *Moderní revue*, and, prior to World War II, it was often staged in this version; apart from the National Theatre, it was performed by the *Vinohradské divadlo* (Vinohrady theatre) in Prague in 1928, and there were also three different productions in Brno in 1906, 1908 and 1924. Moreover, before Krecar published his own rendering in 1918, two more translations of the play had appeared in book form: one by a mysterious Adi-Hidári-Ho in 1905 and the other by Julius Schmitt in 1911. Preceding all these is an anonymous rendition that appeared in the *Divadelní listy* (Theatre gazette) in 1902. This is the earliest known translation of a Wilde play into Czech and, together with the three post-war translations (Ivo Fleischmann's, 1959; Drahoslava Janderová's, 1988; and Michal Láznovský's, 2000), it makes *Salomé* the most frequently translated among Wilde's works. FT was staged at the Prague National Theatre in 1909 and then again in Ostrava in 1928. In both cases the translation used was the one made by Jaroslav Kvapil under the pen name Jarmila Dušková.[14]

Krecar's translations are literary, not dramatic ones. The essay he attached to the edition of *Salomé*, and later included in the collection of essays *Glossy do cizích knih* (My notes in other people's books), is again a typical example of how the Czech Decadents treated Wilde. Unlike Václav Tille's introduction to Theer's translation, which maps all the difficulties of an objective approach to and assessment of Wilde, Krecar's is a psychological study of an artist fully absorbed in his theme. Krecar sees Wilde's achievement mainly in his ability to create in the characters of a virgin and a prophet 'eternal types of irrepressible [sex] drive and divine mission' ('věčné typy nezdolného pudu a božského poslání'), whose fates are unavoidable and who are destroyed by life's blind will 'with which the outer reality controls people, their great passions as well as their great dreams' ('jímž vnějšek ovládá lidi, i jejich velké vášně a velké sny'). The play, according to Krecar, is semantically open to allow anyone to identify with the heroine and to understand her unique position (Krecar 1924, 39).

There are inaccuracies and inconsistencies both in Krecar's account of the theme's context and in his interpretation of the play, but they are less relevant

---

[14]   Kvapil, who was director of the National Theatre since 1900, directed the Prague production of FT himself, as well as the National Theatre production of *Salomé*. FT was also staged in Brno in 1911 (directed by Josef Fišer) and, although it is not certain whose translation was used there, it is highly probable that it was Kvapil's again. Kvapil's translation, unlike Krecar's, has not been published and it is thus difficult to say how much the two versions differed. Kvapil's own early poetry (from around 1890) was written in the Decadent manner, but he abandoned this tendency very soon in favour of more traditional verse. SCo, a short, fragmented text, has never been staged in Czech.

in his 'imaginary portrait' than in an academic piece of writing. What seems striking, however, is the fact that Krecar's text is in some basic details almost identical with the *Salomé* passage in Richard Ellmann's biography of Wilde, written seven decades later. Ellmann's passage on Wilde's obsession with the story sounds like an echo of Krecar (see Ellmann 1988, 323). This only testifies to the fact that both authors depended on the same source, Robert Ross's introductory note to the 1912 English edition of the play. To question the reliability of this single source is, however, outside the scope of this article.

Another contributor to the *Moderní revue*, Miloš Marten (1883–1917), was influenced by Wilde's formal innovations rather than his ideas. One of the first texts Marten published in the magazine was his review of Marie Jesenská's translation of Wilde's fairy tales, *Dvě knihy pohádek* (1904), in which he characterized the publication and translation as 'acts of artistic choice and taste' ('činy uměleckého výběru a taktu') and praised highly the charm of these 'sweet and sad legends' ('sladké a smutné legendy') (Marten 1904, 409). Marten's, as well as Wilde's, interest in style drew upon the same source, Walter Pater. Some of Marten's texts are written in the same dialogue form with which Wilde experimented in the two major essays of *Intentions*, especially the 'testament' (Marten's term) 'Nad městem' (Over a city). Yet Marten's talent was too great to be limited by the narrow preferences of the *Moderní revue*. In 1916 he left the review and in the following year he died.

Among the poets, artists, critics and translators inclined towards the Decadent programme, Arthur Breisky (1885–1910), for one, was indisputably a Wilde figure. Breisky was an extreme individualist who loved exquisite moments, dandiacal postures and mystifying gestures. In his monograph *Fragment zastřeného osudu* (Fragment of an obscure life), Jaroslav Podroužek tells the story of the young ambitious critic's first encounter with Karásek. On this occasion, Breisky told the poet that he had a house of his own in North Bohemia where he lived alone with his old servant, protected from any contact with other people (Podroužek 1945, 66–67). But in actual fact Breisky's life was very far from the Des-Esseintes image with which he presented himself to his Decadent idol. He worked as a clerk at a customs and excise office in Teplice, a small North Bohemian town, lived in a small room and used all his spare time to read, write or visit his intellectual friends in Dresden or in Prague.

Breisky's life was a life of dreams. Intellectually he was influenced by Nietzsche, who inspired his extreme individualism and his ambition to become 'Great'. He wrote to his girlfriend Božena Dapeciová: 'I said to myself: either you will achieve what you want and become Great, or you will fall and die, and this would be much better for you than to crawl around just like every common man. For my soul abhors Mediocrity [...]. *Be hard!* is what Nietzsche said' (Breisky 1997a, 21).[15] At the same time he loved Wilde and it

---

[15] 'A řekl jsem si: buď dojdeš a dosáhneš toho, co chceš, a budeš Velikým, anebo padneš, zhyneš, a bude ti lépe, než by ses měl plaziti jako tuctový člověk tímto životem. Neboť duše má se hrozí Prostřednosti [...]. *Buďte tvrdí!* řekl Nietzsche.'

was because of Wilde that he learned English.[16] After the crisis which followed his parting with Božena Dapeciová, Wilde became ever more important for him as a teacher of emotional detachment. During his stay in Teplice (mainly in the year 1905), Breisky became an ardent student of Wilde: he admired his paradoxes, his art of lying, his elegance, dandyism and his desire to be applauded by those whom he disdained. It was not philosophical depth that Breisky was looking for in Wilde, but inspiration for how he should organize his public life. He did not imitate him, rather he became like him by circumstances (Podroužek 1945, 52).

A rare photograph shows Breisky as Wilde with a big white flower in his buttonhole. His essays, especially 'Kvintesence dandysmu' (The quintessence of dandyism) and 'Harlekýn – kosmický klaun' (The Harlequin – a cosmic clown), are written in the vein of Wildean individualism and are perhaps the most refined examples of Breisky's purple prose. 'Oscar Wilde', the concluding short story of his only book, *Triumf zla* (Triumph of evil) (1910), is a mystification based on the assumption that Wilde did not die in 1900, but only staged his death so that he could watch the reactions of the world. The story, which takes place in 'the corridors of the Vatican gallery', consists almost entirely of a dialogue, reminiscent of PMWH, between Wilde and a young English writer, Harry Good. Jiří Karásek exalted Breisky's courage and 'art of lying' (the book includes seven 'imaginary portraits') in his introductory note;[17] but Breisky's method seems to lag far behind the art of his model. The dialogue hardly does more than present the material that was published after Wilde's death in books or essays by Gide, Sherard or Ross, and one feels just how much Breisky wanted to show that he was acquainted with these posthumous Wildeana (cf. Breisky 1997b, 89–107). This is exactly the shortcoming of the whole book: Breisky seems to be impressed so much by the sources he has studied that he is not able to select them properly and adapt them to his goal. Instead of creating and presenting delightful mental pictures of the figures he includes in the book

---

[16]   He comments on this in a letter to Božena Dapeciová of 5 February 1904: 'Believe me, it is for Wilde that I want to learn English. Though I know nothing yet and often look up a verb in a dictionary, I already have his essays – real wine of ideas, sweet and noble –, *Intensions,* and his excellent novel *The Picture of Dorian Gray*.' ('Věř, jen kvůli Wildovi se chci naučiti angličtině. Ač neumím ještě nic, často hledám sloveso ve slovníku, přece již mám jeho eseje – pravé to sladké a ušlechtilé myšlenkové víno – Intentions a jeho skvělý román The Picture of Dorian Gray') (Breisky 1997a, 204). Two months later he writes to Karel Scheinpflug: 'I can speak German, French and partly English' ('Ovládám německý, francouzský a částečně anglický jazyk') (Breisky 1997a, 224).

[17]   Although both Karásek and Breisky indulged in creating dreamy worlds, it is worth noting that Breisky's conception of the dream was very different from Karásek's. They were both dreams of beauty but Karásek's idea of beauty, as it was presented in his play *Sen o říši krásy* (Dream of the empire of beauty), is organic and physiological: his hero can be an emperor only while young and beautiful; on the other hand, Breisky's idea includes the active participation of the subject: one creates himself beautiful by one's dandiacal gestures.

(which range from Tiberius and Nero to Baudelaire and Wilde), what he offers is sometimes too close to mere instruction in disguise. There seems to be more Wildean flavour in his other mystifications, especially in the two tales he published together with his translation of the first part of Robert Louis Stevenson's *The Suicide Club* as two 'newly discovered miniatures by Stevenson': 'Báseň v próze' (A poem in prose) and 'Zpověď grafomanova' (The confession of a graphomaniac). The reader finds in them much less Stevenson than Wilde combined with Poe (Breisky 1997b, 110–28). It is paradoxical that the *Čas* hailed the two texts written by Breisky as Stevenson's most famous stories and praised them over the original one (Podroužek 1945, 92).

Breisky's career was too short and too precocious. If the circumstances had been more favourable, he might have matured into a unique Wildean type. Instead he was held back by the realities of life, like and yet unlike Wilde himself. He was never rich enough to do the only thing he longed for: leave the provincial towns of North Bohemia and join the literary and artistic circles of Prague. Exasperated by the office drudgery, he left for the United States only to find his untimely death there. He was killed in a New York hospital, where he was employed as a lift operator. This fatal accident, in which his face was crushed beyond recognition, was the origin of a new mythology according to which Breisky had not died but was instead living in hiding – the fate he had attributed to Wilde in the above-mentioned story. If Life ever imitated Art, then it was in the fate of the unfortunate Arthur Breisky.

1910, the year of Breisky's death, was also a turning point in the development of Wildean themes in Czech art. An analysis of these themes provides a fitting epilogue to the story of Wilde in the Czech cultural context of this period. Art, especially painting and engraving, had gradually absorbed the most frequent Decadent elements and motifs since the turn of the century and Czech art critics nowadays recognize Decadence as a crucial phase in the modern history of art. In 1907, Wilde was portrayed by Jan Konůpek (1883–1950), a prolific Symbolist painter, engraver and book designer. He poses as an aesthete in a rich fur coat with a golden chain and several jewelled rings on his fingers, an image inspired by the photographs from his American lecture tour. The exquisitely lush background and the expression on Wilde's face reflect not only the influence of Joris-Karl Huysmans's *À Rebours*, Edward Burne-Jones and James McNeill Whistler, but also of the contemporary Austrian artists Gustav Klimt and, especially, Egon Schiele. It may be of some interest that there is a clear affinity between this painting and Konůpek's black-and-white drawing of Hamlet from the following year.

In 1910, Konůpek revived his interest in Wilde in a series of pictures representing Salome, the most famous one of which is a charcoal drawing of a reclining girl with the head of John the Baptist suspended over her body and blood trickling onto her breasts. Around this time Wilde's *Salomé* provided a predominant theme among Czech and Czech-German artists. Like Aubrey Beardsley in his famous illustrations to the play, Czech artists aimed to intensify Wilde's meanings in their works (cf. Larvová 1998, 30–32). The question, of course, is what stimulated this interest. I believe that there is a clear connection to the theatrical productions of *Salomé*, especially in Prague.[18] Otakar Theer's translation of the play, directed by Jaroslav Kvapil, was premiered at the National Theatre on 15 April 1905. The production ran for eleven years, featuring such stars as Eduard Vojan as Herodes and Anna Sedláčková as Salomé. One and a half years later, Strauss's *Salome* was staged in Prague.[19] If there were only very occasional pictures of Salome before 1905 (by Josef Jakší, ca. 1900, or Hugo Boettinger, after 1900), during the play's presence on the National Theatre stage, the Biblical *femme fatale* was portrayed by numerous artists, as diverse as Josef Wenig (1905), Otty Schneiderová (after 1905), Josef Váchal (1909 and 1913), Jan Zrzavý (1910), Emil Filla (1911), František Kobliha (1913), František Drtikol (1913) and František Tavík Šimon (before 1920). The representations are very different indeed, as the uniting moment of Decadent art was thematic rather than formal (cf. Urban 2006, 11). They range from the exotic, Schiele-esque, art-nouveau dancer of the almost forgotten Schneiderová, through Konůpek's and Váchal's expressionist scenes, to Filla's cubist assembly of contrasting facets in the quivering light of dance and music. In the photographs of František Drtikol (1883–1961), Salome is an insane, hysterical woman with wide-opened eyes and full breasts, clutching possessively the bloody head of Jokanaan (1913). František Kobliha (1877–1962), who became one of the most important artists and art critics of the *Moderní revue*, made Salome one of his *Women of My Dreams* – a series of woodcuts from 1913 in which women appear as half-naked somnambulist creatures amid the solitude of starry nights and limitless space. The works of the Czech artists add to the many representations of diabolical women, which characterize European *fin-de-siècle* art. Characteristically, after the disappearance of *Salomé* from the stage, the theme disappears from art as well.

The popularity of the play might also have inspired Jindřich Hořejší – one of the most important lyric poets of a later period and a translator of French poetry and drama – to write the sonnet 'U hrobu Oscara Wilda' (At the grave of Oscar Wilde), in which the Salome motif is once again dominant (the poem was published in the *Moderní revue* in February 1911). But in fact the theme had been exploited even earlier, by yet another poet connected with the magazine, Stanislav Kostka Neumann. Neumann published his 'Salome' in the *Almanach na rok MCM* (Almanac for 1900) and later included the poem in his *Sen o zástupu zoufajících a jiné básně* (A dream about the despairing multitudes and other poems).

---

[18] The popularity of the play in those years is evident from its successful parody by one of the most famous Prague cabarets, Červená sedma (The seven of hearts, or better, The red seven, as it was named after its founder Jiří Červený, whose name means 'red'). In 1910 the group staged a parody written by the pianist František Hvižďálek, in which Salomé is finally presented with a pig's head on a plate and marries Narraboth. However, when the cabaret restaged the play in 1921, the attempt ended in failure (cf. Červený 1959, 22, 268).

[19] Strauss's opera received the cold shoulder from the *Moderní revue* reviewer Kamil Fiala, who called it 'a double monster' ('podvojná zrůda') (1907, 99).

Salomé is the nexus of Oscar Wilde's presence in Czech Decadence. It is a point where literature, theatre and art meet. In later years, Wilde would be reduced mostly to the author of four brilliant conversational comedies, a development of which the Decadents would certainly disapprove.[20] But Wilde was a Protean figure – and this is perhaps why he is still so much alive.

---

[20] In the last sixty years, two comedies especially have never left the stage: *IBE* and *IH*, both produced mostly in the ingenious translations of J. Z. Novák (as *Jak je důležité míti Filipa* and *Ideální manžel*, respectively). *Salomé* has, by contrast, been staged only occasionally in the post-war period, and almost certainly not before the mid–1980s. Novák also translated *PDG* (as *Obraz Doriana Graye*) in 1958, the tales (1965) and the fairy tales (1981); these translations have been published repeatedly. The successful TV adaptations of *IBE* (1979), *IH* (2001) and *CG* (1989) prove that in recent years the public's preference has been for the light-hearted, entertaining Wilde, the more so as Jiří Věrčák's TV film based on *Salomé* (1993) is nowadays almost forgotten.

17 The 'Byron of Kipling's England': Oscar Wilde in Croatia

Irena Grubica

From the beginning of the twentieth century to this day, the continued presence of Oscar Wilde in Croatia is testified by the translations of all his major works, the frequent performances of his plays, critical articles and various adaptations of his works by Croatian writers. The paradigms of reception and critical debate around his life and work have however changed over time. A few years after Wilde's death, which went unnoticed by Croatian literary journals, his Croatian reputation began to flower, reaching its peak in the following two decades. It seems certain, however, that a number of prominent Croatian intellectuals had already become familiar with Wilde's controversial personality and aesthetic views during his lifetime, even if they did not write about him until later. This resulted in a kind of tacit reception. On 14 October 1900, a few days before Wilde's last birthday and only a month before his death, the progressive literary review *Svjetlo* (Light) published Wilde's prose poem 'The Artist', translated by the versatile young intellectual Vladimir Jelovšek, who would later gain some fame as a Decadent poet. The translation was printed without commentary or critical assessment. But it is telling that, only one year earlier, this same poem had been rendered into Polish by Arnošt Procházka in the Czech magazine *Moderní revue* (for an extensive treatment of the important role of this periodical in Wilde's Czech reception see Zdeněk Beran's essay in this volume). Jelovšek, who was at the time a medical student in Prague and frequented Czech literary circles, is likely to have been familiar with Procházka's translation, which might have been the source, or at least an incentive, for his own. During the *fin de siècle* many young Croatian intellectuals left their country for various European cultural centres, predominantly Vienna, Munich and Prague, in order to be educated there. Their endeavours to catch up with European artistic movements fuelled their own creative work, which remained, at the same time, deeply connected with their homeland. Knowledge about Wilde travelled within this cosmopolitan context and was inflected by the different dynamics of his reception in these cities.

Croatia was part of the Austro-Hungarian Empire until 1918 and, as a result, there was a flourishing cultural exchange between Vienna and

Zagreb. Wilde first became known in Croatia predominantly via Vienna, where his ideas and works were circulated among the Croatian student intelligentsia gathered around *Mladost* (Youth), a periodical on modern literature and art launched in 1898. The aim of the journal was to break away from the national and political activism which other Croatian literary journals promoted overtly or indirectly and to focus instead on the dissemination of modern literature. *Mladost* printed both writing by contemporary Croatian authors and avant-garde and modernist works in translation, especially by Slavonic, Scandinavian and French writers. It provided first-hand information about distinguished literary figures of the *fin de siècle*, and published works by Marcel Prévost, Gabriele D'Annunzio, Knut Hamsun and Arthur Schnitzler among others. Although there are no references to Wilde in the six volumes that make up the life span of the journal, the editors and readers of *Mladost* certainly aided the dissemination of the Wilde myth in Croatia by their keen interest in Wilde's cultural context, their Francophile tendencies and their engagement with Viennese literary life at the time of Wilde's release from prison and of the first German translations of his works.

The overt disregard for Wilde at this stage might be due to the great influence of the critics Hermann Bahr and T. G. Masaryk on the nation's mainstream cultural opinion. *Mladost*'s editorial board was highly influenced by Bahr, whom they considered the spiritual leader of the modernist movement and whose derogatory remarks on Wilde's art might have determined the absence of his name from the pages of the journal. Masaryk, who sometimes quotes Wilde's aphorisms, had similarly small regard for Wilde's artistic achievements. In this light, it is not so surprising that no obituary of Wilde was published in the Croatian press; the more so as even the influential German broadsheet *Die Zeit* (The time), edited by Bahr, did not publish an obituary on Wilde's death. As English was not widely read in Croatia at this time, Wilde's works were largely mediated through German translations. In Germany, the year 1897 had seen a translation of CG by Anna Marie von Boehn, published in Munich. In 1891 *Intentions* came out in the original English edition, which, for linguistic reasons, appears to have had an insignificant impact on Croatian readers.

Of greater relevance were the first-hand and up-to-date accounts of Wilde from Paris. Antun Gustav Matoš gave a vivid portrayal of Wilde in a long letter from Paris dated 1 January 1901 which was published in the Zagreb newspaper *Hrvatsko pravo* (Croatian law) from 17 to 19 January. Matoš, a poet, journalist and essayist who would soon become the central figure of the Croatian Moderna (modernism), was living in Paris at the time. In the early twentieth century he would play a fundamental role in the introduction of European (mainly French) modern literary currents such as Symbolism and Impressionism into Croatian literary culture. The tone of the 1901 piece, which displays Matoš's characteristic sharp wit and ironic stance, played a crucial role in moulding the early reception of Wilde in Croatia. Matoš painted an ambivalently compassionate image of Wilde, describing him as the 'victim of modern hypocrisy', the 'Byron of Kipling's England' and a rebel against social and artistic conventions who was ultimately 'killed by scandal'

(Matoš 2003, 260–61).[1] Matoš drew attention to the fact that even Heine's Paris funeral (1856) had been attended by more people than Wilde's and took the opportunity to inform Croatian readers that Lina Munte, rather than Sarah Bernhardt, was currently playing the title role of *Salomé* in the *Theatre Libre* (Matoš 2003, 260–61).

On 23 July of the following year, just a few months before the premiere of Max Reinhardt's *Salomé* at the *Kleines Theater* (Small theatre) in Berlin (discussed in this volume by Rainer Kohlmayer and Lucia Krämer), a belated obituary came out in the journal *Narodne novine* (National newspaper). It was again written by Matoš, who had sent it directly from Paris where he had come across Gide's article on Wilde published that month in *L'Ermitage* (Matoš 1902).[2] Matoš summarizes Gide, interspersing his article with excerpts from Gide's essay in an attempt to give Croatian readers the first authentic account of Wilde the man as well as Wilde the artist. Matoš's article remained the most extensive Croatian text on Wilde for several years. Therefore, while information about Wilde had until then come to Zagreb predominantly from Vienna, it now also started to be disseminated from Paris. It is significant that, in this early reception of Wilde in Croatia, Gide's writing and his views played an intermediary role, since Gide enjoyed great fame and popularity among Croatian men of letters and his judgements had a strong influence on the early reception of many English and Irish modernist writers, including Joyce. The full version of Gide's article on Wilde would be translated into Croatian by Višnja Machiedo in the second half of the twentieth century (Gide 1980). In more recent years it has also served as an afterword to Luko Paljetak's translation of Wilde's PP, *Pjesme u prozi* (Wilde 2002), in a bilingual edition illustrated by the renowned artist Duško Šibl, whose illustrations were also shown at a solo exhibition in Dubrovnik in 2003.

Matoš lived in Montmartre and some biographical sketches hint at the fact that he met or at least came across Wilde. The writer Tin Ujević remembered that Matoš sometimes used to boast in public that Wilde was his neighbour (Ujević 1967, 52, 70), but there is no reliable evidence of this. Matoš was also the first Croatian writer to engage in a creative dialogue with Wilde. On 1 October 1902 he published the short story 'Ugasnulo svjetlo' (The extinguished light) in the Zagreb journal *Mlada Hrvatska* (Young Croatia), in which Wilde appeared as one of the characters. The short story was subsequently republished in the collection *Umorne priče* (Tired stories) in 1909. In his essays and letters Matoš praised the aestheticism of Walter Pater but he was often more ambivalent in his admiration for Wilde, whose work he discussed in relation to Poe and Byron (Matoš 1911, Matoš 1940b).

Croatian men of letters now started to deal more thoroughly with Wilde's literary works, prompted by the examples of several of his friends and admirers on the Continent. In 1902 there were two more references

---

[1]   'žrtva modernog prijetvorstva [...] Byron Kiplingove Engleske [...] Ubio ga "škandal"'.

[2]   For a full account of Gide's writings on Wilde see Victoria Reid's essay earlier in this volume.

to Wilde in Croatian journals. On 19 April, the Zagreb German-language daily *Agramer Zeitung* (Agram [Zagreb] newspaper) published a feuilleton by Otto Kraus which discussed Wilde's *PDG*, Rudyard Kipling's *The Jungle Book* and Mathilde Malling's *Donna Isabel* (Kraus 1902). In the same year, literary historian Vladoje Dukat, who played a pioneering role in the introduction of English literature in the country, published a short note in *Nada* (Hope), a Sarajevo-based review, in which he informed readers about current perform-ances in London theatres. In this note he mentions Wilde's plays and gives a passing reference to his recent death in Paris (Dukat 1902). Two years later, in 1904, in an overview of English literature that remained the only one in Croatia until the second half of the twentieth century, Dukat wrote a passage on Wilde in a chapter entitled 'The Age of Queen Victoria'. He presented Wilde primarily as a playwright because he considered his plays, in particular his comedies, the most relevant of all his works (Dukat 1904). Dukat's emphasis on Wilde's theatrical achievements was representative of the early reception of Wilde by Croatian critics.

The sensational aura of Wilde's popularity in those years boosted interest in his works. Literary journals started to report more thoroughly on the events that contributed to the imprint of Wilde on the European cultural landscape, especially after the first public performances of *Salomé* and the early German translations of his works. In 1903, shortly before the play's premiere at the *Deutsches Volkstheater* (German people's theatre) in Vienna (see Sandra Mayer's chapter in this volume), *Vienac* (Wreath), one of the leading Croatian literary journals, printed an account of censorship in Germany, which discussed plays forbidden in England but staged in German theatres. The author mentioned *Salomé* along with plays by Paul Heyse and Max Dreyer, which were also struggling with German censorship laws at that time (Milčinović 1903). Croatian readers were acquainted with the troubled history of *Salomé* in the German context: the private stagings of the play in Brussels and Munich in 1901, followed by Berlin in 1902 and then by the first public stagings in Stuttgart and Hamburg. They were also acquainted with Hedwig Lachmann's German translation of the play, which was influential in the early reception of Wilde in the region. Nevertheless, it took some time before Wilde's critical reputation was high enough to prompt a series of translations and stagings of his works in Croatia.

In 1905 a series of important events contributed to the popularization of Wilde's works. The increasing number of notes and sweeping commentaries on Wilde in Croatian dailies often mention Robert Ross's publication of *DP* and its German translation by Max Meyerfeld, as well as Richard Strauss's operatic adaptation of *Salomé*. On 27 May of that year *Salomé* was premiered at the Croatian National Theatre in Zagreb, an event which inaugurated an enduring presence of Wilde in Croatian theatres over the next few decades. It is telling that one of the newspaper critics who reported on the event, alluding to the Wilde 'renaissance' in Germany that had such a strong reverberation in Croatia, observed that Wilde was now so widely discussed in Croatia that even the Germans ought to be jealous (Ogrizović 1905). The date chosen for the Croatian premiere roughly coincided with the tenth anniversary of Wilde's notorious conviction, giving the production the air of a symbolic homage to the author. The premiere was announced in a long article published in the Zagreb newspaper *Obzor* (Horizon) earlier in the day, which described the play as perhaps the most interesting work of European drama performed during that season (J. B. 1905). 'The "perverse" Wilde' (Ogrizović 1905), the 'King of Life' and 'man of paradoxes [...] killed by the English Philistines' (J. B. 1905),[3] as some of the first Croatian articles described him, had finally conquered the Croatian audience with a touch of glamour. On 5 November of this same year the play was also staged at the Slovenian National theatre in Ljubljana. The production was directed by the Czech Adolf Dobrovolny and featured Josipina Kreisova, an invited Czech actress, in the leading role. It is likely that Dukat's critical views, which were held in high esteem by Slovene theatre manager Govekar, influenced the inclusion of *Salomé* in the Slovene repertory (Stanovnik 1970, 128). But unlike the Croatian *Salomé*, which was a great success, the Slovene production was not well received by either audience or critics, and was repeated only once (Stanovnik 1970, 150).

Fran Galović, who was seventeen at the time and was to become one of the most important and prolific modernist writers in the country, saw the play in Zagreb and took notes about it in the notebook in which he kept records of his theatre attendance. Galović is one of the Croatian writers whom we can certainly identify as being engaged in a creative dialogue with Wilde's works. During his formative years as a writer, he was an eager reader of Wilde and reworked some of his motifs in his own works, such as the poem 'Salome' written in 1905 inspired by the performance of *Salomé* he saw in Zagreb, which he reworked and published in 1911, the one-act play *Tamara* (1906), rewritten in verse in 1907, which bears a significant resemblance to Wilde's *Salomé*, and the story 'Začarano ogledalo' (Spellbound mirror), written in 1912 and published in 1913, which is sprinkled with Wildean motifs. Galović also translated one of Wilde's fairy tales, YK (1913).

The premiere of *Salomé* in Zagreb was an outstanding achievement. The Zagreb-born actress Hermina Šumovska, who was at the peak of her popularity, was invited as an internationally acknowledged guest actress to play the leading role. She had started her career in Zagreb but had then left for Berlin and Zurich. From 1897 she was a distinguished member of Berlin's *Schillertheater* (Schiller theatre) and later joined Zurich's *Stadttheater* (City theatre). The role of Wilde's Salomé was one of her greatest successes. The play had been translated from the German (most probably from Lachmann's translation). A note in the manuscript says that because of time pressure two translators were engaged: the first part of the play was translated by Julije Benešić, a renowned Croatian scholar, writer, editor and translator from the Polish, and the second by a scholar, editor, translator and, as the note particularly emphasizes, drama-turge Nikola Andrić. Both of them played an active role in the activities of the Croatian National Theatre in Zagreb. Andrić, who would go on to publish more of Wilde's work in 1913, was also one of the founders of the Croatian National Theatre in Osijek and the school of acting in Zagreb. The translation

---

[3]   '"perverzni" Wilde'; 'kralj života [...] čovjek paradoksa [...] ubijen od engleskih filistara'.

was completed in May, just in time for the play to be rehearsed for the stage. The performance was directed by renowned director Josip Bach, who also served as director of the Croatian National Theatre from 1908 to 1920 and who was eager to modernize the Croatian stage and to familiarize Croatian theatre goers with the latest European cultural movements. It is important to stress the German connection: the Croatian staging of *Salomé* did not follow the first performance in Paris but, rather, the one in Berlin, which had profound reverberations throughout Central Europe; moreover, some of the actors and directors engaged in performances of Wilde in Croatia, at this point and later, had had previous professional experience in Berlin theatres, the Berlin repertory having long been influential in Croatian theatrical circles.

The audience was mesmerized by Šumovska, who studied her role meticulously and brought it to perfection. All the newspapers carried vivid and flamboyant accounts of her breathtaking performance. One reviewer reported on how 'her voice freely and graciously sails through that night full of bloody noise and secret premonitions and her movements are almost visionary', concluding that her voice 'completely fuses with poetry' (Ogrizović 1905).[4] Her dance, in particular, was praised with elaborate expressions of admiration. Another critic pointed out that Šumovska had modelled her performance on the impressionist Berlin school and that her stylized creation resembled those of Gertrud Eysoldt and Tilla Durieux (*Narodne novine* 1905).

The Zagreb *Salomé* continued to enjoy widespread success for several years. The director and cast mostly remained the same (Ignjat Borštnik as Herod, Milivoj Barbarić as the young Syrian, Josip Štefanac as Iokanaan, Marija Ružička Strozzi as Herodias) but the leading role was entrusted to different, carefully selected, guest actresses. The Croatian press referred to it as 'the most sensational play staged in the last few years, the climax of the so called *Stimmungskunst* (art of moods)', displaying 'inventive and colourful linguistic variations and richness of light effects' ('Oskar Wilde, pjesnik "Salome" na hrvatskoj pozornici' 1905).[5] It was described as 'brimming with dramatic energy and poetic spirit' ('pune dramatske vatre i pjesničkoga daha') (Ogrizović 1905), and as 'a great poem' ('velika pjesma') ('Saloma od Oskara Wildea' 1905). The play was very popular: Hećimović records that there had been twelve stagings by the year 1920 (1990, 11). In each theatrical season the performance of *Salomé* was remembered by the peculiar artistic achievements of guest actresses from acclaimed central European stages. Although Šumovska was undoubtedly the most celebrated, in 1906 the newspapers carried enthusiastic reports of the performance of the Czech actress Isa Grégrova, who was at the time a member of the National Theatre in Prague, and who became famous for her interpretations of Wilde's Salomé and Henrik Ibsen's Hedwig in *The Wild Duck*. Critics agreed that her dance, at the climax of the play, was

---

[4] 'njezin glas, slobodno i raskošno jedri kroz onu noć punu krvavoga šuma i tajnih slutnja, a kretnje su joj gotovo već visionarne [...] taj isti glas [...] se sasvim sljubi s poezijom'.

[5] 'najsenzacionalnije pozorišno djelo posljednjih godina, vrhunac tzv. Stimmungskunsta'; 'originalno šarenilo jezika i bogatstvo svjetlosne udesbe'.

not as suggestive as Šumovska's, but Grégrova had a peculiar capacity for subtle psychological characterization and a superior ability to penetrate into the most intricate feminine aspects of the character (Lunaček 1906). The difficulty lay in portraying Salomé's perversity without spoiling the aesthetic pleasure and reducing it to vulgarity (Sv. 1906). In 1908 the young actress Anka Kernic, later an outstanding member of the regular cast of the Croatian National Theatre, was entrusted with the leading role. Critics agreed that Kernic was very talented and performed well but complained that, in comparison to Šumovska and Grégrova, her acting was not suggestive enough and that she was perhaps too young to understand thoroughly all the aspects of the complex woman whom she had to portray (Canić 1908, Livadić 1908a, Ogrizović 1908). The early reception of Wilde on the Croatian stage was thus marked by the suggestive performances of strong female actresses, each of whom brought with her a new style and different subtleties of interpretation. However, most of these performances remained overshadowed by the memorable acting of Šumovska, whom one critic called 'a passing meteor leaving a brilliant trace' ('meteorska pojava blistava traga') on the Croatian stage (Livadić 1943). In 1920 Ljerka Trauttner played the role of Salomé in a performance directed by Ivo Raić.

LWF was the second play by Wilde to be staged at the Croatian National Theatre in Zagreb. It was performed on 20 April 1907 in a translation by Milan Šrabec, better known as Milan Bogdanović, to whom Croatian culture was indebted for the first translations of some of Shakespeare's dramas. Wilde's popularity in this period is reflected in the fact that some of the leading figures of Croatian cultural life were engaged in stagings of his works which often received rave reviews. The role of Lord Windermere was played by Andrija Fijan, who was then a director of drama and who also remains famous in the history of Croatian theatre as the most outstanding interpreter of Shakespeare; while Ljerka Šram, one of the most charismatic actresses on the Croatian stage, played the role of Lady Windermere. Critics particularly emphasized the excellent acting of Marija Ružička Strozzi in the role of Mrs Erlynne (Lunaček 1907). In November 1907 *LWF* was staged in Osijek with a cast of actors from Osijek, two weeks before the official opening of the Croatian National theatre in Osijek took place on 7 December. Two more productions of this light-hearted comedy successfully energized the National Theatre repertory in Zagreb in the 1920s, a period which saw a burgeoning interest in Wilde. *LWF* had renewed success at the National Theatre three decades later, in the season of 1953–54. It was premiered again on 15 April 1954, when Bela Krleža, the wife of the leading Croatian writer Miroslav Krleža, played the role of Mrs Erlynne. In 1967 the Komedija theatre in Zagreb successfully staged *Lady iz Pariza* (The lady from Paris), a musical in two parts composed by Peter Kreuder, based on Karl Farkaš's *Lady aus Paris*, an adaptation of *LWF*. Two outstanding contemporary Croatian writers and translators, Ivan Slamnig and Antun Šoljan, also ventured into translating *LWF* for the stage. The typescript of their translation is held at the Croatian Academy of Sciences and Arts. As in the case of all successful stagings of Wilde's society comedies, the strength of this production lay in the effective linguistic and cultural adaptation of the author's humour and paradoxes.

The third of Wilde's plays to be premiered in Zagreb was FT. The play had been staged in Berlin on 12 January 1906 and the German translation by Max

Meyerfeld published in 1907. These two events had a strong impact on the Croatian reception of the play, which was obviously influenced by the wider reception of Wilde in the Austro-Hungarian Empire. It is interesting to note that Marcell Benedek's first translation of the play into Hungarian also dates from 1907. FT was staged in Zagreb primarily because of the active interest of Ivo Vojnović, a distinguished modernist writer who is considered to be one of the founders of modern Croatian drama, and who also served as a drama-turge at the Croatian National Theatre at that time. Vojnović translated the play, which was premiered at the Croatian National Theatre in Zagreb on 15 September 1908. It is significant that in his translation, published in the review *Ilustrirani Obzor* (Illustrated horizon) on 14 February 1909 (and reprinted in *Dubrovnik* in 2001), Vojnović included a note on the Berlin premiere, revealing how closely he followed the repertory of Berlin theatres. Fijan directed the play and also played the role of the merchant Simone. However, the cooperation between the two competing national theatre stars, Vojnović and Fijan, did not survive long and the play was staged only twice. Critics who reported on the performance pointed out that this play could be easily compared to *Salomé* in terms of its refined poetic quality (Livadić 1908b). It is possible to argue for Wilde's creative influence on Vojnović's literary works but it is often difficult to determine whether his use of 'Wildean' motifs should be attributed to the specific influence of Wilde or of the wider literary heritage of the *fin de siècle*. Miroslav Krleža, for instance, commented on the occurrence of Wildean thematic motifs in some Vojnović's works (Krleža 1932a, Krleža 1961, 62–63).

The popularity of Wilde's plays and the increasing number of translations of his works soon called for a more informed account of his life. In 1906, R. H. Sherard's *Life of Oscar Wilde* came out in London. Although this publication was not recorded in the Croatian press, it seems that it was well-known to Croatian intellectuals at that time. The biography, which was soon translated into German and published in Vienna later in 1906, remained for a long time an important source of information about Wilde's life. German translations of Wilde's works played an important intermediary role in his early reception in Croatia – in particular those published by Wiener Verlag in the series *Oscar Wildes Werke in deutscher Sprache* (Vienna and Leipzig, 1906–08) and those in the Tauchnitz Collection of British Authors, which included an eleven-volume collection of Wilde's works issued in Leipzig from 1906 to 1908. Around this time PDG had become Wilde's best-selling book in Germany, with thirteen editions and reprints recorded between 1901 and 1927 (Schlösser, 1937; O'Neill 1985, 266). The German popularity of Wilde's novel, fuelled also by the sensational accounts of his life, found immediate reverberation in Croatia. Artur Schneider's first Croatian translation of the novel was, as a note in the contents says, serialized in the Zagreb journal *Hrvatska smotra* (Croatian review, in 1907[6]) and then came out in book form the following year. This translation

---

6   In the contents of the second volume of *Hrvatska smotra* for 1907 there is a note which informs readers that about sixteen pages of PDG, in a translation by Artur Schneider, were enclosed with each volume of the journal. Unfortunately, there is no copy of this enclosed translation in any Croatian library.

was to become a best-seller, probably circulating among readers alongside the popular 1908 Tauchnitz edition. In 1908 *Hrvatska smotra* also published a translation of Wilde's story NR under the title 'Crvena ruža' (Red rose), and the following year the review carried the unsigned article, 'Has Oscar Wilde died?', which reported rumours that Wilde might still be alive and that somebody else might have been buried in his grave ('Je li umro Oscar Wilde' 1909).

Two more of Wilde's plays were premiered at the Croatian National Theatre in Zagreb before 1910. The Zagreb production of *IH* was staged on 18 May 1909. Before that *IH* had been staged in Osijek in the German language on 6 March 1907. The play was written, as one critic commenting on the Zagreb performance noted, 'in the manner of Sardou' ('u Sardouvoj maniri') (Ld. 1909), displaying a fine realism and containing plenty of intrigues, paradoxes and dramatic effects that provided a bitter commentary on English public morals. The play for the Zagreb production was translated by the prolific Croatian translator Milan Šenoa and directed by Josip Bach. *IBE* was premiered on 22 February 1910. This 'trivial comedy for serious people' obviously appealed to the taste of the audience in Zagreb: Hećimović records nineteen performances by 25 April 1919 (1990, 110). The play was directed by Ivo Raić and translated by Milan Begović. Begović was a renowned novelist and playwright of the Croatian Moderna, who also took an interest in Wilde in his acclaimed theatre criticism, reviewing performances of some of Wilde's plays, including *Salomé* (Begović 1920, 1921, 1930). *IH* and *IBE* were staged in different productions again in the 1920s and early 1930s and regained their popularity in the 1980s. *IBE* continued to be staged in the '90s and, more recently, in 2007.

In 1911, *Priče* (short stories including HP, NR, SG, DF and RR along with some poems in prose) came out in Zagreb, translated and published by August Harambašić. The translator wrote a very short foreword in which he pointed out Wilde's relevance in the context of contemporary literature and emphasized the fact that his tragic destiny had served as an incentive for his popularity. Although he drew on second-hand sources, his account of Wilde's life was no longer as vague and ambivalent as the first references to Wilde earlier in the century. In the same year the Zagreb newspaper *Obzor* published an article by Matoš on Wilde and Whistler (Matoš 1911), and Arsen Wenzelides, at the time an acknowledged literary critic, wrote a longer article on Wilde and his works published in the magazine *Savremenik* (Contemporary) (Wenzelides 1911) which, by his own admission, draws on various essays on Wilde, in particular German sources and essays by Leconte de Lisle, Henri de Régnier and Ernest La Jeunesse. Wenzelides was attacked by an anonymous critic who insisted that he had lifted many passages of his article from an essay on Wilde by the Italian Enrico Aresca. This debate throws light on the sources early Croatian criticism on Wilde relied on in the first decade of the twentieth century.

In 1913 Alfred Douglas sued Arthur Ransome for the allegedly libellous report of his homosexual relationship with Wilde in Ransome's *Oscar Wilde: A Critical Study* (for a more detailed account of these events see Joseph Bristow's essay in this volume). The trial was the breaking news appearing on the front page of *Obzor* on 25 April, reported in a long unsigned article interspersed with some excerpts from letters read at the court sessions ('Tragika Oscara

Wildea' 1913). The Zagreb German-language daily *Agramer Tagblatt* (Zagreb daily news) also published an article on the issues of guilt and responsibility in the court case against Wilde, presenting the trials from an ethical point of view (Vernić 1913). The trial Crosland Ross was also reported in Croatian newspapers. However, Wilde's homosexuality never received specific treatment by Croatian critics and was only briefly mentioned or discreetly alluded to in some passing references.

In 1913 *IBE* was still popular with the audience in Zagreb and the Croatian National Theatre in Osijek decided to host this production along with some other plays, but the guest performance of *IBE* in Osijek that took place on 25 March 1913 was not very well attended. That year Nikola Andrić founded the series *Zabavna biblioteka* (Entertaining library), which aimed to publish bestselling works by renowned authors. By the year 1941 it published more than 400 volumes. He devoted the fourth volume to works by Wilde, including *Salomé,* based on the 1905 translation for the stage with minor linguistic modifications, CG and some other stories and poems in prose, which were accompanied by an extensive and well-informed but not completely accurate foreword in which he noted that all of Wilde's major works had by that time appeared in Croatian translation, either in print or on the stage. In 1913, however, this was only partially true. The same year saw an early, but incomplete, attempt at a translation of *BRG* by Krešimir Kovačić, which was published in the review *Karlovac,* as well as a fine translation of 'Mladi kralj' (YK) by Fran Galović, published in the magazine *Prosvjeta.*

In this period of Wilde's increased popularity, the leading Croatian writer Miroslav Krleža was just about to write the first fragment of his play *Salomé.* His thematic preoccupation with the Biblical story resulted in several drafts written in different literary genres. He showed one of these drafts to the director Josip Bach already in 1914, hoping to attract his interest. But Bach rejected it, commenting that, although this was indeed a 'new' *Salomé,* the dialogues were not dramatic enough and therefore unsuitable for a play, and that the work was altogether too poetic. In 1918, Krleža published his long poem 'Saloma' in the magazine *Savremenik* (Contemporary). The final version of Krleža's work, the one-act play *Saloma,* was published in 1963. Krleža did not have a very good command of English and, by his own admission, he first read Wilde in Hungarian in 1911. Although it is impossible to deny the existence of intertextual relations between Wilde's *Salomé* and Krleža's *Saloma,* the influence of Wilde on Krleža is a complex issue that needs to be examined in a broader context. At the beginning of the century the development of Croatian Modernism went hand in hand with the ongoing process of formation of a Croatian national identity. The creation of national mythologies was therefore sometimes mediated through Symbolism and Aestheticism. This is the case, for instance, with allegorical tales and fables by Vladimir Nazor, especially 'Šuma bez slavuja' (The wood without the nightingale) and 'Albus kralj' (King Albus), which share some formal and stylistic aspects with fables by Wilde and Maurice Maeterlinck.

In the meantime *Salomé* continued to be staged in Zagreb and in 1914 newspapers carried news about the performance of the leading guest actress, the Czech Anna Suchánková, acting in Croatian (Ogrizović 1914, 'Drugo gostovanje Hane Suchánkove. "Saloma". Wilde' 1914). On 15 May 1915, Strauss's operatic adaptation of Wilde premiered at the Croatian National Theatre in Zagreb in a translation by Andro Mitrović. It was also published in *Biblioteka opernih i operetnih tekstova* (A library of opera and operatic texts), which specialized in the publication of translations of librettos. The opera was directed by Ivo Raić, who had worked in some of the theatres that had hosted ground-breaking performances of Wilde's works in Europe, such as the *Neues Theater* (New theatre) in Berlin, *Narodni Divadlo* (National Theatre) in Prague and the *Stadttheater* (City theatre) in Hamburg. His previous experience in these places might have helped him to establish a link between their productions and the one in Zagreb – in particular his acting in some plays directed by Max Reinhardt during his stay in Berlin and the adoption of his modernist poetics. The opera was conducted by Fridrik Rukavina and the leading role was entrusted to Vinka Engel who had already played the role of Salome in the Viennese *Volksopera* in 1912. Strauss's opera gradually but steadily took over the play version of *Salomé*, which almost completely disappeared from theatres' repertories. Unlike the dramatic version of *Salomé*, directed for several years only by Josip Bach, the opera has been directed by a number of renowned Croatian directors including Branko Gavella in 1922, Petar Raičev in 1934, Tito Strozzi in 1955, Daniel Marušić in 1969, Tobias Richter in 1988, Petar Selem in 1996 and Christian Romanowski in 1999. Wilde's play also inspired two ballet versions: Florent Schmitt's 'The Tragedy of Salome', first performed in Paris in 1907, was premiered in Croatia as *Tragedija Salome* on 17 June 1953 by the ballet of the Croatian National Theatre in Zagreb, conducted by Mladen Bašić and choreographed by the superb Croatian ballet master Nenad Lhotka; and *Salomé*, choreographed by Miljenko Štambuk and based on music by Richard Strauss, Erik Satie, Luciano Berio, Boris Papandopulo and Igor Fjodorovič Stravinsky, which was premiered at the Croatian National Theatre 'Ivan pl. Zajc' in Rijeka on 26 February 1988 and attracted wide critical attention.

The year 1915 also saw a translation of *DP* by the renowned Serbian writer Isidora Sekulić-Stremnicka, which circulated among readers as the only complete translation in the region for more than a decade.

In 1918, Mirko Breyer edited a new selection of Wilde's short stories, *Mladi kralj i druge pripovijesti* (The young king and other stories) translated by Iso Velikanović, one of Croatia's finest translators and skilfully illustrated by the Croatian artist Ljubo Babić. This edition was reprinted in 1920. By 1920 Wilde's popularity in Croatia had reached its peak. Alongside Breyer's second edition of Wilde's stories, three editions of *PDG* came out that year, two in Zagreb and one in Vukovar. The two Zagreb editions were reprints of the 1908 translation by Arthur Schneider, one of them hastily rendered in Cyrillic with many imperfections. The other was a new translation of the novel by David S. Pijade, with a long introduction by Miloš Crnjanski. In addition to these, *Zločin lorda Artura Savilea* (*LASCOS*) came out in Koprivnica in a translation by Milan Drvodelić. Two new productions of *Salomé* took place in different Croatian theatres. On 15 October 1922 the play, translated by Radmilo Jovanović, was premiered at the Croatian National Theatre in Osijek, directed by Zlata Markovac, and on 5 May 1923 it received its premiere at the Croatian National Theatre in Split, directed by Niko Bartulović. Wilde became part of the Split theatrical repertoire in the early 1920s, with his plays premiered in each theatrical season: in 1922 (*IBE*), in 1923 (*Salomê*), in 1924 (*LWF*) and in 1926 (*IH*).

In the following year Wilde's presence in Croatian culture was revived by a number of newspaper articles and a few interesting obituaries commemorating the anniversaries of his death (V.R. 1925, P. v. P. 1930; '40. godišnjica smrti Oscara Wildea' [Fortieth anniversary of the death of OW] 1940), one of which drew a parallel between Wilde's destiny as an outcast from society and the destiny of the Croatian poet and bohemian Tin Ujević (Vučetić 1925). Wilde's plays continued to be staged every year, but the sensational force of their impact lessened. Some of his stories, which enjoyed immense popularity, were also put on the stage. In 1923 and 1925 two different productions of SG took place. In 1927, *Zvjezdan* (SC) was adapted for the stage by Mladen Širola and published in the series *Dječje pozorište* (Children's theatre). It was staged only once, at *Malo kazalište* (Little theatre) in Zagreb in 1931. In the 1930s the interest in Wilde's plays was revived thanks to two outstanding guest performances. On 11 December 1930, Harry Liedtke, a film star in full bloom, along with a cast of Berlin actors, most of them veterans of silent film – including Max Landa, Carola Toelle and Arthur Schröder – performed *IH* at the Croatian National Theatre in Zagreb in a performance directed by Eugen Robert. Critics, including Milan Begović, particularly praised the acting of Traute Carlsen in the role of Mrs Cheveley. Begović also recalled her brilliant achievement in Herman Bahr's play *Josephine* performed in Mannheim several years earlier when she was entrusted the title role (Begović 1930). On 14 April 1939, The Gate Theatre Company from Dublin performed *IBE* at the Croatian National Theatre in Zagreb.[7] The production was announced the previous day in *Obzor* by Josip Torbarina, a renowned scholar of English and comparative literature. In 1933 a new translation of *DP* came out in the series *1000 najljepših novela* (The thousand best stories). In these years there are references to Wilde in Miroslav Krleža's criticism (Krleža 1932) and Tin Ujević's essays (Ujević 1965 and 1967). It is possible to note a considerable shift from a biographical interest in Wilde to more elaborate, albeit brief, critical comments on his art, which help identify Wilde's impact on the work of Croatian authors and his role within the wider context of Croatian literary culture. Matoš's essays and letters, including those with references to Wilde, were now reprinted in several volumes in the first edition of his collected works (Matoš 1938 and 1940a).

In the 1940s, beside a few fine translations of poems and fragments by some excellent Croatian poets such as Tin Ujević and Ivan Goran Kovačić, there were no major publications or performances of Wilde's works. After World War II, Communist ideology established clear preferences for the types of literature that would best represent and shape the official ideas declared by the State. However, brave attempts by some publishing houses in the early 1950s resulted in the publication of a large variety of books, mainly pivotal texts of

---

7   As Noreen Doody notes in this volume, the Gate Theatre played a crucial role in the reception of Wilde on the Irish stage.

world literature, that did not necessarily fit the framework of socialist doctrine. *PDG* was published in 1953 in a translation by Zlatko Gorjan, a renowned Croatian translator who also rendered Joyce's *Ulysses* a few years later.[8] This translation was reprinted several times (1969, 2000, 2008). The 1953 edition contains an afterword written by the scholar Ivo Hergešić, 'Oskar Wilde ili tisuću i jedan paradoks' (Oscar Wilde or the hundred and one paradoxes), which was reprinted separately in 1955 in his book *Književni portreti* (Literary portraits). This well-informed essay, which heralded new academic approaches to Wilde, contains valuable, though to some extent incomplete, notes on Wilde's critical reception in Croatia. The novel has since then seen two other fine translations by Zdenko Novački (1987, reprinted in 1989) and Vesna Mlinarec (2003).

Gorjan also produced the first complete translation of 'Balada o Readingu' (*BRG*), published in the November 1961 issue of the Split review *Mogućnosti* (Possibilities) together with Hergešić's introduction. In 1965, Slavko Ježić translated the three stanzas of the sixth part of *BRG* and published them in *Antologija svjetske lirike* (An anthology of world lyrics). Nobel prize winner Ivo Andrić had also translated thirteen stanzas (about 150 lines) from the second part of *BRG* during his imprisonment for political activism, having been accused of involvement in the assassination of Archduke Francis Ferdinand of Austria in Sarajevo in 1914. The case was eventually dropped due to lack of evidence and Andrić was released after spending three years in various prisons (Split, Šibenik, Maribor, Zenica). His prose translation of *BRG*, entitled *Balada o redinškoj tamnici*, was eventually published in the review *Književnost* (Literature) in 1978.

SMUS, translated and published in Croatia in 1956 (reprinted in 1968), met with the sympathy of the dominant political and intellectual elite. The views expressed in that essay were easily absorbed into the political discourse of the time. From the 1960s onwards there was also a blossoming of interest in Wilde's stories. Many of these were reprinted and retranslated several times (translators included Harabamašić, Velikanović, Drvodelić, Krešić, Gregorić, Paljetak, Juričić, Perić, Raos, Zebić and Bauer) and some of them staged (SG in 1946, 1985, 2001; SC in 1979, 1995; HP in 1962, 1975, 1980, 1984, 2003, 2006; NR in 1980). The renowned Croatian composer and conductor, Boris Papandopulo, composed an opera in three acts based on CG, which was staged at the Croatian National Theatre in Osijek in 1979. Luko Paljetak, one of the most prolific among contemporary Croatian translators and poets, drew renewed attention to Wilde when, in 1987, he published a translation of *BRG* which stands out as one of the finest recent translations in Croatia. Interestingly, aiming to preserve the ballade form of the poem, Paljetak opted for a metrical scheme that is similar to that of the first translation by Kovačić, rather than to the one used in the more recent translation by Gorjan; however, the overall effect of his translation brings the poem closer to the linguistic sensibility of contemporary readers. 1987 also saw new translations of SMUS and *DP* by Zlatko Crnković (reprinted in 2001). *DP* was accompanied by Vyvyan

---

[8]   See Bašić 2004, 181.

Holland's introduction. Some years later a new translation of *Salomé* (1989) and, subsequently, a translation of *VN* (1997) were published in the literary review *Forum*. The year 1998 saw a revived interest in *Salomé*, performed by the theatrical troupe *Dream Team Theatre* in the old ruins of Paromlin in Zagreb which provided an ideal setting for the play, featuring the decay of industrial civilization. The cast consisted of promising Croatian actors (Ivana Boban in the title role, Mladen Vulić as Iokanaan, Ranko Zidarić as Horod, Helena Buljan as Heordias, Sven Šestak as the young Syrian, Marinko Prga as the soldier, etc.). It was directed by Aleksandra Broz and the dramaturge of the play was Vladimir Stojsavljević. It was an attempt to explore various layers of symbolism in Wilde's *Salomé* by positioning them within the ambivalent moral framework of contemporary society and by decoding the meaning of Salomé's dance in relationship to contemporary views on dominion, usurped authority and the decay of moral values.

The reception of Wilde in recent years has taken a different turn, as his image and works have started to be absorbed by popular culture and the Wilde 'myth' has acquired new dimensions. The afterword to the recent 2000b edition of Grojan's translation of *PDG* explicitly aims at a wide popular readership by introducing Wilde with the telling title 'Oscar Wilde: Pop idol prije pop glazbe' (Oscar Wilde: pop idol before pop music). The author discusses the subversive cultural roles played by a number of pop cultural icons and their relation to Wilde.

Within the wider context of the reception of Wilde in Croatia, academic criticism did not play a particularly influential role. Rather than constituting a solid body of work, it consists mainly of some valuable insights put forward in articles and books that briefly deal with Wilde within the broader context of *fin-de-siècle* aestheticism. There are some fruitful comparisons that hint at the creative influence of Wilde on a number of Croatian authors, mostly as part of the broader dialogue with world literature. The articles by comparatist Ivo Hergešić, based on informed biographical criticism (1955, 1961), and Tatjana Blažeković's unpublished doctoral thesis, *Engleska književnost i njene veze s Hrvatskom Modernom (1900–1914)* (English literature and its relation to the Croatian Moderna (1900–1914)) (1957), hint at some biographical and creative links between Wilde and Croatian authors, in particular Matoš and Krleža. The influence of Wilde on Matoš is also the subject of Višnja Sepčić's article 'Matoš između Wildea i Poea' (Matoš between Wilde and Poe) (1976), in which she suggests that the content of Matoš's story 'Ugasnulo svjetlo' (The extinguished light) might have been partly inspired by his interest in Wilde's aestheticism, but that it was written in the manner of Edgar Alan Poe whom she underlines as more significant influence. Ivo Vidan, in his article on Krleža and George Bernard Shaw, argues that Shaw's plays influenced formal and stylistic aspects of Krleža's *Saloma* much more than Wilde, whose reverberations are merely thematic (1988). In his later book, *Engleski intertekst hrvatske književnosti* (The English intertext of Croatian literature) (1995), which remains one of the most important comparative studies in the field, Vidan pursues analogies between Croatian and English authors, highlighting occasional intertextual references to Wilde. Along the same lines, in several of his comparative studies dealing with the *fin de siècle*, the renowned scholar Viktor Žmegač discusses

Wilde's role in the formation and dissemination of the dominant poetics of the time (see for instance 1990). Ljiljana Ina Gjurgjan puts forward valuable ideas on Croatian writers' creative dialogue with Wilde in her examination of the role of turn-of-the-century art in shaping the national mythologies in the Croatian Moderna (1995). Two eminent scholars and drama critics, Nikola Batušić and Darko Gašparović, have also embarked on a brief examination of Wilde's works in their respective articles on *Salomé* (Batušić 2000 and Gašparović 1989). Paljetak has proved to be not only an excellent translator but also the author of four fine essays on Wilde. These pieces are included in his two collections of essays *Engleske teme* (English themes) (1997a & b) and *Vanjski rub: studije i ogledi o stranim književnostima i književnicima* (The outer border: studies and essays on world literature and authors) (2007a & b), and are of considerable significance for readers in Croatia and beyond. Paljetak's own literary works are occasionally permeated with creative echoes of Wilde, forging layers of subtle allusion.

The most concrete echoes of Wilde in contemporary Croatian literature can be found in the play *Dandy ili san glavosječke noći* (Dandy or the dream of the head-severing night) by playwright and scholar Boris Senker, published in 2004 as the second part of his trilogy *Tri glavosjeka* (Three beheadings). The three plays are centred on the figures of Judith, Salome and Gloriana, whose respective involvements in narratives of decapitation epitomize moments of apocalyptic change. *Dandy* is dense with over-aestheticized Decadent imagery and undertones of subtle perversity through which it forges an atmosphere of modern morbidity, anxiety and decay of values. The protagonist, Dandy, is a fictional Wilde who is engaged in highly elevated intellectual discussions monitored by his alter ego, a prophetic voice that is meant to embody Nietzsche. An extremely tense dialogue unfolds between these two controversial *fin-de-siècle* figures, who are driven by their competing desires for power. *Salomé* is present as a play within the play performed in the style of the Theatre of Shadows. The whole play becomes a palimpsestic postmodern theatrical simulacrum, in which characters are reduced to voices and deceiving shadows, some of ambiguous gender identity.

After highlighting some general aspects of the reception of Wilde in Croatia and some changes in the paradigms of reception, it seems fitting to conclude that although Wilde's works initially came to Croatia indirectly – through Paris and Vienna – they had an immediate and strong impact on Croatian culture, opening up the potential for various modes of cross-cultural influence and integration. Wilde's plays made up a significant part of the repertory of the Croatian National Theatre, which, if we consider the practices of censorship in other central European theatres, showed very liberal tendencies even when compared to the Viennese theatrical scene. Although the creative influence of Wilde, the dissemination of the Wilde 'myth' and the formation of particular patterns of discourse about his life and his poetics have changed over time, the reception of Wilde in Croatia has been a continued feature of the literary and cultural life of the country. His writings have been assimilated both by the mainstream and the subcultural milieus.

18 'Next to Christ': Oscar Wilde in Russian Modernism

Evgenii Bershtein

Oscar Wilde was and has remained the most popular representative of early European modernism in Russian culture.[1] Hundreds of editions of his prose works (many aimed at children and teenagers), widely-read translations of his poetry, Soviet-era films based on his plays, as well as numerous popular and scholarly works on his life and art, all testify to the impact Wilde has had on Russian literature and culture. Literary influences aside, scholars stress that 'Wilde's contribution to Russian modernist culture lies primarily in the crucial concept of life as art, *zhiznetvorchestvo*,' central to Russian modernism (Moeller-Sally 1990, 469). This essay will argue that, in addition to artistic lives, Wilde's biographical legend shaped the formation of sexual identities and ideologies in *fin-de-siècle* Russia. First, I will show how detailed and sensational news reports of Wilde's fall preceded his literary fame in Russia, arguing that the way in which the Wilde narrative initially reached Russia coloured his subsequent reception there. Second, I will investigate how the Wilde myth acquired strong Christological connotations in Russia and how his reputation as a Decadent sufferer translated into a quasi-religious sainthood. Third, I will consider the reputation of the poet Mikhail Kuzmin (1872–1936) as 'the Russian Wilde'. Although Kuzmin emphatically rejected the scenario of gay martyrdom suggested by the Wilde myth, his very condemnation of this myth confirmed its inescapable relevance as a symbolic framework for homosexuality in the Russian culture of the Silver Age.

---

[1] Parts of the present essay are based on my earlier work: Bershtein 2000. For general surveys of Wilde's reception in Russian literature, see: Moeller-Sally 1990; Pavlova 1991; Polonsky 1998. Roznatovskaya's annotated bibliography *Oskar Uail'd v Rossii* (Oscar Wilde in Russia) is a particularly valuable source, despite some lacunae (Roznatovskaya 2000).

How the Russians found out about Wilde: the London trials and Prince Meshcherskii's trumpeters

Despite his widespread fame throughout most of Western Europe during his lifetime, Wilde was practically unknown in late nineteenth-century Russia. Like other European cultural and literary fashions, aestheticism made a belated arrival in Russia, reaching full strength only in the early 1900s. Nonetheless, Russian newspapers followed the example of their British and French counterparts, covering the trials extensively (cf. essays by Emily Eells and Richard Hibbitt in this volume). In particular, the mass-circulation national daily *Novoe vremya* (New time), published by A. S. Suvorin (1834–1912), devoted eighteen reports to the court proceedings. One of Russia's most influential papers, *Novoe vremya* essentially created the Wilde trials as a news event for the Russian public. The question of how and why Suvorin's newspaper did this deserves consideration. Since only five of the eighteen reports were received by telegraph, and the rest brought by mail (which usually took eight days), the narrative was serialized in a curious way: the telegrams provided the reader with previews of the story and the outcome of the three trials; somewhat later, longer articles clarified psychological and factual details. At the end of this 'soap opera', the paper published the only signed article on the topic, giving an overview and analysis of the trials.

The first telegram, dated 25 March, London, explained how Wilde had come to stand trial 'for actions offensive to public morality'. It concluded with the story of Wilde's arrest and reported the rumor that this would soon be followed by the arrest of Alfred Douglas, as well as 'others among Wilde's friends, mostly from the ranks of servants, grooms, trumpeters and persons repeatedly convicted in the past' (*Novoe vremya* 1895, 6851: 1).[2] *Novoe vremya* published subsequent reports in its international news section. On 27 March, it provided a detailed account of the first day of the trial and full translation of the major piece of evidence against Wilde, his love letter to Douglas. The issue of 28 March contained the text of Edward Carson's interrogation of Wilde almost verbatim and described the heartbreaking family drama that accompanied the reading of the insulting telegrams which the marquis and his son had exchanged. The next report emphasized the gravity of the offence which, in English law, stands 'only one step below murder' ('tol'ko odnoi stupen'yu nizhe ubiistva'). It speculated that, if found guilty, Wilde may be sentenced to as long as ten years' hard labour or even life (*Novoe vremya* 1895, 6854: 2). The newspaper also reported that during the trials

> a change took place in Wilde himself. His self-confidence had all but evaporated. When he was taken into the 'dock' – that is, the cage for defendants – his former friends and acquaintances could no longer recognize the author who had previously been so self-confident and somewhat of a fop. He sat down heavily on the defendant's bench, not daring to lift his eyes to the court and the public. Pale, his

---

[2]   'drugikh druzei Vil'de, bol'sheyu chast'yu iz razryada molodykh lakeev, grumov, trubachei i lits, mnogo raz sudivshikhsya.'

hair uncombed, unwashed and dressed sloppily, Wilde was, indeed, unrecognizable. (*Novoe vremya* 1895, 6867: 2)[3]

After describing the proceedings of the third trial and reporting the jury's guilty verdict, the paper published an analysis by its London correspondent, G. S. Veselitskii–Bozhidarovich, writing under his usual pen name of 'Argus'. In 'Oscar Wilde and Oscar-Wilde-ism' ('Oskar Uail'd i oskar-uail'dizm'), Argus stressed the gravity of Wilde's offence ('an unprecedented trial, more horrible, as the judge who pronounced the sentence said, than the most horrible murder') and he concluded that the trial had a very profound significance as 'not simply a trial of individuals, but one of England's hereditary aristocracy' (Argus 1895, 2).[4]

This last point was more than just the expression of the author's personal opinion. Rather, it reflected the political line taken by the paper's publisher, Suvorin.[5] In the field of international politics, *Novoe vremya* took a strongly anti-English and pro-French position. In the field of the Russian Empire's internal affairs, it opposed aristocratic exceptionalism while exalting the monarch as the centre of national statehood. One of Suvorin's important opponents and his main competitor in the struggle for influence in governmental spheres was Prince Vladimir Meshcherskii (1839–1914), the publisher of the daily *Grazhdanin* (Citizen). Meshcherskii's diplomatic line was Francophobic and Anglophile, and his ideology was aristocratic. While Suvorin's paper was an incredibly successful commercial venture, Meshcherskii's *Grazhdanin* was secretly subsidized by the government on the order of Alexander III, during whose reign Meshcherskii enjoyed enormous influence at court.[6] However, after the death of Alexander in 1894, Nicholas II – who had reservations about Meshcherskii's personality – was less willing to employ his publication as a mouthpiece for conservative views, and it took several years for Meshcherskii to restore his authority.

It is within the context of the polemic between Suvorin's *Novoe vremya* and Meshcherskii's *Grazhdanin* that the coverage of Wilde must be seen. Alongside reports of the trials, *Novoe vremya* carried editorials on the role of the aristocracy in Russia and on Meshcherskii's anti-French views (*Novoe vremya* 1895, 6907 and 6904). Furthermore, the nature of Wilde's crime provided a direct link to Meshcherskii, who was a notorious homosexual. Memoirists agree that no educated person in St Petersburg was unaware of Meshcherskii's reputation

---

3   'Proizoshla peremena i v samom Vil'de. Samouverennost' ego kak-to sovsem uletuchilas'. Kogda Vil'de vveli v 'dock' [English in the original], t.e. kletku dlya podsudimykh, ego byvshie druz'ya i znakomye bolee ne uznavali prezhnego khlyshchevatogo i samouverennogo pisatelya. On grustno opustilsya na skam'yu podsudimykh, ne smeya podymat' glaza na sud i publiku. Blednyi, nechesanyi, nemytyi i neryashlivo odetyi, Vil'de byl deistvitel'no neuznavaem.'

4   'nebyvalyi protsess, bolee uzhasnyi, po vyrazheniyu proiznesshego prigovor sud'i, nezheli, uzhasneishee ubiistvo [...] ne prosto sud nad lichnostyami, a nad rodovoi aristokratiei Anglii.'

5   On Suvorin and his paper, see Solov'eva, Shitova 1977.

6   Prince Meshcherskii's persona, career and reputation are discussed in Mosse 1981.

(Feoktistov 1929, 247; Vitte 1960, 582). E. K. Pimenova, a *Grazhdanin* staff member in the 1880s, wrote that 'everyone on the newspaper knew about his vices';[7] then she crossed out the words 'on the newspaper' (Pimenova, 59). In the 1880s satirical poems played on the name of Meshcherskii's periodical. One anonymous epigram (in the manuscripts collection of the Russian National Library in St Petersburg) puns on the title of Meshcherskii's paper, claiming that the publisher was 'a citizen of Sodom' (grazhdanin Sodoma) ('Ego S–vu Kn. Meshcherskomu' [n.d.]). The philosopher Vladimir Solov'ev also wrote a series of epigrams depicting Meshcherskii as a proud and shameless Sodomite (Solov'ev 1974, 148, 255–60). In putting Wilde's offence in the limelight, Suvorin may have had two goals. First, by publishing a long psychological narrative on sexual vice, he provided entertainment for his readers; second, by alluding to Meshcherskii and *his* vice, he tried to deliver a political blow to his competitor, also implicating the latter's aristocratic ideology and his Anglophilia.

The parallel between Wilde and Meshcherskii might, however, have escaped the attention of contemporaries, not to mention later scholars, had *Novoe vremya* not included a direct allusion to the best-known of Meshcherskii's sex scandals in its first telegram on the Wilde affair. As we have seen, the telegram described Wilde's 'friends' as drawn 'from the ranks of servants, grooms, trumpeters and persons repeatedly convicted in the past'. Yet there were no *trubachi* (trumpeters) among those of Wilde's compromising acquaintances whose testimonies Queensberry solicited. Neither were there *trubochisty* (chimney sweeps), a word related to the former and more appropriate in the context of a list of lower-class vocations. However, in 1887 Meshcherskii had been compromised by a relationship with a trumpeter from the Infantry Battalion of the Guards. The soldier's visits to Meshcherskii at his St Petersburg home became known to his superior, Colonel Keller. The soldier was reprimanded and further visits were banned. Meshcherskii responded in *Grazhdanin* with a smear campaign against the colonel. As a result, Keller was dismissed, then, upon further investigation, recalled to service.[8]

Unlike *fin-de-siècle* England and Germany, where a number of homosexual scandals resulted in legal prosecution and were covered by the press, nothing comparable occurred in Russia. In the words of Laura Engelstein, '[o]n the [Russian] public stage, homosexuality never served as vehicle for symbolic politics, as it did in England and Germany during the same period' (Engelstein 1992, 58). She adds that 'the obvious candidate to the Russian Eulenburg was Prince Vladimir Meshcherskii' (Engelstein 1992, 58n). If Suvorin's coverage of the Wilde scandal was an attempt to draw attention to moral corruption in upper governmental spheres, he did not succeed. That would have required the greater development of an independent press and legal system. In Russia, cases like Meshcherskii's were settled at the Tsar's discretion. For instance, when in 1903 the newspaper *Znamya* (Banner) published an article that almost openly satirized Meshcherskii's sexual vice, the Tsar ordered a temporary closure of the

---

7   'poroki <Meshcherskogo> byli khorosho izvestny vsem nam v redaktsii'.
8   The 'istoriya s trubachem' (trumpeter story) is recalled by several memoirists. See, for instance, Vitte 1960, 582.

paper and consoled Meshcherskii in a private letter (Nicholas II 1903, see also Viktorovich 1999). Given Meshcherskii's closeness to the Imperial family, it is reasonable to presume that, even in 1895, any public criticism of his character was not an entirely safe enterprise. Suvorin could not have failed to understand this. In paying such extraordinary attention to the Wilde affair, Suvorin's most likely design was to hurt Meshcherskii's already tainted credibility. Still, Meshcherskii's *Grazhdanin* could not afford to ignore the Wilde trials entirely. Long after *Novoe vremya* started its coverage, *Grazhdanin* published several Reuters telegrams, all very short, about the trials. Curiously, these telegrams contained not the slightest hint as to the character of Wilde's crime.[9]

'Next to Christ': interpretations of Wilde in Russian Symbolism

The Russian search for an ideological interpretation of the Wilde scandal began right after the trials and continued for two decades. No Russian newspaper named Wilde's actual transgression but, except for *Grazhdanin*, they all found indirect ways to communicate its nature. The conventions of decency adopted by the Russian press did not, however, prevent the name of Wilde from turning into the standard euphemism for modern homosexuality, as expressions such as 'Oscar Wilde's tastes' and 'Oscar Wilde's inclinations' became common figures of speech which placed the transgressive sexual practice in the West. In 1897, when Wilde was still serving his prison term, and while his name was still taboo in the English press, a journalist of the St Petersburg weekly *Knizhki nedeli* (Books of the week) noted that the scandal did a service to Wilde's fame (N. V. 1897, 5). This was certainly true in Russia, where the scandal unleashed a flood of publications on the previously unknown writer and his work (see Pavlova 1991).

Zinaida Gippius's society tale '*Zlatotsvet*' (Oxeye), published in the leading modernist St Petersburg periodical, *Severnyi vestnik* (Northern herald), eight months after the trial, provides a lively satirical picture of the St Petersburg artistic circles that had begun to discuss both Wilde's writings and his reputation. The story's main character, the Decadent Zvyagin, presents a paper on Wilde's aesthetic theory (apparently based on *Intentions*) to a circle of wealthy literary dilettantes. His talk provokes opposition in Pavel Vasil'evich Khamrat. A true philistine, Khamrat pits himself against Wilde's aestheticism and objects to the idea that one can get a complete picture of Wilde without touching on his life. But the expected analysis of Wilde's life never follows. 'Gentlemen, we are in the company of ladies – I don't have the opportunity to touch upon certain subjects,' says Khamrat. Instead, as the sarcastic narrator reports, he 'started a long, passionate, even raging debate about and condemnation of the most modern themes' (Gippius 1896, 229–30).[10] Khamrat's argument underscores the paradoxical side of the early perception of Wilde

---

9   *Grazdanin* 1895, no. 113 (26 April), no. 128 (11 May), no. 132 (15 May). See also *Nedelya* 1895, no. 15 (9 April), no. 18 (30 April).

10   "Gospoda, ya izvinyayus' my v damskom obshchestve. Mnogikh predmetov ya ne

in Russia: for almost a decade it was precisely Wilde's life, rather than his writings, that enjoyed renown, yet the public transgression that made Wilde famous could be discussed in print only in the most equivocal terms.

A distinct feature of the development of Wilde's public image in Russia was the tendency of commentators to draw analogies between him and Nietzsche. In *Degeneration* (1892), Max Nordau placed Wilde next to Nietzsche in a subcategory of modern degenerates whom he called 'Egomaniacs'; while André Gide states in his memoirs that when he began to read Nietzsche, he was 'astonished less' because he had already heard similar ideas from Wilde (Gide 1949, 15; for a full treatment of Gide's writings on Wilde, see Victoria Reid's essay in this volume). In the Russian context, in his influential treatise *Chto takoe iskusstvo?* (*What is Art?*) (1897–98), Lev Tolstoy invoked Wilde side by side with Nietzsche as a 'prophet' of a false and, therefore, immoral attitude toward art: 'Decadents and aesthetes of Oscar Wilde's sort choose the rejection of morality and the celebration of depravity as the theme of their works' (Tolstoy 1951, 172).[11]

Preceding Tolstoy's treatise, the leading modernist St Petersburg journal *Severnyi vestnik* (Northern herald) was the first periodical to stress the parallel. Akim Volynskii (1861–1926), the editor, reviewed Wilde's *Intentions* in December 1895, half a year after Wilde's final trial. In his review, he outlined the connections between Wilde's theories and Nietzsche's philosophy. He did not hide the enormous impression made on him by Wilde's spectacular downfall: 'All of a sudden, his life, glamorous from the outside, but containing inner sores, played itself out in a depressing drama with a repulsive criminal finale' (Volynskii 1895, 312–13).[12] The notion of a play evokes the Nietzschean ideal of creating one's life as a work of art, so consonant with Wilde's own aesthetic statements. Transposed from the realm of aesthetic and philosophical thought into biographical analysis, the Nietzschean concepts of 'play' as the artistic creation of life and 'morality' as the instrument of control used by the inferior human majority gave Volynskii a key to understanding Wilde's fate.

In September 1896, Volynskii published another article in *Severnyi vestnik* in which he mobilized his sarcasm against the hypocrisy of the English judicial system and a society that kept Wilde at hard labour. In the article, Volynskii mocks the liberal intelligentsia's idea of equality before the law. There can be no doubt that Volynskii's anti-liberal and pro-Wildean stance was Nietzschean in its ideological roots:[13]

---

imeu vozmozhnosti kosnut'sya"'; 'pustilsya v dlinnye, zharkie, dazhe pylayushchie rassuzhdeniya i osuzhdeniya na samye novye temy'.

[11] 'Dekadenty i estety, vrode Oskara Uail'da, izbirayut temoyu svoikh proizvedenii otritsanie nravstvennosti i voskhvalenie razvrata.'

[12] 'Vdrug zhizn' ego, blestyashchaya snaruzhi, no taivshaya v sebe vnutrennie yazvy, razygralas' v gnetushchuyu dramu s otvratitel'nym ugolovnym finalom.'

[13] See Volynskii's articles on Nietzsche published in *Severnyi vestnik* in that same period: 'Apollo and Dionysus' (Apollon i Dionis, Volynskii 1896b) and 'Literary Notes' (Literaturnye zametki, Volynskii 1896a).

The immoral Wilde has been imprisoned, and thus moral people have punished a vice soiling the reputation of the whole of English society. This, of course, consists entirely of highly moral people, and Wilde, untidy in his personal life, should be driven out of this world. To trample and spit on him before the whole world is to reveal one's own moral infallibility. To subject him to the strictest of regimes is to sow terror in the hearts of those who may be inclined to abandon the path of virtue. There should be no doubt that the law, which deals severely with any moral sin, could not treat Wilde in any other way. To subjugate people to itself, it must be merciless [...]. Wilde's health has deteriorated. But how could it be otherwise? Do you think that an English prison must serve as a cooling Eldorado for those who have broken the moral law as it is understood by the English parliament? [...] When imprisoning its criminals, the English government will not think of their nerves, their health and their literary talent [...]. *Fiat justitia!* [Let Justice be done!] For Wilde – sickly, nervous, pitiful in his helplessness – no mitigation has come. From the heights of its juridical grandeur, the English law is deaf and dead to the insane pestering of people who are incapable of subtle thought. (Volynskii 1896, second pagination, 57–58)[14]

In Volynskii's accounts, the once-glamorous Wilde is made to seem pitiful by his severe punishment and the resulting illness. The expectation that 'the sickly, the nervous, the pitiful' will utter the final truth is quite within the spirit of the Russian literary tradition. It was not by chance that *Severnyi vestnik* began its campaign to bring Nietzsche to the Russian public by publishing Lou Andreas–Salomé's biography of the German philosopher, where his sufferings, caused by debilitating disease, were described in vivid detail (Andreas-Salomé 1896). As many Russian followers of Nietzsche later contended, his sufferings put the stamp of truth on his writings and gave him the moral right to preach amorality. The pain he had undergone sanctified both his philosophy and his public image, and many Russian Symbolists perceived Nietzsche as a Christ-like figure (see Shestov 1992, 5–61 and Belyi 1911, 69–90).

---

14 'Beznravstvennyi Uail'd zasazhen v tyur'mu – eto znachit, chto v nem nravst-vennymi lyud'mi nakazan porok, marayushchii reputatsiyu tselogo angliiskogo obshchestva. Konechno, vse ono sostoit iz vysokonravstvennykh lyudei, i Uail'd, kotoryi okazalsya neopryatnym v svoei lichnoi zhizni, dolzhen byt' izgnan iz ego sredy. Zatoptat' i oplevat' ego v obshchestvennom mnenii tselogo mira – eto znachit obnaruzhit' svoyu sobstevnnuyu nravstvennuyu nepogreshimost'. Zamuchit' ego strogim rezhimom – eto znachit vyzvat' strakh v serdtsakh lyudei, sklonnykh, byt' mozhet, svorotit' s nravstvennogo puti. Ne dolzhno byt' nikakikh somnenii, chto zakon, surovo otnosyashchiisya ko vsyakomu nravstvennomu grekhu, ne mog postupit' s Uail'dom inache. Chtob podchinit' sebe lyudei, on dolzhen byt' besposhchaden [...]. Uail'd rasstroil svoe zdorov'e. No kak zhe byt' inache: razve angliiskaya tyur'ma dolzhna sluzhit' prokhladitel'nym el'dorado dlya lyudei, povinnykh v narushenii nravstvennogo zakona, kak ego ponimaet angliiskii parlament? [...] Zatochaya v tyur'mu svoikh prestupnikov, angliiskoe pravitel'stvo ne stanet dumat' ob ikh nervakh, ob ikh zdorov'e, ob ikh literaturnom talante [...]. Fiat justitia! Dlya boleznennogo, nervnogo, zhalkogo v svoei bespomosh-chnosti Uail'da ne posledovalo do sikh por nikakogo oblegcheniya. Na vysote yuridicheskogo velichiya zakon glukh i mertv k bezumnomu pristavaniyu ne tonko myslyashchikh lyudei.'

Wilde's perceived 'Nietzscheanism', a peculiar combination of amorality and saintly 'superhumanness', gradually became a commonplace in turn-of-the-century Russian literary discourse. The philosopher Lev Shestov (1866–1938) noted the following in his 1898 book *Dobro i zlo v uchenii Grafa Tolstogo i F. Nitsshe* (Good and evil in the teaching of Count Tolstoy and F. Nietzsche):

> The opinion that Wilde can be justified and elevated into an ideal by the philosophy of Nietzsche can be heard everywhere. Moreover, all kinds of people, tempted by Wilde's amusements, now consider it their duty to go about their business in the conviction that they are the precursors of the *Übermensch* and, therefore, the best workers in the field of human progress. (Shestov 1992, 140)[15]

The first years of the twentieth century saw a great increase in Wilde's translations and popularity in Russia (see Pavlova 1991). The focus of public discussion, however, remained constant: as before, the life and personality of Wilde, rather than his creative writing, dominated the debate. Konstantin Bal'mont (1867–1942), a major Symbolist poet, translator and popularizer of Wilde, laid the foundation for the Symbolist interpretation of Wilde. Bal'mont's 1903 lecture 'Poeziya Oksara Uail'da' (The poetry of Oscar Wilde) produced a noticeable scandal and was printed in the first issue of the main Symbolist journal *Vesy* (Libra). Its position, following the editor Valerii Bryusov's manifesto 'Klyuchi tain' (The keys of mysteries), reflects Wilde's stature in the hierarchy of literary authorities recognized by the Russian Symbolists. Bal'mont refuses to talk about Wilde's work, however; by 'the poetry of Wilde' he understands 'the poetry of his personality, the poetry of his fate' (Bal'mont 1904, 25).[16] More importantly, Bal'mont reinforces the parallel between Wilde and Nietzsche. He sees in Wilde's *life* a phenomenon analogous to Nietzsche's *writing*:

> In the sense of being an interesting and original person, he cannot be compared to anyone except Nietzsche. However, while Nietzsche's personality marks the absolute impetuosity of literary work, combined with asceticism of personal behaviour, the reckless Oscar Wilde is as chaste as air in his artistic work [...], but in his personal behaviour he went so far from commonly accepted rules that he spent two years at hard labour despite all his enormous influence, despite all his fame. (Bal'mont 1904, 37)[17]

---

[15] 'mnenie, chto O. Uail'd opradyvaetsya i chut' li ne vozvoditsya v ideal filos-ofiei Nitsshe, vy uslyshite povsyudu. Bolee togo, raznogo roda lyudi, kotorykh soblaznyayut uail'dovskie zabavy, teper' schitayut svoim dolgom predavat'sya svoim zanyatiyam s ubezhdeniem, chto oni predtechi Übermensch' a [German in original] i, sledovatel'no, luchshie rabotniki na pole chelovecheskogo progressa.'

[16] 'tol'ko o poezii ego lichnosti, o poezii ego sud'by.'

[17] 'v smysle interestnosti i original'nosti lichnosti on ne mozhet byt' postavlen v uroven' ni c kem, krome Nitsshe. Tol'ko Nitsshe oboznachaet svoei lichnost'yu polnuyu bezuderzhnost' literaturnogo tvorchestva v soedinenii s asketizmom povedeniya, a bezumnyi Oskar Uail'd vozdushno-tselomudren v svoem khudoz-hestvennom tvorchestve [...], no v lichnom povedenii byl nastol'ko dalek ot obshchepriznannykh pravil, chto, nesmotrya na vse svoe orgomnoe vliyanie, nesmotrya na svoyu slavu, on popal v katorzhnuyu tyur'mu, gde provel dva goda.'

Wilde's story became further mythologized in the numerous responses to Bal'mont's article. Russian critics now considered his life as a failed super-human effort to overcome morality; and in his attempt to create life artistically they saw a revolt doomed to punishment.

The works of Wilde's that were first translated and widely discussed in Russia contributed to such an interpretation of his life story. These were neither his sophisticated essays nor his witty society plays that had made him famous in Britain. In Russia's Silver Age, Wilde's best-known texts were his prison writings. *BRG* was issued in a translation by Bal'mont in 1904 (as early as November 1903 Bal'mont read his translation at the meeting of the Moscow Literary-Artistic Circle; his lecture accompanied the reading). *DP* was promptly translated into Russian by E. Andreeva and printed in the March 1905 issue of *Vesy* with a sympathetic editorial introduction. In this work, Wilde famously admits that in his life before the trials he had been misled by the constant pursuit of pleasure, and that he had not understood the importance of suffering, which he realized only later in prison. 'Suffering – curious as it may sound to you', he writes to Douglas, 'is the means by which we become conscious of existing' (Wilde 1986, 113). He also speaks at great length about Christ, of whom he claims to have approached an understanding while in prison.

By 1905, when Wilde's Nietzscheanism appeared to be a proven fact in Russia, the discovery of his later Christian inclinations caused an enthusi-astic response in modernist circles. As Kornei Chukovskii noted, 'there is no Russian article devoted to Wilde that does not speak of his repentance, rebirth, catharsis' (Chukovskii 2001, 409).[18] Having always suspected a Christian basis to Nietzsche's embrace of suffering, Russian culture now found material confirmation in the Nietzschean life of Wilde. Presenting a mystical and philosophical interpretation of Wilde's *Salomé*, the Symbolist writer Nikolai Minskii saw that in this drama, while still being a prophet of demonic aesthet-icism, Wilde had already had the 'presentiment of a new light' ('predchuvstvie novogo sveta') that revealed itself to him at the depth of his ostracism and suffering (Minskii 1908, 56).

Led by Valerii Bryusov's journal *Vesy* and his publishing house *Skorpion*, the Russian Symbolists made Wilde into a banner of their own aesthetic movement. At the same time, translating Wilde became an industry and readers began to discover Wilde in more and more accessible translations and editions. For instance, in the first two decades of the twentieth century, *BRG* and *DP* were rendered into Russian five times each, *Salomé* had six Russian translations and *PDG* seven (Pavlova 1991, 102). A twelve-volume edition of Wilde's collected works issued by the publisher Sablin (Uail'd 1905–09) and notable for many substandard translations was followed by the competent four-volume set edited by Kornei Chukovskii (Uail'd 1912), which aimed at correcting this problem. Both editions comprised *PDG*, *Salomé*, the fairy tales, critical essays, short stories, comedies and prison writings. Chukovskii's

---

[18] 'Net takoi russkoi stat'i, posvyashchennoi Uail'du, v kotoroi ne tverdili by o ego raskayanii, pererozhdenii, katarsise.'

1912 edition also featured a selection of Wilde's poetry translated by Russia's leading modernist poets, such as Fedor Sologub, Nikolai Gumilev, Bal'mont and Kuzmin, among others. A competition of sorts took place to achieve the most effective rendition of *BRG*. Bal'mont's popular version was seen as too ornate for this sombre text, and *Vesy's* critic Mikhail Likiardopulo translated it in prose for Wilde's first collected works (Uail'd 1905–09, 8). When Bryusov undertook his own poetic translation for the 1912 collected works, he aimed at preserving both the rhythmic and lexical structure of Wilde's original (Uail'd 1912, 2; Roznatovskaya 2000, 335). This competition continued into the Soviet period and produced at least nine different Russian versions of the poem (Roznatovskaya 2000, 85–86).

The prominence of the prison works helped shape Wilde's literary reputation in a peculiar way: not only did the biographical narrative remain central to Wilde's reputation in Russia, but it also acquired some strongly idiosyncratic features, such as the aura of voluntary suffering added to his self-destructive behaviour immediately before and between the trials. In 1904, Grigorii Petrov, a priest and journalist writing in the newspaper *Russkoe slovo* (Russian word) under the pen name V. Artaban, described Wilde as a latter-day Raskol'nikov (the hero of Dostoevsky's *Crime and Punishment*):

> He feels that he is a criminal and he sends himself to hard labour, he executes himself. One can say with confidence that the horrors of Reading Gaol [...] were no more dreadful for him than the torture that he bore within himself at the end of his life, long before the trial. (Artaban 1904, 1)[19]

Petrov entitled his article – devoted to Nietzsche, Wilde and Bal'mont's lecture – 'Gnilaya dusha' (The rotten soul), and built it around the metaphor of 'the apple of Sodom'. By this, Petrov explained, he meant a particular fruit that grew in Palestine in the place where Sodom had stood. The fruit looked quite beautiful from the outside but was rotten within. Such, in his opinion, was Wilde. Though Petrov's view of him is clearly negative, he nevertheless persists in describing Wilde, on the model of Raskol'nikov, as redeeming himself through voluntary suffering.

In February 1906, in the midst of revolutionary upheaval in the country and soon after the publication of *DP*, the official journal of the St Petersburg Theological Academy, *Khristianskoe chtenie* (Christian reading), printed Vasilii Uspenskii's article 'Religiya Oskara Uail'da i sovremennyi asketizm' (Oscar Wilde's religion and contemporary asceticism). Uspenskii, a former professor of the Academy and a member of the St Petersburg Religious Philosophical Meetings (a series of meetings organized by Vladimir Merezhkovskii and Zinaida Gippius, designed to encourage collaboration between intellectuals and members of the clergy), believed that there was a religious meaning in

---

[19] 'On chuvstvuet, chto on prestupnik, i sam posylaet sebya na katorgu, sam kaznit sebya. Mozhno smelo skazat', chto uzhasy Redingskoi tyur'my [...] dlya nego ne byli strashnee toi katorgi, kotoruyu on pod konets zhizni, zadolgo do suda, nosil v sebe.'

the call to tragic pleasure, emblematized in contemporary culture by Wilde and Nietzsche. Comparing Wilde to a saint, Uspenskii describes the writer's suffering as 'great and profound – and not only because of the external circumstances of his life. He knew more horrible, internal torments. His blood merged with those streams of blood through which mankind acquired profound religious thought' (1906, 225).[20] Most Russian critics focused on Wilde's life during and after the trials and interpreted it as the apotheosis of voluntary suffering. The critic Zinaida Vengerova, who did much to bring English aestheticism to the attention of Russian readers around the turn of the century, echoed this view: 'Now, amidst the tortures of the legal proceedings, his spirit was triumphant, for [...] fate gave him the opportunity to incarnate the tragic truth of being, the law of suffering' (1912, 174).[21]

However, even in suffering Wilde appeared ambiguous – Christian with distinctly pagan overtones. In his *Birth of Tragedy* (1872), Nietzsche had presented the Dionysian element in Greek art as a symbol of the tragic liberation from the control, responsibilities and moral restrictions imposed by the world of fixed forms. The leading ideologue of Russian Symbolism, Vyacheslav Ivanov (1866–1949), saw an absolute metaphysical principle in Nietzsche's distinction between Dionysian and Apollonian elements. As a scholar of antiquity, Ivanov concentrated on the study of the cult of Dionysus and finally arrived at the conclusion that the Greek cult of the suffering god was a major source for early Christianity (Ivanov 1904, 1905). This hypothesis had important consequences for the philosophical foundations of Russian Symbolism: it proved that the Dionysian element, with its always implied unbridling of sexual drives, and the Christian ideal of suffering were not mutually contradictory (Ivanov 1971–87, 1: 720). By extension, the orgiastic, or Dionysian, side of Wilde's reputation only complemented his saintliness. As Ivanov announced in 1909, 'the whole life of the noble singer and humble martyr of Reading Gaol has turned into the religion of the universal Golgotha' (Ivanov 1971–87, 3: 564–65).[22]

The explanation for the remarkable vitality of Wilde's Russian mythologies seems to be in the easy adaptability of Wilde's life story to the discursive resources of Russian culture. Particularly relevant is the Russian nineteenth-century novelistic model of a hero's 'remaking his own essence' ('peredelka sobstvennoi suti'), to use Yuri Lotman's expression, through moral crisis, self-sacrifice and suffering (Lotman 1993, 102). Rooted in mythology and hagiography, this model proved to be incredibly productive in Russian literary fictions; it spread into cultural mythologies and eventually shaped the modern and modernist conceptualizations of sexuality. Thus, besides providing a

---

[20] 'Uail'd mnogo i gluboko stradal, i ne tol'ko ot vneshnikh obstoyatel'stv zhizni. On znal bolee strashnye, vnutrennie muki. Ego krov' priobshchilas' k potokam krovi, kotorymi chelovechestvo priobretalo uglublennuyu religioznuyu mysl'.'

[21] 'Teper', stredi terzanii sudebnogo razbiratel'stva, dukh ego likoval, ibo [...] sud'ba dala voplotit' i tragicheskuyu pravdu mira – zakon stradaniya.'

[22] 'vsya zhizn' blagorodnogo pevtsa i smirennogo muchenika "Redingskoi tyur'my" obratilas' v religiyu Golgofy vselenskoi.'

forum for discussing sexuality, literary discourse influenced the forming of sexual identities. The case of Wilde was a crucial instance.

Kuzmin: the Russian Wilde?

For certain modernist artists in Russia, the Wilde story assumed great personal significance, constituting an important phase in the development of turn-of-the-century discourses on modern sexuality. For instance, one day in the summer of 1906, Wilde became the subject of a heated discussion at Vyacheslav Ivanov's St Petersburg apartment on Tavricheskaya Street, known as *Bashnya* (The tower), the very heart of the Russian Symbolist movement. Besides Ivanov and his wife Lidiya Zinov'eva-Annibal, three men were present in the Tower: the poet Mikhail Kuzmin, the young artists Konstantin Somov (1869–1938) and Leon Bakst (1866–1924). In his diary Kuzmin reported how 'V[yacheslav] I[vanov] places this snob, hypocrite, bad writer and most faint-hearted man, this man who dirtied the very thing he was tried for, next to Christ – this is downright horrible' (Kuzmin 2000, 166).[23] A week later the same dispute was repeated in the same setting (Kuzmin 2000, 171). What made this exchange so passionate and fraught with symbolic significance was its context, since everyone in attendance belonged to Ivanov's inner circle, that is, to the so-called Hafiz society which had first assembled at the Tower in May 1906 and continued to meet there until November of that year.[24] The group included several of Ivanov's close friends who were homosexual (Kuzmin, Somov and Val'ter Nuvel') as well as several other young men, talented and handsome, including the philosopher Nikolai Berdyaev (1874–1948), the poet Sergei Gorodetskii (1884–1967) and the writer Sergei Auslender (1886–1943). With the exception of Zinov'eva-Annibal, the group consisted exclusively of men. The location of the apartment near the Tauride Garden added to the attractiveness of these gatherings: the Tauride was St Petersburg's central area for homosexual cruising, and several members of the Hafiz society were in the habit of checking out its paths before or after the meetings, at which reports of recent escapades featured prominently. At their gatherings, the participants immersed themselves in what they perceived as instances of the Dionysian: they drank wine, dressed up, played flutes, flirted and kissed. They also read aloud their diaries, as well as erotic poetry.

Eros was the main topic in the Hafizites' conversations. In these talks, Ivanov formulated his views on homosexuality, as recorded in his diary:

> [Kuzmin] is a sort of pioneer of the coming age when, with the growth of homosexuality, humanity will no longer be maimed and crippled by the modern

---

[23] 'V. I. Stavit etogo snoba, litsemera, plokhogo pisatelya i malodushneishego cheloveka, zapachkavshego to, za chto byl sudim, ryadom s Khristom – eto pryamo uzhasno.'

[24] On the Hafiz society, see Bogomolov 1995, 67–99. On Kuzmin circa 1906, see Malmstad and Bogomolov 1999, 92–124.

aesthetic and ethic of the sexes, understood as 'men for women' and 'women for men' [...]. This aesthetic of savages and this biological ethic, which blind every 'normal' person to an entire half of humanity and cut off an entire half of its individuality in favour of the continuation of the species. Homosexuality is inseparably linked to humanism; but, as a one-sided principle that excludes hetero-sexuality, it contradicts humanism, in respect to which it is transformed into *petitio principii*. (Ivanov 1971–87, 2: 750)[25]

The question of homosexuality was far from theoretical for Ivanov. His affair with Gorodetskii took place that very summer. Ivanov conceptualized this relationship as mystical and Dionysian: it was supposed to clear the way to the superhuman for both participants. From its very beginning Ivanov expected his love for Gorodetskii to be 'tragic' in the Nietzschean sense of utter, illumi-nating suffering (Bershtein 1998, 40–57).

Mikhail Kuzmin's novel *Kryl'ya* (*Wings*) offered a different account of the relationship between art and life. Published in 1906, *Kryl'ya* is the first attempt in Russian literature at portraying same-sex love extensively and sympatheti-cally. Kuzmin's contemporaries noticed the novel's radicalism – a few with approval, many with opprobrium (Malmstad 2000). Some Russian modernist readers saw Kuzmin's social daring as unparalleled anywhere else in Europe, and this consideration may have in turn motivated Bruisov's unprecedented decision to devote an entire issue of *Vesy* to the novel. The subsequent scandal propelled Kuzmin to fame, earning him the reputation of 'the Russian Oscar Wilde' – a title that Kuzmin disliked. But, retrospectively, one can agree with the intuition of Kuzmin's contemporaries: just like Wilde in Britain, Kuzmin stood in Russia at the origin of the modern cultural trend to emancipate and legitimize male homosexuality.

In *Kryl'ya*, Kuzmin presents the story of Vanya Smurov, a middle-class teenage boy who befriends an older man named Larion Dmitrievich Shtrup. Throughout the novel, Shtrup is referred to as either English or half-English or a British subject, and he is portrayed as the central figure within the St Petersburg circle of homosexual aesthetes. At their gatherings, Vanya learns the programme for the aesthetic transformation of life which these new 'Hellenes' are attempting to realize (Kuzmin 1972, 33). Vanya begins to fall in love with Shtrup but soon discovers that the Englishman has hired a young bathhouse attendant, Fedor, as a live-in servant. From the same overheard conversation, Vanya finds out that it is the custom of bathhouse attendants to fool around

---

[25] '[Kuzmin] v svoem rode pioner gryadushchego veka, kogda s rostom gomoseksual'nosti ne budet bolee bezobrazit' i rasshatyvat' chelovechestvo sovre-mennaya estetika polov, ponimaemykh kak "mushchiny dlya zhenshchin" i "zhenshchiny dlya mushchin" [...], – eta estetika dikarei i biologicheskaya etika, osleplyayushchie kazhdogo iz "normal'nykh" lyudei na tseluyu polovinu chelovechestva i otsekayushchie tseluyu polovinu ego individual'nosti v pol'zu prodolzheniya roda. Gomoseksual'nost' nerazryvno svyazana s gumanizmon: no kak odnostoronnee nachalo, isklyuchayushchee geteroseksual'nost', – ono zhe protivorechit gumanizmu, obrashchayas' po otnosheniyu k nemu v *petitio principii* [Latin in the original].'

with their clients for a fee. It becomes clear to him that Fedor is hired to provide sexual services to Shtrup. Vanya is jealous and bitterly disappointed by the apparent contradiction between Shtrup's lofty ideals regarding life and his practice of keeping a lower-class lover. Additionally, Vanya finds it difficult to accept the physical side of love in general. Through many twists of the plot and philosophical dialogues, Vanya gradually learns to embrace his love for Shtrup, with the implication that he is also accepting the physical component of sexual desire. The book ends on an ecstatically optimistic note: having decided to join Shtrup in his travels and evidently in a life together, Vanya throws open the window 'onto a street flooded with sunlight' ('na ulitsu, zalituyu yarkim solntsem') (110).

The programme for a new, aesthetically transformed way of life, which Shtrup and his friends formulate and Vanya absorbs, has three main elements. First, this new life is based on the sensual intensification of experience; second, it is a Hellenic life, shaped by patterns of classical beauty; and third, it incorporates the classical pederastic *eros* that links man to boy, teacher to disciple, wisdom to beauty. In Shtrup's salon, Vanya hears the following speech:

> And when they say to you 'unnatural,' be content to look at the blind fool who has said such a thing and go your way [...]. People go about like the blind, like the dead, when they might create for themselves a life burning with intensity in every moment, a life in which pleasure would be as poignant as if you had just come into the world and might die before the day were done [...]. Miracles crowd upon us at every step: there are muscles, sinews in the human body which one cannot look upon without a tremor! And those who bind the idea of beauty to the beauty of a woman seen through the eyes of a man – they reveal only vulgar lust and are furthest of all from the true idea of beauty. We are Hellenes, lovers of the beautiful, the bacchants of the coming day. (Kuzmin 1972, 33)[26]

From Kuzmin's diary, one gets the sense that the aesthetic and erotic philosophy formulated in *Kryl'ya* corresponded very closely to his personal quest. In an entry of 27 August 1905 he wrote that he 'would like to convey to people all that delights me, so that they could drink the slightest beauty with the same intensity, with their flesh, and, through that, be as happy as none of them dreams of being' (Kuzmin 2000, 32).[27] Kuzmin continues this entry by daydreaming of finding a friend with whom he could share a

---

[26] 'I kogda vam skazhut: "protivoestestvenno", – vy tol'ko posmotrite na skazavshego sleptsa i prokhodite mimo [...]. Lyudi khodyat kak slepye, kak mertye, kogda oni mogli by sozdat' plamenneishuyu zhizn', gde vse naslazhdenie bylo by tak obostrenno, budto vy tol'ko chto rodilis' i seichas umrete [...]. Chudesa vokrug nas na kazhdom shagu: est' muskuly, svyazki v chelovecheskom tele, kotorye nevozmozhno bez trepeta videt'. I svyazyvayushchie ponyatie o krasote s krasatoi zhenshchiny dlya muzhchiny yavlyayut tol'ko poshluyu pokhot', i dal'she, dal'she vsego ot istinnoi idei krasoty. My – elliny, liubovniki prekrasnogo, vakkhanty gryadushchei zhizni.'

[27] 'Kak ya khotel by peredat' lyudyam vse, chto menya vostorgaet, chtoby i oni tak zhe intensivno, plot'yu, pili maleishuyu krasotu i cherez eto byli by schastlivy, kak nikto ne smeet mechtat' byt'.'

physical love as well as the delights of artistic life – a friend who could be both his comrade and disciple, with whom he would travel in Italy, 'bathing in beauty' ('kupayas' v krasote'), enjoying music and so on. In this long list of delights, the sensual and sexual are interlaced with the aesthetic. Kuzmin envisions a new Renaissance, and the 'new man' ('novyi chelovek') of *Kryl'ya* is also the *Renaissance-Mensch* – the German term employed by his close friend Georgii Chicherin in a letter to Kuzmin, written just as Kuzmin was working on *Kryl'ya* (November 1904; Bogomolov and Malmstad 1995, 105). To the first readers of *Kryl'ya*, Kuzmin's use of this loaded notion triggered memories of the socialist utopia depicted in Nikolai Chernyshevskii's influential 1863 novel *Chto delat'* (*What Is to Be Done?*). While the new men of Kuzmin's novel are certainly no socialists, they nevertheless share an important trait with Chernyshevskii's revolutionaries: they are people of the future, who not only embody an ideal but also proselytize in order to create even more new people. Thus in *Kryl'ya*, the Greek teacher Daniil Ivanovich, a member of Shtrup's circle, helps enlighten Vanya largely through classical culture and Socratic dialogues.

The question of what sources Kuzmin had for this vision has long interested scholars. In their seminal biography of Kuzmin, Malmstad and Bogomolov find a number of striking parallels between Kuzmin's thinking and early German Romanticism, specifically the works of the German philosopher Johann Georg Hamann and the writer and critic Johann Jacob Wilhelm Heinse (Malmstad and Bogomolov 1999, 72–79). These parallels, however persuasive, do not answer the question of why Kuzmin makes Larion Dmitrievich Shtrup, the hero who most fully embodies the principles of new Hellenism and the artistically transformed life, an Englishman.

Clearly drawing on the writings of Wilde and Walter Pater, the influential critic Zinaida Vengerova declared in 1905 that England was the birthplace of an aesthetic Renaissance that had spread throughout Europe over the preceding ten to fifteen years (Vengerova 1905, 267). England's association with a new Renaissance is registered in Kuzmin's diary on 13 September 1905: '[i]n the library I was reading *Italian Renaissance in England,* precisely that which inspires me' – literally, that which gives me wings ('imenno to, chto […] menya okrylyaet') (2000, 41).[28] It is noteworthy that in the sunlit ending of *Kryl'ya*, Vanya joins the *Englishman* Shtrup for a journey in *Italy*.

Wilde, the best-known representative of English aestheticism, was a familiar character not only to Kuzmin, but also to his lover Grigorii Murav'ev, despite the fact that the eighteen-year-old Murav'ev had no education whatsoever (in all likelihood he was a bathhouse attendant, and Kuzmin certainly paid him for their intimate time together). In September 1905, when Kuzmin shaved off his Russian beard and adopted a European look, Murav'ev immediately suggested that Kuzmin had done so in order to resemble the exiled Englishman [*sic*], that is, Wilde (Kuzmin 2000, 45). After the publication of *Kryl'ya* a year later, everyone would see in Kuzmin 'the Russian Wilde'.

---

[28] 'V biblioteke chital "Ital'yanskoe Vozrozhd\<enie\> v Anglii", imenno to, chto oba menya okrylyaet.'

Yet the mythology of redemptive suffering associated with Wilde and, by extension, with the entire phenomenon of same-sex love, did not attract Kuzmin. In *Kryl'ya*, he provides a scenario for finding ecstatic happiness. How could the tragic prisoner Wilde fit into Kuzmin's utopian universe of unbounded sensual and aesthetic bliss? In his aesthetic thinking, Wilde was much indebted to Pater. Rachel Polonsky has suggested that 'Shtrup is a Paterian figure, a Russian transposition of the Oxford tutor, as conceived by Victorian Hellenism' (1998, 176). Indeed, the statements made by the St Petersburg aesthetes in *Kryl'ya* closely resemble certain passages from 'The Conclusion' to *The Renaissance* (a work much admired by Wilde), in which Pater calls for a new Renaissance modelled on aspects of ancient Greek culture. In his characterization of the German art historian Johann Joachim Winckelmann in this same book, Pater also hinted that this Hellenic ideal included pederastic relations. Both in spirit and in detail, Kuzmin's Hellenic utopia resembles Pater's Hellenism. Even the epigraph of Pater's *Renaissance* ('Yet shall ye be as the wings of a dove', Psalms 68. 13) sounds, retrospectively, Kuzminian (both writers were obliquely drawing on Plato's suggestive image of love lending wings to the soul in the *Phaedrus*).

Pater worked and died before Wilde's tragic downfall. Wilde's much-publicized trials drastically changed the terms of the discussion of homosexuality: his *aesthetic* defence against the *moral* and *legal* charges filed against him failed spectacularly in the courtroom. In the subsequent decades, scientific and legal approaches to homosexuality came to the fore. Even the emerging gay emancipation movement adopted the dual conceptual frameworks of science and law. While Kuzmin's borrowing of the English aesthetes' abstract intellectual constructions was certainly a radical step, in Europe the aesthetically grounded advocacy of homosexuality had already had its day. By 1905 it could appear archaic and even quaint. The true originality of Kuzmin's novel is therefore in its attempt to transplant a primarily English aesthetic ideology onto the Russian tradition of social utopia. In the spirit of this Russian tradition, the novel describes, albeit obliquely, a sect-like group of devotees to the new ideal and also provides a naturalist perspective onto the seedy side of life in St Petersburg – in this case, the seedy side of gay life. This apparently incongruous mixing of high intellectual discourse and naturalism was mocked in the press (for a full account of the contemporary Russian reception of *Kryl'ya* see Malmstad 2000).

In the final analysis, Kuzmin, 'the Russian Wilde', opposed the very key element of the Wilde myth in Russia: the notion that the modern homosexual was inclined to tragic rebellion and voluntary suffering, in order to be rewarded by a kind of sainthood. Kuzmin rejected the Wilde myth and built his own utopian vision of blissful and ecstatic same-sex love, which he based on the twin notions of life's artistic transformation and its sensual intensification. While featuring a number of distinctly Russian ideological elements, this utopia paralleled certain tenets of English aestheticism: it mirrored Pater's and Wilde's aesthetic pronouncements but disregarded St Oscar's catastrophic and much mythologized end.

Bibliography

Introduction

Adorno, Theodor W. (2003) *Ästhetische Theorie*, Frankfurt a.M.: Suhrkamp.

Bann, Stephen (ed.) (2004) *The Reception of Walter Pater in Europe*, The Reception of British and Irish Authors in Europe, series ed. Elinor Shaffer, London; New York: Continuum.

Beckson, Karl (1970) *Oscar Wilde: The Critical Heritage*, London: Routledge.

Borges, Jorge Luis (1999) 'On Oscar Wilde', *The Total Library: Non-Fiction 1922–1986*, London; New York: Penguin, pp. 314–16.

Dowling, Linda (1996) *The Vulgarization of Art: The Victorians and Aesthetic Democracy*, Charlottesville: University of Virginia Press.

Evangelista, Stefano (2009) *British Aestheticism and Ancient Greece: Hellenism, Reception, Gods in Exile*, Basingstoke; New York: Palgrave Macmillan.

Gide, André (1902) 'Hommage à Oscar Wilde', *L'Ermitage* [Paris], June, 401–29.

Holland, Vyvyan (1954) *Son of Oscar Wilde*, London: Rupert Hart-Davis.

Hurtley, Jacqueline A. (2006) 'Lands of Desire: Yeats in Catalonia, Galicia and the Basque Country, 1920–1936', in Jochum, Klaus Peter (ed.) *The Reception of W. B. Yeats in Europe*, London; New York: Continuum.

Keilson–Lauritz, Marita (1997) *Die Geschichte der eigenen Geschichte: Literatur und Literaturkritik in den Anfängen der Schwulenbewegung*, Berlin: Verlag Rosa Winkel.

Jochum, Klaus Peter (2006) *The Reception of W. B. Yeats in Europe*, The Reception of British and Irish Authors in Europe, series ed. Elinor Shaffer, London; New York: Continuum.

Langlade, Jacques de (1975) *Oscar Wilde écrivain français*, Paris: Stock.

Lernout, Geert (2004) 'Introduction', in Lernout, Geert and Wim Van Mierlo (eds) *The Reception of James Joyce in Europe*, The Reception of British and Irish Authors in Europe, series ed. Elinor Shaffer, 2 vols, London; New York: Continuum, 1: 3–13.

Mann, Thomas (1947) *Nietzsche's Philosophy in the Light of Contemporary Events*, Washington: [Library of Congress]; 'Address delivered [...] in the Coolidge Auditorium in the Library of Congress on the evening of April 29, 1947'.

Quilter, Harry (1895) 'The Gospel of Intensity', *Contemporary Review*, June, 761–82.

Ross, Robert Baldwin (Robbie) (1908) 'Unpublished speech made at a dinner in the speaker's honor at the Ritz Hotel, London', William Andrews Clarke Memorial Library, University of California Los Angeles, Wilde Papers, Box 58, Folder 3.

Stutfield, Hugh E. M. (1895) '"Tommyrotics"', *Blackwood's Magazine*, 157 (June): 833–45.

Wilde, Oscar (2000) *The Complete Letters of Oscar Wilde*, eds Merlin Holland and Rupert Hart-Davis, London: Fourth Estate.

Yeats, W. B. (1891) 'Oscar Wilde's Last Book', *United Ireland*, 26 September, 5; quoted in Beckson 1970, 111.

Chapter 1. Picturing His Exact Decadence: The British Reception of Oscar Wilde

'A.E.R.' (1912) 'Views and Reviews', *New Age* [London], 27 June, 207–08.

Arata, Stephen (1996) *Fictions of Loss in the Victorian Fin de Siècle*, Cambridge: Cambridge University Press.

Beckson, Karl (ed.) (1970) *Oscar Wilde: The Critical Heritage*, London: Routledge and Kegan Paul.

Beerbohm, Max (1900) 'A Satire on Romantic Drama', *Saturday Review*, 8 December, 719–20.

Betjeman, John (1937) *Continual Dew: A Little Book of Bourgeois Verse*, London: John Murray.

'The Bookworm' (1900) 'Bibliographical', *Academy* [London], 8 December, 542.

Brasol, Boris (1938) *Oscar Wilde: The Man, the Artist, the Martyr*, New York: Charles Scribner's.

Bristow, Joseph (2004) 'Biographies: Oscar Wilde: The Man, the Life, the Legend', in Roden, Frederick S. (ed.) *Oscar Wilde Studies*, Basingstoke: Palgrave Macmillan.

Bristow, Joseph (2008) 'Introduction', in Bristow, Joseph (ed.) *Oscar Wilde and Modern Culture: The Making of a Legend*, Athens, OH: Ohio University Press.

Calder, Charles (1995) 'Hesketh Pearson', in Serafin, Steven (ed.) *Late Nineteenth- and Early Twentieth-Century British Literary Biographers*, DLB (*Dictionary of Literary Biography*) 149, Detroit, MI: Gale Research, pp. 189–96.

'Commemoration of Oscar Wilde' (1954) *Times*, 18 October, 8.

Cooper-Prichard, A(rthur) H(enry) (1931) *Conversations with Oscar Wilde*, London: Philip Allan.

Coppa, Francesca (2008) 'The Artist as Protagonist: Wilde on Stage', in Bristow, Joseph (ed.) *Oscar Wilde and Modern Culture: The Making of a Legend*, Athens, OH: Ohio University Press.

Croft-Cooke, Rupert (1967) *Feasting with Panthers: A New Consideration of Some Late Victorian Writers*, London: W. H. Allen.

Douglas, Alfred (1914) *Oscar Wilde and Myself*, London: John Long.

Ellmann, Richard (1988) *Oscar Wilde*, New York: Knopf; 1st US edn.

Ervine, St John (1951) *Oscar Wilde: A Present Time Appraisal*, London: George Allen and Unwin.

Forster, E. M. (1971) *Maurice*, London: Edward Arnold.

Gibbons, Tom (1973) *Rooms in the Darwin Hotel: Studies in English Literary Criticism and Ideas, 1880–1920*, Nedlands: University of Western Australia Press.

Gide, André (1905) *Oscar Wilde: A Study*, trans. Stuart Mason [Christopher Sclater Millard], Oxford: Holywell Press.

Guest, F. Haden (1907) 'The Last of Wilde', *New Age*, 30 May, 75.

Hale, Keith (ed.) (1998) *Friends and Apostles: The Correspondence of Rupert Brooke and James Strachey, 1905–1914*, New Haven, CT: Yale University Press.

Harris, Frank (1916) *Oscar Wilde: His Life and Confessions*, 2 vols, New York: privately pub.

Hichens, Robert (1894) *The Green Carnation*, London: William Heinemann.

Holland, Vyvyan (1954) *Son of Oscar Wilde*, New York: E. P. Dutton.

Housman, Laurence (1923) *Echo de Paris: A Study from Life*, London: Cape.

'H.T.P.' (1901) 'The Death of Oscar Wilde', *Bookman*, 12.5: 452–53.

Hunter, Ian (1987) *Nothing to Repent: The Life of Hesketh Pearson*, London: Hamish Hamilton.

Hyde, H. Montgomery (1948) *The Trials of Oscar Wilde*, London: William Hodge.

Hyde, H. Montgomery (1973) *The Trials of Oscar Wilde*, 2nd edn, New York: Dover.

Ingleby, Leonard Cresswell [C. Ranger Gull] (1907) *Oscar Wilde*, London: T. Werner Lauries.

Joyce, James (2000) 'Oscar Wilde: The Poet of "Salomé"', in *Occasional, Critical, and Political Writing*, ed., intro. and notes Kevin Barry, trans. from Italian Conor Deane, Oxford: Oxford University Press, pp. 148–51.

Kaplan, Sydney Jane (1991) *Katherine Mansfield and the Origins of Modernist Fiction*, Ithaca, NY: Cornell University Press.

Kettle, Michael (1977) *Salome's Last Veil*, London: Hart-Davis, MacGibbon.

Kemp, Richard W. (1906) 'Mr. R. H. Sherard's "Life of Oscar Wilde"', *Bookman*, 24.4: 365–67.

Kermode, Frank (1987) 'A Little of This Honey', *London Review of Books*, 29 October, 12–13.

Kingsmill, Hugh (1938) 'The Intelligent Man's Guide to Oscar Wilde', *Fortnightly Review*, 144: 296–303.

Le Gallienne, Richard (1921a) 'What's Wrong with the Eighteen-Nineties?', *Bookman*, 54.1: 1–7.

Le Gallienne, Richard (1921b) 'Oscar Wilde and "Willie Hughes"', *Bookman*, 564.2: 162–64.

Le Gallienne, Richard (1926) *The Romantic '90s*, New York: Doubleday, Page.

Lewis, Wyndham (1915) 'The Art of the Great Race', *Blast* [London], 2: 70–72.

'LM' [Ida Constance Baker] (1971) *Katherine Mansfield: The Memories of LM*, London: Michael Joseph.

Mansfield, Katherine (1927) *Journal*, ed. John Middleton Murry, London: Constable.

Mansfield, Katherine (1984–2008) *Collected Letters*, ed. Vincent O'Sullivan and Margaret Scott, 5 vols, Oxford: Clarendon Press.

Mansfield, Katherine (2002) *Selected Stories*, ed. Angela Smith, Oxford: Oxford University Press.

Mason, Stuart [Christopher Sclater Millard] (1905) 'Oscar Wilde Bibliography', *Notes and Queries*, 10th series, 30 September, 266.

Nicholson, Steven (2003) *The Censorship of British Drama, 1900–1968, vol. 1: 1900–1932*, Exeter: Exeter University Press.

Nordau, Max (1895) *Degeneration*, trans. anon., London: William Heinemann.

Orage, A. R. (1909) 'The New Romanticism', *New Age*, 4 March, 379.

O'Sullivan, Vincent (1936) *Aspects of Wilde*, New York: Henry Holt.

O'Sullivan, Vincent (1975) 'The Magnetic Chain: Notes and Approaches to K. M.', *Landfall* [Christchurch], 114: 95–111.

Pearson, Hesketh (1946) *The Life of Oscar Wilde*, London: Methuen.

Powys, John Cowper (1916) *Suspended Judgements: Essays on Books and Sensations*, New York: G. Arnold.

Ransome, Arthur (1912) *Oscar Wilde: A Critical Study*, London: Martin Secker.

Review of Leonard Cresswell Ingleby's *Oscar Wilde* (1907) *New Age*, 30 November, 93–94.

Review of *LASCOS* (1909) *New Age*, 23 September, 400.

Review of G. Constant Lounsbery's *PDG* (1913) *Times*, 29 August, 7.

Review of Stuart Mason's *Bibliography of Oscar Wilde* (1914) *Nation*, 8 August, 716.

Review of *Salome*, Gate Studio Theatre, London (1931a) *Times*, 28 May, 10.

Review of *Salome*, Savoy Theatre, London (1931b) *Times*, 6 October, 10.

Ricketts, Charles (1932) *Oscar Wilde: Recollections*, London: Nonesuch Press.

Robertson. W. Graham (1931) *Time Was*, London: Hamish Hamilton.

'St James's Theatre' (1895) *Times*, 15 February, 5.

Schroeder, Horst (2002) *Additions and Corrections to Richard Ellmann's 'Oscar Wilde'*, Brunswick: privately pub.

Shaw, George Bernard (1908) 'Letter', *New Age*, 19 January, 223–24.

Shellard, Dominic, and Steve Nicholson (2004) *The Lord Chamberlain Regrets: A History of British Theatre Censorship*, London: British Library.

Sherard, Robert Harborough (1902) *Oscar Wilde: The Story of an Unhappy Friendship*, London: Hermes Press.

Sherard, Robert Harborough (1906) *The Life of Oscar Wilde*, London: T. Werner Laurie.

Smith, Hester Travers (1924) *Psychic Messages from Oscar Wilde*, London: Psychic Book Club.

Stokes, Leslie and Sewell Stokes (1938) *Oscar Wilde*, New York: Random House.

Symons, Arthur (1930) *A Study of Oscar Wilde*, London: Charles J. Sawyer.

Tanitch, Robert (1999) *Oscar Wilde on Stage and Screen*, London: Methuen.

Tydeman, William and Steven Price (1996) *Salome*, Cambridge: Cambridge University Press.

Vidal, Gore (1987) review of Richard Ellmann's *Oscar Wilde*, *Times Literary Supplement*, 2–8 October, 1063–64.

Wilde, Oscar (1905) *De Profundis*, London: Methuen.

Wilde, Oscar (1908) *Collected Works*, ed. Robert Ross, 14 vols, London: Methuen.

Wilde, Oscar (2000) *The Complete Letters*, eds Merlin Holland and Rupert Hart-Davis, London: Fourth Estate.

Wildeblood, Peter (1955) *Against the Law*, London: Weidenfeld and Nicolson.

Yeats, W. B. (ed.) (1936) *The Oxford Book of Modern Verse*, Oxford: Clarendon Press.

Yeats, W. B. (1999) 'The Tragic Generation', in *Autobiographies*, eds William H. O'Donnell and Douglas N. Archibald, New York: Scribner.

Chapter 2. Performance and Place: Oscar Wilde and the Irish National Interest

Articles in The Irish Times
(1877) 'Catholic University Literary and Historical Society', 25 May, 6.
(1878) 'Notes of the Times', 17 June, 4.
(1879) 'At Home', 5 March, 4.
(1882a) 'Our London Letter', 11 March, 9.
(1882b) 'Our London Letter', 6 April, 5.
(1882c) 'Our London Letter', 12 April, 5.
(1882d) 'Our London Letter', 15 April, 5.
(1885) 'Mr. Oscar Wilde on Dress', 6 January, 6.
(1891a) 'Notes of the Day', 25 May, 6.
(1891b) 'Literary Notes', 28 December, 7.
(1893a) 'A Woman of No Importance', 23 September, 5.
(1893b) 'Lady Windermere's Fan', 19 October, 5.
(1893c) 'A Woman of No Importance', 7 November, 5.
(1894a) 'London Correspondence', 21 September, 5.
(1894b) 'London Correspondence', 24 September, 5.
(1895a) 'The Charge against Lord Queensberry', 4 April, 5.
(1895b) 'Arrest of Mr. Oscar Wilde', 6 April, 6.
(1895c) 'The Charge against Wilde', 8 April, 6.
(1905) 'Auction of Valuable Books', 21 November, 10.
(1906a) 'Platform and Stage', 15 December, 9.
(1906b) 'Echoes from "Kottabos"', 21 December, 7.
(1907) 'Public Amusements', 3 September, 6.
(1908a) 'London Correspondence', 26 September, 4.
(1908b) 'Gaiety Theatre: "Lady Frederick"', 6 October, 5.
(1938a) 'Death of a Poet', 8 March, 3.
(1938b) 'Irishman's Diary', 4 June, 6.
(1946) 'Rainy Saturday in a Paris Graveyard', 19 February, 2.

(1949) 'For Sale by Private Treaty', 10 September, 10.

(1954a) 'Place Names', 11 September, 4.

(1954b) 'Irish Wilde', 17 September, 8.

(1954c) 'London Letter', 18 October, 5.

(2008) Isabel Morton, 'Talking Property', 21 August, 30.

Secondary sources

Coakley, Davis (1944) *Oscar Wilde: The Importance of Being Irish*, Dublin: Town House and Country House.

Cocks, Harry G. (2003) 'Respectability, Blackmail and the Transformation of Scandal', in *Nameless Offences: Homosexual Desire in the Nineteenth Century*, London: I. B. Tauris, pp. 115–56.

Ellmann, Richard (1987) *Oscar Wilde*, London: Hamish Hamilton.

Doody, Noreen (2002) ' "An Echo of Someone Else's Music": The Influence of Oscar Wilde on W. B. Yeats', in Böker, Uwe, Richard Corballis and Julie A. Hibbard (eds) *The Importance of Reinventing Oscar: Versions of Wilde during the Last 100 Years*, Amsterdam: Rodopi, pp. 175–82.

Doody, Noreen (2001) 'An Influential Involvement: Yeats, Wilde and the French Symbolists', in Kelly, Aaron and Alan Gillis (eds) *Critical Ireland*, Dublin: Four Courts, pp. 48–55.

Doody, Noreen (2003) 'Oscar Wilde: Landscape, Memory and Imagined Space', in Sanchez, Jose Fernandez and M. Elena Jaime de Pablos (eds) *Irish Landscapes*, Almeria: University of Almeria, pp. 179–84.

Doody, Noreen (2004) 'Wilde: Nation and Empire', in Roden, Frederick (ed.) *Palgrave Advances in Wilde Studies,* New York: Palgrave, pp. 246–66.

Doody, Noreen (2000) 'Wilde, Yeats: Nation and Identity', in Mathews, P. J. (ed.) *New Voices in Irish Criticism*, Dublin: Four Courts, pp. 27–33.

James, Dermot (2008) *From the Margins to the Centre: A History of 'The Irish Times'*, Dublin: The Woodfield Press.

Kiberd, Declan (1995) *Inventing Ireland*, London: Cape.

Killeen, Jarlath (2005) *The Faiths of Oscar Wilde: Catholicism, Folklore and Ireland*, Houndmills: Palgrave Macmillan.

Kingsmill, Hugh (1977) 'Meeting with Yeats', in Mikhail, Edward Halim (ed.) *W. B. Yeats: Interviews and Recollections*, 2 vols, London: Macmillan, 2: 294–96.

Leahy, Aoife and David Rose (2008) 'Oscar Wilde: An Irish Scenography', *The Oscholars*, <http://www.oscholars.com/TO/Appendix/Scenographies/Ireland/ireland.htm#_The_Importance_o> [accessed 30 September 2008].

MacCormack, Jerusha (ed.) (1998) *Wilde the Irishman*, New Haven; London: Yale University Press.

Ní Chuilleanáin, Eiléan (ed.) (2003) *The Wilde Legacy*, Dublin: Four Courts.

O'Brien, Mark (2008) *'The Irish Times': A History*, Dublin: Four Courts.

O'Toole, Fintan (2008) 'A Reflection on the Times', review of *'The Irish Times': A History*, *Irish Times*, 25 October, 3.

Shaw, George Bernard (1962) 'Oscar Wilde', in *The Matter with Ireland*, trans. Felix F. Strauss and Mr Laurence, London: Hart-Davis, p. 30.

Slote, Sam (1995) 'Wilde Thing: Concerning the Eccentricities of a Figure of Decadence in *Finnegan's Wake*', in Hayman, David (ed.) *Genetic Criticism and Joyce*, European Joyce Studies 5, Amsterdam: Rodopi, pp. 101–22.

Walshe, Éibhear (2005) *Éire-Ireland*, 40: 3 & 4 (Fall/Winter): 38–57.

Walshe, Éibhear (forthcoming) *Oscar's Shadow: Wilde, Homosexuality and Modern Ireland*.

Wilde, Oscar (1922) *De Profundis*, London: Methuen
Yeats, W. B. (1970) 'Oscar Wilde's Last Book', in *Uncollected Prose of W. B. Yeats: First Reviews and Articles, 1886–1896*, 1, ed. John Frayne, London: Macmillan, p. 204.
Yeats, W. B. (n.d.) '1903 American Lecture', National Library of Ireland TS, W. B. Yeats Collection, microfiche 30, 627.

Chapter 3. The Artist as Aesthete: The French Creation of Wilde

Primary sources

Adam, Paul (1895) 'L'assaut malicieux', *La Revue blanche* [Paris], May; repr. in Brunet 1994, 29–36.
Bahr, Hermann (1968) 'Décadence', in Wunberg, Gotthart (ed.) *Zur Überwindung des Naturalismus*, Stuttgart: Kohlhammer, pp. 167–72 ; orig. pub. 1894.
Bauër, Henry (1895a) 'Les Grands Guignols', *L'Echo de Paris*, 6 April, 1.
Bauër, Henry (1895b) 'Oscar Wilde en prison', *L'Echo de Paris*, 15 June; repr. in Brunet 1994, 41–44.
Bauër, Henry (1895c) 'Pour Oscar Wilde', *L'Echo de Paris*, 3 December; repr. in Brunet 1994, 73–75.
Bec, George (1895) 'Pastel Cruel', *L'Echo de Paris*, 11 April, 1.
Brunet, Catherine (ed.) (1994) *Pour Oscar Wilde: Des écrivains français au secours du condamné*, Rouen: Librairie Elisabeth Brunet / Association des Amis d'Hugues Rebell.
Brunetière, Ferdinand (1892) 'La Critique impressionniste', in *Essais sur la littérature contemporaine*, Paris: Calmann-Lévy, pp. 1–30; 1st pub. 1891.
Coppée, François (1895) 'Une pétition', *Le Journal* [Paris], 30 November, 1.
'Courrier de Londres' (1892) *Le Temps* [Paris], 25 February, 1–2.
Daurelle, Jacques (1891) 'Un poète anglais à Paris: Oscar Wilde', *L'Echo de Paris*, 6 December, 2 ; incl. short interview with Wilde.
de la Bretonne, Raitif [pseud. Jean Lorrain] (1895) 'Pall-Mall Semaine', *L'Echo de Paris*, 27 April, 2.
de la Bretonne, Raitif [pseud. Jean Lorrain] (1900) 'Convoi de victimes', *Le Journal*, 6 December, 1.
Deschamps, Léon and Paul Merrill (1895) 'Tribune libre: L'affaire Oscar Wilde', *La Plume* [Paris], 1 December, 559–60; launch of petition to Queen Victoria, repr. in Brunet 1994, 64–67.
Douglas, Lord Alfred (1896) 'Une introduction à mes poèmes, avec quelques considérations sur l'affaire Oscar Wilde', *La Revue blanche* [Paris], May, 484–90.
'Echos: Esthètes' (1895) *Le Figaro*, 7 April, 1.
F. O. (1895) 'Deux comédies de M. Oscar Wilde', *Le Petit Temps* [Paris], 20 February, 1.
France, Anatole (1888) 'Préface', in *La Vie littéraire*, 2 vols, Paris: Calmann-Lévy, 1st series, 1: iii–iv.
France, Anatole (1893) 'Courrier de Paris', *L'Univers illustré* [Paris], 10 June, 318–19.
Goldemar, Ange (1895) 'Oscar Wilde à la prison de Pentonville', *Le Gaulois* [Paris], 13 June, 1.
Goncourt, Edmond de (1956) *Journal: Mémoires de la vie littéraire*, 22 vols, ed. Robert Ricatte, Paris: Fasquelle and Flammarion.
Goncourt, Edmond (1891) 'Journal de 1883', *L'Echo de Paris*, 15 December, 2.
Huret, Jules (1895) 'Petite Chronique des Lettres', *Le Figaro*, Supplément Littéraire, 13 April, 58–59.

La Jeunesse, Ernest (1900) 'Oscar Wilde', *La Revue blanche* [Paris], 15 December, 589–96.

Le Roux, Hugues (1891) 'Oscar Wilde', *Le Figaro*, 3 December, 3.

Lormel, Louis (1895) 'À M. Oscar Wilde', *La Plume* [Paris], 15 April, 164–65.

Mallarmé, Stéphane (1973), 'Correspondance', vol. 4, eds Henri Mondor and Lloyd Austin, Paris: Gallimard.

Merrill, Stuart (1893) 'Oscar Wilde', *La Plume* [Paris], 15 March, 116–18.

Merrill, Stuart (1895) 'Tribune libre' (letter to M. Léon Deschamps), *La Plume* [Paris], 15 November, 507–08; repr. in Brunet 1994, 62–63.

Merrill, Stuart (1896) 'Pour Oscar Wilde: Epilogue', *La Plume* [Paris], 1 January, 8–10; repr. in Brunet 1994, 68–72.

Merrill, Stuart (1900) 'Oscar Wilde', *La Plume* [Paris], 15 December, 738–39.

Mirbeau, Octave (1895) 'A propos du "Hard Labour"', *Le Journal* [Paris], 16 June; repr. in Brunet 1994, 45–49.

Mirbeau, Octave (1983) *Le Journal d'une femme de chambre*, Paris: Folio; 1st pub. 1900.

Muhlfeld, Lucien (1900) 'Courrier de Paris', *Le Journal* [Paris], 21 December, 1.

Rachilde [Marguerite Eymery] (1896) 'Questions brûlantes', *La Revue blanche* [Paris], September, 193–200.

Rebell, Hugues (1895) 'Défense d'Oscar Wilde', *Le Mercure de France*, August ; repr. in Brunet 1994, 13–23.

Régnier, Henri de (1895) 'Souvenirs sur Oscar Wilde', *La Revue blanche* [Paris], 15 December; repr. in Brunet 1994, 82–86.

Roché, Paul (1895) 'Oscar Wilde jugé par le Dr Max Nordau', *Le Gaulois* [Paris], 10 April; repr. in Brunet 1994, 24–28.

Sougenet, Léon (1899) 'Ballade de la geôle de Reading' (review), *La Plume* [Paris], 1 February, 86.

Tailhade, Laurent (1895a) 'Un martyr', *L'Echo de Paris*, 29 May; repr. in Brunet 1994, 37–40.

Tailhade, Laurent (1895b) 'Echec aux Pharisiens', *L'Echo de Paris*, 4 December; repr. in Brunet 1994, 76–81.

Villars, P. (1895a) 'Tribunaux Etrangers; M. Oscar Wilde et le marquis de Queensbery' [*sic*], *Le Figaro*, 5 April, 3.

Villars, P. (1895b) 'Tribunaux Etrangers; Le scandale de Londres: M. Oscar Wilde accuse Queensbery [*sic*]; Un coup de théâtre', *Le Figaro*, 6 April, 2–3.

Wilde, Oscar (1889) 'L'Anniversaire de la petite infante', [trans. Stuart Merrill], *Paris illustré*, 30 March, 203–09.

Wilde, Oscar (1891a) 'A propos du Journal des Goncourt: Lettre de M. Oscar Wilde', *L'Echo de Paris*, 19 December, 2.

Wilde, Oscar (1891b) 'Le Géant Egoiste', trans. Marcel Schwob, *L'Echo de Paris*, 27 December, 2–4.

Wilde, Oscar (1979) *Selected Letters of Oscar Wilde*, ed. Rupert Hart-Davis, Oxford: Oxford University Press.

Wyzewa, Téodor de (1892) 'M. Oscar Wilde et les jeunes littérateurs anglais', *La Revue bleue* [Paris], April, 423–29.

Secondary sources

Acquien, Pascal (2006) *Oscar Wilde: Les mots et les songes*, Paris: Aden.

Camus, Albert (1952) 'L'artiste en prison', preface to Oscar Wilde, *La Ballade de la geôle de Reading*, trans. Jacques Bour, Paris: Falaize.

Clive, H. P. (1969) 'Pierre Louÿs and Oscar Wilde: A Chronicle of Their Friendship', *Revue de Littérature Comparée*, 43.3: 353–84.

Clive, H. P. (1970) 'Oscar Wilde's First Meeting with Mallarmé', *French Studies*, 24, 145–49.

Ellmann, Richard (1987) *Oscar Wilde*, London: Hamish Hamilton.

Erber, Nancy (1996) 'The French Trials of Oscar Wilde', *Journal of the History of Sexuality*, 6.4: 549–88.

Hartley, Kelver (1935) *Oscar Wilde: L'influence française dans son œuvre*, Paris: Sirey.

Jullian, Philippe (1971) *Oscar Wilde*, trans. Violet Wyndham, London: Paladin.

Langlade, Jacques de (1975) *Oscar Wilde: Ecrivain français*, Paris: Stock.

Langlade, Jacques de (1994) *La Mésentente Cordiale: Wilde – Dreyfus*, Paris: Julliard.

Lemonnier, Léon (1931) *Vie d'Oscar Wilde*, Paris: Éditions de la Nouvelle revue critique.

Merle, Robert (1957) *Oscar Wilde*, Classiques du XIXe siècle, Paris: Editions universitaires.

Robinson, Christopher (1995) *Scandal in the Ink: Male and Female Homosexuality in Twentieth-Century French Literature*, London: Cassell.

Sartre, Jean-Paul (1951) *Saint Genet*, Paris: Gallimard.

Wright, Thomas (2008) *Oscar's Books*, London: Chatto & Windus.

Yourcenar, Marguerite (1929) 'Abraham France traducteur de Virgile: Oscar Wilde', *La revue bleue*, October, 621–27; rev. version pub. as 'Wilde rue des Beaux-Arts', in Yourcenar (1989) *En pèlerin et en étranger*, Paris: Gallimard, pp. 121–35.

Chapter 4. Naturalizing Oscar Wilde as an *homme de lettres*: The French Reception of *Dorian Gray* and *Salomé* (1895–1922)

Early translations into French, productions and works published in France

(1889) 'L'anniversaire de la naissance de la petite princesse', trans. [Stuart Merrill], *Paris illustré*, 30 March, 203–09.

(1891) 'Le Géant égoïste' (SG), trans. Marcel Schwob, *L'Echo de Paris*, 27 December, 2.

(1892) *L'Eventail de Lady Windermere* (*LWF*), trans. Gaston Bonnefont, extract from *La Revue britannique* [Paris], 93–159.

(1893) *Salomé,* Paris: Librairie d'Art Indépendant ; original French pub.

(1895) *Le Portrait de Dorian Gray*, trans. [Eugène Tardieu and Georges Maurevert], Bibliothèque cosmopolite, Paris: Albert Savine éditeur; 1st repr. 1904, Bibliothèque cosmopolite 12, Paris: P.-V. Stock; 2nd repr. 1920 with woodcut illus. Fernand Siméon, Paris: Mornay.

(1898) *Ballade de la geôle de Reading* (*BRG*), trans. Henry D. Davray, bilingual edn, Paris: Société du *Mercure de France*; entitled 'transcription française'; reviewed in *La Plume*, 1 February 1899.

(1899) *Poèmes en prose* (*PP*), trans. Henry D. Davray, *La Revue blanche*, 19 (May): 43–46.

(1900) 'Le Rossignol et la rose' (NR), extract trans. Stuart Merrill from *HPOT*, *La Plume*, 15 December, 738–45.

(1902) *La Maison des grenades* (HOP), trans. Georges Khnopff, Paris: éditions de la Plume, incl. 'Le jeune roi' (YK), 'L'anniversaire' (BI), 'Le Pêcheur et son âme' (FHS), 'L'enfant étoile' (SC); BI 2nd trans.

(1905) *Le Crime de Lord Arthur Savile* (*LASCOS*), trans. Albert Savine, Paris: éditions Stock.

(1905) *De profundis*, trans. Henry D. Davray, preceded by letters to Robert Ross written in prison, followed by *La Ballade de la geôle de Reading*, Paris: Mercure de France.

(1905) *Intentions*, trans. Jean-Joseph Renaud, Paris: P.-V. Stock; reviewed Davray 1905.

(1906) *Intentions*, trans. Hugues Rebell [Georges-Joseph Grassal], pref. Charles Grolleau, Paris: C. Carrington; dated 1906, but reviewed Davray 1905.

(1906) *L'âme de l'homme* (SMUS), trans. Paul Grosfils, Bruges: Anne Herbert.

(1906) *Poèmes en prose*, trans. Charles Grolleau, pref. Jacques Desroix, Paris: C. Carrington; PP 2nd trans.

(1906) *Le Portrait de Monsieur W. H.* (PMWH), trans. Albert Savine, Bibliothèque cosmopolite 20, Paris: P.-V. Stock; incl. trans. of *contes*: 'Le Fantôme de Canterville' (CG), 'Un sphinx qui n'a pas de secret' (SWS), 'Le modèle millionnaire' (MM); *Poèmes en prose* (PP), 3rd trans.: 'L'artiste', 'Le Faiseur de bien', 'Le Disciple', 'Le Maître', 'La Maison du jugement' (HJ), 'Le Maître de Sagesse'; *L'âme humaine sous le régime socialiste* (SMUS).

(1906) *Trois comédies: L'Eventail de Lady Windermere* (LWF); *Un mari idéal* (IH); *Une femme sans importance* (WNI), trans. Arnelle [pseud.], Paris: Dujarric; *LWF* 2nd trans.; *IH* 1st trans.; *WNI* 1st trans.

(1907) *Poèmes*, trans. and pref. Albert Savine, Bibliothèque cosmopolite 21, Paris: P. V. Stock.

(1907) *Le Prêtre et l'acolyte* (PA) *et Etudes d'art et de littérature*, trad. Albert Savine, Bibliothèque cosmopolite 23, Paris: P. V. Stock.

(1908) *The Picture of Dorian Gray*, illus. Paul Thiriat and Eugène Dété, Paris: Carrington; issued 1910.

(1909–11) *Théâtre*, trans. Albert Savine, Bibliothèque cosmopolite 33, 41 and 48, 3 vols, Paris: P.-V. Stock; 1.33: Les drames: *Véra, La Duchesse de Padoue* (DOP), 1st trans.; 2.41: Comédies (1910): *Une femme sans importance* (WNI) 2nd trans.; *L'Eventail de Lady Windermere* (LWF) 3rd trans.; 3.48: Comédies (1911): *De l'importance d'être sérieux* (IMP), 1st trans.; *Un mari idéal* (IH), 2nd trans.

(1911) *Une maison de grenades*, trans. Albert Savine, Bibliothèque cosmopolite 49, Paris: Stock; *HOP* 2nd trans.; *BI* 3rd trans.

(1912) *Essais de littérature et d'esthétique 1877–1885: L'œuvre de Wilde appréciée par lui-même*, trans. Albert Savine, Bibliothèque cosmopolite 60, Paris: P.-V. Stock; incl.: Lettre à Joaquin Miller; A propos de Dorian Gray (30 pp. of letters defending the novel in the press); Notes sur Whistler; Une doléance anglo-indienne; Une maison de Grenades; Pantins et acteurs; L'Eventail de Lady Windermere; Salomé; Le Club des Treize; L'éthique du journalisme; L'œillet vert (letter to *Pall Mall Gazette*); *Essais et Critiques* (mostly extracts from the press): La tombe de Keats; La Galerie Grovesnor (1877); La Galerie Grovesnor (1879); L'Envoi; Hester Grazebrook; Le costume de la femme; D'autres idées radicales sur la réforme du costume; Le Ten o'clock de M. Whistler; Le rapport entre la toilette et l'art; Diners et plats; Un poème épique moderne; Shakespeare et la mise en scène; Une volée de poètes; Le Parnasse contre la Philologie; Hamlet au Lyceum; Deux romans nouveaux; Henri IV à Oxford; Poésie grecque moderne; Olivia au Lyceum; Comme il vous plaira à Coombe-House; Un manuel du mariage.

(1912) *Un mari idéal*, trans. Georges Bazile, Paris: *Comœdia*, 8 July; in section 'Feuilleton de *Comœdia*'; *IH* 3rd trans.

(1913) *L'Éventail de Lady Windermere*, trans. Georges Bazile, Paris: *Comœdia*, 20 October; *LWF* 4th trans.

(1913) *Une femme sans importance*, trans. Georges Bazile, Paris: *Comœdia*; *WNI* 3rd trans.

(1913) *Derniers essais de littérature et d'esthétique 1887–1890*, trans. Albert Savine, Bibliothèque cosmopolite 68, Paris: P.-V. Stock.

(1914) *Opinions de littérature et d'art*, trans. Jeanne Cantel, Paris: l'édition moderne.

(1918) *Une tragédie florentine (FT)*, trans. Cecil Georges-Bazile, preceded by G. Bernard Shaw 'Mes souvenirs d'Oscar Wilde', pref. Robert Ross, wash drawing Aubrey Beardsley (Salomé: 'A Woman in the Moon'), in *Les Cahiers britanniques et américains*, 10–11, trans. and ed. Cecil Georges-Bazile, Paris: C. G.-Bazile.

(1919) *La maison de la courtisane* and prose fragments (letters to *The Daily Chronicle* on living conditions in prison), trans. Albert Savine, Bibliothèque cosmopolite 72, Paris: éditions Stock.

(1920) *Le portrait de Dorian Gray*, trans. Eugène Tardieu [and Georges Maurevert], illus. Fernand Siméon, Paris: Mornay.

(1924) *Le Portrait de Dorian Gray*, Edmond Jaloux and Félix Frapereau. Paris: Stock; DG 2nd trans.

(1925) *Théâtre à lire*, trans. Cecil Georges-Bazile, illus. André Utter, Paris: Delpeuch; incl. *La Duchesse de Padoue (DOP)*, 'Une tragédie florentine' (FT), 'La Sainte courtisane', *Le Cardinal d'Avignon*; repr. Georges-Bazile's 1918 trans. of 'Une tragédie florentine'.

(1942) *Il importe d'être constant (IBE)*, trans. Guillot de Saix, production at Théâtre de l'Humour, Paris, dir. Paul Raynal; text pub. *Paris-théâtre* (1954), vol. 90.

(1954) *Il est important d'être aimé (IBE)*, trans. Jean Anouilh and Claude Vincent, production at Théâtre de la Comédie des Champs-Elysées; text pub. *Avant-Scène* (1955), vol. 101.

Secondary sources

Adelswärd-Fersen, Jacques (1909) 'Sur la glorification du vierge dans la religion d'Oscar Wilde', *Akademos* [Paris], 10 (15 October): 547–50.

Bauër, Henry (1892) 'La Ville et le Théâtre', *L'Echo de Paris*, 2 July, 1.

Bauër, Henry (1896a) 'Premières représentations', *L'Echo de Paris*, 13 February, 3.

Bauër, Henry (1896b) *L'Echo de Paris*, 8 June, 1.

Bernard, Tristan (1896) *Le Grand Journal* [Paris], 12 February, 2.

Bernard-Derosne, Léon (1896) 'Premières représentations', *Gil Blas* [Paris], 13 February, 3.

Berr, Emile (1908) 'Une « Salomé » française', *Le Figaro* [Paris], 25 February, 3.

Blum, Léon (1909) review of *Lady Windermere's Fan*, *Comœdia* [Paris], 8 May, 2.

Bonnefont, Gaston (1892) 'L'Eventail de Lady Winderemere', *La Revue britannique* [Paris], March–April, 93–159.

Boyer, Georges (1896) 'Critique dramatique', *L'Evénement* [Paris], 12 February, 3.

Céard, Henry (1896) 'Les Théâtres', *Le Matin* [Paris], 12 February, 3.

'The Censure and "Salomé": An Interview with Mr. Oscar Wilde' (1892) *Pall Mall Gazette* [London], 29 June, 1–2.

Christensen, Peter G. (1986) 'Three Concealments: Jean Cocteau's Adaptation of *The Picture of Dorian Gray*', *Romance Notes*, 27.1 (Autumn): 27–35.

Cocteau, Jean (1950) 'Eloges des Pléiades', *Œuvres complètes*, vol. 10, Geneva: Marguerat, pp. 237–41.

Cocteau, Jean (1978) *Le portrait surnaturel de Dorian Gray*, Paris: Oliver Orban.

Davray, Henry-D. (1905) review article of the translations of *Intentions*, *Mercure de France*, 57 (15 September): 305–07.

Davray, Henry-D. (1910) review article of Laurent, *Mercure de France*, 88 (1 November): 172–73.

Du Tillet, Jacques de (1896) review of *Salomé*, *La Revue bleue* 7 [Paris], 4th series, 5 (15 February): 219.

Eells, Emily (2004) '*Influence occulte*: The Reception of Pater's Works in France before 1922', in Bann, Stephen (ed.) *The Reception of Walter Pater in Europe*, The Athlone Critical Traditions Series: The Reception of British and Irish Authors in Europe, series ed. Elinor Shaffer, London: Continuum, pp. 111–13.

Eells, Emily (2010) *Two Tombeaux to Oscar Wilde: Jean Cocteau's* Le Portrait surnaturel de Dorian Gray *and Raymond Laurent's Essay on Wildean Aesthetics*, High Wycombe, Bucks: Rivendale Press.

Ellmann, Richard (1987) *Oscar Wilde*, London: Hamish Hamilton.

[H. F.-C.] (1896) 'Courrier des théâtres' (review of *Salomé*), *Journal des débats politiques et littéraires* [Paris], 13 February, 3.

Gachons, Jacques de (1896) review of *Salomé*, *L'Ermitage* [Paris], March, 203.

Geffroy, Gustave (1896) 'Critique dramatique' (review of *Salomé*), *Paris*, 13 February, 2–3.

'Grosclaude' (1895) 'Chronique Fantaisiste: Les pattes de Mouche' (review of *Dorian Gray*), *Le Journal* [Paris], 6 April, 1.

Guillot de Saix, Léon (1950) trans. 'Il importe d'être constant', *Les Œuvres libres* [Paris], 1 September, 233–314.

Le Journal (1895) unsigned report on the trials, 6 April, 1.

Le Journal (1896) unsigned review of *Salomé*, 12 February, 2.

Lalo, Pierre (1908) review of Mariotte's *Salomé*, *Le Temps* [Paris], 25 November, 3.

Langlade, Jacques de (1975) *Oscar Wilde: écrivain français*, Paris: Stock.

Laurent, Raymond (1910) *Etudes anglaises*, Paris: Bernard Grasset.

Le Senne, Camille (1896) 'Premières représentations', *Le Siècle* [Paris], 12 February, 3.

Lorrain, Jean (1895) 'Pall-Mall Semaine', *L'Echo de Paris*, 28 June, 1.

Lorrain, Jean (1896a) 'Salomé et ses poètes', *Le Journal*, 11 February, 1–2.

Lorrain, Jean (1896b) 'Pall-Mall Semaine', *Le Journal*, 1 November, 1.

Lounsbery, Grace Constant (1913) *The Picture of Dorian Gray*, London: Simpkin Marshall.

Magnan, Jean-Marie (1979) 'Jean Cocteau et le double peint de Dorian Gray', *Cahiers Jean Cocteau*, Paris: Gallimard, 8: 185–92.

Marrot, Paul (1896) 'Les Premières' (review of *Salomé*), *La Lanterne* [Paris], 13 February, 2.

Mason, Stuart (1908) *Art and Morality: A Defence of 'The Picture of Dorian Gray'*, London: J. Jacobs.

Matzneff, Gabriel (1973) review of *Salomé* at the Théatre du Globe, Paris, Spring 1973, *Les Nouvelles littéraires* [Paris], 1 May, 24.

Mauclair, Camille (1895) review of *Dorian Gray*, *Mercure de France*, August, 237–38.

Mendès, Catulle (1896) 'Premières représentations' (review of *Salomé*), *Le Journal*, 12 February, 2.

Mercey [also Mercet], Suzanne (1922) *Dorian Gray: drame en un prologue et cinq actes*, Paris: Figuière.

Mikolyzk, Thomas A. (1993) *Oscar Wilde: An Annotated Bibliography*, Westport, CT: Greenwood Press.

Mille, Pierre (1912) 'Salomé', *Petit Marseillais* [Marseilles], 22 June, 1.

Mirbeau, Octave (1895a) 'A propos du Hard Labour', *Le Journal*, 16 June, 1.

Mirbeau, Octave (1895b) 'Sur un livre' (review of *Dorian Gray*), *Le Journal*, 7 July, 1.

'M.P.' (1973) review of *Salomé* at the Théâtre du Globe, Paris, Spring 1973, *Combat* [Paris], 26 March, 12.

'Le Pompier de service' (1896) 'La Soirée parisienne' (review of *Salomé*), *La Paix* [Paris], 12 February, 3.

'L.V.' (1912) review of musical adaptation of *Salomé* at the *Théâtre du Châtelet*, Paris, *Comœdia*, 14 June, 3–4.

Proust, Marcel (1971) *Contre Sainte-Beuve*, eds Pierre Clarac and Yves Sandre, Edition Pléiade, Paris: Gallimard.

Proust, Marcel (1988a) *A la recherche du temps perdu: Le Côté de Guermantes II*, ed. Jean-Yves Tadié, Edition Pléiade, vol. 2, Paris: Gallimard.

Proust, Marcel (1988b) *A la recherche du temps perdu: Sodome et Gomorrhe I*, ed. Jean-Yves Tadié, Edition Pléiade, vol. 3, Paris: Gallimard.

Proust, Marcel (1988c) *A la recherche du temps perdu: Sodome et Gomorrhe II*, ed. Jean-Yves Tadié, Edition Pléiade, vol. 3, Paris: Gallimard.

Proust, Marcel (1988d) *Against Sainte-Beuve and Other Essays*, trans. John Sturrock, London: Penguin Classics.

Proust, Marcel (1992) *In Search of Lost Time*, trans. C. K. Scott Moncrieff and Terence Kilmartin, rev. D. J. Enright, 4 vols, London: Chatto & Windus.

Raffalovich, Marc André (1896) *Uranisme et unisexualité: Etude sur différentes manifestations de l'instinct sexuel*, Lyons: Stork.

Ransome, Arthur (1912) *Oscar Wilde: A Critical Study*, London: Martin Secker.

Rebell, Hugues (1895) 'Défense d'Oscar Wilde', *Mercure de France*, August, 182–90.

Retté, Adolphe (1895) 'Chroniques des livres' (review of *Dorian Gray*), *La Plume* [Paris], 15 October, 474.

Review of musical adaptation of *Salomé* at the *Théâtre du Châtelet*, Paris (1912) *Comœdia*, 15 June, 3.

Review of *Salomé* at the Théatre du Globe, Paris, Spring (1973) *Le Monde*, 24 March, 29.

Saint-Paul, Georges (1896) *Perversion et perversité sexuelle: Tares et poisons*, Paris: G. Carré.

Sarcey, Francisque (1896) review of *Salomé*, *Le Temps*, 17 February, 2.

Segard, Achille (1896) review of *Salomé*, 'Théâtres', *La Plume*, 1 March, 164.

Tailhade, Laurent (1895) review of *Dorian Gray*, *L'Echo de Paris*, 29 May, 1.

Tinan, Jean de (1896) review of *Salomé*, *Mercure de France*, March, 415–17.

'Les Treize' (1896) review of *Salomé*, *Le Grand Journal*, 13 February, 1.

'Tribunaux' (1895) anon. report on the trials, *Le Temps*, 6 April, 3.

'Two Vavass Sisters' (1895) 'Métamorphoses d'Oscar Wilde', *La Lanterne, Supplément illustré*, 16 June, 1–2.

Vanor, George (1896) 'Les Premières' (review of *Salomé*), *La Paix*, 12 February, 3.

Wilde, Oscar (1894) *Salome, A Tragedy in One Act: Translated from the French of Oscar Wilde; Pictured by Aubrey Beardsley*, London: Elkin Matthews and John Lane.

'Willy' [Henry Gauthier-Villars] (1895) 'Old England', *L'Echo de Paris*, 17 April, 1.

Chapter 5. André Gide's 'Hommage à Oscar Wilde' or 'The Tale of Judas'

Apter, Emily (1987) *André Gide and the Codes of Homotextuality*, Saratoga, CA: ANMA Libri.

Bloom, Harold (1973) *The Anxiety of Influence*, New York: Oxford University Press.

Brown Downey, Katherine (2004) *Perverse Midrash: Oscar Wilde, André Gide, and Censorship of Biblical Drama*, London; New York: Continuum.

Delaveau, Philippe (1985) 'André Gide et Oscar Wilde', in Pollard, Patrick (ed.) *André Gide et l'Angleterre*, London: Birkbeck, pp. 60–66.

Delay, Jean (1957) *La Jeunesse d'André Gide*, vol. 2: *D'André Walter à André Gide, 1890–1895*, Paris: Gallimard.

Dollimore, Jonathan (1991) *Sexual Dissidence: Augustine to Wilde; Freud to Foucault*, Oxford: Oxford University Press.

Durosay, Daniel (1993) 'Ménalque à Marseille', *Bulletin des amis d'André Gide*, 21.98: 361.

Durosay, Daniel (2000) 'Gide et Wilde, Paradoxe de l'In memoriam: éloge et procès du reprouvé', *Bulletin des amis d'André Gide*, 28.125: 155–68.

Gide, André (1902) 'Hommage à Oscar Wilde', *L'Ermitage* [Paris], June, 401–29.

Gide, André (1903a) 'Oskar [*sic*] Wilde', trans. Berta Franz, *Rheinisch Westfälische Zeitung* [Essen], 8, 12 & 15 July.

Gide, André (1903b) 'Oscar Wilde', in *Prétextes*, Paris: Mercure de France, pp. 265–305.

Gide, André (1904) *In memoriam Oscar Wilde*, ed. and trans. Franz Blei, Leipzig: Insel-Verlag.

Gide, André (1905a) 'Le "De Profundis" d'Oscar Wilde', *L'Ermitage* [Paris], August, 65–73.

Gide, André (1905b) *Oscar Wilde: A Study*, ed. and trans. Stuart Mason, Oxford: Holywell Press.

Gide, André (1910a) *Oscar Wilde*, Paris: Mercure de France.

Gide, André (1910b) 'Oscar Wilde', *Le Figaro, Supplément littéraire*, 7 May, 1; extracts from Gide 1902 without Wilde's biblical tales.

Gide, André (1918) *Oscar Wilde: In memoriam*, trans. Otokar Levý, Prague: Alois Srdce.

Gide, André (1921) 'Oscar Wilde', in *Morceaux choisis*, Paris: Nouvelle Revue Française, pp. 405–19.

Gide, André (1924) *Corydon*, Paris: Nouvelle Revue française.

Gide, André (1929) *Vzpomínky na osobní styky s Oscarem Wildem: Úryvek z paměti: Jestliže zrno nezakrní* (Personal Reminiscences of Oscar Wilde: Fragments of a Memoir: If It Die), trans. Z. Šmíd, in *Rozpravy Aventina* [Prague], 5.13/14 (December): 150–52.

Gide, André (1933) *Œuvres complètes*, 15 vols, ed. Louis Martin-Chauffier, Paris: Nouvelle Revue Française.

Gide, André (1951) *Oscar Wilde*, trans. Bernard Frechtman, London: William Kimber; incl. passages referring to Oscar Wilde from *If It Die* and *The Journals*.

Gide, André (1955) *André Gide–Paul Valéry Correspondance, 1890–1942*, ed. Robert Mallet, Paris: Gallimard.

Gide, André (1958) *Romans: Récits et soties: Œuvres lyriques*, eds Yvonne Davet and Jean-Jacques Thierry, Paris: Gallimard.

Gide, André (1968) *André Gide–Roger Martin du Gard Correspondance, 1913–1951*, ed. Jean Delay, 2 vols, Paris: Gallimard.

Gide, André (1970) 'Soixantenaire de l'*Oscar Wilde* d'André Gide' (unpub. letter by Gide to 'Bertha Franzos' [Franz Blei]), *Bulletin des amis d'André Gide*, 1.6: 3–4.

Gide, André (1988) *Correspondance avec sa mère 1880–1895*, eds Claude Martin and Henri Thomas, Paris: Gallimard.

Gide, André (1996) *Journal 1887–1925*, ed. Eric Marty, Paris: Gallimard.

Gide, André (1997a) *André Gide–Henri de Régnier, Correspondance, 1891–1911*, eds David J. Niederauer and Heather Franklyn, Lyon: Presses universitaires de Lyon.

Gide, André (1997b) *Journal 1926–1950*, ed. Martine Sagaert, Paris: Gallimard.

Gide, André (1999) *Essais critiques*, ed. Pierre Masson, Paris: Gallimard.

Gide, André (2001) *Souvenirs et voyages*, ed. Pierre Masson, incl. contribs by Daniel Durosay and Martine Sagaert, Paris: Gallimard.

Guillot de Saix, Léon ([n.d.]) *Collection Guillot de Saix (1885–1964)*, Bibliothèque nationale française, Département des Arts du spectacle, 4°-COL–31/224 and 4°-COL–31/301.

Hutchinson, Hilary (1992) 'André Gide et Oscar Wilde, une nouvelle perspective', Bulletin des amis d'André Gide, 20.94: 135–42.

Kohlmayer, Rainer (1996) *Oscar Wilde in Deutschland und Österreich: Untersuchungen zur Rezeption der Komödien und zur Theorie der Bühnenübersetzung*, Tübingen: Niemeyer.

Langlade, Jacques de (1975) 'André Gide et la philosophie païenne', in *Oscar Wilde: écrivain français*, Paris: Stock/Monde ouvert, pp. 141–96.

Laurent, Raymond (1910) *Etudes anglaises*, Paris: Bernard Grasset.

Masson, Pierre (1978) '*Monsieur de Phocas*, ou Quand Gide et Wilde se rencontrent chez Jean Lorrain', *Bulletin des amis d'André Gide*, 7.42: 51–57.

Masson, Pierre (1988) 'Pour une relecture de l'*Oscar Wilde* d'André Gide', *Littératures*, 19: 115–19.

Masson, Pierre (2002) 'Wilde dans *Les Caves*', in Cabioc'h, Serge and Pierre Masson (eds) *Gide aux miroirs: le roman du xxème siècle*, Caen: Presses universitaires de Caen, pp. 69–76.

Maurois, André (1927) *Etudes anglaises: Dickens, Walpole, Ruskin, Wilde, la jeune littérature*, Paris: Bernard Grasset.

Mouret, François J.-L. (1975) 'Quatorze Lettres et billets inédits de Lord Alfred Douglas à André Gide, 1895–1929', *Revue de Littérature comparée*, 49.3: 483–502.

Pagels, Elaine and Karen L. King (2007) *Reading Judas: The Gospel of Judas and the Shaping of Christianity*, London: Allen Lane.

Pollard, Patrick (2004) *Littérature et culture de langue anglaise*, in *Répertoire des lectures d'André Gide*, vol. 2, London: Birkbeck College.

Pollard, Percival (ed. and trans.) (1905) *In Memoriam Oscar Wilde*, Greenwich, CT: The Literary Collector Press.

Rank, Otto (1971) *The Double*, trans. Harry Tucker Jr., New York: Meridian.

Reid, Victoria (2009) *André Gide and Curiosity*, Amsterdam: Rodopi.

Renard Jules (1960) *Journal 1887–1910*, eds Léon Guichard and Gilbert Sigaux, Paris: Gallimard.

Segal, Naomi (1998) *André Gide: Pedagogy and Pederasty*, Oxford: Oxford University Press.

Sherard, Robert Harborough and G. J. Renier (1933) *André Gide's Wicked Lies about the Late Mr. Oscar Wilde in Algiers in January, 1895*, Calvi: Vindex.

Wilde, Oscar (1942) *Le Chant du cygne: contes parlés d'Oscar Wilde*, ed. Léon Guillot de Saix, Paris: Mercure de France.

Wilde, Oscar (1969) *A Collection of Critical Essays*, ed. Richard Ellmann, New Jersey: Prentice-Hall.

Wilde, Oscar (1996) *As De Profundis: Cu cateva amintiri despre Oscar Wilde ale lui André Gide* (*De Profundis* presented with some recollections of Oscar Wilde by André Gide), trans. Irina Izverna, Bucharest: Allfa.

Wilde, Oscar (2000) *The Complete Letters of Oscar Wilde*, eds Merlin Holland and Rupert Hart-Davis, New York: Henry Holt.

Wilde, Oscar (2005a) *De Profundis; 'Epistola: In Carcere et Vinculis'*, ed. Ian Small, in *The Complete Works of Oscar Wilde*, vol. 2, Oxford: Oxford University Press.

Wilde, Oscar (2005b) *The Picture of Dorian Gray*, 1890, ed. Joseph Bristow, in *The Complete Works of Oscar Wilde*, vol. 3, Oxford: Oxford University Press.

Chapter 6. 'Astonishing in my Italian': Oscar Wilde's First Italian Editions, 1890–1952

Translations

(1901) *Salomé*, trans. Giuseppe Garibaldi Rocco, *Rassegna Italiana*, 9.1.

(1904) *Il principe felice* (HP), trans. Francesco Bianco, *Il Marzocco* [Florence], 28 August, 2–3.

(1905) *De Profundis: seguito da alcune lettere inedite di O. Wilde*, trans. Olga Bicchierai, Venice: S. Rosen.

(1905) *Doriano Gray Dipinto* (*PDG*), trans. Biagio Chiara, Naples: Bideri.

(1905) *Il ritratto di Doriano Gray* (*PDG*), Milan; Palermo: Remo Sandron Editore.

(1906) *Doriano Gray dipinto* (*PDG*), trans. Biagio Chiara, Palermo: privately pub. by the trans.

(1906) *Intenzioni*, trans. and intro. Raffaello Piccoli, Turin: Bocca.

(1906) 'The House of Judgement', trans. Biagio Chiara, *Tavola Rotonda* [Naples], 16.22 (20 May): 2.

(1906) *Il ventaglio di Lady Windermere* (*LWF*), trans. Carlo Castelli and Ferruccio Bernardini, Rome: E. Voghera.

(1907) *La ballata della prigione di Reading* (*BRG*), trans. Giuseppe Vannicola, pref. André Gide, Rome: Lux.

(1907) *La casa dei melograni* (*HOP*), trans. Biagio Chiara, Naples: Bideri.

(1907) *Sàlome: poema drammatico*, trans. Giuseppe Garibaldi Rocco, Naples: Bideri.

(1907) *Una donna qualunque* (*WNI*), trans. Carlo Castelli and Ferruccio Bernardini, Rome: E. Voghera.

(1907) *Un marito ideale* (*IH*), trans. Giovanni. Battista. Palmieri, Bologna: Brugnoli.

(1908) *Il dovere del delitto* (PPP), trans. Federigo Verdinois, Naples: Società Editrice Partenopea.

(1908) *Salomé*, trans. Giuseppe Vannicola, Rome: Lux.

(1912) *L'anima dell'uomo e Sebastiano Melmoth* (SMUS), ed. Antonio Agresti, Lanciano: Carabba.

(1912, 1919) *Il principe felice* (HP), trans. 'Misa', Palermo: Sandron.

(1913, 1947) *L'anima umana in regime socialista* (SMUS), ed. Luigi Fabbri, Bologna: 'La Controcorrente'.

(1913) *Il prete e l'accolito* (PA), trans. Biagio Chiara, Naples: Bideri

(1914) *'De Profundis' seguito dalla 'Ballata del Carcere di Reading'* (*DP* & *BRG*), trans. Giovanni Frasca De Naro, Milan: Sonzogno.

(1914) *Il delitto di Lord Savile* (LASC), trans. Giuseppe Vannicola, Genoa: A. F. Formiggini.

(1914) *Il fantasma di Canterville* (CG), trans. Giuseppe Vannicola, Naples: Bideri.

(1914) *Poemi in Prosa* (PP), trans. Franz W. von Tigerström, pref. Marco Slonim, Florence: Quattrini.

(1914) *Una tragedia fiorentina* (*FT*), comp. Carlo Ravasenga, libretto Ettore Moschino, Turin: Tipografia Subalpina.

(1916) *L'amore e le donne: aforismi, idee, paradossi*, ed. Francesco Stocchetti, Genoa: Libreria Editrice Moderna.

(1919) *De Profundis, La ballata del carcere di Reading* (*BRG*), *Lettere dalla prigione*, trans. Adelina Manzotti–Brignone, Milan: Facchi.

(1919) *Una tragedia fiorentina e la santa cortigiana* (FT & SCo), ed. Ettore Moschino, Naples: Editrice Italiana.

(1922) *L'importanza di far sul serio* (*IBE*), trans. Irene Nori Giambastiani, pref. Carlo Pellegrini, Ferrara: Taddei.

(1928) *La Duchessa di Padova* (*DOP*), trans. Luigi Motta, Milan: Pervinca.

(1931) *HPOT*, ed. Luigi Pratesi, Livorno: Giusti; reissued 1934, 1938, 1946.

(1945) *L'anima dell'uomo sotto il socialismo* (SMUS), ed. Antonino Repaci, Turin: Libreria Editrice Eclettica.

(1945) *L'anima umana in regime socialista* (SMUS), trans. Maria Rodano, pref. Alberto Cento, Spoleto: Panetto e Petrelli.

(1945) *L'anima dell'uomo sotto il socialismo* (SMUS), trans. Enrico Vaquer, Florence: La Voce.

(1945) *Individualismo e Socialismo* (SMUS), trans. Guglielmo Zatti, Brescia: Studio Editoriale Vivi.

(1946) *L'anima dell'uomo in regime socialista* (SMUS), trans. Ugo Bianchelli, Rome: Edizioni Europa.

(1948) *Tutto il teatro del maggior drammaturgo dell'età vittoriana*, pref. Carlo Franzero, intro. Lorenzo Gigli, I Capolavori: Collana delle opere teatrali di autori di risonanza mondiale, ed. Lucio Ridenti, Turin: Società Editrice Torinese.

(1949) *Il mistero del Signor W. H. e altre prose*, trans. Longino Valbia, Milan: Bolla; incl. PMWH, LASC, CG, SWS, MM

(1951–52) *Tutte le opere*, ed. Aldo Camerino, Rome: Casini.

(1979) *Opere*, ed. Masolino D'Amico, Milan: Mondadori.

(1994) *Tutte le opere*, ed. Masolino D'Amico, Rome: Newton-Compton.

(1997) *Il Quinto Vangelo*, ed. Rita Severi, Palermo: Novecento.

Secondary sources

Andreucci, Franco and Tommaso Detti (1976) *Il movimento operaio italiano: Dizionario Biografico*, 2: 1853–1943, Rome: Editori Riuniti.

Antonini, Sandro (2008) *Sem Benelli: Vita di un poeta: dai trionfi internazionali alla persecuzione fascista*, Genoa: De Ferrari.

Bianco, Francesco (1904) 'Il principe felice' (HP), *Il Marzocco* [Florence], 28 August, 2–3.

Biblioteca Estense di Modena, *Archivio Editoriale Formiggini*, file: Giuseppe Vannicola.

Chiara, Biagio (1906) pref. to trans. of *HOP*, *Tavola Rotonda* [Naples], 13 May, 1–2.

Chiara, Biagio (1903) *L'Umano Convito*, Palermo: F. Ganguzza-Lajosa.

D'Ambrosio, Matteo (1990) *Nuove Verità Crudeli: Origini e sviluppi del Futurismo a Napoli*, Naples: Alfredo Guida.

D'Amico, Masolino (1994) 'Oscar Wilde in Naples', in Sandulescu, C. George (ed.) *Rediscovering Oscar Wilde*, Princess Grace Irish Library 8, Gerrards Cross: Colin Smythe, pp. 76–81.

D'Amico, Masolino and Rita Severi (2001) *La vita come arte: Oscar Wilde, le arti e l'Italia*, pref. Merlin Holland, Palermo: Novecento.

Ellmann, Richard (1987) *Oscar Wilde*, London: Hamish Hamilton.

Falchi Picchinesi, Simona (1985) 'Le riviste di Giuseppe Vannicola', *Inventario*, new series, 14.2: 45–48.

Gallo, Claudio and Paola Tiloca (2007) *Luigi Motta scrittore d'avventure*, Zevio (Verona): Perosini editore.

Gerra, Ferdinando (1978) *Musica, letteratura e mistica nel drama di vita di Giuseppe Vannicola*, Rome: Bardi Editore.

Giammattei, Emma (2003) *Il romanzo di Napoli: geografia e storia letteraria nei secolo XIX e XX*, Naples: Guida.

Govoni, Corrado (1943) 'Sergio Corazzini', *Il Popolo d'Italia* [Milan], 25 March, [n.p.].

Holland, Merlin (2003) '*De Profundis*: The Afterlife of a Manuscript', in Keane, Robert N. (ed.) *Oscar Wilde: The Man, His Writings, and His World*, papers presented at Oscar Wilde Centennial Conference, Hofstra University (April 2000), New York: AMS Press; London: Eurospan, pp. 251–67.

Horodisch, Abraham (1954) *Oscar Wilde's BRG*, New York: Aldus Book Co.

Index Bibliographicus Notorum Hominum (1985), Osnabruck: Biblio Verlag.

Limentani, Uberto (1997) 'Leone and Arthur Serena and the Chair of Italian, 1919–1934', *Modern Language Review*, 92.4: 877–92.

Lipparini, Giuseppe (1905) '*De Profundis* di Oscar Wilde', *Il Marzocco* [Florence], 2 July, 2.

Livio, Gigi (1992) *La scrittura drammatica: Teoria e pratica esegetica*, Milan: Mursia.

Ojetti, Ugo (1898) review of *BRG*, *Il Marzocco* [Florence], 4 December, 1–2.

Rovito, Teodoro (1922) *Dizionario dei Letterati e Giornalisti Italiani Contemporanei*, Naples: Rovito.

Severi, Rita (1981) 'Oscar Wilde e il mito di Salomé', *Rivista di Letterature Moderne e Comparate*, 34.1: 59–74.

Severi, Rita (1985) 'Oscar Wilde, la femme fatale and the Salomé Myth', in Balakian, Anna (ed.) *Proceedings of the Tenth Congress of the International Comparative Literature Association*, vol. 2: *Comparative Poetics*, ed. Claudio Guillen, New York: Garland, pp. 53–64.

Severi, Rita (1998) *L'anima dell'uomo: Oscar Wilde in Italia*, Palermo: Novecento.

Sylvester, Paul [Miss Pauline Schletter] (1889) 'Matilde Serao', *The Woman's World*, 552–57.

Vitaletti, Guido (1908) *Salome nella leggenda e nell'arte*, Rome: Lux.

Wilde, Oscar (2000) *The Complete Letters of Oscar Wilde*, eds Merlin Holland and Rupert Hart-Davis, New York: Henry Holt.

Chapter 7. 'Children of Pleasure': Oscar Wilde and Italian Decadence

Alastor [Emilio Bodrero] (1903) 'Arte e Democrazia', *Leonardo*, 7 (29 March): 5–7.

Andreoli, Annamaria (2000) *Il vivere inimitabile: vita di Gabriele D'Annunzio*, Milan: Mondadori.

Audoli, Armando (2002) 'Le prime di Vannicola', *Wuz*, 5 (June): 22–31.

Barini, Giorgio (1908) 'La morale nelle opere di Oscar Wilde (con un ritratto)', *Nuova Antologia di lettere, scienze ed arti* [Rome], 218.66 (1 March): 66–75.

Benadusi, Lorenzo (2005) *Il nemico dell'uomo nuovo: l'omosessualità nell'esperimento totalitario fascista*, Milan: Feltrinelli.

Cecchi, Emilio (1976) 'Il mito di O. Wilde', in *Scrittori inglesi e americani: saggi, note e versioni*, Milan: Alberto Mondadori, 5th edn, 1: 181–86.

Ceccuti, Cosimo (ed.) (1979) *Carteggio D'Annunzio-Ojetti*, Florence: Le Monnier.

Conti, Angelo (1911) *Dopo il canto delle sirene*, Naples: Riccardo Ricciardi.

Conti, Angelo (2007) *Giorgione*, ed. Ricciarda Ricorda, Novi Ligure: Città del Silenzio.

Conti, Angelo (1931) *San Francesco*, Florence: Vallecchi.

Crucitti Ullrich, Francesca Bianca (ed.) (1985) *Carteggio Cecchi-Praz*, Milan: Adelphi.

D'Amico, Masolino (1973) *Oscar Wilde: il critico e le sue maschere*, Rome: Istituto dell'Enciclopedia Italiana.

D'Amico, Masolino (1977) *Vita di Oscar Wilde attraverso le lettere*, Turin: Einaudi.

D'Amico, Masolino and Rita Severi (eds) (2001) *La vita come arte: Oscar Wilde, le Arti e l'Italia*, Palermo: Novecento.

D'Annunzio, Gabriele (1887) 'Cronaca Bizantina: Un poeta d'autunno', *La Tribuna* [Rome], 8 October, 2.

D'Annunzio, Gabriele (1895) 'Proemio', *Convito*, 1 (1 January): 3–7.

D'Annunzio, Gabriele and Giuseppe Saverio Gargano (1896) 'Prologo', *Il Marzocco* [Florence], 2 February, 1.

D'Annunzio, Gabriele (1988) *Prose di romanzi*, ed. Annamaria Andreoli and Niva Lorenzini, 2 vols, Milan: Mondadori.

Dall'Orto, Giovanni (2000) 'Il paradosso del razzismo fascista verso l'omosessualità', in Burgio, Alberto (ed.) *Nel nome della razza: il razzismo nella storia d'Italia 1870–1945*, Bologna: Il Mulino, 515–28.

de Lisle, Arnaldo (1908) 'Oscar Wilde', in Oscar Wilde, *Il dovere del delitto: racconto con strane rivelazioni sulla psiche morbosa dell'autore*, Naples: Partenopea, pp. 7–51.

De Michelis, Eurialo (1979) 'Giuseppe Vannicola fra D'Annunzio e Wilde', *Quaderni del Vittoriale*, 3.14: 55–74.

'Il *De Profundis* di Oscar Wilde' (1905) *Il Marzocco* [Florence], 7 May, 5.

Doderet, André (1956) *Vingt ans d'amitié avec Gabriele D'Annunzio*, Paris: Imprimerie du Cantal.

Ellmann, Richard (1982) *James Joyce*, New York: Oxford University Press.

Ellmann, Richard (1987) *Oscar Wilde*, London: Hamish Hamilton.

Franci, Giovanna (1977) *Il sistema del dandy: Wilde-Beardsley-Beerbhom*, Bologna: Patron.

Gamberale, Luigi (1912a) 'Il processo e l'estetica di Oscar Wilde', in *Scritti vari*, Agnone: Sammartino and Ricci, pp. 37–81.

Gamberale, Luigi (1912b) 'Un più reale Oscar Wilde', in *Scritti vari*, Agnone: Sammartino and Ricci, pp. 83–122.

Gargano, Giuseppe Saverio (1906) 'Precetti di estetica wildiana', *Il Marzocco* [Florence], 2 December, 2–3.

Joyce, James (1959a) 'The Day of the Rabblement', in Mason, Ellsworth and Richard Ellmann (eds) *The Critical Writings of James Joyce*, New York: Viking Press, pp. 68–72.

Joyce, James (1959b) 'Oscar Wilde: the poet of *Salomé*', in Mason, Ellsworth and Richard Ellmann (eds) *The Critical Writings of James Joyce*, New York: Viking Press, pp. 201–05.

Joyce, James (1979) 'Oscar Wilde: il poeta di *Salomé*' in Corsini, Gianfranco and Giorgio Melchiori (eds) *James Joyce: scritti italiani*, Milan: Mondadori, pp. 60–66.

Lipparini, Giuseppe (1905) '*De Profundis* di O. Wilde', *Il Marzocco* [Florence], 2 July, 2.

Luperini, Romano (1976) *Gli esordi del Novecento e l'esperienza della 'Voce'*, Rome; Bari: Laterza.

Maggiore, Giuseppe (1929) 'Maschilità del fascismo', in *Un regime e un'epoca*, Milan: Treves, pp. 138–47.

Marabini Moevs, Maria Teresa (1976) *Gabriele D'Annunzio e le estetiche della fine del secolo*, L'Aquila: Japadre.

Marabini Moevs, Maria Teresa (2001) 'Su sentieri paralleli: Oscar Wilde e Gabriele D'Annunzio', in D'Amico, Masolino and Rita Severi (eds) *La vita come arte: Oscar Wilde, le Arti e l'Italia*, Palermo: Novecento, pp. 87–117.

Mariano, Emilio (1978) 'Il San Francesco di Gabriele D'Annunzio', *Quaderni del Vittoriale*, 2.12: 9–82.

Marjanovic, Alexandra (2005) 'Introduzione alla vita e alle carte di Raffaello Piccoli: un racconto', *Cartevive: bollettino dell'Archivio Prezzolini e degli archivi di cultura contemporanea della Biblioteca cantonale di Lugano*, 16.1 (June): 26–84.

Marinetti, Filippo Tommaso (2005) 'Futurist Speech to the English', in Rainey, Lawrence (ed.) *Modernism: An Anthology*, Maldon; Oxford: Blackwell, pp. 6–9.

Marucci, Franco (1996) 'The Forms of Modernity and the Modernity of Form', in Bizzotto, Elisa and Franco Marucci (eds) *Walter Pater (1839–1894): Le forme della modernità / The Forms of Modernity*, Milan: Cisalpino, pp. 11–29.

Marucci, Franco (2006) 'Wilde', in *Storia della letteratura inglese*, Florence: Le Lettere, 4: 858–922.

Miracco, Renato (1985) 'Ancora sul caso Wilde', *Sodoma*, 2.2: 102–07.

Miracco, Renato (ed.) (1998) *Oscar Wilde, Verso il sole: cronaca del soggiorno napoletano*, Naples: Colonnese; 3rd edn 2000, with appendix 'Oscar Wilde e Sorrento'.

Ojetti, Ugo (1897) 'Dialoghi dei vivi: della critica e dell'Entusiasmo', *Il Marzocco* [Florence], 21 November, 2–3.

Ojetti, Ugo (1898) 'La Ballata del Carcere di Reading', *Il Marzocco* [Florence], 4 December, 1–2.

Papini, Giovanni and others (1913) 'Introibo', *Lacerba*, 1: 1.

'Perversioni' (1926) *Il Popolo d'Italia* [Milan], 7 November, 3.

'La psicologia di Cristo' (1905) *Leonardo*, 3.2 (June–August): 131–33.

Raffalovich, Mark André (1896) *L'uranismo, inversione sessuale congenita: osservazioni e consigli; Il processo di Oscar Wilde*, trans. D. Bruni, Turin: Fratelli Bocca.

Re, Lucia (2002) 'D'Annunzio, Duse, Wilde, Bernhardt: il rapporto autore/attrice fra decadentismo e modernità', *MLN*, 117.1 (January): 115–52.

Ricorda, Ricciarda (1993) *Dalla parte di Ariele: Angelo Conti nella cultura di fine secolo*, Rome: Bulzoni.

Rosadi, Giovanni (1911) 'Oscar Wilde in carcere', *Nuova Antologia*, 239 (1 October): 407–26.

Sartorio, Giulio Aristide (1895–96) 'Esposizione di Venezia: Nota sulla pittura in Inghilterra', *Convito*, 7 (July–March): LVIII–LXIII.

Severi, Rita (1998) *L'anima dell'uomo: Oscar Wilde in Italia*, Palermo: Novecento.

Slawinski, Maurizio (1990) 'La metamorfosi di Ariele: D'Annunzio, il romanzo inglese e la voce del vate', in Nerozzi Bellman, Patrizia (ed.) *Gabriele D'Annunzio e la cultura inglese e americana*, Chieti: Solfanelli, pp. 45–70.

Soffici, Ardengo (1918) *Giornale di bordo*, Florence: Libreria della Voce.

Sorani, Aldo (1911) 'Oscar Wilde e sua madre', *Il Marzocco* [Florence], 14 May, 3–4.

Sorani, Aldo (1920) 'Le recensioni di Oscar Wilde', *Il Marzocco* [Florence], 31 October, 5.

Valera, Paolo (1909) *I gentiluomini invertiti: echi dello scandalo di Milano; Il capo-scuola Oscar Wilde al processo con i suoi giovanotti*, Milan: Floritta.

Veronesi, Matteo (2000a) 'Da Poe a Wilde. Intorno ad alcune fonti del concetto di critica tra il *Convito* e il primo *Marzocco*', *Poetiche: rivista di letteratura*, 1: 37–57.

Veronesi, Matteo (2000b) '"Un solitario e tacito concerto": Dal poème critique simbolista al "saper leggere" vociano', in Pieri, Piero and Giuliana Benvenuti (eds) *Quando l'opera interpella il lettore: poetiche e forme della modernità letteraria; studi e testimonianze offerti a Fausto Curi per i suoi settant'anni*, Bologna: Pendragon, pp. 189–206.

Veronesi, Matteo (2004) 'D'Annunzio e Wilde', *Cartapesta: libri e/o idee*, 10: 8–9.

Veronesi, Matteo (2006) *Il critico come artista dall'estetismo agli ermetici. D'Annunzio, Croce, Serra, Luzi e altri*, Bologna: Azeta.

Weiss, Roberto (1968) 'D'Annunzio e l'Inghilterra', in Mariano, Emilio (ed.) *L'arte di Gabriele D'Annunzio*, Milan: Mondadori, pp. 463–70.

Wilde, Oscar (1962) *The Letters of Oscar Wilde*, ed. Rupert Hart-Davis, New York: Harcourt, Brace and World.

Zanetti, Giorgio (1996) *Estetismo e modernità: saggio su Angelo Conti*, Bologna: Il Mulino.

Zanotto, Sandro (1996) *Filippo de Pisis ogni giorno*, Vicenza: Neri Pozza.

Chapter 8. The Strange Adventures of Oscar Wilde in Spain (1892–1912)

Translations

For a listing of translations into Castilian and Catalan see A. Palau y Dulcet (1977) *Manual del librero hispanoamericano*, vol. 28, Barcelona: Antonio Palau y Dulcet.

(1909) 'El príncipe feliz' (HP), trans, Ricardo Baeza, *Promoteo*, 2. 7 (1 May): 31–43.

(1909) *Balada de la cárcel de Reading* (*BRG*), trans Ricardo Baeza, *Promoteo*, 2.10 (1 August): 46–64.

(1909) *La casa de las granadas* (*HOP*), trans. Emeterio Mazorriaga, pref. Enrique Díez-Canedo, Madrid: Hijos de Gómez Fuentenebro.

(1910) 'Poemas en prosa' (PP), trans. Ricardo Baeza, *Prometeo*, 3.15 (1 March): 30–42.

(1910) 'El ruiseñor y la rosa' (NR), trans. Ricardo Baeza, *Prometeo*, 3.23 (1 November): 811–17.

(1911) 'Frases y filosofías para el uso de los jóvenes' (PPUY), trans. Ricardo Baeza, *Prometeo*, 4.33 (1 September): 807–10.

(1911) *Balada de la cárcel de Reading* (*BRG*), trans. Ricardo Baeza, Madrid: Helénica.

(1911) *Una mujer sin importancia* (*WNI*), trans. Ricardo Baeza, Madrid: Fernández Arias.

(1912?) *La decadencia de la mentira: La importancia de no saber nada* (DL), trans. Miguel Guerra Mondragón, Madrid: Helénica.

(1917) *El príncipe feliz y otros cuentos* (HP and other tales), trans. Ricardo Baeza, Madrid: Imprenta Clásica Española.

(1918) *El retrato de Dorian Gray* (*PDG*), trans. Ricardo Baeza, 2 vols, Madrid: Biblioteca Nueva.

(1919) *El crimen de Lord Arturo Savile* (LASC), trans. Julio Gómez de la Serna, afterword Ramón Gómez de la Serna, Madrid: Biblioteca Nueva

(1919) *De Profundis, El alma del hombre bajo el socialismo* (*DP* & SMUS), trans. Armando Vasseur, Madrid: Pueyo.

(1919) *Intenciones (Ensayos de literatura y estética)* (*Intentions*), trans. Julio Gómez de la Serna, afterword Ramón Gómez de la Serna, Madrid: Pueyo.

(1920) *Renacimiento del arte ingles y otros ensayos* (ERA and other essays), trans. León Felipe, Madrid: Editorial Americana.

(1930) *El alma del hombre y otros ensayos* (SMUS and other essays), trans. Ricardo Baeza, Madrid: La Nave.

(1936) *La Duquesa de Padua y otras obras inéditas* (*DOP*), trans. Julio Gómez de la Serna, Madrid: Editorial Biblioteca Nueva.

(1937) La balada de la presó de Reading (BRG); seguida dels Poemes en prosa, trans. Josep Janés i Olivé, Biblioteca de la Rosa dels Vents 35, Quaderns literaris 182, Barcelona: Edicions de la Rosa dels Vents; in Catalan.

(1941) *El fantasma de Canterville* (CG), trans. Julio Gómez de la Serna, Barcelona: Editorial Nausica.

Secondary criticism

Baudelaire, Charles (1961) *Curiosités esthétiques; L'Art romantique et autres oeuvres critiques*, ed. Henri Lemaître, Paris: Pléiade.

Cardwell, Richard A. (1972) critical edn and intro., Ricardo Gil, *La caja de música*, Exeter Hispanic Texts, Exeter: University of Exeter Press.

Cardwell, Richard A. (1984) critical edn and intro., Francisco A. de Icaza, *Efímeras & Lejanías*, Exeter Hispanic Texts, Exeter: University of Exeter Press.

Cardwell, Richard A. (1998a) 'El premodernismo español', in Romero, Leonardo (ed.) *Historia de la literatura española: Siglo XIX (II)*, Madrid: Espasa-Calpe, pp. 309–43.

Cardwell, Richard A. (1998b) 'Los raros de Rubén Darío y los medicos chiflados finiseculares', in Cueva, Cristóbal (ed.) *Rubén Darío y el arte de la prosa: Ensayo, retratos y alegorías,* Actas del XI Congreso de Literatura Española Contemporánea, 10–14 de noviembre de 1997, Málaga: Publicaciones del congreso de literatura española contemporánea, pp. 55–77.

Cardwell, Richard A. (1999) 'Poetry and Culture, 1868–1936', in Gies, David T. (ed.) *The Cambridge Companion to Modern Spanish Culture*, Cambridge: Cambridge University Press, pp. 175–86.

Cardwell, Richard A. (2003) 'Madman, Martyr and *Maudit*: Oscar Wilde and Spain; Medicine, Morals, Religion and Aesthetics', in Bonaddio, Federico and Xon de Ros (eds) *Crossing Fields: Studies in Modern Hispanic Cultures*, Oxford: Legenda, pp. 35–53.

Cardwell, Richard A. (2004) 'The Poetry of *Modernismo* in Spain', in Gies, David T. (ed.) *The Cambridge History of Spanish Literature*, Cambridge: Cambridge University Press, pp. 500–12.

Davis, Lisa E. (1973) 'Oscar Wilde in Spain', *Comparative Literature*, 25: 136–52.

Darío, Rubén (1950) *Obras completas*, Madrid: Afrodisio Aguado.

Ellmann, Richard (1987) *Oscar Wilde*, London: Hamish Hamilton.

'Los estetas' (1898) *Vida Nueva*, 21 (30 October), n.p.

Fernández, Pura (1995) *Eduardo López Bago y el Naturalismo radical: La novela y el mercado literario en el siglo XIX*, Amsterdam: Rodopi.

Gómez Carrillo, Enrique (1891) *Sensaciones de arte*, Paris: Imprimerie de G. Richard.

Gómez Carrillo, Enrique (1892) *Esquisses, Siluetas de escritores y artistas*, Madrid: Imprenta de la Viuda de Hernández y Cia.

Gómez Carrillo, Enrique (1894) 'Notas sobre las enfermedades de la sensación, desde el punto de vista de la literatura', in *Obras completas*, 20 vols, Madrid: Editorial Mundo Latino, 11: 83–145.

Gómez Carrillo, Enrique ([1920?]) *En plena bohemia*, in *Obras completas*, 20 vols, Madrid: Editorial Mundo Latino, 16: 190–98.

Lombroso, Cesare (1864) *Genio e follia: Prelezione al corso di clinica-psychiatrica*, Milan: Chiusi.

Lombroso, Cesare (1876) *L'uomo delinquente*, Milan: Hoepli.

Lombroso, Cesare (1887) *L'Homme criminel*, Paris: Alcan.

Lombroso-Ferrero, Gina (1911) *Criminal Man according to the Classification of Cesare Lombroso*, New York: G. Putnam's Sons.

Maristany, Luis (1973) *El gabinete del doctor Lombroso (Delincuencia y fin de siglo en España),* Barcelona: Editorial Anagrama.

Martínez Sierra, Gregorio (1905) *Teatro de ensueño; con melancólica sinfonía de Rubén Darío e ilustraciones líricas de Juan R. Jiménez*, Madrid: Renacimiento.

Nordau, Max (1968) *Degeneration*, intro. George L. Mosse, New York: Howard Fertig; reprint of 1895 American edn.

Nordau, Max (1892–93) *Entartung*, Berlin: C. Dunker.

Nordau, Max (1894) *Dégénérescence*, trans. Auguste Dietrich, Paris: Paul Brodad.

Nordau, Max (1895) *Degeneration*, trans. from 2nd German edn, New York: D. Appleton.

Nordau, Max (1902) *Degeneración*, trans. Nicolás Salmerón, Madrid: Jubera y Jeramnos.

Potter, Helen (1891) *Impersonations*, New York: Edgar S. Werner.

Quinn, Patrick F. (1957) *The French Face of Edgar Poe*, Carbondale: Southern Illinois University Press.

Wolfgang, Marvin E. (1960) 'Cesare Lombroso', in Mannheim, Hermann (ed. & intro.) *Pioneers in Criminology*, Library of Criminology 1, London: Stevens & Sons, pp. 168–227.

Chapter 9. The Reception of Wilde's Works in Spain through Theatre Performances at the Turn of the Twentieth and Twenty-first Centuries

Early Spanish translations of Wilde's plays

(1902?) *Salomé*, trans. J. Pérez Jorba and B. Rodríguez, Madrid: Rodríguez Serra.

(1910) *Salomé: drama en un acto*, trans. J. Pérez Jorba, Barcelona: Biblioteca Teatralia.

(1911) 'Una mujer sin importancia' (*WNI*), *Prometeo*, 26, 27 and 28.

(1914) *Un marido ideal (IH)*, trans. Román Jori, Barcelona: Doménech.

(1918) *Un marido ideal (IH)*, trans. Ricardo Baeza, Madrid: Atenea.

(1920) *El abanico de Lady Windermere (LWF)*, trans. Ricardo Baeza, Madrid: Atenea.

(1920) *La importancia de llamarse Ernesto (IBE)*, trans. Ricardo Baeza, Madrid: Atenea.

Other translations

Catalan or Catalonian publications/productions (Barcelona)

(1908) *Salomé*: drama en un acte, trans. Joaquim Pena, Barcelona: Fidel Giró.

(1923) *El vano de Lady Windermere: comedia dramàtica en quatre actes* (*LWF*), trans. Josep M. Jordà and Francesc Pujols, Collecció La Escena catalana 121, Barcelona: Salvador Bonavía.

(1938) *La importància d'ésser Fidel* (*IBE*), trans. Eduard Artells, Biblioteca de la Rosa dels Vents 56, Barcelona: Edicions de la Rosa dels Vents.

(1998) *La importància de ser Frank* (*IBE*), trans. and prologue by Jaume Melendres, Barcelona: Institut del Teatre.

(1998) *Salome*, libretto Hedwig Lachmann and Richard Strauss, music Richard Strauss. trans. Jordi Ibáñez, Barcelona: Consorci del Gran Teatre del Liceu, D.L.; pub. on the occasion of the opera *Salome*, Palau de la Música (Barcelona), dir. Peter Schneider and Frank Beermann, Barcelona: Generalitat de Catalunya, Ajuntament de Barcelona, Ministerio de Cultura, Diputació de Barcelona.

(2002) *Salome / Ramala*, trans. Terenci Moix, dir. and dramaturg Antonio Morcillo, asst dir. and movement Núria Legarda, Barcelona; 2 videocassettes, Taller de 4rt curs de direcció escènica, curs 2001–2002 (4th-year workshop on theatre direction 2001–02), l'Institut del teatre, dir. Antonio Morcillo. Recording carried out at the Teatre Estudi (Barcelona), 12 December 2002.

Galician

(1999) *Ernest: Comedia frívola para xente seria (IBE)*, ed. and trans. Miguel Pérez Romero, illus. Felipe Criado, Collecció Biblioteca Arquivo Teatral Francisco Pillado Mayor, Outras literaturas dramáticas 4, A Coruña: Universidade da Coruña, Departamento de Filoloxías francesa e galego-portuguesa.

Criticism and reviews

Alcalá Galiano, Álvaro (1919) 'Oscar Wilde: una semblanza', in *Conferencias y ensayos*, Madrid: Pueyo, pp. 151–208.

Amestoy, Ignacio (1997) 'Una Salomé sexual y turbadora abre el Festival de Mérida', *El Mundo: Cultura*, 2 July, [n.p.]; <http://www.elmundo.es/1997/07/02/cultura/02N0101.html> [accessed 7 September 2009].

Amorós, Andrés (1988) 'La investigación teatral en España: hacia una historia de la escena', *Boletín informativo de la Fundación Juan March*, 33 (February): 3–12.

Anderson, Andrew A. (1994a) 'Ricardo Baeza y el teatro', *Anales de la literatura española contemporánea*, 19.3 (Drama/Theatre): 229–39.

Anderson, Andrew A. (1994b) 'Una iniciativa teatral: Ricardo Baeza y su compañía dramática "Atenea" (1919)', in Gabriele, John. P. (ed.) *De lo particular a lo universal: El teatro español del siglo XX y su contexto*, Frankfurt: Vervuert, pp. 29–40.

Anderson, Andrew A. (2000) 'La campaña teatral de Ricardo Baeza e Irene López Heredia (1927–1928): historia externa e interna de una colaboración', *Revista de Literatura*, 62.123 (January-June): 133–53.

Aszyk, Urszula (1986) 'Los intentos de renovación teatral en España ante la reforma teatral en Europa en las primeras décadas del siglo XX', *Gestos: Teoría y práctica del teatro hispánico*, 1 (April): 73–85.

Bird, Alan (1977) *The Plays of Oscar Wilde*, New York: Barnes and Noble.

Bloom, Harold (ed.) (1985) *Oscar Wilde,* Modern Critical Views, New York: Chelsea House Publishers.

Centeno, Enrique (1992) '100 años de Oscar Wilde', *Diario 16* [Madrid], 1 October, [n.p.].

Centeno, Enrique (1995) 'Oscar Wilde se merece algo más', *Diario 16* [Madrid], 17 September, [n.p.].

Centeno, Leopoldo (2004) 'Sin pena ni Gloria: Comentario: "El retrato de Dorian Gray"', *La Voz de Galicia* [Pontevedra], 30 October, [n.p.]; <http://www.lavozde galicia.es/hemeroteca/2004/10/30/3161090.shtml> [accessed 9 September 2009].

Ciurans, Enric (2001) *Adrià Gual*, Barcelona: Infiesta Editor, Gent Nostra 123.

Coletes, Agustín (1985) 'Oscar Wilde en España, 1902–1928', *Cuadernos de Filología Inglesa*, 1: 17–32.

Cortina, Álvaro (2008) ' "La importancia de llamarse Ernesto": Daniel Pérez y Eduardo Galán presentan en el Teatro Maravillas su versión libre', *El Mundo*, 10 June <http://www.elmundo.es/elmundo/2008/06/10/cultura/1213116785. html> [accessed 31 July 2009].

Constán, Sergio (2009) *Wilde en España. La presencia de Oscar Wilde en la literatura española, 1882–1936*, León: Akrón.

Davis, Lisa E. (1973) 'Oscar Wilde in Spain', *Comparative Literature*, 25.2: 136–52.

Dougherty, Dru and Maria Francisca Vilches (1990) *La escena madrileña entre 1918 y 1926: Análisis y documentación*, Madrid: Editorial Fundamentos.

Ellmann, Richard (1988) *Oscar Wilde*, New York: Alfred A. Knopf; 1st US edn.

Galindo, Carlos (1995) 'Las tres dimensiones de Óscar Wilde en *La importancia de llamarse Ernesto*', *ABC*, 8 September, 79.

Gómez de la Serna, Julio (1991) 'Gloria e infortunio de Oscar Wilde (Su vida y su obra): Coloquio imaginario en el umbral', in Oscar Wilde, *Obras Completa*s, comp., trans., pref. and annotations Gómez de la Serna, Mexico City: Aguilar, pp. 9–84; 1st pub. 1943.

Haro Tecglen, Eduardo (1992) 'Convenciones: *El abanico de Lady Windermere. . . o la importancia de llamarse Wilde*', *El País*, 2 October, 36.

Haro Tecglen, Eduardo (1995) 'El querido tío Oscar: *La importancia de llamarse Ernesto*', *El País*, 17 September, 'Cultura, Crítica, Teatro': [n.p.].

Haro Tecglen, Eduardo (1996) 'Lo que no son los ingleses: *Un marido ideal*', *El País*, 14 September, 'Cultura, Crítica, Teatro': [n.p.].

Haro Tecglen, Eduardo (2005) '*El retrato de Dorian Gray*. La moral contraria', *El País*, 14 February, 'Espectáculos, Crítica: Teatro': [n.p.].

Huerta Calvo, Javier (ed.) (2003) *Historia del teatro español*, 2 vols, Madrid: Gredos.

Juan, José Luis de (2000) 'La fulgurante eternidad de Wilde', *El País: Babelia*, 25 November, 9.

López Sancho, Lorenzo (1995) '"La importancia de llamarse Ernesto": Oscar Wilde al "ralentí"', *ABC*, 16 September, 74.

Lorés, Maité (1977) 'Introducción', in Oscar Wilde, *Un marido ideal*, trans. and ed. Maité Lorés, Barcelona: Bosch, pp. 54–70.

Macklin, John (n.d.) 'La recepción de la literatura y cultura inglesas en la España del fin de siglo' in *Enciclopedia Fin de Siglo* <http://findesiglo.net/archivos/capitulo9/3. html> [accessed 23 September 2008].

Mateo, Marta (1995) *La traducción del humor: Las comedias inglesas en español*, Oviedo: Universidad de Oviedo, Servicio de Publicaciones.

Mateo, Marta (2005) 'La traducción de *Salomé* para distintos públicos y escenarios', in Merino, Raquel, Jose M. Santamaría and Eterio Pajares (eds) *Trasvases Culturales: Literatura, Cine y Traducción 4*, Bilbao: Servicio Editorial de la Universidad del País Vasco, pp. 225–42.

Mateo, Marta (2009) 'El juego pragmático como eje del humor de Oscar Wilde en inglés y en español', in Chamosa, José Luis and others (eds) *Lengua, traducción, recepción: en honor de Julio César Santoyo / Language, translation, reception: To honour Julio César Santoyo*, Leon: Universidad de León, Secretariado de Publicaciones, pp. [to be inserted].

Merino Álvarez, Raquel (1994) *Traducción, tradición y manipulación: Teatro inglés en España 1950–1990*, León: Universidad de León and Universidad del País Vasco, Servicio de Publicaciones.

Merino Álvarez, Raquel (2007) 'La homosexualidad censurada: estudio sobre corpus de teatro TRACEti (desde 1960)', in Merino (ed.) *Traducción y censura en España (1939–1985): Estudios sobre corpus TRACE: cine, narrativa, teatro*, Bilbao: Servicio Editorial de la Universidad del País Vasco, pp. 243–86; <http://www.ehu.es/ p200-content/es/contenidos/libro/se_indice_literatura/es_literatu/adjuntos/trace. pdf> [accessed 31 July 2009].

Mira, Alberto (2003) 'La importancia de no ser fiel: a propósito de una nueva traducción de Oscar Wilde', *Vasos comunicantes: Revista de ACE Traductores*, 27 (Winter): 92–99.

Moreno, Maria Sol (2008) 'Oscar Wilde "con vaqueros"', *El Mundo*, 5 June, 13 <http://www.elmundo.es/papel/2008/06/05/madrid/2411191.html> [accessed 31 July 2009].

'Notas teatrales: Princesa, "Una mujer sin importancia"' (1917a) *ABC*, 3 October, 14.

'Notas teatrales: "Nuevo pleito literario" and "Príncipe Alfonso; Inauguración y estreno"' (1917b), *ABC*, 18 November, 13.

Palau y Dulcet, Antonio (1990) *Manual del librero hispanoamericano*, 7: T-Z, Madrid: Julio Ollero Editor.

Pérez de Ayala, Ramón (1924) 'Las comedias modernas de Oscar Wilde' and 'Oscar Wilde o el espíritu de la contradicción', in *Las máscaras II*, Madrid: Renacimiento, pp. 7–18, 26.

Pérez-Rasilla, Eduardo (1995) 'La importancia de llamarse Ernesto: Una versión íntegra', *Reseña de Literatura: Arte y Espectáculos*, 266 (November): 18.

Portusach, Ramón (1910) 'Teatro principal de Barcelona: *Salomé*; Poema dramático de Oscar Wilde', *Comedias y Comediantes*, 9 (15 February): 24.

Rodríguez Clusella, Montse (2002) 'Herodias: Salome' (unpublished dissertation, Institut del Teatre, Escola Superior d'Art Dramàtica [Barcelona]).

Rodríguez Fonseca, Delfina (1997) *Salomé: la influencia de Oscar Wilde en las literaturas hispánicas*, Oviedo: KRK.

Ruiz Contreras, Luis (1930) *Medio siglo de teatro infructuoso*, Madrid: Sociedad General Española de Librería; 1st pub. 1920.

Soldevilla-Durante, Ignacio (1992) 'Ramón Gómez de la Serna: Entre la tradición y la vanguardia', in Dougherty, Dru and Maria Francisca Vilches (eds) *El teatro en España: Entre la tradición y la vanguardia, 1918–1939*, Madrid: CSIC, pp. 69–78.

Toro Santos, Antonio Raúl de (2007) *La literatura irlandesa en España*, Irish Studies Series of Instituto Universitario de Estudios Irlandeses 'Amergin', Oleiros (La Coruña): Netbiblo; 2nd edn, contains list of Spanish translations of Irish authors incl. Wilde in appendix.

Umbral, Francisco (1992) '*El abanico de Lady Windermere*: Oscar Wilde en persona', *El Mundo*, 1 October, 38.

Vilches, Maria Francisca and Dru Dougherty (1997) *La escena madrileña entre 1926 y 1931: Un lustro de transición*, Madrid: Editorial Fundamentos.

Villán, Javier (1995) '"Bunburysmo" puro', *El Mundo*, 16 September, 92.

Villena, Luis Antonio de (1983) 'Introducción', in Oscar Wilde, *El retrato de Dorian Gray*, intro. and trans. de Villena, Barcelona: Planeta, pp. ix-xxv.

Víllora, Pedro Manuel (2000) 'Un fascinante Oscar Wilde en *Salomé: La hija de Herodías*', *ABC*, 24 December, 72.

Chapter 10. Tragedy and the Apostle of Beauty: The Early Literary Reception of Oscar Wilde in Germany and Austria

Translations

(1894) 'Der Verfall des Lügens', [trans. Hermann Bahr], *Die Zeit* [Vienna], 1.6 (November 10): [n.p.].

(1900) 'Salome. Tragödie in einem Aufzug', trans. Hedwig Lachmann, *Wiener Rundschau* [Vienna], 4.12: 189–212.

(1901) *Dorian Gray*, trans. Johannes Gaulke, Leipzig: Max Spohr.

(1902) *Das Bildnis des Dorian Gray*, trans. Felix Paul Greve, Minden: J. C. C. Bruns.

(1902) *Lady Windermeres Fächer: Das Drama eines guten Weibes* (*LWF*), trans. Isidore Leo Pavia and Hermann Freiherr von Teschenberg, Leipzig: Max Spohr.

(1902) *Lehren und Sprüche für die reifere Jugend*, trans. Felix Paul Greve, Munich: In Commission J. Littauer Kunstbuchhandlung.

(1902) *Fingerzeige* (*Intentions*), trans. Felix Paul Greve, Minden: J. C. C. Bruns.

(1902) *Eine Frau ohne Bedeutung* (*WNI*), trans. Isidore Leo Pavia and Hermann Freiherr von Teschenberg, Leipzig: Max Spohr.

(1902) *Salome: Tragödie in einem Akt*, trans. Hedwig Lachmann, Leipzig: Insel.

(1903) *Das Bildnis des Mr. W. H.* (PMWH)*; Lord Arthur Saviles Verbrechen* (LASC), trans. Felix Paul Greve, Minden: J. C. C. Bruns.

(1903) *Bunbury (IBE): Eine Komödie*, trans. Felix Paul Greve, Minden: J. C. C. Bruns.

(1903) *Dorian Grays Bildnis*, trans. Felix Paul Greve, Minden: J. C. C. Bruns.

(1903) *Ein idealer Gatte* (*IH*), trans. Isidore Leo Pavia and Hermann Freiherr von Teschenberg, Leipzig: Max Spohr.

(1903) *Salome: Drama in einem Aufzuge*, trans. Isidore Leo Pavia and Hermann Freiherr von Teschenberg, Leipzig: Max Spohr.

(1904) *Salome*, trans. Dr Kiefer, Leipzig: Reclam [UB 4497].

(1905) *Das Granatapfelhaus* (*HOP*), trans. Felix Paul Greve, Leipzig: Insel.

(1905) 'De Profundis / Aufzeichnungen und Briefe aus dem Zuchthause in Reading', *Die neue Rundschau* [Berlin], 16.1 (January): 86–104; 16.2 (February): 163–91.

(1905) *De Profundis / Aufzeichnungen und Briefe aus dem Zuchthause in Reading*, Berlin: S. Fischer.

(1905) *Intentionen*, trans. Arthur Roeßler, Leipzig: Friedrich Rothbart.

(1906–08) *Sämtliche Werke in deutscher Sprache*, Vienna; Leipzig: Wiener.

(1907) *Die Ballade vom Zuchthaus zu Reading* (*BRG*), trans. Walther Unus, Leipzig: Reclam [UB 4864].

(1907) *Ernst sein!* (*IBE*)*: Eine triviale Komödie für seriöse Leute*, trans. Hermann Freiherr von Teschenberg, Leipzig: Max Spohr.

(1908) *Das Bildnis des Dorian Gray*, trans. Margarete Preiß, foreword Johannes Gaulke, Leipzig: Reclam [UB 5008].

(1910) *Die Erzählungen und Märchen*, trans. Felix Paul Greve and Franz Blei, Leipzig: Insel.

(1930) *Werke in zwei Bänden*, ed. Arnold Zweig, Berlin: Knaur.

Secondary sources

Alewyn, Richard (1967) 'Hofmannsthals Wandlung' [1949], in *Über Hugo von Hofmannsthal*, Göttingen: Vandenhoeck und Ruprecht.

Altenberg, Peter (1905) 'Der Sozialismus und die Seele des Menschen, von Oscar Wilde', *Die Fackel* [Vienna], 173 (16 January): 12–15.

Altenhofer, Norbert (1978) 'Hugo von Hofmannsthal und Gustav Landauer: Eine Dokumentation', *Hofmannsthal-Blätter*, 19–20: 43–72.

Arlaud, Sylvie (2000) *Les références anglaises de la modernité viennoise*, Bibliothèque d'études germaniques, hébraïques et juives de l'Université Paris 8: série d'études germaniques 7, Saint-Denis: Suger.

Bahr, Hermann (1894) 'Décadence', *Die Zeit* [Vienna], 1.6 (10 November): 87–89.

Bahr, Hermann (1996) *Tagebücher, Skizzenbücher, Notizhefte*, vol. 2: *1890–1900*, ed. Moritz Csáky, Vienna; Cologne; Weimar: Böhlau Verlag.

Barboni, Benedetta (2001–2002) 'Oscar Wilde nella letteratura tedesca di fine Ottocento', *Studi urbinati, B: Scienze umane e sociali*, 71–72: 531–42.

Blei, Franz (ed.) (1904) *In Memoriam Oscar Wilde*, Leipzig: Insel.

Blei, Franz (1930) 'Oscar Wilde', in *Männer und Masken*, Berlin: Rowohlt, pp. 171–98.

Blei, Franz (1995) *Das große Bestiarium der Literatur*, ed. Rolf-Peter Baacke, Hamburg: Europäische Verlagsanstalt.

Bridgwater, Patrick (1999) 'Oscar Wilde and Germany: Germany and Oscar Wilde' and 'Masked Men: Nietzsche, Pater and Wilde', in *Anglo-German Interactions in the Literature of the 1890s*, Oxford: Legenda, pp. 43–72; 226–54.

Bridgwater, Patrick (2002) 'Some German Oscar Wildes', in Böker, Uwe, Richard

Corballis and Julie Hibbard (eds) *The Importance of Reinventing Oscar: Versions of Wilde during the last 100 Years*, Amsterdam: Rodopi.

Brittnacher, Hans Richard (1996) '"Der Geck war tragisch": Hofmannsthals Nachruf auf Oscar Wilde', *Forum Homosexualität und Literatur*, 26: 27–41.

Brod, Max (1937) *Franz Kafka: Eine Biographie (Erinnerungen und Dokumente)*, Prague: Heinrich Mercy.

Davis, W. Eugene (2001) 'Oscar Wilde, *Salome*, and the German Press 1902–1905', *English Literature in Transition*, 44.2: 148–80.

Dormer, Lore Muerdel (1977) 'Die Truggestalt der Kaiserin und Oscar Wilde: Zur Metaphorik in Hofmannsthals Drama *Der Kaiser und die Hexe*', *Zeitschrift für Deutsche Philologie*, 96: 579–86.

Ellmann, Richard (1988) *Oscar Wilde*, Harmondsworth: Penguin; orig. pub. 1987, London: Hamilton.

Ernstmann, H. (1906) *Salome an den deutschen Hofbühnen: Ein Kulturbild*, Berlin: Hermann Walther.

Frisch, Efraim (1903–04) 'Aus Berliner Theatern', *Das Theater* [Berlin], 1: 29–31.

Gaulke, Johannes (1896) 'Oscar Wilde', *Die Gegenwart* [Berlin], 49: 184–87.

George, Stefan and Hofmannsthal, Hugo von (1953) *Briefwechsel zwischen George und Hofmannsthal*, Munich; Düsseldorf: Küpper.

Gide, André (1947) *Prétextes: Réflexions sur quelques points de littérature et de morale*, Paris: Mercure de France.

Gilman, Sander L. (1988) 'Opera, Homosexuality, and Models of Disease: Richard Strauss's *Salome* in the Context of Images of Disease in the Fin de siècle', in *Disease and Representation: Images of Illness from Madness to AIDS*, Ithaca; London: Cornell University Press.

Greve, Felix Paul (1903) *Randarabesken zu Oscar Wilde*, Minden: J. C. C. Bruns.

Hammond, Charles Henry (2006) 'Blind Alleys: Hugo von Hofmannsthal, Oscar Wilde and the Problem of Aestheticism' (unpublished doctoral thesis, University of California, Irvine).

Hänsel-Hohenhausen, Markus (1999) *Die frühe deutschsprachige Oscar-Wilde-Rezeption (1893–1906)*, Frankfurt a.M.: Deutsche Hochschulschriften.

Harris, Frank (1923) *Oscar Wilde: Ein Lebensbeichte*, Berlin: S. Fischer.

Herzfeld, Marie (1898) 'Ibsen und seine Landsleute', *Die Zeit* [Vienna], 14.181 (19 March): 186–87.

Hofmannsthal, Hugo von (1893) 'Algernon Charles Swinburne', *Deutsche Zeitung* [Vienna], 5 January, [n.p.]; repr. in Hofmansthal 1979b, pp. 143–48.

Hofmannsthal, Hugo von (1935) *Briefe 1890–1901*, Berlin: S. Fischer.

Hofmannsthal, Hugo von (1979a) *Erzählungen, Erfundene Gespräche und Briefe, Reisen*, Frankfurt a.M.: Fischer Taschenbuch.

Hofmannsthal, Hugo von (1979b) *Reden und Aufsätze I: 1891–1913*, Frankfurt a.M.: Fischer Taschenbuch Verlag.

Hofmannsthal, Hugo von (1979c) *Reden und Aufsätze III: 1925–1929; Aufzeichnungen*, Frankfurt a.M.: Fischer Taschenbuch.

Hofmannsthal, Hugo von (1982) *Sämtliche Werke III: Dramen 1*, eds Götz Eberhard Hübner, Klaus-Gerhard Pott and Christoph Michel, Frankfurt a.M.: S. Fischer.

Hofmannsthal, Hugo von (1988) *Sämtliche Werke II: Gedichte 2*, eds Andreas Thomasberger and Eugene Weber, Frankfurt a.M.: S. Fischer.

Kassner, Rudolf (1969) *Sämtliche Werke*, ed. Ernst Zinn [and Klaus E. Bohnenkamp], Pfullingen: Neske.

Keats, John (1987) *Letters of John Keats: A Selection*, ed. Robert Gittings, Oxford: Oxford University Press.

Knoenagel, Alex (1986) 'Greve's First Translation', *Canadian Literature*, 111: 214–20.

Kohlmayer, Rainer (1996) *Oscar Wilde in Deutschland und Österreich: Untersuchungen zur Rezeption der Komödien und zur Theorie der Bühnenübersetzung*, Tübingen: Niemeyer.

Kraus, Karl (1903) 'Salome', *Die Fackel*, 150 (23 December): 1–14.

Kraus, Karl (1904a) 'Das Bildnis Dorian Gray's', *Die Fackel*, 151 (4 January): 18–21.

Kraus, Karl (1904b) 'Oscar Wilde über die Presse', *Die Fackel*, 167 (26 October): 9–13.

Landauer, Gustav (1906) 'Drei Dramen und ihre Richter', *Die Schaubühne*, 2.6 (8 February): 151–59.

Le Rider, Jacques (1993) *Modernity and Crises of Identity: Culture and Society in Fin-de-Siècle Vienna*, trans. Rosemary Morris, New York: Continuum.

Mann, Thomas (1960) *Betrachtungen eines Unpolitischen*, in *Gesammelte Werke in zwölf Bänden*, vol. 12, Frankfurt a.M.: S. Fischer.

Mann, Thomas (1997) 'Nietzsches Philosophie im Lichte unserer Erfahrung', in *Essays*, vol. 6: *Meine Zeit. 1945–1955*, eds Hermann Kurzke and Stephan Stachorski, Frankfurt a.M.: S. Fischer.

Mayer, Ernst (1901–2) 'Von den Londoner Theatern', *Bühne und Welt* [Berlin], 4: 1047–57.

Mayer, Sandra and Pfeifer, Barbara (2007) 'The Reception of Oscar Wilde and Bernard Shaw in the Light of Early Twentieth-Century Austrian Censorship', *Platform*, 2.2: 59–75.

Meyerfeld, Max (1903) 'Erinnerungen an Oscar Wilde', *Neue deutsche Rundschau*, 14: 400–07.

Meyerfeld, Max (1905) 'Wilde, Wilde, Wilde', *Das litterarische Echo: Halbmonatschrift für Litteraturfreunde* [Berlin], 15: 985–90.

Mitterbauer, Helga (2003) *Die Netzwerke des Franz Blei: Kulturvermittlung im frühen 20. Jahrhundert*, Tübingen; Basel: A. Francke.

Musil, Robert (1981) *Briefe 1901–1942*, ed. Adolf Frisé with Murray G. Hall, 2 vols, Reinbek bei Hamburg: Rowohlt.

Nietzsche, Friedrich (1954–6) *Werke*, ed. Karl Schlechta, 3 vols, Munich: Carl Hanser.

Polgar, Alfred (1905) 'Oscar Wildes Lustspiele', *Die Schaubühne*, 1.16 (21 December): 457–60.

Polgar, Alfred (1925) 'Die Frau ohne Bedeutung', *Die Weltbühne*, 21.51 (22 December): 954.

Price, Lawrence Marsden (1932) *The Reception of English Literature in Germany*, Berkeley, CA: University of California Press.

Rizza, Steve (1997) *Rudolf Kassner and Hugo von Hofmannsthal: Criticism as Art; The Reception of Pre-Raphaelitism in* fin de siècle *Vienna*, Frankfurt a.M.: Peter Lang.

Schlösser, Anselm (1937) *Die englische Literatur in Deutschland von 1895 bis 1934 mit einer vollständigen Bibliographie der deutschen Übersetzungen und der im deutschen Sprachgebiet erschienenen englischen Ausgaben*, Jena: Verlag der Frommannschen Buchhandlung W. Biedermann.

Schroeder, Horst (n.d.) 'The "Definitive" Edition of Oscar Wilde's *De Profundis*' <http://horst-schroeder.com/DeProfundis.htm> [accessed 20 July 2009].

Sternheim, Carl (1988) *Briefe*, ed. Wolfgang Wendler, 2 vols, Darmstadt: Luchterhand.

Stillmark, Alexander (1981) 'Hofmannsthal and Oscar Wilde', in Yuill, W. E. and Patricia Howe (eds) *Hugo von Hofmannsthal: Commemorative Essays*, London: University of London, pp. 9–20.

Timms, Edward (1986) *Karl Kraus, Apocalyptic Satirist: Culture and Catastrophe in Habsburg Vienna*, New Haven; London: Yale University Press.

Vilain, Robert (2000a) *The Poetry of Hugo von Hofmannsthal and French Symbolism*, Oxford: Clarendon Press.

Vilain, Robert (2000b) 'Temporary Aesthetes: Decadence and Symbolism in Germany and Austria', in McGuinness, Patrick (ed.) *Symbolism, Decadence and the 'fin de siècle'*, Exeter: Exeter University Press, pp. 209–24.

Vilain, Robert (2002) 'The Reception of Walter Pater in Germany and Austria', in Brake, Laurel, Lesley Higgins and Carolyn Williams (eds) *Walter Pater: Transparencies of Desire*, Greensboro, NC: ELT Press, pp. 63–72.

Weber, Eugene (1971) 'Hofmannsthal und Oscar Wilde', in *Hofmannsthal-Forschungen: Referate der zweiten Tagung der Hugo von Hofmannsthal Gesellschaft*, Basel: Hofmannsthal Gesellschaft, pp. 9–106.

Weinzierl, Ulrich (2005) *Hofmannsthal: Skizzen zu seinem Bild*, Vienna: Zsolnay.

Wilde, Oscar (1962) *The Letters of Oscar Wilde*, ed. Rupert Hart-Davis, London: Hart-Davis.

Wunberg, Gotthart (ed.) (1976) *Das junge Wien: Österreichische Literatur- und Kunstkritik 1887–1902*, 2 vols, Tübingen: Niemeyer.

Chapter 11. *Bunbury* in Germany: Alive and Kicking

Translations

(1900) *Salome: Tragödie in einem Aufzug von Oscar Wilde (London)*, trans. Hedwig Lachmann, *Wiener Rundschau*, 4: 189–212.

(1902a) *Lady Windermere's Fächer: Das Drama eines guten Weibes* (*LWF*), trans. Isidore Leo Pavia and Hermann Freiherr von Teschenberg, Leipzig: Spohr.

(1902b) *Eine Frau ohne Bedeutung* (*WNI*), trans. Isidore Leo Pavia and Hermann Freiherr von Teschenberg, Leipzig: Spohr.

(1903a) *Salome*, trans. Isidore Leo Pavia and Hermann Freiherr von Teschenberg, Leipzig: Spohr.

(1903b) *Ernst sein!* (*IBE*), trans. Hermann Freiherr von Teschenberg, Leipzig: Spohr.

(1903c) *Ein idealer Gatte* (*IH*), trans. Isodore Leo Pavia and Hermann Freiherr von Teschenberg, Leipzig: Spohr.

(1906–08) *Sämtliche Werke in deutscher Sprache*, 10 vols, trans. Otto Hauser and others, Vienna; Leipzig: Wiener Verlag.

(1930) *Werke in zwei Bänden*, ed. Arnold Zweig, trans. Otto Hauser and others, Berlin: Knaur.

(1934a) *Eine Frau ohne Bedeutung: Schauspiel aus der Gesellschaft* (*WNI*), trans. and adapt. Karl Lerbs, Bad Kissingen: Vertriebsstelle und Verlag Deutscher Bühnenschriftsteller und Bühnenkomponisten.

(1934b) *Lady Windermeres Fächer: Eine Komödie, die von einer guten Frau handelt* (*LWF*), trans. and adapt. Karl Lerbs, Berlin: Felix Bloch Erben.

(1935a) *Ein idealer Gatte: Schauspiel aus der Gesellschaft* (*IH*), trans. and adapt. Karl Lerbs, Berlin: Verlag Deutscher Bühnenschriftsteller und Bühnenkomponisten.

(1935b) *Vor allem Ernst! (Bunbury): Komödie in drei Akten* (*IBE*), free trans. and adapt. Ernst Sander; Library of the Vienna Burgtheater.

(1970) *Werke in zwei Bänden*, ed. Rainer Gruenter, vol. 2: *Theaterstücke*, trans. Paul Baudisch and Edith Landmann [*sic*] [Hedwig Lachmann], Munich: Hanser.

(1971) *Sämtliche Theaterstücke*, trans. Siegfried Schmitz, Munich: Winkler.

(1971) *Keine Hochzeit ohne Ernst (Bunbury): Komödie in drei Akten* (*IBE*), trans. and adapt. Kurt Jung-Alsen, East Berlin: Henschelverlag.

(1975) *Sämtliche Dramen*, trans. Christine Hoeppener, Leipzig: Insel.

(1981) *Bunbury oder Ernst sein ist wichtig: Eine triviale Komödie für ernsthafte Leute* (*IBE*), trans. Rainer Kohlmayer, Stuttgart: Reclam; 2nd edn 1993, 3rd edn 2004.

(1986) *Ein idealer Ehemann: Eine Gesellschaft-Komödie* (*IH*), trans. Hans Wollschläger, Zürich: Haffmans.

(1990) *The Importance of Being Earnest: A Trivial Comedy for Serious People*, ed. Manfred Pfister, Stuttgart: Reclam.

(1991) *Ein idealer Gatte: Komödie in vier Akten (IH)*, trans. Rainer Kohlmayer, Stuttgart: Reclam.

(2005) *Ernst ist das Leben (Bunbury) (IBE)*, adapt. Elfriede Jelinek, trans. Karin Rausch, Reinbek: Rowohlt Theater Verlag.

Criticism and reviews

[A.] (1935) review of *Bunbury* (*IBE*) at Neues Theater Hamburg, *Altonaer Tageblatt*, [n.d.], [n.p.]; source: Sander-Archiv, Brunswick.

Barcata, Louis (1938) review of *Bunbury* (*IBE*) at Burgtheater Vienna, *Neue Freie Presse* [Vienna], 28 October, 9.

Blackburn, Robert (1995) '"The Unutterable and the Dream": Aspects of Wilde's Reception in Central Europe 1900–1922', *Irish Studies Review*, 11: 30–35.

Bridgwater, Patrick (2002) 'Some German Oscar Wildes', in Böker, Uwe, Richard Corballis and Julie A. Hibbard (eds) *The Importance of Reinventing Oscar: Versions of Wilde During the Last 100 Years*, Amsterdam; New York: Rodopi, pp. 237–47.

C.O.E. (1936) review of *Eine Frau ohne Bedeutung* (*WNI*) at Nationaltheater Mannheim, *Neue Mannheimer Zeitung*, 31 March, 7.

Davis, W. Eugene (2001) 'Oscar Wilde, Salome, and the German Press 1902–1905', *English Literature in Transition (1880–1920)*, 44: 149–80.

Deuter, Ulrich (1998) review of *Bunbury* at Kammerspiele Bonn, *Der Tagesspiegel*, 19 November, 35.

Eloesser, Arthur (1902) 'Theater und Musik', *Beilage zur Vossischen Zeitung*, 16 November, n.p..

Epstein, Max (1984) 'Max Reinhardt bis zur Gründung des Deutschen Theaters', in Boeser, Knut and Renata Vatková (eds) *Max Reinhardt in Berlin*, Berlin: Edition Hentrich; Fröhlich & Kaufmann, pp. 56–63.

Fiedler, Leonhardt M. (1975) *Max Reinhardt in Selbstzeugnissen und Bilddokumenten*, Reinbek: Rowohlt.

Gide, André (1903) 'Oskar [*sic*] Wilde', trans Berta Franz, *Rheinisch Westfälische Zeitung* [Essen], 8, 12 & 15 July, n.p..

Gilman, Sander L. (1988) *Disease and Representation*, Ithaca: Cornell University Press.

Giovanopoulos, Anna-Christina (2001) 'Censorship and the Institutionalisation of Meaning: Oscar Wilde in East Germany', in Böker, Uwe and Julie A. Hibbard (eds) *Processes of Institutionalisation: Case Studies in Law, Prison and Censorship*, Essen: Blaue Eule, pp. 111–40.

Giovanopoulos, Anna-Christina (2002) 'Wilde in the East: Processes of Mediation', in Böker, Uwe, Richard Corballis and Julie A. Hibbard (eds) *The Importance of Reinventing Oscar: Versions of Wilde During the Last 100 Years*, Amsterdam; New York: Rodopi, pp. 275–83.

Göpfert, Peter Hans (1980) review of *Bunbury* (*IBE*) at Freie Volksbühne Berlin, *Die Welt*, 28 April, 25.

Goetz, Wolfgang (1937) 'Oscar Wilde: Sein Leben und Werk', in Oscar Wilde, *Werke in zwei Bänden*, Berlin: Knaur, 1: 5–40.

Hänsel-Hohenhausen, Markus (1999) *Die frühe deutschsprachige Oscar-Wilde-Rezeption (1893–1906): Bibliographie*, 2nd edn, Egelsbach: Hänsel-Hohenhausen.

Hagemann, Carl (1904) *Oscar Wilde*, Minden: Bruns.

Höfele, Andreas (1999) 'Oscar Wilde, or, The Prehistory of Postmodern Parody', *European Journal of English Studies*, 3: 138–66.

Jacobs, Monty (1929) review of *Bunbury* (*IBE*) at Tribüne Berlin, *Vossische Zeitung* [Berlin], 11 October, [n.p.].

Kaiser, Joachim (1984) review of *Bunbury* at Kleine Komödie Munich, *Süddeutsche Zeitung*, 15 February, [n.p.].

Kohl, Norbert (1980) *Oscar Wilde: Das literarische Werk zwischen Provokation und Anpassung*, Heidelberg: Winter.

Kohlmayer, Rainer (1990) 'Ein Dandy "bester Zucht": Oscar Wildes Gesellschaftskomödie *An Ideal Husband* in Karl Lerbs' Bühnenbearbeitung aus dem Jahre 1935', in Schultze, Brigitte, Erika Fischer-Lichte, Fritz Paul and Horst Turk (eds) *Literatur und Theater: Traditionen und Probleme der Dramenübersetzung*, Tübingen: Narr, pp. 273–311.

Kohlmayer, Rainer (1991) 'Ambiguität und Ideologie als Probleme deutscher Wilde-Übersetzungen', in Forstner, Martin and Klaus von Schilling (eds) *Interdisziplinarität: Deutsche Sprache und Literatur im Spannungsfeld der Kulturen*, Frankfurt a.M.: Peter Lang, pp. 421–64.

Kohlmayer, Rainer (1993) 'Sprachkomik bei Wilde und seinen deutschen Übersetzern: Normalisierung, Konfliktdämpfung und Selbstzensur in den frühen Komödienübersetzungen', in Paul, Fritz, Wolfgang Ranke and Brigitte Schultze (eds) *Europäische Komödie im übersetzerischen Transfer*, Tübingen: Narr, pp. 345–84.

Kohlmayer, Rainer (1994) 'Oscar Wilde's Society Comedies and the National Socialist Message', *New Comparison*, 17: 11–22.

Kohlmayer, Rainer (1996a) *Oscar Wilde in Deutschland und Österreich: Untersuchungen zur Rezeption der Komödien und zur Theorie der Bühnenübersetzung*, Tübingen: Niemeyer.

Kohlmayer, Rainer (1996b) 'Oscar Wildes Einakter *Salome* und die deutsche Rezeption', in Herget, Winfried and Brigitte Schultze (eds) *Kurzformen des Dramas: Gattungspoetische, epochenspezifische und funktionale Horizonte*, Tübingen: Francke, pp. 159–85.

Kohlmayer, Rainer (1997) 'Wildes *Bunbury* auf braunen Bühnen: zwischen Zeitkritik und Eskapismus', in Fritz, Bärbel, Brigitte Schultze and Horst Turk (eds) *Theaterinstitution und Kulturtransfer I: Fremdsprachiges Repertoire am Burgtheater und auf anderen europäischen Bühnen*, Tübingen: Narr, pp. 361–72.

Krünes, Erik (1937) review of *Bunbury* (*IBE*) at Staatstheater Berlin, *Berliner Illustrierte*, night edn, 10 April, n.p..

Krug, Hartmut (2005) review of *Bunbury* (*IBE*) at Akademietheater Vienna, *Der Tagesspiegel*, 21 February, 24.

Küster, Otto (1935) review of *Ein idealer Gatte* (*IH*) at Thalia-Theater Hamburg, *Hamburger Nachrichten*, 13 November, [n.p.]; source: Hamburger Theatersammlung, University of Hamburg.

Landau, Isidor (1902) review of *Salome* and *Bunbury* at Kleines Theater Berlin, *Berliner Börsen-Courier*, 16 November, [n.p.].

Lerbs, Karl (1935) 'Warum spielen wir heute Wilde?' and 'Der zeitnahe Wilde', *Ein idealer Gatte* Staatstheater Berlin programme, December.

Mahn, Paul (1902) review of *Bunbury* (*IBE*) and *Salome* at Kleines Theater Berlin, *Tägliche Rundschau* [Berlin], 16 November, 3.

Meyerfeld, Max (1903) 'Oscar Wilde in Deutschland', *Das litterarische Echo*, 5: col. 458–62.

Meyerfeld, Max (1905) 'Wilde, Wilde, Wilde...', *Das litterarische Echo*, 7: col. 985–90.

Niessen, Carl (1984) 'Max Kruse', in Boeser, Knut and Renata Vatková (eds) *Max Reinhardt in Berlin*, Berlin: Edition Hentrich; Fröhlich & Kaufmann, pp. 254–55.

Nordau, Max (1892) *Entartung*, Berlin: Duncker.

Otte, Paul (1937) review of *Bunbury* (*IBE*) at Staatstheater Berlin, [n. pub.], 10 April, [n.p.]; source: Archive of the Akademie der Künste, Berlin.

Pfister, Manfred (1986) *Oscar Wilde: 'The Picture of Dorian Gray'*, Munich: Fink.

Pinthus, Kurt (1929) review of *Bunbury* (*IBE*) at Tribüne Berlin, *8-Uhr-Abendblatt* [Berlin], 10 October, 12.

Pitsch, Ilse (1952) 'Das Theater als politisch-publizistisches Führungsmittel im Dritten Reich' (unpublished doctoral thesis, University of Münster).

Rainalter, Erwin H. (1936) review of *Eine Frau ohne Bedeutung* (*WNI*) at Staatstheater Berlin, *Völkischer Beobachter* [Munich], Berlin edn, 26 July, [n.p.].

Reinhardt, Max (1987) Conversation with Arthur Kahane (1901), in Fuhrich, Edda and Gisela Prossnitz (eds) *Max Reinhardt: 'Ein Theater, das den Menschen wieder Freude gibt': Eine Dokumentation*, Munich; Vienna: Langen Müller, pp. 29–31.

Schlösser, Anselm (1937) *Die englische Literatur in Deutschland von 1895 bis 1934: Mit einer vollständigen Bibliographie der deutschen Übersetzungen und der im deutschen Sprachgebiet erschienenen englischen Ausgaben*, Jena: Verlag der Fromannschen Buchhandlung Walter Biedermann.

Schramm, Wolf (1935) review of *Bunbury* (*IBE*) at Neues Theater Hamburg, *Hamburger Anzeiger*, 1 November, n.p..

S[ervaes], F[ranz] (1929) review of *Bunbury* (*IBE*) at Tribüne Berlin, *Berliner Lokal-Anzeiger*, 10 October, n.p..

Sternheim, Carl (1964) *Oskar* [sic] *Wilde: Sein Drama*, in *Gesamtwerk*, vol. 3, ed. Wilhelm Emrich, Berlin; Neuwied a. Rhein: Luchterhand, pp. 263–374.

Wahl, Christine (2006) review of *Bunbury* (*IBE*) at Deutsches Theater Berlin, *Der Tagesspiegel*, 3 May, 26.

Wilde, Oscar (1908–22) *Works*, 14 vols, ed. Robert Ross. London: Methuen.

Wirsing, Sibylle (1980) review of *Bunbury* (*IBE*) at Freie Volksbühne Berlin, *Frankfurter Allgemeine Zeitung*, 28 April, 25.

[ze.] (1935) review of *Bunbury* (*IBE*) at Neues Theater Hamburg, *Völkischer Beobachter* [Munich], northern German edn, 5 November, [n.p.].

Zweig, Arnold (1930) 'Versuch über Oscar Wilde' in Oscar Wilde, *Werke in zwei Bänden*, ed. Zweig, Berlin: Knaur, 1: 5–39.

Chapter 12. When Critics Disagree, the Artist Survives: Oscar Wilde, an All-Time Favourite of the Viennese Stage in the Twentieth Century

'Adele Sandrock in "Bunbury"' (1931) *Neues Wiener Tagblatt*, 4 May, 5.

Antropp, Theodor (1907) 'Rundschau: Wiener Theater', *Österreichische Rundschau*, 10.1: 311–12.

Augustin, Claudia (2004) '"Die Übersetzung schmiegt sich an das Original wie das Lamm an den Wolf": Elfriede Jelinek im Gespräch mit Claudia Augustin', *Internationales Archiv für Sozialgeschichte der deutschen Literatur*, 29.2: 94–106.

Bahr, Hermann (1894) 'Décadence', *Die Zeit* [Vienna], 10 November, 87–89.

Basil, Otto (1955) 'Burgtheater: "Bunbury"', *Neues Österreich* [Vienna], 1 February, 5.

Basil, Otto (1958) '"Eine Frau ohne Bedeutung" im Akademietheater', *Neues Österreich* [Vienna], 24 January, 6.

Bridgwater, Patrick (1999) *Anglo-German Interactions in the Literature of the 1890s*, Oxford: Legenda.

Daviau, Donald G. (2001) 'Der "Austropäer" Hermann Bahr als Anreger und Vermittler der Moderne im europäischen Kontext', in Lachinger, Johann (ed.)

Hermann Bahr: Mittler der europäischen Moderne, Jahrbuch des Adalbert Stifter Institutes 5, Linz: Land Oberösterreich, pp. 13–26.

'Deutsches Volkstheater' (1905) *Deutsches Volksblatt* [Vienna], 10 December, 9–10.

Dössel, Christine (2005) 'Froh zu sein bedarf es wenig', *Süddeutsche Zeitung*, 21 February, 17.

Fontana, Oskar Maurus (1955) 'Wildes Paradoxon vom Ernstsein', *Die Presse* [Vienna], 1 February, 4.

Gilman, Sander L. (1988) 'Strauss, the Pervert, and Avant Garde Opera of the Fin de Siècle', *New German Critique*, 43: 35–68.

Gordon, David J. (1998) 'Shavian Comedy and the Shadow of Wilde', in Innes, Christopher (ed.) *The Cambridge Companion to George Bernard Shaw*, Cambridge: Cambridge University Press, pp. 124–43.

Grossmann, Stefan (1905) 'Theater und Kunst: Deutsches Volkstheater', *Arbeiter-Zeitung* [Vienna], 10 December, 7.

Guy, Josephine and Ian Small (2006) *Studying Oscar Wilde: History, Criticism, and Myth*, Greensboro, NC: ELT Press.

Hevesi, Ludwig (1905) 'Feuilleton: Deutsches Volkstheater', *Fremden-Blatt* [Vienna], 10 December, 17.

Hirschmann-Altzinger, Elisabeth (2005) ' "Wer hören will, der höre": Interview', *Die Bühne* [Vienna], 2: 32–33.

Honegger, Gitta (2006) 'How to Get the Nobel Prize without Really Trying', *Theater*, 36.2: 4–19.

Huish, Louise Adey (1998) 'An Austrian Comic Tradition?', in McKenzie, John R. P. and Lesley Sharpe (eds) *The Austrian Comic Tradition: Studies in Honour of W. E. Yates*, Austrian Studies IX, Edinburgh: Edinburgh University Press, pp. 3–23.

Jelinek, Elfriede (2005) 'Oscar Wilde', in *Ernst ist das Leben (Bunbury)*, Burgtheater im Akademietheater (Vienna) theatre programme, pp. 4–6.

Kaplan, Joel (1997) 'Wilde on the Stage', in Raby, Peter (ed.) *The Cambridge Companion to Oscar Wilde*, Cambridge: Cambridge University Press, pp. 249–75.

Kauer, Edmund Theodor (1955) ' "Bunbury" im Burgtheater', *Volksstimme* [Vienna], 1 February, [n.p.].

Kohlmayer, Rainer (1996) *Oscar Wilde in Deutschland und Österreich: Untersuchungen zur Rezeption der Komödien und zur Theorie der Bühnenübersetzung*, Tübingen: Max Niemeyer.

Lindner, Anton (1903) 'Gute und schlechte Frauen', *Fremden-Blatt* [Vienna], 20 January, 12.

Lohs, Lothar (2005) 'Lügner aus Prinzip', *Die Bühne* [Vienna], 2: 32+.

Lothar, Rudolph (1905) 'Vom Theater', *Die Wage* [Vienna], 8.2: 1204–06.

Lothar, Rudolph (1907) 'Von den Wiener Theatern 1906/07', *Bühne und Welt* [Hamburg], 9.1: 387–89.

Mayer, Sandra and Barbara Pfeifer (2007) 'The Reception of Oscar Wilde and Bernard Shaw in the Light of Early Twentieth-Century Austrian Censorship', *Platform*, 2.2: 59–75.

Michalzik, Peter (2005) 'Im Moosi-Sakko', *Frankfurter Rundschau*, 22 February, 16.

Newman, Ernest (1970) 'Oscar Wilde: A Literary Appreciation', in Beckson, Karl (ed.) *Oscar Wilde: The Critical Heritage*, London: Routledge, pp. 202–10.

O'Brien, George M. (1982) 'Cothurnus to Extempore: Theater in Austria since 1945', in Wright, William E. (ed.) *Austria since 1945*, Minneapolis: Center for Austrian Studies at the University of Minnesota, pp. 133–45.

Petsch, Barbara (2005) 'Geschlechter-Gewurl im Whirlpool', *Die Presse* [Vienna], 21 February, 15.

Petsch, Barbara (2006) 'Miss Schenk und Domina Lohner', *Die Presse* [Vienna], 28 January, [n.p.].

Pfister, Manfred (1990) 'Nachwort', in Oscar Wilde, *The Importance of Being Earnest: A Trivial Comedy for Serious People*, Stuttgart: Reclam, pp. 109–40.

Pohl, Ronald (2005a) 'Wohllebenskünstler in der Armutsfalle' (interview with Falk Richter), *Der Standard*, 20 February, 25; also at <http://derstandard.at/> [accessed 15 August 2009].

Pohl, Ronald (2005b) 'Luftbläschen in Oscars Wasserbad', *Der Standard*, 21 February, 24; also at <http://derstandard.at/> [accessed 15 August 2009].

Rathkolb, Oliver (2006) 'Ernst Lothar, Rückkehr in eine konstruierte Vergangenheit: Kulturpolitik in Österreich nach 1945', in Thunecke, Jörg (ed.) *Echo des Exils: Das Werk emigrierter österreichischer Schriftsteller nach 1945*, Wuppertal: Arco, pp. 279–95.

Richter, Falk (2005) 'Pointenporno: Notizen zu Bunbury', in *Ernst ist das Leben (Bunbury)*, Burgtheater im Akademietheater (Vienna) theatre programme, pp. 66–75.

Rollett, Edwin (1955) 'Faschingspremiere des Burgtheaters: "Bunbury" neu inszeniert', *Wiener Zeitung*, 1 February, 3.

Sammells, Neil (2004) 'Oscar Wilde and the Politics of Style', in Richards, Shaun (ed.) *The Cambridge Companion to Twentieth-Century Irish Drama*, Cambridge: Cambridge University Press, pp. 109–21.

Schneeberger, Peter (2005) 'Der Agit-Popper', *Profil*, 14 February, 122–23.

Shaw, Bernard (1905) 'Oskar Wilde', trans. Siegfried Trebitsch, *Neue Freie Presse* [Vienna], 23 April, 38.

Singer, Herta (1955) 'Lachstürme im Burgtheater: Die Komödie des Froh-Seins', *Der Abend* [Vienna], 31 January, [n.p.].

Stadelmaier, Gerhard (2005) 'Vom Kopf auf den Fummel', *Frankfurter Allgemeine Zeitung*, 21 February, 39.

Stokes, John (1994) 'Wilde Interpretations', *Modern Drama*, 37: 156–74.

Stokes, Leslie and Sewell (1937) *Oscar Wilde*, London: Martin Secker and Warburg.

Tartarotti, Guido (2006) 'Zwischen Kammerspielen und Löwinger-Bühne', *Kurier*, 28 January, 33.

'Theater- und Kunstnachrichten' (1905) *Neue Freie Presse* [Vienna], 10 December, 13.

'Theaterzeitung: Deutsches Volkstheater' (1905) *Illustrirtes Wiener Extrablatt* [Vienna], 10 December, 9.

Villiger Heilig, Barbara (2005) 'Unernst ist das Theater', *Neue Zürcher Zeitung*, 21 February, 18.

'Volkstheater' (1945) *Kleines Volksblatt* [Vienna], 25 December, [n.p.].

Weiss, Rudolf (1999) 'Terra Incognita, Populärkultur, intellektuelle Akrobatik: Das englische Drama im Wiener Theater der Jahrhundertwende', in Bachleitner, Norbert (ed.) *Beiträge zur Rezeption der britischen und irischen Literatur des 19. Jahrhunderts im deutschsprachigen Raum*, Amsterdam; Atlanta: Rodopi, pp. 345–405.

'Wiener Bürgertheater' (1907) *Illustrirtes Wiener Extrablatt* [Vienna], 6 January, 9.

Wilde, Oscar (2005) *Ernst ist das Leben (Bunbury)*, German stage version Elfriede Jelinek, trans. Karin Rausch, Burgtheater im Akademietheater (Vienna) theatre programme, pp. 7–62.

Yates, Willliam Edgar, Allyson Fiddler and John Warren (2001) 'Introduction', in Yates, Fiddler and Warren (eds) *From Perinet to Jelinek: Viennese Theatre in Its Political and Intellectual Context*, Oxford: Peter Lang, pp. 9–22.

Chapter 13. Composing Oscar: Settings of Wilde for the German Stage

Adler, Felix (1917) review in *Bohemia*, 30 January 1917, quoted in Mikuláš Bek (1995) 'On the Dramaturgy of Zemlinsky's 'Eine florentinische Tragodie'', *Cambridge Opera Journal*, 7.2: 165–74, p. 173.

Beaumont, Antony (2005) *Alexander Zemlinsky: Biographie*, trans. Dorothea Brinkmann, Vienna: Paul Zsolnay.

Blaukopf, Herta (ed.) (1988) *Gustav Mahler/Richard Strauss: Briefwechsel 1888–1911*, Munich; Zurich: Piper.

Bülow, Bernhard von (1930) *Denkwürdigkeiten*, Berlin: Ullstein.

Carpenter, Tethys (1989) 'Tonal and Dramatic Structure', in Puffett, Derrick (ed.) *Salome*, Cambridge: Cambridge University Press.

Engelbert, Tina (ed.) (2003) 'Mad, Scarlet Music: A Monthly Page Dedicated to Oscar Wilde and Music' (January), <http://www.irishdiaspora.net/ids/exhibits/239/Mad_Scarlet_Music.doc> [accessed 22 December 2008].

Flury, Philipp and Peter Kaufmann (1979) *O mein Papa... Paul Burkhard: Leben und Werk*, Zurich: Orell Füssli.

Flury, Richard (1950) *Lebenserinnerungen*, Derendingen: Habegger.

Heindl, Christian (2002) 'Biographie', in Heindl (ed.) *Paul Walter Fürst: Werke bei/Music published by Doblinger*, Vienna: Doblinger, pp. 3–4.

Lewinski, Wolf-Eberhard von (1964) review of Sutermeister's *Das Gespenst von Canterville*, *Allgemeine Zeitung* [Mainz], 9 September, [n.p.].

Mahler-Werfel, Alma (1963) *Mein Leben*, Frankfurt a.M.: Fischer.

'Musical notes from abroad' (1939) *The Musical Times*, 80.1157: 546–48.

Röhl, John (1994) *The Kaiser and His Court*, Cambridge: Cambridge University Press.

Röhl, John (ed.) (1979) *Philipp Eulenburgs politische Korrespondenz 1892–1895*, vol. 2, Boppard a.R.: Boldt.

Röhl, John (ed.) (1983) *Philipp Eulenburgs politische Korrespondenz 1895–1921*, vol. 3, Boppard a.R.: Boldt.

Schaeuble, Hans, diary MS in Zentralbibliothek Zürich.

Sombart, Nicolaus (1982) 'The Kaiser in His Epoch: Some Reflections on Wilhelmine Society, Sexuality and Culture', in Röhl, John and Nicolaus Sombart (eds) *Kaiser Wilhelm II: New Interpretations*, Cambridge: Cambridge University Press.

Strauss, Richard (1989) '"Salome"', in *Betrachtungen und Erinnerungen*, ed. Willi Schuh, Munich; Mainz: Piper & Schott, pp. 224–29.

Tschiedel, Joachim (2005) *Bernhard Sekles 1872–1934: Leben und Werk des Frankfurter Komponisten und Pädagogen*, Schriftenreihe zur Musik 33, Schneverdingen: Verlag für Musikbücher Karl Dieter Wagner.

Várkonyi, Mátyás, website: <http://3rdproof.com/matyasvarkonyi/navi.php?lang=en&page=cv> [accessed 22 December 2008].

Walton, Chris (2005) 'Beneath the Seventh Veil: Richard Strauss's *Salome* and Kaiser Wilhelm II', *The Musical Times*, 146.1893: 5–27.

Wolfer, René (1988) 'Spielpläne 1933–1987', in Riess, Curt (ed.) *Das Schauspielhaus Zürich: Sein oder Nichtsein eines ungewöhnlichen Theaters*, Munich; Vienna: Langen Müller, pp. 397–437.

W.P. (1964) review of Sutermeister's *Gespenst von Canterville*, *Süddeutsche Zeitung* [Munich], 9 September, [n.p.].

Zoppi, Rosina (ed.) *Die Oper im Knopfloch, Bunbury: Produktion 2004*, <http://www.operimknopfloch.ch/oik2004/pressestimme.html> [accessed 24 December 2008].

Chapter 14. From Continental Discourse to 'A Breath from a Better World': Oscar Wilde and Denmark

Translations

(1903) *Salomé*, trans. Paul Sarauw, Copenhagen: Dagmar Teateret.

(1905) *Dorian Grays Billede: Fantastisk Roman*, trans. Sten Drewsen, Copenhagen: Gyldendal; re-issued 1918 (under the title *Dorian Gray*), 1930 and 1962.

(1910a) *Den ideelle Ægtemand (IH)*, trans. Edgard Høyer, Copenhagen: Det Ny Teater.

(1910b) *Hvad hedder Han? (IBE)*, Copenhagen: Frederiksberg Teater.

(1910c) *Kvadet om Reading Tugthus (BRG)*, trans. Oskar V. Andersen, Copenhagen: Th. Johansens Forlag; re-issued 1928, 1944, 1994.

(1911) *Æventyr*, trans. Oskar V. Andersen, Copenhagen: Th. Johansens Antikvariats Forlag.

(1919) *Salomé* (libretto for Strauss's opera), trans. Julius Lehmann, Copenhagen: Kongelige Teater.

(1922) *Bunbury (IBE)*, trans. Niels Th. Thomsen, Copenhagen: Dagmar Teateret.

(1924) *En Kvinde uden Betydning (WNI)*, trans. Niels Th. Thomsen, Copenhagen: Dagmar Teateret.

(1927) *De Profundis*, trans. Marguerite Gamél, Copenhagen: Gyldendalske Boghandel.

(1944a) *Canterville Spøgelset og Lord Arthur Savilles Forbrydelse (CG and LASC)*, trans. K. Robert Adamsen, Copenhagen: Thaning & Appels Forlag; reissued 1970.

(1944b) *Eventyr*, trans. A. C. Normann, Odense: A. C. Normanns Forlag.

(1946) *Bunbury (IBE)*, trans. Mogens Lind, Copenhagen: Libri elegantiarum.

(1952) *Kapitalismen, Socialismen og Mennesket (SMUS)*, trans. and intro. Henning Kehler, Copenhagen: [n. pub.].

(1953a) *Kritikeren som Kunstner (CA)*, trans. and intro. Henning Kehler, Copenhagen: [n.pub.].

(1953b) *Dorian Grays billede*, trans. Grethe Juel Jørgsensen, Copenhagen: Hirschsprung; re-issued 1984.

(1955) *Balladen om Reading Tugthus (BRG)*, trans. Frederik J. Geddebro, Bjergby: Forlaget Bien.

(1962) *De Profundis*, trans. Ingeborg Buhl, Copenhagen: Steen Hasselbalchs Forlag.

(1991) *Fortællinger for børn* (Fairytales), trans. Knud Holst and Susanne Grønborg, Bagsværd: Carlsen.

(1993) *Eventyr*, trans. Jens Peder Agger, Copenhagen: Bogfabrikken.

(2000) *Den lykkelige prins og andre eventyr (HP* and *HOP)*, trans. Gerd Have, Copenhagen: Hernov.

(2006) *Billedet af Dorian Gray*, trans. Karen Dinesen, Frederiksberg: Det lille Forlag.

Criticism and reviews

Bang, Herman (1904) *Mikaël*, Copenhagen: Gyldendal.

Bang, Herman (1907) *Sælsomme Fortællinger*, Copenhagen: Gyldendal.

Bang, Herman (1922) *Gedanken zum Sexualitätsproblem*, ed. Dr Max Wasbutzki, preface Dr Siegfried Placzek, Bonn: A. Marcus & E. Weber.

Bang, Herman and Sven Lange (2008) *Mikaël: Skuespil i 5 Akter af Herman Bang og Sven Lange (efter romanen "Mikaël")*, ed. Knud Arne Jürgensen, Copenhagen: C. A. Reitzel.

Barfod, Thorkild (1944) review of the Royal Theatre production of *IBE*, *Fædrelandet* [Copenhagen], 11 November, [n.p.].

Bertz, Edvard (1905) 'Walt Whitman: Ein Characterbild', *Jahrbuch für sexuelle Zwischenstufen*, VII: 153–289.

Borg, Merete (1986) *Sceneinstruktøren Bang: Teatersyn og metode*, Copenhagen: Nyt Nordisk Forlag.

C., Hj. (1910) review of the Frederiksberg Theatre production of *IBE*: *Hvad hedder Han?*, *Politiken*, 5 October, [n.p.].

Gaulke, Johannes (1901) 'Oskar Wildes Dorian Gray', *Jahrbuch für sexuelle Zwischenstufen*, III: 275–92.

Geismar, Otto (1944) review of the Royal Theatre production of *IBE*, *Kristeligt Dagblad* [Copenhagen], 11 November, [n.p.].

Gnudtzman, Albert (1903) review of the Dagmar Theatre production of *Salomé*, *Teateret*, III: [n.p.].

Gregaard, Peer (1959) *Et Teater blev til: Det Ny Teater*, Copenhagen: Det Ny Teaterforlag.

'Hansen, Albert' [pseud. Carl Albert Hansen Fahlberg] (1901) 'H. C. Andersen: Beweis seiner Homosexualität', *Jahrbuch für sexuelle Zwischenstufen*, III: 203–31.

Hauch, A. F. (1944) review of the Royal Theatre production of *IBE*, *Børsen* [Copenhagen], 11 November, [n.p.].

Heede, Dag (2003) *Herman Bang: Mærkværdige læsninger; Toogfirs tableauer*, Odense: Syddansk Universitetsforlag.

Heede, Dag, Torben Lund, Knud Arne Jürgensen and Sten Rasmussen (2007) *Stoppet i Farten: Herman Bang i karikaturens troldspejl*, postscript Mette Winge, Copenhagen: Gyldendal.

Hending, Arnold (1942) *Valdemar Psilander*, Copenhagen: Urania.

Hirschfeld, Magnus von (ed.) (1899–1908) *Jahrbuch für sexuelle Zwischenstufen unter besonderer Berücksichtigung der Homosexualität*, Leipzig: Max Spohr.

Houmark, Christian (1950) *Timer der blev til Dage: Udgivet efter hans Død af Horatio*, Copenhagen: Thaning & Appels Forlag.

Jacobsen, Harry (1966) *Den tragiske Herman Bang*, Copenhagen: H. Hagerup.

Jensen, Johannes V. (1906) [n. title], *Politiken*, 30 November, [n.p.].

Jørgensen, Johannes (1910) review of Oskar V. Andersen's Danish translation of *BRG*, *Nationaltidende* [Copenhagen], 18 September, [n.p.].

Krohg, Christian (1999) *Fire Portretter/ Four Portraits*, trans. Jennifer Lloyd, Lysaker: Geelmuyden Kiese.

Levin, Paul (1905) review of Sten Drewsen's Danish translation of *PDG*, *Politiken*, 7 April, [n.p.].

Lindeballe, Poul (1944) 'Klunketidens sorte Faar', *Berlingske Aftenavis* [Copenhagen], 7 November, [n.p.].

Lindemann, Kelvin and Kai Normann Andersen (1936a) *Musen paa Bordet: En musikalsk Komedie frit efter Oscar Wildes Farce*, Copenhagen: Apolloteateret.

Lindemann, Kelvin (1936b) *Musen paa Bordet*, music Kai Normann Andersen, Copenhagen; Leipzig: Wilhelm Hansen Musik-Forlag.

Mikhail, E. H. (1978) *Oscar Wilde: An Annotated Bibliography of Criticism*, London: Macmillan.

Mikhail, E. H. (ed.) (1979) *Oscar Wilde: Interviews and Recollections*, 2 vols, London: Macmillan.

Nelson, Walter W. (1966) *Oscar Wilde in Sweden and Other Essays*, Dublin: Dublin University Press.

Østermark-Johansen, Lene (1998) *Sweetness and Strength: The Reception of Michelangelo in Late Victorian England*, Aldershot: Ashgate.

Prätorius, Numa (1901) 'Oskar Wilde: Ein Bericht', *Jahrbuch für sexuelle Zwischenstufen*, III: 265–75.

R., Christian (1910) review of Oskar V. Andersen's Danish translation of *BRG*, *Politiken*, 7 December, [n.p.].

Review of the Dagmar Theatre production of *Salomé* (1903) *Politiken*, 11 December, [n.p.].

Review of *Musen paa Bordet* (1936) *Berlingske Tidende* [Copenhagen], 15 November, [n.p.].

Review of the Ny Teater production of *IH* (1910) *Politiken*, 3 January, [n.p.].

Rosen, Wilhelm von (1993) *Månens kulør: Studier i dansk bøssehistorie 1628–1912*, 2 vols, Copenhagen: Rhodos.

Schmidt, Albrecht (1937) *I Liv og Kunst,* Copenhagen: H. Hagerup.

Schyberg, Frederik (1933) *Walt Whitman*, Copenhagen: Gyldendal.

Soya (1944) review of the Royal Theatre production of *IBE*, *Ekstra Bladet*, 11 November, [n.p.].

Thomsen, Ejnar (1948) 'Besættelse og Befrielse', in Henriques, Alf, Torben Krogh, Henry Hellsen, Poul Linneballe, Robert Neiiendam, Julius Clausen, Svend Erichsen and Ejnar Thomsen, *Teatret paa Kongens Nytorv 1748–1948*, Copenhagen: Berlingske Forlag, pp. 279–316.

Thomsen, Niels Th. (1920) *Oscar Wilde: Literaturbilleder fra det Moderne England*, Copenhagen: Privattryk.

Thomsen, Niels Th. (1932) *Oscar Wilde (1856–1900): An Introduction to the Performance of 'The Importance of Being Earnest'*, Copenhagen: Dansk Skolescene.

Tydeman, William and Steven Price (1996) *Wilde: Salome*, Plays in Production, Cambridge: Cambridge University Press.

Chapter 15. An Ideal Situation? The Importance of Oscar Wilde's Dramatic Work in Hungary

Translations (1st editions and major later editions)

(1903) *Lady Windermere legyezője* (*LWF*), trans. Tamás Moly, Budapest: Lampel.

(1904) *A boldog herceg. Modern mesék* (*HPOT*), trans. Imre Iván, Budapest: Sachs.

(1904) *Dorian Gray arczképe* (*PDG*), trans. Tivadar Konkoly, Budapest: Országos Irodalmi R. T.

(1905) *De Profundis*, trans. Géza Sztankay, Budapest: Országos Irodalmi R. T.

(1907) *Aforizmák* (Aphorisms), ed. and trans. Teréz Radó, Budapest: Lampel.

(1907) *Bunbury* (*IBE*), trans. Lajos Mikes, Budapest: Lampel.

(1907) *Az eszményi férj* (*IH*), trans. József Mihály, Budapest: Lampel.

(1907) *Flórenczi tragédia* (FT), trans. Marcell Benedek, Budapest: Lampel.

(1907) *Salomé*, trans. Géza Battlay, Budapest: Révai-Salamon.

(1908) *Gránátalmaház* (*HOP*), trans. Lajos Mikes, Budapest: Lampel.

(1908) *A readingi fegyház balladája* (BRG), trans. Antal Radó, Budapest: Lampel.

(1910) *A páduai hercegnő* (*DOP*), trans. Dezső Kosztolányi, Budapest: Lampel.

(1911) *Vera, a nihilista lány* (*VN*), trans. Kálmán Rozsnyay, Békéscsaba: Tevan.

(1912) *Az ember lelke* (SMUS), trans. Anna Winkler, Losoncz: Kármán.

(1916 [1922]) *Wilde Oszkár verseiből* (From the poems of Oscar Wilde), trans. Mihály Babits, Budapest: Athenaeum.

(1918) *A kritikus, mint művész* (*Intentions*), trans. Andor Halasi, Budapest: Athenaeum.

(1920) *A canterville-i kísértet* (CG), trans. Judit Tímár, Budapest: Genius.

(1921) *A readingi fegyház balladája* (BRG), trans. Árpád Tóth, Budapest: Dante.

(1922) *Bunbury* (*IBE*), trans. Sándor Hevesi, Budapest: Genius.
(1922) *Az eszményi férj* (*IH*), trans. Sándor Hevesi, Budapest: Genius.
(1922) *Lady Windermere legyezője* (*LWF*), trans. Sándor Hevesi, Budapest: Genius.
(1922) *Lord Arthur Savile bűne* (LASC), trans. Judit Tímár, Budapest: Genius.
(1923) *Dorian Gray arczképe* (*PDG*), trans. Dezső Kosztolányi, Budapest: Genius.
(1923) *Firenzei tragédia* (*FT*), trans. Dezső Kosztolányi, Budapest: Genius.
(1923) *A jelentéktelen asszony*, trans. Sándor Hevesi, Budapest: Génius.
(1923) *Salomé*, trans. Dezső Kosztolányi, Budapest: Génius.
(1923) *A szent parázna* (SCo), trans. Dezső Kosztolányi, Budapest: Genius.
(1924) *Bunbury* (*IBE*), trans. Frigyes Karinthy, *Színházi élet*, 41: 109–41.
(1924) *Versek* (Poems), trans. Antal Radó, Budapest: Lampel.
(1926) *Költemények* (Poems), trans. Dezső Kosztolányi, Budapest: Genius; repr. 1957, Budapest: Szépirodalmi.
(2000) *Oscar Wilde összes művei* (Complete works), ed. Zsolt Szántai, Szeged: Szukits.
(2006; 2007) *Dorian Gray arcképe* (*PDG*), trans. Dezső Kosztolányi, Szeged: Lazi; Budapest: Ulpius-ház.
(2008) *Az élet titka a művészet: Oscar Wilde füveskönyve* (The secret of life is art: Oscar Wilde's book of ideas), ed. and trans. Miklós Molnár, Szeged: Lazi.

Criticism and reviews

Ady, Endre (1987) *Publicisztikai írások*, Budapest: Szépirodalmi Kiadó.
Csík, István (1971) 'Hazudj igazat!', *Szolnok Megyei Néplap* [Szolnok], 30 December, [n.p.].
Czigány, Lóránt (2000) *A History of Hungarian Literature from the Earliest Times to the Mid–1970s* <http://mek.oszk.hu/02000/02042/html/> [accessed 25 August 2008].
Darvas, Szilárd (1949) 'Eszményi férj', *Világosság* [Budapest], 18 May, [n.p.].
Douglas, Alfred (1919) *Wilde és én*, trans. Dezső Kosztolányi, Budapest: Kultúra.
Egri, Péter (1983) *Törésvonalak: Drámai irányok az európai századfordulón*, Budapest: Gondolat.
Ézsaiás, Erzsébet (1981) 'Egy előadás paradoxonjai: Oscar Wilde bemutató Veszprémben', *Színház*, 14.4: 19–20.
Faludy, György (1949) '*Az eszményi férj*: Wilde-repríz a Kis Kamaraszínházban', *Népszava* [Budapest], 18 May, [n.p.].
Gajdó, Tamás (ed.) (2001) *Magyar Színháztörténet 1873–1920*, Budapest: Magyar Könyvklub, OszMI.
Gide, André (1925) *Oscar Wilde*, trans. Viktor Lányi, Budapest: Kultúra.
Hermann, István (1959) '*Lady Windermere legyezője*: Oscar Wilde darabjának felújítása a Madách Kamara Színházban', *Magyar Nemzet* [Budapest], 20 December, [n.p.].
Ignotus, Pál (1929) 'Faj és művészet', *Nyugat*, 22.11: 715–18.
Kállai Katalin (1995) 'Helyzet, jelentés. Oscar Wilde: *Salomé*', *Színház*, 28.3: 15–16.
Koltai, Tamás (1995) 'Fin de siècle', *Kritika*, 39.3: 16.
Kontler, László (1999) *Millennium in Central Europe: A History of Hungary*, Budapest: Atlantisz.
Kosztolányi, Dezső (1978) *Színházi esték*, vol. 1, Budapest: Szépirodalmi Könyvkiadó.
Lajosi, Krisztina (2002) 'The Reception of Oscar Wilde in Hungary: Translator as Critic - Critic as Artist – Translator as Artist', in Böker, Uwe, Richard Corballis and Julie A. Hibbard (eds) *The Importance of Reinventing Oscar: Versions of Wilde during the Last 100 Years*, Amsterdam; New York: Rodopi, pp. 257–67.
Langgaard, Halfdan (1907) *Wilde Oszkár*, trans. Tamás Moly, Budapest: Lampel.

Lemle, Géza (1959) '*Bunbury*: a Kamaraszínház évadnyitó előadása', *Napló* [Budapest], 23 September, [n.p.].

Lengyel, Menyhért (1909) '*Padua hercegnője*', *Nyugat*, 2.19: 386–87.

Lőcsei, Gabriella (1995) 'Szenvedélye a színház: Gábor Miklós rendez', *Magyar Nemzet* [Budapest], 7 January, pp. 19–20.

Lukács, György (1911) *A modern dráma fejlődésének története*, Budapest: Magvető.

Lukács, György (1977) *Ifjúkori művek (1902–1918)*, Budapest: Magvető.

Mészáros, Tamás (1978) 'Könnyű győzelmeink?', *Magyar Hírlap* [Budapest], 12 August, [n.p.].

Osvát, Ernő (1945) *Összes írásai*, Budapest: Nyugat Kiadó és Irodalmi R. T.

P. (1906) '*A jelentéktelen asszony*', *Budapest Hírlap*, 68.

Müller, Péter P. (1996) 'Oscar Wilde: *Salomé*', *Kritika*, 40.5: 43.

Rademacher, Jörg W. (2001) *Oscar Wilde*, trans. István Balázs, Budapest: M. Kvklub.

Rajk, András (1968) '*Bunbury*: Wilde operettszínészekkel', *Népszava* [Budapest], 9 February, [n.p.].

Schöpflin, Aladár (1926) '*Az eszményi férj* a nemzeti Színházban', *Nyugat*, 19.9: 842–43.

Schöpflin, Aladár (1928) 'Bunbury a Kamaraszínházban', *Nyugat*, 21.19: 494–95.

Simon, István (1960) '*Hazudj igazat*: Oscar Wilde vígjátéka a Szegedi Nemzeti Színházban', *Délmagyarország* [Szeged], 19 January, [n.p.].

Sn. (1907) '*Salomé*', *Budapesti Hírlap*, [n.d.], p. 69.

Szabó, Lőrinc (1921) 'Tóth Árpád Wilde-fordítása', *Nyugat*, 14.10: 790–93.

Szántó, Judit (2004) 'A Patyolat kevés. Oscar Wilde: *Az ideális férj*', *Színház*, 37.2: 34–35.

Szász, Zoltán (1908) 'Wilde Oszkár', *Nyugat*, 1.13: 650–78.

Szilágyi, Géza (1902) 'Wilde Oszkár', *Magyar Géniusz* [Budapest], 22 June, pp. 419–21.

Szini (1908) 'A mese alkonya', [n. pub.].

Szini, Gyula (1902) 'Wilde Oszkár', *Magyar Géniusz*, 30 August, pp. 582–83.

Török, András (1989) *Oscar Wilde világa*, Budapest: Európa Könyvkiadó.

Vass, László (1949) 'Független kritika *Az eszményi férj*-ről', *Független Magyarország* [Budapest],10 May, [n.p.].

Vámos, Anna (2004) 'Egy pompás "mai" színdarab', *A Radnóti szín Lapja*,13.1.

V. L. (2003) 'A kegyes csalás művészei', *Kisalföld* [Győr], 17 February, [n.p.].

Vöő, Gabriella (2009) 'A Congenial Race: Reflections on Irish Literature and National Character in the Hungarian Literary Journal *Nyugat*', in Kurdi, Mária (ed.) *Literary and Cultural Relations: Ireland, Hungary, and Central and Eastern Europe*, Dublin: Carysfort Press. pp. 139–62.

Chapter 16. Oscar Wilde and the Czech Decadence

Translations

(1895) 'Úpadek Lhaní' (DL), trans. Hugo Kosterka, *Moderní revue*, 2.3: 49–51, 2.4: 83–8, 2.5: 105–15, 2.6: 128–37.

(1896) 'Předmluva k románu Portrait Doriana Graye' (Preface to *PDG*), trans. Arnošt Procházka, *Moderní revue*, 3.1: 2–3.

(1899) 'Básně v prose: Umělec, Učedník' (PP: The Artist, The Disciple), trans. Arnošt Procházka, *Moderní revue*, 10.2: 59–60.

(1900) 'Mistr' (The Master), trans. Arnošt Procházka, *Moderní revue*, 11.7: 224–25.

(1901) *Ballada o žaláři v Readingu* (*BRG*), trans. Jiří Almar [Jiří Živný], Prague: Hugo Kosterka.

(1902) *Salome*, trans. anon., *Divadelní Listy*, 3.9: 235–38, 3.10: 263–66, 3.11: 287–90, 3.12: 317–18, 3.13: 345–52, 3.14: 371–72, 3.15: 391–94, 3.16: 423–24, 3.17: 447–50, 3.18–19: 473–38, 3.20: 515–18.

(1903–04) 'Kritik umělcem' (CA), trans. F. X. Šalda, *Volné směry*, 8.3: 77–81, 8.4: 111–18, 8.5: 159–66, 8.6: 187–92, 8.8: 251–57.

(1904) *Dvě knihy pohádek* (*HPOT, HOP*), trans. Marie Jesenská, intro. Josef Bartoš, Prague: J. Otto.

(1905) *Obraz Doriana Graye* (*PDG*), trans. Antonín Tille and Jaromír Borecký, Prague: Máj.

(1905) *Salome*, trans. Adi-Hidári-Ho, Prague: K. S. Sokol.

(1905) *Salome*, trans. Otakar Theer, intro. Václav Tille, Prague: J. Otto.

(1906) *De profundis* (*DP*), trans. Antonín Starý, intro. Miloš Marten, Prague: Kamilla Neumannová.

(1908) *Básně v prose* (PP), trans. Arnošt Procházka, Knihovna Moderní revue 46, Prague: Moderní revue.

(1908) *Dvě povídky* (SWS, MM), trans. Norbert Fomeš [Arnošt Procházka], Knihovna Moderní revue 47, Prague: Moderní revue.

(1908) *Úpadek lhaní* (DL), trans. Jaroslav Novák, Prague: Adámek.

(1908) *Zločin lorda Arthura Savila* (LASC); *Strašidlo Cantervillské* (CG), trans. Norbert Fomeš [Arnošt Procházka], Prague: Kamilla Neumannová.

(1909) *Portrait Mr. W.H.*, *Sfinga bez tajemství, Vzorný milionář, Básně v prose, Ballada o žaláři v Readingu* (PMWH, SWS, MM, PP, *BRG*), trans. Jiří Živný (*BRG*) and Norbert Fomeš [Arnošt Procházka], Prague: Kamilla Neumannová.

(1909) *Essaie* (SMUS, ERA, L'Envoi, Personal Impressions of America), trans. Norbert Fomeš [Arnošt Procházka], Prague: Kamilla Neumannová.

(1909) *Kritik umělcem* (CA), trans. Jaroslav Novák, Prague: Adámek.

(1910) *Básně* (*Poems*), trans. Antonín Klášterský, Prague: J. Otto

(1911) *Pravda masek* (TM), trans. Jaroslav Novák, Prague: A. Hynek.

(1911) *Salome*, trans. Julius Schmitt, Prague: O. Štáfl.

(1911) *Vévodkyně Padovská* (*DOP*), trans. Arnošt Procházka, Prague: Kamilla Neumannová.

(1918) *Florencká tragedie a Svatá kurtisana aneb Žena pokrytá drahokamy* (FT, SCo), trans. Jarmil Krecar, Prague: Ludvík Bradáč.

(1918) *Salome*, trans. Jarmil Krecar, Prague: Ludvík Bradáč.

(1918) *Slavík a růže* (NR), trans. anon., Knihovna Moderní revue 65, Prague: Moderní revue.

(1919) *Kněz a ministrant a nevydané dosud fragmenty z De profundis* (PA and extracts from *DP*), trans. Jan Rey, Prague: Grosman a Svoboda.

(1919) *Vějíř lady Windermereové* (*LWF*), trans. Jan Havlasa, Prague: Máj.

(1921) *Oscar Wilde před soudem* (The Oscar Wilde Trial: Records), trans. Jarmil Krecar, Prague: K. Jánský.

(1930) *Strašidlo cantervillské* (CG), trans. Arnošt Procházka, Prague: E. Janská.

Secondary criticism

Bednaříková, Hana (2000) *Česká dekadence*, Brno: Centrum pro studium demokracie a kultury.

Blümlová, Dagmar (1999) 'Václav Tille – historik lidské duše', in Blüml, Josef, Dagmar Blümlová and Bohumil Jiroušek (eds) *Jihočeši v české historické vědě*, České Budějovice: Jihočeská univerzita, pp. 59–77.

Breisky, Arthur (1997a) *V království chimér: korespondence a rukopisy z let 1902–1910*, ed. Luboš Merhaut, Prague: Thyrsus.

Breisky, Arthur (1997b) *Triumf zla: Dvě novely*, eds Gabriela M. Zemanová and Aleš Zach, Prague: Thyrsus.

Chaloupka, Bohuslav (1895) 'Budoucí umění', *Moderní revue*, 1.6: 121–26.

Červený, Jiří (1959) *Červená sedma*, Prague: Orbis.

Ellmann, Richard (1988) *Oscar Wilde*, London: Penguin; orig. pub. 1987, London: Hamilton.

Fiala, Kamil (1907) 'Wilde a Strauss', *Moderní revue*, 13.2: 99–100.

Herben, Jan (1936) *Kniha vzpomínek*, Prague: Družstevní práce.

Karásek ze Lvovic, Jiří (1895a) 'O kritice jako žánru uměleckém', *Moderní revue*, 1.6: 130–33.

Karásek ze Lvovic, Jiří (1895b) untitled article, *Literární Listy*, 16.16: 274.

Karásek ze Lvovic, Jiří (1901) 'Oscar Wilde', *Moderní revue*, 7.2: 119–21.

Karásek ze Lvovic, Jiří (1905) *Apollonius z Tyany*, Prague: Hejda & Tuček.

Karásek ze Lvovic, Jiří (1923) *Zastřený obraz*, Prague: Aventinum.

Karásek ze Lvovic, Jiří (1924) *Román Manfreda Macmillena*, Prague: Aventinum.

Karásek ze Lvovic, Jiří (1925) *Ganymedes*, Prague: Aventinum.

Karásek ze Lvovic, Jiří (1926) *Renaissanční touhy v umění*, Prague: Aventinum.

Karásek ze Lvovic, Jiří (1994) *Vzpomínky*, Prague: Thyrsus.

Klincman, Miloš (1918) 'Knižní úpravy', *Moderní revue*, 24.6: 294.

Krecar, Jarmil (1917) *Sňaté masky*, Prague: Ludvík Bradáč.

Krecar, Jarmil (1924) *Glossy do cizích knih*, Prague: Ludvík Bradáč.

Larvová, Hana (1998) 'A Pilgrim to Infinity', in Larvová (ed.) *Jan Konůpek: A Pilgrim to Infinity*, trans. Jan Valeška and Ivan Vomáčka, Prague: Galerie hlavního města Prahy, pp. 15–69.

Lipanský, Jetřich (1929) *Jiří Karásek ze Lvovic: Essay*, Veselí pod Čepí: Edice Izmael.

Marten, Miloš (1904) 'Měsíční přehled', *Moderní revue*, 10.9: 409–10.

Merhaut, Luboš (2006) 'A Summit and Abyss in One', in Urban, Otto M. (ed.) *Decadence: In Morbid Colours; Art and the Idea of Decadence in the Bohemian Lands 1880–1914*, Prague: Obecní dům; Arbor vitae, pp. 41–57.

Niva (1895) 5.18: 291, 5.19: 314.

Novák, Arne, Rudolf Havel and Antonín Grund (1946) *Stručné dějiny literatury české*, Olomouc: R. Promberger.

'Oscar Wilde' (1895) *Čas*, 9.18: 276–77, 9.20: 309.

Podroužek, Jaroslav (1945) *Fragment zastřeného osudu*, Prague: ELK.

Procházka, Arnošt (1895) 'Immoralita v umění', *Moderní revue*, 1.5: 115–18.

[Procházka, Arnošt and Jiří Karásek ze Lvovic] (1895) 'Kritika', *Moderní revue*, 1.3 (June): 70–72.

Reichmann, Jan (1919) 'Oscar Wilde a české písemnictví', in Oscar Wilde, *Vějíř lady Windermerové*, trans. Jan Havlasa, Prague: Nakladatelství Jana Havlasy.

'Rozhledy časopisecké' (1895) *Studentský sborník strany neodvislé*, 1: 11–12.

Schauer, Hubert Gordon (1917) *Spisy*, Prague: Kamilla Neumannová.

Soldan, Fedor (1941) *Jiří Karásek ze Lvovic*, Prague: Prokop Toman.

'Sursum' [Tomáš Garrigue Masaryk, Josef Svatopluk Machar and František Václav Krejčí] (1895) 'Rozhledy časopisecké', *Naše Doba*, 2.8: 752–53, 2.9: 846.

Šalda, František Xaver (1963) 'Orientace staré a nové' [1925], in *Soubor díla F. X. Šaldy*, gen. eds Jan Mukařovský and Felix Vodička, vol. 22: *Kritické projevy – 13, 1925–1928*, ed. Emanuel Macek, Prague: Československý spisovatel, pp. 18–28.

Šalda, František Xaver (1949) 'Synthetism v novém umění' [1892], in *Soubor díla F. X. Šaldy*, gen. eds Jan Mukařovský, Václav Černý, Felix Vodička and Jiří Pistorius, vol. 10: *Kritické projevy – 1, 1892–1893*, ed. Jiří Pistorius, Prague: Melantrich, pp. 11–54.

Šld [Šalda, František Xaver] (1908) *Wilde, Oscar*, in *Ottův slovník naučný*, Prague: J. Otto, 27: 233–36.

Thomas, Alfred (1999) 'Sadomasochistický národ: Umění a sexualita v české literatuře 19. století', in Petrbok, Václav (ed.) *Sex a tabu v české kultuře 19. století*, Prague: Academia, pp. 172–84.

Tille, Václav (1904) 'Oskar Wilde', *Nová česká revue*, 4: 267–76.

Urban, Otto M. (2006) 'Introduction: The Space of Decadence', in Urban (ed.) *Decadence: In Morbid Colours; Art and the Idea of Decadence in the Bohemian Lands 1880–1914*, Prague: Arbor vitae, pp. 11–17.

Vévoda, Rudolf (1999) 'Sodoma: Předtím a potom', in Petrbok, Václav (ed.) *Sex a tabu v české kultuře 19. století*, Prague: Academia, pp. 217–26.

Chapter 17. The 'Byron of Kipling's England': Oscar Wilde in Croatia

Translations

(1897) *Der Geist von Canterville* (CG) trans. Anna Marie von Boehn, Munich: Max von Boehn.

(1899) 'Básně v prose: Umělec; Učedník' (PP: The Artist, The Disciple), trans. Arnošt Procházka, *Moderní revue* [Prague], 10.2: 59–60; in Czech.

(1900) 'Umjetnik' (The Artist), trans. Vladimir Jelovšek, *Svjetlo* [Karlovac], 14 October, 9.

(1905) *Salomé*, trans. Julije Benešić and Nikola Andrić, MS at Croatian Academy of Sciences and Arts, Zagreb.

(1906) 'Pjesme u prozi: Umjetnik, Dobrotvor, Učitelj' (PP: The Artist, DG, The Master), trans. Mel, *Novi srbobran* [Zagreb], 3/16 August, 1; in Cyrillic.

(1906) 'Pjesme u prozi: U kući sudišta, Učitelj nauke' (PP: HJ, The Teacher of Wisdom [1st instalment]) trans. Mel, *Novi srbobran* [Zagreb], 4/17 August, 1; in Cyrillic.

(1906) 'Pjesme u prozi' (PP), trans. Mel, *Novi srbobran* [Zagreb], 5/18 August, 1–2; 2nd instalment of 'The Teacher of Wisdom' in Cyrillic.

(1906–07) 'Učenik' (The Disciple), trans. Laetus [Miroslav Schlesinger], *Domovina*, 18.6: 95–96.

(1907) 'Dies irae', trans. B. D., *Srđ* [Dubrovnik], 15 September, 772.

(1908) 'Iz pjesama u prozi: Umjetnik, Dobrotvor, Učenik, Učitelj, Na sudu' (From PP: The Artist, DG, The Disciple, The Master, HJ), *Narodne novine* [Zagreb], 29 May, 1.

(1908) *Dorian Gray*, trans. Artur Schneider, Zagreb: Hrvatska smotra.

(1908) 'Crvena ruža' (NR), *Hrvatska smotra* [Zagreb], 4: 350–51.

(1909) *Fjorentinska tragedija* (FT), trans. Ivo Vojnović, *Ilustrovani obzor* [Zagreb], 14 February, 97–107.

(1909) 'Učitelj mudrosti' (The Teacher of Wisdom), *Ilustrovani Obzor* [Zagreb], 7 November, 732–34.

(1910) 'Doživjela priča' (Recollected story), 'Umjetnik' (The Artist), 'Posrednik' (DG), trans. Filip Stilinović, *Mi* [Osijek], 1: 99–100. The 1st is a story from Gide's recollections of Wilde beginning: 'There was once a man who was beloved in his village for the tales he told. [...] I have seen nothing'.

(1911) *Priče*, trans. August Harambašić, Zagreb: the trans.; short stories incl. HP, NR,

DF, SG, and PP: The Artist, DG, The Disciple, The Master, HJ, The Teacher of Wisdom, MM.

(1913) 'Balada o tamnici u Readingu' (*BRG*), trans. Krešimir Kovačić, *Karlovac*, 2.46: 1, 47: 1–2; trans. incl. parts 1, 2 and 6 stanzas of part 3, totalling 210 lines.

(1913) 'Pjesme u prozi: Umjetnik, Dobročinilac, Učenik, Meštar, Sudna kuća' (PP: The Artist, DG, The Disciple, The Master, HJ), *Hrvatska rieč* [Šibenik], 6 May, 1–2.

(1913) 'Pjesme u prozi: Učitelj mudrosti' (The Teacher of Wisdom), *Hrvatska rieč* [Šibenik], 10 May, 1–2.

(1913) 'Sretni kraljević' (HP), *Hrvatska rieč* [Šibenik], 27, 29 and 31 May, 1.

(1913) 'Model i milijunaš' (MM), *Hrvatska rieč* [Šibenik], 12 and 14 June, 1.

(1913) 'Sebični div' (SG), *Hrvatska rieč* [Šibenik], 19 June, 1–2.

(1913) 'Mladi kralj' (YK), trans. Fran Galović, *Prosvjeta, tečaj XXI*, September, 628–42; repub. in Fran Galović (1942) *Članci i kritike (1902–1914)* (Articles and criticism 1902–1914), Zagreb: Izdanje Hrvatskog izdavačkog bibliografskog zavoda, pp. 302–15.

(1913) *Sablast od Cantervilla* (CG), Knjižnica Zabavna 4, Zagreb: Nakladom Kr. Zem. Tiskare; incl. *Salomé*, 'Sfinga bez tajni' (SWS), 'Ribar i njegova duša' (FHS), 'Slavuj i ruža' (NR), 'Sretan kraljević' (HP), some poems in prose and aphorisms.

(1915) *De profundis*, trans. Isidora Sekulić. Belgrade: S. B. Cvijanović; in Serbian.

(1915) *Saloma*, trans. Andro Mitrović, Biblioteka opernih i operetnih tekstova 42, Zagreb: Nakladom Adademske knjižare Gjure Trpinca; trans. of the libretto of Strauss's opera.

(1917) 'Mladi kralj' (YK), *Hrvatska njiva* [Zagreb], 1.29: 525–26; 1.30: 540–42.

(1918, 1920) *Mladi kralj i druge pripovijesti* (*HPOT*), trans. Iso Velikanović, ed. and illus. Ljubo Babić, Zagreb: Naklada knjižare Mirka Breyera.

(1920) *Dorian Gray*, trans. Artur Schneider, Zagreb: Naklada St. Kugli, Knjižara Kr. Sveučilišta i Jugoslavenske akademije.

(1920) *Slika Dorijana Greja* (*PDG*), trans. Artur Schneider, Zagreb: Naklada St. Kugli, Knjižara Kr. Sveučilišta i Jugoslavenske akademije; in Cyrillic.

(1920) *Slika Dorijana Graya* (*PDG*), trans. David S. Pijade, foreword Miloš Crnjanski. Vukovar, Belgrade: Savremena biblioteka.

(1920) *Zločin lorda Artura Savilea* (*LASCOS*), trans. Milan Drvodelić, Svjetska biblioteka vol. 37–38, Koprivnica: Knjigotiskara V. Vošicki; incl. SWS and some poems in prose.

(1920) 'Činilac dobra' (DG), trans. Nikola Karlić, *Nezavisnost: glasilo organizacije hrvatske zajednice za gradove Bjelovar, Križevac i okolicu* [Bjelovar], 22 May, 1–2.

(1922) 'Umjetnik', 'Kuća suda' (The Artist, HJ),*Vjerni drug* [Zagreb], 1 May, 17–18.

(1923) 'Tri pjesme u prozi: Umjetnik, Učenik, Učitelj' (Three poems in prose: The Artist, The Disciple, The Master), *Lipa* [Zagreb], 1.8: 57–58.

(1923) 'Pjesme u prozi: Učitelj, Učenik' (PP: The Master, The Disciple), *Dom i svijet* [Split], 15 December, 429.

(1925) 'Sud' (HJ) *Podravska oblast* [Varaždin], 24 December, 1.

([1927]) *Zvjezdan* (SC), adapted for stage and ed. Mladen Širola, Dječje pozorište 9, Zagreb: Naklada Knjižare St. Kugli.

(1928) 'Kuća suda' (HJ), 'Dobročinitelj' (DG), *Hrvatska sloboda* [Karlovac], 1 June, 2.

([1920s]) *Dvije priče* (Two stories: HP & NR), Zagreb: Naklada Ivana Smojvera.

(1933) *De profundis*, trans. V. M., Tisuću najljepših novela 52–54, Zagreb: Slovo.

(1937) 'Requiescat', trans. Ton Smerdel, *Obitelj*, 9.44: 828.

(1945) 'Kuća bludnica' (The Harlot House) trans. Ivan Goran Kovačić), *Republika* [Zagreb], 1.3 (December): 186–87.

(1947) 'Impression du matin', 'Uskrs' (Easter day), 'Kuća bludnica' (The Harlot

House), trans. Ivan Goran Kovačić, in *Prijevodi strane lirike* (Translations of world lyrics), Zagreb: Nakladni zavod Hrvatske, pp. 77–80. repr. in Ivan Goran Kovačić (1983) *Sabrana djela, 4: Pjesme; Prepjevi* (Collected works, 4: Poems, translations), ed. Dragutin Tadijanović, Zagreb: Jugoslavenska akademija znanosti i umjetnosti, Nakladni zavod Matice hrvatske, Globus, Sveučilišna naklada Liber, pp. 442–45.

[1930s–40s] 'Sonet slobodi' (Sonnet to Liberty) [1st 7 lines only], 'Simfonija u žutom' (Symphony in Yellow), trans. Ivan Goran Kovačić, unpub.

(1953) *Slika Doriana Graya* (*PDG*), trans. Zlatko Gorjan, afterword Ivo Hergešić, Zagreb: Zora.

(1954) *Three Stories* (NR, HP and DF), eds Mira Vodvarka-Kočonda and Ivana Jonke-Gajer, Zagreb: Školska knjiga; incl. interpretations and dictionary; repr. 1958, 1963, 1965, 1967, 1972, 1974, 1986.

(1955) *Bajke: Sretni kraljević i druge bajke; Kuća mogranja* (Fairy tales: *HPOT, HOP*), trans. Stjepan Krešić, Zagreb: Mladost, Svjetski klasici; texts in Croatian and English.

(1956) *Bajke* (Fairy tales), trans. Smiljana Kršić, Sarajevo; Zagreb: Svjetlost, printed Zavod Ognjen Prica Zagreb, Biblioteka Proljeće; incl. HP, NR, SG, DF, RR; repr. 1963.

(1956) *Duša čovjeka u socijalizmu* (SMUS), trans. Staniša N. Kostić, Zagreb: IBI.

(1956) 'Javna kuća' (The Harlot House), in Slamnig, Ivan and Antun Šoljan (trans. and eds) *Suvremena engleska poezija: antologija*, Zagreb: Lykos, p. 9.

(1961) 'Balada o Radingu' (*BRG*), trans. Zlatko Gorjan, intro. Ivo Hergešić, *Mogućnosti* [Split], 11: 1126–44.

(1965) 'Requiescat', trans. Mira Šunjić, in Ježić, Slavko (ed.) *Antologija svjetske lirike*, Zagreb: Naprijed, p. 541.

(1965) 'Impression du matin', trans. Ivan Goran Kovačić, in Ježić, Slavko (ed.) *Antologija svjetske lirike*, Zagreb: Naprijed, p. 542.

(1965) 'Balada o Readinškoj tamnici' (*BRG*), trans. Slavko Ježić, in Ježić, Salvko (ed.) *Antologija svjetske lirike*, Zagreb: Naprijed, p. 542; last 3 stanzas of part 6 only.

(1965) *Saloma* [excerpt], trans. Dubravka Matošić, 'Jutro' (Impression du matin), trans. Ivan Goran Kovačić, in Matošić, Joe (ed.) *Izbor remek-djela svjetske erotske ljubavne literature: proza-drama-poezija* (A selection of masterpieces of the erotic literatue and the literature of love: prose-drama-poetry), Zagreb: Vjesnik, pp. 458–64.

(1966) 'Ave Maria gratia plena', trans. Tin Ujević [1940–55], in Ujević, *Postuma I: Pjesme, pjesničke proze, prepjevi* (Poems, poems in prose, translations), Zagreb: Znanje, p. 598.

(1966) 'Sebični div' (SG), *Mali koncil* [Zagreb], December, pp. 12–14.; repr. in Wilde 2007.

(1968) *Duša čovjeka u socijalizmu* (SMUS), trans. Staniša N. Kostić, Sisak: Jedinstvo.

(1969) 'Sebični div' (SG), trans. Stjepan Krešić, in Šoljan, Antun (ed.) *100 najljepših svjetskih bajki* (100 of the world's best fables), Zagreb: Stvarnost, pp. 149–52.

(1969) *Slika Doriana Graya* (*PDG*), trans. Zlatko Gorjan, foreword and afterword Ivo Hergešić, Zagreb: Stvarnost.

(1970) 'E tenebris, Iz "Sjena" ' (E tenebris), trans. and ed. Krešimir Mlač, in Mlač (ed.) *U tlocrt urisan: prepjevi duhovne lirike* (Inscribed into the ground plan: translations of spiritual lyrics), Zagreb: the author, p. 38.

(1970) 'E tenebris', trans. Krešimir Mlač, in Kokša, Đuro (ed.) *Zapadna duhovna lirika* (Western spiritual lyrics), Rome: Alma Roma, p. 242.

(1978) 'Balada o redinškoj tamnici' (*BRG*), trans. Ivo Andrić, *Književnost* [Belgrade], 10: 1701–02.

(1986) *Slavuj i ruža i druge pripovijesti* (NR and other stories), trans. Iso Velikanović, illus. Ljubo Babić, Zagreb: Sveučilišna naklada Liber, Rijeka: Liburnija; repr. 1987.

(1987) *Slika Doriana Graya* (*PDG*), trans. Zdenko Novački, Zagreb: Mladost; repr. 1989.

(1987) *Balada o tamnici u Readingu i druge pjesme* (*BRG* and other poems), trans. Luko Paljetak, Zagreb: Znanje.

(1987) *Socijalizam i ljudska duša; De profundis* (*SMUS; DP*), trans. Zlatko Crnković, Zagreb: Grafički zavod Hrvatske; foreword to *DP* by Vyvyan Holland, pp. 69–76.

(1989) *Saloma*, trans. Boris B. Horvat, *Forum* [Zagreb], 28.7/8 (July–August): 51–72.

(1993) 'Samoživi div' (SG), in Težak, Dubravka (ed.) *Priče o dobru, priče o zlu: priručnik za razvijanje moralnog prosuđivanja u djece* (Tales about good and evil: a handbook for developing moral judgement in children), Zagreb: Školska knjiga, pp. 177–79; repr. 1996, 2005.

(1993) *Sretni kraljević i druge pripovijesti* (*HPOT*), trans. Pavel Gregorić, Zagreb: EMINEX; repr. 1995.

(1994) *Sretni kraljević i druge pripovijesti* (*HPOT*), trans. Luko Paljetak, Biblioteka Stribor, Zagreb: Znanje; repr. 1997, 2nd edn 2004, repr. 2007, repr. 2009, Zagreb: Tisak, Vjesnik.

(1997) *Vera ili nihilisti* (*VN*), trans. Dominick Andreas Varga, *Forum* [Zagreb], 36.69 (11/12): 1455–1503.

(1998) 'Slavuj i ruža' (NR), 'Sretni kraljević' (HP), trans. Stjepan Krešić, in Težak, Dubravka (ed.) *Bajke: antolgija* (Fairy tales: an anthology), Zagreb: Divič, pp. 199–213; repr. 2001.

(1999) *Bajke* (Fairy tales: SG, HP), trans. and ed. Dinka Juričić, Zagreb: Školska knjiga.

(1999) *Sretni kraljević i druge bajke* (*HPOT*)*; Kuća mogranja* (*HOP*), trans. Stjepan Krešić, Zagreb: DiVič.

(1999) *Priče za djecu* (Fairy tales for children), trans. Vesna Perić, Zagreb: Egmont; incl. NR, DF, SG, RR, YK, HP.

(1999) 'Aforizmi' (Aphorisms), *Europski glasnik*, 4.4: 260, 276, 322, 354, 378, 558, 578, 586, 612, 714, 812, 862, 905, 911, 912, 925, 926, 944, 952.

(2000a) *Slika Doriana Graya* (*PDG*), trans. Zlatko Gorjan, afterword Ivo Hergešić, Biblioteka Svjetski klasici, Split: Marjan knjiga.

(2000b) *Slika Doriana Graya* (*PDG*), trans. Zlatko Gorjan, afterword Darko Glavan, Biblioteka Stranci u noći, Koprivnica: Šareni dućan.

(2000) *Sretni princ i druge bajke* (*HPOT*), trans. Luko Paljetak, Zagreb: Školska knjiga, Grafički zavod Hrvatske; repr. 2002, 2004.

(2000) *Sebični div* (SG), trans. Luko Paljetak, Biblioteka List, Zagreb: Kašmir promet.

(2000) *Zločeste misli* (Epigrams and aphorisms), trans. Sado Terzić, Biblioteka Mali mrav, Koprivnica: Šareni dućan.

(2001) *Sretni kraljević i druge bajke* (*HPOT*), trans. Pavel Gregorić, Biblioteka Lektirna knjiga, Zagreb: ABC naklada.

(2001) *Sretni kraljević i druge bajke* (*HPOT*), trans. Dubravko Zebić, Biblioteka Učilišno štivo: lektira, Zagreb: Zagrebačka stvarnost.

(2001) *De profundis*, trans. Zlatko Crnković, Zagreb: V. B. Z.

(2001) *Fjorentinska tragedija* (FT), trans. Ivo Vojnović, *Dubrovnik*, 12.1: 43–66.

(2002) *Pjesme u prozi* (PP), trans. Luko Paljetak, afterword André Gide, trans. from French Višnja Machiedo, illus. Duško Šibl, Biblioteka Salona, Zagreb: Ceres; texts in Croatian and English.

(2002) *Sretni princ i druge priče* (*HPOT*), trans. Predrag Raos, Zagreb: Mozaik knjiga, Grafomark; repr. 2004 in special edn of *Večernji list*.

(2003) *Slika Doriana Graya* (*PDG*), trans. Vesna Mlinarec, Split; Široki Brijeg: Hercegtisak.

(2006) *Sretni princ* (HP), trans. Ludwig Bauer, Biblioteka list, Zagreb: Kašmir promet.

(2005) 'Sfinga bez tajne' (SWS), trans. Nataša Demirović, in Boban, Vjekoslav (ed.) *Irske kratke priče: antologija* (Irish short stories: an anthology), Zagreb: Naklada Jurčić, Grafocentar, pp. 119–27.

(2007) 'Sebični div' (SG), in Tomić, Sonja (ed.) *Vatrene ptice: 100 odabranih priča iz Makove škrinje* (Fire-like birds: 100 stories selected from Mak's box), Zagreb: Glas koncila, pp. 20–24.

(2008) *Slika Doriana Graya* (*PDG*), trans. Zlatko Gorjan, Zagreb: Europapress.

(2008) *Bajke* (Fairy tales), trans. Ludwig Bauer, Zagreb: Profil; incl. HP, NR, SG in Croatian and English.

(2008) *Sretni kraljević i druge bajke* (*HPOT*), trans. Pavel Gregorić, Biblioteka ABC, Varaždin: Katarina Zrinski.

(2009) *Intencije* (*Intentions*), trans. Damjan Lalović, afterword Lada Čale Feldman, Biblioteka Književna smotra, Zagreb: Hrvatsko filološko društvo, Disput, Feroproms.

(2009) *Sretni kraljević i druge pripovijesti* (*HPOT*), trans. Luko Paljetak, Biblioteka Stribor, special ed. Book 7, Zagreb: Znanje, Jutarnji list, Vjesnik.

(2010) *Aristotel uz popodnevni čaj: ogledi, rasprave, recenzije* (Ad dies vitae – five o'clock tea), trans. Robertino Bartolec, Varaždin: Modernist.

(2010) *Balada o tamnici u Readingu* (*BRG*), trans. and afterword Luko Paljetak, Biblioteka Psyche, Book 4, Dubrovnik: Matica hrvatska, Ogranak; Zagreb: Durieux.

(2010) *Duh iz Cantervillea* (*CG*), trans. Luka Posarić, Zagreb: Partenon, Grafix.

(2010) *Idealan muž* (*IH*), trans. Đuro Roić, Zagreb: Kašmir promet; Čakovec: Zrinski.

(2010) 'Sebični div' (SG), in Tomić, Sanja (ed.) *Vatrene ptice: odabrane priče iz Makove škrinje, Mali koncil –MAK 1966-2009*, (Fire-like birds: stories selected from Mak's box, Mali koncil – MAK 1966-2009), Zagreb: Glas Koncila; Lukavec: Grafika Markulin, pp. 20-24, 2nd enlarged edition.

(2010) Udovičić Pleština, Željka. *Saloma* (*Salomé*) based on the motifs of Oscar Wilde's play, adapted for the stage by Željka Udovičić and Damir Zlatar Frey, Biblioteka INK, Pula: Istarsko narodno kazalište, Gradsko kazalište; Pula: MPS.

(2012) 'Cantervilleski duh' (CG), in Matković, Tomislav (ed.) *Horor priče za laku noć 3* (Horror Stories for Good Night 3)*,* Zagreb: Zagrebačka naklada, De Ve De, pp. 339-63.

(2012) *Sretni kraljević i druge pripovijesti* (*HPOT*), trans. and afterword by Luko Paljetak, Biblioteka Stribor, Zagreb: Znanje, 3rd ed.

Selected secondary works

'40. godišnjica smrti Oscara Wildea' (1940) *Hrvatska revija*, 13.12: 671–72; signed 'an.'.

Barbieri, Marija (2003) 'Neki aspekti recepcije glazbeno-scenskog opusa Richarda Straussa u Hrvatskoj, I. dio: *Salome* i *Der Rosenkavalier*' (Some aspects of the reception of music and stage works by Richard Strauss in Croatia, part 1: *Salomé* and *Der Rosenkavalier*), *Arti musices: Hrvatski muzikološki zbornik*, 34.1–2: 133–68.

Batušić, Nikola (2000) 'Galovićeva *Tamara* i Wildeova *Saloma*', in Hećimović, Branko (ed.) *Krležini dani u Osijeku 1999*, Zagreb: Zavod za povijest hrvatske književnosti, kazališta i glazbe HAZU, Odsjek za povijest hrvatskog kazališta; Osijek: Hrvatsko narodno kazalište, Pedagoški fakultet, pp. 50–54.

Begović, Milan (1920) 'Wilde: *Saloma*', *Novosti* [Zagreb], 21 September, 1–2; repub. in Begović (2003) *Sabrana djela*, 17: *Studije i kritike*, Zagreb: Naklada Ljevak, 17: 76–80.

Begović, Milan (1921) 'Nanovo uvježbana drama jedne dobre žene: *Lepeza Lady*

Windermerove od Oscara Wildea, režija Ivo pl. Raić 19. ožujka 1921', *Novosti*, 22 March, 4; repub. in Begović 2003, 104–06.

Begović, Milan (1930) 'Gđa Traute Carlsen u Zagrebu: *Ein idealer Gatte* od Oscara Wildea, režija Dr. Eugen Robert', *Novosti*, 14 December, 10; repub. in Begović 2003, 321–25.

Begović, Milan (2003) *Sabrana djela*, 18.1: *Theatralia I: Prikazi kazališnih predstava (1909–1944)*, Zagreb: Naklada Ljevak, Hrvatska akademija znanosti i umjetnosti.

Benešić, Julije (1909) 'Oscar Wilde: Idealan muž', *Narodne novine* [Zagreb], 19 May, 5; repub. Julije Benešić (1943) *Kritike i članci*, Zagreb: Izdanje Hrvatskog izdavalačkog bibliografskog zavoda, pp. 26–29.

Blažeković, Tatjana (1957) 'Engleska književnost i njene veze s Hrvatskom Modernom (1900–1914)' (unpublished doctoral thesis, University of Zagreb).

Bridgwater, Patrick (1999) *Anglo-German Interactions in the Literature of the 1890s*, Oxford: Legenda.

Canić, Josip (1908) [Izvedbe djela Saloma O. Wildea i Oprosna večera A. Schnitzlera u Zagrebu (HNK)], *Hrvatstvo* [Zagreb], 11 May, 3.

Corballis, Richard and Julie Hibbard (2002) *The Importance of Reinventing Oscar: Versions of Wilde during the Last 100 Years*, New York; Amsterdam: Rodopi.

Čengić, Enes (1985) *S Krležom iz dana u dan (1980–1981): U sjeni smrti* (With Krleža day by day (1980–1981): In the shadow of the death), Zagreb: Globus.

Čuljat, Sintija (2002) 'Stilotvorni učinak Wildeovih "Phrases and philosophies for the Use of the Young"' (The stylistic effect of Wilde's PPUY), *Riječ: časopis za slavensku filologiju*, 8.2: 7–15.

'Drugo gostovanje Hane Suchánkove: "Saloma": Wilde' (The second guest performance of Hana Suchánková: *Salomé*: Wilde) (1914), *Novosti* [Zagreb], 30 May, 4.

Dukat, Vladoje (1902) 'Engleske literarne sitnice. Iz pozorišnog svijeta', *Nada*, 8.8: 112.

Dukat, Vladoje (1904) 'Doba kraljice Vikotorije', in *Slike iz povijesti engleske književnosti*, Zagreb: Matica hrvatska, pp. 301–02.

'Der Fächer' (1907) *Slavonische Presse* [Osijek], 26 November, 3.

Flaker, Vida (1978) 'Vladimir Nazor i evropska moderna', in Flaker, Aleksandar and Krunoslav Pranjić (eds) *Hrvatska književnost u evropskom kontekstu*, Zagreb: Zavod za znanost o književnosti Filozofskog fakulteta Sveučilišta and Liber, pp. 451–59.

Galović, Fran (1907) 'Tamara', *Hrvatska smotra* [Zagreb], 3: 303–19; in verse, repr. in Fran Galović (1942) *Djela Frana Galovića* (The works of Fran Galović), ed. Julije Benešić, 3: *Drame (1903–1906)*, Zagreb: Hrvatski izdavalački bibliografski zavod, 3: 107–28.

Galović, Fran (1911) 'Saloma', *Mlada Hrvatska*, 4.9: 260; an elaborated version of the poem 1st written in 1905; repr. (1943) *Djela Frana Galovića*, ed. Julije Benešić, *Pjesme I* (Songs), 2nd edn, Zagreb: Hrvatski izdavalački bibliografski zavod, p. 36.

Galović, Fran (1913) 'Začarano ogledalo' (The spellbound mirror), Savremeni hrvatski pisci 25, Zagreb: Društvo hrvatskih književnika; written from 23 March to 14 April 1912; repr. in (1942) *Djela Frana Galovića*, ed. Julije Benešić, *Pripovijesti* (Stories), 1: *1903–1912*, Zagreb: Hrvatski izdavalački bibliografski zavod, 1: 152–266.

Galović, Fran (1940) 'Saloma' [1905], in *Djela Frana Galovića*, ed Julije Benešić, *Pjesme I* (Songs), Zagreb: Binoza, pp. 135–36.

Galović, Fran (1942) *Tamara, scena po motivu Lermontovljeve pjesme* (Tamara, a scene on a motif from Lermont's poem), one–act play written in prose 1–3 May 1906, in *Djela Frana Galovića*, ed. Julije Benešić, 3: *Drame (1903–1906)*, Zagreb: Hrvatski izdavalački bibliografski zavod, 3: 94–106.

Gašparović, Darko (1989) 'O Wildeovu apokrifu', *Forum*, 28.7/8 (July/August): 73–79.

Gide, André (1980) 'Oscar Wilde', in *Povodi i odjeci: kritike, članci i eseji*, trans. Višnja

Machiedo, Rijeka: Otokar Keršovani, pp. 112–35. repr. in Wilde (2002) *Pjesme u prozi* (PP), trans. Luko Paljetak, afterword Andre Gide trans. from French Višnja Machiedo, illus. Duško Šibl, Zagreb: Ceres, pp. 59–78.

Gjurgjan, Ljiljana Ina (1995) *Mit, nacija i književnost 'kraja stoljeća': Vladimir Nazor i William Butler Yeats*, Zagreb: Nakladni zavod Matice hrvatske.

Hećimović, Branko (ed.) (1990) *Repertoar hrvatskih kazališta: 1840–1860–1980*, 2 vols, Zagreb: Globus.

Hećimović, Branko (ed.) (2002) *Repertoar hrvatskih kazališta (1981–1990)* (Repertory of Croatian theatres, 1981–1990), AGM 3, Zagreb: Hrvatska akademija znanosti i umjetnosti.

Hergešić, Ivo (1955) 'Oscar Wilde ili Tisuću i jedan paradoks', in *Književni portreti*, Zagreb: NIP, pp. 107–28; rev. edns: 1967, Zagreb: Stvarnost, pp. 521–40; 2005, Zagreb: Ex libris; also pub. in Wilde 1953, Wilde 1969, Wilde 2000a.

Hergešić, Ivo (1961) 'Oscar Wilde ili život kao umjetnina', *Mogućnosti* [Split], 11: 1175–85.

J. B. (1905) 'Oscar Wilde', *Obzor* [Zagreb], 27 May, 1–2.

'Je li umro Oscar Wilde?'(1909) *Hrvatska smotra* [Zagreb], 5.1: 43.

Kraus, Otto (1902) 'Streifzüge in der ausländischen Literatur', *Agramer Zeitung* [Zagreb], 19 April, 1–3.

Krleža, Miroslav (1918) 'Saloma: fragmenat iz eposa 'Smrt Ivana Preteče' (Saloma: a fragment from the epos 'The death of Ivan Preteča'), *Savremenik* [Zagreb], 13: 331–32.

Krleža, Miroslav (1932a) *Sabrana djela* (Collected works), *Eseji* (Essays), vol. 1, Zagreb: Minerva.

Krleža, Miroslav (1932b) *Moj obračun s njima*, Zagreb: the author.

Krleža, Miroslav (1956) *Davni dani* (Olden days), Zagreb: Zora.

Krleža, Miroslav (1961) 'O Marcelu Proustu', in *Eseji I*, Zagreb: Zora, pp. 53–92.

Krleža, Miroslav (1963) 'Saloma: legenda u jednom činu' (Salome: a one-act legend), *Forum* [Zagreb], 2.4 (October): 499–522.

Krleža, Miroslav (1967) 'Saloma', in *Legende* (Legends), Zagreb: Zora, pp. 277–313.

Krleža, Miroslav (1973) 'Saloma', in *Legende* (Legends), Sarajevo: NIP Oslobođenje, pp. 229–58.

Krleža, Miroslav (1982) 'Wilde Oscar: Pjesnik snobova', in *Panorama pogleda, pojava i pojmova*, Sarajevo: NIŠRO, «Oslobođenje», 5: 410–12.

Ld. (1909) on the production of *IH* and other plays at the Croatian National Theatre in Zagreb, *Savremenik* [Zagreb], 4.6: 343–45.

Livadić, Branimir (1908a) 'Gostovanje gđice A. Kernicove: Saloma' (Anka Kernic's guest performance: Salomé), *Obzor* [Zagreb], 12 May, 1–2.

Livadić, Branimir (1908b) 'Tri aktovke', *Obzor* [Zagreb], 16 September, 1–2.

Livadić, Branimir (1943) 'Hermina Šumovska umjetnički lik iz sjajnog razdoblja hrvatskog kazališnog života', *Spremnost*, 75: 9.

Lunaček, Vladimir (1906) 'Gostovanje gđice Ise Gregrove', *Obzor* [Zagreb], 24 May, 9.

Lunaček, Vladimir (1907) 'Oskar Wilde: Lepeza Lady Windermerove', *Obzor* [Zagreb], 21 April, 3.

Matoš, Antun Gustav (1902) 'Oskar Wilde', *Narodne novine* [Zagreb], 23 July, 1.

Matoš, Antun Gustav (1902) 'Ugasnulo svjetlo', *Mlada Hrvatska* [Zagreb], 1 October, 129–34; repr. in Matoš (1909) *Umorne priče*, Zagreb: Breyer Mirko, pp. 7–15.

Matoš, Antun Gustav (1911) 'Wilde i Mac Neill Whistler', *Obzor* [Zagreb], 21 November, 3–4.

Matoš, Antun Gustav (1938) *Dojmovi*, Zagreb: Binoza, nakladni zavod.

Matoš, Antun Gustav (1940a) *Iz stranoga svijeta*, Zagreb: Binoza, nakladni zavod.

Matoš, Antun Gustav (1940b) untitled letter to Vladimir Lunaček, *Obzor* [Zagreb], 1 October, 5.

Matoš, Antun Gustav (1955) *Misli i pogledi A.G. Matoša*, ed. M. Ujević, Zagreb: Leksikografski zavod FNRJ.

Matoš, Antun Gustav (2003) 'Pismo iz Pariza, *Impromptu*, Pariz, 1. siječnja 1901', in Tadijanović, Dragutin (ed.) *Dojmovi; Ogledi*, Samobor: 'A. G. Matoš', pp. 260–67; 1st pub. 1901 in *Hrvatsko pravo* [Zagreb], 17–19 January, 3.

Milčinović, Andrija (1903) 'Zabranjene drame na njemačkim pozornicama', *Vienac* [Zagreb], 35.12: 387–90.

Narodne novine (1905) review of Wilde's *Salomé* and Hartleben's *The Moral Demand* at the Croatian National Theatre in Zagreb, 29 May, 4.

Nazor, Vladimir (1913) *Istarske priče*, Zagreb: Matica hrvatska.

'Oskar Wilde, pjesnik "Salome" na hrvatskoj pozornici' (Oscar Wilde, a poet of *Salome* on the Croatian stage) (1905) *Narodne novine* [Zagreb], 24 May, 3–4.

Ogrizović, Milan (1905) 'Wilde: Saloma i Hartleben: Zahtjevi morala', *Hrvatsko pravo* [Zagreb], 29 May, 3.

Ogrizović, Milan (1908) 'Prvo gostovanje gđice: Anke Kernicove; Oskar Wilde: Saloma' (Anka Kernic's first guest performance; Oscar Wilde: Salomé), *Hrvatsko pravo* [Zagreb], 11 May, 3.

Ogrizović, Milan (1914) 'Drugo gostovanje g-đice Suchankove (Saloma)', *Narodne novine* [Zagreb], 29 May, 4.

O'Neill, Patrick (1985) *Ireland and Germany: A Study in Literary Relations*, New York: Peter Lang.

P. v. P. [Petar Preradović jr.] (1930) '"Das Schicksal Oscar Wildes": Zum 30. Todestag des Dichters', *Morgenblatt* [Zagreb], 30 November, 9.

Paljetak, Anamarija (2001) 'Tragovi Oscara Wildea u djelu Srećka Kosovela', *Dubrovnik*, 12.1: 78–84.

Paljetak, Luko (1997a) 'Oscar Wilde, gospodin sa suncokretom', in *Engleske teme*, Rijeka: Izdavački centar, pp. 224–34; also pub. in Wilde 1987 (*BRG and other poems*), pp. 131–45.

Paljetak, Luko (1997b) 'Oscar Wilde i njegove bajke', in *Engleske teme*, Rijeka: Izdavački centar, pp. 235–37; also pub. in Wilde 1994, pp. 71–73.

Paljetak, Luko (2007a) 'Ljepota i stvaranje u bajkama Oscara Wildea', in *Vanjski rub: studije i ogledi o stranim književnostima i književnicima*, Zagreb: Naklada Ljevak, pp.116–29; repr. in Wilde 2000, 2002, 2004, pp. 199–212.

Paljetak, Luko (2007b) 'Fi(jo)rentinska tragedija, dodirna točka Wildea i Vojnovića', in *Vanjski rub: studije i ogledi o stranim književnostima i književnicima*, Zagreb: Naklada Ljevak, pp. 130–41; repr. in *Dubrovnik* (2001), 12.1: 67–77.

Primorac, Antonija (2006) 'Dvije Salome: Saloma Oscara Wildea i Saloma Miroslava Krleže', *Književna smotra* [Zagreb], 38.3/4 (141/142): 123–30.

Raby, Peter (ed.) (1997) *The Cambridge Companion to Oscar Wilde*, Cambridge: Cambridge University Press.

'Saloma od Oskara Wildea: Zahtjevi morala od O. A. Hartlebena' (Wilde's *Salomé* and O. A. Hartleben's *The Moral Demand*) (1905) *Obzor* [Zagreb], 29 May, 3.

Sv. (1906) 'Hrvatsko kazalište. Oskar Wilde: Saloma', *Hrvatstvo* [Zagreb], 23 May, 3.

Sepčić, Višnja (1976) 'Matoš između Wildea i Poea', *Croatica*, 7.7/8: 135–51.

Senker, Boris (2004) 'Dandy ili san glavosječke noći', in *Tri glavosjeka*, Zagreb: Disput, pp. 53–114.

Schlösser, Anselm (1937) *Die englische Literatur in Deutschland von 1895 bis 1934*, Jena: Biedermann.

Spillern, Edmund (1907) '*Ein idealer Gatte*: Komödie in 4 Akten von Oskar Wilde; Deutsch von Isidore Leo Pavia und Herm. Freih. v. Teschenberg; Zur

Erstaufführung in Esseg am 6 März 1907', *Slavonische Presse* [Osijek], 6 March, 1–2.

Stanovnik, Majda (1970) '*Oscar Wilde* v slovenskem tisku do leta 1914 / Oscar Wilde in the Slovene Press up to 1914', in *Razprave / Dissertationes*, Ljubljana: Slovenska akademija znanosti in umetnosti (SAZU), Razred za filološke in literarne vede/ Academia Scientiarum et Artium Slovenica, Classis II: Philologia et Litterae, 7: 113–51; in Slovene, incl. summary in English.

Španić, Stjepko (1919) 'Prorok', *Savremenik* [Zagreb], 14.5: 238–39.

Tabain-Šantić, Vicko (1914) 'Letimični potezi: (U očekivanju drugog Wildeovog procesa...)' [about the 2nd Wilde trial in London], *Naše jedinstvo* [Split], 21 and 23 July, 1.

Torbarina, Josip (1939) '**Gostovanje irskog ansambla The Gate Theatre Company**', *Obzor* [Zagreb], 13 April, 1.

'Tragika Oscara Wildea: Novi proces u Londonu; Od *De profundis* do pisama Lordu Douglasu' (1913), *Obzor* [Zagreb], 25 April, 1.

Ujević, Tin (1965) *Eseji, rasprave, članci*, vol. 1, Zagreb: Znanje.

Ujević, Tin (1967) 'Studija o Antunu Gustavu Matošu', in *Postuma II*, Zagreb: Znanje, pp. 33–108; 1st pub. 1963 as 'Studija o Matošu' (A study on Matoš), *Mogućnosti* [Split], March–May, 10.3: 250–67, 10.4: 354–71, 10.5: 489–504.

V. R. (1925) 'Oskar Wilde: 25-godišnjica njegove smrti', *Večer* [Zagreb], 18 November, 4.

Vernić, Zdenko (1913) 'Epilog', *Agramer Tagblatt* [Zagreb], 30 April, 1–2.

Vidan, Ivo (1988) 'Krleža i G. B. Shaw', *Književna smotra* [Zagreb], 21.69–72: 72–80.

Vidan, Ivo (1995) *Engleski intertekst hrvatske književnosti*, Zagreb: Zavod za znanost o knji`evnosti Filozofskog fakulteta u Zagrebu.

Vollmer, Hans (1910) 'Oscar Wilde: Zur 10-jährigen Wiederkehr seines Todestages (30. November 1900)', *Agramer Zeitung* [Zagreb], 29 November, 2–4.

Vučetić, Mate (1925) 'Dvadesetpeta godišnjica smrti Oscara Wildea', *Obzor* [Zagreb],25 December, 9.

Wenzelides, Arsen (1911) 'O Oskaru Wildeu', *Savremenik* [Zagreb], 6.11: 651–58, 705–10.

Xenyl [pseud. Arsen Wenzelides] (1912) 'Suvišno otkriće', *Narodni list* [Zadar], 20 March, 1.

Žmegač, Viktor (1990) 'Zbilja oponaša umjetnost: o jednom mentalnom motivu na prijelomu stoljeća', *Umjetnost riječi* [Zagreb], 34.1: 51–61.

Chapter 18. 'Next to Christ': Oscar Wilde in Russian Modernism

Translations

(1897) 'Zagadochnaya zhenshchina (Veer ledi Uindermer)' (*LWF*), trans. Vladimir V. Vasil'ev, *Teatral*, 130: 3–84.

(1898) 'Predannyi drug' (DF), trans. M., *Detskii otdykh*, 11: 75–88.

(1898) 'Schastlivyi prints' (HP), trans. M., *Detskii otdykh*, 9: 89–100.

(1899) 'Upadok lzhi' (DL), trans. O. M. Solov'eva, *Novyi zhurnal literatury, iskusstva i nauki*, 4: 40–47, 5: 155–66.

(1901) 'Iskusstvo kritiki' (CA), trans. O. M. Solov'eva, *Novyi zhurnal literatury, iskusstva i nauki*, 5: 439–57, 6: 554–74.

(1903) *Ballada Ridingskoi tyur'my*, trans. N. Norm, St Petersburg: [n. pub.].

(1903) 'Den' rozhdeniya infanty' (BI), trans. O. F. Sherstobitova, *Yunyi chitatel'* [St Petersburg], 15 September, 89–108.

(1903) 'Solovei i roza' (NR), trans. Z. T., *Novyi zhurnal literatury, iskusstva i nauki*, 3: 218–21.

(1904) *Ballada Redingskoi tyur'my*, trans. Konstantin D. Bal'mont, Moscow: Skorpion.

(1904) *Salomeya*, trans. Vladimir and Leonid Andruson, ed. Konstantin D. Bal'mont, Moscow: Grif.

(1905) *De profundis*, trans. Ekaterina A. Andreeva, *Vesy*, 3: 1–42.

(1905) *Pamyati Uail'd* [In memory of Wilde], ed. Ekaterina A. Andreeva, Moscow: Grif; includes Gide's memoir of Wilde and *DP*.

(1905) *Portret Doriana Greya*, trans. A. T., *Novyi zhurnal literatury, iskusstva i nauki*, 7: 1–16, 8: 17–32, 9: 33–48, 10: 49–80.

(1905–09) *Polnoe sobranie sochinenii* (Complete works), 8 vols, Moscow: Sablin.

(1906) *Zamysly* (*Intentions*), trans. Anna Mintslova, Moscow: Grif.

(1907) *Dusha cheloveka pri sotsialisme* (SMUS), trans. M. A. Golovkina, Moscow: Diletant.

(1907) *Florentinskaya tragediya* (*FT*), trans. Mikhail Likiardopulo and A. Kursinksky, *Vesy*, 1: 17–38.

(1907) 'Ideal'nyi muzh' (*IH*), trans. O. N. Popova, *Biblioteka 'Teatra i iskusstva'*, 8: 41–57.

(1908) *La Sainte courtisane, ili Zhenshchina, uveshannaya dragotsennostyami*, trans. Mikhail Likiardopulo, *Vesy*, 11: 22–31.

(1908) *Portret mistera W. H.* (PMWH), trans. S. A. Berdyaev, Moscow: [n. pub.].

(1908) *Trivial'naya komediya dlya ser'eznykh lyudei* (*IBE*), trans. G. Popilov and Z. von Minkvits, Moscow: Izd. Teatr. biblioteki M. A. Sokolovoi.

(1909) *Nigilisty: P'esa iz russkoi zhizni* (*VN*), trans. N. Solov'ev, Moscow: Problemma.

(1912) *Polnoe sobranie sochinenii* (Complete works), 4 vols, ed. Kornei Chukovskii, St Petersburg: Marks.

(1960) *Izbrannye proizvedeniya* (Selected works), 2 vols, ed. Kornei Chukovskii, Moscow: Goslitizdat; 1st post-Stalin collection.

Secondary sources

Andreas–Salomé, Lou (1896) 'Fridrikh Nitsshe v svoikh proizvedeniiakh', *Severnyi vestnik* [St Petersburg], 3,4, 5.

Argus [Gavriil S. Veselitskii-Bozhidaroich] (1895) 'Oskar Uail'd i oskar uail'dizm', *Novoe vremya* [St Petersburg], 6907 (24 May/ 5 June): 2.

Artaban, V. [Grigorii Petrov] (1904) 'Gnilaya dusha', *Russkoe slovo* [Moscow], 43 (12 February): 1.

Bal'mont, Konstantin (1904) 'Poeziya Oskara Uail'da', *Vesy*, 1: 22–40.

Belyi, Andrei (1911) 'Fridrikh Nitsshe', *Arabeski*, Moscow: Musaget, pp. 69–90.

Bershtein, Evgenii (1998) 'Western Models of Sexuality in Russian Modernism' (unpublished doctoral dissertation, University of California, Berkeley).

Bershtein, Evgenii (2000) 'The Russian Myth of Oscar Wilde', in Engelstein, Laura and Stephanie Sandler (eds) *Self and Story in Russian History*, Ithaca: Cornell University Press, pp. 168–88.

Bogomolov, Nikolai A. (1995) *Mikhail Kuzmin: stat'i i materialy*, Moscow: Novoe literaturnoe obozrenie.

Bogomolov, Nikolai A. and Dzhon Malmstad (1995) *Mikhail Kuzmin: iskusstvo, zhizn', epokha*, Moscow: Novoe literaturnoe obozrenie.

Chukovskii, Kornei (2001) *Sobranie sochinenii*, vol. 3, Moscow: Terra–Knizhnyi klub.

'Ego S–vu Kn. Meshcherskomu' ([n.d.]) MS, Russian National Library, fond 391, item 81.

Engelstein, Laura (1992) *The Keys to Happiness: Sex and the Search for Modernity in Fin–de-Siècle Russia*, Ithaca: Cornell University Press.

Feoktistov, Evgenii M. (1929) *Vospominaniya E. M. Feoktistova: za kulisami politiki i literatury: 1848–96*, ed. Yuri G. Oksman, Leningrad: Priboi.

Gide, André (1949) *In Memoriam (Reminiscences): De Profundis*, trans. Bernard Frechtman, New York: Philosophical Library.

Gippius, Zinaida (1896) 'Zlatotsvet', *Severnyi vestnik* [St Petersburg], 2.

Grazhdanin [St Petersburg] (1895).

Ivanov, Vyacheslav (1904) 'Ellinskaya religiya stradayushchego boga', *Novyi put'*, 1: 110–34, 2: 48–78; 3: 38–61, 5: 28–40, 8: 17–26, 9: 47–70.

Ivanov, Vyacheslav (1905) 'Religiya Dionisa: Ee proiskhozhdenie i vliyanie', *Voprosy zhizni*, 6: 185–220, 7: 122–48.

Ivanov, Vyacheslav (1971–87) *Sobranie sochinenii*, 4 vols, eds Dmitry V. Ivanov and Olga Deschartes, Brussels: Foyer Oriental Chrétien.

Kuzmin, Mikhail (1972) *Wings; Prose and Poetry*, Ann Arbor, MI: Ardis.

Kuzmin, Mikhail (2000) *Dnevnik 1905–1907*, eds Nikolai Bogomolov and Sergei Shumikhin, St Petersburg: Izdatel'stvo Ivana Limbakha.

Lotman, Yurii (1993) 'Syuzhetnoe prostranstvo russkogo romana XIX stoletiya', *Izbrannye stat'i*, Tallinn: Aleksandra, 3: 91–106.

Malmstad, John (2000) 'Bathhouses, Hustlers, and Sex Clubs: The Reception of Mikhail Kuzmin's *Wings*', *Journal of the History of Sexuality*, 9.1–2: 85–104.

Malmstad, John and Nikolai Bogomolov (1999) *Mikhail Kuzmin: A Life in Art*, Cambridge, MA: Harvard University Press.

Minskii, Nikolai (1908) 'Smysl Salomei', *Zolotoe runo*, 6: 56–58.

Moeller-Sally, Betsy (1990) 'Oscar Wilde and the Culture of Russian Modernism', *The Slavic and East European Journal*, 34.4: 459–72.

Mosse, Werner E. (1981) 'Imperial Favorite: V. P. Meshchersky and the *Grazhdanin*', *The Slavonic and East European Review*, 4: 529–47.

N. V. (1897) 'Oskar Uail'd i angliiskie estety', *Knizhki nedeli*, June, 5–25.

Nedelya [St Petersburg] (1895).

Nicholas II (1903) letter to Prince Vladimir Meshchersky, 21 June, Bakhmeteff Archive, Rare Book and Manuscript Library, Columbia University, New York.

Novoe vremya [St Petersburg] (1895) 6851: 1, 6854: 2, 6867: 2, 6904 and 6907.

Pavlova, Tat'yana (1991) 'Oskar Uail'd v russkoi literature (konets XIX–nachalo XX vv.)', *Na rubezhe XIX I XX vekov: iz istorii mezhdunarodnykh svyazei russkoi literatury: sbornik nauchnykh trudov*, ed. Yu. D. Levin, Leningrad: Nauka.

Pimenova, Emiliya K. ([n.d.]) 'Dni minuvshie', manuscript, Russian National Library, St Petersburg, f. 1000, l. 2, no. 1054.

Polonsky, Rachel (1998) *English Literature and the Russian Aesthetic Renaissance*, Cambridge: Cambridge University Press.

Roznatovskaya, Yuliya A. (2000) *Oskar Uail'd v Rossii: bibliografacheskii ukazatel', 1892–2000*, Moscow: Rudomino.

Shestov, Lev (1992) *Sochineniya*, Moscow: Khudozhestvennaia literatura.

Solov'ev, Vladimir (1974) *Stikhotvoreniia i shutochnye p'esy*, ed. Z. Mints, Leningrad: Sovetskii pisatel'.

Solov'eva, I. and V. Shitova (1977) 'A. S. Suvorin: portret na fone gazety', *Voprosy literatury*, 2: 162–99.

Tolstoy, Lev (1951) *Polnoe sobranie sochineii*, vol. 30, Moscow: Gosudarstvennoe izdatel'stvo khudozhestvennoi literatury.

Uspenskii, Vladimir (1906) 'Religiya Oskara Uail'da i sovremennyi asketizm', *Khristianskoe chtenie*, February, 204–25.

Wilde, Oscar (1986) *De Profundis and Other Writings*, London: Penguin Books.

Vengerova, Zinaida (1905) *Literaturnye kharakteristiki: kniga vtoraya*, St Petersburg: Tipo-litografiia A. E. Vineke.

Vengerova, Zinaida (1912) 'Sud nad Oskarom Uail'dom', *Novaya zhizn'*, 11: 157–79.

Viktorovich, V. A. (1999) 'Meshcherskii Vladimir Petrovich', *Russkie pisateli, 1800–1917: Biografiheskii slovar'*, Moscow: Bol'shaya rossiiskaya entsiklopediya, 4: 44–46.

Vitte, Sergei Yuri (1960) *Vospominaniya*, vol. 3, Moscow: Izdatel'stvo sotsial'no-ekonomicheskoi literatury.

Volynskii, Akim (1895) 'Oskar Uail'd', *Severnyi vestnik*, 12: 311–17.

Volynskii, Akim (1896) 'Oskar Uail'd', *Severnyi vestnik*, 9: 57–58; 2nd pagination.

Volynskii, Akim (1896a) 'Literaturnye zametki', *Severnyi vestnik*, 10: 223–55.

Volynskii, Akim (1896b) 'Apollon i Dionis', *Severnyi vestnik*, 11: 232–55.

Index